Honoring All Life

A Practical Guide To Exploring A New Reality

Shaktari L. Belew

First Edition, 2005

ISBN: 0-9744391-4-2

Published in the U.S.A. by:

Honoring All Life Foundation

Ashland, Oregon 97520

For information and purchasing, please visit our website:

<u>www.HonoringAllLife.org</u>

Write the Author at: <u>Shaktari@HonoringAllLife.org</u>

Design, layout and printing in the U.S. by

Interactive Media Publishing

Phoenix, OR 97535

<u>www.i-mediapub.com</u>

*Printed on 100% post consumer fiber recycled paper
using a chlorine free process and recycled toners and inks.*

Simple Gratitude

In celebration of and gratitude for the magnificence of All That IS ...

We Are !

When all the noise has died down,

when all the tears have been cried,

when all the letters have been written,

who will stand and speak

the silence of the heart?

Who will see the light

emanating from all,

when our focus is on the

loudly shouting voices of conflict?

To see light

one must focus on LIFE.

To hear the heartbeat of All-That-Is

one must be willing to be still.

To honor one Self

one must be willing to soften,

to not-know

and in that not-knowing.

to humbly perceive the perfection of all.

CONTENTS

PREFACE

Much of my life has been spent studying the way we perceive. The illusion that I know much of anything has faded as I have learned more about the perceptual filters through which I have narrowly viewed life. This book is a journey into an awareness of the perceptual filters through which we all perceive our unique experience of "reality". As you read, I invite you to become aware of the perceptual filters that are presented to you as "facts".

Not only will you be showered with my own perceptual filters – as the author – but even the "facts" that are scattered throughout the book can be seen as examples of selective information gathered by those who were focusing on specific aspects of life, within their own highly subjective experience of "reality." Just as physicians of the past failed to see the connection between hand-washing and the infection-rate while they went about facilitating the very deaths they were attempting to prevent, our focus of attention determines what we allow ourselves to perceive. So please hold any statistics lightly.

Why then, are they included? Because in order for me to understand what I want, I need to differentiate what I don't want. Following the old axiom that "you get what you focus on", I then chose to focus all my attention on creating the life experience I wanted.

But what *did* I want?

As the realization that my highly subjective perceptual filters (forged through my thoughts, beliefs, judgments, and experiences) literally establish my experience of "reality", I determined to choose a perceptual filter that produced a reality that pleased me. I started asking myself some important questions: Why am I here? What is my purpose? To explore the answers to these questions, I played a game with myself. I asked myself what I would say to everyone I knew, if I only had 30 seconds left to live. This was my response:

> **Thank you for BEing YOU**. (Thank you for all I have learned by being with you, interacting with you, having you in my life – whether I experienced it as fun or difficult; positive or negative; challenging to everything I embrace, or as an ecstatic affirmation of what I embrace as real. Everything I experienced from you has been a gift and has provided value and context in my life.)

> **I love you**. (Underneath everything that has been said and done between us, is love. I recognize that the core of our being IS love. I appreciate the richness and magnificence I experience in both you AND me when I allow myself to simply and fully be present with you.)

> Or more simply "**I HONOR the gift you are to me**."

Through playing this game and discovering this truth for myself, I got in touch with the essence of what is most important to me. Once I realized this statement embodied who I wanted to be in my life – one who *honors all (including Self)* - the only thing left for me to do, was to live my life *from* this statement. But I didn't know how.

This book is a chronicle of my process of discovery. It is offered as a gift with the intention that, if you so wish, it assist you in your own perception-expanding exploration.

Shaktari L. Belew

June 2005

FIRST THINGS FIRST

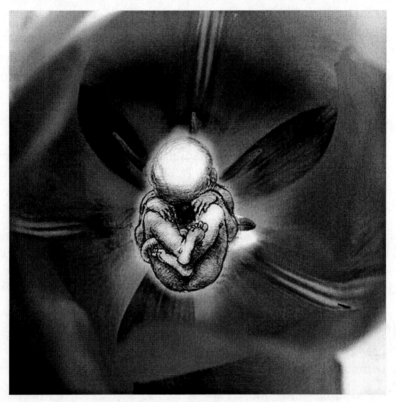

(Fetus drawing courtesy of Leonardo Da Vinci)

Honoring All Life asks,
"Who are you willing to BE in the context of this (or any) subject?"
And then it explores the choices available
as seen through a multitude of perceptual filters. It asks,
"What world do you want to create?"
And then networks those who envision similar ideas.
This book is the beginning
Of a continuous co-creative effort to explore and articulate
The magnificence of human expression.

FIRST THINGS FIRST

A Perceptual Shift

Our choices in life are dictated by the way we perceive reality. Yet few of us take the time to really explore the personal way in which we perceive, assuming that everyone sees the same reality we do. But that's not true. As we shall see, studies in perception reveal that each person sees uniquely.

This book appeals to the intrepid explorer in you. It invites you to explore your own personal habits of perception and how they affect your life choices. In a broader scope, it is about how we, as a species, view our role on this planet.

We just completed the bloodiest century of recorded history. When you look at the status of life on Earth, the narrow analysis upon which we base our decisions, the lack of common sense and logic, the emphasis on material gain over quality of life ... are you satisfied? Or do you yearn for deeper connection? Are you longing to contribute? Do you ask yourself, "Is this the best we can do?"

It seems we have become "human doings" instead of "human beings." This book is a step toward becoming human *beings*, by exploring some of the underlying concepts, beliefs, and judgments that directly affect our perception of who we are and what is possible. In a shift of focus it asks, **"Who do we choose to BE?"**

More precisely, it examines what life would be like if we consciously chose to honor all life in our daily decisions. This is not a pie-in-the sky dream, but a reality that is being explored and developed on every continent – right now – by thousands just like you. It touches every aspect of our daily lives.

It requires both an inner and outer exploration, as it acknowledges the truth that anything we want to manifest into the world must first be present within ourselves. This is important, because each of us has a vital role to play in this gentle transformation of our way of life on Earth.

I have to admit this is not an easy path. In the years since I promised myself that I would explore living a life that honors all, every aspect of my life that wasn't honoring raised it's head in a direct challenge. Yet this journey of self discovery has been such a celebration of Life, that I can no longer imagine living any other way.

This shift in perception has allowed me to be effective in the world, in a way I've never experienced before. When I view the wake of destruction and pain that trails behind humanity's choices in the past several hundred years, it has offered me hope for the future well-being of my children and all life on this planet.

This book explores an intentional shift of focus. Although it can be seen as a brief introduction to many new (and old) ways of seeing life, it is not about religion or philosophy, but about perception. It explores some of the most prominent and profoundly different concepts through which we view ourselves and our place in the cosmos - and how those perceptions color our choices. Each chapter can be considered an introduction to a topic that deserves volumes. They are intended to act as a sort of catalyst for your own exploration.

I must be the change I wish to see in the world.

M. K. Gandhi

Moving to Wholeness

Human beings are amazingly magnificent creatures. We are driven by love, highly adaptable, possess brilliant wisdom, and are always learning. Although we may not recognize ourselves as such, nor often act in a way that reflects this innate beauty, our actions reveal more of a need for a shift in the way we perceive ourselves and our place in the living systems of life, than a shift in who we are.

We no longer have the luxury of spending decades "improving" ourselves for the day when we can finally make a contribution to the world. (I don't doubt the value of inner-work and its healing potential. It is the underlying premise that we need to "fix" ourselves, that I am questioning.) We have always had the option of seeing ourselves as whole and complete, because that is who we are.

What has been missing is a perceptual shift from seeing ourselves as sinners or less-than, to seeing ourselves as whole, creative, and competent beings. This subtle shift of perception allows us to finally see the possibility of acknowledging our interdependent world, and then living in a way that honors all life. One in which we care for each other - not because we have to - but because we can't help but do so. It is an expression of who we are.

Assessing Who We Are

When we self-assess we hone our skills with the intention of becoming as efficient and effective as possible. Yet individually and as a species, we rarely self-assess. We rarely question the basic assumptions that constitute the foundation upon which we base our decisions. Are we willing to ask simple questions and then listen within for the answers? In the post-9/11 world, perhaps more importantly, are we willing to ask any questions at all? Most fundamental of all is the question:

What do we want?

We are surrounded by evidence that many of our assumptions and subsequent actions no longer support Life. If I am completely honest, and ask myself if my own choices in life contribute to the best possible expression of life on Earth, my answer is "No." Somehow I've allowed the busy pace of my life to compromise my core values. You know, the ones we all share: love, peace, harmony, unity, honesty.

We say we want peace. Yet instead of seeing conflict as a gift that leads us to discuss deeper underlying issues that can lead to genuine healing; we barely hesitate before using force whenever conflict arises. I'm not just referring to our penchant for war, I'm referring to something much closer to home – the difficulty most of us have in simply looking at conflict (even with our own children or within our own hearts) as a tool with which to discover more about ourselves and life in general.

Instead of supporting life in all its diverse manifestations, we pick and choose which portion of life we are willing to support - while decimating the rest (whether deliberately or through ignorance) – failing to understand that life is a living whole, none of which can be harmed without injuring ourselves and all life in the process.

We say we want our communities based on love, but even in the richest nations we fail to take care of all community members equally. At the same time we ignore or degrade the commons – those aspects of life we all share that are essential for

Picasso said: 'I don't develop; I am.'

Life is not about becoming something, but about making real the image already there. We are obsessed with personal growth, reaching towards some imaginary heaven, but instead of trying to transcend human existence, it makes more sense to 'grow down' into the world and our place in it.

Tom Butler-Bowdon
50 Self-Help Classics
http://www.butler-bowdon.com/soulscode.htm

survival (unpolluted arable land, clean air, vibrantly alive potable water, biodiversity, to name a few).

We say we care about others, yet our choices often place profit over well-being, contribute to unhealthy pollution, the unjust treatment of many, and the continued use of domination and control in almost every aspect of our lives.[1]

These are not the symptoms of a "sinful" and "bad" species, but of a *way of perceiving* that no longer serves anyone.

PART ONE – A WILLINGNESS TO EXPAND PERCEPTION

This section explores two aspects of perception. **First, *how* we perceive.** This includes a deep exploration of the ways in which our beliefs, concepts, and experiences impact our perceptions, and actually contribute to the perceptual filters through which we create our sense of reality. Once we are aware of them, we are free to change them.

Second, it explores ways of perceiving that empower you – the perceiver – to expand the quality of your perceptual experience, and hence your experience of life itself. Each chapter explores an important perceptual filter (or way of seeing) that significantly shifts our sense of the possible – and hence the choices available at any given moment. Understanding these perceptual filters will greatly assist in understanding Part Two.

As I have learned to let go of my own beliefs and ideas about life in a desire to allow new and more expanded perceptions to enter my experience, what I see is also expanding. Life has again become that awe-filled open-hearted exploration that defines the experience of the young child.

PART TWO – HONORING ALL LIFE

Honoring Self

As I practiced the ability to perceive multiple points of view and to shift perceptual awareness at will, I experienced life as layers of reality, each one valid within its context. Each moment was alive with possibilities. I began to realized that even though perceptual cues may seem to take place outside of me, all of the processing takes place within me – *nothing happens outside of me.*

Most of us have been taught just the opposite. We are taught that we have the ability to impartially observe life, and to participate only when we want to. However, from a perceptual stand point, we can't help but participate – we are the space in which everything we experience happens. To understand life then, you must first understand yourself. In short, you need to learn to honor you. By doing so, you open the doorway to honoring all. [2]

Finding Practical, Livable Solutions

A Collective Quest

Allowing myself to "re-perceive" life through various perceptual filters has also allowed me to see many of our social structures with fresh eyes. I am not alone in this process. As the evidence has mounted that our ways of living on Earth no longer serve humanity, nor life in general, we are collectively beginning to ask ourselves important questions about our role on Earth as a species.

Incredible books have been written, conferences have been convened, think-tanks have thought, and all have developed more accurate methods for discerning our current status as well as suggested plans of action. One of the best – and highly recommended - is Lester R. Brown's 2003 book, Plan B – <u>Rescuing a Planet under Stress and a Civilization in Trouble</u>, in which he both outlines a plan for restructuring our economy and argues for the need to do so in "wartime speed." He points out:

> Time is running out. Whereas historically we lived off the interest generated by the earth's natural capital assets, we are now consuming those assets themselves. We have built an environmental bubble economy, one where economic output is artificially inflated by overconsumption of the earth's natural assets. The challenge today is to deflate the bubble before it bursts. [3]

Even though thousands are working on "deflating" that bubble, we have just begun to move the discussion from a general level, to address these complex issues within our own *selves*. In other words, how can we begin to move the discussion from "out there in the world at-large" to a personal dialog within each participant?

Bringing it home

I noticed in my own life, that I was willing to make *some* changes, but was I ready to shift my living style in a grand way? How "bad" did things have to get before I was willing to address the underlying beliefs, concepts, and assumptions that harbored my resistance? Even amidst overwhelming evidence that our current choices determine the quality of our experience, many of us are reluctant to acknowledge that evidence. Even fewer are ready to act.

The intention of this book is to encourage a shift of perception that allows this change to be experienced as a joyous celebration of the best of who we are, instead of a dismal experience of reluctantly letting go of perceived comforts we enjoy. To accomplish that goal we will examine three things:

- how we perceive our available choices,
- what currently works and doesn't work – without judgment,
- and what possible alternative choices exist right now. (There are many!)

As Lester R. Brown and so many other scientists and concerned citizens have stated, push has come to shove. The time to act is now. **I would like to suggest that the feeling of urgency is more a reflection of our own dissatisfaction with our individual and life choices – ones that consistently feel less than joyful.** We cannot live in peace and enjoy happiness if there is a contant war going on between our daily choices and our hearts. While many perceptual filters claim that we are all "doomed" if we don't make more ecologically sustainable choices, I wonder if those choices could more easily be embraced if they were chosen because they truly bring us joy, instead of choosing them out of fear.

Part Two of this book is an exploration of practical ways in which "honoring all" can be accomplished. Ways in which we can make small, somewhat painless changes in our everyday lives that have global repercussions. These are changes that can actually increase our own joyous experience of life, while at the same time include all of Earth's inhabitants in the scope of our decisions.

The second part is also a celebration of those who are already making this choice. Ultimately it is a celebration of the possible human – who we choose to be – not in some far off future, but right now, in this next moment.

Fear of Change

This entire book celebrates our ability to choose the quality of our experience – to self-assess and constantly make changes. But change doesn't have to be a gut-wrenching devastating experience. It can be gentle, similar to Buckminster Fuller's Trimtab[4] concept, where small incremental adjustments yield huge results.

Those of us who live privileged lives compared to most of humanity, usually feel fear whenever the idea of making changes is broached in conversation. We fear that we will have to give up something we truly enjoy; so either the conversation never gets started, or it is met with strong resistance. But we don't always feel that way.

When it comes to our children, we are ready to make whatever changes necessary to provide them with the best life possible. We do everything in our power to keep them from experiencing starvation, violence, or poverty – it is a boundary we are unwilling to cross.

I realize that I am also unwilling to cross that boundary for myself. I love myself enough to know that I – like everyone else – deserve to have my needs met, my voice heard, and my gifts shared. I have found my worthiness, and with it came a quality-of-life boundary I am unwilling to cross. It is my *intention* that keeps me from crossing that boundary.

> **Loving yourself means you are willing to set bottom-line boundaries for both yourself and the world you live in.**

I now realize that love expresses in this same manner – everywhere. When I feel loving towards myself, I make sure that my needs are met. When I love others, I insist their needs also be met – that is my bottom line. So why not carry this same principle out regarding the entire planet?

I am unwilling to watch our beloved Earth be destroyed – and so I constantly envision my planet as the whole, balanced, healthy place it naturally is. And I choose to live in a way that honors that conviction as much as possible. I am unwilling to treat others as "collateral damage" in my quest to accomplish some goal – and so I carefully examine other points-of-view, aware that there is always more to perceive beyond my current understanding. And I actively choose to see others as an integral part of the interconnected whole of which I am part. I am unwilling to create wars in my heart in order to conform to someone's need to dominate or control through fear – and so I pay attention to the quality of *feeling* that accompanies my choices in life, always striving to make decisions that bring a sense of inclusiveness and expansion to my heart. These may seem like political statements, but they reach into every facet of our daily lives.

It is a lack of self-love, I believe, that keeps us mired in complacency in the midst of overwhelming evidence that change is necessary for our own well-being. Because once self-love exists, the capacity to love everything and everyone blossoms – and also the commitment to live in a way that supports those we love.

The myth of separation

What keeps us from seeing our *entire* planet as home, and not just the ground beneath our feet? What keeps us from seeing ourselves when we gaze into each other's eyes?

I believe it's the misperception of separation. When we break things down into parts we tend to see them as separate entities, complete unto themselves. This focus fails to take into consideration the relational impact those seemingly separate items have with each other, and their overall interdependence. It perpetuates the idea that you can harm or remove any item and not affect the rest.

A simple shift of focus reveals an entire world of relationships previously overlooked. For example, how do you explain water without including the entire cycle of precipitation or the fact that most of the planet surface – even your own body – is made up of water?

"Honoring All Life" is a perceptual shift that takes us from our traditional mechanistic way of perceiving to a systems-based perception.

It is a shift sourced from the most current findings in biology, chemistry, economics, quantum physics, ecology, and – perhaps surprisingly – the ancient spirituality of almost all religions. It is the model of life that has always been present in every aspect of nature; but because our focus was elsewhere, many of us missed it entirely.

This isn't to say that the lessons of the mechanistic separation-based perspective haven't been valuable. On the contrary, they have taught us much – and continue to do so. But it is now time to step into another perception and learn as much as we can *within that context* as well. We humans are incredibly adaptable and this is simply another step in the thrill of human exploration.

How do you separate oxygen from the entire respiratory cycle in nature, in which we all breathe each other? Where does my breath end and yours or the forest's begin?

Terms Used...

To ensure that we share the same vocabulary, we need to agree on a few basic definitions. Please understand that the entire book could also be considered a definition of "honoring all." Let's delve into the title: "Honoring All Life".

Honoring

By "honor", I mean something beyond "respect." The dictionary uses both words as synonyms, but there is a nuance of difference that I'd like to examine. In comparison to "Honor," "Respect" often reflects a hierarchical role as in "respecting elders," simply because they are assumed to be more – in some way – than those doing the respecting. Those receiving respect may not necessarily reciprocate - it implies an element of *exclusivity*.

"Honoring" means to accept and allow without judgment, because you humbly recognize there is always a bigger picture than the one you see at any given moment. Honoring implies openness — a willingness to expand awareness and embrace new possibilities. This willingness to embrace new possibilities is grounded in recognition – even a celebration – of a shared essence with whatever or whomever you honor. Honoring is always relaxed, open, expansive, and *inclusive*. "Honoring" acknowledges that life always creates balance.

In Robert Heinlein's classic science-fiction novel, <u>Stranger In a Strange Land</u>, the main character greets everyone with the words, "Thou art God." Honoring means accepting each person and thing with that same sort of reverence, as if all is God. It is similar to the tradition of greeting people with "Namaste," which roughly means, "the God in me greets the God in you." It honors the divine in everything.

All Life

Understanding the phrase, "All life," requires a larger perceptual shift. Our traditional, mechanistic view of the world categorizes things as "living" or "inert." Based on my own expanded perceptual experience in which everything seems to vibrate, and several theories in both quantum physics and systems analysis; I'm not sure I can tell the difference between them anymore. Even when acknowledging a difference in degree of complexity, for simplicity's sake I now include all of creation – flowers, rocks, birds, and their interrelated systems - everything – as alive.[5]

Perceptual

Online Etymology states that *perceptual* is taken directly from the Latin *percipere,* meaning to "obtain, gather," or metaphorically, "to take entirely." [6] I like that definition. It is similar to the word that most closely defines perception in the way I experience it - Robert Heinlein's "grok," (also from <u>Stranger In A Strange Land</u>.) To grok something is "to drink it fully," or "to be one with it".

To explore this perceptual possibility requires thoroughly understanding and embracing – being one with. It is a shift in perception so substantial that everything viewed through the lens of "honoring all" necessitates new assumptions about our roles, thoughts, and actions on this planet.

The Possible Human

This is an exciting time to be alive. As a species, we are at cusp. Perhaps consciously for the first time, we have the opportunity to re-define who we are, what we stand for, and how we want to live. In every moment, we have the opportunity to step fully into being the possible human. This book is intended as a catalyst for this process.

Acknowledging the scope of his work, Lester R. Brown ends the preface of his book with these words:

> *And, finally, I do not have the credentials for writing this book. Nor do I know anyone who does. But someone had to give it a try.* [3]

I'd like to echo his statement.

An Invitation

This is not a how-to book. Living life in a way that honors all is new territory for the human species – at least for most of us. I invite you to join me in creating this experience.

In a way, it could be said that this invitation offers a method for filtering one's choices in life. Once you determine if honoring all life is a fundamental expression of Who you are, then you can use this simple question as a means for making choices that align with your essence. Simply ask yourself, **"Does this choice honor ALL life?"** If your choice produces a feeling of joy, then it honors YOU. How could you possibly honor life more?

Notes

1. On December 6th 2004 Oxfam International released its report entitled, Paying the Price, offering a perfect example of our mixed-up priorities:
    "A new report from international agency Oxfam today reveals that 45 million more children will die needlessly by 2015, because rich countries are failing to provide the necessary resources they promised to overcome poverty. The report, *Paying the Price*, finds that rich countries' aid budgets are half what they were in 1960 and poor countries are paying back a staggering $100 million a day in debt repayments. Oxfam also calculates that 97 million more children will be out of school by 2015 unless urgent action is taken. Jeremy Hobbs, Oxfam's Executive Director, said: "The world has never been wealthier, yet rich nations are giving less and less. Across the globe, millions of people are being denied the most basic human needs - clean water, food, health care and education. People are dying while leaders delay debt relief and aid." In 1970 rich countries agreed to spend just 0.7 percent of their incomes on aid. Thirty-four years later, none of the G8 members have reached this target and many have not even set a timetable.
    In addition, only 40 percent of the money counted officially as aid actually reaches the poorest countries, and when it does it is often seriously delayed. For example, 20 percent of the European Union's aid arrives at least a year late and 92 percent of Italian aid is spent on Italian goods and services.
    At only 0.14 percent of national income, the US spending on foreign aid in 2003 was one-tenth of what it spent on Iraq. The US won't reach the aid target needed to halve world poverty until 2040.
    Germany won't reach the target until 2087 while Japan is decreasing its aid commitments."
    From their press release of the same date, "Oxfam: Poor Are Paying the Price of Rich Countries' Failure, http://www.oxfam.org/eng/pr041206_MDG.htm.
2. As we shall see in the discussion of physics, especially the theories on holography, all information is available at all times, but our ability to *perceive* it is what can always be expanded. Additionally, according to the holographic theory of both the brain and the universe, all parts of the whole contain the whole.
3. Lester R. Brown's, Plan B – Rescuing a Planet under Stress and a Civilization in Trouble, Preface.
4. A trimtab refers to the mechanism for steering a ship. The rudder is small compared to the ship, but at times it is still difficult to turn. The trimtab is a sort of rudder on the rudder, that allows the larger rudder to be turned more easily. The significance is that the trimtab can be shifted slightly, but the result is much larger by comparison.
5. "I propose that there is reason to see the whole universe as alive, self-organizing endless fractal levels of living complexity as reflexive systems learning to play with possibilities in the intelligent co-creation of complex evolving systems." Elisabet Sahtouris, Ph.D. A Tentative Model for a Living Universe, Part One
6. http://www.etymonline.com/ http://www.etymonline.com/p4etym.htm also for quantum, http://www.etymonline.com/index.php?search=quantum&searchmode=none

WHY HONOR ALL LIFE?

The question is...

If we get what we focus on... what do we want to create?

If we focus on what we don't want... that is what we'll get.

If we focus on the core of what we want...

lives filled with Joy and a sense of Well-Being...

in which we know our needs will always be provided for

- and those of everyone else -

that is what we will create.

But it requires a shift of focus,

From judgment, denial, and scarcity,

To co-creative pleasure...

allowing inner-joy to be our guide every step of the way.

WHY HONOR ALL LIFE?

The way to reduce population is to have all people feel honored.

Paul Hawken
Brother, Can You Spare a Paradigm?, by Paul Hawken, from Nature's Operating Instructions, edited by Kenny Ausubel with J.P. Harpignies, 2004, page 159

I could offer you all kinds of reasons why "honoring all" is essential to our survival on this planet, and why you *should* do it. In fact, from many perceptual filters, it seems imperative that we do. But no matter what I say or what evidence I provide, you will either agree with me or not based on your own experience. We already assail ourselves with "shoulds" in life. The last thing any of us needs is another reason for feeling guilty about not doing something we *should* be doing.

There is absolutely no reason to "honor all life" unless you want to. Period. In fact, if it is done from anything other than the joy it brings you – it will not work.

If it's done from fear – fear will permeate all you create.

If it's done from guilt – it will not satisfy, and resentment will result.

In fact, if it's done from anything less than your whole-hearted embracing of 'honoring all' as an expression of YOU - it will not honor *you*.

Does It Make Your Heart Sing?

How can you go about making that choice? My favorite way of ascertaining if a choice resonates within me is to ask, "Does it make my heart sing?"

But simply asking the question requires that I pause and check for the answer. I may have to gather more information, do some research into alternative points-of-view, etc. Ultimately, no matter what information I find, (especially if it is ambiguous), the answer is *my* choice. So I check within to see…

- If the answer is accompanied by a feeling of lightness and joy
- If I feel a sense of both expansion and inclusion
- If the answer opens up a field of possibilities in life
- If the answer is a resounding, "YES!" in capital letters, then my choice is made.

Don't do it out of fear, do it out of "YES!" Do it precisely *because* it resonates with Who You Are. Do it because you can't possibly *not* do it. Because when honoring all life - you honor yourself by expressing the fundamental magnificence at the core of your BEing.

A Short Cut

To display the lantern of soul in shadowy times like these -- to be fierce and to show mercy toward others, both, are acts of immense bravery and greatest necessity. Struggling souls catch light from other souls who are fully lit and willing to show it.

Clarissa Pinkola Estes, Ph.D.

If you are like most of us, you lead an extremely busy life, often feeling pulled in multiple directions at once. Within that experience, we are asked to make instant decisions that have potentially long-range consequences. I call those moments, "Choice-Points." In the best of all worlds, it would be wonderful to be able to pause for a moment, take a deep breath, and go deeply within before making a decision at each Choice-Point. Yet we often perceive that luxury as not available.

I wanted to find a sort of "short cut" method of decision making that allowed me to meet Choice-Points in my life with decisions that honored the deepest part of my Inner Being.

We each experience our Inner Being in those moments when all of life seems to vibrate as interconnected and unconditionally loving. Whenever I make decisions from that place, the result is always deeply joyful and fulfilling.

By asking the question, "How can I honor all life?" this book hopes to offer that short-cut tool. It proposes that by simply answering this question, we can more consciously begin to think and act *from* our Inner Being – our Essential Self. Here's how it works for me...

When I explore "honoring all," I am automatically forced to examine if my choice honors:

- Myself – does it resonate deeply with my inner truth?
- Others – does it come from a place of non-judgmental acceptance?
- Aliveness – does it support the experience of expansion and openness we feel when vibrantly alive?
- All Life – does it promote life in all its diverse and interconnected expressions, not just now, but for many future generations as well?

If so, then my decision will resonate with who I know myself to be. The criteria above are mine. I invite you to find your own.

Ultimately, the greatest gift that the practice of "honoring all life" can offer is the ability to live life's day-to-day moments *from* our innermost Being – that magnificent source of connection with All-That-Is that we all carry within.

Revolutionary change does not come as one cataclysmic moment (beware of such moments!) but as an endless succession of surprises, moving zigzag toward a more decent society. We don't have to engage in grand, heroic actions to participate in the process of change. Small acts, when multiplied by millions of people, can transform the world.

Howard Zinn

PART ONE-PERCEPTION

Our subjective senses perceive only what we allow them to perceive.
We can choose - through intention - the quality and depth
of our perceptual experience.

PART ONE – PERCEPTION

Before we can explore *what* is possible, we need to know *how* we determine the scope of the possible. This section explores the process of perception. It also explores some of the most vibrant perceptual filters we humans use in the course of making decisions. Since those filters determine our experience of reality, their understanding is essential to the process of making intelligent choices. Each chapter will offer a different veil, or filter, through which we can perceive our world. Some of them may be quite new, and will stretch your sense of the possible.

Seeing Symbols

When I teach art classes to children, even the youngest children in my classes mistake the symbol of a tree for the tree itself. If I sit my students in front of a conifer and ask them to draw, they almost always draw a large triangle with a rectangle at the bottom center. When I ask them to point to the triangle in the live tree, their jaws usually drop in surprise, so certain are they that trees consist of large triangles. In a similar manner, we all bring our life experiences, judgments, thoughts, and beliefs to our perceptual experiences.

I remember one day when my daughter showed me page after page of instructions she received from school on "how to draw *a* nose, how to draw *a* mouth, etc." I felt shock as I suddenly realized that this is the legacy we hand down to each generation of children – **we teach them to see the symbols of things *instead of the actual things themselves*.** Even though seeing symbols can be highly useful and is definitely necessary for survival; the *exclusive* use of this type of perception can also keep us from seeing what stands before our eyes. Have we unwittingly created a world in which children grow to be adults - all carefully taught *not to see*? No wonder there is so much conflict in the world!

It's time to take a much closer look at the process of perception. Most of us take our senses for granted, figuring that we can perceive just fine, thank you very much. We dismiss the need or desire to understand the process and to explore perceptual options as unnecessary for survival. Yet experience has taught me just the opposite. On a survival basis alone, our need to re-perceive our world and our role within life on Earth has never been greater.

How would we have designed our world if we had been encouraged from a very early age to perceive fully, to constantly explore deeper experiences of perception, and to honor each person's unique perceptual experience?

Some first-nation languages have over twenty words to describe nuances of a certain color. What if all languages contained such highly descriptive words to match our unique perceptions - words that fleshed out form, texture, value, tone, their relationships, and any number of other subtleties?

Part One of this book consists of a deep exploration of perception, perceptual filters, and several ways of perceiving that literally shift our experience to such a degree that reality alters dramatically. As you read, imagine how you would design economic, societal, agricultural, educational, and legal systems *through* each perceptual filter. How would that change our world?

Perception is participation. The more we perceive, the more we participate. The more we participate, the more we are connected. With connection comes caring.

Adam Wolpert,
Painting is practice
from Ode Magazine ssue 14, originally from Resurgence (March/April 2004),
www.adamwolpert.com

We see what we believe and accept that we ourselves are. The qualities of gratitude, thankfulness, gentleness, and appreciation are themselves powerfully transforming. Our experience of the world and life is totally the result of inner beliefs and positionalities.

Dr. David R. Hawkins,
The Eye of the I,
page 228.

1

<u>PERCEPTION</u>

My Mother-In-Law & My Wife by W.E. Hill 1915

The ability to perceive or think differently
is more important than the knowledge gained.
Dr. David Bohm
Physicist

PERCEPTION

Empathic Seeing – the ability to perceive the breadth, depth, and infinite possibilities of life - is the invitation to see All Life in the same way that we look into the eyes of our Beloved.

I received an e-mail recently. It told the story of two men in a hospital room, both seriously ill. One had the bed next to a window and the other's bed was on the opposite side of the room. He couldn't sit up and had no hope of seeing out the window.

The man near the window was allowed to sit up once a day for an hour to drain the liquid from his lungs. Every time he was allowed to sit up, he would pass the time by describing all the things outside the window to his roommate. It became their shared ritual, and the other man eagerly anticipated it with joy.

After many weeks, the man at the window peacefully died. The other man asked to be moved to the bed by the window. Once there, he managed to prop himself up high enough to see out. The window faced a blank wall.

When he asked the nurse what could have compelled his friend to make up such detailed stories, she told him that the man was blind and could not even see the wall.

This e-mail illustrates the power of perception. Both men created their world based on what they were *willing* to perceive. The blind man realized that the power to perceive reality in a way that brought him joy *was his own choice.* Isn't this true for all of us?

Holistic Perception

If the two men in the story had a choice about how they perceived reality, what choices are we making right now that limit or expand our perceptual awareness? A willingness to constantly expand perceptual awareness and to move from a narrow focus to a more holistic perception - one that expands our circles of inclusivity - profoundly changes our perceptual options.

I give a workshop series called The Power of Perception, in which we explore this new perceptual world. I like to call this holistic perception Empathic Seeing, or Seeing From the Heart, because the process of expanding perception requires empathy – an intentional openness or willingness to be aware of and sensitive to, the feelings, thoughts, and experience of another.

It includes all possible sensory input, and can only be explored through the willingness to first identify and then see beyond our perceptual filters – the concepts, thoughts, beliefs, and judgments through which we perceive.

How do we Perceive?

Our understanding of the complex process of visual perception is still minimal, but scientists understand there are two basic types of visual information being processed at any given time. They are simply called the "What" and "Where" systems, as described below:

> The more primitive half of the visual system begins with large ganglions having big, bushy, dendritic arbors. This part perceives motion, depth, and spatial organization. Known as the Where system, it is colorblind but keenly sensitive to small differences in brightness. We share

the Where system with other mammals, but only primates have evolved the more refined What system. The What system starts with smaller ganglion cells. It sees color well but not contrast. It has vision that is three times sharper than the Where system. Both systems cover the entire visual field. The Where system sees a person moving toward us; the What system tells us it is Aunt Emily. The Where system sees the forest; the What system sees the trees.[1]

But what do we do with the information obtained through the What and Where systems? How do we process it? There are many theories on the reliability of sensual input, but we still have a long way to go before we fully understand what happens. Scientists ask not only what and how we *receive* information, but also how we *process* that information once it is received. In other words, what do we *allow* ourselves to perceive? We know that one function, very obviously, is to perceive biologically useful information – that which aids our survival. Yet what other criteria do we use to assess what is useful information worthy of our attention?

Attention

Our ability to process perceptual input is directly related to our perceptual filters. I have witnessed as many perceptual filters as there are moments in the day, for our filters are always evolving to match our experiences. This constantly flowing process provides us with the opportunity to shift our perceptions at any moment.

I have dedicated much of the last few years to exploring and stretching beyond my own perceptual filters into greater possibilities. The workshop I give offers a hands-on exploration of that process, and it is always an honor to witness our unfolding awareness of what initially seems so mundane and unworthy of further exploration. In fact, when I tell others that I give a workshop on how we perceive, often the reply is "Why?" Most people assume they perceive just fine, and see no reason to pursue the matter any further. They are not aware of perceptual filters, so they see no reason to give the *quality* of their perception much attention.

Interestingly, studies by Arien Mack and Irvin Rock, detailed in their book, Inattentional Blindness, gives evidence that perception *requires* attention. They write:

> The interim conclusion we reached was that the perception of shape, unlike the perception of motion, color, location, and numerosity, requires attention… The consistency of this result made it difficult to ignore, and before long it was clear that it was a highly predictable, robust phenomenon, which was potentially of great theoretical significance... we labeled this phenomenon inattentional blindness (IB)…

> The discovery of IB raised serious questions about whether in fact anything at all is perceived without attention and ultimately led us to adopt the working hypothesis that there is no perception without attention… but it is essential to bear in mind at the outset that the term perception here refers to explicit conscious awareness and is to be distinguished from what is referred to as subliminal, unconscious, or implicit perception, that is, perception without awareness. Thus the hypothesis that we believe the evidence presented in this book supports is that there is no conscious perception without attention.[2]

Further studies using tactile and auditory stimulus showed a similar affect. They summarize:

> Subjects reported that they did not hear a tone or a word that was presented to one ear while they carried out a version of a shadowing task with stimulation in the other ear. Similarly, subjects were unaware of a puff of air delivered to one forearm while they were attempting to report what letter was being written upon the other. In both these cases, subjects had no difficulty localizing and describing the unexperienced stimulus under conditions of both full and divided attention.

Man can learn nothing except by going from the known to the unknown.

Claude Bernard

When the criticalness and discrimination of dualistic perception are set aside, the absolute perfection and beauty of everything stands revealed.

Dr. David R. Hawkins
The Eye of the I, *page 9*

19

It's true that we evolve our technology as we understand more, but our understanding of life has been limited by the pretense that nature is complex machinery. We have failed to investigate living systems in their own right, without the assumption that they are mechanical, until very recently. For example, we used to think the brain functioned like an input-output plumbing system -- a system of pipes and valves in which things got jammed up and had to be released and flushed: the Freudian model of the brain. Then we invented the telephone and suddenly the brain was a telephone system. The neurons were wires relaying the messages down the wires, and things like that. Then we invented the computer and, lo and behold, the brain became a computer. Then it became a holographic camera and projector. Then we invented parallel processing. So the brain became a parallel processor. In other words, as technology comes closer to emulating our observation of life, we continue to project the latest technology onto life itself, ever confusing our models with natural reality.

Elisabet Sahtouris, Living Systems, the Internet and the Human Future Talk presented 13 May 2000 at Planetwork, Global Ecology and Information Technology Conference held at the San Francisco Presidio

These data, which must be considered preliminary, suggest that attention may be necessary for perception in all sensory modalities. [2]

This is a significant finding. It supports the The Power of Perception workshop experience. Not surprisingly, participants notice there is a direct correlation between their level of awareness and the focus of their attention.

The quality of our perceptual exploration determines everything about how we perceive reality, and thus how we determine our actions in the world. A diagram of this relationship and how it affects our sense of reality is illustrated below:

The Spiral of Perception

We determine our unique sense of reality through our perceptions.

All perceptions are filtered through these beliefs, concepts, and judgments.

We create beliefs, concepts, and judgments based on our experience of that uniquely filtered reality.

This process is described as a spiral because it builds upon itself. We constantly change our perceptual filters based on our unique experience. Those perceptual filters, in turn, determine what we *allow* ourselves to experience in each situation. How can we begin to speak a common language about a shared experience when we each perceive uniquely? How can we bridge the perceptual gap between your experience and mine?

The answer seems obvious. If we can each discover our own filtering process, then we would be free to change it in any way we chose.

Types of Awareness

Even though our perceptual filters determine our level of awareness, these are areas of exploration for which there seems to be little vocabulary. I was therefore thrilled to find the work of Dr. Claus Otto Scharmer, co-founder of both the MIT Leadership Lab and the Global Institute for Responsible Leadership. He describes three levels of awareness involved in what he calls "presencing," a word he created by combining "pre-sensing" and "presence," meaning to "pre-sense and bring into presence one's highest future potential." The potential to activate this capacity is an innate capability of every human being and social system. In his draft paper entitled, Presencing: Illuminating the Blind Spot of Leadership, Dr. Scharmer describes this process of presencing as follows:

> The U-process of presencing involves moving through three fundamentally different gestures of awareness:
>
> • opening up to the world outside: becoming one with the world (sensing),

- opening up to the world inside: becoming one with one's deepest source of future potential (presencing),
- and bringing the future potential into reality (actualizing).
- Whenever I have seen a group going through the deep process of presencing—that is, shifting the place of operating to their deepest source of creativity—three things happenfrom an experiential point of view:
- a transformation of social space: decentering and collapsing social boundaries;
- a transformation of social time: slowing down to stillness; and
- a transformation of self: collapsing the boundaries of the ego ("self") and bringing into reality one's highest future potential ("Self"). [3]

Presencing, as described, is also a beautiful description of what is meant by "honoring," both the self and the creative potential of a group (described in more detail in the chapter on Co-creating). This act of opening to an infinite field of self-possibilities (presencing) and then consciously choosing, what Scharmer calls "bringing the future potential into reality *(actualizing)*," is the intended outcome of honoring all. As he so aptly points out, the process involves a deep sensing, both of what we commonly call the "exterior" and our "interior" worlds.

I love the way he describes sensing as "becoming one with the world," because that is exactly what is necessary to fully sense anything – you must open to the point of merging. To do so, you must also be willing to open to your Self – your essential or core BEing found at the still-point of all experience. When one is willing to make this journey, to open fully to both exterior sensation and interior BEing, a profound shift in reality potential occurs. Not only are perceptual filters revealed, but on the sensory level, possibilities arise that were previously closed to our awareness – an expansion of perceptual experience from symbolic to holistic-perception.

Seeing without Eyes

As difficult as it is for those of us with functioning eyes to perceive fully, there is growing evidence that perhaps eyes aren't even necessary for vision to take place. Jacques Lusseyran was a blind French resistance fighter in World War II who lost his vision at age eight. He wrote many books about his experiences of "seeing:"

The limits of the possible can only be defined by going beyond them into the impossible.

Arthur C. Clarke

> The light I saw changed with my inner condition. ...The true changes depended on the state of my soul. When I was sad, when I was afraid, all shades became dark and all forms indistinct. When I was joyous and attentive, all pictures became light. Anger, remorse, plunged everything into darkness. A magnanimous resolution, a courageous decision, radiated a beam of light. By and by I learned to understand that love meant seeing and that hate was night.

> I had the same experience with space. When I became blind, I found out that an inner space existed. This space also changed its dimensions in accordance with the condition of my soul. Sadness, hate, or fear not only darkened my universe, but also made it smaller. The number of objects I could encompass within myself with one glance decreased. In the truest sense of the word, I knocked against everything. Objects and beings became obstacles within myself. Outwardly I could not avoid running against doors and furniture. I was punished very thoroughly and very quickly.

> Conversely, however, courage, attention, joy, had the immediate effect of opening up and illuminating space. Soon everything existed in me abundantly: a great many objects, pictures, beings. .. At the same time, my physical adroitness increased; I found my way and moved with assurance. In short, there were two possibilities: to reject the world – and that meant darkness, reversals – or to accept it, and that meant light and strength. [4]

We are endowed with five senses and more: we have sensory nerves which make us aware of the body position and movement in relation to a space (kinaesthesia); we have thermal receptors which register warmth and cold; we have visible and involuntary micro-muscular responses that psychologists have recorded when we watch sports or look at paintings, (haptic muscular sensitivity); a 'third eye' (intuition) and much else. It is in the interaction of all our senses that we can begin to really see – to experience.

Victor Papanek
The Green Imperative,
Natural Design
for the Real World
page 76

Lusseyran is offering us clues to an expanded experience of perception. Evidently his experience isn't unique amongst the blind. More recently, a blind Turkish artist name Esref Armagan, visited the United States to undergo a series of tests to see how he is able to paint two-dimensional representations of three-dimensional objects so well that sighted people easily recognize them.[5]

John Kennedy, a psychologist at the University of Toronto, tested Armagan in various ways. He had him feel a solid cube, cone, and ball. Then he asked the artist to draw them as though he were sitting at various positions in relation to the objects. He was also asked to draw two rows of glasses, extending off into the distance. This kind of spatial awareness is difficult for most sighted people to translate onto a two dimensional surface, and is seemingly impossible for a blind person. Yet Armagan succeeded beautifully:

> … he asked him to draw a cube, and then to rotate it to the left, and then further to the left, Armagan drew a scene with all three cubes. Astonishingly, he drew it in three-point perspective - showing a perfect grasp of how horizontal and vertical lines converge at imaginary points in the distance. "My breath was taken away," Kennedy says. [5]

Kennedy's studies have shown that congenitally blind people can understand outline drawings just like sighted people do. They can understand and draw in three dimensions. He has even shown that blind children can learn to draw if given the opportunity. His tests with Armagan also revealed some surprises.

Armagan's brain lit up in the area of the visual cortex – where we process vision - while drawing, indicating that his brain processes the act of drawing and painting very similarly to a sighted person's act of seeing. The evidence was so strong that one researcher conjectured that a casual viewer of the brain scan would assume Armagan was sighted.

Armagan seems to have developed a "mind's eye" without physical visual input. I wonder what perceptual possibilities await us when we release any limiting beliefs about our senses?

Discovering our Senses

Since our senses provide us with most of the information from which we create our own story of reality, it is important to know what sensory input is available. We have been taught that we only have five senses, but science has identified many more.

The list below specifies only those senses that we are aware of *at this time*. The list is evolving rapidly. As we begin to expand our willingness to explore the senses, perhaps we will find that our sensory knowledge has just begun to scratch the surface of what is possible.

The satiated man and the hungry one do not see the same thing when they look upon a loaf of bread.

Jalaluddin Rumi

- **Seeing** or **Vision** The ability to detect light, which includes the reception of color (frequentcy), brightness (energy), depth, and movement.
- **Hearing** The ability to detect sound at various frequencies.
- **Taste** The ability to receive certain chemical stimuli, usually classified as sweet, salt, sour, bitter, umami (confirmed in 2000 – it detects the amino acid glutamate).
- **Smell** The ability to receive chemical stimuli through the nose. This sense is tied to taste.

- **Tactition** The ability to sense **pressure**.
- **Thermoception** The ability to sense **heat** and the absence of heat (**cold**). This is a highly complex sense. The substance of an object contributes to the sensation of heat or cold we experience. A cold piece of metal feels colder than the same temperature of wood, for example.
- **Nociception** The ability to perceive **pain**. There are thee types of pain senses: skin, joint and bone, and body organ pain.
- **Equilibrioception** The ability to perceive **balance**
- **Proprioception** The ability to be aware of your body part locations. (You can close your eyes and still know where everything is.) [6]

The following are other senses that currently are considered non-human. However I question the thoroughness of our investigation into the validity of this conclusion.

- **Electroception** The ability to detect electrical fields. Fish, sharks, rays, and platypus have demonstrated this ability. This is a strong candidate for further research, in my opinion, as many humans are becoming more aware of electronic fields and their own ability to perceive them in some way. Could this be an example of consciously removing a perceptual filter, one that says humans cannot do this?
- **Magnetoception** The ability to detect fluctuations in magnetic fields, as demonstrated most commonly by birds. This also seems to be an excellent candidate for further human research.
- **Echolocation** The ability to determine one's orientation through reflected sound. Most commonly identified in dolphins and bats, my former husband (who is blind) also demonstrated a surprising ability in this area, though not in the same way. He could easily tell where openings were located in a room simply by listening to an echo. [6]

It is the way in which we *allow* ourselves to process sensory information that determines the qualities inherent in each of our individual experiences of reality.

The same stimulus could elicit vastly different sensual experiences depending upon the manner in which the person *receiving* the stimulus accepts it into his/her world. For example, during childbirth I noticed that if I called the strong stimulus rolling like an unleashed volcanic eruption through my body by the word "pain", it was strongly painful. However, when I referred to it as a "stimulus," without attaching a descriptive adjective to how I perceived the experience, it became much more tolerable and I was able to ride it like a surfer rides a wave. Could this be true of all life's experiences?

Labels and Language

We humans seem to enjoy classifying and labeling everything. This process can be both beneficial and limiting depending on its use. One very common use of labels helps us identify our environment so that we can then focus our attention on what seems important. For example, once I conclude that the cylindrical object on the table is a cup, I cease seeing the object. I now see a symbol, "cup", instead of the object itself. This type of labeling, while simplifying life, also keeps us from seeing deeply into whatever we are perceiving. When we stop this habit long enough to allow each sensual experience to simply BE what it is, received in the fullness of the

I've noticed that to look outside yourself is to look inside yourself… When you look deeply into the natural world you look deeply into yourself— when you describe nature, you describe yourself.

We create the world with our senses as much as it makes us.

Adam Wolpert,
Painting is practice

from Ode Magazine issue 14, originally from Resurgence (March/April 2004), www.adamwolpert.com

WORD WISDOM:
You are what you speak

Deep in the Amazon, a tribe lived in a shadowy light of the forest ceiling. The anthropologist who was studying them discovered they didn't have a word for the color red.

If the hue was closer to purple that is what it was called. If it was closer to orange, that is what it was called.

Like any good modernist, ever on the lookout for how to alter an indigenous culture as quickly as possible, this researcher created a word for the color red that the tribe's member could use.

Once they had this new word, suddenly they saw a new color.

A new word created a new perception.

Mikela and Philip Tarlow Authors of Digital Aboriginal… from their Newsletter Shape Shifter News – Volume One

October 20, 2002

moment *without* descriptive (and therefore instantly limiting) labeling, the opportunity for a richer experience unfolds.

A second use for labeling is outlined by Diane Ackerman in her book, A Natural History of the Senses. She reveals that even though most humans can identify between 150 and 200 colors, many languages have developed very few words to describe those colors. For example, until very recently the Japanese language used the word "aoi" to describe the range of colors between green and violet. She states,

> Primitive languages first develop words for black and white, then add red, then yellow and green; many lump blue and green together, and some don't bother distinguishing between other colors of the spectrum.[7]

I wonder if this means they simply are not labeling the colors they see, or does it mean they haven't *allowed* themselves to see them?

Further on, she suggests that even English, overflowing – by comparison – with color words, could use a more detailed palette of words to really honor the glory of our sensory world. For example, she writes:

> We need to follow the example of the Maori of New Zealand, who have many words for red – all the reds that surge and pale as fruits and flowers develop, as blood flows and dries. We need to boost our range of greens to describe the almost squash-yellow green of late winter grass, the achingly fluorescent green of the leaves in high summer, and all the whims of chlorophyll in between. We need words for the many colors of clouds, surging from pearly pink during a calm sunset over the ocean to the electric gray-green of tornadoes. We need to rejuvenate our brown words for all the complexions of bark. And we need cooperative words to help refine colors, which change when they're hit by glare, rinsed with artificial light, saturated with pure pigment, or gently bathed in moonlight.[8]

In this type of labeling, the precision and careful nuance of meaning demands a closer more refined focus of attention on the object described for both the user and listener. And isn't that what we are seeking here… a deeper and richer experience of life?

Empathic Seeing

Empathic Seeing is the *intention* to honestly see beyond the surface to the deeper totality of being expressed, *without judgment*. It encourages you to be open and see beyond the obvious – to use both your interior and exterior vision. It is always a choice.

I use the word "empathic" because it honors the fact that we do not live in an observable world, but instead impact everything with which we interact. In a sense, it can be said that we empathically join and become one with whatever we perceive to the point that the distinction between observer and observed melts away.

Here is an example. When I paint a portrait, I loose my "self" (my identity) in the process. When looking at the finished painting, I cannot in all honesty, separate what part of the finished painting is me and what part is the sitter. From one standpoint you could argue that the finished painting is technically *all* me, because I took the image of the sitter as I saw it filtered through my perceptual filters, and then produced a recognizable image on the canvas.

"Looking at an object feels simple,: says Jacopo Annese, a neuroscientist at the Laboratory of Neuro Imaging at UCLA. "But the brain is processing very complex information in parallel." The image is broken down into information about color, form, and orientation by segregated modules in the visual cortex. The resulting output is sent along to specialized areas that analyze the components and interpret more comprehensive aspects of the image. "In the old days, people said the brain is like a computer," says Arthur Toga, the lab's director. "I'd say no. Images get decomposed and then recomposed. It's very distributed, closer to the Internet."

James Shreeve
The Blink of an Eye section of Beyond the Brain - The Mind is What the Brain Does
from
National Geographic
March 2005

I have never failed to fall in love with the subject of anything I am painting. I've even tried painting when I was angry with the subject, and yet by the time the painting was finished, I was in love with that person. Why is this?

There is something very invasive about viewing anything with the intention to see it as deeply and completely as possible. It is as if the subject has given me permission to see into his total being. I believe that permission creates an opening that allows our energies to merge. It does not matter if the subject of my attention is alive or what we call 'inanimate". Everything is energy; and from my own personal experience, everything is alive with the energy of life.

Empathic seeing consists mainly of acutely focused attention on levels or depths of awareness. By their very nature these experiments cannot rely on traditional Newtonian scientific methods that recognize only certain kinds of empirical data. However quantum physics is beginning to offer substantial scientific support for these ideas. String theory, among others, suggests that everything in our universe is simply energy expressing. How difficult, then, is the concept of one energy expression merging with another? In <u>The Holographic Universe,</u> Michael Talbot presents a strong argument that our brains, our bodies, and in fact the *entire* universe operates holographically. Talbot states:

> In a universe in which the consciousness of a physicist affects the reality of a subatomic particle, the attitude of a doctor affects whether or not a placebo works, the mind of an experimenter affects the way a machine operates, and the imaginal can spill over into physical reality, we can no longer pretend that we are separate from that which we are studying. In a holographic and omnijective universe, a universe in which all things are part of a seamless continuum, strict objectivity ceases to be possible. [9]

Omote and Ura

This was elegantly expressed by Tachi Kiuchi when he described his perceptual transformation regarding rainforests and all life:

> In Japan, we have two terms to describe this: *omote* and *ura*.
> *Omote* is the surface or front of an object, *ura* is its back or invisible side.
> *Omote* and *ura* . External reality and underlying reality.[10]

Empathic Seeing includes both omote *and* ura, in a way that everyday vision doesn't. Peter Russell describes the profundity of this awareness in <u>Reality and Consciousness: Turning the Superparadigm Inside Out</u> , in which he writes:

> We tacitly assume that things are as they appear, and that we are experiencing the world as it is. We think that the tree we see is the tree in itself.

> When we realize that they are not the same thing at all, but are very different indeed, a revolutionary new model of reality emerges. Space, time and matter fall from their absolute status, to be replaced by light in the physical realm, and by consciousness (the inner light) in the world of experience. Instead of matter being primary, and the source of everything we know, including mind; <u>consciousness becomes primary, and the source of everything, including matter, as we know it</u>. For a second time, the universe has been turned inside out.[11]

Intention is the force that opens the door to this world of expanded possibilities. In Marshall Rosenberg's Nonviolent Communication, the *intention* to hear the feelings and needs behind the "story" or narrative of the expressions voiced; and the intention to fully understand them leads to deep connection. It is one of the most powerful ways we can honor each other... by simply *intending* to understand

Likewise, intention results in the bodily gaze being focused on the near side of an object, whereas love results in the dilation of the pupils and the eyes focus on the far side of an object or person so as to include them.

Dr. David R. Hawkins
<u>*The Eye of the I*</u>*, page 207*

In the Cheyenne language there is no "it." There is no "he" or "she," either. Third person singular is indicated by words that specify, that speak of others respectfully as "thou." These words translate roughly into something like "this one, that one." I try to imagine living within this language. No it. Always I-thou; never I-it. No inanimate or soul-less beings.

Marya Grathwohl <u>*Planetary Spirituality and Berry Picking in Northern Cheyenne Country*</u> *Timeline Magazine Nov/Dec 2003*

another's experience. The same is true of Empathic Seeing. Our intention determines the depth and quality of our experience.

Opportunities

What opportunities of choice do we possess regarding perception? More than we can imagine. Diane Ackerman's beautiful prose reveals the richness of the possible:

> People who dowse for water are probably responding to an electromagnetic sense we all share to a greater or lesser degree. Other animals, such as butterflies and whales, navigate in part by reading the earth's magnetic fields. It wouldn't surprise me to learn that we, too, have some of that magnetic awareness. We were nomads for so much of our history. We are as phototropic as plants, smitten with the sun's light, and this should be considered a sense separate from vision, with which it has little to do. Our experience of pain is quite different from the other worlds of touch. Many animals have infrared, heat-sensing, electromagnetic, and other sophisticated ways of perceiving. The praying mantis uses ultrasonics to communicate. Both the alligator and the elephant use infrasonics. The duckbill platypus swings its bill back and forth underwater, using it as an antenna to pick up electrical signals from the muscles of the crustaceans, frogs, and small fish on which it preys. The vibratory sense, so highly developed in spiders, fish, bees, and other animals, needs to be studied more in human beings.

> We have a muscular sense that guides us when we pick up objects – we know at once that they are heavy, light, solid, hard, or soft, and we can figure out how much pressure or resistance will be required. We are constantly aware of a sense of gravity, which counsels us about which way is up and how to rearrange our bodies if we're falling, or climbing, or swimming, or bent at some unusual angle. There is the proprioceptive sense, which tells us what position each component of our bodies is in at any moment in our day. If the brain didn't always know where the knees or the lungs were, it would be impossible to walk or breathe. There seems to be a complex space sense that, as we move into an era of space stations and cities and lengthy space travel, we will need to understand in detail. Prolonged Earthlessness alters our physiology and also the evidence of our senses, in part because of the rigors of being in zero gravity, and in part because of the lidless sprawl of deep space itself, in which there are few sensory handrails, guides or landmarks, and everywhere you look there is not scene but pure vista.[12]

With all these options available on which to focus our perceptual attention, the world can truly be seen as a cacophony of sensory input. Science argues that we filter our sensory input down to that which provides us with the best opportunity of survival, relying on our other sensory information only in those rare instances when necessary for survival, or through conscious choice. Yet perhaps it is the very fact that we have a choice that has been missing from our awareness. **Believing ourselves to be limited to five senses, and then drastically limiting our use of those five, has led us to narrow our perceptual experience of what we believe is possible**. It is a self-fulfilling argument in which we only perceive that which we *believe* we can perceive. But it is based on an illusion. Diane Ackerman writes,

> When scientists, philosophers, and other commentators speak of the real world, they're talking about a myth, a convenient fiction. The world is a construct the brain builds based on the sensory information it's given, and the information is only a small part of all that's available…. Physicists explain that molecules are always moving. The book in front of you is actually squirming under your fingertips. But we don't see this motion at that molecular level, because it's not evolutionarily important that we do. We're given only the sensory information crucial to our survival. [13]

If this is true, then we now stand at a wonderful moment in history. We have the opportunity to be aware of and to choose where we focus our attention and *intention*

Margin notes (left column):

I was shocked, for instance, to discover that a sighted person sitting in a lawn chair can look down and see individual blades of grass, weeds, and other plants, perhaps even crawling and hovering insects, while all I would see is an expanse of green. It might seem that this discovery would lead to sadness--what else have I been missing all these years? In fact, it has inspired a kind of perplexed wonder—what do sighted people do with all this visual detail?

Georgina Kleege
Sight Unseen

When we speak of "the material world", we think we are referring to the underlying reality, the object of our perception. In fact we are only describing our image of reality.

Matter is not to be found in the underlying reality; atoms turn out to be 99.99999999% empty space, and sub-atomic "particles" dissolve into fuzzy waves. Matter and substance seem, like space and time, to be characteristics of the phenomenon of experience.

Peter Russell
Reality and Consciousness: Turning the Superparadigm Inside Out
http://twm.co.nz/prussell.htm

regarding our sensorial input. We can choose to experience beyond what mere survival dictates.

Possibilities

As a species, we humans have made some very poor decisions regarding how we treat ourselves and our planet. In fact, in the last two hundred years our choices have been anything but survival-based. We have brought our planet to the brink of the first planet-wide mass extinction ever created through the actions of a single species. This "sixth" extinction provides us with one of several possibilities of planetary destruction. Yet it also provides us with that survival-based inspiration to look beyond our old ways of seeing, our old concepts and beliefs that have led us to this moment.

When Diane Ackerman describes the vibratory sense of the spider or the phototropic sensibility of plants, she is describing sensory possibilities long available on this planet. **We experience something much greater than our individual selves when we allow our experience to expand to the point where we resonate with *all life*,** an experience many call transformative, similar to experiencing oneself as all that is. Quantum physics tells us that there is no definable edge between one "object' and another. Could there also exist the possibility of experiencing life through all the sensory experiences available on our planet?

It is helpful to realize that nothing can be described or experienced except from outside itself. All descriptions, no matter how elegant, are nothing more than perceptual measurements and definitions of imputed qualities which have no self-existence. Nothing is as it can be described; therefore, all descriptions are of what a thing is not.

David R. Hawkins
The Eye of the I, page 109

When you think about the shared commonality of all Earthly matter, which is estimated to be far greater than any differences between us, this concept is not so far-fetched. Theories from holographic explanations of life to the idea that *all* perception is vibratory, are being actively investigated by science. With so many possible explanations of how we perceive and *what* we perceive, we humans have the opportunity to perceive our world as we have never done before. Perhaps a willingness to open our perceptual experience of life – and hence reality – is one of the greatest gifts we can give ourselves. It requires humility – as in a sense of "not-knowing" - and both an open heart and mind.

It also requires a willingness to be tender with yourself. Just like the fish whose sense of reality is completely altered when he finally sees water for the first time, seeing your own perceptual filters – especially those upon which you have based your life assumptions – can be extremely jarring. As the waves of realization wash over you, please be *unconditionally* loving with yourself. You will have just stepped beyond your customary level of consciousness into a new frontier. Everything will look different, similar to the way removing dark glasses suddenly makes all life look brighter.

So it comes down to this. I am free to decide how much of life's banquet of sensory experiences I am willing to receive. In this realm we are all pioneers. If we throw out the theory that life's experience – and hence what we call reality – is only determined by a limited use of our traditional five senses, we open the doors to uncharted territories. Are you willing to begin this exploration together with me? It is the essence of Empathic Seeing.

There is one more thought I wish to share. We have spent the last several millennia focused on religious beliefs that usher us away from our physical experience, promising "heaven" if only we deny "Earthly pleasure" for the promise of spiritual rewards. Yet my experience has been just the opposite.

When I allow myself to open my sensory experience, I also allow myself to share in an experience of physical reality that goes beyond anything I've experienced when focused only on our traditional five senses. Life comes alive in ways I never imagined. Simply opening to the possibility of experiencing the vibrations of molecules, for example, immediately alters the possibilities of my experience. Instead of seeing the physical world as a stepping stone to an after-life, I now explore the physical world as an expression of "heaven on Earth". Can you imagine a better way to honor all life? I invite you to join me in this exploration.

The following Goals and Guidelines are handouts at the The Power of Perception Workshop. They are included to offer assistance in your own journey to Empathic Seeing. If you wish to find out more about the workshop, go to www.HonoringAllLife.org.

The Power of Perception^(SM) Goals

No human has ever had a direct (real) experience except in the eternally present Now moment; all the rest can only be stories that weave particular and more general past experience into the present.

Elizabet Sahtouris,

A Tentative Model for a Living Universe - Part One

Connect with yourself, such that you access your own feelings and motivations. They are the filters through which you perceive. Once you are aware of them, the possibility exists to let go, open, and choose how you intend to experience life. To do so, you must be willing to allow your sense of perception to expand beyond your present beliefs of what is possible. Those beliefs keep your sensory experience limited to the confirmation of what you perceive as your limits. For example, if you believe that those who claim to see auras are charlatans, you will not allow yourself to see auras even though your senses may actually perceive them. Let go of your conceptions of what is possible, and simply allow yourself to be open to the possibilities of life. What you experience then becomes a function of what you are willing to experience.

Connect with your subject. Regardless of whether your subject is considered "animate" or "inanimate", the possibility exists of joining and exploring your energies. This is an invitation to experience life's energy in a new way. When you allow yourself to merge or connect energetically with a subject, you access worlds of information beyond those perceived traditionally alone. Your willingness to do so opens the door.

Be fully present with your subject. When you open fully and place your complete awareness on your subject in this present moment, you can experience an exchange of energy. And when that merging occurs, you become One. The energy experienced is as much your own energy as that of the subject.

Trust the experience. As you open to deeper sensory perception, you will find that your subjective experience does not always match that of others. Honor yourself by trusting your experience. Honor the experience of others by fully understanding the subjective nature of perception.

Enjoy the connection. With the acknowledgment of how little we know, comes the willingness to open and learn. When your focus holds the intention of accessing and grokking all that is available in life, you open to a deeper experience of reality.

With practice, Empathic Seeing becomes not only comfortable, but a natural, fulfilling, and enjoyable way of perceiving life.

The Power of Perception(SM) Guidelines

- **You see what you intend to see.** As in all life, what we focus on is what we get.
- **The intention to connect builds trust.** Most people can tell when someone is looking at them with an open and loving intention, a desire to know more about them, to connect. The more open you are, the more revealing your subject will be. Transparency creates trust.
- **The attitude of "Not-Knowing" allows greater perception.** If you already think you know about something, you bring all those pre-conceived thoughts to your experience. They can keep you from seeing what is really going on. Try to remember how selective and subjective perception truly is. Allow yourself to experience a state of "not-knowing." At the same time, this "not-knowing" can open your heart to the "field of possibilities" that is the expression of *all* life. Your "opening" allows access to that field of KNOWINGNESS that is experienced beyond the limited scope of scientific proof.
- **Honesty creates connection.** The more honest you are about what you perceive, the more you open to seeing deeper. It is as if you go from initially seeing only 'omote', the surface; to seeing deeply within, or 'ura' – the "field of possibility" that is the totality of what your subject. Yet because it is you doing the looking, it is very much your "field of possibilities" (what you are willing to allow) that you see as you gaze at another. Becoming aware of your filters provides the opportunity of seeing without them. It requires your full presence in this moment of now.
- **People who cannot see something simply have not learned to see.** Often when things are pointed out, they exclaim in surprise and wonder how they failed to see it before. As young children we revel in awe at the wonder of life. It seems we can see all of its magic and glory. Yet as we age, we often learn to selectively see. As a result, seeing openly and empathically must sometimes be relearned in adulthood.
- **There is always more to perceive than you are yet perceiving.** As we learn more about the selectivity of perception, we become keenly aware that there is always more to perceive, far more than just through the traditional five senses and the conditioned way we allow ourselves to use them.

Love starts out as conditional and a feeling state, but it progresses. It becomes apparent that love is a way of seeing, experiencing, and interpreting life. Later, it becomes apparent that it is a state of being.

Life itself becomes the expression of love, and that love is the way to realizing that one's life is love. In the final realization, the divinity of love transforms perception into spiritual vision, and the presence of God as All That Is becomes self-revealing. All existence radiates forth the divinity of its essence as creation, which is the manifestation of the love of God.

Dr. David R. Hawkins, The Eye of the I, page 225.

Notes

1. Carol Cruzan Morton, <u>Science Illuminates Art - Dual Nature of Seeing Accounts for Brain's Double Take on Visual World</u> FOCUS May 17, 2002, http://focus.hms.harvard.edu/2002/May17_2002/neurobiology.html This article is a review of the book, <u>Vision and Art: The biology of Seeing,</u> by Margaret Livingston, Harvard Medical School Professor of Neurobiology.

2. <u>Inattentional Blindness – An Overview</u> By Arien Mack & Irvin Rock, Arien Mack Department of Psychology, New School for Social Research, USA, and Irvin Rock, Department of Psychology, University of California, Berkeley USA, Copyright I MIT 1998 http://psyche.cs.monash.edu.au/v5/psyche-5-03-mack.html

3. Dr. Claus Otto Scharmer, Presencing: Illuminating the Blind Spot of Leadership, (http://www.generonconsulting.com/Publications/PresencingIntro.pdf) A draft paper.

4. From <u>What One Sees Without Eyes</u>, selected writings of Jacques Lusseyran, © 1999 by Parabola Books, published in the UK by Floris Books.

5. Alison Motluk, <u>Senses special: The art of seeing without sight</u> (http://www.newscientist.com/channel/being-human/mg18524841.700) 29 January 2005 from <u>New Scientist</u> magazine, Print Edition, issue 2484, 29 January 2005, page 37. (When drawing, he creates raised lines on paper, allowing him to feel his way through the experience.)
To view Armagan's art see http://www.anatolia.com/anatolia/Gallery/armagan/room2/esref98_3.htm.

6. http://en.wikipedia.org/wiki/Senses The information included was inspired by Wikipedia and other sources, but not directly quoted. I urge further use of this wonderful resource.

7. <u>A Natural History of the Senses</u>, Diane Ackerman, Vintage Books, Random House, 1991, page 253.

8. IBID, page 253

9. Talbot, Michael *The Holographic Universe.* Page 297. New York: HarperCollins Publishers, 1991.

10. Kiuchi, Tachi *Keynote address to the World Future Society* July 19, 1997. At the time of this speech Kiuchi was the Managing Director of Mitsubishi Electric Corporation, General Manager of Global Communications, Former Chairman and CEO of Mitsubishi Electric America. His entire speech was a remarkable exploration of systems theory and perception entitled, "What I learned from the Rainforest".

11. Peter Russell,<u>Reality and Consciousness: Turning the Superparadigm Inside Out</u> http://twm.co.nz/prussell.htm

12. Ackerman, Diane *A Natural History of the Senses.* Page 302. New York: Vintage Books, 1991.

13. Ibid. Page 304

14. Fritjof Capra, <u>The Web of Life – A New Scientific Understanding of Living</u> Systems, page 28 and 30.

15. <u>The Ethics of Interdependence -An interview with H.H. the Dalai Lama,</u> Copyright © 1998-2004 What Is Enlightenment? Press. All rights reserved. FROM: http://www.wie.org/j24/DalaiLama.asp

16. Riane Eisler, <u>Sacred Pleasure – Sex, Myth, and the Politics of the Body – New Paths to Power and Love</u>, Harper Collins Publishers 1995. The entire book.

2

<u>BEAUTY</u>

Beauty, then, is not a fact.
It is not something you either have or don't have.
Beauty is a state of being...
It is the intentional process of choosing to perceive Beauty.

BEAUTY

When humans allow themselves to
release all judgments
regarding how things should
look, act, feel, and be,
Then the opportunity arises
to see the light
emanating from the depths of form,
the essence of the being perceived.
It is this vibratory awareness,
This radiant light energy
That stands as the essence of beauty.

And when the perceiver looks deeply
into the perceived
At the core of perception
beyond form, beyond concept,
Stands the context that holds
them both…
Like a mirror it reflects back into
the eyes of the perceiver
All that s/he allows to be perceived.

Thus the act of perceiving anything
Takes place only through the
permission of the perceiver —
Who determines what is allowed,
and who determines the level of
awareness possible.

Who then is perceiving
and what is perceived?

At the core of perception,
Perceiver and perceived are One.

This then, is the secret of beauty…
To see all from the choice of beauty
To pre-conceive that the beauty
within oneself
Is reflected in the beauty of
All That Is.

To see the world as beauty
Simply because it reflects the love
that is the essence of All.
Beauty, then, is not a fact.
It is not something you either have
or don't have.
Beauty is a state of being…
It is the intentional process of
choosing to perceive Beauty.

When you allow yourself to
experience beauty as the love that
holds the very molecules together,
That IS all,
When you allow yourself to
BE that beauty,
Then you allow your awareness to
perceive the same
in all that is perceived.

Then the dance of the
perceiver and perceived
Comes full circle,
The Mirror's surface
reflects the reflection,
And the circle is complete.

3

SEEING THE WHOLE
Systems Theory

General system theory, therefore, is a general science of "wholeness..."

The meaning of the somewhat mystical expression,

"The whole is more that the sum of its parts"

is simply that constitutive characteristics are not explainable

from the characteristics of the isolated parts.

The characteristics of the complex, therefore, appear as "new" or "emergent"

Ludwig von Bertalanffy
Biologist, founder of General System Theory

Seeing the Whole: Systems Theory

A Holistic perception of life...

System dynamics is a set of techniques for thinking and computer modeling that helps its practitioners begin to understand complex systems—systems such as the human body or the national economy or the earth's climate. Systems tools help us keep track of multiple interconnections; they help us see things whole. Because much of conventional wisdom comes from seeing things in parts and focusing on one small part at a time, system dynamicists tend to have surprising points of view.

Donella H. Meadows
System Dynamics Meets the Press The Global Citizen, 1991

While perceptual filters can block our ability to perceive more fully, they can also offer us new ways to view life that expand our sense of the possible.

As mentioned earlier, we have traditionally been taught to see objects. We see a chair or a cup and believe we know each item clearly. Yet there is another way of perceiving that sees the chair as a part of a larger whole, less of an object and more as a *flow* or *process.*

In simplest terms, imagine drawing the chair. You could draw the legs and the complex pattern they make on a flat piece of paper, or you could choose to focus on the space *between* the legs, thereby defining the legs by defining their *interaction* with their environment. This comes very close to defining Systems Theory, except that Systems Theory embraces more than just the relationship between the chair and the space surrounding it.

Imagine that you could also see the molecular interaction between the chair, the table, the person sitting in the chair; the pressure of the chair on the floor; the air pressure, heat, and energy interaction of the chair and its environment; the electron clouds around the nucleus of each atom of every item named and their interaction, etc. In short, focus on the *systems* interacting instead of the objects.

When you focus on the systems, you begin to see the multiple systems involved and their processes. You see, for example, the entire lifecycle of the chair – the concept, gathering of raw materials, production, marketing, sales, purchase, use, eventual breakage, recycling of materials or disposal, the eventual breakdown of the molecules into their smallest possible components, and the eventual re-cycling of those components into something else. When you do so, you move from seeing everything as separate and contained within itself to seeing everything as related and interacting, all part of concentric wholes, and all affecting each other. **Nothing is separate and isolated. From a systems perspective, *everything* matters.** Fritjof Capra explains:

> What the early systems thinkers recognized very clearly is the existence of different levels of complexity and different kinds of laws operating at each level. Indeed, the concept of "organized complexity" became the very subject of the systems approach. At each level of complexity the observed phenomena exhibit properties that do not exist at the lower level. For example, the concept of temperature, which is central to thermodynamics, is meaningless at the level of individual atoms, where the laws of quantum theory operate. Similarly, the taste of sugar is not present in the carbon, hydrogen, and oxygen atoms that constitute its components...Systems thinking is "contextual," which is the opposite of analytical thinking. Analysis means taking something apart in order to understand it; systems thinking means putting it into the context of a larger whole.[1]

This perceptual filter helps tremendously to understand the concept of honoring all. When we say ALL, we are not referring to individual items alone, or even combined; but the whole – and the whole within the whole within the whole – that is revealed through systems thinking.

This shift from focusing on objects to their relationships is being applied to all areas of life, and it is yielding surprising results. For example, Elisabet Sahtouris addressed its impact in biology at the 2000 Planetwork Conference. She cites Barbara McClintock's evidence that "DNA reorganizes itself intelligently in response to events *outside* the organism," and Eshel Ben Jacob's work that "concludes… bacteria not only alter their individual genomes intelligently but display group mind in doing so." She cleverly describes the short comings of research that concentrates solely on our traditional mechanistic filter:

> As an illustration of the failure to understand life, take the human genome project. I like to say that when they map the human genome they're going to know as much about a human body as you would know about New York City looking at its telephone directory; or as much you would know about a beautiful Peruvian hand-knit sweater if you unraveled it and measured the kinks in the yarn. Would you be able to reconstruct it from those kinks? -- from that string of kinks, from that series?

> By the way, the only part of the DNA that scientists know anything about is the protein-coding part, and that's about three to five percent. The other ninety-five to ninety-seven percent, they don't talk about, or if they do, they often call it garbage, or junk DNA. Now, as far as I know, junk is a human invention. If you look very carefully at nature, you will not find any junk. So it likely has a lot to do with the organization and maintenance of this highly intelligent system of cells in a body. And we don't know anything about it yet. [2]

The humility of her words echo the scientists who have begun research using a systems theory perceptual filter. But what an exciting concept, to re-visit all that we have learned through the power of traditional science, adding a new layer of understanding through this simple shift of focus!

Fritjof Capra has developed five criteria for systems perception:

1. Shift from the parts to the whole. The properties of the parts can be understood only from the dynamics of the whole. In fact, ultimately there are no parts at all.
2. Shift from the structure to the process. In the new paradigm, every structure is seen as a manifestation of an underlying process.
3. Shift from objective to epistemic science. In the new paradigm, it is believed the epistemology - the understanding of the process of knowledge - has to be included explicitly in the description of natural phenomenon…
4. A shift from building to networks as a metaphor of knowledge. In the new paradigm, the metaphor of knowledge as a building is being replaced by that of the network.
5. Shift from truth to approximate descriptions. This insight is crucial to all modern science…in the new paradigm, it is recognized that all scientific concepts and theories are limited and approximate…

One of the most important insights of the new systems theory is that life and cognition are inseparable. The process of knowledge is also the process of self-organization, that is, the process of life. [3]

This last point is crucial. Instead of seeing knowledge as individual facts; in Systems Theory, knowledge is an ever-evolving process. Capra calls this a "dialog between the subject and object," which describes the process of perception beautifully! When comparing our present society, built as it was on the perceptual filter of traditional physics, to one that more closely reflects Systems Theory, Capra states:

> I believe that the world view implied by modern physics is inconsistent with our present society, which does not reflect the interrelatedness we observe in nature. To achieve such a state of dynamic balance, a radically different social and economic structure will be needed; a cultural revolution in the true sense of the word. The survival of our whole civilization may depend on whether we can bring about such a change. It will depend ultimately, on our ability to…experience the wholeness of nature and the art of living with it in harmony. [1]

In some sense man is a microcosm of the universe; therefore what man is, is a clue to the universe. We are enfolded in the universe.

Dr. David Bohm,
Physicist

According to (Harlow) Shapley,… "Air exits your nose to go right up your neighbour's nose. In everyday life we absorb atoms from the air that were once a part of birds and trees and snakes and worms, because all aerobic forms of life share that same air (aquatic life also exchanges gases that dissolve back and forth at the interface between air and water)."

Our next breaths, yours and mine, will sample the snorts, sighs, bellows, shrieks, cheers and spoken prayers of the prehistoric and historic past.

David Suzuki
The Sacred Balance,
1997, p.37
http://www3.open.uogue lph.ca/de/ideaExchange /zoo1500/cwork/unit8 /connection.html

Evidently Sahtouris and many other systems thinkers would agree with Capra. She captures the essence of this perspective when she says:

> We need to think more loosely and largely than our current paradigms. We need to think about the possibility that many other human cultures were right in perceiving a cosmic consciousness that creates itself as it goes and that is intelligent at every step of the way. We need to go way beyond asking "Is a bacterium intelligent at that lowly stage of evolution?" and ask "Are *all* bacteria and their planet Earth and our physical Universe and the entire Cosmos of material and non-material realms intelligent as a whole, as a whole intelligent unity or Oneness?"

> I believe that this is what we are finding out: that consciousness is the *source* of evolution, rather than a late product of an evolution in which dumb mud bootstrapped itself into intelligence. [2]

"Honoring ALL life" is the recognition that the process described through Systems Theory is alive in every aspect of our lives. It honors the consciousness that Sahtouris refers to as the "source of evolution" by offering a simple and feasible method of catalyzing:

- the gentle transformation of our ability to perceive - from seeing within the familiar contextual view of the world to seeing an expansion of possibilities;
- the subtle but all-pervasive shift from making choices that avoid something to making choices that create something;
- the willingness to approach all life as a student – acknowledging that there is always more to learn;
- the celebration of all life, no matter what perceptual filter you use, as alive with the divinity or intelligent ONEness that unifies us all.

A human being is part of the Whole...He experiences himself, his thoughts and feelings, as something separated from the rest...a kind of optical delusion of his consciousness. This delusion is a kind of prison for us, restricting us to our personal desires and to affection for a few persons nearest us. Our task must be to free ourselves from this prison by widening our circle of compassion to embrace all living creatures and the whole of nature in its beauty. Nobody is able to achieve this completely, but the striving for such achievement is, in itself, a part of the liberation and a foundation for inner security.

Albert Einstein
Ideas and Opinions
http://www.newciv.org/ISSS_Primer/asem10tm.html

Notes

1. Fritjof Capra, *The Web of Life – A New Scientific Understanding of Living Systems*, page 28 and 30.

2. Elisabet Sahtouris, <u>Living Systems, the Internet and the Human Future</u> Talk presented 13 May 2000 at the Planetwork, Global Ecology & Information Technology Conference held at the San Francisco Presidio

3. http://www.newciv.org/ISSS_Primer/seminare.html, from *An Inquiry at the Beginning of History* by Tom Mandel, quoting Fritjof Capra, The Role of Physics in the Current Change in Paradigms in *The World View of Contemporary Physics*. Edited by R.F. Kitchener, New York, State University of New York Press

4

PARTNERSHIP - Yin Yang Balance

We have examined the consequences incurred by the repression of the Great Mother archetype and found that many of our core emotional problems are enforced by the resulting archetypal imbalance. Our claim is that this imbalance influences, either directly or indirectly, major issues facing our world and humankind today: from global concerns such as pollution and third-world debt, to social issues such as women's rights and civil liberties; from cultural behaviors such as consumerism and violence to our relationships with others and the world at large; and finally, to our hopes for the future and our very own sense of self.

Bernard A. Lietaer and Stephen M. Belgin
Of Human Wealth – Beyond Greed and Scarcity

PARTNERSHIP

*When the goal shifts from taking to giving-receiving,
balance prevails, and Beauty awakens...*

What is balance?

There will be stories about how we humans are conceived in delight and rapture, not in sin. There will be images spiritualizing the erotic, rather than eroticizing violence and domination. And rather than myths about our salvation through violence and pain, there will be myths about our salvation through caring and pleasure.

*Riane Eisler
Sacred Pleasure
page 399*

As our perceptual filters are identified and embraced such that they no longer control us, but instead are tools of knowledge, one of the strongest must now be addressed. The balance between male and female energy has been tipped for approximately the last 10,000 years. Male energy (Yang) has been left to seek balance alone - an impossible task. Psychologists refer to this imbalance using the metaphor of human archetypes.

The concept of archetypes was introduced into psychology by Carl Jung, and was used to study the collective unconscious. Basically, an archetype is a recurring image that represents patterns of human behavior, usually observed over time and across cultures. For example, the familiar characters of mythology all represent aspects of particular human archetypes. Jung felt that all of the most powerful ideas in history, including religious, scientific, philosophical, and ethical issues were all sourced from the basic human archetypes.

Archetypal images are useful in explaining and predicting consistent human behavior. An essential aspect of archetypes is their shadow, which represents those characteristics that manifest when the archetype's particular aspects are repressed. For example, the archetype of the Higher Self is the Sovereign, one who is self-governing, independent, and possessing supreme rank or power. The shadow of the Sovereign presents as either the Tyrant (abuse of power) or the Weakling (lack of autonomy). When fear steps beyond being a healthy reaction, the archetypal shadows emerge, each harboring an innate fear of the other. Therefore, the deepest fear of the Tyrant is weakness, while the deepest fear of the Weakling is to become a Tyrant. When a person is stuck in a particular shadow pattern, he will tend to attract those who demonstrate the opposite shadow. Thus, Tyrants are usually surrounded by Weaklings, while Weaklings tend to be dominated by Tyrants. Additionally, whatever the person rejects about himself, he will tend to project on others.

It is important to note that throughout this chapter, whenever the "masculine" or "feminine" aspects are referred to, they are not tied to gender or sexual orientation. They refer to the archetypal aspects of the masculine (Yang) and feminine (Yin) that we all carry, regardless of our gender.

The shadow side of the Sovereign could be seen as the extreme Yang (Tyrant) or the extreme Yin (Weakling). Therefore, balance could be thought of as that in-between state in which both masculine/feminine aspects are equally balanced. In other words, in terms of the human archetypal pantheon, a man cannot be fully male without a balance of YinYang energy. Likewise, a woman cannot be fully female without a similar YinYang balance. *Both* must be present, balanced, and acknowledged. Yet that has not been the case within the last 7-10,000 years of human culture.

Historically there is profuse evidence that the image of the "Great Mother," that nurturing, life-giving, life-taking aspect clearly and abundantly represented in the upper Paleolithic to early Bronze Age images of the divine, was systematically eliminated. This significant change from the worship of God as a unifying force at-one-with nature, to God as a powerful force in **control** of nature cannot be underestimated. This gradual shift, over thousands of years, from archetypal balance to the extreme expression of masculine and feminine energies, resulted in the culture we experience today; in which all vestiges of the Great Mother archetype have been eliminated: God is male, creation is a male-driven force despite the evidence of our own bodies, and power is hierarchical.

It is vitally important to see this perceptual evolution without judgment of right or wrong. One of the wonderful services provided by archetypal shadows is the ability to help us clearly see our blind spots. In doing so, we eventually awaken from any unbalanced points of view, and gradually move towards wholeness. That is the process we are experiencing today, as we gradually begin to acknowledge those parts of ourselves that we have ignored in the last few millennia.

We have now, as a species, traveled far enough through that experience that we can no longer pretend that domination in any form brings us joy. We are moving from the enshrinement of the mind-as-supreme (Yang) to an embracing of our heart/mind (YinYang). That process brings with it a new humility, as we recognize how little we know, how we have been blinded by our own illusions, and how much we long for healing. Embracing the Great Mother back into the archetypal pantheon of humanity is part of the next step in our conscious exploration of life, and what it means to be human.

But if everything familiar is enmeshed in the imbalance of the extreme Yang, (also called "patriarchy"), what does balance look like? As we explore this question, we begin to see that healing the illusion of patriarchy is similar to peeling an onion. Each layer reveals another deeper layer beneath, yet each must be dealt with before the next can be revealed. The onion in this analogy is, first of all, our individual self — all the ways in which each of us have absorbed and made the perceptual filter of patriarchy our own.

The traditional YinYang symbol graphically represents balance.[1] Note that in balance, the Yin contains the Yang, and the Yang contains the Yin. All is embraced and cherished, all contributes to wholeness. Thus, contrary to the belief of some, we are not seeking the opposite of Patriarchy, (called "Matriarchy"), but instead the dance of balanced energy perhaps best called "Partnership" by author Riane Eisler.

This chapter is an exploration of the impact - both individually and on the culture at large - of embracing the Great Mother, (called Yin from now on), back into our lives. As you read this book, try to imagine seeing each subject through the perceptual filter of Partnership. What would a Partnership economy look like? How would Partnership education differ from our current system? What would change in the business world, or our judicial system?

To begin our exploration, I'd like to re-visit the story of Sleeping Beauty, focusing on the aspects within the story that make it a wonderful metaphor for the awakening of the Yin within us all.

Taoists see Yin-Yang as connected to each other, as necessary components to make the whole possible. That is why they never refer to "Yin or Yang" but always to "Yin-Yang." In this way, they point to the link between them rather than the space that separates them. Yin is black only to the extent that Yang is white...The difference in world-view is subtle, but critical. The Taoists look at the whole at the same time as the parts. Each part exists only because of the interface they create in the whole. In contrast, we tend to take one part and oppose it to the other.

Bernard Lietaer
The Future of Money
page 269

Sleeping Beauty as Metaphor

On the surface, the storyline seems to be dripping with classic patriarchal messages: Beauty, (also known as both Rose and Aurora in the Disney version), the victim of an evil woman's wrath, lies helplessly asleep while the handsome Prince Charming risks his life and flexes a lot of muscles to battle a fire-breathing dragon and a forest of thorns so that he can awaken her with his kiss. She, of course, falls instantly in love with her hero and lives happily ever after, as his prize.

As in all good tales, there are multiple levels of deeper meaning within this story. In his murder mystery, The Da Vinci Code, author Dan Brown suggests that Disney deliberately planted Goddess-worship symbolism throughout the film. He suggests that Beauty's name, Rose, is a direct reference to the Goddess, who's symbol throughout history has been the rose. While I'm not convinced Disney *consciously* included Goddess symbology in this film, Brown's analysis encouraged me to take a deeper look.[2] When I remove the perceptual filter of our common patriarchal viewpoint and replace it with that of the Great Mother/Yin Archetype – that nurturing, birthing, surrendering, accepting, loving, cyclical, all-inclusive symbol of nature that occurs in almost all indigenous cultures – this is what I see.

The Yin of Sleeping Beauty

The story begins with a celebration of the birth of the young princess. All but one person has been invited. Scorned, this person arrives uninvited to punish the King and Queen for ignoring her, by declaring that the princess will prick her finger on a spindle and die. Another magical person shifts the curse so that the princess will not die, but instead fall into a deep sleep, along with everyone in the kingdom. She can only be awakened by the kiss of "true love," perhaps more accurately called *unconditional* love.

At her 16th birthday celebration, the Princess pricks her finger and the entire kingdom falls into a magical sleep. Thorn bushes grow up around the castle, which is guarded by a fire-breathing dragon who is really the uninvited guest transformed.

All is Self

Imagine that the kingdom and all its inhabitants represent the Self. Each person in the kingdom represents a different aspect of Self, and the uninvited guest represents those parts of ourselves that we dismiss, ignore, or even consciously reject.

As we all know, what we resist… persists. Here is a beautiful example of that saying in action. The King and Queen resisted embracing and including the uninvited guest, a part of Self that was underappreciated, unpleasant, or even judged unworthy. She swore revenge and her sabotage almost succeeded. However another aspect of Self – the magical part (perhaps what we would call "Grace" or the "Essential" Self) – intervenes and offers an opportunity for *growth instead of death*. This opportunity is available to us all in every circumstance. We can choose to perceive our daily circumstances as struggle (ultimately leading to death) or as opportunities for growth. On an archetypal level, the uninvited guest could be seen as the aspects of the Yin that are powerful and difficult to fully understand – those that require surrender, that deal with life (birth) and death (the crone) - and are therefore a bit scary for the King and Queen (conscious awareness) to embrace.

Yin Aspect

Aurora, who's name means "dawn", does indeed represent the Goddess, the Divine Feminine, or the Yin Archetype. She represents the "dawning" of a new age. She embodies our Yin aspect: the deep and silent part of Self that is connected to All, that processes in the mystery or "dream time", that sees holistically, and that represents who we choose to BE.

Yang Aspect

The Prince, representing the Yang aspect, experiences life through DOing, and sees life as a linear process. Thus, his actions proceed predictably through a series of battles with those concepts that act as obstacles (dramatic events, thoughts, and beliefs that distract him) to accomplishing his goal (awakening the Yin aspect within). This Yang aspect of Self - regardless of whether we are describing a male or female – is searching for *balance* by joining with the Yin.

In our culture, when we become aware that we carry self-defeating concepts and beliefs, we often become overly zealous in our warrior-like attempts to track-down and eradicate every last belief that keeps us from experiencing ourselves as whole. This is a very Yang approach to healing. It is the path followed by the Prince.

Releasing the Illusion of Evil

As he succeeds in releasing old concepts that no longer serve him (painful thorn bushes), he faces the dragon. This is the part of Self that was dismissed, ignored, and rejected. The uninvited guest has transformed into a fire-breathing dragon (a dangerous misrepresentation of "power" as force). The guest has grown into a dragon in order to be noticed. Another way of saying this, is that the "Universe has turned up the volume," by forcing an extreme situation in which the Prince can't help but notice and deal with the dragon/unacknowledged guest.

The illusion that the dragon represents some kind of evil *outside of self* must be destroyed. By slaying the dragon he releases the dismissed parts of himself from the illusion of evil, allowing healing to take place. (Those dismissed parts could also be seen as a projected illusion representing the Prince's fears of confronting that part of himself he has avoided for so long, and the unknown world of balance he longs to create.)

Approaching the Goddess

Once past the thorn bushes and the dragon, the Prince searches the castle for the Princess. Finding her at last, he leaves his sword and shield at the door, removes his helmet, and enters the stillness of her space. This is important. The warrior must leave all warrior-like behavior and implements outside this holy space. It contains the stillness of our essence BEing, a rose growing within an often protected fortress. She is both highly vulnerable and the seat of *true* power. In other words, her power does not come from the use of force, but from a deeply centered, loving, and open flexibility. One might even call it a form of surrender or adaptablility in harmony with the energy of the moment.

In order to awaken her, the Prince must approach with openness, gentleness, and absolute authenticity. This is no place for the Ego' illusions.

The entire creation flowing from the Source is an incredible and fascinating interplay or "dance of the polarities," summed up in the ancient symbol of sacred marriage, the ✡ which represents the sacred marriage of the opposites, the heiros gamos of antiquity.

The entwined triangles of the ✡ represent the archetypes of masculine and feminine, the "blade" and the "chalice." They are also occasionally called the "fire" and "water" triangles respectively, and correspond to the Yang and Yin of Oriental philosophy.

Margaret Starbird
Imaging God as Partners

The feminine grows spiritually by learning to live as love rather than by hoping for it.

The masculine grows spiritually by learning to live as freedom rather than by struggling for it.

David Deida
http://www.livereal.com/sexual_arena/intro_david_deida.htm

41

CEDAW - The Treaty for the Rights of Women is often described as an international "Bill of Rights" for women. Consisting of a preamble and 30 articles, it defines what constitutes discrimination against women and sets up an agenda for national action to end such discrimination.

The Treaty requires regular progress reports from ratifying countries but it does not impose any changes in existing laws or require new laws of countries ratifying the treaty. It lays out models for achieving equality but contains no enforcement authority.

As of Dec 2004,179 countries have ratified the 1979 Treaty.

With U.S. Senate action blocked by extremists for so many years, momentum for ratification has begun to come from the states. To date, legislatures in 10 states have endorsed U.S. ratification: California, Hawaii, Iowa, Maine, Massachusetts, New Hampshire, New York, North Carolina, Rhode Island and Vermont. The Connecticut and Wisconsin Senates and the House of Representatives in Florida, Illinois and South Dakota also have endorsed U.S. ratification.

http://www.un.org/womenwatch/daw/cedaw/ and http://www.womenstreaty.org

Finding Balance

Bending on one knee, the Prince gently kisses the Princess awake. Because she is approached with unconditional love, she awakens and joins the Prince as a YinYang expression of beauty, perfection, and wholeness. This is what is meant by Partnership, that perfect balance of male/female, yang/yin. It is a union that shifts contexts, allowing for a new and exciting experience in every aspect of life. Where separation once ruled, now everything is transformed into an expression of inclusion, love, and unity. In this all-inclusive moment of wholeness embraced, the entire kingdom finally awakens.

Sex as Partnership

At the most intimate level, how does partnership affect sex? Can we relate in a way that truly honors both partners? As our relationship to sex has rapidly evolved over the last 50 years, we have questioned many aspects of our traditional roles. Yet those questions have taken place within the same cultural assumptions we have held for thousands of years.

As Dr. Yvette Abrahams, of South Africa, points out; at times our "liberated" sexual society is anything but liberated. She sees a woman's willingness to freely participate in sex without demanding love and nurturing in return, as the greatest illusion of them all: the mistake of seeing a total lack of responsibility as freedom. **As long as we operate within the same context – one that is decidedly yang in outlook – our ability to heal our relationship to our bodies, our planet, and our partners remains questionable.** She pointedly reminds us of the perceptual cloud of our sexual illusions, and the opportunity to celebrate ourselves and all of life through the erotic and sensual experiences available as physical beings:

I love female sexual organs. I love to hold them, feel them, touch their moistness, and smell their delicious scents. I love them so much I plan to retire early and devote my life to the enjoyment and admiration of vulvas and vaginas of every size and colour. Hoy, I will die of pleasure!

Now the funny thing is that if I say I want to retire and be a gardener, nobody will be shocked. In fact, it sounds quite respectable. But when I phrase it like I did at first, people get quite horrified. It sounds like I might even be (shock! horror!) a lesbian. Suddenly I change from a person who is quite respectable to somebody they wouldn't want teaching their children. Me, I find it a matter of abiding interest that human beings have this obsession with the sexual organs of plants. …Yet we don't talk about this. Freud would no doubt have a lot to say about it, and the words "subconscious" and "repressed" would inevitably come up…

In the service of liberating our minds from mental slavery, then, I think we must agree that western capitalist culture has an atrocious relation to sex. First, they tried to suppress it, then demonize it, and then spent the 1960s and 1970s making up for lost time. ..

In discovering the joys of sex without guilt, …people forgot the pleasures of the erotic as part of the all-embracing, life-celebrating, Creation-worshipping act we call love. Audre Lorde, of course knew this. She wrote of the erotic as a powerful, life-fulfilling force that would affirm us in doing many things, including liberation... She knew that good sex is everywhere, not just in our sexual organs, but in our minds, in our hearts, and (my addition) in our gardens. That even hard-working Black struggle women need this power in our lives. And that limiting the erotic to the pleasures of the body is really short-changing ourselves. We deserve, and can get, so much more than that. [3]

So much more! That is what we are longing for — sex as an all-encompassing expression of the love we experience when our hearts are fully open to *all* aspects of life lived — seeing and expressing it all as unabashed love.

In the quest to balance the YinYang aspects within ourselves so that our hearts can fully open, Marnia Robinson offers tools she feels can make it possible to heal —on many levels — through sex. She outlines her discoveries in her book, <u>Peace Between the Sheets,</u> which she wrote with her husband, Gary Wilson. In it she shares 10 years of research and personal experience.

Hit and Run Programming

Robinson and Wilson explain that our biological blueprint contains an "intimacy sabotaging device that is hard-wired into the primitive part of the brain." Pointing out that most mammals are not monogamous, they remind us that from a biological standpoint, the more partners we have, the more genetic diversity is supported. Diversity increases the survival of the species.

Using the latest findings in brain chemistry, Robinson shows how our biology has deliberately evolved to promote short-term relationships. In other words, sex drives our physical chemistry to release certain chemicals that at first draw us together; and then upon orgasm, pull us apart. She calls this, "cupid's poisoned arrow." It's a great plan if your intention is to guarantee a genetically diverse population, but not so great if your intention is to experience long-term intimate relationships.

Wilson explains that the chemical changes at climax can:

> …lead to multiple behavioral and emotional symptoms, which, in our experience, can arise over the next two weeks. During this time, our behavior may change for the worse. More importantly, our perception of each other can shift dramatically for the worse. If we feel depleted, our partner will seem overly demanding; if we feel needy, our partner will seem selfish and uncaring. Of course, few people ever avoid orgasm for two weeks. Most of us ride this roller coaster over and over, never really experiencing balanced brain chemistry.[4]

Additionally, they describe the "The Coolidge Effect," which is also linked to this post-orgasm hangover. Observing the affects of these chemicals on rats, Wilson states:

> The reason the rat loses interest is that he's not getting any more dopamine surge from Partner No. 1. Low dopamine, no interest. The same thing happens to humans. The thrill is gone, and Partner No. 1 looks like Brussels sprouts. Now you're primed for anything that will jack up your dopamine again. Partner No. 2 appears, and your dopamine soars. As if by magic, your blues are gone, and you have that heady feeling of anticipation, that sense of uninhibited aliveness. In short, No. 2 looks like chocolate cake. [4]

Luckily, if you want a long-term intimate relationship there is a solution. It has been mentioned in many cultures and spiritual practices for thousands of years. However, as Robinson points out, we've been biologically programmed to reject it, or at least find it unappealing. The solution is to "tiptoe around cupid's poisoned arrow," by avoiding orgasm.

Here's how it works. It involves oxytocin, also called the "cuddle" or "bonding" hormone. It is one of the primary hormones involved in the neurochemical experience of falling in love, but unlike dopamine, which contributes to craving;

At last we can observe humanity's circumstances with a minimum of religious and social distortion. The picture is not pretty, but at least it is plain. Humanity has a weak link in its design when it comes to mating behavior. It's not a flaw from evolutionary biology's viewpoint, but it routinely erodes our wellbeing and happiness by weakening our capacity for monogamy.

Marnia Robinson & Gary Wilson

http://www.reuniting.inf o/GBwisdom.htm

oxytocin is associated with nurturing, affection, and unconditional love. Wilson writes:

> Oxytocin has various functions in the body, such as inducing labor contractions and milk ejection, but from evolutionary biology's perspective, its main evolutionary function is to bond us to our children for life. It also serves to bond us to our mate…at least long enough to produce a child and get it on its feet. [4]

Robinson and Wilson have gathered considerable evidence that when you consistently raise your levels of oxytocin, you counteract the effect of "cupid's poisoned arrow." How do you do this? Through changing your focus.

From Great Expectations to No Expectations

Before we can discuss how to change focus, we need to discern the focus of traditional sexual behavior. In his article, <u>What is Sex, Anyway?</u>, Reid Mihalko, suggests:

> Sex can be so many things, that to try to define what sex is and what sex isn't is near impossible. But we can define what sexualizing something means… Sexualizing is when you're intention is to get to the next base, really. It's that simple. Are you kissing him or her because you're enjoying the feel of their lips, or are you testing the waters to see if you can get to Second Base?... Are you nuzzling into their embrace because it's comforting and sweet, or are trying to arouse them to reassure yourself that you've "still got it"? In other words, what are your intentions? [5]

As Mihalko indicates, it is *intention* that determines the quality of the experience.

Robinson and Wilson suggest that if your intention (or focus) is to *give without expecting something in return*, you will stimulate oxytocin production – and hence promote unconditionally loving behavior in your partner and yourself. Their research and experience indicates that sex without orgasm increases both partner's pleasure and general wellbeing. It can even lead to the experience described as "sacred sex."

Receptivity

There is another aspect to this approach that I love. It is the conscious willingness to receive. The distinction between "receive" and "take" is important.

- **To receive** is to be willing to accept. It is a state of openness, free from judgment. It acknowledges the gift being offered.

- **To take** is to place focus on what *you* want to obtain, *your* pleasure.

Receptivity can be one of the most honoring and powerful forces on the planet. It lovingly and firmly says, "I trust you;" which instantly shines the light of love and safety into the dark corners of fear and doubt. Because it is non-threatening, its presence can create a sense of safety that instantly opens hearts and creates connection.

Here's an example from one of my workshops. A couple was standing approximately 15 feet apart, facing each other, and focusing their attention on feeling each other's energy. The female was having difficulty with the process. She was frustrated that she couldn't feel her partner's energy, and wanted him to move closer. I suggested that she put her hands up in front of her body, palms facing her partner. He did the same. Instantly she was able to feel his energy.

As you grow spiritually, sex becomes service to others. In the midst of sex, you may occasionally choose to feel and visualize someone to whom you want to send love and healing. Eventually, through practice, you feel all beings through your lover. You love through your lover, as a portal to all beings. Rather than having sex for your own pleasure only, you have sex for the sake of giving love to all beings…

David Deida
Do Sex to Enlighten the World
Adapted from
Finding God Through Sex
http://www.deidacentral.com/articles/sex_to_enlighten.asp

What changed? Several things. She took an openly receptive stance that simultaneously left her less physically vulnerable, allowing her to perceive herself as safe. Her chest and heart were protected by her arms and hands, and her own energy shifted towards her partner. His energy also changed. When he assumed a position of receptivity, he could no longer be perceived as a threat. His path to her was blocked by his own arms and hands that were held openly toward her, expecting her energy to move toward him, instead of the opposite direction.

Receptivity offers another gift as well, especially for those who are used to giving all day long. This may seem obvious, but its worth noting. It is only when you are receptive, consciously opening yourself to receive, that you can fully receive what any one or any thing has to offer. When you willingly receive, you offer others the opportunity to give to you. **In doing so, you empower them to experience and acknowledge their *own* abilities, abundance, and inner magnificence.**

Moreover, if your conscious intention is to always *give*, you are actually pushing your partner's energy away. Ultimately, when the dance of giving and receiving is entered with total consciousness and honor, it is seen as the same energy in a circular flow. Constantly pulsing in balance, it is similar to the expansion/contraction, on/off energy that pulses at the quantum level. **This is the magic of honoring both giving and receiving in balance… the Yin and the Yang - it literally honors the dance of the universe.**

Receiving requires the following:

- You must be willing to release all control;
- You must open your heart and consciously create a space for reception;
- You must forgive yourself for any desire to control, releasing any preconceived ideas you might have about what is going on;
- You must surrender to the moment. This is the biggest challenge of all for many, because it requires that you be fully present, without attaching stories to the moment. This means you cannot cling to the moment – no matter how enjoyable - but instead simply allow it to flow through you, gently witnessed and caressed with your heart, but always released to the next manifestation in the next moment. It also means you cannot attach any stories about the next moment to this one. This is important. You cannot decide anything about a future moment or you will instantly be taken out of the current moment altogether.
- The last step is to TRUST completely and let go of the details of how it happens… simply allow.

This change in attitude, from goal-oriented sex to giving-oriented sex in which you consciously create a space of honoring and receptivity within both partners; can provide some surprising side effects.

Sex as Healing

According to Robinson, studies show that elevated oxytocin levels can help heal addictions and counter stress which improves immunity. Both she and her partner grew healthier and more harmonious, while chronic illnesses, long-term addictions, and depression fell away. Wilson's own words best convey the significance of their findings:

> This allows making love without orgasm to be completely satisfying. The affection is always there, flowing between you and your partner. When we tiptoe around dopamine's highs and lows, we encourage more oxytocin receptors and actually re-wire our brain, getting pleasure from a

Sacred sex, which is the experience of ecstasy, is the real sexual revolution. Sacred sexuality is about love – not merely the positive feeling between intimates, but an overwhelming reverence for all embodied life on whatever level of existence. Through sacred sexuality, we directly participate in the vastness of being – the mountains, rivers, and animals of the Earth, the planets and the stars, and our next-door neighbors.

Sacred sexuality is about recovering our authentic being, which knows bliss beyond mere pleasurable sensations. It is a special form of communication, even communion, that fills us with awe and stillness.

Rabbi Zalman Schachter-Shalomi & Eve Ilsen
Sacred Sex
YES! Magazine
Winter 1997/1998
Reprinted from YES! magazine, PO Box 10818, Bainbridge Island, WA 98110. Subscriptions: 800/937-4451 Web: www.yesmagazine.org

different cocktail of neurochemicals. Best of all, understanding the power of oxytocin shows how sexual relationships can heal. [3]

Contrary to what you'd expect, there's no sexual frustration or feeling of "missing out on something." Quite the opposite….we make love a lot. Everything about my life is immeasurably better as a result of being in love and staying in love. [3]

The story of healing and deeply fulfilling love that Robinson and Wilson experience is detailed in her book. Robinson thoughtfully includes a set of practices for any couple wishing to re-wire their neurochemical programming by increasing their levels of oxytocin. Their support group, website, and newsletter contain volumes of additional history, science, and fascinating information. [6] Best of all, however, are the testimonials from couples who have taken the plunge and committed themselves to re-creating their sexual relationship as a statement of balanced partnership that honors all.

PARTNERSHIP IN CULTURE

How did we get here?

How does the story of Sleeping Beauty fit our own present state of human cultural evolution? Like a glove! As Riane Eisler and other scholars have pointed out, we are just beginning to emerge from what she terms our "Dominance Trance", the overarching cultural perception that the only way to survive life is through domination and pain. She presents us with an alternative option, that of "Partnership" in which both the Yin and Yang aspects of our culture are honored *equally*.

This results in a culture in which behavior that supports life is *rewarded*, as opposed to a culture in which undesired behavior is *punished*. Life-affirming behaviors include choosing co-creation over control, and communication over judgment and assumption. Eisler's books trace the origins of our dominator culture to several factors. Before we examine them, it is important to understand what she means by "dominator" and "partnership" models.

> She refers to the "partnership/pleasure" model because evidence has suggested that our earlier cultures were based on the idea of rewarding socially accepted behavior with pleasure. This concept is difficult for us to comprehend, because we live in what she calls a "dominator/pain" cultural model, or one that punishes socially unacceptable behavior.

Pause for a moment and allow yourself to fully take in the significance of these polarities of perception. Let's explore tem in detail.

The Partnership-Pleasure Model

In a partnership/pleasure model, both genders are equally valued, with non-violent conflict resolution preferred. The cultural structure does not support violence, and values diversity as a primary source of creativity. Freedom of choice is encouraged in all aspects of life. Sex is seen as both a pleasurable experience - often spiritual in nature, as well as a means of procreation. Spirituality is expressed through empathy, equality, and unconditional love. Relationships are held together through pleasure-bonds that take the form of caretaking, love-making, and other pleasurable and sacred expressions. Power is expressed as the ability to give and nurture, with love being the highest expression as well as the unifying element of the universe. Life is lived in a way that sustains *all*.

The Dominator-Pain Model

A dominator/pain based model has the following characteristics: The male gender is seen as superior to the female, with the accompanying masculine traits seen as more highly valued than female traits. The cultural structure incorporates violence and abuse; in fact, it often supports it as necessary. Social structures are hierarchical and authoritarian, with males at the top.

Women are seen as tools or property, not as equals. Manipulation and coercion are strong elements of both mate selection and sex.   Erotic pleasure is repressed, while domination is glorified. Sex is primarily a method of procreation and male sexual release.

Man and religion (stories that defend domination as a God-given right) are ranked over women and nature. Because of this perception, God is perceived as a judging being, scrutinizing all of man's activities and calling forth punishment upon those who do not submit to domination.

Pain (psychological, emotional, mental, and physical) is used by parents to control their children, which in turn teaches them that it is ok to inflict pain and to force domination on others (often while *voicing* the contrary message). As a result, touch is often associated with pain. Pain is seen as sacred in some religions ("you must suffer to grow"), as is death. An example is the glorification of the martyrdom of saints and the choice of the symbol of Jesus' death to represent the entire religion.

The world is seen as a commodity, given to man to use in any way he chooses.

Power is expressed as the ability to dominate, with war being chosen above non-violent means of conflict resolution. Pain and death are seen as the ultimate solutions for those who deviate too far from society's structure, and it is often performed in the name of a deity.[5]

It is important to remember that these descriptions are extreme, and that many current and past cultures expressed these models in differing proportions, including our own.

Dominator Politics

The relevance of how these subtle but highly pervasive cultural assumptions create perceptual filters that define our vision of reality – and thus the choices we make, on the individual, cultural, and species-wide levels, cannot be underestimated.   David C. Korten, Nicanor Perlas, and Vandana Shiva discuss the dominator/partnership models' impact on our experience in their comprehensive paper, <u>Global Civil Society: The Path Ahead, A Discussion Paper – (Summary)</u> in which they state:

> The outward political expression of this conflict mirrors an inner psychic tension that resides within each of us. On the one hand, we experience the pull of love, trust, a joyful sense of connection to the whole of life grounded in a perception of the world as a nurturing, caring, and cooperative place overflowing with creativity and abundance. On the other hand, we experience the opposing pull of fear, distrust and alienation grounded in a perception of the world as a threatening place filled with human and natural enemies that must be physically controlled or destroyed to make ourselves secure. At a more primitive level of experience the former pull is associated with the feminine predisposition to bond for mutual protection in the face of danger and the latter with a masculine predisposition to fight or flight.

Hitler's Germany (a technologically advanced, Western, rightist society), Stalin's USSR (a secular leftist society), fundamentalist Iran (an Eastern religious society), and Idi Amin's Uganda (a tribalist society) were all violent and repressive. There are obvious differences between them. But they all share the core configuration of the domination model. They are characterized by top-down rankings in the family and state or tribe maintained through physical, psychological, and economic control; the rigid ranking of the male half of humanity over the female half; and a high degree of culturally accepted abuse and violence—from child- and wife-beating to chronic warfare.

How a society structures the primary human relations— between the female and male halves of humanity, and between them and their children—is central to whether it is violent and inequitable or peaceful and equitable

Riane Eisler
<u>*Spare the Rod*</u>
Winter 2005
Reprinted from YES! magazine, PO Box 10818, Bainbridge Island, WA 98110. Subscriptions: 800/937-4451 Web: www.yesmagazine.org http://www.saiv.net/docs/32 YesEisler150dpi.pdf

While one tendency or the other may be more fully expressed in a given individual or society, both reside in each of us — both male and female — which helps to account for the wide variety of the human experience. In societies where love, trust, and sense of connection prevail, we are more likely to find cooperative partnership models of social organization that favor deeply democratic self-organizing processes mediated by an ethical culture that values equality, justice, the creative freedom of the individual, and the willingness of each individual to act with a sense of responsibility for the interests of the whole.

In societies where fear, distrust, and alienation prevail, we may find more competitive dominator models of social organization that extend rights and freedoms to those on the top that are denied to those on the bottom — and a legitimating culture that extols the virtues of the powerful winners and condemns the vices of slothful losers. Societies so organized are likely to exhibit persistent patterns of exploitation, injustice, and scarcity, a climate of fear and insecurity, perceptions of real or imagined threats, political demagogues who play to these fears, violence against suspect groups, and the embrace of coercive institutions that specialize in the use of force to impose order. Such societies easily become trapped in a self-reinforcing cycle of violence and competition for power that provides a fertile ground for demagogues who build their power base on fear and violence by appealing to those who long for vengeance and to those who seek the protection of a powerful leader. [7]

Does any of this sound familiar? Many of our dominator-based choices are destroying life on Earth —not just some of it —all of it, cultures, people, languages, entire bioregions. At the same time we are finally becoming aware, individually and collectively, that we are free to choose how we want to live our lives and whether we want to use fear-based or love-based motivations when making those choices.

Before this awareness, we simply assumed that the dominator model was "human nature," and an inevitable consequence of living on Earth. This perceptual filter was so pervasive, in fact, that it colored our perception of *everything*. We saw nature as competitive - "survival of the fittest" – which is currently understood to mean something significantly different and more complex than how it is casually used in conversation today. We are beginning to understand that the abilities to *co-create* and *adapt* are equally important to survival in the natural world.

How can we harness this new-found awareness to make healing choices from this point on? Perhaps understanding what prompted the change from the partnership cultures of 10-12,000 years ago to the dominant cultures of today might help.

How and why did we change?

There are many theories regarding the huge perceptual shift in humanity's approach to life that took place so long ago. Riane Eisler offers several explorations into this perceptual change. I'll concentrate on a few of her suggestions. First, she suggests that the discovery of agriculture, the awareness that we could influence nature by planting, tending, and gathering specific cultivars emboldened us. It facilitated our survival. The context in which this change took place was important. Previous to the advent of agriculture, evidence indicates that humans lived as hunter-gatherers, and nature was seen as sacred. Up to that point, the idea of manipulating nature in any way, was foreign.

The next step was to notice that animals could be domesticated and, in a sense, handled in the same way as plants. This was a huge step, for it necessitated the willingness to dominate and control another animal life form. Again, the significance of this choice must be seen from the standpoint of a previous partnership/pleasure

Throughout sub-Saharan Africa the death of a father automatically entitles his side of the family to claim most, if not all, of the property he leaves behind, even if it leaves his survivors destitute.

In an era when AIDS is claiming about 2.3 million lives a year in sub-Saharan Africa - roughly 80,000 people last year in Malawi alone - disease and stubborn tradition have combined in a terrible synergy, robbing countless mothers and children not only of their loved ones but of everything they own.

Sharon Lafraniere
AIDS and Custom Leave African Families Nothing
New York Times
February 18, 2005

culture that saw nature as a manifestation of God, with females fully honored for their life-giving and life-nurturing qualities that emulated God/Goddess itself. *All* was seen as sacred. In that context, the willingness to dominate animals and even to go so far as to control every aspect of their breeding *with the ultimate intent of killing them* was a huge change. Even though humans had hunted for thousands of years, the shift to suppressing one's natural expression of love and nurturing in order to kill one's pet, (which was how domesticated animals were treated), was great. Eisler concludes

> Because once empathy and love are in any context habitually suppressed, this tends to result in what psychologists call blunted affect—a reduced and highly compartmentalized capacity to respond to feelings (affect) other than anger, contempt, and similar "hard" emotions.[8]

This is a crucial point. Something happened to human beings when they willingly chose to deaden their feelings in order to survive. It is important to remember that they were already surviving - in a different way - before they took this step. Yet at some point their perception of life shifted from a willingness to live in harmony and gratitude with nature, to a willingness to dominate nature.

Furthermore, she suggests that when humans started seeing animal females as nothing but "breeding stock", the switch to seeing *human females* in the same light was not that difficult. Likewise, the willingness to dominate and virtually enslave animals could eventually lead to a willingness to enslavement humans too.

Moving from Unity to Competition

There is another factor to consider. With the onset of the last ice age, significant changes in the amount of grazing land and available water took place. Eisler suggests that competition for these perceived scarce commodities, which often instigated mass migration of human populations, could have led to the desire to dominate one's neighbor.

However, again one must try to view this change from the standpoint of a partnership culture, and *not* through the dominate culture with which we are all familiar. To our acculturated eyes, competition seems natural. There is a winner and a loser. Sometimes you win, and sometimes you loose. But to people living in a partnership culture, the idea that some people loose at the expense of others would be alien. In a partnership culture, solutions are found in which everyone unites so that everyone can survive. This can only take place in a culture in which each person's unique value is acknowledged and seen as contributing to the whole.

Moving from the Inner-Leader to a Dominant Leader

Today, when circumstances seem to create a life-and-death emergency situation which requires a quick response, civil liberties are willingly dispensed with so that a leader may dominate and quickly control the situation. We call this "Marshall Law." Eisler suggests that the shift to a dominator culture was made more easily because those embracing this new lifestyle perceived their survival as dependent upon a sort of permanent 'Marshall Law" - the quick and controlled response of a leader - one who could defend them in their competition for grazing land, water, and natural resources.

The Tao begot one, one begot two, two begot three. The three begot the ten thousand things. The ten thousand things embrace Yin and express Yang. Harmony is achieved by combining these forces.

Lao Tzu
Tao Te Ching

49

In a partnership culture, however, even if there were leaders or a Council of Elders, their power was given and taken by the people. Leadership was seen differently than we use it today. For example, most of our leaders are seen symbolically as a father-figure, with the general public seen as the children (often in need of protection). It is this perception that contributes to the tendency of many adults today, to deny full responsibility for their choices, their lives, and the condition of our planet.

In a partnership model, each person is encouraged to develop his/her own leadership skills in whatever healthy way they manifest. There isn't as much of a clear division between the "leader" and those he/she leads. (See the chapter on Co-creation for additional details.) The term, "Inner-Leader," refers to the concept that each person has access to a deep inner-knowing – the sacred Oneness shared with all life - and it is from that connection through the Essential-Self that each person experiences an "Inner-Leader." Thus *all* voices are considered important and worthy of being heard, for they all come from the Oneness (what physicist David Bohm called the Implicate Order) that unifies us all.

Moving from Equality and Pleasure to Fear and Domination

All of these elements combined to ease the transition from a partnership culture in which they held a reverence for all nature and life (with an emphasis on the creative and nurturing gifts of the female); to a willingness to live in a culture driven by domination of nature, the enslavement of animals, and ultimately leading to the enslavement of women and other human beings. Eisler concludes,

> This willingness to release age-old partnership models of equality and pleasure-based religions for survival-based, fear-laden newer models of dominance/pain ushered in a transformation for the entire planet. For once dominator/pain model cultures thrived, they had no qualms about dominating their peace-loving unprotected neighbors, and forcing them to embrace the new dominator model of living, or die.[9]

Moving from Enjoyment to Avoidance Motivations

Our choices are always based on our perceptions of life. When humanity perceived all life as sacred and basically pleasurable, those choices seemed motivated by love and acceptance. The change in humanity's choices seems to have been brought about by survival-based fear. In other words, people made the choices they did in an effort to *avoid* pain and death, not in an effort to *enjoy* pleasure. We seem to have moved from actively seeking pleasure to perhaps meekly avoiding pain. The entire cultural structure grew from those motivations… fear or pleasure. This is still true today. If we are to allow ourselves, as a species, to shift again towards a partnership model, we will need to address and resolve those fears, both individually and collectively.

Compassion

As my perception of the extent to which our dominator culture manipulated sex roles grew, I first experienced anger. Then, as I allowed myself to move from a stance of victimhood, I began to see all the ways in which we (women and men) allowed and even encouraged the perpetuation of the dominator culture in which we live. I began to feel great compassion for women *and* men, both caught in the limiting boxed-in roles that we have mutually created over the last 10,000 years of dominator culture.

In their wonderful article entitled, Parenting Partnerships, Tera Abelson and Greta Cowan offer a brief glimpse into their book, The Good News About Family: An Uplifting Collection of New Family Portraits. They describe the stories of partnership families, including partnership marriages, divorces, and parenting partnerships that "support creative conflict resolution and innovative family building."

Their list of Sustainable Partnership Family attributes include:

o *Prioritize Children*

o *Rethink Work – develop flexibility, demand flexibility*

o *Share the Care of Infants and Children*

o *Honor Autonomy – harmonize commitment to self and family*

o *Be Generous – accept the worst and expect the best of one another*

o *Move Beyond Blame – be willing to grow*

o *Open the Family Circle – rely on a community of significant others*

o *Be Creative – design the family that works for you.*

YES! Magazine Fall 1998

Reprinted from YES! magazine, PO Box 10818, Bainbridge Island, WA

As Riane Eisler so movingly points out, the human desire to deeply connect at an intimate soul-level, is severely restricted for both men and women by our dominator culture. Both sexes are boxed into roles that keep them for experiencing themselves fully and celebrating each person's uniqueness. It is a no-win situation for all involved.

So how do we emerge from the trance we have lived, collectively, for thousands of years? By choice. By placing our attention and intention on awakening to the nuances of how dominator control has permeated every aspect of our lives. And then, as our awareness grows, by consciously choosing a partnership path. We will have to invent it together as we go along, co-creating our culture and ourselves as expressions of the best we know ourselves to be.

Partnership and Abortion

When I began writing this book, I was surprised at the reaction I sometimes received to the title, "Honoring All Life." Every once and awhile someone would ask me if it was an anti-abortion book. Perhaps I was naïve, but it always startled me to think that the idea of honoring *all* life would instantly be seen as supporting an issue that clearly does *not* honor all. To me, the essence of honoring is *allowing*. This means that I allow others to make their own choices *without judgment*.

Abortion is not a simple issue. It has become a hot issue precisely because we fail to honor each other and the complexities involved in such a personal decision. We women are hardwired to desire and nurture our offspring, and the decision to terminate a pregnancy is never taken lightly. I have yet to meet a woman who has contemplated abortion without feeling the weight and responsibility of that choice. And it *is* a choice, whether we make it difficult to obtain or not. Women have aborted pregnancies throughout human history. The degree to which we make abortion difficult to obtain merely determines how many women will suffer and die in the process. When we finally begin to honor each other fully, we will let go of the need to control each other; and replace mistrust with faith in the magnificence of each person and their ability to make choices that honor all, including themself.

Energy Flows

Many people see life as energy, it may transform but never ends. Like many, I also experience life as eternal energy. Thus birth and death are seen more as gateways instead of end points. When held in this context, life is a constant flow of energy, and the fear associated with the concept of death disappears. Seen in this light, abortion is more about honoring *both* the mother and the child and their choice to manifest together at a specific time.

Welcoming the Yin back into the rich pantheon of human archetypes means including all her aspects. Traditionally she is the doorway to both birth and death, for she represents the cycles of life. It is time for us to begin trusting in those cycles again - not as something outside of humanity that we merely witness - but as an integral part of the nature that runs through us all. When we remember that what appears as death in winter returns as life in spring, we honor the natural energy flow of life. It is a matter of trust, and nature is our best teacher.

If each person is looking out for their own interest within, say, a family, how does family integrity happen? There have to be negotiations that recognize family integrity as having its own self-interest at its own level of holarchy. Couplehood is a simple, two-level holarchy where the individuals are not only negotiating with each other, but with their couplehood, that second level of the holarchy. The integrity of couplehood demands certain sacrifices, doesn't it? It demands certain times when you have to back down and not get your way in order for couplehood to flourish. ….. And it goes on as long as life goes on because we are always in some holarchy and this tension, as I said earlier, is the fundamental source of all creativity.

Elisabet Sahtouris, Living Systems, the Internet and the Human Future Talk presented 13 May 2000 at Planetwork, Global Ecology and Information Technology Conference held at the San Francisco Presidio http://www.ratical.org/ LifeWeb/Articles/LSin etHF.html

Dominator Trace Today

When I had my first child, a daughter, I chose to stop shaving my legs and underarms. I also stopped using deodorant. I wanted my child to celebrate the perfection of her own body, without feeling the need to alter it to another's view of what was beautiful and acceptable. I stopped using deodorant because I wanted to smell like the woman that I am. These seemingly small but forthright steps helped me begin the process of reclaiming my sense of "self" from the myths I had been spoon-fed as a child by my entire culture.

I began to awaken from what Riane Eisler calls the "Dominator Trance". She writes,

> These were all major changes. However, they are part of a much larger drama that can only be understood within the broader context of modern history and, even beyond this, the history of consciousness. For, as we will see, they represent only the latest phase in our gradual awakening—as if from a long, painful trance—from the mind-and-body-numbing effects of millennia of recorded, or dominator, history.[10]

In her more recent article, Spare the Rod, she describes cultural indicators of whether a country or cultural group embraces a dominator or partnership model. Surprisingly, there are many examples of partnership models still in existence, they just don't normally make our drama-laden news. Her analysis shows:

> Where the rights of women and children are protected, nations thrive. In fact, a study of 89 nations by the organization I direct, the Center for Partnership Studies, shows that the status of women can be a better predictor of the general quality of life than a nation's financial wealth. Kuwait and France, for example, had identical GDPs (Gross Domestic Product). But quality of life indicators are much higher in France, where the status of women is higher, while infant mortality was twice as high in Kuwait.

> An important lesson from these cultures is this: How a society structures the primary human relations— between the female and male halves of humanity, and between them and their children—is central to whether it is violent and inequitable or peaceful and equitable.[11]

Eisler continues by offering examples of cultures in which women are seen as equals, partners in the co-creation of society, and their subsequent prosperity. Finland is a good example. She reminds us that Finland was considered very poor at the dawn of the 20th century. But then the country invested heavily in its own human capital, by providing for childcare, healthcare, family planning, and paid parental leaves. Now, according to the UN, Finland ranks high in their Human Development Reports, and far ahead of the USA, Saudi Arabia, and other "wealthy" nations. Finland's legislature if filled with a more balanced ratio of men to women. It has a strong men's movement intent on freeing them from the shackles of the dominant male model, and the government no longer turns a blind eye to the physical discipline of children. Their support of peace-based education, not surprisingly coincides with a low crime rate, and their developing expertise as international mediators. And unlike in the USA, Finland's strong support of developing nations is seen as a worthwhile, logical, and beneficial investment for all involved.

Partnership and Parenting

Our questions reflect how we perceive Ourselves

As the dominator trance begins to fade, and our perceptions expand, our questions will also undergo a transformation: How do we each perceive our own body, and

---

At the dawn of feminism, there was an assumption that women would not be as severely judged on their looks in ensuing years. Phooey. It's just the opposite. Looks matter more than ever, with more and more women spending fortunes turning themselves into generic, plastic versions of what they think men want, reaching for eerily similar plumped-up faces and body shapes.

Maureen Dowd
Where's the Road Beef?
New York Times
February 20, 2005

In spite of the Ulemas' rebellion, the country commits itself to oppose female genital mutilation...

For a number of the Ulemas, Koranic commandments to respect the body and preserve health must carry the day. That's also the opinion of the Djiboutian government, which, by ratifying the Maputo Protocol, became the ninth African country to commit to the rights of women and their physical integrity.

Claude Guibal
Djibouti Comes Out against All Excisions,
Libération
Tuesday 15 March 2005

how do we want our children to perceive theirs? What beliefs do we hold regarding the limitations of behavior allowed men and women, and how do those beliefs affect our kids? How do we teach discernment while also teaching our children to be non-judgmental? How do we perceive our culture's obsession with sex, and particularly the objectification of women's and men's bodies; and what do we do, say, and think that perpetuates that obsession? How do we feel about sex, and how do we want our children to feel about it? What are the hidden messages behind TV commercials? Why are women dressed in skimpy outfits while surrounded by fully dressed men in most of our films and TV shows? Why are women always being rescued by men, and rarely the other way around? And why is the mother dead, missing, or converted to evil in some way, in almost all of our children's stories? And so on...

Every aspect of the parent-child relationship will be reassessed through the new ever-evolving perceptual filters of "honoring all" and "partnership."

Re-Thinking Cultural Assumptions about Parenting and Children

Investigating our cultural assumptions brought me to question everything about motherhood. Since there were few guideposts, I learned to trust my own feelings about what was nurturing and loving in decisions regarding my own experiences and those I had control over as a mother. In my efforts to live in partnership instead of the traditional dominance-trance, I made the following realizations and decisions:

- **Pregnancy is a gift, not an illness**. When we honor ourselves, we trust our bodies to handle all they were designed to handle. Humans have been delivering healthy babies as long as they have existed on this planet. Delivery requires no intervention except in those cases in which problems arise. What they do require is support, trust, and experienced, knowledgeable assistance.

- **Humans require nurturing touch to survive.** Honoring the need for children to feel safe and fully nurtured, it is natural and healthy to sleep with your children.

- **Breast feeding is best.** Even though pollutants are now found in the breast milk of even the most remote humans, it is still by far the healthiest food for infants. Cow milk was designed for the special needs of calves, not humans.

- **Children need to experience their own bodies**, to explore without shame, to celebrate the unique magnificence of the vessel in which they live, and their place within the interdependent systems of life. They need to feel their own empowerment as they challenged their bodies to respond to greater and greater feats of physical prowess. Honoring the wisdom of children can sometimes mean that the parent must find that fine line between ensuring safety and owning one's own fears. Honoring children means allowing them to learn to *trust themselves.*

- **We need to encourage both boys and girls to explore and express their feelings, free from judgment**. The focus is on experiencing their own inner wisdom and soft loving heart. The best method of producing a world

The Yin-Yang way of looking at reality is not about competing ways to relate and interpret reality, no more than your right eye competes with the left one. Instead, because of their differences, together they provide you with range and depth of vision, something which neither one can do by itself.

*Bernard A. Lietaer &
Stephen M Belgin
Of Human Wealth,
page 231*

that honors all is to live that intention ourselves, by consciously honoring our own deepest Inner Wisdom, and modeling that choice for our children.

- **We need to encourage children to clearly state their needs and to assert themselves when necessary,** to draw unambiguous boundaries regarding how they are willing to be treated and about what feels honoring. At the same time we must encourage them to focus on how to best honor others and all life around them. These are not separate focuses. Once the interconnectedness of all life is understood, the idea of honoring one part of life but not another no longer works. All life is seen as One.

- **Adults need to model openness and transparency in our relationships with each other and children.** When a child asks about a particular topic, then it is time to discuss it in the most honoring, honest, and open manner, yet fully mindful of the *amount* of information requested. Role modeling transparency offers the best hope for establishing it as a cultural trait. This goes way beyond not telling lies. It includes the willingness to discuss the shadow parts of ourselves and our culture: money, sex, hidden agendas, etc.

- **Life is a field of possibilities.** Participating in a huge range of events, performances, gatherings, etc. with the goal of stretching awareness of the possible, allows creativity to flow. This includes different cultures, ways of thinking, perceptual filter explorations, beliefs, etc. Most importantly, we want to encourage a love of learning about life – all life. And not simply the experience of exterior-learning "out there;" but also inner-learning, that deep experience of the Essential Self. On one level of awareness, any concept of external learning ceases to exist, as all learning and all experience, becomes an exploration of Self.

- **We need to assist Children in being aware of any manipulation or media assault aimed at them, so they can avoid abuse.** With the global market view of children as tools of commercial gain, children need to learn to perceive hidden agendas and motives in others; and then to think and act out of a declaration of the highest statement of who they know themselves to be – not out of someone else's ideas of who they are.

- **Children need to know that self love and self honor are the foundation upon which their ability to love and honor others grows.** This means learning to identify and nurture their needs; to cherish, thank, and honor their growing bodies; and to enter puberty from a standpoint of always honoring themselves and others.

- **Sex is a sacred event.** When they reached the age where sex becomes a possibility, children need to be taught how to proceed safely *and* lovingly. We need to encouraged them to make their first experience a loving and honoring one, knowing it will be a memory they will hold their entire lives.

- **Offering pleasure instead of punishment.** Instead of disciplining our children with forms of punishment – grounding them, withholding affection, shouting, even physically hitting them – we now have the ability to choose a different path. Since it is new for most of us, we will have to experiment with what works best in each situation and with each child, but simply changing our intention from control to *partnership with* the child will allow creative ideas to spring forth. We are all pioneers on this path, but the joy and honoring we all feel in the process makes the effort more than worth while.

As we collectively awaken from our dominator trance, we will continually discover new ways of honoring ourselves and our children. Our shifting perceptions will facilitate the awareness of new possibilities, the repercussions of which will reflect in all aspects of our lives.

Yin and Our Species

Coming Home — The Story Of Sarah Bartmann

It is often difficult to grasp just how much the dominator trance has affected our choices and our history. The ideas of colonization and slavery –with the accompanying assumption that no one "of value" was adversly affected – was one of the most obvious dominator behaviors in human history. We'd like to think that era of human-to-human cruelty is over, but is it? Our current global economic policies amount to covert slavery and colonization by multinational corporations, yet because they are hidden behind powerful organizations and government leaders, they go unnoticed. [12] But their damage is just as great. It is time we step into a more partnering relationship with each other, and openly seek to heal the wounds of all forms of domination.

The following story represents a significant step towards healing the complex wounds of the dominator trance in which we have all been living. It is Sarah's story, but it is also the story of humanity. [13] In many ways, it is the beginning of a welcoming home party – that of the Yin and Yang as equal partners at last.

Sarah Bartmann was taken from her native South Africa in November 1809 by an Englishman who proceeded to display her as a novelty in a freak exhibit in London. Her steatopygia — enlarged buttocks — and elongated labia, a genital feature typical of some Khoisan women of the time, evidently facinated those who paid to view her naked performance. The humiliation and violence (mental, physical, spiritual, and emotional) that she endured on a daily basis is hard to imagine. Records exist of her abuse because, in 1810, the Englishman was brought to court for his mistreatment of her. Although the case was ostensibly a trial of *his* behavior; it was she who was on trial, as the issue discussed was the question of her humanity. The case garnered much media attention and made her possibly the most famous Khoekhoe of European history, though it did not end favorably.

She was eventually sold to a Frenchman, who continued to abuse her. She died in 1815. Less than 24 hours after her death, her body was subjected to "scientific inquiry." Her brain and genitalia were preserved and her skeleton was placed on display at the Musee de l'Homme until 1974.

In 1994 Nelson Mandela asked France to return her remains. It took eight years of negotiating. During that time her people won recognition at the UN as indigenous

On May 26th 1998 Australians participated in a public-led event of deep significance - Sorry Day - in which they expressed their sorrow for the forced removal of Aboriginal children from their families. This attempt at assimilating the children into the dominant white culture took place throughout the last century until the early 1970's. According to John Bond, in his article, Aussie Apology, the policy's aim was genocide, as defined by the Convention on Genocide ratified by Australia in 1949.

What made this event particularly meaningful was that it was carried out by the citizens without the government's sanction. Some even created "Sorry Books" filled with blank pages in which everyone had the chance to express their own feelings regarding the forced removal policy. Eventually over 1,000 books with half a million messages were presented to members of the "stolen generations."

What an beautiful example of the willingness to heal from our dominance trance and begin to explore a more partnership-oriented existence — one that honors the peaceful essence within us all.

YES! Magazine Fall 1998 Reprinted from YES! magazine, PO Box 10818, Bainbridge Island, WA 98110. Subscriptions: 800/937-4451 Web: www.yesmagazine.org

"First Nation" people. A law was finally passed on March 6th, 2002 allowing for the return of her remains. In her speech at the enrobement ceremony on August 4th, 2002, the Deputy Minister of Arts, Culture, Science and Technology, Ms. B.S. Mabandla celebrated the implications of the occasion:

> There is something hugely significant in the national and international action and co-operation that took place in ensuring that Sarah Bartmann's remains traveled back to her land. In taking this step, there is an implicit acknowledgement that earlier world-views no longer have a place in our world.
>
> As the President has said, Sarah Bartmann's return is profoundly significant, as her experience symbolizes the inter-relationship of gender oppression, colonialism and racial exploitation. Consequently the restoration of Sarah Bartmann's dignity through this enrobement ceremony and through a proper burial is a powerful statement about the need to restore and safeguard the dignity of all the women of Africa and the world. In this, the African Millennium, let us not forget the need for a strong Nation to be built on values of dignity, human rights and freedom for all.
>
> Kom ons vat mekaar se hande en werk saam vir 'n beter Suid-Afrika waarop ons nog meer trots kan wees. [14]

Sarah Bartmann, (Saartjie Baartman), is a perfect symbol of human domination. She represents those who were on the receiving end of the human willingness - in the context of the domination trance - to subjugate and de-humanize others, especially those clearly representing the Yin archetype. Her repatriation represents not only the recognition of her humanity and dignity as a First Nation woman, but, on many levels, the conscious symbolic return and embracing of the Yin archetype into humanity's Being once more.

What will life look like when we fully embrace Yin into our hearts? That is ours to create, but Riane Eisler offers us a glimpse in her book, <u>Sacred Pleasure – Sex, Myth, and the Politics of the Body – New Paths to Power and Love</u>. The chart below was adapted from that found on pages 403-405, showing a clear comparison between the world viewed through the perceptual filter of the Dominator Model and one viewed through the Partnership Model.

We're sometimes told violence is "human nature." But findings from sociology, psychology, and neuroscience show that a major factor in whether people commit violence is what happens during a child's early formative years. As research from Harvard University and Maclean Hospital shows, the brain neurochemistry of abused children tends to become programmed for fight-or-flight, and thus for violence.

When children experience violence, or observe violence against their mothers, they learn it's acceptable— even moral—to use force to impose one's will on others. Indeed, the only way they can make sense of violence coming from those who are supposed to love them is that it must be moral.

Riane Eisler
Spare the Rod
YES! magazine Winter 2005

Reprinted from YES! magazine, PO Box 10818, Bainbridge Island, WA 98110. Subscriptions: 800/937-4451 Web: www.yesmagazine.org http://www.saiv.net/docs/32 YesEisler150dpi.pdf

Component	Dominator Model	Partnership Model
Gender Relations	Male ranked over Female	Female and Males are Equal
Violence	High degree of Social Violence. Abuse is institutionalized	Violence and Abuse are NOT structural components
Social Structure	Predominantly Hierarchic and Authoritarian	Generally egalitarian
Sexuality	Coercion is a major element. Erotization of dominance, and/or repression of erotic pleasure.	Mutual respect and freedom of choice for both males and females.
Spirituality	Man and spirituality are ranked over woman and nature	Both woman's and natures' life-giving and sustaining powers are recognized and valued
Pleasure and Pain	Infliction or threat of pain is integral to systems maintenance	Human relations held together more by pleasure bonds than by fear of pain
Power and Love	Highest power is the power to dominate and destroy	Highest power is the power to give, nurture, and illuminate life

Acknowledgment begins the Healing

The pain endured by Sarah Bartmann and the millions who have suffered under dominator culture need to be acknowledged. Both victim and perpetator suffered – we all did. And it continues today, in every instance where multinational corporations claim the commons (water, air, land, natural resources) — those vital gifts of the Earth that belong to all who inhabit her — as their own. In every place where AIDS runs rampant and disease is allowed to flourish due to lack of clean food, sanitation, inexpensive drugs and creative remedies. Everywhere that economic structures demand scarcity in order that the few can benefit from the unacknowledged slavery of the many (whether through the promotion of mass illusion, through gender-related roles and inequalities, or actual slavery in the traditional sense.) In all places where voices are silenced, muffled, disrespected, or merely dulled through misinformation and the feeding of distractive brain candy instead of straight transparent truth. It is alive in every instance where we see anything other than magnificent wholeness when we look into each other's eyes, or see less-than when we peruse any aspect of life on Earth, or look into the mirror.

We have the choice to be colonists of each other or interdependent advocates for the aliveness that we all share. When we choose to honor all, we choose life.

One might say that macular, or central vision, is "Yang" as compared to peripheral vision, which is "Yin". The intellect is Yang; the Self is more comparable to Yin. (Although it includes the Yang, it does so in a Yin manner!)

Dr. David R. Hawkins

The Eye of the I, page 207

Notes

1. Originally, the Yin Yang symbol was the result of the ancient Chinese tracking of the cycle of the seasons, by noting the shadow of an 8 foot stick placed in the center of a 24 sectioned circle. Throughout the year the position of the shadow, as it fell on the circle, was noted. The spots on this circle that represented the summer and winter solstices corresponded to the shortest and longest shadows.

    By rotating the Sun chart and positioning the Winter Solstice at the bottom, it will look like this . The light color area which indicates more sunlight is called Yang (Sun). The dark color area has less sunlight (more moonlight) and is called Yin (Moon). Yang is like man. Yin is like woman. Yang wouldn't grow without Yin. Yin couldn't give birth without Yang. Yin is born (begins) at Summer Solstice and Yang is born (begins) at Winter Solstice. Therefore one little circle Yin is marked on the Summer Solstice position. Another little circle Yang is marked on the Winter Solstice position. These two little circles look like two fish eyes.

    In general, the Yin Yang symbol is a Chinese representation of the entire celestial phenomenon. It contains the cycle of Sun, four seasons, 24-Segment Chi, the foundation of the I-Ching and the Chinese calendar.

Summer Solstice

Vernal Equinox *Autumnal Equinox*

Winter Solstice

The qualities associated with Yang are: white, active, creative, warm, light, full, muscle, bone, male, extroversion, sun, south, and summer.

The qualities most associated with Yin include: black, passive, receptive, cold, dark, empty, fat, female, introversion, moon, north, and winter.
Although these associations have been translated through many languages and were created in the context of a specific time and culture, the general concept – with slight variations – has been found in diverse cultures throughout history. There are many other qualities I would add to both lists, such as "birthing, being, and co-creation" to Yin; and "doing" to yang. Inspired by Allen Tsai's wonderful website::
http://www.chinesefortunecalendar.com/yinyang.htm

2. While I have difficulty believing these assertions, I may have to re-think my resistance after recently reading the compelling essay The "Little Mermaid" and the Archetype of the Lost "Bride." , by Margaret Starbird, 1999. I found it at http://members.tripod.com/~Ramon_K_Jusino/littlemermaid.html
3. Yvette Abrahams, So How Come We're Not Talking About Love Anymore? (A Kukummi) http://www.fito.co.za/april_2004/articles/abrahams_so_how_come.htm
4. Gary Wilson, Sex IN the Brain, FROM: http://www.reuniting.info/RAsexbrain.htm This is the same neurochemical dance comically portrayed in the wedding scene from the hit movie, "What the Bleep Do We Know?" (see www.whatthebleep.com).
5. What is Sex, Anyway? By ReiD Mihalko http://cuddleparty.com/articles/whatissex.html
6. Marnia Robinson, Peace Between the Sheets, throughout the book. http://www.reuniting.info/GBabout.htm
7. David C. Korten, Nicanor Perlas, and Vandana Shiva Global Civil Society:The Path Ahead (Summary) http://www.pcdf.org/civilsociety/path.htm#Democracy
8. See Riane Eisler, Sacred Pleasure – Sex, Myth, and the Politics of the Body – New Paths to Power and Love pages 403-405 for a more detailed comparison of the dominator and partnership models.
9. Riane Eisler, Sacred Pleasure – Sex, Myth, and the Politics of the Body – New Paths to Power and Love page 96
10. Riane Eisler, Sacred Pleasure – Sex, Myth, and the Politics of the Body – New Paths to Power and Love page 96
11. Riane Eisler, Spare the Rod, Yes! Magazine, Winter 2005, http://www.yesmagazine.com/article.asp?ID=1167 Reprinted from YES! magazine, PO Box 10818, Bainbridge Island, WA 98110. Subscriptions: 800/937-4451 Web: www.yesmagazine.org Also see Riane Eisler, Sacred Pleasure – Sex, Myth, and the Politics of the Body – New Paths to Power and Love page 179
12. See the Reference Section for detailed statistics from multiple sources that back up this claim.
13. The main source of Sarah Bartmann's story was this article: http://www.gwsafrica.org/knowledge/yvette.html Feminist Knowledge | Identities, Culture & Religion Colonialism, disjuncture and dysfunction: Sarah Bartmann's resistance By Yvette Abrahams (Paper presented at the AGI informal seminar series 6 November, 2001)
14. Speech By The Deputy Minister Of Arts, Culture, Science And Technology, Ms Bs Mabandla, At The Enrobement Of The Remains Of Sarah Bartmann, Cape Town Civic Centre, 4 August 2002 http://www.info.gov.za/speeches/2002/02080611461001.htm

5

AVOIDING THE VOID
Quantum Physics

This state was utterly void in one sense and utterly full in another.

It contained nothing we could possibly perceive,

yet the potential for everything resided here.

As the Vedic seers declared,

neither existence nor nonexistence could be found,

since those terms apply only to things that have a beginning, middle, and end.

Deepak Chopra

How to Know God, page 31

If consciousness is not some emergent property of life, as Western science supposes, but is instead a primary quality of the cosmos - as fundamental as space, time, and matter, perhaps even more fundamental - then we arrive at a very different picture of reality. As far as our understanding of the material world goes, nothing much changes; but when it comes to our understanding of mind, we are led to a very different worldview indeed. I realized that the hard problem of consciousness was not a problem to be solved so much as the trigger that would, in time, push Western science into what the American philosopher Thomas Kuhn called a "paradigm shift."... I now believe that rather than trying to explain consciousness in terms of the material world, we should be developing a new worldview in which consciousness is a fundamental component of reality.

Peter Russell
Mysterious Light: A Scientist's Odyssey
From Noetic Sciences Review
#50, pp. 8-13,44-47

Avoiding the Void

As I began to expand my perceptual experience, I wanted to know if there was a field of science that could explain my new and evolving perceptual awareness. I didn't need to look far. This chapter is an exploration of that connection between science, perception, and the personal experience I call, "the void."

Diving into the Unknown

Over the last century physics has developed several new branches, perhaps none more exciting than quantum mechanics. One of the most famous physicists, Niels Bohr, who won the Nobel Prize in 1922, stated:

If quantum mechanics hasn't profoundly shocked you, you haven't understood it yet.

He was right. Not only does it turn much of classic physics on it's head, it is constantly changing with new theories and interpretations. Most lay people just shake their head when trying to comprehend its complexities, and even many scientists are confused. It humbles us all. It is precisely this aspect of quantum mechanics — its tendency to dwell in the realm of the "not known" - that captivates me, for I come from a culture that reveres science as absolute (even though the best scientists don't). The humility to enter that place of "not knowing" is essential to creative inquiry.

Scientists use experiments and math to substantiate the validity of their theories, but in the realm of quantum mechanics and cosmology, how can you finally prove anything? The nature of the subject matter makes it difficult to track, measure, and quantify. In that way, it is somewhat analogous to life. Stephen Hawking offers an extremely clear discussion of theories in his book, <u>A Brief History of Time (The Updated and Expanded Tenth Anniversary Edition),</u> when he writes:

> I shall take the simpleminded view that a theory is just a model of the universe, or a restricted part of it, and a set of rules that relate quantities in the model to observations that we make. It exists only in our minds and does not have any other reality (whatever that might mean). A theory is a good theory if it satisfies two requirements. It must accurately describe a large class of observations on the basis of a model that contains only a few arbitrary elements, and it must make definite predictions about the results of future observations...Any physical theory is always provisional, in the sense that it is only a hypothesis: you can never prove it. No matter how many times the results of experiments agree with some theory, you can never be sure that the next time the result will not contradict the theory. On the other hand, you can disprove a theory by finding even a single observation that disagrees with the predictions of the theory. [1]

Our society has placed scientists on such a high pedestal that it is refreshing to hear such a revered scientist acknowledge the inability to prove physical theories. I find it humbling to know that ultimately, in this physical world, nothing can be proved true — even through scientific methodology.

A Quantum Physics Perceptual Filter

Both subtle and physical worlds remain in possibility until consciousness self-referentially collapses the possibility structure into actuality.

Amit Goswami
Physicist

Quantum mechanics is a dynamically evolving area of scientific theory, one in which many minds are eagerly searching for answers to life's basic questions. It consists of many theories — many contradictory — based on the best evidence science has been able to acquire so far. It is important to understand that this field of study changes so quickly even the theorists have a hard time keeping up. Therefore please understand that anything I quote here could be out of date by tomorrow.

But what an exciting field of discovery! I like to think of these theories as perceptual filters, similar to a pair of glasses through which to observe life. Scientists seem to be trying on many filters very rapidly right now (and discarding them just as quickly). This adds a light-hearted, highly creative air to the adventure. Let's check some out.

Atoms Revisited

Quantum mechanics offers a different picture of the atom than the simple traditional solar-system model often taught in school. It's focus is the study of the sub-atomic particles that make up an atom. Surprisingly, the smaller the particle, the less solid everything becomes. Deepak Chopra does one of the best jobs of explaining one common theory to the layperson. He begins:

> But in fact an amazing transformation happens beyond the atom – everything solid disappears. Atoms are composed of vibrating energy packets that have no solidity at all, …or (definite*) size, nothing of the senses to see or touch. The Latin word for a packet or package is *quantum*, the word chosen to describe one unit of energy inside the atom, and, as it turned out, a new level of reality.

> At the quantum level nothing of the material world is left intact. It is strange enough to hold up your hand and realize that it is actually, at a deeper level, invisible vibrations taking place in a void. Even at the atomic level all objects are revealed as 99.9999 percent empty space. On its own scale, the distance between a whirling electron and the nucleus it revolves around is wider than the distance between the earth and the sun. But you could never capture that electron anyway, since it too breaks down into energy vibrations that wink in and out of existence millions of times per second. Therefore the whole universe is a quantum mirage, winking in and out of existence millions of times per second. At the quantum level the whole cosmos is like a blinking light. There are no stars or galaxies, only vibrating energy fields that our senses are too dull and slow to pick up given the incredible speed at which light and electricity move. *(The word "definite" added by Shaktari for clarification.)* [2]

We cannot "see" any fundamental particles, they are far below the limits of our retinal perception. What we do see is the manifestation of zillions of these particles. That is what we call "reality." Chopra likens our perception of reality to the science behind the making of movies. The name, "movie," refers to the fact that films are actually made up of 24 still pictures flashed before our eyes every second, with a gap of blackness in between each picture. Since our eyes cannot detect 48 stop-motion events in a second, the illusion of a moving picture results. He states:

> Now speed this up by many powers of ten and you get the trick of the movie we call real life. You and I exist as flashing photons with a black void in between each flash – the quantum light show comprises our whole body, our every thought and wish, and every event we take part in. In other words, we are being created, over and over again, all the time. Genesis is now and always has been. [3]

According to this theory then, we are actively re-creating ourselves new each moment, with every pulse of our quantum vibration. In fact, everything is in that same state of newness.

The Objectivity Illusion

Another surprising theory is Heisenberg 's Uncertainty Principle of 1927. The Uncertainty Principle states that one can determine the position or velocity of an electron, but not both *simultaneously* with unlimited accuracy, no matter how good

Psychiatrist Stanislav Grof (1985, 1988) has developed a cartography of human consciousness that summarizes his extensive research into nonordinary states of consciousness. He has noted a close correspondence between the holomovement and his research findings. More than thirty years of clinical research and observation have led Grof to the viewpoint that "each of us is everything." meaning that every human being has potential access to all forms of consciousness (Grof 1990). His data provide a kind of phenomenological evidence for a holographic model of consciousness.

Will Keepin, PhD
Life Work of David Bohm – River of Truth

your instrumentation. Dr. Hawking remarks that the implications of this Principle regarding how we view the world are rarely appreciated, even after over seventy years. They are still highly controversial. For example, he points out that the dream of developing a grand theory of science that would be completely deterministic and able to predict future events exactly, can no longer be sustained if you can't even measure the present state of the universe with any precision. The result of this principle, however, was the birth of quantum mechanics. He writes,

> In general, quantum mechanics does not predict a single definite result for an observation. Instead, it predicts a number of different possible outcomes…(it) introduces an unavoidable element of unpredictability or randomness into science. [4]

Without going into much detail, the conclusion drawn - in layperson terms, is that the *observer affects the observed.* A sub-atomic particle exists as a wave *and* a particle. When it is observed, it collapses into a particle that expresses as form. If your attention is withdrawn, it again becomes a wave – a potential unexpressed.   Think about this for a moment. It completely contradicts everything we learned in school about science being an impartial observer of life. On the quantum level, it seems there is no impartiality. The mere act of observation results in change. Observation takes a potentiality and collapses it into what we perceive as reality. What does this say about the power of perception itself?

…quantum theory forced them to accept the fact that the solid material objects of classical physics dissolve at the subatomic level into wavelike patterns of probabilities. These patterns, moreover, do not represent the probabilities of things, but rather probabilities of <u>interconnections</u>.

Fritjof Capra
<u>The Web of Life</u>
page 30.

The Separation Illusion

There is more. The concept of Nonlocality was derived from studies of particle spins within a single system. The spin of a particle cannot be determined until a measurement is made, but once the spin of particle 1 is determined, the spin of particle 2 is also determined. In other words, particle 2 will respond instantly to the state of particle 1, no matter their distance. The question is, how does particle 2 know the spin of particle 1? We haven't been able to discover any method by which information has been transferred, yet evidence shows that once particles have interacted at any time, this connection remains – even if they are on opposite sides of the universe. Alain Aspect's experiments of 1982 have been refined and repeated to the point that they seem to strongly substantiate the existence of quantum nonlocality, also sometimes called "nonseparability."

This suggests that our traditional view of objects as separate independently existing entities is no longer valid. For example, if everything in the universe was created in one huge "big bang," then *everything* is related in a similar manner to particles 1 and 2. Every particle is "aware" of every other particle in the universe – suggesting a profound cosmological holism. Furthermore, at the quantum level of reality, it seems that *everything* affects everything else.

If this conclusion is valid, it means that *you personally influence* the world and *the world influences you* in the most intimate manner possible. In experiment after experiment, science is showing that your thoughts and feelings actually impact others over varying distances. As a result, science is beginning to explain what was previously seen as inexplicable psychic phenomenon, including prayer.

Take for example, the work of Dr. Larry Dossey, who offers experimental evidence that consciousness and intention are unifying forces in nature. His studies of the impact of intercessory prayer on humans with AIDS and pregnancy show highly impressive results. But it is his work with replication rates of bacteria in test tubes, fungi growth in petri dishes, and germination rates of seeds that has really convinced the scientific community to take notice – specifically because the experiments were done in laboratory settings with rigorous precision. These non-human experiments offer evidence that non-locality of consciousness is active throughout nature. He writes:

> You see these intentionality and prayer effects from the micro or atomic-molecular level through the meso or middle world, where bacteria live, up to the macro world inhabited by human and plants and animals. This linkage, this so-called concatenation of coming together of effects, unifying these vastly different domains of nature, is one of the most compelling aspects of this field. This sort of concatenation is a highly valued feature of valid science. It suggests that we're dealing with a general principle that is embedded throughout all nature, and that we're not fooling ourselves about the existence of the phenomenon…
>
> I would suggest that these healing and fertility studies ought to function as a wake-up call for the entire eco-environmental movement, because what are we involved in if not the fertility and healing of the earth?[5]

Dr. Dossey's influence has been so great, that this field of study has been added to 80 of the 125 medical schools in the USA; up from only three just six years ago.

You can probably think of many instances where you experienced this non-local phenomenon in your own life. Have you ever felt something was "off," but you had no explanation for it, no proof? Yet later you found you were right? We often call this "intuition" but perhaps these studies are finally placing this common phenomenon in a scientific context.

Since 1998, the Global Consciousness Project, located at Princeton University, has been monitoring 40 random number generators around the world. The Institute of Noetic Sciences Review #58 states:

> Preposterous though it may sound, *significant deviations have been noted in the randomness of data from these RNGs around times of major events in the world.* Immediate questions, of course, include "Is this a real effect?" and, if so, "What is going on?"… It appears that consciousness may sometimes produce something that resembles, at least metaphorically, a nonlocal field of meaningful information.

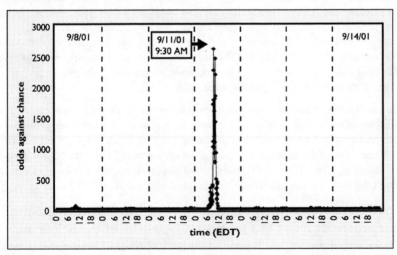

It isn't that the world of appearances is wrong; ;it isn't that there aren't objects out there, at one level of reality. It's that if you penetrate through and look at the universe with a holographic system, you arrive at a different view, a different reality. And that other reality can explain things that have hitherto remained inexplicable scientifically: paranormal phenomena, synchronicities, the apparently meaningful coincidence of events.

Karl Pribram, PhD.
Creator of the Holographic Model of the Brain

In an interview in Psychology Today, quoted by Michael Talbot in his book, The Holographic Universe, page 11.

This graph was created by Dean Radin, PhD, and first appeared in IONS Review #58 (Dec. 2001-Feb. 2002). Reprinted by permission of the Institute of Noetic Sciences (IONS), www.noetic.org. Copyright © 2001 IONS. All rights reserved.

This picture (above) shows a remarkable correlation between the behavior of the GCP's random event generators (REG) and an event that intensely focused mass attention worldwide. The graph plots the odds against chance associated with data generated by all 36 REGs running in the GCP network from September 8 through 14. The large spike on **September 11, 2001**, which began to rise around 6 AM EDT, peaked during the midst of the terrorist attacks on the World Trade Center and the Pentagon. This indicates that the GCP network—and, by hypothesis, the collective psyche—responded to and possibly anticipated the attacks... We don't yet know how to explain the subtle correlations between events of importance to humans and the GCP data, but they are quite clear...The results are evidence that the physical world and our mental world of information and meaning are linked in ways that we don't yet understand. [6]

What is especially worth noting is that the spike in the graph began 3 hours *before* the event actually occurred. This phenomenon has repeated on many dates in which historical events of significance took place, both peaceful and traumatic. We don't yet know what this means, but perhaps it is compelling evidence for the Oneness experienced in what Dr. David Bohm calls, the Implicate Order, that field of infinite possibilities to which ALL is connected.

Explicate, Implicate, and Superimplicate Orders

Physicist David Bohm's model of reality includes the concept of a dynamic holomovement made up of three levels of manifestation: the Explicate Order, which consists of what we perceive to be everyday normal reality; the Implicate Order, which acts as a field of infinite possibility from which all manifestation arises; and the Superimplicate Order, a highly complex and subtle realm likened to an eternal order outside of time - neither static nor everlasting – that is the source of creativity. In his homage to Bohm entitled, River of Truth, Will Keepin explains:

The quantum potential, the superquantum potential, the implicate order, and superimplicate orders are all names given to realms that are invisible to ordinary perception, yet for Bohm, they constitute the true structure of reality. For Bohm, the holomovement is the nature of reality, and the implicate order and superimplicate order are its primary structural features, with the explicate order being the surface appearance. Superimplicate orders may be involved in innumerable physical and natural processes. In evolution, for example, superimplicate orders could guide the emergence of a bird, which must not only develop wings but aerodynamically adapted feathers, appropriate musculature, shifted center of gravity, lighter bones and appropriate changes in metabolism--all at the same time. Otherwise, any one of these changes by itself would likely decrease chances of survival... All of these terms are just labels for subtle orders or forces that remain hidden to empirical science, and hence they are resisted by mainstream scientists, sometimes vehemently. However, just because they have not been directly observed does not mean that they do not exist. In his postulate of the implicate order, Bohm clearly demonstrates how such realms could exist and be very fundamental, while being missed altogether by mainstream science in its focus on the explicate order only.

Consciousness is much more of the implicate order than is matter. . . Yet at a deeper level [matter and consciousness] are actually inseparable and interwoven, just as in the computer game the player and the screen are united by participation in common loops. In this view, mind and matter are two aspects of one whole and no more separable than are form and content. "Deep down the consciousness of mankind is one. This is a virtual certainty because even in the vacuum matter is one; and if we don't see this, it's because we are blinding ourselves to it. [7]

Bohm, used the term "holomovement" to describe the dynamic flux of energy inherent in all three orders. It refers to a unique characteristic of the hologram, in which no matter how you divide it, each individual part contains the information of the whole. A holomovement is an undivided whole in perpetual dynamic flow from which all arises and to which all returns, merging into One. Keepin writes:

It's only in physics that we're beginning to talk about the deep reality of non-locality, which means that every point in the universe has access to the information at any other point. There will probably also be acknowledged, if not already, such a thing as non-temporality, in which anything at any given time in the universe (linear time) has access to the information at any other time. Because the basis of the universe is turning out to be a non-time-space "something" that is really "everything" -- precisely what the ancient Greeks called the Plenum. It isn't limited by time-space constraints. It doesn't have to worry about linear time. And as the deep reality of our universe, it is of course the deep reality of every one of our cells! It's the deep reality of each one of our molecules. It's the deep reality of each of us.

Elisabet Sahtouris, Living Systems, the Internet and the Human Future Talk presented 13 May 2000 at Planetwork, Global Ecology and Information Technology Conference held at the San Francisco Presidio http://www.ratical.org /LifeWeb/Articles/L SinetHF.html

Similarly, living and nonliving entities are not separate. As Bohm puts it, "The ability of form to be active is the most characteristic feature of mind, and we have something that is mindlike already with the electron." Thus, matter does not exist independently from so-called empty space; matter and space are each part of the wholeness…

In analogy to holography but on a much grander scale, Bohm believes that each part of physical reality contains information about the whole. Thus in some sense, every part of the universe "contains" the entire universe.

Evidence for this kind of holographic structure in nature has emerged recently in the burgeoning field of chaos theory and its close cousin, fractal geometry… As Bohm puts it, the holomovement refers to "the unbroken wholeness of the totality of existence as an undivided flowing movement without borders" (Bohm 1980, 172). [7]

Perhaps now we can begin to answer the earlier question, regarding how our physical reality is perceived as the same moment to moment even though it consists – as described by Chopra – of "flashing photons with a black void in between each flash… a quantum light show comprised of our whole body, our every thought and wish, and every event we take part in."

Bohm explains physical reality through the action of electrons. He sees them as "enfolded ensembles" that are usually without location, but instead exist as clouds of potentiality. At any moment, one of the ensembles may unfold, causing it to localize. Another may enfold, then another unfold, each time localizing adjacent to the previous one, giving the illusion of continuous motion, similar to the 48 frames of flashing stills per second that create the illusion of movies. To understand this process more clearly, Will Keepin asks us to imagine the twirling propeller of an airplane, that gives the illusion of a solid disc. He quotes Bohm:

> ". . . fundamentally, the particle is only an abstraction that is manifest to our senses. *What is,* is always a totality of ensembles, all present together, in an orderly series of stages of enfoldment and unfoldment, which intermingle and inter-penetrate each other in principle throughout the whole of space" (Bohm 1980, 183-184). [7]

Keepin reminds us that the implicate and superimplicate orders, though invisible, are the fundamentals of reality. He calls the explicate order – that which we perceive as reality - "a set of 'ripples' on the surface of the implicate order". The implicate and explicate orders interpenetrate everything. He again quotes Bohm:

> "[I]n the implicate order the totality of existence is enfolded within each region of space (and time). So, whatever part, element, or aspect we may abstract in thought, this still enfolds the whole and is therefore intrinsically related to the totality from which it has been abstracted. Thus, wholeness permeates all that is being discussed, from the very outset." (p. 172) [7]

The implicate is everywhere and of everything, similar to the way light and air surround and fill us – or in the way that water is so much a part of everything that we cease to be aware of it. I like to refer to the Implicate order as the "field of infinite possibilities," because no limitations exist in this realm.

It is important to note that our *intentions* are the tool through which we impact and affect the Implicate Order – and thus reality. Your intentions *and* mine. We literally create each other through our thoughts, feelings, and intentions. If we combine Bohm's implicate order and the principle of nonlocality, one could conclude that *we are all ONE, there is no separation.* Chopra poetically describes this Oneness:

> But are we being dreamed by a single divine intelligence, by God, or are we being dreamed by the collective consciousness of all things – by all the electrons, Z particles, butterflies, neutron stars,

What is needed is a relativistic theory, to give up altogether the notion that the world is constituted of basic objects or building blocks. Rather one has to view the world in terms of universal flux of events and processes.

Dr. David Bohm
Physicist

It is as if consciousness rests upon a self-sustaining and imagining substrate -- an inner place or deeper person or ongoing presence -- that is simply there even when all our subjectivity, ego, and consciousness go into eclipse. Soul appears as a factor independent of the events in which we are immersed. Though I cannot identify soul with anything else, I also can never grasp it apart from other things, perhaps because it is like a reflection in a flowing mirror, or like the moon which mediates only borrowed light.

James Hillman
Re-visioning Psychology
http://www.mythosandlogos.com/ Hillman.html

To appreciate the relationship between parts and wholes in living systems, we do not need to study nature at the microscopic level. If you gaze up at the nighttime sky, you see all of the sky visible from where you stand. Yet the pupil of your eye, fully open, is less than a centimeter across. Somehow, light from the whole of the sky must be present in the small space of your eye. And if your pupil were only half as large, or only one quarter as large, this would still be so. Light from the entirety of the nighttime sky is present in every space —no matter how small.

This is exactly the same phenomenon evident in a hologram. The three-dimensional image created by interacting laser beams can be cut in half indefinitely, and each piece, no matter how small, will still contain the entire image. This reveals <u>what is perhaps the most</u> mysterious aspect of parts and wholes: as physicist Henri Bortoft says, "Everything is in everything."

Peter M.Senge, C.Otto Scharmer, Joseph Jaworski, and Betty Sue Flowers

<u>*Awakening Faith in an Alternative Future*</u>

www.dialogonleadership.org. and Reflections The SoL Journal on Knowledge,Learning,and Change, Vol 5 Number 7. (See "Conversation with Henri Bortoft: Imagination Becomes an Organ of Perception," interview by C.O. Scharmer London, July 14,1999)

sea cucumbers, human and nonhuman intelligences in the universe? Here again we collide headlong into the bars of our own conceptual limitations, for in a holographic universe this question is meaningless. We cannot ask if the part is creating the whole, or the whole is creating the part because *the part is the whole.* So whether we call the collective consciousness of all things "God," or simply "the consciousness of all things," it doesn't change the situation. The universe is sustained by an act of such stupendous and ineffable creativity that it simply cannot be reduced to such terms. Again it is a self-reference cosmology. Or as the Kalahari Bushmen so eloquently put it, "The dream is dreaming itself." [8]

Quality of your Life

How does life change when you suddenly realize that you alone determine the quality of your reality through your use of thoughts and intention? Life becomes an adventure, and each moment is pregnant with possibilities.

You can still find yourself voting as to whether or not you like the choices you've made and the circumstances you find yourself currently experiencing. But when you take full responsibility for those choices, the illusory burden of being a victim *of anything* disappears. It is replaced with the joy of creativity.

It's as if your life is a canvas and you are the painter, free to choose the quality of your artistic statement in every moment. When you find that you don't like something you've painted, you can simply change it. And because you are open to the flow of life's energy, serendipitous experiences become the norm. Ultimately, when in this state of Oneness, all elements of life seem to co-create together.

The Void

Soon after I realized my ability to create the quality of my life through my own thoughts and intentions, a new experience began. It was an experience, I soon realized, I had avoided at all cost. As I have allowed myself to experience life as choice, I have begun to glimpse what I can only call a sort of background field, a kind of landscape from which choice emerges. I call it "the VOID", and perhaps Dr. Bohm would call it the "Superimplicate," while Dr. Chopra would use "Virtual Domain." Unlike the experience of ONEness-with-All (the Implicate Order) that fills me with indescribable joy, the experience of the VOID holds no emotion, it simply is.

Meaning

Just as there are no words to accurately describe the experience of being ONE with everything, we also have no language to describe the VOID. When I am in touch with the VOID, life is experienced as a neutral field in which *nothing matters*, because I experience humans as eternal beings playing our chosen roles, all of which can change with the next choice. *Therefore the only meaning anything has is the meaning I give it.* And regardless of what choice I make, ultimately *nothing matters – or everything matters,* because *all* experiences offer valuable lessons to those willing to receive them. I had intellectually understood this concept for years, but until I allowed myself to experience the VOID, I had never actually lived it.

The effect of this realization was tremendous. Since it didn't matter what I chose, simply making a choice became meaningless and unimportant. I no longer judged certain choices as better than others, because they were all simply choices, and each held as much significance as choosing what clothes I would wear that day. As a result, I spent several months barely functioning. My daughter forced me to play my role as mother, but behind everything was a detachment, a sort of witnessing of myself playing my chosen roles. Yet this same feeling of being un-attached to the outcome of any decision paradoxically allowed me to simply enjoy the moment without an investment in what would come next.

Nothing but Choice

I also found that my *desire* and passion for any activity disappeared. It seemed to me that it didn't matter if I ever DID anything, including finish this book. After allowing myself to wallow in the VOID for a while, I got to the point where actively choosing became more exciting than the choice to not choose.

Consciously choosing became my expression of passion and aliveness in life. Choosing became my vote for who I am (who I choose to be) in any given moment. I had to smile inwardly, for the actions I undertook looked the same to an observer, but my *experience* of them had been transformed.

The gift of the VOID

Allowing myself to finally experience the inactive state of the VOID, provided me with an enormous gift – the gift of taking full responsibility for everything. By taking full responsibility for the choices I make, I acknowledge my power as a co-creator in life. We all have this ability, and when we consciously choose to co-create our world together, it can truly be an expression of the unconditional love that lies at the heart of humanity, it can truly honor all.

Will Keepin summarizes the difference between our experience of reality and the underlying truth that all religions, philosophies, and physics seek to reveal:

> There is a gulf between truth and reality; they are not the same thing.
>
> Illusion and falsehood are certainly part of reality, but they are not part of truth.
>
> Truth includes all that is; it is one.
>
> Reality is conditioned and multiple. Truth is beyond reality; it comprehends reality,
>
> but not vice versa.
>
> Reality is everything; truth is no-thingness
>
> We need truth, but our minds are occupied with reality.
>
> We seek security in reality, but authentic security comes only in complete nothingness,
>
> that is, only in truth.
>
> The seed of truth is a mystery that thought cannot encompass; it is beyond reality. [9]

I like Dr. Keepin's distinction between reality as everything (All-That-Is or Oneness) and Truth as no-thingness (the Void). Humanity has struggled with these concepts forever. No language can describe truth, for it is outside the descriptive possibilities of linear language. The minute you label it – it is no longer truth. It is a label of a concept. Perhaps that is why poetry best illuminates that which words can merely dance around but never actually touch.

Truth simply is. The constant unfolding joy of life is the pleasure of allowing that experience – found deep within our hearts - to illuminate our daily choices.

There are suggestive, intriguing parallels between the universe of the new physics and the universe of the timeless mystics. The deep sense of interconnectedness and privileging of consciousness over matter supports – indirectly – the worldview of nonviolence…

That world of material mechanics, which still holds sway over most minds and is the official science 'story' of the mass media, is a world of scarcity (because matter is finite, because it has a limited capacity to fulfill us). It spawns violence by telling us that we are separate: "I can hurt you without hurting the larger whole that includes myself - and since there isn't enough for both of us, we have a reason to fight each other."

Michael Nagler
Compassion – The Radicalism of this Age
Yes! Magazine Fall 1998

Notes

1. Stephen Hawking, A Brief History of Time -The Updated and Expanded Tenth Anniversary Edition, page 10.
2. How to Know God, Deepak Chopra, pages 29-30.
3. How to Know God, Deepak Chopra, page 30.
4. Stephen Hawking, A Brief History of Time -The Updated and Expanded Tenth Anniversary Edition, page 58.
5. Larry Dossey, Think Globally, Act non-locally: Consciousness beyond Time and Space, from Ecological Medicine – Healing the Earth, Healing Ourselves, edited by Kenny Ausubel, with J.P. Harpignes, pages 220-221. See also the work of Dr. Larry Dossey, author of Healing Words and Prayer Is Good Medicine. Dr. Dossey's meticulous research backs up his claim that the effects of nonlocal healing (as in prayer and other non-traditional modalities) are too persuasive to ignore.
6. This graph was created by Dean Radin, PhD, and first appeared in IONS Review #58 (Dec. 2001-Feb. 2002). Reprinted by permission of the Institute of Noetic Sciences (IONS), www.noetic.org. The quote is from the same issue.   (http://noosphere.princeton.edu/)
7. Will Keepin, Lifework of Quantum Physicist David Bohm – River of Truth, http://www.vision.net.au/~apaterson/science/david_bohm.htm#HOLOMOVEMENT
8. How to Know God, Deepak Chopra, page 31.
9. Will Keepin, Lifework of Quantum Physicist David Bohm – River of Truth, http://www.vision.net.au/~apaterson/science/david_bohm.htm#HOLOMOVEMENT

In a sense, the seed is a gateway through which the future possibility of the living tree emerges.

Peter M.Senge, C.Otto Scharmer, Joseph Jaworski, and Betty Sue Flowers <u>Awakening Faith in an Alternative Future</u> *Reflections The SoL Journal*

on Knowledge,Learning,and Change, Vol 5 Number 7

In this same way, we are each the gateway through which our highest expression of life and love emerges.

6

<u>VICTIM to VISIONARY</u>

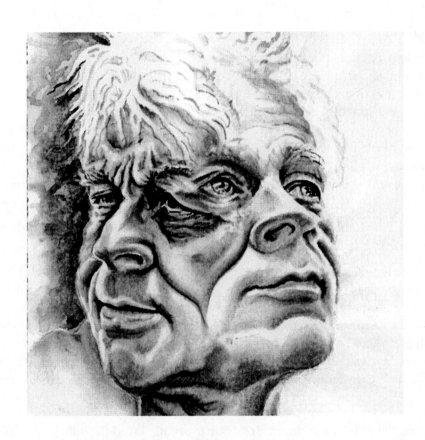

It requires the slightest shift of focus,
from concentrating on Lack,
to focusing on Gratitude for what is...
to move from the helpless feeling of the Victim
to the creative expression of the Visionary.

VICTIM TO VISIONARY

Our focus determines the field of the possible. Visionary creator or Victim, it is always a choice...

A human being is a part of the whole, called by us, "Universe," a part limited in time and space. He experiences himself, his thoughts and feelings as something separated from the rest -- a kind of optical delusion of his consciousness.

This delusion is a kind of prison for us, restricting us to our personal desires and to affection for a few persons nearest to us. Our task must be to free ourselves from this prison by widening our circle of compassion to embrace all living creatures and the whole of nature in its beauty.

- Albert Einstein

Because I was not independently wealthy, I chose to mortgage the only asset I owned – my home – in order to write this book. My home is the culmination of a lifetime of design, and it was my first public artistic expression. Risking it was a step I took with great reluctance. However, the energy of the universe flowed so freely in that direction, that when there seemed to be no other way to finance the writing of this book, the refinancing of my home proceeded relatively smoothly.

After a year, the book was still not complete. Luckily the real estate market had appreciated quickly, so I was again able to refinance. However this second loan gifted me more than just money.

When I designed my home, I went back to one of my first ventures in home design, completed at the age of ten. Back then, I had the revolutionary thought (at least so I thought) of creating a round home. Using that as my springboard, I designed a small home inspired by the idea of living inside a tree. I lovingly designed every aspect of this home, and most people feel that love upon entering. Unfortunately, lenders do not take kindly to creativity. They prefer low risk (design for conformity) loans. So even though my home appraised for more than was necessary, the paperwork was complete, and loan approval was given, the lender refused to fund the loan.

What was going on for me during this time? I was praying that my home and I would be found worthy of their approval, because I really needed that money. I remember feeling shock when I realized how I was playing the role of a victim. Me?

It hadn't occurred to me that perhaps it was the lender who should feel honored for the privilege of carrying my loan. Instead I felt helpless waiting for their "approval" of me and my heartfelt design. And because I was so caught up in what I perceived as the need for them to approve of me (the loan), I reacted with anger. It seemed highly illogical for them to withhold funding of a home that was already approved and had met all requirements. My anger kept me from seeing the many people, including my lender, who were working day and at night to complete my loan.

The power of Gratitude

I finally walked out on my deck one morning, faced the sun, and consciously connected my heart to all those who were working so hard for my loan. I began by thanking them for all their hard work and asking forgiveness if I had failed to acknowledge their efforts. Then I consciously connected with the one person upon whose desk my loan now rested. I joined hearts and repeated my gratitude. I stayed connected until I felt a shift in energy – a joining of purpose in the larger scheme of life – and a recognition of our shared Oneness.

As I turned to go back inside my house, I looked up. There on the back two-story interior wall was the shape of a perfect heart made out of sunlight coming through the ceiling skylight. I grabbed my digital camera, took the picture, and sent it to the lender with a note of gratitude sharing my realizations.

Within five minutes he called to say that the funding had gone through. When I replied, "I know," he asked how I knew. I told him, "I got out of the way."

Then I asked if he'd seen the heart photo on my e-mail and he said, "What e-mail?" When he check the time it came in to his computer, it matched the time when he received the phone call telling him the loan was complete. I was not surprised. **When we shift our energy from that of helpless victim to the energy of gratitude and creative visioning, the field of the possible also shifts.**

How does this work in everyday life? Take a look at your own life. Are there places in which you can clearly see yourself as a victim? This is subtle, because the perceptual filter of victimhood is built into our society just as strongly as the dominator-trance. In fact, they go hand in hand.

An Example…

Our culture teaches us to focus on what we dislike about ourselves and others instead of what we like. When you look into a full length mirror, do you like what you see? If you take off your clothes, does your approval level go up or down? Do you find yourself nit-picking what you like and don't like about your face? ("I have good eyes, but my cheekbones aren't high enough, etc." or similar stories about your physical presentation to the world?)

These are all symptoms of victimhood – focusing on what we don't like or want, and than evaluating life from that space. It is easy to spy because it is never creative and joyful. It often starts with the statement, "If only…"

I propose that victimhood is one of our most prevalent and socially supported perceptual filters, especially in the developed world. Strange as it seems, those of us who enjoy the most privileged lives on Earth also seem to have the most difficulty appreciating our bounty.

Lack

Notice how easily we commiserate with each other; but how difficult it is, at times, to truly celebrate another's good fortune without feeling jealous. The feeling of lack that permeates our lives seems to keep us from seeing that the good fortune of one *always* leads to the good fortune of us all. Only the illusion of separation makes it seem otherwise.

Abundance

As with all perceptual filters, once we are aware of it, we can choose the quality of our experience. Are you willing to focus on the abundant life before your eyes, the gift of each moment; or do you prefer to focus on the lack of some desired goal?

It is said that heaven and hell are only a perceptual shift apart, as exemplified in the following simple story. Both heaven and hell consist of a banquet set with very long forks. At one, the diners starve because they cannot reach their own mouths with the long utensil. At the other, all are fat and happy as the diners take turns feeding each other. Lack and abundance/gratitude are the tools of focus that determine the outcome. **By focusing on who we choose to BE instead of what we want, we all win.**

The emerging new superparadigm accounts for consciousness—an intractable anomaly for the old model… It offers radically new perspectives on some of the most perplexing problems in contemporary physics. And, most significantly, points towards a resolution of one of the oldest challenges of all—the reconciliation of the scientific worldview with the spiritual.

Peter Russell
Reality and Consciousness: Turning the Superparadigm Inside Out

PART TWO: HONORING ALL LIFE

Life Is nothing but possibilities...

THE PARABLE OF THE CATERPILLAR

A caterpillar was born. He slowly crawled out of his egg, saw that it was good, and ate it. Then he started on the leaf on which he stood. Gradually making his way along the edge, he ate and ate, always in a straight line, always one bite after another. Soon the leaf was nothing but the bony ridge of stem connecting it to the branch. Looking up, he realized that the world was nothing but leaves on stems, all for his pleasure. Consuming everything in his path, he felt comfortable in his cozy life. His days became one leaf after another as he ate his way to the moment when he suddenly no longer felt a drive to constantly consume.

Noticing the monotonous and somehow unfulfilling patterns of his life, he felt for the first time that something was wrong. When unable to discern the source of this "wrongness," he felt utterly helpless. Eating ceased to be his major life focus, as he slowly realized that there were other choices in life, other ways of being to explore. With the sudden swiftness of a lightning strike he realized that his way of seeing life was just one possible way and that he had been stuck in a single perspective his entire life. "There must be more to life than just eating everything in sight," he thought, "but what?"

Feeling angry that he had not seen the limitations of his own life, he now had the courage to search for an answer. As he sat in silence, he heard an inner voice that grew gradually louder the more listened. He chose to follow his inner voice, no matter where it might lead him, for he felt an overwhelming urge to experience life in a different way. No longer was his life described by leaves, stems, and eating. Pausing in that moment, without knowing quite what he was doing, he started spinning a cocoon. As the darkness of the closing cocoon and the confines of his now very limited world engulfed him, he was able to see his old way of living with new eyes. For the first time he was able to see that fear of lack had been a driving force in his life. The impulse to continue on his journey overwhelmed him. Merging with his fear, he felt that death was imminent. Yet he could not stop himself. Consumed with an overpowering drive to finish what he had started, he persevered. Finally the last remaining rays of light were locked out as he sealed the cocoon and his own fate in one sweeping motion.

With new-found feelings of self-compassion and with a sigh, he surrendered to the end, allowing his body to break apart into genetic soup. Stillness surrounded him, and for the first time, something else… peace and joy. Time disappeared as well. All was perceived as never-ending moments of now. No longer a caterpillar, he had no identity, and felt as if he was part of everything. A vast void opened up before him, and he seemed to float in a field of possibilities.

Gratitude flooded his being and he became aware that life was nothing but possibilities. All he had to do was choose. Empowered by this thought, he felt paradoxically both vulnerable and invincible. Feeling joyous to the point of bursting, he flung open the confining walls of the cocoon and stepped out into the dawn of a new day. Sunlight caressed his every cell as he slowly pumped life into his new expression of Self. Embracing the peace and unity he now felt with all of life, he rose and flew off to co-create the next moment as part of All-That-Is.

Moving away from our center into the limitations of our manifestations, we have forgotten. With a conscious shift of our attention from the path we are walking back toward the source of our Being, we remember... and laugh.

Sri Aurobindo
The Life Divine

When we know what we are, it no longer matters who we have thought we were.

Rainer Maria Rilke
Selected Poems of Rainer Maria Rilke

7

BEING SEEN

Deafened by the voice of desire
you are unaware the Beloved lives
in the core of your heart.
Stop the noise and you will hear
His voice in the silence.

Rumi

BEING SEEN

What alienated and dismissed parts of ourselves
Need to be called home — into our hearts,
In order to embrace the fullness of our magnificence?

Throughout most of this book we are exploring the nuances and opportunities of perceptual choices. Those choices absolutely determine our experience of "reality".

Willingness

There is another aspect of perception to explore, and it has to do with the *willingness* to be seen. In the chapter on "Honoring Self" we will explore some choices involved in consciously choosing to honor Self. Those choices determine not only our experience of Self, but ultimately our experience of everything else.

There is a distinction between Identity Self, which is the body, name, and personality into which you were born; and your Essential Self, the core of your being that is larger than your daily concerns. Your Essential Self always sees the larger picture, encompasses everything about you, and includes that special experience when you feel One with All.

How you perceive yourself, whether small and incompetent or an expression of divinity, is reflected in how others perceive you. When you are feeling small you are choosing to be your Identity Self. When you are playing full-out and are clear about your own magnificence, then you are coming from your Essential Self, and that magnificence radiates for all to see. **When aware of your Essential Self, not only do you recognize your own magnificence, but you can't help but see the same in everyone and everything you meet.** Those around may not be aware of what draws their attention, but one who radiates Self-love is like the sparkle of a mirror reflecting sunlight in a crowd. And because we are all mirrors for each other, when you truly experience Self-love, you set an example for others to experience their own magnificence too.

The Gift of Self-Love

Today, as I was walking through the local Grower's Market, I caught sight of a very unusually dressed large man. He wore a gray monk's cassock with a red heart topped by a Christian cross emblazoned on his chest. He carried an air of peace as he eagerly encountered each seller's wares. I couldn't help but approach him, his energy was radiating such acute awareness and presence. When I asked him who he was, he willingly shared his story. None of those details matter. I found I had met a master of self-love, inner peace, and joy — and his gift was to reflect that joy for all to share. My gift to him was to see and acknowledge who he was… a reflection of us all.

Focusing on Pain

I sometimes experience just the opposite. I have become keenly aware of how tender we all are, particularly adults in their 40's and 50's. I've noticed that many of us are newly single after decades of experiencing life as a couple, that many of us have become dissatisfied with our lives, and have focused our attention on passionately wanting to make a contribution in life. Yet we have placed ourselves on the edge of a precipice, with the old and familiar behind, the unknown ahead, and only our self-love and trust to offer us wings with which to fly.

Many of us are wounded and in pain. As a result, we seem so ready to focus on the pain instead of the open heart beneath the pain. We seem so ready to feel alone instead of recognizing that all of us are feeling the same loneliness together.

I am sometimes overcome with sadness when I look into our eyes. We all have so much to offer… so much wisdom, so much love, so much joy and creativity. Yet the pain that remains unhealed, unspoken, unseen, is what shouts over whatever love we are bursting to share. And because of that, we often fail to see ourselves and each other when we look into our eyes… any eyes.

Time and again I have experienced this. I want my every action to convey the love I experience myself to be, yet my expression can often be unloving. I find myself thinking, saying, and acting in ways that reveal my own unhealed wounds. And even though I know that embracing those wounds in love, instead of resisting or denying them, will lead to healing… I often don't know where or how to begin.

Seeing Fully

Slowly, I am beginning to see that it is ME I have failed to see. Not just the easy-to-see lovingness of me, but also those aspects I would prefer to deny have anything to do with me.

As long as I am willing to judge anything - good or bad - that very judgment keeps me from experiencing openly, from accepting "what is" fully, with unblinking eyes. And it is in that very moment when I finally (and with great humility) dissolve the need to be better-than, to be right, to protect myself because I am not embracing the fullness of my own magnificence - (and am thus feeling small and weak) - *it is in that very moment when the wall of judgment comes tumbling down*, that I can finally embrace myself – and all life – fully.

It is also in that moment when I finally allow myself to see ME; unveiled, full, richly textured, multi-colored, many-specied, multi-languaged, infinitely complex, and delightedly simple ME. The ME that encompasses All-That-Is, because I AM that. We all are.

Calling Home

I call this process of healing the abandoned parts of myself "calling home." I picture myself calling those parts of myself that have been hidden from my awareness back home to my heart. Then I cradle them in my arms, just as I did my own children, and nurse them with the love and acceptance of my heart, into wholeness and joy. I nurse them as often as necessary until they no longer require the reminder that they/we *are* love.

I realize now that when I can see and honor all aspects of myself, even those that I judge as negative, then I can finally see and honor ALL life. In that moment, all illusions of separation fall away revealing what has always been…the oneness and unity of all.

Here is an example…

Being George W. Bush

As I started focusing more thoroughly on the parts of myself I routinely rejected, I realized that our President represented many of the attitudes and choices I tended to judge the most. I often found it difficult *not* to react with anger or sadness whenever his administration made a decision – a sure sign of unacknowledged issues that I needed to explore and welcome home.

So I played a game with myself. I wrote a story in which I was having a conversation with the President, and since I was the author, I got to play all the roles:

Once upon a time there was a girl who loved life. She loved everything about it and explored it fully.

She looked at the President of her country and wondered why he couldn't see life as she did. He seemed so certain that his way of seeing things was absolutely the one and only right way, and he surrounded himself with people who agreed with him. Not only that, he seemed determined to force his vision on everyone else.

"What was the matter with these seemingly "stuck" and inflexible people, have they no humility at all?" she thought.

Then a friend taught her a trick that totally altered her perception. He suggested she try imagining that every person she saw was a reflection of something inside *her*. He also suggested that she try imagining that every voice she heard was really *her own voice* coming through another. It was like a universal "turning up of the volume", so that she could see something within herself that she resisted or refused to see before… not to make her feel wrong or bad, but to help her learn to love herself even more… to grow.

So she decided to give it a try. Since the person who represented the most difficulty for her was the President, he was an obvious first choice. Every time he opened his mouth to encourage others to embrace HIS vision, a vision that was almost entirely the opposite of hers, she imagined that it was her own voice speaking directly to her.

This is what she heard:

President: We need to invade this other country to protect ourselves, and we have to strike first before they strike us. Translation: I am scared for our survival and my usual and comfortable method for dealing with fear is to strike first to protect myself.

President: We need to give a tax break to the wealthy, not the poor, because the poor will benefit from the stimulus to the economy that the wealthy will create. *Translation: I fear for a lack of money (survival) at all times. I will make sure that my friends and I are well taken care of because I fear there is no way that I can help the desperately poor… so why bother. If I do, then we will all suffer. Besides, we deserve to be treated the best because of who we are.*

President: We must have the option of using weapons of mass destruction to ensure that no one else uses them against us. Translation: If I make sure that I am more protected with bigger weapons than those I fear, I will survive. Survival is more important than anything. I am afraid of dying.

President: The world and all its resources are here for the benefit and domination of mankind. Translation: I am scared that my needs won't be met, so I will take what I want now. I do not trust life to provide for my needs.

It is important to realize that she allowed herself these translations because she saw that they were coming from her about *herself*, and they had *nothing* to do with the President. She could still strongly disagree with him, but the message contained within her translations was *hers*.

Bush's Gift

It was the girl who was scared about her own survival; and whether the fear was over a direct physical assault or economic survival, made no difference. It was the girl who saw money from a stand point of lack at all times. It was the girl who saw life as one in which she felt she could never help the truly poor and so she felt defeated before she ever began. It was the girl who felt as if she was a victim and therefore needed extreme protection at all times. And finally, it was the girl who didn't trust life.

The girl wasn't consciously aware of these thoughts and feelings, but she noticed that because the President always aroused a STRONG reaction within her emotions, she was somehow tied to these issues. She was not neutral or unattached. (If she had merely disagreed with the President, it would have indicated that she simply had a different perception of the issues.) The fact that she had a strong and almost violent reaction to both the content of his words and him, indicated that her feelings came from a deeper issue *within herself*. She was as much a participant – from an energy level – as the President seemed to be. She realized the gift her friend was offering her- a chance to heal a part of her own self.

So she thanked her friend for helping her see places within herself that still reacted from fear instead of trust and love. She saw that it was *she* who was inflexible and righteous. She began to look deeper within to find the source of her fears. She discovered beliefs and concepts she held that no longer served her desire to live life as an expression of love. She was finally able to silently thank the President for his gift of helping her become more aware of places within herself that needed healing and love – even though she still disagreed with his policies and vision.

She was able to see that his role was to help her understand herself better, for she understood that who the President was *in her life* was always a product of her own perceptions, and that they had nothing to do with who he really was.

Yet once she was no longer seeing through the filter of judgment and righteousness, she was finally able to see who he really was. He was a fear-laden being struggling for survival… just as she was. In fact, from her standpoint, in a very real sense, he *was* her.

So from that point on, instead of just feeling angry whenever the President said or did things that ran directly contrary to her own choices, she also offered him a silent prayer of understanding and compassion. Instead of sending him hate and anger, which she now realize healed no one, she sent him love. She hoped that somehow the energy of love would reach him, not so he would change his opinion and agree with her (because that isn't *unconditional* love), but so that he could perhaps learn to love himself just a little bit more. So that he could learn to stand in front of the mirror and see the compassionate person she knew he was at the core of his being. And she knew this because now, when she looked at herself in the mirror, she saw the compassionate, magnificent being that she realized had always been there.

Most of all, she now saw that the President's role in her life had been pivotal. She saw that he filled an important role in the lives of many people, and she was able to finally thank all such people in her life – **for those with whom we have a strong reaction, are our greatest teachers about ourselves**. It's as if they volunteer to be the catalyst for a great self-exploration that ultimately leads to our own self-embrace and forgiveness. Eventually it leads to humility, compassion, and gratitude. What a gift!

Thanks, Dubya!

Now, about your policies…

Calling Home Our Fear

If I were to choose one word to describe the Bush administration's policies, I'd say they were driven by FEAR. Only the fearful strike first, play bully, use force to get their way, and refuse to seek understanding of the deeper motivations behind their actions or the actions of others. Only fear leads people to look out only for themselves at the expense of others. Only fear drives people to operate from a belief in scarcity.

Fear is a strong motivator. I carries the illusion of strength, and is often so convincing and effective that we cower before it. Yet it is possible to move beyond fear-motivated perceptual filters and actions.

If we can humble ourselves enough to explore the idea that the fear-laden Bush policies are a reflection of our own societal fears, then the work no longer rests outside ourselves in the actions of some "other." The work rests within our own perceptions, beliefs, and actions. That doesn't negate the necessary work of creating societal structures that are no longer fear-driven, but it means that the first step to healing our dominant society lies within.

So how do we begin to heal the fear-driven perceptions within ourselves? Perhaps we can begin by simply acknowledging our fears – no small task - and then beginning the process of calling those fearful parts of ourselves back home. Once we are willing to see the fear motivating much of our policies and choices, how do we embrace the fullness of who we are (including the fear) and re-perceive each other?

The First Step…

Look into the mirror. See your own beauty and magnificence. See the loving heart yearning to contribute to the aliveness and beauty of life. Allow self-tenderness and self-compassion to fill your heart. Then, with that same tender compassionate vision, turn your gaze on others and the world.

Here is what one person wrote when he allowed himself to see George W. Bush through the eyes of tenderness. His words are a prime example of the compassion available in us all – not in some distant future after we all heal ourselves – but now, in our next breath…

Subject: Open Letter to George W. Bush

Dear George W, Bush,

I am writing to you with little hope you will ever read this letter. So, I am sending this out as an open letter to the George W. Bush inside myself and most other Americans, if not most people in the world. You see, because of the position you occupy, you are in all of us. There is a man inside our minds that is you. I am trying to reach that man.

I'm doing this, because the other day, on T.V., I finally saw you. I mean that I finally allowed myself to see you. You made it a little easier. You were talking to reporters in the Oval Office, and for a moment seemed to slip out of role. The Presidential mask came off and you said "Look, I'm a loving guy". Your voice quivered a bit and your face muscles strained to hold back emotion as you slid back into stern face and said, "But, I have a job to do.... and I'm going to do it." Once again, you were the man in charge, but still visibly holding back emotion. So, I saw the little boy that you are, and the ordinary man. An ordinary man caught in an impossibly complex position.

This is a big shift for me. Up until now, I must confess, I have been mostly angry at you, holding you with contempt, disrespect and even hatred. Being a "political progressive", my ideas and agendas strongly conflict with your actions and policies.

I now see you as a man; a man trapped in a steel grid of the most powerful forces on this earth. The most powerful human created institutions are weighing in on you at all times, telling you, "this is what you must do", "this is what you must say". The intensity of their commanding opinions is heightened by the world-wide perception, that you hold the keys to the fate of the world. Lord, what a load on the shoulders. As I began to recognize you as imprisoned in a pattern that the little man in me also shares, I felt a need to remind you (and me) of your (our) rights:

You have the right to remain silent. You have a right to walk into the woods, or into your room, turn off all phones, t.v.s, and other communication devices, place guardians at all the doors, and go inside your self. You may release all thoughts of terrorism, counter-terrorism, CIA, FBI, Taliban, Saddam Hussein, Osama Bin Laden, Afghanistan, Republicans, Democrats, opinion polls, and even your role as President, and just experience what is going on in your heart and body.

You have the right to whatever feelings you are having. It's hard to imagine being in your place and not being somewhat afraid. I'm out here and I'm scared. Afraid of what will happen next. Afraid of what you must do. Afraid of not knowing what to do, of doing the wrong thing, of being judged by your Father, Mother, Wife, associates, the masses of people watching your every move. Also, if you are indeed opening your heart to the people and families directly hurt by the terror, the grief is profoundly heavy to bear. And of course, you are entitled to feel frustration, rage, and the urge for revenge.

You have the right to feel the pain in your body. The position you are in must be absolutely gut wrenching. Having to pose as strong and determined, confident in the face of what you yourself believe is EVIL. It's hard to imagine facing evil without trembling, without tremendous tension in the neck and shoulders, a tight knot in the belly. You have a right to just feel your own pain in the midst of this.

You have the right to not know what to do. Even with your advisors and associates and media pundits strong proclamations of what must be done, you are the one who must choose, and you may not really know what is right. This is an immensely difficult situation, to put it mildly. Your slightest gestures and utterances ripple across the globe. You are the Commander in Chief of the most powerful humanly driven forces on this planet (second only to the powers of Mother Nature herself). How can you possibly KNOW what to do? What will serve the greatest good? (and I trust that this is the intention of your deepest self). It's ok if you don't know, if your not sure.

You have the right to ask for help. This is critical. In the sanctity of your silent place, in touch with your pain and not knowing, you may ask with your most authentic voice for help from that which brings life and peace to this world. It will be a balm for your hurt, fear and anger. You may also be given guidance on what to do. For you, it may come from Jesus, truly a Light unto us all. No matter that for others it will have different names and forms. In this presence you are indeed an ordinary man, and I'm sure you will be grateful for that.

You have the right to choose PEACE. With all the pressures for hate and rage and vengeance, pressures to try to control the situation, you have a choice in this moment. You can choose to breathe . And when you exhale, exhale peace and justice; to make your next words, your next step, your next actions supportive of peace and the justice that sustains peace. And to continue that with each breath. And when you forget, go back to the beginning, find the quiet place, and remember your rights.

A couple of further thoughts: Please do not try to "rid the world of evil". I know you said that in a moment of trying to appear strong and on top of things, but I just want to remind you that that is not your job. You have a very big job, but not that big.

Second, in case you didn't receive it, I am sending below the message the Dalai sent you. He is a very wise man, with great humility, and loves you in a way that few living beings are capable of.

With great respect for the divine presence manifesting as you, President George W. Bush, and all the rest of us. May we find the wisdom, courage and will to do the right thing.

--Alan Levin, alevin@holosinst.org, www.holosinst.org

This is who we are. Let us shout it from the rooftops. Let it infuse our every thought and perfume the breath of our spoken words. Let our actions reflect the grace within our hearts, for we are birthing ourselves anew.

Instead of using the English word of "labor", which connotes a difficult transition and hard work; I prefer the Spanish word for birthing, "dar la luz", which means to "give light." Isn't that exactly what we are doing? We are birthing our perceptional awareness of what we have always been, but never acknowledged. It is time. May our light shine brightly.

8

CO-CREATION

One doesn't discover new lands
without consenting to lose sight of the shore for a very long time.
—Andre Gide

CO-CREATION

Co-creation is the reality of the universe, and thus a perfect model for the new human reality.
There is no separation in true co-creation, only unity.
There is no ego involvement, because in true co-creation, all voices are the voice of God.
All events are equally important on a present moment basis.
All is honored in co-creation.

Cocreator. In this path the Essential Self incarnates, comes in the whole way. We shift our identity from egoic selves seeking the Divine to the Divine incarnate guiding the whole being. In this path the Essential Self seeks to express in creative action that itself evolves the person and the world.

Barbara Marx Hubbard in a conversation with Alan Sasha Lithman Feb. 12, 2004. Foundation for Conscious Evolution.

The term, co-creation, has been used and miss-used so much in the last few years, that I wanted to focus acute attention on discerning exactly what it means. Beyond all the *talk* about "co-creation", I wanted to explore the application of it in my everyday life. That experience has strongly colored the contents of this chapter.

What it is NOT.

Co-creation is not collaboration or compromise. According to Dictionary.com their meanings are:

Collaborate: To work together, especially in a joint intellectual effort.

Compromise: To settle by concessions.

Neither collaboration nor compromise fill the participant with a sense of expansion and joy. In fact, as used today, compromise means that each party gives up part of their vision in order to find common ground. Both parties leave the discussion feeling diminished in some way. *That is the exact opposite of co-creation.*

A new Paradigm of Group Communication

There are several excellent examples of co-creation in action today, one of the best is Jim Rough's "Choice-Creating" process in the Dynamic Facilitation methods as outlined in his book, Society's Breakthrough! In order to better understand this process I took his 4-day training to be a facilitator. What an experience! People from highly diverse backgrounds came together with the express intent of learning how to empower creative group communication and problem-solving. Jim explains the difference between two types of change below:

Type 1: Manageable change

This model has explained the universe for hundreds of years. It holds that extrinsic forces, or causes, make change happen. Because of this change can be predetermined, measured and controlled. This model views the universe as though it is a giant machine following natural laws. Goals can be set and procedures followed to achieve the goals. Ultimately this view means accepting the idea that the universe is predetermined. Our culture traditionally views this Newtonian model as truth, common sense.

Type 2: Self-organizing change

Self-organizing change is more like a garden than a machine. Things are growing all the time by themselves, drawn out by an inner life quest for quality and efficiency. This growth is transformational, things can radically change their course spontaneously. Aspects can be planned, and growth can be anticipated, but fundamentally, this change process is not plannable. Type 1 methods are used, but it is recognized that they are not always applicable. In this model success is sought in the quality of relationship with nature, not power over it. (see chart below)[1]

Two Models of Change

	Manageable (Type 1) e.g. a machine, monarchy, traditional meeting	Self-Organizing (Type 2) e.g. a living organism, democracy, dialogue
How order is determined	**It is organized by someone** (extrinsic forces) Build it / Do it... with no mistakes Closed boundaries Mostly stable with periodic disorder	**Order comes from within** (intrinsic energy) Explore / trial and error Open boundaries Dynamic... between chaos and order
Thinking	**Stay rational** ....avoid the unconscious mind Decide on goals ... avoid feelings Discern and analyze Stop things from going wrong	**Be creative** ....work with the unconscious mind Energy driven... include feelings Generate and synthesize Seek what's right ... i.e. quality
Leadership	**Manage to get results** Can measure progress Emphasize extrinsic motivation ....(rewards) Static process... step by step	**Facilitate the process** Use milestones to reflect on progress Emphasize intrinsic motivation ....(mission, vision) Dynamic process... the flow
Orientation	**Stop things from going wrong** There are objective constraints All is measurable Eliminate chaos	**Help things go right** Expect breakthroughs Measuring everything can mess things up Some chaos is essential

The big cycle I see over and over throughout evolution is this: Some unity individuates, as you saw with the sea breaking up into waves, or as we know the homogenous early Earth individuated into core and crust, the crust then individuating into a myriad bacteria, and so forth.

This individuation always leads to the tension and conflict we have already discussed several times, in couples and in the world economy as everywhere in nature.

What comes out of that -- if the parties don't split up or kill each other? Negotiations, which come to the kind of resolutions that end in cooperation, with a new unity eventually forming itself at a higher level.

Elisabet Sahtouris, <u>*Living Systems, the Internet and the Human Future*</u> *Talk presented 13 May 2000 at* <u>*Planetwork, Global Ecology and Information Technology*</u> *Conference held at the San Francisco Presidio* http://www.ratical.org/LifeWeb/Articles/LSinetHF.html

Every Vision Honored

The change created by Jim's Self-Organizing Model honors the participants and their contributions fully. Unlike compromise, there is no desire to diminish each person's dream for the sake of agreement. On the contrary, each person is encouraged to stand strongly in her vision until everyone in the room can understand it fully.

Everything Contributes

Darkness isn't a condition apart from light. Darkness is a state of light and light is a state of darkness. Belief in the separation of one thing from another thing is the beginning of fear.
Oneness is the end of it.

Wendell Berry

Every contribution, even those that are blatantly dissenting and disruptive are seen as valid and extremely valuable; as they point to other points of view - issues not yet addressed - and usually sit just on top of a creative breakthrough or solution. Even if only one person in the group expresses a particular opinion, usually others also have somewhat similar thoughts, perhaps just below their level of conscious awareness.

Therefore everything said is recorded in front of the group on paper, so that each person's contribution is shared and honored, ensuring that it is clear beyond a shadow of a doubt. Those statements can later be referred to at any point in the progress of discussion.

Barriers Are Dropped

All of this sounds great on paper, but in real life, the experience goes beyond great to profound. I participated in many discussions ranging from the traffic jams in Seattle to uses for slug slime. What struck me most was the aliveness in the room. Very quickly participants realized that they would be listened to and honored completely, therefore they had no reason to be defensive. The facilitator provided protection for each speaker, making sure each was clearly heard and complete. As a result, barriers came down, and with them, a lot of pre-conceptions about each other.

Core Issues Are Revealed

As each person was encouraged to speak from his deepest passions, the room perked up and was vitally alive. Nothing was boring, no matter what the topic. I mean that literally, as it was quickly apparent that whatever topic we thought we were discussing changed as the group followed the energy of the conversation. In fact, every single time I've participated in this type of dynamically facilitated group communication, the topic we originally thought we were discussing led to one or more deeper underlying issues.

Exponentially Expanded Creativity

I am enough of an artist to draw freely upon my imagination.

Imagination is more important than knowledge. Knowledge is limited.

Imagination encircles the world.

Albert Einstein

Once everyone felt safe, honored, and comfortable with the dynamic energy flow of the conversation, things really got exciting. The creative level of the group seemed to expand beyond anything we could imagine. Ideas were flowing right, left, and in-between as the facilitator struggled to get it all down on paper fast enough to keep up. Participants dropped any ego-based need to stand out and seem important because they knew they were each vitally important to the process.

Solutions Beyond Band-aids

Each participant drew on the previous statements to creatively jump outside the box of common perceptions, beliefs, and concepts. This resulted in some wild ideas that we eventually realized were not so wild after-all. Most importantly, because so much time had been spent in clarifying the issues involved, proposed solutions were never cosmetic.

For example, when discussing the traffic jams in Seattle, we quickly realized that adding freeway lanes would never solve the real problem. And what was the underlying problem that emerged? Within a half hour we realized that the city had been designed around the automobile. We went from a traffic problem to a city planning issue. Once we realized that, we could address interim and long-range solutions that dealt with city design. The potential solutions involved every aspect of city living.

But before we could even begin to do that, we had to determine our common goals. You can see where this led. If we had been a citizens' group from Seattle instead of participants in a workshop, our next logical steps would have been clear… Clarify our goals and then playfully, dynamically, and co-creatively develop solutions with all involved.

Co-Creation as a Way of Life

The description above was intended to give you an idea of the power behind co-creation. It is a quantum leap beyond collaboration and especially compromise. A fundamental part of the experience is that it takes place within you. I mean that in a specific way. When people feel listened to with full attention and a sincere desire to be heard, their defenses drop. They open their hearts and let other visions, other perspectives in. Within that context, incredible growth takes place. When we honor each other, we move from a space of defense and maintenance of the status-quo (what feels familiar and therefore comfortable); to a heightened space of creativity in which our focus is on creating what we want, not defending what already doesn't work.

Co-creation offers the possibility of moving beyond constantly stirring the same arguments around in the same old pot of common perception, to leaping completely out of the pot into a new paradigm of relationship and perception:

- one in which we move from defensiveness to openness,
- from stagnation to growth,
- from a world view of being the victims of circumstance to being the creators of a world that works for everyone and everything
- by taking full responsibility for our choices.

The following Guidelines were created from a desire to facilitate an exploration of co-creation as a way of honoring all. They are inspired by the work of others, and I encourage you to create your own. Then actively choose to live them in your everyday life.

The Honoring All Life Co-Creation Guidelines

Honor Self

I honor myself by expressing my core essence - that deeply grounded BEingness I experience as my true Self.

Be fully present

I intend to be fully present in this moment of NOW. I release any past perceptions or stories that may keep me from honoring the richness of this moment and consciously choose to experience NOW with the innocent awe and openness of the young child.

"A common will," writes Otto Scharmer, "is formed and accessed when a group uncovers the various layers of their present reality and develops a shared image and felt sense of the future. The process of uncovering and accessing common will includes more than what is generally known as 'visioning'." This discovery was more than just significant; it expands our understanding of how groups unleash the capacity to sense and actualize the emerging future.

<u>*Crossing the Threshold*</u>
http://www.generonconsulting.com/Publications/Crossing_the_Threshold.pdf

Dr. C. Otto Scharmer is co-founder of the MIT Leadership Lab, lecturer at the

Massachusetts Institute of Technology, and a visiting professor at the Helsinki School of Economics. He is also co-founder of the Global Institute for Responsible Leadership.

Realize our Potential

I am committed to expressing my magnificence and empowering others to do the same.

Follow my Inner Guidance

I trust my Inner Guidance (by whatever name I choose to call it) to always work for the well-being of the whole – because we are all part of the whole.

Communicate with Integrity

I agree to express what is true for me in this moment, withholding nothing. I agree to express with the full passion of my feelings, for the sake of my own clarity and that of those listening. I do so with compassion for myself and all others.

Act with Integrity

I intend to act with integrity at all times. This means I make agreements that resonate with both my mind and my heart – with all of me. I agree to honor my agreements.

Deep Listening

I intend to compassionately listen to the communication of others and to focus on their needs and feelings – especially the unspoken ones - regardless of their manner of communication. I am aware that when I listen as if the person speaking is me speaking to myself, I allow a deeper meaning to unfold, the gift of the moment has a chance to be revealed.

Honor One Another

I agree to honor each person's process – including my own - acknowledging that everyone is making the best possible choice or decision we are capable of in the moment. Additionally, I honor each person's natural timing, and do not require that their timing match my own.

Appreciate Our Contributions

I take responsibility for acknowledging myself and the gift of my contribution. If I feel the need for acknowledgment, I will ask for it. I am aware that one of the best ways of acknowledging others is to consciously seek the gift available in every encounter and experience, and to openly express gratitude.

Honor Our Diversity

I intend to come from a sense of cooperation and caring in my interactions with others and with all life. I understand that our deeper goals are often the same even though our methods for achieving them may differ. When I am willing to open myself to other points of view, the field of the possible expands. I honor and celebrate the diversity of all life.

Take Responsibility

I take full responsibility for my thoughts, my perceptions, my creations, my reactions, my experience, and my relationships.

I understand that I am in charge of my reactions, even though it may seem that they are triggered by someone else. I take responsibility for handling my problems in a way that honors all involved, to the best of my ability.

Maintain Resonance

I agree to take the time to establish rapport, and then to honestly re-connect with anyone with whom I feel out of harmony, as soon as it may be appropriate.

Resolve Problems at their Source

I will take problems, complaints and upsets to the person or people with whom I can resolve them, at the earliest opportunity.

Learn from Experience

I learn from my experiences, and celebrate those lessons learned – they are some of the greatest gifts of life. Within this context, what I used to call a "mistake" is now an opportunity.

Accept What Is

To the best of my ability, I embrace and accept without judgment, bowing to the wisdom that there is always more to perceive than I am yet perceiving.

Passion

I empower myself and others to know and follow our passions. They are the indicators of our greatest potential contribution.

Service to Aliveness

I open my heart and mind in compassionate service to all life.

Choice

I empower myself to choose, assess the results, and then re-choose as I participate in every aspect of my life. I am always at choice.

Lighten UP!

Because there is always more to perceive than I currently understand, I can trusting that all is happening in perfect timing, even if I don't understand how that is true. I therefore choose to flow with life's energy, and willingly share my joy as I celebrate the mystery of life. [2]

Celebrate your light - the exuberant ONEness that you are - in this and all moments...
Laugh out loud, sing, dance, and celebrate every waking moment.
Life is a celebration, not drudgery.
Show it in your trust, your voice, your walk, you ease of being.
Show it in your unconditional love, embracing all people...
not just those who agree with you.
Celebrate the multifaceted beauty of ALL of life...
There is no difference...it is all rich and full and perfect.

Notes

1. Dynamic Facilitation and the Magic of Self-Organizing Change by Jim Rough (This article appeared in the June 1997 issue of the Association for Quality and Participation Journal.) http://www.tobe.net/papers/facilitn.html Also see Society's Breakthrough! Releasing Essential Wisdom and Virtue in All the People by Jim Rough, 2002

2. These Agreements were adapted from The Cocreators Agreements, from The Co-Creator's Handbook Copyright©2001 Foundation for Conscious Evolution. They, in turn, were adapted from The Geneva Group Agreements, Boulder, CO 1985.

9

PRECAUTIONARY PRINCIPLE

The Precautionary Principle is the active aspect of Honoring All Life.
Where Honoring All Life is a concept you come from
It is a place of BEing —
The Precautionary Principle is the application,
the Doing.

THE PRECAUTIONARY PRINCIPLE – FORECARING FOR LIFE

When an activity raises threats of harm to human health or the environment, precautionary measures should be taken even if some cause and effect relationships are not fully established scientifically. In this context the proponent of an activity, rather than the public, should bear the burden of proof. The process of applying the Precautionary Principle must be open, informed and democratic and must include potentially affected parties. It must also involve an examination of the full range of alternatives, including no action.

—*Definition created at the Wingspread Conference on the Precautionary Principle, January, 1998*

Precautionary Action

• *Anticipatory and preventive*

• *Increases rather than decreases options*

• *Can be monitored and reversed*

• *Increases resilience, health, integrity of whole system*

• *Enhances diversity (one size does not fit all)*

*Carolyn Raffensperger
SEHN*

What do the City of San Francisco, the counties of Marin, California and Multnomah, Oregon (including the city of Portland, Oregon), the State of New York, as well as the Los Angeles School District Pest Management Policy, the preamble to the 1992 Rio Declaration, and many organizations and governments in Europe have in common? They all embrace something called the Precautionary Principle, using it as a filter before making decisions. The Precautionary Principle is simple to define yet complex to apply, because it offers an entirely different way of perceiving our available options when making decisions. Nancy Myers explains:

> The precautionary principle is an emerging principle of international law but has only recently been proposed in North America as a new basis for environmental policy. On the surface it is a simple, common sense proposition: in the face of possible harm, exercise precaution. But the enthusiasm the principle has stirred among public advocates suggests it has a deeper appeal. It is, in fact, based on values related to "forecaring for life" and the natural world. The principle cannot effectively be invoked without stating these values up front. The principle makes it clear that decisions and developments in science and technology are based first of all on values and only secondarily on scientific and technological fact and process. Moreover, a precautionary approach is best carried out in the context of goals that embody the values of communities and societies. [1]

Far from denying science, the Precautionary Principle asks us to use science in the service of the common good. Kenny Ausubel, creator of the Bioneers Conference, the annual forum in which new ideas are exchanged, writes:

> There is a global effort afoot today to replace the risk paradigm with the precautionary principle, which is based on a recognition that the ability of science to predict consequences and possible harm is limited. The precautionary principle acknowledges that all life is interconnected. It shifts the burden of proof (and liability) to the parties promoting potentially harmful technologies, and it limits the use of those technologies to experiments until they are proven truly safe… It's a new understanding of health and illness that has begun to move away from treating only the individual. Instead, good health lies in recognizing that each of us is part of a wider web of life. When the web is healthy, we are more likely to be healthy… But an ecological approach to healing also looks to deeper tenets embedded in nature itself and how it operates. [2]

It is the concept of "Risk Assessment," (what Kenny Ausubel calls 'risk paradigm') that comes into question here. Not only because the criteria often used in Risk Assessment ignores so many other factors that common sense requires us to include – like ethics, morality, common good, financial and safety concerns, etc. – but also because the assumptions underlying the Risk Assessment methodology are now subject to re-evaluation in light of systems theory and any number of other

If this burgeoning movement (the Precautionary Principle) succeeds, the next great scientific advance won't be another wonder drug or feat of genetic engineering. It will be putting a stop to our habits of technological recklessness and the damage that results from valuing efficiency and profit over a healthy world.

*Karen Olsen
"Our Planet Our Selves"
Utne Reader
July 20, 2001*

perceptual filters through which we examine life. Risk Assessment methodology is just too narrow a focus to get the job done.

The Problem

The words, "Precautionary Principle" originated from the German concept of *Vorsorgeprinzip,* in which *Vorsorge* translates roughly to "forecaring", meaning "to care into the future." Though the concept isn't new, the way it is being applied is. It's simplest definition is very familiar, "First do no harm;" but the application of this simple statement reverses many of our current policies.

Chemical Body Burden

For example, the proof that a pesticide is dangerous to human health currently lies on the shoulders of the general public. In other words, the public must document that a certain number of people have gotten sick or died as a direct result of this particular chemical before it will be removed from the market. (Yet how likely is it that those affected will have the funds and time available to legally prove wrong-doing?) In the meanwhile, the manufacturer is free to wreck havoc on the environment and people's lives while making a neat profit, all in the name of "freedom."

If the Precautionary Principle were applied, however, it would be the responsibility of the *manufacturer* to prove that the chemical was harmless *before* it would be allowed onto market shelves and into the environment. Ah, you say, but surely we test chemicals for safety before openly using them?

Unfortunately the answer in approximately 90 percent of the cases is NO. In fact, less than 10% of the approximately 85,000 synthetic chemicals currently in use have been tested for their effect on humans; and virtually none have been tested in combination, which is how we receive them in the real world. Even fewer tests have evaluated their effect on the complex interdependent systems that make up our environment. Charlotte Brody, former RN, organizing director of the Center for Health, Environment and Justice and cofounder of Health Care without Harm writes:

> We can't prove that taking action to reduce dioxin, to phase out PVC, to stop using mercury, or to reduce air pollution will reduce a particular patient's disease. It isn't like an appendectomy, a proven cure for a particular patient with a unique set of symptoms. In medicine, what we can't prove, we ignore. In a world where the health of industry matters more than the planet and life upon it, industry keeps raising the bar for how much proof you need before you can take action.[3]

The Precautionary Principle is one answer to this increasingly common dilemma. Furthermore, she points out that with healthcare counting for approximately thirty percent of the Gross National Product, there isn't much financial incentive to change the status quo. Yet there is overwhelming evidence that we must. The facts are alarming:

> The Learning Disabilities Association states that 24 billion pounds of developmental toxicants are released annually in the US, and 17 percent of kids now show developmental learning or behavior disorders.

> High levels of phthalates, an endocrine-disrupter are showing up in women of child-bearing age. The most likely source is cosmetics. This is the chemical suspected in causing early puberty in girls.

Precautionary Responsibilities

• *Industry and business have an obligation:*
– *to test their products*
– *provide the information to the public*
– *take responsibility and pay for any damage they cause*
• *Government has obligations to:*
– *Serve as a trustee for the commonwealth*
– *Protect the commonwealth for this and future generations*
– *Give the benefit of the doubt (of scientific uncertainty) to public health and well-being*
– *Choose the least harmful alternative*
– *Actively promote democracy*
– *The Public has responsibilities to:*
– *Hold government accountable for their trustee responsibilities*
– *Actively participate in democratic decision-making*

Carolyn Raffensperger
SEHN

HOW WILL IT HELP CHANGE THINGS?

Incorporating the Precautionary Principle into laws, regulations, and policies would fundamentally

change the way that environmental, land-use and health decisions are made, so that we can:

·Take more health protective actions in the face of scientific uncertainty;

·Select the safest alternative technologies and materials to meet our needs;

·Require that producers, not the public, demonstrate that they have selected the safest alternative;

·Fully involve the public in making democratic decisions regarding their lives and health;

·Move closer to creating sustainable communities by preventing harm from the outset.

Bay Area Working Group On The Precautionary Principle

Winter 2004

Brominated flame retardants which affect thyroid function and mental abilities are now found in breast milk.

Low levels of dioxin have been shown to interfere with vaginal development.

Humans live near the top of the food chain. Toxin exposure increases fifty to a hundredfold for every step higher that you eat on the food chain.

Breast milk fed babies live even higher on the food chain. One known way to significantly reduce your toxic load is to feed your breast milk to a child, who then receives those same toxins. (Even so, because of many other factors breast milk's health advantages still outweigh any form of infant formula.) A sad recognition of our oneness is the fact that, throughout the world (even in the Inuit people of the Arctic Circle), nursing mothers' breasts have become toxic waste dumps.

We now witness a wide range of animals with gender confusion, while sperm counts are declining in the industrial world. [4]

How is it that we humans have designed our world such that releasing potentially harmful substances into our water, air, land, and food chain is both legal and sanctioned by the government – even as the evidence of their harmful effect mounts? How is it that we have created a way of business that rewards those who disregard public health, while ignoring the effect of that disregard on the lives of millions and the health of the biosphere? How is it that we have given the power to make decisions that affect our health, well-being, and the viability of our existence over to others who clearly have ulterior motives, without demanding a voice in the decision making process? In short, we have focused so strongly on the rights of the individual to do whatever he wants, that we have lost sight of the larger picture.

The Precautionary Principle offers a perceptual shift from blindly supporting blatantly destructive behavior in the name of "individual freedom" to re-thinking our decisions such that they support *all* life. We can no longer afford to hide our heads in the sand, pretending that our actions don't affect us all.

Lack of Feedback Loops

We can also no longer afford to allow our systems of finance, industry, and business to keep us from being able to make informed, honoring, and loving decisions as a species – and as participants in the web of life on this planet. Michael Lerner, President and co-founder of Commonweal, comments on the current situation, and the lack of clear feedback loops present today:

A whole new analytic synthesis is coalescing around issues of globalization, human rights, women's rights, the environment, corporate power and accountability, environmental justice, the unfinished agenda of race, the responsibilities of faith communities, and the question of who owns science. Toxicology is largely owned by the chemical corporations, and we can't have science owned by corporations. If science is owned by corporations, and the media are owned by corporations, we do not have the feedback loops that we need. [5]

Indeed, if our feedback loops are not clear and unbiased how can we possibly make informed decisions about anything? Isn't unbiased feedback the very backbone of scientific methodology?

Alarming Disease Trends

Studies have begun to identify some troubling trends in the patterns of human disease and illness. According to the 2003 San Francisco Precautionary Principle White Paper, the following trends were noted:

- Chronic diseases and conditions affect more than 100 million men, women, and children in the United States—more than a third of the population. Cancer, asthma, Alzheimer's disease, autism, birth defects, developmental disabilities, diabetes, endometriosis, infertility, multiple sclerosis, and Parkinson's disease are becoming increasingly common, and mounting evidence plausibly links these diseases to environmental toxins.

- Nearly 12 million children in the U.S. (17 percent) suffer from one or more developmental disabilities. Learning disabilities alone affect 5-10 percent of children in public schools, and these numbers are increasing. Attention deficit hyperactivity disorder conservatively affects 3-6 percent of all school children, and the numbers may be considerably higher. The incidence of autism appears to be increasing. (Schettler et al., 2000)

- Asthma prevalence has doubled in the last 20 years. San Francisco has one of the highest hospitalization rates for asthma attacks in children under 15 in urban California counties. In the city's Bayview–Hunters Point section, one in six children suffer from asthma, according to the San Francisco Department of Public Health's most recent study.

- The age-adjusted incidence of melanoma, lung cancer in women, non-Hodgkins lymphoma, and cancers of the prostate, liver, testis, thyroid, kidney, breast, brain, esophagus, and bladder has increased over the past 25 years. (SEER 1996) Breast cancer, for example, now strikes more women worldwide than any other type of cancer. Rates have increased 50 percent during the past half century. In the 1940s, the lifetime risk of breast cancer was one in 22. Today's risk is one in eight in the US and rising, (Evans 2002) with Marin County's risk factor at one in seven. Marin County has a cancer rate nearly 40 percent higher than the national average.

In the U.S., the incidence of some birth defects, including male genital disorders, some forms of congenital heart disease, and obstructive disorders of the urinary tract, is increasing. (Pew 2003, Paulozi 1999) Sperm density is declining in some parts of the U.S. and elsewhere in the world. (Swan et al., 1997) [6]

These trends demand a willingness to look facts straight in the eye and re-think our priorities. The health of any aspect of this planet is ultimately tied directly to the health of any individual, they can no longer be seen as separate. The question remains: Will we be willing to see the indications evident in the prevalence of increasing toxins in our bodies and take appropriate measures to cease polluting ourselves? Or will we continue to pretend that there isn't enough "good science" yet available, and therefore fund additional studies, with the hidden intention of stalling any real effort to re-perceive the manner in which we make our decisions? The choice is ours.

"Good Science"

In issues regarding the environment, the Precautionary Principle asks us to re-examine our practice of using science as the *only* basis on which we determine our course of action. While science is essential to making any intelligent decision regarding issues in the environmental, medical, and legal fields; the point, however, is that it shouldn't be the *only* factor considered in decision making.

The health of the oceans depends on the health of rivers; the health of rivers depends on the health of small streams; the health of small streams depends on the health of their watersheds. The health of the water is exactly the same as the health of the land; the health of small places is exactly the same as the health of large places. As we know, disease is hard to confine. Because natural law is in force everywhere, infections move.

We cannot immunize the continents and the oceans against our contempt for small places and small streams. Small destructions add up, and finally they are understood as parts of large destructions.

Wendell Berry
Contempt For Small Places

An Op-Ed piece by Wendell Berry, the author of "The Unsettling of America."
- June 2003

The Precautionary Principle says that our first priority is protecting our health. It asserts our right to air, water, land and food that won't hurt us. It acknowledges that in our complex world, scientists often cannot predict what impact toxic exposures will have on our health.
Bay Area Working Group on the Precautionary Principle Fact Sheet
- Winter 2004
http://www.takingprecaution. org/
http://www.takingprecaution.or g/docs/BAWGFactSheet_12_ 03.pdf

When we as a society have a clear purpose – a demonstrated belief as to what we represent and who we choose to be – then it is imperative that our choices reflect that vision. Decisions must include our values of justice (what is balanced within the given context), morality (how do we want to be treated and how do we want to treat each other), and our vision (who do we want to be) as well as the facts provided by scientific research. Another way of saying this is that our decisions must consider economic, social, health, safety, moral, and ethical issues as well.

Yet often, especially in areas of oversight and regulation where we authorize a given activity – one that potentially affects all life – we rely solely on "good science." Janet Jacobson, in her article entitled, <u>Good Science vs. the Common Good</u>, asks what exactly the words, "Good Science" mean:

> …Good science has been defined for me as scientific research that is independently conducted and subjected to peer review. However, in the real world, good science usually means research that substantiates whatever position one is trying to validate.

> …Science is not totally objective. Researchers are influenced by the interests of their funding source.

> …Laws and regulations must be written to preserve the common good in balance with the rights of individuals.

> Next time someone tells you that you need to use "good science," ask what exactly that means and if that is really the only thing that should be considered. [7]

Contrary to a policy of manipulating or misusing "good science," the **Precautionary Principle encourages the embracing of unbiased, neutrally funded, rigorous scientific methodology** – science intent on finding truth not merely validating a position - to the highest extent possible. Precautionary science involves seeking to offer the public transparent, unbiased scientific information, including the disclosure of scientific uncertainty, so that informed democratic decisions are possible. It includes gathering a wide-range of information and options, while encouraging multiple perceptual viewpoints, especially the complexities of interdependent systems.

Pursuing a Deeper Understanding

Along with the obvious question of whether or not a given decision promotes life and does not compromise safety, the Precautionary Principle urges us to ask deeper questions:

- How do we determine safety? What criteria do we use, and how do we justify what is included and excluded in our determination?
- What perceptual filters are we using? Are there other ways of seeing this same issue that we haven't yet explored, ones that will significantly change the quality and scope of the exploration itself?
- What important questions have we failed to ask? What have we ignored?
- How does this decision impact all life, not just humans?
- Is there a deeper issue we haven't yet addressed?
- What is truly important here?
- Where do we draw the line; and what does where we choose to draw the line say about our priorities?

There's a place where companies can sell products even if they contain ingredients linked to breast cancer. It's called the beauty aisle.

Many beauty products you use every day — shampoo, nail polish and makeup — contain chemicals linked to breast cancer.

And worse, it's perfectly legal for cosmetics companies to sell these products to you.

In Europe, beauty products are now barred from containing any chemicals known or strongly suspected to cause cancer or birth defects. At the Breast Cancer Fund, we're urging U.S. cosmetics companies to

voluntarily eliminate these chemicals from their products, too.

Breast Cancer Fund http://www.breastcancerfund.org

These are questions we generally dismiss as unimportant or even irrelevant when setting policy regarding business, industry, political options, the environment, finance, law, medicine, and any number of other fields. Why? How can we possibly make decisions that truly benefit all, if we are unwilling to vigorously explore all alternatives *and* the assumptions upon which we base our conclusions?

Ignoring Science

There is a disturbing practice that is becoming more common as our country becomes enmeshed in a strategy of fear. It is the suggestion that we must cut corners and "tow the line" when it comes to fighting terrorism and any other "ism" that could possibly befall us. Unfortunately those "cut corners" include documented cases of the intentional misuse, misinterpretation, or outright dismissal of scientific data in order to manipulate public and political response. The Union of Concerned Scientists (http://www.ucsusa.org/), an independent nonprofit alliance of more than 100,000 concerned citizens and scientists, outlines the problem:

> To be a scientist is to investigate, meticulously -- particle by particle, cell by cell, and theory by theory -- the wondrously complex miracle that is the world. To push aside the findings of scientific research that don't support desired policy goals for short-term interests is beyond shortsightedness, beyond narrow-mindedness. It is to look through a lens so small that the very world is lost.

> ...(Climate change is one of thirty examples the Union of Concerned Scientists has documented of distortion of scientific findings.)...

> A fundamental tenet of successful democracies is that citizens and their leaders should make decisions based on the best and most accurate information. If the present attitude in Washington prevails -- that it is okay to give a little here, fudge a little there, remove anyone in the way, call anyone an expert, and discourage the meticulous examination and thought based on the facts -- then we will have deeply compromised the human impulse that both sustains great civilizations and is critical to our very survival. [8]

The Precautionary Principle asks us to cease using "science" to promote any agenda other than what supports life. It asks us to do our homework, face facts, and then take steps that promote the well-being of all.

Mistaking lack of proof for proof of safety

Instead of asking what seems to be a common approach to environmental policy: "How much environmental harm should be allowed?," the Precautionary Principle asks: "How little harm is possible?" [9] Jared Blumenfeld, Director of San Francisco's Department of the Environment writes:

> We acknowledge that our world will never be free from risk. However, a risk that is unnecessary, and not freely chosen, is never acceptable. San Francisco's Precautionary Principle, enacted as part of the Environment Code, insists that environmental decision-making be based on rigorous science -- science that is explicit about what is known, what is not known and what may never be known about potential hazards.

> The costs of not taking precautionary action are often very high, as we've seen in the case of tobacco, lead and asbestos. Early scientific warnings about risks to health went unheeded by government agencies. As a result, billions of dollars have been spent to deal with the consequences of these problems. Costs include health care and health insurance, lost economic productivity, absenteeism, lost wages and cleanup. The Precautionary Principle process also requires decision-makers to consider possible impact to the local economy. ...environmental democracy is deeply ingrained in San Francisco's Precautionary Principle. [9]

UCS's July 2004 report refers to scientists feeling that they are being asked to violate the "ethical code of science." Can you unpack that term?

It speaks to scientists' obligation to report the findings of their research in an objective and unbiased manner, and for them to allow peers to examine and question their methodology -- the whole culture of peer review and publishing your results. The code of ethics is violated when scientists can't publish their results, or are prohibited from speaking at conferences, or are barred from making sure that decision makers have unvarnished access to what the best and the latest science has to say, even if the results are conflicting.

<u>*An interview with Kevin Knobloch, president of the Union of Concerned Scientists*</u>
By Jennifer Weeks
Grist Magazine
05 Jan 2005
http://www.grist.org/news /maindish/2005/01/05/ weeks-knobloch/?source=daily

This concept of "environmental democracy" as embraced by the city of San Francisco, truly expresses the essence of honoring all life - in action. It encourages democracy that spans the breadth of life on this planet, embracing all forms of life and the complex interconnected webs that weave us all together into one living unit.

The Precautionary Principle is Good Economics

Contrary to conventional assumptions, environmental protection actually contributes to job creation. This is partly because some environmentally friendly technologies are more labor intensive than those they replace. But another contributing factor is that a strong Earth-friendly economy stresses local production over imports. This requires that an entire industry evolve locally – serving the community well-being while creating jobs. Simply stated, environmental protection and remediation cannot be out-sourced abroad.

Another myth is that environmental regulations cause companies to relocate outside the USA. Again, the facts do not support the myth. This is because environmental protection does not cost that much to implement, usually less than 2-3% of a company's sales revenue. It is much less a motivator for relocation than taxes, cheaper labor, access to new markets, or political stability. [10]

According to a 2002 study from the Global Development and Environment Institute of Tufts University:

> Technologies employed to control or prevent pollution not only provide public health and environmental benefits; in many cases, they also create relatively high-paying jobs requiring specialized skills. Building, installing, operating and inspecting pollution control equipment create skilled industrial jobs; the money that some industries spend on pollution prevention and controls shows up as payrolls for other industries that produce and install the controls and other new technologies. Economist Eban Goodstein notes that from 1977 to 1991, employment in these areas increased fifty-five percent, making this area of work "one of the most dynamic growth sectors in the US economy." (Goodstein 1999: 18)… Transferring funds from almost any other government program into environmental clean-up will create more, not fewer, skilled industrial jobs. [10]

Not only do strong environmental policies create jobs, according to the same study, but they also create many jobs indirectly associated with those jobs. A 1991 EPA study estimated that around 4,000 people were directly employed in the manufacturing of electrical machinery used in environmental clean-up. They also calculated that an additional 21,500 workers indirectly owed their jobs to environmental spending. Projects such as the cleanup of Boston Harbor create huge numbers of jobs, go on for years, and support the local economy even during times of recession. [10] Statistics also show that complying

with environmental regulations is usually much less expensive than the industry initially estimates.

One unexpected bonus of complying with environmental regulations, evidence shows, is that it stimulates innovation. Invoking the Precautionary Principle will make this especially true, because it urges evaluation of all alternative options. And because attention is placed on creative solutions, the field of possibilities is expanded. Several examples are cited in the Tufts study:

… on March 15th, the EPA issued a rule that allows power plants to continue spewing harmful amounts of mercury for more than a decade to come. Recognizing mercury's health risks, the EPA in 2000 decided to require maximum achievable controls that could reduce mercury pollution by 90 percent by 2008. The EPA's new rule overturns that determination, and instead allows power plants to emit more than seven times as much mercury, for a decade longer, than current law allows.

NRDC's EARTH ACTION: The Bulletin for Environmental Activists March 16, 2005.

- A 1991 recycling law in Japan encouraged businesses to create products that were easier to disassemble. This law stimulated innovations that led to elimination of expensive materials, reduction of unnecessary packaging, and simpler product designs.
- A jewelry company in Attleboro, Massachusetts faced the possibility of having to close down because it had violated permits for discharge of toxic substances into water. The company developed a closed-loop, zero-discharge system for the water used in its jewelry plating process. Water purified through this system was 40 times cleaner than city water. In addition, jewelry plating through this system was of higher quality than before. In this case, the innovations catalyzed by the need to comply with water quality standards made the business as a whole more competitive.
- A study by the environmental research group INFORM looked at actions taken to reduce pollution at 29 chemical plants in California, Ohio, and New Jersey. Of 181 changes that were made at these plants to reduce pollution, only one was found to have increased operating costs. [10]

Perhaps the most obvious benefit to implementation of the Precautionary Principle is the health benefit for both humans and the environment (which directly impacts human health.) Not only do workers enjoy greater health (and thus greater efficiency) once toxins are removed from their environment; but their lower health costs and absenteeism directly impact the bottom line.

Taking early precautionary action can prevent cancers, birth defects, and any number of community health problems. How can anyone begin to place a price tag on the economic impact of eliminating such health and environmental disasters?

The Tufts study highlights the case of benzene, a widely used chemical identified as hazardous as early as 1897. Yet it went unregulated until a 1977 study concluded that the allowed rate of benzene exposure between 1940 and 1971 raised leukemia rates five to tenfold. OSHA stepped in to lower the rate of exposure, but was challenged by the American Petroleum Institute in court. As a result, regulations did not take effect until 1987. [10]

Another example is asbestos, which was identified as hazardous more than 100 years ago. Yet it wasn't banned throughout Europe until 1998, and was still not banned in the USA at the publishing of the 2002 Tufts report. What are the costs of delaying the regulation of known carcinogens? According to one estimate, the combined monetary cost of addressing issues related to asbestos exposure in the Netherlands alone will amount to roughly $2,000 *per person* in the entire country. This does not take into consideration the suffering involved. If asbestos had been banned 28 years earlier, an estimated 34,000 lives would have been saved. [10]

Precautionary Health = Seeing the Big Picture

The Precautionary Principle asks us to look at the individual as part of a complex web of larger interconnected systems. Therefore, one can't merely treat the sick individual. Doing so is like continually hitting your head on a low beam, and treating the injury each time, but never taking action to either move the beam or change your path to keep from hitting your head yet again. Quite obviously, the entire situation must be tended to... the injury, the low beam, and the need for an alternate path around the beam; but also the context in which the beam exists and the multiple ways in which the beam participates within that context (why is it there, what does it support, is this the best placement for it, etc.)

Breast milk is 4 percent fat. As Michele nursed Mikaela and then Rowan, she drained a life's accumulation of pollutants into her children.

That's no reason to stop breast-feeding, cautioned Kim Hooper, the state PBDE expert with Cal EPA who has done extensive work with breast milk. Quite the opposite. Because in addition to fat, breast milk contains essential vitamins, minerals, growth hormones, enzymes, proteins and antibodies.

Plenty of evidence also suggests Rowan and other children get a far bigger dose from their environment.

Douglas Fischer
What's In You?
Inside Bay Area
http://www.insidebay area.com/bodyburden /ci_2600879

As we have learned to broaden our perceptions in regard to all facets of life on Earth, it isn't surprising to see our concept of Healthcare follow suit. Evidence consistently shows direct links between the choices we make as a species and the illnesses we experience. This realization has spurred the development of a field of study called Ecological Medicine, in which the focus is on the entire complex web of systems and how they contribute to the health and illness patterns of *all* involved, not just humans. It represents a fundamental shift from the old mechanistic paradigm of medicine that viewed each human as a separate part of a social machine, a separate entity. Public health addressed the machine as a whole unit. Ecological Medicine goes a step further and focuses attention on the entire complex system, including the room in which the machine sits, and anything else - excluding nothing. The illusion that humans can exist inside a bubble of protection separating them from "nature," can no longer be supported; because this old "us" vs. "them" mindset no longer serves our survival.

In his essay entitled, <u>Reconciling Human Rights, Public Health, and the Web of Life</u>, Ted Schettler describes Ecological medicine:

> … which extends its concerns beyond humans to include other species and the physical and spiritual world more generally. Ecological medicine focuses even more on relationships, and it encounters even more fundamental ethical tensions. Here, we are concerned about our relationships not only with each other, but with other species, landscapes, and ecosystems. [11]

It considers the balance of our relationship - as humans - with the rest of life; and encourages us to work *with* nature, not against it. It says that taking care of the health of *all life* is the most effective way of taking care of human life. It leads to changes in every aspect of how we view health, including the education of our medical practitioners. Perhaps comprehensive medical training will soon include ecology and evolution as fields of study.

This broader context will force us to see through different eyes. For example, when biologist Marge Profet[12] started questioning why pregnant women experience nausea primarily during the first trimester, she assumed that nature would not have evolved such a wide-spread experience unless it had a purpose. Her research showed that the first trimester is the most vulnerable time for the fetus to be exposed to toxins. Women's bodies quite literally tell them what to eat during this critical time! So much so, in fact, that there is evidence that those women who receive anti-nausea medication or who don't experience "morning sickness" at all, actually have a higher risk of birth defects or miscarriage. The best intentions of those doctors who prescribe anti-nausea medication, don't make up for our general lack of knowledge regarding the evolutionary explanation of our bodies' behavior.

Ecological medicine, looks at the way we design our lives – from land use and urban planning, to our use of natural resources, how we develop products to meet our needs, and even how we define and prioritize those needs.

Precautionary Health Care Options

In traditional western medicine, the options for treatment of any particular illness can be extremely narrow. Yet the field of alternative medicine offers widely varying methods of successful treatment, many with decades of sound scientific evidence

We are all, in a sense, subjects of an experiment, with no way to buy your way out, eat your way out or exercise your way out. We are guinea pigs when it comes to the unknown long-term threat these chemicals pose in our bodies and, in particular, our children.

Douglas Fischer
What's In You?
Inside Bay Area
http://www.insidebay area.com/bodyburden /ci_2600879

backing up their efficacy. Unfortunately the narrow focus of western medicine often keeps these success stories from ever reaching our ears.

Nevertheless, the alternative medicine field has steadily grown until today it offers a multitude of choices. Many have benefited from acupuncture, kinesiology, chiropractic, homeopathy, energy work, etc.

Still more is possible. We are just beginning to look seriously at the benefits of herbs and natural remedies. They tend to offer fewer side effects than their synthesized man-made cousins available over the pharmaceutical counter. Dr. Larry Dossey is applying scientific methodology to non-local treatments, including prayer. His findings have been so impressive, that the majority of medical schools in the USA now offer courses on the subject. Likewise, those who have learned to deeply merge with nature and the spiritual realm are discovering or re-discovering ancient energy methodologies and the healing balance that comes from reciprocity.

Hoxsey and the Cancer Industry

Perhaps one of the most dramatic examples of what happens without the Precautionary Principle in effect, is the story of Harry Hoxsey and his family's struggle to share their knowledge of his innovative cancer treatments. Outlined in his book, <u>When Healing Becomes a Crime: The Amazing Story of the Hoxsey Cancer Clinics and the Return of Alternative Therapies,</u> Kenny Ausubel[13] tells the story of their 75 year effort that finally culminated in federal government recognition through a 2001 National Institutes of Health report that found evidence of survival using the Hoxsey herbal treatment for cancer. Finally recognition was achieved, according to Ausubel, after the long-term combined efforts of the AMA, the FDA, the NCI, and the ACS, as well as several large corporations that profit from the cancer "industry," to shut down the successful Hoxsey clinics that had been providing alternative medical treatment for cancer sporadically since 1925. The atmosphere was so charged, that the state of California even passed a law in the 1950's outlawing the use of any cancer treatment except surgery, radiation, and chemotherapy.

Ausubel notes that it wasn't until 1975 that reports were widely published showing that cancer survival rates hadn't progressed since the 1950's. Shockingly, the studies showed that there had been no significant advances in cancer treatment during that time. Not surprisingly, Ausubel points to a "trade war" between Hoxsey and those who profit from the "cancer industry." He reveals that the $110 billion dollar a year cancer industry accounts for ten percent of the national healthcare costs. And in an article in the New York Times, Richard Smith, editor of the British Medical Journal, according to Ausubel, stated that a whopping 85 percent of prescribed standard medical treatments lack scientific validation, only 1% of the articles in medical journals are scientifically sound, and many treatments have never been assessed at all. Additionally, the average cancer patient spends approximately $100,000 on treatment. Ausubel points out that from an economic standpoint, hospital admissions for cancer generate more business, usually producing 2-3 times the billings of a typical non-cancer admission. Finally, he reveals that global sales of chemotherapy drugs in 1997 alone were $30.9 billion, $12 billion of which was generated in the USA. [14]

The Bush dministration has decided to give the oil and gas industry two years to comply with a storm-water regulation that goes into effect across the country Monday, and will consider granting a permanent exemption.

Environmental groups and environmentalists in Congress argued that the administration is granting special rights to a favored industry, at the risk of polluting rivers and lakes…It was written in 1999, but its effective date was delayed for four years.

Elizabeth Shogren
<u>*Bush Administration Exempts Oil Industry From Clean Water Act*</u>
LA Times
08 March 2003

When medical practitioners, patients, and even the scientific research community feel pressured to make decisions based on the economics of business goals, it is time to reassess our healthcare model. We can no longer afford to see ourselves as the victims of those we perceive as more powerful because of their position in our hierarchically structured governments and corporate board rooms. The quality of our healthcare system affects us all, as does the health of the entire planet. It is time to shift our perception and allow for the more holistic, systems-based awareness that Ecological medicine provides.

Additionally, in light of the way in which different perceptual filters dramatically change what is perceived, it would seem highly prudent to apply the full force of creative scientific inquiry into *all* methods of healing; especially those that have a track record of success even though they fall outside the confines of traditional medical practice. The Precautionary Principle stands as an invitation to open the doors of scientific inquiry.

My healing

I'd like to share two stories of healing that represent a broader perception of the possible. The first involves a well slammed car door, that accidentally pinned my hand, violently squishing it to the bone. Before I could find someone to free me from the door, I realized I had a choice to make.

The hand involved was my painting hand, and as an artist, I guarded that hand for the years of fine-motor-tuning that allowed it to be so responsive to my artistic desires. As I stood there waiting for help, I realized I could panic or take a different approach to the situation.

I decided to bathe the hand in unconditional love. I envisioned light enveloping it in love, and thanked it for all the service it had offered me throughout my life. I let go of the outcome, but simply stayed in a state of gratitude.

Once my hand was freed, I elevated it, wrapped it in ice, and took a homeopathic remedy for shock. Within hours the severe dents across my fingers were gone, there was only slight discoloration, and total movement and feeling had returned. By the next day, only a trained eye could tell that anything had happened at all. I believe the quick healing was directly related to my willingness to experience several things:

- I was willing to experience whatever the lesson of this experience held for me, unattached to the outcome
- I was willing to allow for all possibilities, including no harm whatsoever.
- I was filled with gratitude and appreciation, which kept fear from ever forming.

The second story revolves around my lifetime of experiencing strong seasonal hay fever that often led to severe asthma, frequently landing me in the hospital emergency room. When I was 49 I studied kinesiology, and part of the training involved my own deep kinesiological work. During that time, I learned of the underlying beliefs that kept me mired in the experience of hay fever and asthma.

As I released those beliefs, all symptoms of allergies and breathing difficulties disappeared.

The Centers for Disease Control estimates that 434,000 U.S. children under the age of 5 currently have blood-lead levels linked with serious developmental health consequences. Most of them live in the inner cities.

EPA Reverses Key Lead Abatement Rule: Children at Risk BushGreenwatch 22 March 2005 http://www.truthout.org/issues_05/032205EC.shtml

The following year, as the seasonal for hay fever approached, I experienced something I'd never noticed before. I became fearful that the first year of healing was only temporary, and that the old pattern of allergies and asthma would return. Each time I began to feel that old familiar itchiness in the back of my throat, and felt a sneeze coming on, I clearly saw that I had two choices I could make.

It was as if two doors stood before me. If I walked through one, all the past 50 years of familiar asthma/allergy patterns would return. If I chose the other door, the unknown was mine to experience, but it contained one element of which I was certain – no allergies and no asthma. It was as if I was testing my willingness to experience life in a different, healthier way.

I chose the doorway leading to the new path every time. Instantly, the itchiness and desire to sneeze disappeared.

I have been allergy and asthma free for two years now. The freedom I experienced from this healing cannot be underestimated. I feel as if I was suddenly given a brand new highly functional body.

I share these two stories because they both represent unorthodox methods of healing that succeeded brilliantly. The Precautionary Principle asks us to examine all alternatives before making a decision. Even though these two experiences were outside the mainstream of medical practice, they worked. They involved no drugs, and no side effects. They were tender and loving by nature. Most of all, they were a strong affirmation of my own ability to choose the quality of my experience of life.

Precaution and Insurance

Recent statistics show an alarming rise in the cost of health insurance in the USA. As a result, millions are currently uninsured, and the number is growing annually. Additionally, it is estimated that lack of health insurance causes roughly 18,000 unnecessary deaths every year in the United States. While the USA leads the world in spending on health care, it is the only wealthy, industrialized nation that does not ensure that all citizens have health insurance coverage.

Once the Precautionary Principle is embraced nationwide, it will help us reevaluate our healthcare system and slow down the environmental damage that is a major contributor to poor health. In the meanwhile, we need to find creative ways of ensuring that all people have access to quality healthcare. To that end, the Institute of Medicine of the National Academies has created a set of guiding principles for assessing policy options aimed at creating full medical coverage by the year 2010:

The principles for guiding the debate and evaluating various strategies are:

1. Health care coverage should be universal.
2. Health care coverage should be continuous.
3. Health care coverage should be affordable to individuals and families.
4. The health insurance strategy should be affordable and sustainable for society.
5. Health insurance should enhance health and well-being by promoting access to high-quality care that is effective, efficient, safe, timely, patient-centered, and equitable.

Although all the principles are necessary, the first is the most basic and important. The principles are intentionally general, which allows them to be applied in more specific operational and political processes. [11]

I turn back to the chokecherries, trying to pick and think differently. Grandma Nellie's sense of family somehow included birds… I feel myself in a circle of five generations of Northern Cheyenne women. Within this circle, I suddenly see how my world defines everything that exists as resources for people only, and for development and profit. In the industrial world I grew up in, no wild creature was considered family. We never left the best raspberries for the birds. Or even thought that cutting down forested areas for housing destroyed others' homes.

Marya Grathwohl
Planetary Spirituality and Berry Picking in Northern Cheyenne Country

Timeline Magazine Nov/Dec 2003

The USA is one of the last remaining democracies that does not offer its citizens universal healthcare. The Precautionary Principle, with its concept of "forecaring," encourages that all people be cared for.

Precaution and Law

As our society begins to awaken from thousands of years of dominator trance, (see the chapter on Partnership), and move towards a more balanced society, our interpretation of law will also be profoundly affected. A dominator oriented society believes in using punishment to control the behavior of its citizens. As we shift to a partnership oriented society we are beginning to see an emphasis on healing and personal responsibility replace punishment. The Precautionary Principle is a natural outcome of this shift of focus. Laws that consider all life within the scope of deliberation are slowly beginning to appear.

Law Professor Susan Daicoff has spent much of her career studying legal professionals. She noticed how many of her peers seemed unhappy and dissatisfied within their careers. Her analysis of the current legal system is echoed by many:

> What we are doing in our legal system is not working. Clients are unhappy with their lawyers, with the system, and with the outcomes of the process. Lawyers are extraordinarily unhappy or even impaired. Nonlegal dispute resolution mechanisms in society have failed and society is depending on litigative processes to resolve conflict. As a result, society in general is suffering from the effects of law's overly adversarial, other-blaming, position-taking, and hostile approach to conflict resolution. Perhaps in response to these developments, a number of alternative approaches to law practice are emerging to replace the old, out-moded monolithic system. All of these approaches attempt to optimize the wellbeing of the people involved in each legal matter and acknowledge the importance of concerns beyond simply strict legal rights. [16]

Daicoff's study led her to believe that many lawyers would feel more fulfilled if they practiced what she now calls "Comprehensive Law," an alternative approach that she now teaches. Her intention is to offer many lawyers a better fit for their talents, hopefully leading to greater job satisfaction. Most importantly, however, Daicoff feels that Comprehensive Law will offer more courteous and respectful interactions between legal professionals while also offering clients greater satisfaction with the entire system. A brief description of some of the Comprehensive Law "vectors" are outlined below. Daicoff sees these vectors merging into a new form of law, one more in step with the interdependent world today.

As you read them, note the difference in intent. Note also the definition of "harm" that is used. Ultimately, simply expanding that definition to include *all* life will go far towards the implementation of the Precautionary Principle.

Collaborative Law - Collaborative practice helps families resolve divorce issues with dignity and respect. In the collaborative process, all those involved in the divorce - from the actual couple, through their legal representatives and any other professionals - agree to resolve all issues of their case without contentious court proceedings. The resulting agreement is based on thoughtful decisions that work for everyone involved. The intention is to transform family dispute resolution into a healing process. [16]

Restorative Justice – The Restorative Justice movement is another example of the Precautionary Principle at work. Noting the huge recitative rate in our current

Every day we expose millions of people to chemicals and chemical mixtures for which the toxicity is unknown, said Michael Wilson, a research scientist with the Center for Occupational and Environmental Health at the University of California, Berkeley... The EPA receives 108 applications on average per month from companies seeking to introduce new chemicals on the market — 32,559 since 1979...

In the last 25 years, the country's consumption of synthetic chemicals increased 8,200 percent, Wilson said. Looking just at the 100 highest-volume compounds, the United States put 975 billion pounds into our products and environment in 2002, 16 percent more than in 1992.

The law does not require routine testing of chemicals...

*Douglas Fischer
The Great Experiment
Inside Bay Area
March 18, 2005
http://www.insidebayarea.com/bodyburden/ci_26009
03*

criminal justice system and the fact that severe penalties and longer sentences divert funding from much needed crime prevention programs, Restorative Justice seeks to address the harm done to victims while developing accountability and competency in the offender.   It follows the PP policy of seeking to "first do no harm" as it addresses the underlying issues involved.

Gaining favor in many countries, Restorative Justice incorporates greater community involvement, welcomes family input from both victim and offender, and takes a more holistic approach that respects the needs of all involved. The ultimate aim is the reintegration of the offender into the community by emphasizing education, self-esteem, and both social and spiritual support for the victim, offender, their families, and the community. Aligned, also, with the partnership model, it seeks to heal instead of punish. Once the scope of the definition of "harm" is expanded to include all life, Restorative Justice will fully embrace the Precautionary Principle. 20

Transformative Alternative Dispute Resolution[17] – This process, sees all legal conflict as an issue of human interaction rather than "violations of rights" or "conflicts of interest." Inherent in this concept is the belief that people struggle to balance concern for self with connections to others. The result of an imbalance between the two, is alienating and destructive behavior – and this is what bothers people most about conflict. The potential exists to transform conflict itself into a positive and constructive interaction that is connecting, constructive, and satisfying, no matter what the subject.

The mediator's goal is to help identify the opportunities for empowerment and recognition shifts as they arise in the parties' own conversation, to choose whether and how to act upon these opportunities, and to change interaction from destructive to constructive. Instead of measuring success by settlement, it is measured by shifts toward strength, responsiveness and constructive interaction.

Because the focus is on empowerment and perceptual awareness, the opportunity to embrace the Precautionary Principle is lively here. [16]

Therapeutic Jurisprudence[16] – By focusing on the therapeutic or countertherapeutic consequences of the law on all involved, including the community, it attempts to reform law and legal processes in order to promote the psychological well-being of the people they affect. It concentrates on the law's impact on emotional life and psychological well-being. It recognizes law as a therapeutic social force – one that has the potential to be beneficial. However, it does not suggest that therapeutic concerns are more important than other consequences or factors.

Law as a healing therapy is a concept that seems to flow with the intent of the Precautionary Principle. What would our world look like if all of our social structures shared an intention to heal?

Preventive Law [18]– This process proactively seeks to head off conflict by emphasizing relationships and through careful planning. The aim is to minimize legal risks, maximize legal rights and optimize legal outcomes of transactions (deals), relationships (disputes) and opportunities (problems).   Because it acts *before* actual

Studying individual school districts in Texas, the epidemiologists found that those districts with the highest levels of mercury in the environment also had the highest rates of special education students and autism diagnoses.

Thomas H. Maugh II

Possible Mercury, Autism Connection Found in Study

Los Angeles Times March 17, 2005

http://www.latimes.com/news /science/la-sci-autism17mar17,1,1770760.st ory?coll=la-news-science&ctrack=1&cset=true

Infants begin life with detectable levels of PCBs and DDT in their veins. Fire retardants lace mothers' breast milk. A chemical once used to make Scotchgard taints everybody's blood.

As exposures have risen, so, too, have a string of ailments:

Breast cancer incidence rates have climbed 90 percent since 1950. Non-Hodgkins lymphoma, a cancer tied to a weakened immune system, has seen a 250 percent jump in incidence rates.

Sperm counts appear down — by some indications a man born in the 1970s has three-quarters the sperm as a man born in the 1950s. Eight percent of all couples of reproductive age in the U.S. are infertile, according to the U.S. Department of Health and Human Services...

Between 1982 and 1995, the number of women in their prime childbearing years to report some difficulty conceiving increased 42 percent, according to one study.

Douglas Fischer
The Body Chemical
Inside Bay Area
March 18, 2005

conflict arises, Preventive Law closely follows the Precautionary guideline to avoid harm. [19]

Holistic Law - Seeks to find solutions to legal matters in a broader, more holistic approach than is traditionally associated with lawyers, more like holistic medicine. It focuses on the whole picture, and seeks to benefit the greatest good, promote healing, and completion. Holistic lawyers are often trained in other disciplines, including counseling and even energy healing.[21] Renaissance Law, a holistic law firm in Portland, Oregon provides the following vision statement:

> We have a vision of a legal system that is based on problem- solving, healing conflicts, and supporting us all in working and living together in peace. How DO we live together, work together, avoid misunderstandings, resolve those that inevitably come up, and encourage integrity in ourselves and others? What if the legal system is a resource for creating whole, vibrant, loving communities? For healing and transforming? What if lawyers could be honored for their service and we were able to express our creativity and brilliance in working with our clients? What if the goal for the lawyer is to craft a solution where everyone wins?

> There is a movement in the law toward a more visionary, humanistic approach to the law. Lawyers all over the world are hearing the call and many are beginning to explore new options for practicing law and serving their communities.

> The Renaissance Lawyer is here as a support to those who are answering the call, who are ready to begin the journey toward creating the new legal system, a new paradigm where everyone always wins.[21]

The Precautionary Principle's dictum of "first do no harm" is actively explored in these models. Perhaps these are the first baby steps toward the incorporation of the Precautionary Principle into our entire legal system. They offer the following shared features:

- A focus on more than simple legal rights. They consider needs, resources, goals, values, morals, relationships, efficiency, consequences on people and society.
- Avoid dominance over others, people share equal power
- Encourage compassion, reconciliation, forgiveness, and healing.
- Contribute to peace building at all levels.
- Listen intentionally and deeply in order to gain complete understanding.
- Acknowledge the opportunity in conflict.
- Wholly honor and respect the dignity and integrity of each individual
- Focus on the future and reconciling relationships, listening, forgiveness, gaining completion and moving on, rather than looking to the past and punishing past transgressions;
- Legal issues are seen in the context of the relationships between the parties and in the community with the focus on improving connections rather than separating the parties;
- Seeking Win-Win solutions for all parties involved
- Preventive models are common, proactively identifying risks and taking actions that will prevent conflict;
- The desire to create a better world for all that is healthy, diverse, creative, and respectful of human rights and values;

- A law practice where lawyers can change and grow as authentic and honest persons; consistent with Lawyers' own morals
- A belief that the legal system is an organic process that can respond to our needs and those of our clients[20]

Finally, in the process of slowly bringing the Precautionary Principle into our legal system, there is another important issue that must be addressed. Carolyn Raffensperger writes about it in her essay, The Precautionary Principle: Golden Rule for the New Millennium, in which she discusses the traditional practice of using the "Reasonable Person Standard" in all but criminal cases. She proposes the use of a new standard, the "Respectful Person Standard." She argues, in cases where reasonableness doesn't adequately handle the situation – cases like offenses against dignity and scientific uncertainty – we should apply this new standard:

> When we have vast uncertainty and the harm could be great, it would be wise for us to be respectful. If we are, we will be far less likely to blunder our way into big trouble through ignorance and arrogance. The respectful person gives deference to the mysteries of this great and marvelous earth. [22]

How exciting to watch the evolution of our legal system begin!

Precaution in Practice

Our dominance oriented society has always placed a price-tag on inclusion. Transactions are often determined by what a person can get. In other words, how does this transaction benefit me? Those who do not contribute in the prescribed manner simply are not included. The Precautionary Principle asks us to come from a broader view of life, one that humbly acknowledges that there is always more to learn and understand. It therefore entertains all possibilities, and excludes no one. It asks us to make our decisions after considering all possibilities and all contributions, even though we may not yet fully understand them. In that process, we are automatically forced to review our perceptual biases and filters. Thus it offers us a vibrantly alive ever-evolving process of choice making.

What does that look like in reality? Nancy Myers and Carolyn Raffensperger suggested some of the following lessons they've learned as they explored the Precautionary Principle in action:

Lesson one: Apply it early and often.

By the time a company has spent millions of dollars developing a chemical or technology, it is hard to apply the precautionary principle. What agency will say "no" in the face of all that money pressure? Instead, we discovered that it is much more useful to apply the principle before a technology, such as genetic engineering of crops, is a done deal.

Lesson two: Know what you want.

The principle works best when positive goals are set. If your community decides that children's bodies should be free of toxic chemicals, or that it wants to preserve migratory butter-fly routes, the steps to that goal become clearer. The state of Montana has established its citizens' desire for a clean and healthy environment as a constitutional right. As a consequence, citizen groups have been successful in court in preventing the mining industry from being exempted from this general duty. In

A 2004 analysis of PBDEs in the breast milk of Pacific Northwest women found levels 20 to 40 times higher than those found in Japanese and Swedish women. Recent studies found surprisingly high levels of PBDEs in Oregon salmon, both farmed and wild. These chemicals are also showing up in other wildlife, including orcas in Puget Sound and seals from San Francisco Bay.

Viable alternatives, with no reduction in fire safety, are available for these products. Oregon companies such as Intel, HP and Epson have phased or are phasing these chemicals out of their production processes. The best way to reduce our exposure to this class of persistent chemicals is to stop using them. Several states – including California, Maine, Michigan, New York and Washington – have already passed legislation or are otherwise taking steps to phase out the use of these chemicals.

SB 962 bill will ban the penta and octa forms as of January 1, 2006, and phase out the use of the deca form as of January 1, 2008.

Oregon Conservation Network E-Mail supporting the passage of SB 962, April 27, 2005

1992, an International Joint Commission adopted the precautionary principle to set the goal of stopping all persistent organic pollutants from being discharged into the Great Lakes.

Lesson three: Ask bigger questions.

Business as usual is going to get us business as usual. Mary O'Brien's work on assessing alternatives to damaging activities invites a robust creativity. (See Making Better Environmental Decisions, MIT Press, 2000). What alternatives do we have? How do those alternatives help meet our goals? If faced with a Hobson's choice— say a community is asked to choose between a new waste dump and an incinerator— step back and ask a bigger question: How can we cut down the amount of waste we produce? Reframing the question is often the most important step in applying the precautionary principle. It can turn adversaries into cooperative, problem-solving teams.

Lesson four: Many heads are better than one.

In an uncertain world, scientists, corporations, and politicians should not be the only ones to set up the choices or make the decisions. It is important to gather goals and innovative solutions from throughout society. The Health Care Without Harm campaign has brought together environmentalists, medical professionals, researchers, and industry to find substitutes for medical plastics containing phthalates, which have the potential to harm infants in neonatal care and possibly other patients as well. In the meantime, the campaign calls for precautionary action by asking the medical community to go beyond current regulatory requirements and take ethical responsibility for preventing harm.

Lesson five: Lives, not products, come first.

It surprises many people to learn that most chemicals and other products are considered safe until proven otherwise. In courts of law, products (and corporations) are often given the benefit of the doubt over those who claim to have been harmed by them. But this isn't always true. Hudson, Quebec, banned the use of chemical herbicides and insecticides on lawns a decade ago, and the town was subsequently sued by landscaping companies ChemLawn and Spraytech. In June 2001, the Canadian Supreme Court upheld the town's right to ban pesticides, based on the precautionary principle. ("We're thinking about adopting the dandelion as the municipal flower," Hudson Mayor Stephen Sharr told the CBC.)

Lesson six: Make proponents bear the burden of proof.

If project proponents cannot demonstrate to the satisfaction of the public that their actions will not cause harm, they may be legitimately stopped. The NIMBY (not in my backyard) syndrome that government and industry find so frustrating is often a common-sense exercise of the precautionary principle on the part of citizens. Given the choice of being exposed or not exposed to something that shows some possibility of being harmful, and weighing the benefits to themselves and their descendants, people will generally choose not to accept the danger if they believe it provides little benefit and there are better alternatives, or that alternatives have not been sought vigorously enough.

We have the most expensive health-care system in the world, but are 27th in the world in the quality of our health.

We've produced health-care billionaires and millionaires in America, but have 45 million uninsured.

And even health insurance in America is not much damn good - about a quarter of all bankruptcies last year in this nation were among insured people who were wiped out by co-pays, deductibles, and "non-covered" hospital and health care expenses.

Thom Hartmann
Save Andy - And Save America, Too!
May 1st, 2005

Lesson seven: Just do it.

Precautionary action comes in many shapes and sizes. Bans or phase outs may be appropriate, but pre-market testing can also be precautionary. Monitoring of all kinds fits into a precautionary scheme: products already on the market, human effects on ecosystems, the condition of human bodies.

Any action that helps to prevent harm and to protect humans and the environment in the face of scientific uncertainty qualifies as a precautionary action. Even actions after the fact can be in the spirit of the principle. The Agent Orange Act of 1991 instructed scientists and policy makers to give veterans the benefit of the doubt in the absence of full scientific proof that they had been exposed to herbicides or harmed by them. A scientific review committee of the US Institute of Medicine worked out a standard for evaluating harmful effects of a substance based on the weight of the evidence—"more likely than not"—rather than conclusive proof.

Lesson eight: Wise up.

Choosing the right precautionary action requires wisdom. The regulatory systems we have are based on rules that often leave little room for good sense or even good evidence. Rules have their place, but in making decisions that affect our health and future, we need all the wisdom we can muster. That means not only looking at scientific evidence but also practicing flexibility, foresight, fairness, responsibility, and honesty. The Federal Aviation Administration took precautionary action when it banned use of cell phones and electronic devices at takeoff and landing, based on a single study that suggested these devices might interfere with a plane's electronic systems. Scientists have not been able to duplicate that study. Nevertheless, because the costs of continuing the ban are practically nil, and because the potential adverse consequences are so great, it seems sensible to continue the ban unless it is proven unnecessary.

Lesson nine: A little precaution is better than none.

The precautionary principle is not an absolute. Nothing guarantees a risk-free world. But we must get better at predicting harmful side effects and acting on the first signs of harm. We have very far to go, and many changes and decisions will be difficult. Any progress in exercising precaution is worth applauding—and then pushing further.

The Methodist Church adopted the precautionary principle in 2000 as a way of expressing their commitment to be stewards of God's creation.

The Republican Party of Indiana adopted the principle as one of its planks in 1998.

The Los Angeles Unified School District has adopted a pesticide reduction plan based on the precautionary principle. The principle can be adopted and used to good effect by any organization at any level of jurisdiction—even by families.

Lesson ten: Clean up your messes.

The precautionary principle is about preventing damage. But we all know of contaminated sites or bodies, a clear-cut forest, or a channelized stream. Their degraded condition poses risks of both ongoing and future damage. For this reason, restoration is one of the faces of forecaring, or precaution. Citizens of Metropolitan

Chicago are preserving and restoring what remains of the region's oak-savannah prairies. They call their movement "Chicago Wilderness"—an optimistic assertion that it is worth caring for nature even in the most human-dominated landscapes.

These lessons are not easy. Applying the precautionary principle is one of the most challenging tasks facing citizens of the early 21st century. It is not impossible, however, and it is beginning to happen. [23]

When a loving mother nurtures her children, she does so without regard to that child's possible contribution to society. She simply loves and nurtures each child equally because that is how love expresses.

Ultimately, the Precautionary Principle offers us a guideline for honoring all. The intention to honor all includes seeing each other as a loving mother would, nurturing and caring for all life without an ulterior motive; except perhaps survival. It comes with acknowledgment of life's intelligence, honoring this on-going experiment called life, in a way that assumes every aspect of life expressed has value and contributes.

As a tool, the Precautionary Principle offers us a description of what honoring looks like in daily life. It asks us to find balance within as we work to express that balance into our world. It is a profoundly different way of perceiving life, but ultimately highly fulfilling. Think about it. When the intention of society is to do no harm, our needs will automatically be met. Our job will be to find the gifts we can best offer – the ones that make our hearts sing – and then give them whole heartedly to the world.

Notes

1. http://www.sehn.org/ecoeconomics.html and Ethical Economics: Forecaring A PowerPoint presentation by Nancy Myers Nancy is SEHN's Communications Director. A writer and editor, she has been making the precautionary principle a useful tool for activists and policy makers since the 1998 Wingspread Conference. Nancy serves as SEHN's author, co-author, and editor of pithy fact sheets, arguments, statements and articles She writes the network's reports and proposals and co-edits SEHN's electronic newsletter, the Networker, with Carolyn Raffensperger.

2. Kenny Ausubel The Coming Age of Ecological Medicine from Ecological Medicine – Healing the Earth, Healing Ourselves edited by Kenny Ausubel with J.P. Harpignies, pages 4,6, and 8.

3. Charlotte Brody Thinking Like a Girl is Good Medicine from Ecological Medicine – Healing the Earth, Healing Ourselves edited by Kenny Ausubel with J.P. Harpignies, page 24.

4. Michael Lerner Personal Healing and Planetary Healing from Ecological Medicine – Healing the Earth, Healing Ourselves edited by Kenny Ausubel with J.P. Harpignies, pages 15 - 17.

5. Michael Lerner Personal Healing and Planetary Healing from Ecological Medicine – Healing the Earth, Healing Ourselves edited by Kenny Ausubel with J.P. Harpignies, pages 18.

6. WHITE PAPER The Precautionary Principle and the City and County of San Francisco March 2003. http://temp.sfgov.org/sfenvironment/aboutus/policy/white_paper.pdf

7. Good Science vs. the Common Good By Janet Jacobson Op-ed in Cavalier County Republican, January 19, 2004

8. http://www.oriononline.org/pages/om/04-6om/Knobloch.html The War On Science - White House Disinformation In The Face Of Unwelcome Facts Threatens Everyone by Kevin Knobloch, Orion Nov/Dec 2004. Also see http://www.ucsusa.org/rsi_calltoaction/index.php
Kevin Knobloch is president of the Union of Concerned Scientists To date, the UCS statement has been signed by more than 5,000 scientists, including 48 Nobel laureates. UCS issued reports in February and July of last year that documented dozens of cases of alleged tampering with science, including many involving environmental policy decisions.

In order to preserve the core values in science and science-based decision making, our nation's policies should uphold fundamental scientific principles and practices. We call upon the administration and Congress to make a commitment to policies that will support those principles.These policies should:

- Ensure that scientific and health information and reports provided by the government are based on full and informed assessments of all relevant data, done in an independent manner, free of financial conflicts of interest.
- Ensure that scientists are not pressured to delay, suppress, or alter scientific or medical information that may be in conflict with the administration's political position, and are not penalized if they resist such pressure.
- Ensure that the Federal Advisory Committee Act (FACA) is fully enforced, to make certain that scientific advisory committees are able to provide the highest quality independent scientific advice to the government, without political or ideological bias. Ensure that people who do not have adequate scientific qualifications are not appointed to scientific advisory positions.
- Safeguard against subjecting scientists to ideological or political litmus tests for advisory committees and civil service positions.
- Ensure that the President and Congress get scientific advice as early as possible in the decision making process, and that this is done in a transparent fashion.
- Ensure that the lack of complete certainty or irrefutable proof does not erode time-honored precautionary approaches to public health and environmental protections.

- The suppression and distortion of scientific information erodes credibility and public trust in government, and may compromise the health and safety of Americans.

9. New Approaches To Safeguarding The Earth: An environmental version of the Hippocratic oath By Jared Blumenfeld, From the San Francisco Chronicle Open Forum - August 4, 2003

10. PROSPERING WITH PRECAUTION: Employment, Economics, and the Precautionary Principle, by Frank Ackerman and Rachel Massey, Global Development and Environment Institute, Tufts University, August, 2002 http://www.healthytomorrow.org/pdf/prosper.pdf For more information on the Precautionary Principle's economic impact see http://www.sehn.org/ecoeconomics.html and Ethical Economics: Forecaring A PowerPoint presentation by Nancy Myers.

11. Ted Schettler, Ecological Medicine, Human Rights, and the Web of Life from Ecological Medicine – Healing the Earth, Healing Ourselves edited by Kenny Ausubel with J.P. Harpignies, page 75.

12. Anthony Cortese, Redesigning Environmental Health, from Ecological Medicine – Healing the Earth, Healing Ourselves edited by Kenny Ausubel with J.P. Harpignies, page 29.

13. Kenny Ausubel, Hoxsey: When Healing Becomes a Crime, from Ecological Medicine – Healing the Earth, Healing Ourselves edited by Kenny Ausubel with J.P. Harpignies, p92-93.

14. Kenny Ausubel, Hoxsey: When Healing Becomes a Crime, from Ecological Medicine – Healing the Earth, Healing Ourselves edited by Kenny Ausubel with J.P. Harpignies, p101.

15. http://www.iom.edu/report.asp?id=17632 Insuring America's Health: Principles and Recommendations, Project: Consequences of Uninsurance, January 14, 2004

16. Susan Daicoff, http://www.fcsl.edu/faculty/daicoff/law.htm. Her PowerPoint "Lawyer Know Thyself" is located at http://www.fcsl.edu/faculty/daicoff/orientation_files/frame.htm. See also http://www.fcsl.edu/faculty/daicoff/newerslidesaftart399/tsld015.htm, http://www.fcsl.edu/faculty/daicoff/newerslidesaftart399/tsld016.htm, http://www.fcsl.edu/faculty/daicoff/newerslidesaftart399/tsld017.htm, the information on the various vectors of Comprehensive Law was obtained from Brief Description of the Vectors of the Comprehensive Law Movement --and their Points of Intersection by Susan Daicoff (http://www.fcsl.edu/faculty/daicoff/vectors1.htm), Additional information on Collaborative Law can be found at http://collaborativelaw.org/. More information on Therapeutic Jurisprudence can be found at http://www.law.arizona.edu/depts/upr-intj/.

17. Transformative Alternative Dispute Resolution was first described in Robert A. Baruch Bush and Joseph P. Folger in The Promise of Mediation: Responding to Conflict through Empowerment and Recognition (Jossey-Bass, 1994) http://www.transformativemediation.org and http://www.transformativemediation.org/transformative.htm

18. http://www.preventivelawyer.org/main/default.asp?pid=essays/rowley.htm The Matter with Lawyers Why is it that people love to hate lawyers? Just what is the matter? by David Rowley

19. Carolina Academic Press http://www.cap-press.com/books/1014

20. For more information, see the web site at www.restorativejustice.org or www.restorativejustice.com . Also http://2ssw.che.umn.edu/rjp/. On an international level, Daicoff sees Truth and Reconciliation as a possible subset of this vector. http://www.iahl.org/articles/08_Visionary_lawyering.htm Visionary Law: New Approaches to Expanding our Choices in Law Practice, By J. Kim Wright, J.D, who can be reached at http://www.renaissancelawyer.com/

21. http://www.renaissancelawyer.com/Vision&Values.htm Also see http://www.iahl.org/on Holistic Law.

22. Carolyn Raffensperger, The Precautionary Principle: Golden Rule for the New Millennium, from Ecological Medicine – Healing the Earth, Healing Ourselves edited by Kenny Ausubel with J.P. Harpignies, page 52.

23. Nancy Myers and Carolyn Raffensperger A Precautionary Primer, YES! magazine Fall 2001 http://www.mindfully.org/Precaution/Precautionary-Myers-Raffensperger.htm

24. Reprinted from YES! magazine, PO Box 10818, Bainbridge Island, WA 98110. Subscriptions: 800/937-4451 Web: www.yesmagazine.org

10

COMMUNITY

The egocentric ideal of a future reserved for those
who have managed to attain egotistically the extremity of 'everyone for himself'
is false and against nature...
The outcome of the world, the gates of the future,
the entry into the super-human — these are not thrown open to a few of the privileged
or to one chosen people to the exclusion of all others.
They will only open to an advance of all together,
in a direction in which all together can join
and find completion in a spiritual renovation of the earth...
No evolutionary future awaits man except in association with all other men.
~ Pierre Teilhard De Chardin

COMMUNITY
Who are we willing to be?

The first Hamas female suicide bomber, Reem Raiyshi, 22, struck in Israel. As I read her story, I was reminded of another suicide in Cancun, in which fifty six-year old Lee Kyung Hae stabbed himself in protest to globalization policies that he said were killing Korean farmers.

Both took their lives believing passionately in a cause greater than their desire to live. One physically hurt himself but emotionally touched thousands. The other deliberately tried to take as many lives with her as possible, leaving her own children, ages 18 months and 3 years, without a mother, and her grieving husband – who was unaware of her plans - without a wife.

I ask myself what could lead these two people to so passionately believe in their cause that they would be willing to use their own bodies as political statements, especially when they had so much to live for? Ms. Raiyshi left the children she loved without a mother; while Mr. Lee died days before his daughter's scheduled wedding. He was a former president of the Korean Advanced Farmers Federation and led thousands of farmers in protest over the years, including a hunger strike outside the WTO headquarters in Geneva last year. Mr. Lee chose one of Korea's largest national holidays, Chusok, for his suicide. Significantly, Chusok is the day in which family and friends gather to give thanks to their ancestors for the food they have harvested.

How do we, as individuals and community members, consider such passionate actions in a way that truly honors their intended message while still not condoning their method of conveying it?

The Babemba

In her book, <u>Listening with the Heart</u>, Carol Hwoschinsky tells the story of the Babemba tribe of South Africa, who have developed a most extraordinary method for dealing with instances when a person of the community acts irresponsibly, unjustly, or in a way that harms others.

Instead of punishing the person, they assume that the person has simply forgotten who he is. Everyone in the village gathers around him, and one by one each person steps forward and begins to recall all the positive attributes of the person in the center of the circle. Every event is recalled in as much detail and as accurately as possible, without embellishment or exaggeration. They continue, sometimes for several days, until every person has recalled every single example of a good deed, kindness, positive characteristic, and strength of the person throughout his lifetime. Upon completion, they celebrate and welcome the person back into the tribe.[1]

When I first heard of this approach, I was in awe of the beauty, humility, and honor that the community expressed through this process. Each community member was willing to see the person in the center of the circle as whole, lacking nothing except perhaps the remembering of who he was.

I do not know the impact of such community support on the person in the center of the circle, there are no statistics showing the impact of this method on crime. Yet

These groups believe that self-sufficiency is a human right. They imagine a future where producing the means to kill people is not a business but a crime, where families do not starve, where parents can work, where children are never sold, and where women cannot be impoverished because they choose to be mothers. These groups believe that water and air belong to us all, not to the rich. They believe seeds and life itself cannot be owned or patented by corporations. They believe that nature is the basis of true prosperity and must be honored.

Paul Hawken
Brother, Can You Spare a Paradigm?,

by Paul Hawken, from Nature's Operating Instructions, edited by Kenny Ausubel with J.P. Harpignies, 2004, page 158

the approach is so completely different from our own handling of criminals, that I wonder if the statistics would prove far more successful than our own feeble attempts at rehabilitation and punishment

I also wonder if the extreme actions taken by suicidal farmers and bombers would take place if we willingly saw each person with the same accepting and generous eyes as the Babemba. What would our communities look like – both locally and globally – if we insisted that our decisions reflect an honoring of *all involved* as true members of our community family, seen as whole and perfect beings worthy of intentional caring from all community members?

I do not condone murder, but I ask myself how it is that we have allowed the suffering of our world to become so great that some people feel they must resort to violence simply to be seen and heard? If we willingly chose to treat each other as the Babemba, would anyone feel the need to turn up the volume in order to be heard?

Perhaps we could go even a step further than the Babemba. What if we not only helped the person in the center of the circle re-member himself, the parts that are not in pain and the parts that bask in the awe and magic of love and life, but also willingly asked ourselves how we may have contributed to that person's pain?

Global Community Awareness

I wonder what thoughts, words, and actions I have taken that directly or indirectly contributed to the suffering of Mr. Lee and Ms. Raiyshi; and indirectly to those they killed or hurt through their actions? Without going into the complex political issues involved, how have I contributed to their problems?

- I realized that I saw their problems as taking place far from me and my cushy lifestyle of privilege, and therefore not worthy of my attention. I told myself I had more pressing matters to attend to, ones that impact my life in a more direct way.
- I realized that whenever I dismiss someone who performs what I perceive to be an extreme act, as crazy or not worthy of my attention, I contribute to their feeling of not being seen or heard. This can result in their need to "turn up the volume" in order to gain my attention.
- I saw that when ever I fail to speak out about policies my government chooses that do not express who I see myself to be or how I want to relate to others, I abandon both myself and those in need of my support.
- I saw that I literally ignore both myself and those in need when ever I tell myself that there is nothing I can do.
- I realize that I contribute to globalization when ever I purchase products, especially those that make my life easier and more comfortable, without making sure that my comfort doesn't come at the expense of someone else's pain.
- I saw that when ever I allow myself to see an individual as a generalization (as in "those Palestinians") or turn a complex situation into a simplified symbol (for example by lumping the needs of all farmers into what I perceive as one need); I fail to see the individual human being behind the symbol

If an American is concerned only about his nation, he will not be concerned about the peoples of Asia, Africa, or South America. Is this not why nations engage in the madness of war without the slightest sense of penitence? Is this not why the murder of a citizen of your own nation is a crime, but the murder of citizens of another nation in war is an act of heroic virtue?

--Martin Luther King, Jr

Just as the key to a species' survival in the natural world is its ability to adapt to local habitats, so the key to human survival will probably be the local community. If we can create vibrant, increasing autonomous and self-reliant local groupings of people that emphasize sharing, cooperation and living lightly on the Earth, we can avoid the fate warned of by Rachel Carson and the world scientists and restore the Sacred Balance of life.

David Suzuki
The Sacred Balance
1997, p.8

The highest unity is one which respects difference as well as sameness and regards both with equal respect.

--Glenda Green
Love Without End

bleeding before me. In that moment, I fail to see the individual, the complexity of the situation, and my own part in the drama.

- I saw that it is easy for me to assume that the "other" is less-than in some way, or (I assume) this situation would not exist. The assumption of separation between me and those I perceive as "other" forces me to suppress my natural empathy.

- I realize that what ever I dismiss as not pertaining to me, is actually a part of myself and my world that I am unwilling to own and embrace; and that ultimately, I am unwilling to take responsibility for.

Therefore, dear Ms. Raiyshi and Mr. Lee, while I mourn the suffering you have created through the choices you have made, and even though I cannot condone your actions; I want to begin to see them without judgment. I want to begin– as a member of your global community – to welcome you into my heart once more. Please forgive my ignorance of your suffering, forgive my unwillingness to see you, forgive my denial that my actions affect all lives (not just my own), forgive those moments whenever I saw you as less-than in any way, and forgive my complacency and comfort-induced blindness.

We are each members of the same global community. Our political boundaries are as illusory as lines drawn in the shifting sand, and our planet recognizes no boundaries. Why then, should our policies? I invite us to explore until we finally find a way to live together such that the structure of our cultures, our governments, our economies, and our personal interactions express that magnificent essence that sings within our souls. Why not let our relationships in all aspects of life reflect the beauty that is possible?

It is only a choice away, but whose choice? How can we explore what community means to us in a way that all voices are heard? There are many people searching for answers to those questions, some of their stories I've highlighted below.

We may truly say that different human cultures are complementary to each other. Indeed, each such culture represents a harmonious balance of traditional conventions by means of which latent possibilities of human life can unfold themselves in a way which reveals to us new aspects of its unlimited richness and variety."

Niels Bohr
Summer 1938
from
Michael Nagler
Compassion – The
Radicalism of this Age
Yes! Magazine Fall 1998

Living the Experiment

We must be willing to experiment again and again until we find a way that works, a way that allows each person to feel his or her voice is heard, a way that promotes the well-being and creative expression of each community member. In my opinion, the structure used doesn't matter any where near as much as the simple fact that we, as a community, are willing to voluntarily engage in a conversation that goes beyond pointing the finger at what doesn't work; to actively creating the Vision of who we see ourselves to be, and how that is reflected in all of the every day decisions that make up our community. I celebrate the aliveness that is in each of us. Consciously choosing to express that beauty *as community*, is simply another expression of that aliveness, one that quivers with excitement in the possibilities of the moment.

When we consciously take responsibility for the condition of our communities, and decide to step into the creative role of manifesting exactly what we want as an intentional co-creation, then our vision becomes our ultimate reality. I had the privilege of experiencing the power of that creative intention recently, regarding community violence.

Violence in the Community

A group of women gathered to offer healing to one of our circle who had been physically attacked by her boyfriend. The intention of the healing could be held on many levels. First, it was to offer her support as she went through her own healing process. This included letting her know we were there for her as a source of emotional and even physical support – offering her a place of refuge if he chose to violate his restraining order. Second, we were there to encourage her to look within for her healing and not to get caught up in her story, but to take full responsibility for the parts of her own being that were wounded and needed healing – especially any parts she consistently denied. Third, we were there because those parts, both the attacker and the victim lives in all of us… and on some level still remained unhealed or we would not have this level of violence occurring in the circle of our lives. Fourth, to honor the desire for our small community to deal with this age-old issue in a new and perhaps more loving manner. Our desire was not to condemn or condone, but to instead find a way to heal the deep community and personal issues that provided the fertile ground in which this kind of violence could blossom.

It was an honor to participate in this circle. We came together and willingly told our stories of confronting our own worst fears, or as some say, "stepping into the fire". By doing so, we were able to face, clearly see, and ultimately forgive ourselves for carrying those fears – like a guiding star – all our lives. We told of being able to embrace those parts of ourselves that were so wounded many of us had developed life-threatening diseases and almost died before we gathered the courage to touch and ultimately heal our deepest wounds. And the healing continues to this day.

By telling our stories and hearing our sisters speak of their vulnerabilities and previously hidden wounds, we found that we all carry such pain… that we are not alone. We also found the courage to face our common wounds - not as a sisterhood of victims - but as a human species in which there are no victims… only choices.

The choice to face our demons brings about so many rewards. Deep healing leads to forgiveness for ourselves and the choices we've made; and finally for those we have cast as the antagonists in our stories.

But there is another choice at work here, one that leads, I believe, to the growth of our entire species. That choice is to consciously own the idea that any source of violence in our community is ultimately a reflection of unhealed violence within ourselves as community. Therefore, ALL violence is EVERYONE's business. The time to turn our heads and politely pretend that what happens behind closed doors doesn't affect all of us – is gone.

The other aspect of violence that I realize directly affects me is the way in which I speak about it. It is so easy, especially in a small community, to say something that can be interpreted differently than originally intended. In instances of violent behavior, we all have a tendency to judge one person as the victim and one as the perpetrator. While never condoning violence, I can be aware of how I speak about those directly involved. I can imagine what my experience could be if I were playing either role, and how I would want others to speak of me. The minute we label anyone a victim or perpetrator, we cease seeing him or her at all. They simply

Intimate violence and international violence are as tightly bound together as the fingers of a clenched fist.

Riane Eisler
author of *The Chalice and The Blade*
http://www.partnershipway.org/html/saivpage.htm

become a symbol. **Failing to see a person, and honor them for the unique person they are, honors no one; including ourselves.**

Community as Self

One of the best tools I have found for self-awareness is to see my community as a larger extension of me. In other words, everything that happens within my sphere of experience – including my community, any way you define it – is a message to me from me. I like to think that I draw the experience I most need to myself for the express purpose of learning. Therefore, when there is violence present in my community, I know that there are aspects of violence within me that I have not yet healed.

I like this idea because it gives me a candle to hold up when the darkness of community's issues threaten to engulf me. We live in a time of polarities, when the flames of separation and fear are being fanned by many. It is comforting to know that whatever is manifesting in my community is actually a gift to me. It offers a window into areas of myself I want to embrace and heal so that I no longer live life from fear, but rather from the compassionate core and love that I know myself to be.

As we begin to see the community within ourselves and at the same time, the value we each provide to our community; our traditional image of community is shifting. Gone is the old image of community as a group of people who just happen to find themselves living in the same location. We are learning to empower ourselves to create community as a microcosm of the peaceful world we all long for.

Re-Inventing Community

Once one starts looking at everything through the lens of systems theory, not surprisingly, ideas that were originally developed for application in one area of life work equally as well in other seemingly unrelated fields. Systems theory teaches us that all is related, and the work of Peter Block is a perfect example of interrelatedness in action. His work concentrates on how the language we use determines the perceptions and subsequent actions we allow. He theorizes that if we change our public conversation, we change the context, and thus the possibilities. Although his work is applicable in a variety of fields from business to interpersonal relations, he concentrates much of his attention on the restoration of community.

He identifies six conversations we can have within a community that will move us into the role of co-creators actively manifesting our community goals.

First, he invites us to examine our experience of typical community conversation, which he feels lacks both accountability and commitment. He defines both:

> To be **accountable**, among other things, means you act as an owner and part creator of whatever it is that you wish to improve. In the absence of this, you are in the position of effect, not cause; a powerless stance.

> To be **committed** means you are willing to make a promise with no expectation of return; a promise void of barter and not conditional on another's action. In the absence of this, you are constantly in the position of reacting to the choices of others.[2]

Next, he re-defines the issues. Just as Dynamic Facilitation helps groups uncover the underlying issues that drive more readily apparent problems, Block asks us to look

---

I would rather define self as the interiorization of community. And if you make that little move, then you're going to feel very different about things... boundaries would be much less sure...And 'others' would not include just other people, because community as I see it, is something more ecological, or at least animistic.

James Hillman author of Re-Visioning Psychology and co-author of We've Had a Hundred Years of Psychotherapy And the World's Getting Worse

The GDP, however, is not value free. Leaving social and environmental costs and contributions to the economy off the books does not avoid value judgments. On the contrary, it makes the obvious value judgment that things such as the destruction of farm-land and natural resources, underemployment, longer-commute times, and the loss of free time, count for nothing in assessing how the economy is fairing. The GDP does put a value on such factors: Zero. Keep in mind, this is on top of adding in the value of crime, disaster, and war-related expenditures.

Redefining Progress The Genuine Progress Indicator

1950-2002 (2004 Update) page 7
ttp://www.redefiningprogress.org/ publications/vbi march2004ubdat

beyond conventional views of community problems – topics such as public safety, affordable housing, etc. – to see them as symptoms of the un-reconciled and fragmented nature of community. His aim is to shift the context in which those aspects of community are held, so that the vitality of community can be restored.

It is our underlying assumptions, (the context in which we ask ourselves how to best create community), that need to be addressed. For example, he points out that we have a dominant cultural belief that an alternative future can be "negotiated, mandated, and controlled into existence."[3] The underlying assumption is that people need to change. This automatically sets up resistance. It is as if we are affirming that there is something wrong with us.

Block suggests another path, one that empowers the participants, encouraging them to experience themselves and their community in a more creative, wholesome, and vibrantly alive context. He creates this perceptual shift of context through careful use of language, especially questions that build commitment and accountability. These are questions that engage people, especially those of opposing views. The way they are asked creates an experience of freedom and infinite possibility within the process of making a response.

In Jim Rough's Dynamic Facilitation (see the Chapter on Co-Creation), he suggests that the Facilitator's job is to facilitate, not manage. The best facilitator is not invested in the results, but is a neutral supporter of all participants, guiding none, but following the energy flow of the group. The best facilitators, like the best leaders, empower everyone to step into their own Inner-Leader – that confident, clear, articulate, passionate, highly creative, and compassionate core being that dwells within each of us. The Inner-Leader could be seen as one of the many roles sourced from the Essential Self. When co-creating in a room of people who are participating from their Inner-Leader, magic happens. This is the same space that Peter Block seeks within community co-creation.

Block's work is very detailed and easy to understand. I would love to engage my entire community in his work. His final seven questions reveal the depth of inner-work required to participate fully in community. The word in parenthesis indicates the part of his work each question addresses. The seven questions are:

1. To what extent are you here by choice? (*Invitation*)
2. What declarations are you prepared to make about the possibilities for the future? (*Possibilities*)
3. How invested and participative do you plan to be in this meeting? (*Ownership*)
4. To what extent do you see yourself as part of the cause of what you are trying to fix? (*Ownership*)
5. What are your doubts and reservations? (*Dissent*)
6. What promises are you willing to make to your peers? (*Commitment*)
7. What gifts have you received from each other? (*Gifts*) [3]

I would add another question to #8, "*What gifts are you willing to offer the group?*" By answering this last question, you publicly affirm your own talents and your desire to make them available to the community. It is a powerful and empowering affirmation of who you are. Just as all good facilitators seek to empower others and not simply

Just as the key to a species' survival in the natural world is its ability to adapt to local habitats, so the key to human survival will probably be the local community. If we can create vibrant, increasing autonomous and self-reliant local groupings of people that emphasize sharing, cooperation and living lightly on the Earth, we can avoid the fate warned of by Rachel Carson and the world scientists and restore the Sacred Balance of life.

David Suzuki
The Sacred Balance
1997, p.8

manage or direct them, Block suggests that communities use his questions only as guidelines to finding their own.

Gaviotas, Colombia

The future of humanity depends on the integrity of the individual. It is absolutely touch and go. Each one of us could make the difference.

R. Buckminster Fuller

On of the best community experiments has been taking place in the most unlikely location of Gaviotas, Colombia for the past thirty years. The city of Gaviotas was started by Paolo Lugari, who's interest in civic development was sparked as a teen, by a dinner discussion with Father Louis Lebret, a professor at the Paris Institute of Economics and Humanism. He had been invited by Paolo's father, Mariano Lugari, to give a series of seminars on how the new civil government might humanely plan the country's future. Father Lebret asked everyone at the table, "How can we define development?" After each guest defined it according to his or her own field of expertise, Father Lebret finally suggested,

> Development means making people happy. Before you spend your money on roads and factories, you should first be sure that those are what your citizens really need. [4]

All humans share a desire for meaning, community, and purpose. Some find it in love, hope, generosity, compassion, and a sense of spiritual connection to the whole of life. Others seem to find it in fear, despair, cynicism, hatred, violence, greed, and material indulgence. Belief that community will ultimately prevail is grounded in the premise that for the vast majority of people a life of love, hope, generosity, compassion and spiritual connection is more attractive than a life of ruthless competition, fear, violence, and hate — and that it is within our individual and collective means to consciously choose the former.

David C. Korten, Nicanor Perlas, and Vandana Shiva Global Civil Society: The Path Ahead-A Discussion Paper - Summary

Young Paolo took those words to heart. After completing his education, he noticed the suffering brought about by the imbalance of ever increasing human populations in tropical rainforests. While overcrowding was a problem of tropical urban cities, other parts of Colombia and South America had minimal human populations. He determined to design an ideal civilization for the tropics, the world's fastest-filling region - a model that could be used in many of those fairly empty locations. To do so, he searched for the most challenging location he could find, figuring that if he succeeded there, he could then transfer his success to just about anywhere.

Gaviotas is located in the part of Colombia called the Llanos, an area that is mostly thin-soiled, nutrient-poor savanna grassland with very few trees. It has been described as a "big wet desert." Lugari's reply to that description was,

> The only deserts are deserts of the imagination. Gaviotas is an oasis of imagination... Think of it... Gaviotas could be a living laboratory, a chance to plan our own tropical civilization from the ground up. [5]

And that's what he created. Going to the Universities, he offered students the opportunity to complete their dissertations in peace, in a creative environment away from the civil unrest that often forced students to take seven years to complete a course of study that was designed to take only four. Once, when discussing Gaviotas with Dr. Sven Zethelius, a soil chemist at the Universidead Nacional's agricultural chemistry department, Dr. Zethelius suggested that they aim for creating an alternative inhabitable bio-system, a model they could invite the world to participate in, a utopia. Paolo's reply to this concept was typical of his vision,

> Gaviotas isn't a utopia. Utopia literally means 'no place'. In Greek, the prefix 'u' signifies no. We call Gaviotas a *topia*, because it's real. We've moved from fantasy to reality. From *utopia* to *topia*. [6]

Just what is the 'topia' they have created at Gaviotas? Here are a few examples of the technological and cultural experiences available there:

- Because parts of Colombia are overcast more than half the year, they developed a special coating for solar panels that allows energy to be gathered from diffused sunlight. These are now being used on the Presidential palace in Bogotá, on top of condominiums, apartments, convents, hospitals, orphanages, and on the largest public housing complex in the world to use only solar energy to heat its water.

- Colombia's largest hospital also uses solar 'kettles' designed by Gaviotas technicians, to purify drinking water and sterilize instruments even in their sunless days.
- Their reforestation project has succeeded so well that an indigenous tropical forest is regenerating. Amazed biologists have already recorded 240 species probably not seen in the Llanos for millennia, except near streambeds. Some of the native species are now so well established that the Gaviotans have decided to let the native species slowly choke out the non-native *Pinus caribaea* they originally planted. (It was the only species they could find that would grow in the thin nutrient-poor Llanos soil.) They hope to return the Llanos to it's primeval state, an extension of the Amazon. The population of native deer, anteaters, and capybaras are also increasing.
- Socially, the culture that developed was based on a mutual and community-wide commitment to doing what was necessary to survive and succeed. This meant that over time people found their own niche, contributing where they were most suited, or inventing their own job description. Over the years wages equalized, so there were no hierarchies. All salaries were higher than Colombia's legal minimum. Everyone received free housing, food, schooling, and health care. Each person was proud of his contribution, and each was acknowleged for the vital service provided.
- There is no police, no jail, and no mayor.
- Additionally, the children grew up in non-competitive environment. For children with special needs, like Juan David, Gaviotas offered the opportunity to be treated as an equal. No longer were his best friends only animals.
- For over 30 years, in an area awash with revolutionaries, soldiers, insurgents, and guerilla warriors, the people of Gaviotas managed to live a lifestyle without guns, hunting, or domination.
- Instead they concentrated on the daily job of living lightly, creatively, and sustainably on the Earth. A perfect example of their drive for creative perfection is the story about their desire to create a concert hall in the trees. They noticed that the acoustics of their newly planted tropical pine forest were incredible. So they recruited a classically trained opera singer to assist them in finding the most acoustically perfect location within the forest. I believe this level of dedication to every task they faced helped them accomplish so much in such a short time.
- Most recently, Gaviotas has worked with biodiesal pioneers in the USA to develop the first biodiesel plant in Colombia, and the first in the world to use crude palm oil at a semi-industrial scale. As a result, Gaviotas is now completely independent from fossil fuels. It also runs on pure vegetable oil.
- The community is also generating power with turbine engines fueled by their pine tree forest.
- They have discovered that their pine forest can produce twice as much resin as any other resin-tapping forest. Instead of using the traditional sulfuric acid when making incisions, they use an enzyme that seems to benefit the trees. They have found that planting each tree with mycorrhiza fungus on the roots enhances productivity.
- They converted their former hospital to a water purification and bottling center which provides fresh drinking water, reducing the incidence of local gastro-intestinal ailments. The children use unique water bottles they can assemble like Lego blocks.
- They developed a manual sleeve water pump that can be operated while the children play on a see-saw, a solar kitchen, and a solar kettle for sterilizing water.

Over the years Gaviotas encountered many challenges, but they trusted in their ability to creatively solve each problem that arose. This attitude, and their willingness to think outside-the-box at every turn led them to be named "a model of sustainable development" by the United Nations. Gabriel Garcia Marquez refers to Paolo Lugari as the "inventor of the world." [7] Perhaps the best description of what they have created comes from one of their own, Jorge Zapp:

Eva Cox, an Australian academic and public intellectual, defines social capital as a marker of the bonds within a community…As she sees it, high levels of social capital in a community are characterized by:

- *Shared cultural understandings*
- *A power structure that allows for individuals to feel that they have a voice in decision making*
- *An understanding and acceptance of the group's decision-making and problem-solving process*
- *A safe place for the individual to speak out, raise problems, and seek change*
- *A level of interpersonal connection which can bridge differences*
- *Resilience of the group to cope with stress*
- *The capacity to work together towards a common good*
- *The ability to recognize communalities and share values across differences*
- *The capability to resolve conflicts that arise between individual or specific interest groups*
- *The ability to allocate resources civilly.*

…Eva Cox states that when social capital is losing ground, fear of the outsider becomes more widespread. When…threatened, fear of the "other," whether an unknown intruder, or a subgroup of the community itself, is common.

Jenny Ledgar
Social Capital – the Fragile Inheritance of Community Children
from Communities-Journal of Cooperative Living – Spring 2002

At that moment, it struck me that without even trying, we've been creating another kind of world here. It's based on solidarity, one in which no one knows when he'll be paid for what he does, let alone get rich. It may just be survival, but it's survival in the best sense of the word: People surviving as considerate, sharing beings. No one demands anything of anybody except to get along with each other and work hard, in cooperation. We do this simply because we love to. In Gaviotas, we're driven by something different than competition or pecking orders. And we're content here. Whatever this is, it can't be underestimated.[8]

Curitiba, Brazil

Another example of a highly creative community is the city of Curitiba, Brazil, the capital of the state of Paraná, and home to approximately 1.5 million people. Similar to Gaviotas, Curitiba has been the home of a conscious experiment in community since the 1970's. At the time, corporate agriculture had resulted in a mass migration to the cities, where people encountered housing and job shortages. Slums began to surround the crowded city. Pollution was rampant. With tremendous vision, Curitiba turned to a team of young architects and urban planners for solutions.

Among them was Jaime Lerner, who was appointed mayor in 1971. Although his methods might not have won instant approval, his vision prevailed. Here is an example. Noting that Curitiba had more cars per capita than any other city in Brazil, he realized that he needed to create a city center designed more for people than for cars. So one Friday night, he had detour signs placed on the main downtown shopping street while a crew worked all weekend long. When the merchants and shoppers arrived Monday morning, they found a three block long landscaped pedestrian mall. He asked the angry merchants to give it a 30-day trial. By the end of the 30 days, business had boomed so much that they asked him to do the same to the remaining ten blocks.

Another issue he tackled was the lack of waste management in the slums. The streets were too narrow and choked with trash to use the garbage trucks, so he was faced with either widening the roads at great cost or finding a creative solution. Creativity prevailed. He offered a complementary currency, "Cambio Verde", in the form of bus tokens to anyone who brought in a bag of garbage sorted for recycling. The bus tokens allowed the poor in the surrounding slums to travel into the city for work. Later, the program was expanded to include school books and fresh surplus food from local farmers – creating a win-win situation for everyone involved. Though poor, citizens of the "favelas", enjoy both electricity and clean water. As a result of these efforts, the eight percent of Curitibanos living in the favelas have enjoyed a higher level of health than most poor in South America.

By thinking outside the box, paying attention to what worked and what didn't work within city systems, and then trying to create a situation where each problem's solution produced a benefit that would help solve another problem, Lerner and his team managed to come up with many highly creative ideas. Here are a few:[9]

- To stimulate the economy, he created a 17-square-mile industrial city six miles from the downtown with strict anti-pollution regulations. It is so desireable that there is often a waiting list of companies wanting to relocate to Curitiba.
- Laws were passed forcing developers to leave one third of any project as a green area in exchange for zoning concessions. Developers were offered tax breaks in exhange for letting land surrounding existing parks remain undeveloped.

- Citizens were urged to plant trees at a rate of 60,000 pine and native tropical trees per year. Sheep keep the grass trimmed in the city parks. Parks are connected by bicycle paths throughout the city.

- Traffic problems were handled in a most ingenious way. Five main transportation axes were designed leading traffic away from downtown, lined with high-rise office, shops, and housing. This eliminated much of the commute through downtown for many people.

- Desiring to reduce most private transportation, Lerner created articulated buses that carry 270 people. Entry to the buses, after payment, was through a glass tube similar to a railway station. Passengers enter and depart the buses at the same time, allowing for a smooth and very quick flow of passengers. These buses run every four minutes during rush hour, along a 155 mile network. Today approximately 75% of Curitiba's residents use public transporation, more than any other city in both North and South America. Additionally, this system cost 200 times less than a typical underground railway, is as efficient and convenient, and took only six months to create. Best of all, it pays for itself.

- Over 70% of Curitiba's population separates paper, glass, plastic, metal and organic garbage in their homes – the highest percent of any city in the world. Picked up by special recycling trucks and taken to the city-operated recycling plant located in a pine forest, most of the work is done by recovering alcoholics and drug addicts. 80% of the income from this operation is used to aid Curitiba's poor children.

- In one three-year period, more than 100 schools traded 200 tons of garbage for 1.9 million notebooks. The paper-recycling component alone saved the equivalent of 1,200 trees – each day! *

- Eventually, more than 70% of Curitiban households became involved. The 62 poorer neighborhoods alone exchanged 11,000 tons of garbage for nearly a million bus tokens and 1,200 tons of food. The results in purely economic terms are worth noting. From 1975-1995, the Domestic Product of the city of Curitiba increased by some 75% more than for the entire state of Paraná and 48% more than for Brazil as a whole. The average Curitibano makes about 3.3 times the country's minimum salary, but his real total income is at least 30% higher than that (i.e., about 5 times the minimum salary.) This 30% difference is income directly derived in non-traditional monetary forms, such as the food for garbage systems. What the results were in human terms, in the renewal of dignity, honor, pride and faith in the future of these Curitibanos can only be imagined. *

- Infant mortality has dropped to 20 deaths per thousand births.

- Curitiba has the lowest homicide rate of any city in Brazil.

*These particular statistics are from Of Human Wealth – Beyond Greed and Scarcity, by Bernard A. Lietaer and Stephen M. Belgin, page 2.

In 1992, the United Nations named Curitiba an exemplary sustainable city, and awarded Jaime Lerner a scroll of honor by the United Nations Centre for Human Settlements. In November 1994, Lerner was elected governor of the state of Paraná. As creator of the urban-planning think tank, the Jaime Lerner Institute, Lerner continues to problem solve together with mayors from other similar sized cities. Lerner's attitude could be summed up in his own words:

> The dream of a better city is already a vision in the heads of its residents…All a mayor has to do is tap into those dreams. [9]

Community Design

The dreams Lerner refers to are found within the heart of all community members. When people are asked what they most desire in a community, their answers almost always include the following: good paying jobs, recreational facilities, good schools, a sense of safety everywhere, a clean environment providing healthy clean air, soil, and

(On Mother's Day 1998, when asked if she had a message for mothers in America, Ima Nouri, who's child lay dying due to lack of adequate medical care because of the UN Sanctions against Iraq, stated): "First, tell them from Iraqi women that these are our children and we love them so much…Ask them to please try to help us protect them and take care of them. And, for American women, I want them to feel what I am feeling."

The word compassion means literally suffering with others, feeling what they are feeling. Of course it hurts, but isn't it better to suffer with others and expand, then to wall off our humanity from them and die within?

Michael Nagler

water, access to nature and hiking trails, and easy access to mass transit. Most of all, people want to walk more and drive less.

Yet our current designs, centered around the automobile, rarely include these features, and have contributed to the polarization and isolation that many people now consider to be one of the most pressing problems of community life.

Though many wonderful design concepts have emerged as we begin to address this issue, certain ideas are so strongly desired that they show up in almost all designs across the board, and they are the ones I'd like to summarize below. Be sure to check out the links to community planning and design websites in the Reference section for more details.

Daily needs are all found within walking distance of small residential districts.

These include schools, stores, and work places. So, for example, if a large corporation wanted to locate in a given community, their building design could include housing, schools, recreational areas (pools, parks, soccer fields, etc.), shops, and a major transit station – all for the benefit of their employees. The corporation would have to work with the community members and experts within each needed field to co-create together.

Residential areas are ideally designed around a common area

This would include community gardens and recreational parks. Houses should open onto the commons with welcoming front porches and human-scaled design features that fit a variety of people within the neighborhood, instead of segregating the community by race, income, age, or family situation.

The Ahwahnee Principles state that development should be compact but with open space provided in the form of squares or parks. Urban designer Michael Freedman describes this as space-making rather than space-occupying development. Rather than surrounding buildings in the center of unusable landscaped areas (space-occupying development), Freedman says we should use buildings to frame public space (place-making design). [10]

Closed-loop Infrastructure

Infrastructure needs, such as water, power, sewer, waste handling, and computer communications, are all handled locally (closed loop system) with full citizen input and control. This ensures that each community takes responsibility for handling its own needs. It also keeps all costs and profits within the hands of those who use the systems they have developed. And since they are fully responsible for taking care of their own waste, each community is encouraged to design systems that are sustainable, healthy, and efficient.

Emergency infrastructure needs are also handled locally

Within each small neighborhood group the community is mindful to include at least one alternative energy system (solar, wind, or other proven, sustainable, and site-appropriate power), one home or community building that can be efficiently heated

Fortunately, the current balance of power between empire and community tilts less decisively in favor of empire than it at first seems. Empire controls the institutions of political and economic power — including military and police. This control, however, rests on a false legitimacy dependent on empire's ability to perpetuate a falsified and inauthentic cultural trance based on beliefs and values at odds with reality.

As empire's failures mount, the reality is exposed, the cultural trance is broken for increasing numbers of people, and the legitimacy of empire's institutions is called into serious question — creating space for the forces of community as manifest in the new social organism we know as global civil society.

Global civil society is a social expression of the awakening of an authentic planetary culture grounded in the spiritual values and social experience of hundreds of millions of people. The power of authentic culture gives civil society the ultimate advantage.

David C. Korten, Nicanor Perlas, and Vandana Shiva Global Civil Society: The Path Ahead-A Discussion Paper – Summary http://www.pcdf.org/civilso ciety/default.htm

by wood, and one community water well or large underground cistern, all to be used in case of emergency. It would be in the community's best interest to maintain these infrastructure back-up systems for the benefit of all.

Greenbelts and Wildlife Corridors

I've watched with sadness as the open wilderness edged neighborhood that I've called home for almost twenty years has been developed to the point that fences no longer allow for the free movement of the animals who also call this land their home. When we cut nature out of our inhabited areas, we all lose. The animals' ability to fly in the face of danger is restricted, their habits become more dependent on humans, and what was once a balanced and welcome relationship begins to be counter productive for all involved.

Transportation for all

When we design our communities from the very beginning to allow for clean public transportation with stations spaced easy-walking distance from all parts of town, then the public is more inclined to use it. With fewer cars on the road, our air is cleaner and our streets are safer. Additionally, bike paths, nature trails, and all sorts of other transportation can be planned into the community so that they are no longer after-thoughts, but design elements that complement the overall design.

Respect for Diversity

If we plan our communities to follow the natural flow of water and the land, we honor what time has tested as the best overall design for the area. Instead of defying those plans, why not work with them? Preserving trees, forests, estuaries, and wetlands benefits all. Allowing for natural drainage systems benefits everyone. Planning buildings to comply with the path of the sun and the wisdom of the particular bioregion honors all participants in that location, especially the humans.

Abundance Swap

Three years ago, Jeff Golden, one of the most intelligent and honoring radio talk show hosts I've ever heard, came up with an idea that has now become a holiday tradition in my town. It's called the Abundance Swap, and it's purpose is to create new values around gift-giving and receiving, to notice how these new values may challenge old ways of functioning, and to demonstrate these new ways of being with our family and friends.

Here's how it works. Everyone participating brings no more than three items – in good condition - that they no longer fully enjoy or use. The gifts are displayed for all to see. After connecting with others participating, each person takes whatever time necessary to find great gifts for family and friends. Afterward, participants have the option of gathering to reflect on the experience.

Every year my daughter and I look forward to this event. It knits our hearts together within the community. Beyond the thrill of "free" shopping – which the kids particularly enjoy – it offers me the opportunity to recycle gifts that carry the energy and love of those with whom I share community. I know that I am not only supporting my community, family, and friends; I am also supporting the planet by

If you could imagine a place that has the highest crime rates, the largest drug saturation, the greatest welfare recipient population, and the fastest HIV-positive infection rates in one of the richest cities, in the richest state, in the richest country in the entire world, then you could begin to imagine Watts, California—a district in South Central Los Angeles...

We also offer think tank sessions at the Garden Club. Here we plant the seeds of change, knowledge, and remembrance by facing our history and tasting the bitterness of slavery, oppression, injustice, and self-hatred. … we take a full assessment of where we stand today, here in Watts. In a circle, with the help of a facilitator, we have two-hour jam sessions that make the sweetest music— the sound of thinking people who are awakened fully to the calling of addressing our communities' problems and creating viable solutions…

If you look at history, you can see it takes only one person to change an environment—one person who takes a stand, an advocacy, an action. It takes only one person to change the entire world. Once upon a time we were taught here in Watts "Power to the People." I have lived through that to tell you what I know for sure, and that is People are the Power. And it only takes one—you!

Anna Marie Carter a.k.a. The Seed Lady of Watts from Seeds of Justice, Seeds of Hope Yes! Magazine Spring 2003

When the 11/9 tower incident took place, the world was shocked. The media made sure of that! It seems that approximately 3000 people tragically died in the catastrophe. The same day approximately 40,000 people tragically died of starvation in the Third World countries, most of them children. Did you read about that? No. And for years every day before the Sept 11 2001 incident and every day since people are dying of starvation in similar numbers in the Third World countries. Yet, somehow, it does not hit our shock and compassion buttons in the way it should.

Suddenly - on Boxing Day - a tsunami of death sweeps across the ocean, and people die in the many thousands. This 'does' catch our attention. This 'does' hit our shock and compassion button. Kill people slowly and constantly and we can ignore it. Disease, dictators, and wars kill millions of people annually and we somehow ignore it. Yet with the timing, the power, and the shock of the sudden tsunami, we open up to Change as has seldom happened before. Like a miracle, the tidal wave of a tsunami was transformed into a tidal wave of compassion.

Michael J. Roads http://www.michaelroads.com/

giving gifts that don't further diminish our planetary resources, required very little shipping, and contributed to my experience of life as abundant.

And that's the real gift. In order to participate in an Abundance Swap, I have to acknowledge my own abundance. In order to take gifts home from the Abundance Swap, I have to be willing to receive *and* give. For those who find giving easy but receiving a little more challenging, the event offers an opportunity to stretch a little outside your comfort zone and receive as well. By doing so, you honor both yourself and the one who's goods you are receiving. In essence, this event is an affirmation of what we know to be true but so often forget – we are surrounded by abundance. We only have to allow ourselves the joy of perceiving it.

An important part of each swap is a clear holding of the intentions and opportunities involved. Here are the intentions identified and embraced so far by those creating the event:

- To explore and re-create ideas about 'real' gifts and giving,
- To slow down amidst the holidaze to a remembering of community and the SPIRIT of giving,
- To circulate our 'things,', easing the stress on our natural resources,
- A chance to stretch by letting go of 'stuff,' exploring any worries that we might not get back our fair share, and exploring any resistance to receiving,
- To use this event as a model for taking responsibility to build a new culture ourselves. We cannot rely on the power structures in the world to do it. We must do it ourselves, (and thereby become our own power structure). This event is modeling a new way of holding 'giving' and 'receiving;' of using the resources we have to their maximum, and of supporting the regeneration of our environment while easing the footprint we make on our precious Earth. [11]

In My Village

There is one other experiment in Community that I would like to bring to your attention. First, I want to acknowledge that there have been many intentional community experiments within our general social experience as humans. Intentional, in that the members collectively pursued a goal to explore the concept of "community" in a way that was purposeful and creatively different from the mainstream experience of community. We have learned much through their efforts.

What makes this particular experiment different is that it doesn't seek to explore within a closed exclusive community of like-minded members, but instead seeks to re-invent our own sense of community within the existing collective experience.

Like Peter Block, Jim Rough, and members of communities like Gaviotas, it seeks to ask more questions than it answers. The primary question being:

What do you want?

Such a simple question would seem easy to answer until you try to do so with the utmost sincerity, authenticity, and thoroughness. It is the core of what we need to ask ourselves both individually and collectively when we consciously choose to create community.

The In My Village experiment is in its early stages. It began as a four-month experiment in January 2003. Approximately 300 people gathered from within the Ashland, Oregon community to ask themselves who they wanted to be in relationship to community. After self-assessing the results, the creators of the concept learned that more connection between community members was necessary *before* ever embarking on the Doing part of re-creating community. They realized that a *heart connection* was necessary before anything long lasting could pragmatically be accomplished.

So they created a twelve hour workshop entitled, "The In My Village Blueprint Experience," that invites participants to do the necessary inner-exploration before combining as a group to accomplish any outer-manifestation of their vision of community. Participants responded:

> In my professional career, spanning thirty-three years, I have attended more trainings and workshops then I can remember. This workshop is memorable because it puts forth a blueprint for a new social structure that creates the possibility for community based on what we want that brings us joy individually and as community. The premise builds a community based on shared learning, connection, creation of what is wanted and sustainability. I was genuinely impressed.

> As a veteran of many workshops, what I expected of "In My Village" was, at best, another positive workshop experience. What I received was of an entirely different order: an invitation to contribute my values, creativity and deepest yearnings to the process of collectively inventing/discovering the community and ultimately the world I/we most long for. My enthusiasm and creative engagement has sustained and even increased since the beginning largely due to the ongoing connection and support I am experiencing. [12]

With humility they also realized that there is no ONE vision of community, because community is a living evolving entity – just like an individual human – one that is constantly learning, growing, and re-creating itself within every moment. Above all, it is a co-creative expression of who we see ourselves to be. One that hopefully embraces an ever-expanding perception of our potential and possibilities. I look forward to the day when such conscious exploration becomes a common occurrence within all communities so that they truly reflect the inclusive collective vision of community members.

New Localism

As we begin, both locally and throughout the world, to assess what is working well and what still needs fine-tuning within our civil, business, and economic structures such that they truly accomplish a world in which all are honored and basic needs are met (food, shelter, companionship, living-wage work, creative and expressive fulfillment, education, and health care); we have begun to re-create the rules we live by. Rules are made by people for people, yet they in turn help shape the possibilities available to those very same people. Every now and then they need to be tweaked to ensure that they still accomplish their intended outcome.

The New Rules Project seeks to track local legislation that does just that. Their website provides information about what new laws have been enacted that promote a world that honors all, and why they are necessary:

Why New Rules?

Because the old ones don't work any longer. They undermine local economies, subvert democracy, weaken our sense of community, and ignore the costs of our decisions on the next generation.

The Institute for Local Self-Reliance (ILSR) proposes a set of new rules that builds community by supporting humanly scaled politics and economics. The rules call for:

* Decisions made by those who will feel the impact of those decisions.

...They consider themselves lucky to be here. They have a warm place to stay. They have three meals a day. And they have each other. The family is among an estimated 500,000 to 700,000 people who, on any given night in America, lack a real home.

Sharon Cohen
A Day in the Life of the Homeless in America

The Associated Press Sunday 27 February 2005

(She quotes one outreach worker discussing the homeless) "I know that we may seem to be in separate worlds on the surface...but many of them share the same kinds of problems that affect me and everybody else."

- Communities accepting responsibility for the welfare of their members and for the next generation.
- Households and communities possessing or owning sufficient productive capacity to generate real wealth.

These are the principles of "new localism." They call upon us to begin viewing our communities and our regions not only as places of residence, recreation and retail but as places that nurture active and informed citizens with the skills and productive capacity to generate real wealth and the authority to govern their own lives. [13]

Listed here are some of the categories that localism embraces. I highly recommend a visit to their website to see the actual legislation that has already been passed in various communities in the United States:

Agriculture (http://www.newrules.org/agri/index.html)

Agriculture is the foundation of all sustainable wealth. Even today, when agriculture plays a diminishing role, the productivity of the soil and the health of farmers are still a fundamental concern. This section of the New Rules offers information on agricultural policies and a library of local, state, national and international rules that nurture vibrant and diversified rural communities.

Energy (http://www.newrules.org/de/index.html)

Energy is the force of industrial economies, both literally and figuratively. We named this section Democratic Energy and we report on the rapidly growing movement by households, businesses, and local and state governments to democratize the energy system. We offer actual rules, from statutes and zoning codes to utility tariffs, that encourage technologies and ownership forms and systems that decentralize power and energy production and energy policy decision making.

Environment (http://www.newrules.org/environment/index.html)

Without responsibility, authority will be exercised in shortsighted ways. This section of the web site identifies rules that encourage communities to adopt a longer perspective and embrace policies that are responsible to the next generation. The most enduring way to reduce pollution is to extract the maximum value from local resources. The higher the efficiency, the lower the waste, the lower the pollution.

Equity (http://www.newrules.org/equity/index.html)

This section identifies rules that encourage communities to accept responsibility in two areas: towards their own less fortunate members and less fortunate members in other communities, and towards members of the next generation. Among the topics are education, health care and living wage.

Finance (http://www.newrules.org/finance/index.html)

The delinking of money from place and productive investment is not the inevitable result of technological advances or economic evolution. Money is a human invention and the rules that control its dynamic are also a human invention. The rules we have fashioned favor mobility over community, speculation over productive investment, volatility over permanence. This section contains rules that reconnect capital and community, with a special emphasis on those parts of the community that traditionally have been left behind.

Governance (http://www.newrules.org/gov/index.html)

Governance works best when those who feel the impact of the decisions are those involved in making the decisions. That principle works as well in the private sector as the public sector. This section of the web site focuses largely on process. It examines the mechanisms and rules that encourage the most democratic and socially responsible kinds of decision making.

Information (http://www.newrules.org/info/index.html)

Information economies are inherently global in reach. Yet the information economy also holds great promise for dramatically decentralizing the production and dissemination of information in all its forms (e.g. print, video, radio, online). This section explores policies that cities, states, nations, and international bodies are developing to encourage a sense of place and individual autonomy and security in an age of global information systems.

Retail (http://www.newrules.org/retail/index.php)

Retail is where business meets household, where enterprise meets community, where the value-added of the extraction, processing, manufacturing, wholesaling and distribution chain culminates with sales to the final customer. We named this section the Hometown Advantage and we cover news and rules that communities are using to foster local ownership of retail and a more intimate link between commerce and place.

Taxation (http://www.newrules.org/tax/index.html)

Taxation is the most visible and perhaps the most important issue to voters and policymakers around the world. In this section we will be gathering the tax rules from across all sectors and presenting them here. Taxation, often criticized as excessive government, can be an important policy tool to meet community goals. Taxes can be used to level the playing field, to limit size or sprawl, to protect the environment, and to encourage local ownership and production. [13]

The Earth Charter

Finally, as we begin to willingly explore what honoring all life means to each of us personally, and within our communities, we will ultimately learn to embrace the global community into our hearts. One way we can actively participate in that process - individually, and within our communities and organizations – is by endorsing the Earth Charter. Both the Charter itself and a brief history are included at the end of this chapter.

We have the opportunity to live our lives as declarations of who we choose to be. Let's do it!

Notes

1. Hwoschinsky, Carol Listening With The Heart – A Guide for Compassionate Listening, The Compassionate Listening Project, Indianola WA 2001, page 9
2. Peter Block, Designed Learning: http://www.designedlearning.com/Articles/civic%20engagement/TheQuestions.htm Civic Engagement and the Restoration of Community - *Six Conversations That Matter*
3. IBID
4. Alan Weisman, Gaviotas – A Village to Reinvent the World, 1998, page 24.
5. Alan Weisman, Gaviotas – A Village to Reinvent the World, 1998, page 33 and 39.
6. Alan Weisman, Gaviotas – A Village to Reinvent the World, 1998, page 8.
7. http://www.friendsofgaviotas.org/default.htm
8. Alan Weisman, Gaviotas – A Village to Reinvent the World, 1998, page 83.
9. http://www.cdsea.org/archives/Kcontrib/curitiba.htm
10. http://www.lgc.org/freepub/land_use/articles/ahwahnee_article.html See also http://www.cnu.org/aboutcnu/
11. From the Abundance Swap Committee E-Mails
12. From the In My Village Announcements. See their developing website at http://www.honoringalllife.org/Community.php
13. http://www.newrules.org/index.htm

THE EARTH CHARTER

In 1987 the United Nations World Commission on Environment and Development issued a call for creation of a new charter that would set forth fundamental principles for sustainable development. The drafting of an Earth Charter was part of the unfinished business of the 1992 Rio Earth Summit. In 1994 Maurice Strong, the Secretary General of the Earth Summit and Chairman of the Earth Council, and Mikhail Gorbachev, President of Green Cross International, launched a new Earth Charter initiative with support from the Dutch government. An Earth Charter Commission was formed in 1997 to oversee the project and an Earth Charter Secretariat was established at the Earth Council in Costa Rica.

Mission of the Earth Charter Initiative

A new phase in the Initiative began with the official launching of the Earth Charter at the Peace Palace in The Hague on June 29, 2000. The mission of the Initiative going forward is to establish a sound ethical foundation for the emerging global society and to help build a sustainable world based on respect for nature, universal human rights, economic justice, and a culture of peace.

The goals of the Earth Charter Initiative are:

- To promote the dissemination, endorsement, and implementation of the Earth Charter by civil society, business, and government.
- To encourage and support the educational use of the Earth Charter.
- To seek endorsement of the Earth Charter by the UN.

The principles of the Earth Charter reflect extensive international consultations conducted over a period of many years. These principles are also based upon contemporary science, international law, and the insights of philosophy and religion. Successive drafts of the Earth Charter were circulated around the world for comments and debate by nongovernmental organizations, community groups, professional societies, and international experts in many fields.

PREAMBLE

We stand at a critical moment in Earth's history, a time when humanity must choose its future. As the world becomes increasingly interdependent and fragile, the future at once holds great peril and great promise. To move forward we must recognize that in the midst of a magnificent diversity of cultures and life forms we are one human family and one Earth community with a common destiny. We must join together to bring forth a sustainable global society founded on respect for nature, universal human rights, economic justice, and a culture of peace. Towards this end, it is imperative that we, the peoples of Earth, declare our responsibility to one another, to the greater community of life, and to future generations.

Earth, Our Home

Humanity is part of a vast evolving universe. Earth, our home, is alive with a unique community of life. The forces of nature make existence a demanding and uncertain adventure, but Earth has provided the conditions essential to life's evolution. The resilience of the community of life and the well-being of humanity depend upon preserving a healthy biosphere with all its ecological systems, a rich variety of plants and animals, fertile soils, pure waters, and clean air. The global environment with its finite resources is a common concern of all peoples. The protection of Earth's vitality, diversity, and beauty is a sacred trust.

The Global Situation

The dominant patterns of production and consumption are causing environmental devastation, the depletion of resources, and a massive extinction of species. Communities are being undermined. The benefits of development are not shared equitably and the gap between rich and poor is widening. Injustice, poverty, ignorance, and violent conflict are widespread and the cause of great suffering. An unprecedented rise in human population has overburdened ecological and social systems. The foundations of global security are threatened. These trends are perilous—but not inevitable.

The Challenges Ahead

The choice is ours: form a global partnership to care for Earth and one another or risk the destruction of ourselves and the diversity of life. Fundamental changes are needed in our values, institutions, and ways of living. We must realize that when basic needs have been met, human development is primarily about being more, not having more. We have the knowledge and technology to provide for all and to reduce our impacts on the environment. The emergence of a global civil society is creating new opportunities to build a democratic and humane world. Our environmental, economic, political, social, and spiritual challenges are interconnected, and together we can forge inclusive solutions.

Universal Responsibility

To realize these aspirations, we must decide to live with a sense of universal responsibility, identifying ourselves with the whole Earth community as well as our local communities. We are at once citizens of different nations and of one world in which the local and global are linked. Everyone shares responsibility for the present and future well-being of the human family and the larger living world. The spirit of human solidarity and kinship with all life is strengthened when we live with reverence for the mystery of being, gratitude for the gift of life, and humility regarding the human place in nature.

We urgently need a shared vision of basic values to provide an ethical foundation for the emerging world community. Therefore, together in hope we affirm the following interdependent principles for a sustainable way of life as a common standard by which the conduct of all individuals, organizations, businesses, governments, and transnational institutions is to be guided and assessed.

PRINCIPLES

I. RESPECT AND CARE FOR THE COMMUNITY OF LIFE

1. Respect Earth and life in all its diversity.

a.   Recognize that all beings are interdependent and every form of life has value regardless of its worth to human beings.

b.   Affirm faith in the inherent dignity of all human beings and in the intellectual, artistic, ethical, and spiritual potential of humanity.

2. Care for the community of life with understanding, compassion, and love.

a.   Accept that with the right to own, manage, and use natural resources comes the duty to prevent environmental harm and to protect the rights of people.

b.   Affirm that with increased freedom, knowledge, and power comes increased responsibility to promote the common good.

3. Build democratic societies that are just, participatory, sustainable, and peaceful.

a.   Ensure that communities at all levels guarantee human rights and fundamental freedoms and provide everyone an opportunity to realize his or her full potential.

b.   Promote social and economic justice, enabling all to achieve a secure and meaningful livelihood that is ecologically responsible.

4. Secure Earth's bounty and beauty for present and future generations.

a.   Recognize that the freedom of action of each generation is qualified by the needs of future generations.

b.   Transmit to future generations values, traditions, and institutions that support the long-term flourishing of Earth's human and ecological communities.

In order to fulfill these four broad commitments, it is necessary to:

II. ECOLOGICAL INTEGRITY

5. Protect and restore the integrity of Earth's ecological systems, with special concern for biological diversity and the natural processes that sustain life.

a. *Adopt at all levels sustainable development plans and regulations that make environmental conservation and rehabilitation integral to all development initiatives.*

b. *Establish and safeguard viable nature and biosphere reserves, including wild lands and marine areas, to protect Earth's life support systems, maintain biodiversity, and preserve our natural heritage.*

c. *Promote the recovery of endangered species and ecosystems.*

d. *Control and eradicate non-native or genetically modified organisms harmful to native species and the environment, and prevent introduction of such harmful organisms.*

e. *Manage the use of renewable resources such as water, soil, forest products, and marine life in ways that do not exceed rates of regeneration and that protect the health of ecosystems.*

f. *Manage the extraction and use of non-renewable resources such as minerals and fossil fuels in ways that minimize depletion and cause no serious environmental damage.*

6. *Prevent harm as the best method of environmental protection and, when knowledge is limited, apply a precautionary approach.*

a. *Take action to avoid the possibility of serious or irreversible environmental harm even when scientific knowledge is incomplete or inconclusive.*

b. *Place the burden of proof on those who argue that a proposed activity will not cause significant harm, and make the responsible parties liable for environmental harm.*

c. *Ensure that decision making addresses the cumulative, long-term, indirect, long distance, and global consequences of human activities.*

d. *Prevent pollution of any part of the environment and allow no build-up of radioactive, toxic, or other hazardous substances.*

e. *Avoid military activities damaging to the environment.*

7. *Adopt patterns of production, consumption, and reproduction that safeguard Earth's regenerative capacities, human rights, and community well-being.*

a. *Reduce, reuse, and recycle the materials used in production and consumption systems, and ensure that residual waste can be assimilated by ecological systems.*

b. *Act with restraint and efficiency when using energy, and rely increasingly on renewable energy sources such as solar and wind.*

c. *Promote the development, adoption, and equitable transfer of environmentally sound technologies.*

d. *Internalize the full environmental and social costs of goods and services in the selling price, and enable consumers to identify products that meet the highest social and environmental standards.*

e. *Ensure universal access to health care that fosters reproductive health and responsible reproduction.*

f. *Adopt lifestyles that emphasize the quality of life and material sufficiency in a finite world.*

8. *Advance the study of ecological sustainability and promote the open exchange and wide application of the knowledge acquired.*

a. *Support international scientific and technical cooperation on sustainability, with special attention to the needs of developing nations.*

b. *Recognize and preserve the traditional knowledge and spiritual wisdom in all cultures that contribute to environmental protection and human well-being.*

c. *Ensure that information of vital importance to human health and environmental protection, including genetic information, remains available in the public domain.*

III. SOCIAL AND ECONOMIC JUSTICE

9. *Eradicate poverty as an ethical, social, and environmental imperative.*

a. *Guarantee the right to potable water, clean air, food security, uncontaminated soil, shelter, and safe sanitation, allocating the national and international resources required.*

b. *Empower every human being with the education and resources to secure a sustainable livelihood, and provide social security and safety nets for those who are unable to support themselves.*

c. *Recognize the ignored, protect the vulnerable, serve those who suffer, and enable them to develop their capacities and to pursue their aspirations.*

10. *Ensure that economic activities and institutions at all levels promote human development in an equitable and sustainable manner.*

a. *Promote the equitable distribution of wealth within nations and among nations.*

b. *Enhance the intellectual, financial, technical, and social resources of developing nations, and relieve them of onerous international debt.*

c. *Ensure that all trade supports sustainable resource use, environmental protection, and progressive labor standards.*

d. *Require multinational corporations and international financial organizations to act transparently in the public good, and hold them accountable for the consequences of their activities.*

11. *Affirm gender equality and equity as prerequisites to sustainable development and ensure universal access to education, health care, and economic opportunity.*

a. *Secure the human rights of women and girls and end all violence against them.*

b. *Promote the active participation of women in all aspects of economic, political, civil, social, and cultural life as full and equal partners, decision makers, leaders, and beneficiaries.*

c. *Strengthen families and ensure the safety and loving nurture of all family members.*

12. *Uphold the right of all, without discrimination, to a natural and social environment supportive of human dignity, bodily health, and spiritual well-being, with special attention to the rights of indigenous peoples and minorities.*

a. *Eliminate discrimination in all its forms, such as that based on race, color, sex, sexual orientation, religion, language, and national, ethnic or social origin.*

b. *Affirm the right of indigenous peoples to their spirituality, knowledge, lands and resources and to their related practice of sustainable livelihoods.*

c. *Honor and support the young people of our communities, enabling them to fulfill their essential role in creating sustainable societies.*

d. *Protect and restore outstanding places of cultural and spiritual significance.*

IV. DEMOCRACY, NONVIOLENCE, AND PEACE

13. *Strengthen democratic institutions at all levels, and provide transparency and accountability in governance, inclusive participation in decision making, and access to justice.*

a. *Uphold the right of everyone to receive clear and timely information on environmental matters and all development plans and activities which are likely to affect them or in which they have an interest.*

b. *Support local, regional and global civil society, and promote the meaningful participation of all interested individuals and organizations in decision making.*

c. *Protect the rights to freedom of opinion, expression, peaceful assembly, association, and dissent.*

d.   Institute effective and efficient access to administrative and independent judicial procedures, including remedies and redress for environmental harm and the threat of such harm.

e.   Eliminate corruption in all public and private institutions.

f.   Strengthen local communities, enabling them to care for their environments, and assign environmental responsibilities to the levels of government where they can be carried out most effectively.

14. Integrate into formal education and life-long learning the knowledge, values, and skills needed for a sustainable way of life.

a.   Provide all, especially children and youth, with educational opportunities that empower them to contribute actively to sustainable development.

b.   Promote the contribution of the arts and humanities as well as the sciences in sustainability education.

c.   Enhance the role of the mass media in raising awareness of ecological and social challenges.

d.   Recognize the importance of moral and spiritual education for sustainable living.

15. Treat all living beings with respect and consideration.

a.   Prevent cruelty to animals kept in human societies and protect them from suffering.

b.   Protect wild animals from methods of hunting, trapping, and fishing that cause extreme, prolonged, or avoidable suffering.

c.   Avoid or eliminate to the full extent possible the taking or destruction of non-targeted species.

16. Promote a culture of tolerance, nonviolence, and peace.

a.   Encourage and support mutual understanding, solidarity, and cooperation among all peoples and within and among nations.

b.   Implement comprehensive strategies to prevent violent conflict and use collaborative problem solving to manage and resolve environmental conflicts and other disputes.

c.   Demilitarize national security systems to the level of a non-provocative defense posture, and convert military resources to peaceful purposes, including ecological restoration.

d.   Eliminate nuclear, biological, and toxic weapons and other weapons of mass destruction.

e.   Ensure that the use of orbital and outer space supports environmental protection and peace.

f.   Recognize that peace is the wholeness created by right relationships with oneself, other persons, other cultures, other life, Earth, and the larger whole of which all are a part.

THE WAY FORWARD

As never before in history, common destiny beckons us to seek a new beginning. Such renewal is the promise of these Earth Charter principles. To fulfill this promise, we must commit ourselves to adopt and promote the values and objectives of the Charter.

This requires a change of mind and heart. It requires a new sense of global interdependence and universal responsibility. We must imaginatively develop and apply the vision of a sustainable way of life locally, nationally, regionally, and globally. Our cultural diversity is a precious heritage and different cultures will find their own distinctive ways to realize the vision. We must deepen and expand the global dialogue that generated the Earth Charter, for we have much to learn from the ongoing collaborative search for truth and wisdom.

Life often involves tensions between important values. This can mean difficult choices. However, we must find ways to harmonize diversity with unity, the exercise of freedom with the common good, short-term objectives *with long-term goals. Every individual, family, organization, and community has a vital role to play. The arts, sciences, religions, educational institutions, media, businesses, nongovernmental organizations, and governments are all called to offer creative leadership. The partnership of government, civil society, and business is essential for effective governance.*

In order to build a sustainable global community, the nations of the world must renew their commitment to the United Nations, fulfill their obligations under existing international agreements, and support the implementation of Earth Charter principles with an international legally binding instrument on environment and development.

Let ours be a time remembered for the awakening of a new reverence for life, the firm resolve to achieve sustainability, the quickening of the struggle for justice and peace, and the joyful celebration of life.

(All information on the Earth Charter was obtained from *www.EarhtCharter.org.* Please see the website for additional information and an opportunity to endorse the Earth Charter either individually or through your organization. The formal Endorsement Statement is below.)

Endorsement Statement:

We, the undersigned, endorse the Earth Charter.
We embrace the spirit and aims of the document.
We pledge to join the global partnership for a just, sustainable, and peaceful world and to work for the realization of the values and principles of the Earth Charter.

We pledge to join the Global Partnership in Support of the Earth Charter Initiative for a sustainable way of life AND urge all governments to endorse the Earth Charter.

11

<u>NATURE</u>

Living systems evolve in variety, resilience, and intelligence;
they do this not by erecting walls of defense
and closing off from their environment,
but by opening more widely to the currents of matter-energy and information...
They integrate and differentiate through constant interaction,
spinning more intricate connections and more flexible strategies.
For this they require not invulnerability, but increasing responsiveness.
Such is the direction of evolution.
—Joanna Macy

NATURE

*In the deepest sense, our perception of nature
is the reflection of our own relationship with ourselves.
We are not Earth's stewards, we are co-creators in this interdependent dance of Life.*

Nature as Flow

Almost everyone loves nature. Yet I wonder if our definitions of "nature" actually match? I used to define nature as the natural world outside the human sphere, but that definition no longer works for me. Now, everything is part of nature. Every single object we've created came from natural resources. Every interaction we have in the world – no matter how much we may delude ourselves into thinking it is isolated and separate from nature – actually impacts the entire world in a profound, often subtle, but highly effectual way. More importantly, our perceptual filters are changing. Instead of seeing "things" and "objects", we are learning to see *interacting systems*. From that standpoint, nature isn't a "thing" at all, it is a *flow*. Paul Hawkin describes it beautifully:

> Today we have an expanded and different sense of what nature is. Most important, we understand nature as a flow of services that cannot be commodified – services that are not bought or sold but that absolutely influence and dictate the quality of our life on this planet, and from which all so-called economic value is derived. These flows of services, which we mostly take for granted, include pollination, oxygen, global climatic stability, riparian systems, fisheries, soil fertility, topsoil, erosion control, flood catchment, and so on.[1]

When I moved to Oregon, I left behind a vibrantly abundant and beautiful yard – the kind of yard that inspired questions from strangers passing by. My new yard, however, was over an acre in size, and offered only overgrown remnants of a garden. It took a lot of planning and plain old-fashioned labor to heal that neglected landscape. Eventually flower and vegetable gardens were cleared. I intended to feed my children organic produce from our garden, but I soon learned of the challenge most Ashland gardeners face – deer.

Co-Creative Gardening

While many resorted to high fences, I wanted to find a more nature-friendly solution. Then I discovered Machaelle Wright's Perelandra theories, in which she taught that one could communicate with nature using muscle-testing (kinesiology). She encouraged her students to co-create their gardens with nature, by asking – through kinesiology - where and how various plants wanted to be planted to enhance the optimum health of all.

I loved the idea of gardening co-creatively. It was such a shift from the old methods I had learned, under the theory that man should dominate and tame nature. Yet the problem of the deer still remained. I finally decided that I would try co-creating an agreement with the deer over what they could and could not eat on our property. Surprisingly, making such an agreement was easy. I simply asked the deer what they wanted – what would work for them – and then I told them what I was willing to do within those parameters. The deer kept our agreement for eight years, never once eating in my vegetable garden even though I watched them walk through it many times.

The egocentric ideal of a future reserved for those who have managed to attain egotistically the extremity of 'everyone for himself' is false and against nature... The outcome of the world, the gates of the future, the entry into the super-human -- these are not thrown open to a few of the privileged or to one chosen people to the exclusion of all others. They will only open to an advance of all together, in a direction in which all together can join and find completion in a spiritual renovation of the earth... No evolutionary future awaits man except in association with all other men.

Pierre Teilhard De Chardin
French Jesuit, paleontologist, biologist, and philosopher

Everything in the universe is a pitcher brimming with wisdom and beauty.

Mevlana Rumi

(1207-1273)

Oddly enough, when my husband and I started the painful process of divorce, the deer broke our agreement and decimated the garden. Somehow they could tell that my energy was no longer peaceful and open.

Merging

Throughout that time, I was reading the works of the Australian metaphysical author, Michael J. Roads. Finally, in the summer of 2001, I was thrilled to participate in a Nature Seminar and Workshop with him and his wife, Treenie.

On the first day of the Nature Seminar, he sent us outdoors to sit anywhere with nature, and just BE. Those of you who meditate know how frustrating this experience can be until you learn to let go of expectations, stop trying to control the mind, and just BE with whatever is happening. Michael recommended using the old trick of seeing the mind as the sky with thoughts as the clouds. He suggested drawing our attention back to the blue sky whenever we noticed that our thoughts had drifted to the clouds.

At first difficult, I found I was able to eventually slip into the "space between my thoughts," and *surrender* to the experience. Everything was transformed, and I was able to experience the utter perfection of nature. Not a twig, not a leaf was out of place. Sensuous lines meandered with perfect form through vibrantly alive space, combining utter stillness with a sense of intense purpose. I noticed that anything I merged with was equally a part of the ONE, the perfection…bird, insect, plant, stone…they were all the same. I was infused with an intense feeling of joy.

From that moment on, I practiced merging on a regular basis. It became my form of prayer and meditation, resonating deeply with who I am. I learned much from Nature.

I want to clarify what I experienced when "merging" with nature. I didn't actually hear words, but my mind translated the clear Knowing that I received during these sessions into the language I could most easily understand.

Grass

I remember merging with newly mowed grass, the pollen of which had been a trigger for hay fever and asthma symptoms most of my life. I asked, "How does it feel to be cut by Humans and not allowed to ever flower and reproduce, to finish your life-cycle?" The response was unexpected. Grass said that it didn't mind serving humanity when there was an equal exchange of energy. However most of the time humans tended to mow the lawn with anger and frustration in their hearts…not gratitude. Rarely did anyone cut the lawn in joy. I asked how I could change my relationship with grass. I was told, "Honor me and yourself…co-create with me, do it with joy."

Later, as I walked along a path in the garden, I had another insight. I was shown that there is a connection between how humans treat grass (poisoning it with chemicals, weed killers, and caustic petroleum-based fertilizers), which creates an energy discord. One of the physical manifestations of that discord is the increasing incidence of grass allergies in humans. (Noting that most of our diet consists of grasses or grass seeds, this allergy increase is a bit alarming.)

A human being is part of the Whole…He experiences himself, his thoughts and feelings, as something separated from the rest…a kind of optical delusion of his consciousness. This delusion is a kind of prison for us, restricting us to our personal desires and to affection for a few persons nearest us. Our task must be to free ourselves from this prison by widening our circle of compassion to embrace all living creatures and the whole of nature in its beauty. Nobody is able to achieve this completely, but the striving for such achievement is, in itself, a part of the liberation and a foundation for inner security.

Albert Einstein

The tree which moves some to tears of joy is in the eyes of others only a green thing that stands in the way. Some see nature all ridicule and deformity … and some scarce see nature at all. But to the eyes of the man of imagination, nature is imagination itself.

Judy Pratt-Shelly

Later, as I made merging a daily habit, the voice that spoke was less identified with a particular part of nature, and more an entire segment of nature. For example, trees spoke for all trees. Eventually there was no attachment to form at all. Nature merely spoke, and I could enter the discussion through any means. For me, simply touching any part of "nature" brought me almost instantly into the Oneness of what IS.

Forest Fires

During the summer of 2002, there were forest fires raging around three sides of my small Southern Oregon town. The air was smoky for weeks and the sun was red. I merged with a granite boulder to ask for insight into this experience. I was filled with sadness as I watched the beloved forests burn. I asked to join Earth, and to understand fire. I was gently given a small piece of the experience of Nature's awe-inspiring, knee-buckling, totally surrendering FORCE, the rawness of which we humans spend lifetimes avoiding. Then I was told...

> This energy that wipes clean the landscape and allows a new one to emerge is exactly the same as the shift in perception that takes place when one shifts from living the illusion to BEing unconditional love.
>
> Hold it, know it, feel the difference, this is not a gentle cleansing, but a scouring of your every nuance of known way of Being. Do not take this experience lightly ... it is all-transforming, all-encompassing, it will consume you totally and you will die to the new moment of now.
>
> These fires, this smoke that chokes your lungs and burns your eyes, is a reminder. Face it with the love in your heart that is YOU, open-eyed, fully conscious, welcoming the new day...not in the future, but NOW in this very breath. Choose, in the next breath, and the next, to BE the unconditional love that you are, that truly is all that IS.
>
> It is an easy path; the secret is to follow your heart. Notice what flows naturally and what is struggle. Look deeply into the struggle in your life, for there is the gift, the lesson that will allow you to release into THIS MOMENT, and to die to the illusion. YOU choose, for you are part of the divine spark of God – there is no separation.
>
> Celebrate your own magnificent love, celebrate it in your relationships, in your every footstep, in the touch of your hand upon the self that looks separate but is not, look into the eyes of another and see yourself.

This "cleansing" of the landscape is a metaphor for the transformation taking place in the human species...it is a lesson in letting go of the old and welcoming the new expression of loving humans on this planet...it is a physical manifestation of the cleansing fire burning within all humanity at this very moment. Look around you...it is everywhere...it touches everything. WE ARE ONE and we are birthing ourselves anew.

Oneness

I no longer merge with nature as if it is a separate entity from me. My relationship to All-That-Is has evolved such that I no longer require that illusion. The voice I previously identified as "nature" I now recognize as the Inner Wisdom vibrating in me and All-That-Is, the voice of Oneness. It is as accessible as my next breath. All I need to do is shift my focus and let go of whatever is streaming through my mind. Sometimes I shift my focus to my heart, sometimes I just close my eyes… and there it is. It is a voice of infinite tenderness and unconditional love.

Just as nature is now an experience of unity for me, I have also started to feel the energy vibrating from everything, both animate and inanimate objects alike. This surprised me at first, until I learned that subatomic particles obey entirely different rules from Newtonian physics. At the subatomic particle level, *everything* vibrates with energy.

Wildness

I would like to share one more experience of merging. I do so because it illustrates an important issue regarding how we relate to and heal nature.

A friend of mine owned two adjacent building lots. One was vacant, and contained a huge poplar with multiple trunks. This tree was the epitome of a jungle, and it was clear that it housed an entire village of wildlife.

She eventually decided to sell her house and build on the lot next door, necessitating the removal of this tree. The tree held a special place in her heart, as she had spent many hours communing with it over the years, and it had seen her through some very tough emotional times. She held a small ceremony to thank the tree for its presence in her life, and asked me to merge with it to receive one last message.

When I did, I immediately felt the symbiotic relationship between my friend and this tree. Their mutual love and respect bound them together in many beautiful ways. The tree indicated that it was not attached to its physical form and that it would quite willingly release form to make way for her house. Because of their close relationship it suggested she use part of one of the trunks in the construction of her new home. (It now stands as one of the support pillars for her front porch.)

It suggested one last thing. It told me that it stood as the last remaining wild place in that neighborhood – a haven for wildlife. It asked that she be aware of the pivotal role this particular tree played in the balance of nature, and asked her to create another spot for the wildlife once it was cut down.

Look around our cities, suburbs, and even our country homes. We have removed the wild places. In ancient England, each farm was surrounded by hedgerows. Those hedgerows provided hiding, breeding, and traveling space for the native wild animals. They are being removed as large mono-crop agricultural corporations have moved onto the land. In the USA we eliminated the concept of hedgerows long ago.

What happens when we remove the wild places in our environment, relegating them to distant locations we visit for vacation only? I wonder if our systematic elimination of the wild places – even within our own neighborhoods – isn't a direct reflection of our collective (and perhaps even personal) fear to face our own wildness?

When I followed the Perelandra gardening methods, I always made sure to leave a section of the yard free from human intervention. It was my way of humbly admitting my lack of knowledge about nature's systems while also honoring the consciousness of nature.

Conservationist Dave Foreman talks of the need to "re-wild" the United States. So much habitat has been lost that we can no longer support large carnivore populations. At first that may seem great, but it is short sighted. With large carnivores eliminated, smaller animals overpopulate and quickly upset the ecological

Today the network of relationships linking the human race to itself and to the rest of the biosphere is so complex that all aspects affect all others to an extraordinary degree. Someone should be studying the whole system, however crudely that has to be done, because no gluing together of partial studies of a complex nonlinear system can give a good idea of the behaviour of the whole."

Murray Gell-Mann
Physicist

This absence of vision as to what happens when you foul your nest puzzles me.

Bill Moyers
from an August 2003
interview with Grist Magazine

The fundamental issue is really the difference between monoculture and diversity, not GMOs and conventional hybrids.

Michael Pollan
Genetic Pollution: A Life of Its Own, from Nature's Operating Instructions edited by Kenny Ausubel with J. P. Harpignies, 2004, page 143.

balance. Its happening everywhere. He sites examples from the San Diego coastal sage canyons, where the elimination of the coyote also affects the native bird population; to the absence of mountain lions and wolves leading to the subsequent loss of neotropical migrant song birds in the eastern United States. He writes:

> All over the world we are finding that when we remove large carnivores, the whole system begins to unravel. Large carnivores need big core habitats and they need connections between them… In the United States, we simply no longer have wild areas large enough to maintain habitat for large populations of jaguars, grizzlies, or wolves. What we need to do is link wildlands together so that animals can disperse…To do our work, we have to look across national borders and across the borders between public and private land.[2]

Perhaps its time to "re-wild" ourselves as well. When we stop trying so hard to convince ourselves that we've risen above the "lowly" animals, and allow for the possibility that we have a wild side – a twin spirit with nature – that connects with the deepest part of our BEing; we open the door to the possibility of living in communion experiencing partnershp with all. In doing so, we drop all judgments about "lower" or "higher" life forms and simply see life, in all its glorious splendor.

Humans as Keystone Species

Bioneer Conference founder Kenny Ausubel's recent book, <u>Nature's Operating Instructions</u>, contains articles contributed by both historian Malcolm Margolin and restoration ecologist **Dennis Martinez**. Both men write on the emerging awareness that the human species has consciously co-created our fertile "natural" landscape for the last 12,000 years or more, through her indigenous peoples. Contrary to popular belief that humans simply lived off the "fat of the land" like parasites, their surprising evidence shows that indigenous people actively participated in creating and maintaining a fertile and abundant landscape, even up to the present day. Of course, this is only news to the western-enculturated mind. Indigenous people have always understood their co-creative relationship with nature.

Their use of fire is a perfect example. When non-native settlers arrived they couldn't understand why the native people set forest fires. According to Dennis Martinez, here's what a fire accomplishes:

- stimulates germination of hard seeds;
- opens closed-cone conifers to release seeds that germinate following the fire;
- increases water retention by removing excess vegetation that sucks up groundwater and emits it into the atmosphere through evapotranspiration;
- breaks up the overwintering cycle of insects that prey on important wildlife and cultural plants like oaks;
- decreases forest soil acidity, thereby making more nutrients available to plants.[3]

Because most non-natives do not recognize the vital role the First People played in creating the "pristine wilderness" they inherited or their ancestors conquered, many well-meaning ecologists often create laws that are counter productive to the bioregion's well being, even today. Martinez writes:

> Why are past Indian burning regimes and selective harvesting, for example, important? Because the millennia-long co-evolution of Indians and their environment built a relationship that undoubtedly affected the abundance and distribution – and probably the very DNA – of many species favored by Indian management. To ignore this fact is to risk doing poor ecological science.[4]

To be a human being in this way, to learn such practices, required more than one generation. Among California's Native Americans, this knowledge was learned and transmitted over many generations, and a lot of it is still around. Perhaps above all, it gives us a view of humanity as not living apart from nature and being destructive to the natural world. These traditions and peoples show us splendidly how, by our way of living, we can actually be a blessing to the world.

Malcolm Margolin

<u>The Human-Nature Dance: People as a Keystone Species from Nature's Operating Instructions,</u> *page 79.*

May we all trace our roots to the great Tree of Peace. May we honor the wisdom of our grandparents and care take that wisdom for our grandchildren unto seven generations. Let us recognize the sacredness of this time of transformation and choice, that we may truly manifest the beauteous family of humanity.

Dhyani Ywahoo
from the <u>Journey to the Heart</u> website http://journeytotheheart.org/

In light of the extent to which First People co-evolved the landscape over the past 12,000+ years, how do we answer the question: what is nature? If we wish to restore and heal the landscape of the 21st century, what do we restore to? Perhaps its time to re-evaluate not only our methods, but our goal as well. Martinez concludes:

> In other words, how do we participate in an accelerated creation and re-creation process in the midst of rampant destruction?

> Restoration writ large is not just a landscape restoration project. It's a community-based intergenerational endeavor. It's more a process than a product. It's about relationships. It's about our responsibility as human beings to participate every day in the re-creation of the earth. [5]

Relationships

Restoring our relationship with nature, and understanding and honoring the wisdom of the First People, requires opening our hearts and minds, while we re-think our goals and methodologies. It entails reconsidering our own personal relationship with the wild in nature, as well as reaching out a hand of reconciliation to those who'sviews we have judged.

When we remove the perceptual filter of LACK that seems to color almost everything we see, nature's bountiful design is revealed. In Cradle to Cradle, William McDonough and Michael Braungart successfully argue that we can design humanity's impact on Earth to beneficially *contribute* to the well-being of the environment by studying and applying the natural abundance inherent in nature's designs. We can humbly choose to honor the 3.4 billion years of self-assessment and self-correction that this Earth-experiment has provided. All we have to do is joyfully receive the banquet of knowledge offered, and apply it to our daily lives. Here are a few of the pioneers of this new wave of Earth co-creators and a brief description of their work:

Janine Benyus – Developed the concept of **Biomimicry** by asking the question: What would nature do? She explains Biomimicry's importance:

> We can decide as a culture to listen to life, to echo what we hear, to not be a cancer on the earth. Having this will and the inventive brain to back it up, we can make the conscious choice to follow nature's lead in living our lives. The good news is that we have plenty of help. We're surrounded by geniuses. They are everywhere with us, breathing the same air, drinking the same water, moving on limbs built from blood and bone. Learning from them will take some stillness on our part, so we can hear their symphony of good sense. What biomimicry offers us, in learning *from* nature instead of just *about* nature, is the opportunity to feel a part of, rather than apart from, this genius that surrounds us. [6]

She suggests that even deeper mimicry involves not only studying nature's forms, but also its processes and ecosystem strategies. This is a significant shift in our perceptual awareness of what nature has to offer. It means that we begin to focus our attention on the interrelationships of nature's systems.

As we shift our intention to designing products as sustainments (see the DESIGN chapter), biomimicry offers us the opportunity to study successful sustainments in action, merely by focusing our attention on the nested systems already successfully conceived of and tested in nature. It is a shift from viewing content to focusing on context. As Janine skillfully points out, out design challenges are already solved. All we need to do is humbly shift our own perception of ourselves from dominators of nature to students of nature.

If we put these images together, the resemblance to the hologram is striking...We are constituted by the intersection of two flows — one direct, from the divine, and one indirect, from the divine via our environment. We can view ourselves as interference patterns, because the inflow is a wave phenomenon, and we are where the waves meet.

Dr. George F. Dole,
as quoted by Michael Talbot in The Holographic Universe page 259.

John Todd and Nancy Jack Todd, authors of several books on Ecological Design and co-founders of the New Alchemy Institute in 1969, concentrate much of their energy today on ecological water purification through Ocean Arks International, which they founded in 1981. In a discussion of the difference between "eco" and "inert" machines, as designed to clean up waste-water, John writes:

> But the difference between the eco-machine and the inert machine is that the living one is made up of hundreds, occasionally thousands, of species of life forms ranging from microorganisms to mollusks and fish to higher plants, including trees. All these species work together symphonically as part of a dynamic integrated system. As a consequence, eco-machines have attributes most machines do not. They have limits, but like natural ecosystems they also have the ability to self-design, self-organize, and self-repair. If the human guide is clever enough, they can even self-replicate. A living technology can, in theory, last for hundreds, possibly thousands, of years. It can behave like a forest.[7]

Just in case you are scratching your head at the moment and wondering if you read correctly, let me assure you that you did. John, and many others are designing living systems - called eco-machines or living technologies – to address many of our needs, especially in the areas of waste management, ecological emergencies (like oil spills) and restoration. He optimistically concludes:

> The path I have traveled has led me to conclude that humanity can reduce its negative footprint on the planet by 90 percent. I also believe it's possible to create a culture where vibrant wilderness permeates nearly every locale, even urban settings. It would be an extraordinary world if we could give 90 percent of it that we've damaged back to the world.[8]

Paul Stamets is obsessed with mushrooms, and rightly so. His studies have revealed amazing attributes of fungi that could be essential to the survival of our planet. From the study of overlapping mycelial mats that, he states, "actually permeate all land masses on the planet in the first two to four inches of soil,"[9] to the use of oyster mushrooms to clean up oil spills, mushrooms seem to offer us valuable gifts every time we bother to look deeply at them. He even draws a parallel between human neural structures and mycelial networks, exploring the possibilities that both represent forms of natural intelligence. He states,

> About 465 million years ago, humans shared a common ancestry with fungi. We share about 30 percent of our genes with fungi, giving us more in common genetically with them than any other kingdom. So perhaps it's not such a leap to speculate that mycelial networks might display a form of natural intelligence.[10]

Mushrooms offer so many gifts to humanity in the form of possible medicines and pollution clean-up, that Stamets spends much of his time collecting species before they go extinct. At a time when the threat of terrorist attacks occupy much of our government's attention, Stamets notes that mushrooms offer a unique potential to mitigate the effects of a chemical attack. He suggests they should be protected as a matter of national security.

Dan Dagget deals in paradox. His work in rangeland restoration has yielded amazing results while shooting down some basic assumptions about the process of restoration. He agrees that the essential component of any restoration project is relationship. He writes:

> ...being an effective environmentalist must be more about creating and sustaining healthy, functional relationships than it is about dealing with things.[11]

In 1998, in China's Yangtze Basin, deforestation caused flooding that killed 3,700 people and dislocated more than live in the United States, as well as inundating sixty million acres of cropland. It was a $30 billion disaster that forced China into a $12 billion crash program of reforestation. That's the economic price tag on the loss of an ecosystem service in just one relatively small place.

Hunter and Amory Lovins Where the Rubber Meets the Road from Nature's Operating Instructions edited by Kenny Ausubel with J.P. Harpignies, 2004, page 163.

I would second that motion and then take it a step further. I'd say relationship has everything to do with not just being an effective environmentalist, but living an effective life. Quantum physics and Systems Theory are teaching us that from a very literal scientific meaning, life is nothing but relationships. By "relationship' we mean something specific. It means co-creation, win-win situations, and adaptability such that everyone survives, because ultimately life supports life. Darwin stressed the adaptability of life over a cut-throat type of "survival of the fittest," but his works were misinterpreted by the perceptual filter of his cultural times. That is what makes this perceptual shift so exciting. We are beginning to see in fundamentally new ways, and as a result, an infinite field of possibilities is opening up. All we have to do is pay attention.

Dan Daggert knows this well. In studying our mining wastelands and dying rangelands, he has seen the impact our lack of relating has had. Since humans divorced themselves from nature, stopped taking responsibility for their place as a keystone species in the environment, and subsequently ceased co-creating a balanced nature we have failed to acknowledge the impact of our actions. He points out that we no longer take responsibility for the relationships we impact as both prey and predator, water engineer and fire-starter, seed spreader and animal breeder, all the other roles we used to consciously fill as a keystone species and crucial relationship networker.

Michael J. Roads once shared a story about his metaphysical experience as a young kangaroo joey who was suddenly attacked by an eagle. Dying in the eagle's strong talons while being flown to its nest, he got to experience the ease with which the joey released physical form and the energy transfer that took place as the young eagles consumed the remaining form. There was a perfection of balanced energy on multiple levels, as each species acknowledged its role. In the same way, Daggert points out, the fleetness of the deer was developed because of the skill of its predator, and the complexities of the deer's meadow meal were developed through the direct impact of the deer's eating methods, fertilization, and foraging habits.

Using this knowledge, Daggert has developed rangeland restoration techniques that make the most of the ancient relationship between grasses, grazers, soils, and humans. His results have been exemplary. In one study, a deliberate effort was made to choose the most challenging barren site possible. Even so, with a focus on relationships instead of things, the grass yield was higher than the neighbors' cultivated and irrigated fields. Dan Daggart's work is a testament to the power of co-creative relationships in action.

As we explore new points-of-view and ways of perceiving ourselves in nature, one cannot overlook the work of **Michael Pollan**, author of The Botany of Desire: A plant's-eye view of the world. When asked how he came upon this idea, he described working in his garden. As he noticed the bees busy pollinating the plants, he started wondering how a plant would see the bee. Suddenly his perspective shifted:

> And like the bumblebee, I thought these plants were here for my benefit, you know, all the plants in the garden I was growing. But in fact, I realized maybe they had induced me to help them, because, you know, the bumblebee breaks into the flower, finds the nectar, thinks he's making off with the goods and thinks he's getting the better of the deal with the flower. But, in fact, it's the flower that has tricked the bumblebee into doing the work for him, to take his pollen from

…we don't live in a world of things. We live in a world of relationships.

Dan Dagget
Have a Cow: The Paradox of Rangeland Restoration, *from* Nature's Operating Instructions, *edited by Kenny Ausubel with J.P. Harpignies, 2004, page 100.*

In each case, the Forest Service rejected the "environmentally preferred alternative" identified in the required review under the National Environmental Policy Act even though the environmentally preferred alternative was significantly less costly. *Instead, the Forest Service selected the more intensive and expensive alternatives favored by the timber industry.*

Public Employees for Environmental Responsibilities Press Release
For Immediate Release: Monday, January 31, 2005
Contact: Chas Offutt
(202) 265-7337

http://www.peer.org/press/56 4.html

flower to flower to flower. And then I realized well, what if... So from the flower's point of view, the bumblebee is this credulous gullible animal, and how would we look to our plants... from our plant's point of view? And I realize we're much the same; we're more like the bumblebee than we think. [12]

He concludes that nature is shaping our evolution as much as we shape nature. There is no separation:

> But what I realized when you look at domesticated species, we are in that web. These species have changed us. The invention of agriculture, I think, is a very, kind of, self-centered phrase that implies that we did it, we're the subjects acting on the passive objects. In fact, the invention of agriculture is also something plants did to us. They got us to settle down, start farming, cut down trees all over the world so they could have more habitat. It makes just as much sense to look at the adventure of agriculture as something that the grasses did to us as we to them... they domesticated us as much as we domesticated them. [12]

This mutually beneficial interconnectedness of intentions could offer a new insight into the work of Dan Daggert too. Like Daggert, **Wes Jackson** also addresses the condition of our soils, prairies, and the cumulative damage caused by thousands of years of agriculture. Founder of the **Land Institute** in Salinas, Kansas, Jackson's goal is to pioneer an agriculture that mimics nature's prairie ecosystems, what he calls "perennial polyculture." His accumulated knowledge of soils underscores their importance. He, too, offers a new perspective of agriculture. He writes:

> Soil is as much a nonrenewable resource as oil. When we perceive a need for them, we can and do bring soil or minerals from someplace else, usually at a fossil fuel cost. Agriculture is a mining operation. [13]

Seeing agriculture as a mining operation represents a huge shift in how we approach soil. I imagine Jackson is referring to both the mining involved in that "fossil fuel cost," and the stripping of soil minerals and nutrients that takes place during traditional agricultural practices. This practice of depleting our soil stands in direct contrast to the systems nature has established in native prairie grasslands, where the soil is as rich as the diversity of plant life.

According to Jackson, 70% of the calories humans consume are from grasses. (He calls us "grass-seed eaters.") Yet if you compare the way we traditionally grow our grasses (wheat, rye, sorghum, corn), to nature's prairie ecosystems, you begin to understand why our soils are depleted. Prairie perennials are never plowed, regrow each year without seeds, and dance to a timetable of exquisite complexity – with timing, height, pollination, and species diversification all working together like the multiple voices within a symphony. Additionally, prairie root systems act as an ecological bank, storing what Jackson terms "ecological capital," as they recycle minerals and nutrients, stabilize soil, and hold water.

The Land Institute's 25-years of research have shown that it is possible to grow grasses using a prairie model that is sustainable. It is possible to grow the quality of our soil, expand and support nature's diverse eco-systems, and feed humans; creating a new paradigm in agriculture that truly honors all. The Land Institute's mission statement reflects that intention:

> When people, land, and community are as one,
> all three members prosper;
> when they relate not as members
> but as competing interests,

But even the salesmen are predicting a weaker American economy in 2005 than in 2004.

The biggest global economic uncertainty is the price of oil. Oil producers failed to anticipate the growth of demand in China. Supply side problems in the Middle East (and Nigeria, Russia, and Venezuela) are also playing a role, while George Bush's misadventure in Iraq has brought further instability.

High oil prices are a drain on America, Europe, Japan, and other oil-importing countries. America's oil-import bill over the past year alone is estimated to have risen by around $75bn. If there were any assurance that prices would remain permanently above even $40 a barrel, alternative energy sources would be developed. But we are now in the worst of all worlds - prices so high that they damage the global economy, but uncertainty so severe that the investments needed to bring prices down are not being made.

This Can't Go On Forever - So It Won't
By Joseph Stiglitz
Professor of economics at Columbia University and a Nobel prize winner.
The Guardian U. 01 January 2005

146

all three are exploited.
By consulting Nature as the source
and measure of that membership,
The Land Institute seeks to develop an agriculture
that will save soil from being lost or poisoned
while promoting a community life at once
prosperous and enduring. [14]

Paul Hawken is one of those people who perceives so clearly that his remarks tend to instantly bring what was previously out of focus, sharply into focus for millions. As a pioneer of Natural Capitalism, Paul has worked tirelessly to shift our perceptions towards a systems theory of ecology and to create projects that ease the transition into that new vision. Perhaps more powerfully than anyone else, he articulates the need to embrace that perceptual shift in every facet of life today:

> If we are to save what is wild, what is irreplaceable and majestic in nature, then ironically we will have to turn to each other and take care of all the human beings here on earth. It is not mere industry that must reform; it is our sense of each other. We have the responsibility to create a world of equals. The first rule of ecology is that everything is connected. The first rule of earth-saving is that we are all connected as a species. The economy that destroys the tundra is the same one that creates tens of millions of refugees, that causes families to sell their daughters or compels an Asian farmer to hock his kidney. There is no boundary that will protect an environment from a suffering humanity. [15]

Natural Capitalism, (http://www.natcap.org/), developed together with Hunter and Amory Lovins of the Rocky Mountain Institute, (http://www.rmi.org/), is explained in greater detail in the chapter on Business. It remains one of the most healing economic models today precisely because it shifts our perception from a narrowly focused exclusive and highly competitive model in which few win and many loose, to one that includes the support of *all life* as an indicator of success.

As I type this, I can hear a discussion on the radio regarding the poisoning of our environment (and our bodies) through the huge development of synthetic chemicals taking place today. The talk show host is reading a letter from a representative of Dow Chemical, explaining why they declined to participate in the discussion, and justifying what they perceive to be their positive environmental record. Despite an avalanche of statistics contrary to their position, Dow's executives believe that they are behaving in a responsible manner, so much so that they refuse to publicly discuss the matter. In their opinion, it is a non-issue.

How can this be? How can various groups look at Dow's impact on the world and come to polar-opposite conclusions? Because each chooses to see through a specific perceptual filter that selects certain evidence and disregards the rest. Dow chooses to focus on steps they have taken and awards they have received as evidence that their behavior has been exemplary. Their critics focus on contradictory evidence. Within their perceptual contexts, both are true.

As our awareness of perceptual filters grows, we can begin to see the game we are all playing in which no one sees the same reality, and thus contradictory conclusions can easily be drawn and justified within their perceptual contexts. If asked, I would guess that most people working at Dow would say they want to go to bed at night knowing they have made a positive contribution to their children's health and future. Yet the very premise on which their company exists – the idea that we can synthetically

Those who are inspired by a model other than Nature, a mistress above all masters, are laboring in vain.

Leonardo da Vinci

Consider Japan. In the 1600's, the country faced its own crisis of deforestation, paradoxically brought on by the peace and prosperity following the Tokugawa shoguns' military triumph that ended 150 years of civil war. The subsequent explosion of Japan's population and economy set off rampant logging for construction of palaces and cities, and for fuel and fertilizer...

Japan's isolation at the time made it obvious that the country would have to depend on its own resources and couldn't meet its needs by pillaging other countries. Today, despite having the highest human population density of any large developed country, Japan is more than 70 percent forested.

The Ends of the World as We Know Them
By Jared Diamond
The New York Times Saturday 01 January 2005

duplicate aspects of nature (which is what most chemicals are) without addressing the overall impact those aspects play in the interrelated network of systems that make up life on Earth – is no longer scientifically viable except through the archaic perceptual filter of an object-oriented mechanistic world, one in which everything is seen as separate from everything else. And even then, the evidence is overwhelmingly negative. Natural Capitalism offers us a model that can assist companies like Dow to step through the transition into a systems-oriented world. It will require a huge amount of creativity on Dow's part, but that has never been in short supply within their workforce.

Near the end of the 1980's, Walter Schmid started to develop a method of converting fermented organic waste into a source of energy. The Swiss Federal government and the canton of Zurich decided to financially support the project. The first solid-fuel fermentation plant started in 1992. The end products obtained are compost to VKS guidelines, CO_2 neutral fuel, gas, electric power and heat. Today **Kompogas** (http://www.compogas.com/) stations are located throughout Switzerland, with additional stations located in Italy, Japan, Germany, and England.

With the automobile industry already offering environmentally-friendly cars in Europe that run on natural gas and heavy goods vehicles run on CNG (Compressed Natural Gas), upgraded Kompogas is being added to the already existing natural gas network (e.g. Erdgas Zürich). Their website states:

> A Kompogas plant with an annual processing capacity of 20,000 metric tonnes of biogenous waste will supply the energy needed by about 2000 passenger cars traveling about 10,000 kilometres a year. This translates into about 20,000,000 (20 million) environmentally-friendly kilometres by car. If all organic waste produced in Switzerland was fermented, it would be possible to operate some 10 percent of all low-consumption vehicles using clean Kompogas fuel. What could be better for the environment?

> …The exhaust pipe discharges only that amount of carbon dioxide (CO_2) that the plants which will one day become biogenous waste extracted from the air for their growth. The give and take is balanced, and the natural cycle is closed. For traveling a distance of 100 kilometres, a mid-sized car consumes the amount of energy contained in 100 kilograms of biogenous waste.[16]

Best of all, the biogenous waste used to make Kompogas consists of the following common household organic waste: grass, tree clippings, mixed plant remainders, mixed garden waste, cemetery waste, vegetable and fruit parings, all left-overs from meats (meat, fish, cheese, bread, pasta), tea leaves and coffee grounds (including filter paper), balcony and pot plants, cut flowers, wool remainders, feathers and hair droppings from pets, cat litter including sand, household paper, mowing waste from road banks, and leaves.

Nestled in the beautiful countryside of Cottage Grove, Oregon, is the twenty-year research project known as **Aprovecho Research Center**, located on the web at (http://www.aprovecho.net/). Committed to finding an alternative stove design that uses far less wood while removing smoke from the living area and kitchen, Aprovecho aims to significantly reduce the millions of deaths caused by smoke-inhalation from the open, chimney-less cooking fires used daily by approximately two billion people worldwide. Aprovecho Research Center has been commissioned by the World Food Program to develop cooking stoves that will make use of the tin packing containers food aid is delivered in, ensuring that communities receiving food aid will be able to build low cost, fuel-efficient cook stoves from the discarded

- *In one year, a single tree can absorb as much carbon as is produced by a car driven 26,000 miles.*

- *Trees provide shade and shelter, reducing yearly heating and cooling costs by 2.1 billion dollars.*

- *Two mature trees can provide enough oxygen for a family of four. One tree produces nearly 260 pounds of oxygen each year.*

- *One acre of trees removes up to 2.6 tons of carbon dioxide each year.*

International Society of Arboriculture 2003

http://www.treesaregood. com/funfacts/funfacts.asp

containers. Because they insist on working with the local community in the design phase to ensure that *their* needs are honored, while also using local materials at hand to design a highly efficient stove that transforms most of the smoke into heat, Aprovecho's methods strive to honor all involved.

The Apollo Alliance (http://www.apolloalliance.org/) is a coalition of labor, environmental, business, urban, and faith communities who see energy independence as a source of good jobs. Endorsed by the AFL-CIO and 23 international labor unions, and a host of national environmental organizations, the Alliance focuses on public education campaigns aimed at building public policy dedicated to achieving energy independence. The name comes from the JFK inspired intention to place a human on the moon in a decade's time. That goal was reached eight years later when Apollo 11 landed on the moon providing humanity with a unifying view of our interrelatedness. It is a fitting image for us to embrace as we unify once more to accomplish a task just as formidable – to create a world in which clean renewable energy use is the norm, not the exception.

They have developed a Ten-Point plan that includes: the promotion of advanced technologies and hybrid cars to increase consumer choice and strengthening the viability of the US auto industry; increasing the efficiency of manufacturing factories; encourage construction of "green buildings" and energy efficient homes and offices; increasing the use of energy efficient appliances; updating and modernizing the electrical infrastructure; diversifying energy sources and ambitiously increasing clean renewable generation; increasing clean mobility options from bikes to high-speed rail; re-designing urban centers and infrastructures to revitalize the community in cities; long-term research and clean, renewable development of hydrogen fuel; preserving regulatory protections to ensure energy diversity and reliability, while protecting workers and the environment, and encouraging localization.

Sustainable Robertsfors, Sweden In August 2001 a five year experiment began in the tiny Swedish town of Robertsfors, (population 2,200 with another 5,000 in surrounding villages.) The main income sources are forestry, farming, and tourism. Robertsfors was chosen as a pilot for ecological, economical and social sustainable municipal development.

During the program, all aspects of life will be scrutinized with the intention of creating increased sustainability. This includes economic, ecological, social, and individual practices, as well as formal and informal structures. The intention is to develop democratic, participative processes and cultures that embrace every member in at least one target group; including consumers, producers, children, teachers, and municipal employees. Because the project is based on a democratic process, the desire is to increase participation of community members in key issues, primary among them are Environmental Goals and Sustainable Trade and Industry Development.

The Swedish government has adopted fifteen national environmental goals they hope to reach within the next twenty years, and these same goals are the aim of the Robertsfors project. Additionally, even though Swedish industry tends to be aware of sustainable issues and has an extremely high rate of creative innovations, the *application* of those ideas has become the focus of the Robertsfors project. It is

As summer (2004) comes to the Gulf of Mexico, it brings with it each year a giant "dead zone" devoid of fish and other aquatic life. Expanding over the past several decades, this area now can span up to 21,000 square kilometers, which is larger than the state of New Jersey. A similar situation is found on a smaller scale in the Chesapeake Bay, where since the 1970s a large lifeless zone has become a yearly phenomenon, sometimes shrouding 40 percent of the bay.

*Janet Larsen
Dead Zones Increasing In
World's Coastal Waters
http://www.earth-
policy.org/Updates/
Update41.htm*

They analyzed more than 7 million recordings of ocean temperature from around the world… and compared the rise in temperatures at different depths to predictions made by two computer simulations of global warming…

"In fact we were stunned by the degree of similarity," Dr Barnett said. "The models are right. So when a politician stands up and says 'the uncertainty in all these simulations start to question whether we can believe in these models', that argument is no longer tenable." Typical ocean temperatures have increased since 1960 by between 0.5C and 1C, depending largely on depth. DR Barnett said: "The real key is the amount of energy that has gone into the oceans. If we could mine the energy that has gone in over the past 40 years we could run the state of California for 200,000 years… It's come from greenhouse warming."

Because the global climate is largely driven by the heat locked up in the oceans, a rise in sea temperatures could have devastating effects for many parts of the world.

Ruth Curry, from the Woods Hole Oceanographic Institution, said that warming could alter important warm-water currents such as the Gulf Stream, as melting glaciers poured massive volumes of fresh water into the North Atlantic. "These changes are happening and they are expected to amplify. It's a certainty that these changes will put serious strains on the ecosystems of the planet," Dr. Curry said.

Steve Connor
The Final Proof: Global Warming is a Man-Made Disaster Independent/UK
February 19, 2005

hoped that once these ideas have been successfully developed and tested, they will provide effective models for sustainable development throughout the world.

With a sense of pragmatism, the coordinators of Sustainable Robertsfors acknowledge that powerful sustainable lifestyle changes must occur within the individual first, and then be embraced as a desired lifestyle by the local community. They therefore focus much of their attention on the psycho-social aspects involved in making a personal commitment to sustainable living. We look forward to their findings and results. For more information see their website at http://www.hallbara.robertsfors.se/engelsk/indexeng.html.

Started in 1993 by **Jeanne and Dick Roy** of Portland, Oregon USA, the **Northwest Earth Institute** aims to fill the gap between environmental awareness and the personal daily choices we make that impact the health of our world. Their courses encourage participants to deeply explore personal values, attitudes, and actions through lively discussion that incorporates three key principles:

- An *earth-centered ethic* promoting individual responsibility for the earth.
- The *practice of engaged simplicity* to enrich life and reduce personal impact on the earth.
- A *dedication to living fully in place* and protecting the unique bioregion in which you live.

Their courses are designed to engage people in a variety of settings, including mainstream workplaces, centers of faith, and at home among friends. Offered throughout all fifty United States and in parts of Canada, their total enrollment already exceeded 55,000 by March 2004. I have participated in NWEI courses and events. They have been vital in raising both my awareness of important issues and my personal journey of exploration into how to live in a way that truly honors me (and thus all life).

How can one begin to describe the contributions made to our hearts, our awareness, and our quality of life by **Joanna Macy**? Author or co-author of such monumental works as *World As Lover – World As Self* and *Coming Back to Life,* her work brings aspects of Buddhist teachings, living systems theory, and deep ecology; into our lives in the most honoring and accessible way.

> She introduced us to the **Elm Dance**, whose music, story, and words can be found at her website (http://www.joannamacy.net/html/elmdance.html). Briefly, this simple German dance set to Latvian music deceptively touches each celebrant deeply, as we recommitment to life, the healing of our planet, and the solidarity of all life. In the early 1990's the dance became associated with the area most poisoned by the Chernobyl disaster, Novozybkov. It became an expression of the triumph of life. Macy promised the people of Novozybkov to share their story wherever she went, and she chose the Elm Dance as the vehicle. It has spread throughout the world and helped raise funds to assist the people of Novozybkov by providing radiation monitors for their use. In this way they can reduce their daily danger of contamination.

Together with John Seed she created the **Council of All Beings**, a deeply effective workshop that invites humans to see this planet from the view point of its non-human inhabitants.

Through **The Work That Reconnects** she provides trainings to all who wish to participate consciously in what she terms, "The Great Turning," the transition from an Industrial Growth Society to a life-sustaining, life-promoting civilization. In that light, she offers the concept of a **Nuclear Guardianship Ethic**, a set of guidelines that help us to take full responsibility for the creation of nuclear power and weapons on this planet.

Water

There is the same amount of water on this planet as there always has been, in fact, it is the exact same water. Hard to believe, but the water we drink every day is perhaps the same water that sat within the cells of a dinosaur, rained on our ancient ancestors, and moved across Europe as a vast ice flow during the last Ice Age. With so much water covering our planet, how could there possibly be a scarcity?

It is the way we *perceive* water that contributes to the concept of scarcity. Although the following statistics are alarming, perhaps the most important lesson to draw from them is the blatant disregard for the life-supporting gift of water on our planet. How can intelligent beings miss the integral role clean, potable water plays in the well-being of ALL life? As you read the following statistics from Lester Brown and the Earth Policy Institute, imagine how you would design your own and humanity's relationship to water such that the gift of water was fully honored and acknowledged.

- World water demand has more than tripled over the last half-century.
- Water scarcity has become commonplace, as rivers run dry, wells go dry, and lakes disappear. Among the rivers that run dry for part of the year are the Colorado in the United States, the Amu Darya in Central Asia, and the Yellow in China. China's Hai and Huai rivers have the same problem from time to time, and the flow of the Indus River—Pakistan's lifeline—is sometimes reduced to a trickle when it enters the Arabian Sea. The Colorado River, the largest in the southwestern United States, now rarely makes it to the sea. As the demand for water increased over the years, diversions from the river have risen to where they now routinely drain it dry.
- A similar situation exists in Asia, where the Amu Darya—one of the two rivers feeding the Aral Sea—now is dry for part of each year. Since 1985, China's Yellow River has failed to make it to the Yellow Sea for part of almost every year. Sometimes the river does not even reach Shandong, the last province it flows through en route to the sea. As water tables have fallen, springs have dried up and some rivers have disappeared entirely. China's Fen River, the major watercourse in Shanxi Province, which once flowed through the capital of Taiyuan and merged with the Yellow, no longer exists.
- Another sign of water scarcity is disappearing lakes. In Central Africa, Lake Chad has shrunk by some 95 percent over the last four decades. Reduced rainfall, higher temperatures, and some diversion of water from the streams that feed Lake Chad for irrigation are contributing to its demise. In China, almost 1,000 lakes have disappeared in Hebei Province alone.
- Water tables are falling in several of the world's key farming regions, including under the North China Plain, which produces nearly one third of China's grain harvest; in the Punjab, which is India's breadbasket; and in the U.S. southern Great Plains, a leading grain-producing region.
- With its aquifers being depleted, China is now reconsidering its options for reestablishing a balance between water use and supply. Three possible initiatives stand out: water conservation, diversion of water from the south to the north, and grain imports. A south/north diversion to transport water from the Yangtze River basin will cost tens of billions of dollars and displace hundreds of thousands of people. A comparable investment in more water-efficient industrial practices, more water-efficient household appliances, and, above all, the use of more-efficient irrigation practices would likely yield more water. Since it takes 1,000 tons of water to produce 1 ton of grain, importing grain is the most efficient way to import water.

Lakes are not only being drained dry; they also are dying from contamination. Farm wastes, sewage, and nitrogen fallout from fossil fuel burning fertilize lakes, causing excess algal and plant growth that depletes water oxygen levels and kills aquatic animal life. Such eutrophication plagues more than half the lakes in Europe and Asia, 41 percent of those in South America, and 28 percent in North America.

Earth Policy News
Eco-Economy Update
2005-3
April 7, 2005

Using biofuel -- a mix of vegetable oil and diesel -- to power vehicles is already popular in certain highly vocal circles, but using biofuel to heat homes is just starting to catch on. A recent surge has taken place largely in the U.S. Northeast, where there

remains a large concentration of houses that use heating oil.

Proponents tout the fact that biofuel produces far less soot and thus requires less furnace cleaning, which we're told is a nasty business.

Hearth Warming-Biofuel catching on in the home-heating arena
Daily Grist
24 Mar 2005
http://grist.org

We experience the world through the planetary lens of nature. Because our eye has the same salt concentration as the ocean, we have literally kept the ocean in our eye. Like the one-celled critter of yore, our retina and brain are looking through an ancient sea. We filter light waves from the sun in the same way bacteria did when life began. Part of what this means is that all life shares certain features of a common biological aesthetics.

Peter Warshall
The Eye of the World: Sex, Beauty, Fraud, and Kinship from Nature's Operating Instructions, Edited by Kenny Ausubel with J.P. Harpignies

An increasing number of European countries – the Netherlands, the Nordic 's, and the UK – are using tax reforms to attain environmental objectives. In some countries this has led to CO2 taxes; in others to taxes and levies on highly polluting products (plastic bottles). In practice, environmental taxes still make up a small amount of revenue (less than 0.5% of GDP, although this increases to 2.5% of GDP the energy taxes and taxes on vehicle ownership are taken into account. (The equivalent US Figure is less than 0.9 %). Some countries see here an opportunity for a triple dividend: more revenue; less pollution; less dependence on imported oil.

Jeffrey Owens
Director
Centre for Tax Policy & Administration, OECD
Fundamental Tax Reform: The Experience Of Oecd Countries
Presented at the 67th Annual Meeting of Tax Foundation Washington D.C. November 18, 2004

- Water shortages now plague almost every country in North Africa and the Middle East. Algeria, Egypt, Iran, and Morocco are being forced into the world market for 40 percent or more of their grain supply. As population continues to expand in these water-short nations, dependence on imported grain is rising.

- Iran, one of the most populous countries in the Middle East, with 70 million people, is facing widespread water shortages. In the northeast, Chenaran Plain—a fertile agricultural region to the east of Mashad, one of Iran's largest and fastest-growing cities—is fast losing its water supply. Wells drawing from the water table below the plain are used for irrigation and to supply water to Mashad. The latest official estimate shows the water table falling by 8 meters in 2001 as the demand for water far outstrips the recharge rate of aquifers. Falling water tables in parts of eastern Iran have caused many wells to go dry. Some villages have been evacuated because there is no longer any accessible water. Iran is one of the first countries to face the prospect of water refugees—people displaced by the depletion of water supplies.

- In Yemen, a country of some 19 million people, water tables are falling everywhere by 2 meters or more a year. In the basin where the capital Sana'a is located, extraction exceeds recharge by a factor of five, dropping the water table by 6 meters (about 20 feet) a year. Recent wells drilled to a depth of 2 kilometers (1.3 miles) failed to find any water. In the absence of new supplies, the Yemeni capital will run out of water by the end of this decade.

- Another way of looking at water security is the amount of water available per person in a country. In 1995, 166 million people lived in 18 countries where the average supply of fresh water was less than 1,000 cubic meters a year—the amount deemed necessary to satisfy basic needs for food, drinking water, and hygiene. By 2050, water availability per person is projected to fall below the 1,000-cubic-meter benchmark in some 39 countries. By then, 1.7 billion people will in effect be suffering from hydrological poverty.

- At some point, the combination of aquifer depletion and the diversion of irrigation water to cities will likely begin to reduce the irrigated area worldwide. Data compiled by the U.N. Food and Agriculture Organization, based on official data submitted by governments, show irrigated area still expanding. For example, between 1998 and 1999, the last year for which global data are available, irrigated area grew from 271 to 274 million hectares. [17]

And from YES! Magazine's Winter 2004 issue that was dedicated almost entirely to water scarcity, come these startling facts:

- One third of our rivers, one half of our estuaries, and one half of our lakes are too polluted for fishing or swimming.

- Freshwater animals are disappearing five times faster than land animals.

- One mature tree next to a stream or lake can filter as much as 200 pounds of nitrate runoff per year.

- 3,400 cubic miles of water are locked within the bodies of living things. The average adult is 75 percent water (babies are 90 percent; the elderly, 65 percent).

- Less than 3 percent of the Earth's water is freshwater and over 2 percent is frozen in glaciers or ice caps. That leaves less than 1 percent of all the water on Earth for our agriculture, industries, and communities.

- Large amounts of irrigation water are wasted due to evaporation or run-off. By switching from flood irrigation to drip irrigation, which sends water directly to plant roots, farmers can reduce water use by as much as 60 percent while raising their yields by as much as 50 percent.

- 65 to 70 percent of U.S.A. water is used for irrigation. Industry usees 20 to 25 percent. Drinking and domestic use, 13 percent.

- Thanks to conservation measures, the city of Los Angeles uses the same amount of water it did in 1970, although the city's population is now 30 percent larger. In the 1990's New York City reduced its water use by 14 percent, while Seattle reduced water use by 20 percent.

- Each American uses 153 gallons of water per day. Each Briton uses 88 gallons, each Asian 23, and each African uses 12 gallons. Researchers estimate that 13 gallons per day is the minimum needed to sustain a human life.

- Climate scientists believe global warming is likely to cause severe droughts. In North America, global warming could shift the jet stream, making storms miss most of the continent. Glaciers and snow pack are receding throughout the world; many ecosystems depend on slowly melting ice and snow to provide a source of water throughout the year.
- Research by the NRDC on more than 1000 bottles of water from 103 different companies uncovered microbial content in excess guidelines in one-third of the brands it sampled. They also discovered synthetic orgnic chemicals in one-fifth of the samples.
- EPA guidelines require almost constant monitoring of tap water quality. Bottling facilities are required to test less frequently, and if they find pathogens like E. coli or fecal coliform they can still sell their water with a small disclaimer on the label. [18]

Many people are working to restore the concept of water as a life-right, not a commodity of the free market. Yet while multinational corporations have been diligently moving to control water sources all over the world, few people in the "developed world" seem to be aware of the struggles taking place, especially in undeveloped countries to maintain control of their own water.

Imagine for a moment how you would feel if you were suddenly told that the water in your own area, in the rivers, streams, wells, and even (in some cases) the rain that falls, is no longer yours to use – that you now have to pay a foreign corporation for the privilege of drinking your own local, life-sustaining water. These are not isolated cases, they are corporate policy for many multinationals who leverage greed to buy political influence wherever necessary to pave their way to natural resource control – all at the expense of the people and the environment.

Is this the world we envision when we contemplate "heaven on Earth?" Can this kind of short-sighted behavior lead to anything but war? It's even happening in our own backyards.

I've watched over the last few years as the grocery store shelves have been cleared to make way for an ever-increasing variety of plastic bottles filled with water. It seems that, instead of focusing our attention on ensuring the populace a steady unpolluted flow of inexpensive (and life-sustaining) water, instead of encouraging restraint in the use of water by offering incentives for grey-water and rainwater catchment systems, frugality of use, and laws that discourage pollution; we have simply turned our heads, pretended that potable water is an endless resource, and even encouraged additional pollution. Where do all those plastic bottles go after they are used…recycling?

There is something deeply wrong with our view of ourselves when we are willing to commodify the very natural resources we need to survive. Animals don't naturally destroy their life-sustaining habitat. Yet here we are, a single species on this planet willing to destroy the one natural resource that, to the best of our knowledge, makes our planet unique – water. We are the water planet. Seen from space we are mostly water, approximately 70%. Even our bodies are mostly water, ranging from 70% on up, depending on your age. How can we hold such a precious part of our existence in contempt? What are we missing in our understanding of who we are, and the role we play in the circle of life that we are willing to act in a way that is so obviously detrimental to our long-term survival?

In numbers alone, that means fifty to one hundred species are vanishing every day, approximately 1,000 times faster than natural extinction rates; faster than at any time in the last sixty-five million years. Recently a report from eight of the foremost nature organizations indicates that one in eight plant species worldwide is imperiled; in the United States alone, one in three is endangered. Twenty-four percent of all mammals are endangered. Their diminishment and disappearance goes largely unnoticed by most of us. The magnitude of this loss of life is hard for me to grasp. I know that if current trends in species extinction continue, we may lose half of all Earth's plant and animal species within the next fifty years. But can I imagine that world, that threadbare communion of life? The tiny cerulean warbler's song may fall silent forever within my lifetime. Will I notice?

Marya Grathwohl
Planetary Spirituality and Berry Picking in Northern Cheyenne Country
Timeline Magazine
Nov/Dec 2003

The Message of Water

There is a scene in the movie, <u>What the Bleep Do We Know!?</u>, (www.whatthebleep.com) in which a young woman stands in front of the mirror evaluating herself. She starts screaming, "I hate you!" to herself. How many of us have done the same? We know how painful such self judgment can be, but do we understand how truly harmful such thoughts could possibly be to the entire planet?

Elsewhere in the film, the work of Dr. Emoto is highlighted. He is the pioneer of a way of taking photos of water crystals that he feels reflects the emotions and thoughts of those around the water at the time the ice crystals were formed.

If Dr. Emoto's findings were to be accepted through peer-review, the implications are tremendous.[19] If the quality of water can literally change under the influence of human thought and intention, what does that say about how we think and act on this mostly-water planet? What message is the young girl riddled with self-hate giving to her own body and all life on our planet? What message are we giving water when we treat it with the distain of a multinational corporation who sees water as merely a commodity for profit?

Although the science behind his work is yet to be established, perhaps we can best use his work to begin the process of re-perceiving our relationship to life through water. For example, I love taking baths. I've started consciously connecting with the water in my tub, filling it with my gratitude and love, and choosing to honor water in all its manifestations. Then I imagine that blessing spreading from my little tub of water, throughout Earth, touching every molecule of water - whether visable or not - with acceptance and love. Dr. Emoto suggests we say a simple prayer everytime we see water in any form:

> I thank you, water.
> I love you, water.
> I respect you, water.

I've noticed that treating water with such conscious honor makes me feel wonderful!

How big is your footprint?

It has been difficult to quantifiably measure our human impact on the planet. One of the best and most easily understood measurements yet developed is called Ecological Footprint Analysis (EFA). It measures the amount of renewable and non-renewable ecologically productive land area required to support the resource demands and absorb the wastes of a given population or specific activities. Redefining Progress offers the following explanation:

The ECOLOGICAL FOOTPRINT is a tangible management and communications tool that:

QUANTIFIES: Combines the effect of multiple community's initiatives into one comprehensive, yet easy-to-understand measurement of ecological impact.

SIMPLIFIES: Clearly and visually communicate your community's progress toward sustainability over time.

UNIFIES: Acts an "umbrella" metric that multiple organizations and all individuals can rally around reducing.

Deep in the energy bill that was approved by a House committee this week, under a section titled "Miscellaneous," is a brief provision that could have major consequences for communities struggling to clean up their dirty air.

If it becomes law, it would make one of the most significant changes to the Clean Air Act in 15 years, allowing communities whose air pollution comes from hundreds of miles away to delay meeting national air quality standards until their offending neighbors clean up their own air.

Under the new provision, the "downwind" states would not be required to meet clean air standards until the "upwind" states that were contributing to the problem had done so. Currently, states can get more time but only if they agree to added cleanup measures.

Michael Janofsky
<u>Change to the Clean Air Act Is Built Into New Energy Bill</u>

New York Times
April 16, 2005

From a sustainability perspective, when humanity's Footprint exceeds the amount of renewable biocapacity a draw down in natural capital is required and this is considered unsustainable. Global Footprint accounts over the last forty years indicate a twenty-five year growth trend beyond the amount of renewable biocapacity. In short, humanity's Ecological Footprint appears to have breached ecological limits and is thus unsustainable.

Ecological Footprint Analysis (EFA) also raises several important social equity concerns. When the total amount of ecologically productive land area included in EFA is divided by the human population, there are about 4.5 acres (1.89 hectares) available for each person.[20]

Yet few people in developed countries have an EFA at or below 4.5 acres. Obviously, there is room for improvement, and that is where the EFA becomes an effective tool. By analyzing your own footprint results, you can see exactly where you can adjust your living style to produce a lower footprint. This is true both individually and for communities.

Redefining Progress has found that a combination of this Ecological Footprint Analysis and the Genuine Progress Indicator (GPI – see below) are the best current measures of sustainability. As a result, they offer support in measuring the progress of community and regional efforts toward sustainability. Reports are already completed or in progress for Almada, Portugal; Bermuda; Santa Monica, California; the County of Sarasota Florida; and the San Francisco Bay Area, as well as regional Genuine Progress Indicator calculations for the nine counties in the San Francisco Bay Area.

Results, both individually and community wide can be quite shocking. For example, the results of the Bay Area Regional Footprint shows it is 33 times too large for sustainability.

GPI – Genuine Progress Indicator

The Genuine Progress Indicator was developed by Redefining Progress in 1994 to create a more realistic picture of our economic status. The intention of this nonprofit, nonpartisan public policy institute was to create a better guide for public policy decisions. It is felt by many that a combination of the EFA and GPI tools best indicate our of progress towards sustainability. The Reinventing Progress website offers a wonderful illustration of why the GDP doesn't work:

> Imagine receiving an annual holiday letter from distant friends, reporting the best year ever for their family, because they spent more money this year than ever before. It began during the unusually rainy winter sparked by El Niño, when the roof sprang leaks and their yard in the East Bay hills started to slide: The many layers of roofing had to be stripped to the rafters before the roof could be reconstructed, and engineers were required to keep the yard from eroding away. Shortly after, Jane broke her leg in a car accident: A hospital stay, surgery, physical therapy, and replacing the car took a bite out of their savings. Jane, of course, couldn't maintain her usual routine of caring for their two small children, shopping, cooking, and cleaning duties, so they hired people to help. Then they were robbed and replaced a computer, two TVs, a VCR, and a video camera; they also bought a home security system, to keep these new purchases safe. Essentially, Jane and John's equating money spent with well-being is like using the gross domestic product (GDP) as the barometer of nation's economic health. The GDP is simply a gross tally of money spent--goods and services purchased by households or government and business investments, regardless of whether they enhance our well-being or not. **Designed as a planning tool to guide the massive production effort for World War II, the GDP was never intended to be a yardstick of economic progress; yet, gradually it has assumed totemic stature as the ultimate measure of economic success.** When it rises, the media applaud and politicians rush to take credit. When it falls, there is hand-wringing and general alarm. [21]

There is one measure and one measure only describing the capacity and relationship between human society and living systems: The Ecological Footprint. It is the only standard by which we may calibrate our collective impact upon the planet, and assess the viability of our future. It is "true north" when it comes to sustainability; no report about the environment is complete without it.

Paul Hawken co-author, Natural Capitalism http://www.regionalprogress.org/ EcFootBroch_final.pdf

Consciousness itself is what is fundamental and energy-matter is the product of consciousness… If we change our heads about who we are—and can see ourselves as creative, eternal beings creating physical experience, joined at that level of existence we call consciousness—then we start to see and create this world that we live in quite differently.

Edgar Mitchell, the sixth astronaut to walk on the moon, and founder of the Institute of Noetic Sciences "As the Paradigm Shifts: Two Decades of Consciousness Research" (http://www.ions.org/publicati ons/archive.cfm) Mitchell, Edgar. Noetic Sciences Review # 24 , p.7, Winter 1992.

World production of solar cells—which convert sunlight directly into electricity— soared to 742 megawatts (MW) in 2003, a jump of 32 percent in just one year. With solar cell production growing by 27 percent annually over the past five years, cumulative world production now stands at 3,145 MW, enough to meet the electricity needs of more than a million homes. This extraordinary growth is driven to some degree by improvements in materials and technology, but primarily by market introduction programs and government incentives.

Viviana Jiménez
World Sales Of Solar Cells Jump 32 Percent
http://www.earth-policy.org/Indicators/2004/indicator12.htm

They cite two flaws with the GDP: first, that it measures only monetary transactions and omits services that are usually provided free of charge, like volunteer work, childcare, in-home services, and maintenance. It ignores the value of leisure time and the contribution of the environment, all of which would be expensive if they had to be purchased. Can you imagine paying for clean air or protection from the sun's UV rays? The cost would be incredible! Yet despoiling these same assets isn't taken into consideration – on a cost basis – at all. Common sense and history both demand a more accurate form of accounting, one that places well-being at the center of evaluation, not just exchange of funds.

Second, and most importantly, it fails to differentiate between monetary transactions that contribute to well-being, and those that diminish or degrade the sustainability of life. In fact, those actions that actually contribute to economic growth, such as correcting mistakes of the past, can be seen as a loss instead of a gain; while those that diminish well-being are often counted as pluses:

> … the GDP treats crime, divorce, legal fees, and other signs of social breakdown as economic gains. Car wrecks, medical costs, locks and security systems, and insurance are also pluses to the GDP. [21]

Additionally, the GDP ignores the cost of depleting our natural resources. It can actually count pollution as a gain. For example, oil production is seen as a plus, while cleaning up oil spills is also seen as a plus. Counting the depletion of our natural capital as economic benefit is just plain insane - no one benefits and everyone loses. It violates both basic accounting principles and common sense.

The GPI begins by taking the financial transactions that are relevant to well-being from the GDP. It than makes adjustments for the aspects of the economy the GDP ignores, revealing a relationship between factors conventionally defined as purely economic and those traditionally defined as purely social and environmental. For a thorough explanation of the GPI, see the Redefining Progress website.

The GPI differentiates between positive and negative economic transactions and between the costs of producing economic benefits and the benefits themselves. It adds up the value of products and services consumed in the economy regardless of whether money was involved.

The following graph, provided by Redefining Progress, compares the GNP and the GPI for the years 1950 though 1998.

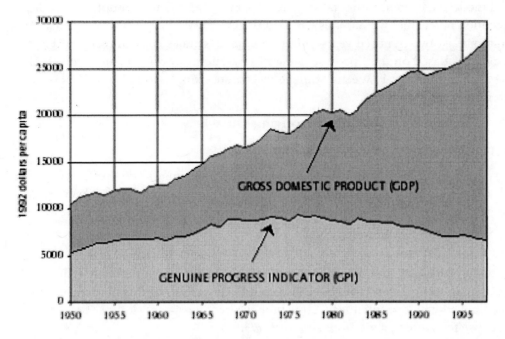

As conventionally measured, 1998 was quite a good year for the economy. The GDP rose by 3.9% (after adjusting for inflation), just as it did in 1997. In per capita terms, this corresponds to an impressive 3% growth rate. These were the two highest growth years in a decade. But before we congratulate ourselves on a highly productive economy, we have to ask what grew, who benefited, and at what cost to our social and environmental health. [21]

Their conclusion reflect what most of us have already surmised regardless of the rosier picture often quoted by traditional economists:

Instead of true progress, our current spending spree reflects a carpe diem mentality. We're buying short-term prosperity with long-term debts. Using the Genuine Progress Indicator to analyze current economic trends uncovers these short-sighted fiscal strategies: consume excessively, borrow from foreign countries, buy on credit, deplete resources, don't invest in future productivity, and distribute the wealth unequally. In effect, let future generations suffer the consequences.

The GPI declined because it includes increasing social, economic, and environmental costs that the continued growth of the GDP ignores. Three main factors help to explain why, despite the claims to a robust economy, many people feel uneasy, less well-off, or left behind by the apparent wave of prosperity. First, the economic growth is not distributed equally: Some have prospered while others work two jobs to get by. Second, this growth is purchased by increasing financial debts to the future, through overseas borrowing and failing to invest enough in future productivity. Third, the costs of growth include degradation of natural assets and depletion of natural resources, an ecological "borrowing" from the future that we can never hope to repay. [21]

Humans as co-creators with Earth

For hundreds of years the image of the indigenous First People held by those Americans of European decent, was that of a community living "off the fat of the land." Recent research has revealed that native human occupants weren't simply benefiting from an Eden-like landscape of bounty, *they were actually active and mindful participants in the creation of that bounty.* They acted in *partnership* with Earth. In fact, their environmental management was key to the creation of what the settlers saw as "pristine untouched wilderness." [22]

Europe is leading the world into the age of wind energy. In its late 2003 projections, the European Wind Energy Association shows Europe's wind-generating capacity expanding from 28,400 megawatts in 2003 to 75,000 megawatts in 2010 and 180,000 megawatts in 2020. By 2020, just 16 years from now, wind-generated electricity is projected to satisfy the residential needs of 195 million Europeans, half of the region's population.

*Lester R. Brown
Europe Leading World Into Age Of Wind Energy*
http://www.earth-policy.org/Updates/Update37.htm

Even modern day environmentalists often operate under that assumption. Studies in perception reveal that we humans will find the evidence to support our beliefs. As a result, our last two hundred years of environmental studies contain many false conclusions based on this "pristine wilderness' assumption. Two commonly held false assumptions are: 1) We are somehow separate from "nature", and 2) Nature is better off without humans.

Re-Perceiving Ourselves

It is time to re-perceive our place on Earth.

Years ago when I learned to use kinesiology (muscle-testing) to co-create my garden with nature, I literally asked nature what worked so that both our needs were met. The garden flourished. Perhaps it is time for us to *consciously* choose to creatively and collectively co-create with nature, and with each other.

I place the word "consciously" in italics because I believe we have been co-creating with nature all along, and the current state of our environment perfectly reflects our lack of awareness. Even though we have not been *conscious* of this process, nature has complied with our intentions. It is time we become aware of those intentions, and chose to create in a way that supports *all* life.

On the deepest of levels there is no separation between humans and what we call "nature." *We are Nature.* There is only the illusion of separation. It is time to acknowledge and honor that truth. In so doing, it becomes obvious that loving ourselves is the first step. Only then can we make choices that honor all.

Life cannot separate itself from itself. Life by its very nature endlessly changes as it flows. It isn't my life or your life or anyone or anything else's life. It is simply life and everything is it.

Sri Aurobindo
Thoughts and Glimpses

Notes

1. Paul Hawken, Natural Capitalism: Brother, Can You Spare a Paradigm? From Nature's Operating Instructions Edited by Kenny Ausubel with J.P. Harpignies, page 148.

2. Dave Foreman, The Green-Fire Wolf: Saving Wildlands with a Wild Heart, from Nature's Operating Instructions Edited by Kenny Ausubel with J.P. Harpignies, pages 95-96.

3. Dennis Martinez, Indigenous Science: The Cultivated Landscape of Native America, from Nature's Operating Instructions Edited by Kenny Ausubel with J.P. Harpignies, page 84

4. Ibid, page 81

5. Ibid, page 91

6. Biomimicry: What Would Nature Do Here?, by Janine Benyus, from Nature's Operating Instructions, edited by Kenny Ausubel with J.P. Harpignies, 2004, page 12. http://www.biomimicry.org/biom_project.html

7. Living Technologies: Wedding Human Ingenuity to the Wisdom of the Wild, by John Todd, from Nature's Operating Instructions, edited by Kenny Ausubel with J.P. Harpignies, 2004, page 20. http://www.oceanarks.org/

8. Living Technologies: Wedding Human Ingenuity to the Wisdom of the Wild, by John Todd, from Nature's Operating Instructions, edited by Kenny Ausubel with J.P. Harpignies, 2004, page 30. http://www.oceanarks.org/

9. Magic Mushrooms: Planetary Healing with Deep Biology, by Paul Stamets, from Nature's Operating Instructions, edited by Kenny Ausubel with J.P. Harpignies, 2004, page 34. http://www.fungi.com/

10. Magic Mushrooms: Planetary Healing with Deep Biology, by Paul Stamets, from Nature's Operating Instructions, edited by Kenny Ausubel with J.P. Harpignies, 2004, page 36. http://www.fungi.com/

11. Have a Cow: The Paradox of Rangeland Restoration, by Dan Dagget, from Nature's Operating Instructions, edited by Kenny Ausubel with J.P. Harpignies, 2004, page 100

12. From the Online NewsHour – June 29th, 2001 Gwen Ifill interview with Michael Pollan, http://www.pbs.org/newshour/conversation/jan-june01/botany_06-29.html#

13. Think Like a Prairie: Solving the 10,000-Year-Old Problem of Agriculture, by Wes Jackson, from Nature's Operating Instructions, edited by Kenny Ausubel with J.P. Harpignies, 2004, page 108

14. http://www.landinstitute.org/vnews/display.v13 http://www.landinstitute.org/vnews/display.v

15. Brother, Can You Spare a Paradigm?, by Paul Hawken, from Nature's Operating Instructions, edited by Kenny Ausubel with J.P. Harpignies, 2004, page 153 http://www.natcap.org/ and http://www.rmi.org/

16. http://www.compogas.com/

17. http://www.earth-policy.org/Indicators/indicator7.htm

18. Carolyn McConnell, Tap Water Takeover, Krista Camernzind, Bottled Water Flimflam,Yes! Magazine Winter 2004, pages 16-18. Reprinted from YES! magazine, PO Box 10818, Bainbridge Island, WA 98110. Subscriptions: 800/937-4451 Web: www.yesmagazine.org

19. http://www.bleepspace.com/download/WTBstudyGuide.pdf

20. http://www.redefiningprogress.org/footprint/

21. http://www.redefiningprogress.org/projects/gpi/updates/gpi1999.html

22. Dennis Martinez, Indigenous Science: The Cultivated Landscape of Native America, from Nature's Operating Instructions – The True Biotechnologies, Edited by Kenny Ausubel with J.P. Harpignies, 2004, pages 80-91.

23. http://www.redefiningprogress.org/footprint/ and http://www.regionalprogress.org/

12

<u>KILLING SPIDERS</u>

What we've discovered, though
—whether or not the conscious awareness breaks surface—
is that blending is the key not only to survival,
but also to calm and harmony.
When we clash with our context,
the chaos and imbalance slip into our souls.
- Eric Alan
<u>Wild Grace: Nature as a Spiritual Path</u>
(White Cloud Press, www.wildgrace.org)

KILLING SPIDERS

How can we expand our experience of "home" to include all life?

My daughter and I had an interesting conversation the other day. She lives in Los Angeles, and was commenting on the reactions of others to her treatment of spiders. Whenever she finds a spider inside her home, she captures and releases it outside, instead of killing it.

I have often received a similar reaction when I do the same. Why?

How more difficult is it to capture a life form and release it outside, rather than hunt it down and then carry the dead body outside (or to the garbage)? One act sets personal boundaries yet honors life, the other thoughtlessly ends it.

This seemingly benign behavior is considered normal in our culture. How have we evolved to the point that killing any life form, especially those that are small, helpless, and harmless, is seen as normal and even sometimes fun?

Home as a Village

When did we loose the ability to see all life as having a right to exist? My home is a world of life. There are wolf spiders, daddy-long-legs, and crickets inside. And those are just the ones large enough for me to see and interact with. Most of the time they are given free reign of the house, for it is their home too. At times when they go where I don't want them, or where their life is threatened (like the bathtub) I remove them to the outdoors, blessing them to have a good life. To me, this isn't sentimental slop – it is a way of life that *honors life*. What would the world look like if we extended that concept of "home" to include the area outside our houses, the cities, the countryside, the wilderness areas, and ultimately the entire planet.

Agreements

I once took an early morning walk around a lake. My head was surrounded by a cloud of mosquitoes eager to land on the only skin I left exposed – my face and my hands. I realized I was going to be covered with bites unless I took immediate action. So I told the mosquitoes that I had an invisible force field around my body that kept them from landing. Even though they continued to swarm around my head, not one of them bit me.

Sometimes the insects in my house develop a symbiotic relationship that benefits us all. We have a nest of paper wasps at either end of our deck. Every summer they rebuild their nest, raise their young, and leave. We live in complete harmony with them. When we eat outdoors in the summer, we sit two feet from their nest, yet they have never bothered us. In exchange for our willingness to provide them with a safe nesting space, their presence seems to have discouraged the yellow-jackets from harassing us.

Recently when I was gone on a long trip, I returned home to find that the black widow spiders had boldly taken over the garden outside the entry to the house. Because I live surrounded by young children, I knew we had to come to an agreement. I sat down and merged with them. Their energy was shockingly deep purple. I asked them what agreement would work such that they would keep out of sight and always leave whenever a human was around. The only boundary I gave them was the inside of my house – it was off limits. In exchange I offered to create a wonderful habitat for them in my garden, complete with lots of stone walls and hiding places. I gave them 48 hours to disappear, telling them I would take that as an indication we were in agreement. Within 48 hours they were all gone. Except for some confusion regarding whether the garage constituted inside or outside the house, I haven't seen them since.

My mother has had a similar experience. She lives in the east part of San Francisco bay, in a housing development nestled in rolling hills. My parents landscaped their home with a natural pond in the backyard, and spend most of their days enjoying the flow of wild nature in and our of their tiny backyard bioregion. Several years ago my mother, who has a unique relationship with wild birds, encountered a wild duck in her pond. They connected on a deep level, and as their relationship grew, they developed their own way of relating to each other. The duck "trained" my mother to come to the glass door whenever she knocked with her beak. Remember, this is a *wild* duck. Because my mother was open and receptive to her, the duck was able to communicate her needs. Now, when the duck knocks, my mother opens the door and feeds her. She will only allow my mother near her, and returns every year during migration, often bringing her mate.

My mother has also had a wild dove nest in the wreath near her front door. The dove felt comfortable and safe enough to tolerate the constant opening and closing of the door. Is my mother unusual? Perhaps, but I believe we all have the ability to live in harmony with each other, she is simply living that reality. She has made the choice to be open and receptive to the birds in her habitat, and as a result, they are open to her. Physicists might say that they are co-creating this special relationship in the implicate order (where they experience themselves as One), and living that choice in the explicate order (where the illusion of separation exists.) No matter what explanation feels "right" to you, the energy around their relationship is loving, inclusive, and highly honoring. Because of that, it touches us all.

The willingness to partner, to co-create such that all needs are met is perhaps one of the most honoring attitudes one can develop. It opens up the field of possibilities, offering ways of living in harmony we are just beginning to explore.

Life is connected at all times. ALL life, even the smallest and seemingly least significant. To see and experience the joy of this connection takes only the willingness to be open and the humility to know that in the grand-scheme of life, we know nothing.

Home as Cosmos

When I got divorced, it seemed as if my world was falling apart. I wanted to pick up the pieces of my life and start anew. I decided to design and build the house I had dreamed of building since I was 10. Because I am an artist, my ideas ran a little beyond the norm, and it was quite a challenge finding builders and sub-contractors willing to be creative on a budget.

Abuse no one and no thing, for abuse turns the wise ones to fools and robs the spirit of its vision.

Shawnee Chief Tecumseh-(1768-1813)

To restore our connection to natural ways, we often have to blend with what is no longer near. We have to use the same potent imagination which has removed the wilderness to find ways to reintegrate small elements of it into our homes.

Eric Alan
<u>*Wild Grace: Nature as a Spiritual Path*</u>
(White Cloud Press, www.wildgrace.org)

I gave every design element my full attention, researching the best materials and methodologies, trying to be as "green" as I could within my budget. For the first time in my life, I allowed myself to listen and act completely from my heart. What a freeing experience!

It was also frustrating, difficult, and challenging beyond anything I'd ever faced – except childbirth – and way beyond my comfort-zone. I developed a sudden admiration for all those who have had the courage to design and complete large projects.

Throughout this experience, I kept one saying as a mantra or affirmation in front of me at all times. It read, "If you have a clear idea of moon, a moon will be born," (from a wall hanging by Dot Fisher-Smith, quoting Dogen-Zenji). This short statement was ultimately what inspired the courage, determination, and intention to complete my home. (Perhaps it allowed me to constantly re-create from the implicate order thought, and manifest in the explicate order of my physical life.)

I now smile with amusement when I think about how careful I was about every aspect of the design and manifestation. I smile because there was so much more going on than I realized at the time. I felt an overwhelming need for certain design aspects to be just "right," without knowing why. It wasn't until I awakened one morning seven months after I moved in, that I recognized the strongly-felt vision that had remained below my conscious perception throughout the creation of my house.

I designed my house to be the inside of a tree. It is round, with vegetative forms in maple and cherry crawling across my birch cabinets. Whole tree trunks hold up the indoor catwalk, tree branches make up the balustrades of the catwalk railing, and the radiant-heat concrete floor is colored to match the rich, deep humus of healthy soil. The sun, moon, and stars pour their illumination through the six-foot round skylight that crowns the central roof peak. The space embodies an aliveness of spriraling energy that culminates in the central sky-lit roof. Not surprisingly, yet completely unplanned on the conscious level, a heart forms on the main room wall at certain times of the year, lit by both the moon and the sun.

My home is the cosmos in microcosm, and it breathes with my every breath – in fact, we breathe each other into being – for where does my house end and me begin? Every night, before sleeping, I thank each molecule for its gift. I, in turn, am blessed with a feeling of total support beyond anything I've previously imagined.

I have begun to *feel* the conscious gift of each piece of wood and every material that make up my house. We are a full and vibrant community of aliveness, no matter what the physical illusion may convey. The wood is not dead, it is merely transformed. The intention and the gift remain, just as they existed when the tree's roots stretched deeply into the earth and photosynthesis actively fed it's form – and then feeding everything in its bio-system in a balanced statement of co-creation.

This is the gift of living *from* the intention to honor all. Harmony and grace radiate throughout my home as much as the sun, stars, and moon fill it with light. In fact, we illuminate each other.

13

<u>DESIGN</u>

Any attempt to separate design, to make it a thing-by-itself,
works counter to the inherent value of design
as the primary underlying matrix of life...
Design is the conscious effort to impose meaningful order.
Victor Papanek

DESIGN

How can we empower ourselves to design a world that honors all?

Many spiritually aware people try to live their lives from the belief that, "We are all ONE." Yet sometimes these same people seem completely unaware of the connection between how we treat the Earth, our daily lifestyle choices, and how we treat each other. There seems to be a disconnect in their minds between humans and all other forms of life.

At the same time, many environmentalists express their passionate love of the Earth from a position that sees polluters as "the enemy." Even those who recognize themselves as part of the problem, often feel victimized to the extent that the choice to do the inner-work necessary to transcend a perception of battle, is not seen as an effective option.

There exists an opportunity here to step beyond the perception of fighting against something or of desperately saving something, to the perception of choosing to design our world in a way that honors all and makes our hearts sing. Why not choose to live sustainably simply because it expresses the magnificence of your deepest being – your Essential Self – and then empower others to do the same?

After living in both worlds - those of the spiritualist and the environmentalist - I have come to the conclusion that if any effort to create sustainability as a lifestyle on this planet comes from fear, guilt, or anything less than an expression of the best of who you know yourself to be, it will ultimately fail. Humans respond to the joy of self-love far more than to guilt or fear. We have the option of perceiving our world as a creative expression, lived in a moment to moment choice of sustainable design.

In the process of working on this book, I came upon the work of Victor Papenek. His 1972 classic, Design for the Real World, literally fell off the book store shelf into my hands. I had long since learned to trust that when a book offers itself to me in such a dramatic manner, I should read it – no questions asked. I have never been disappointed when I trust in this process, and this book was no exception. It was the most illusion free, creative, and honoring book I had ever read.

A New Model For Design

Papenek taught Industrial Design in both the United States and Europe. He realized that his students were being trained to design for a very elite, small percentage of the human population. When he asked, "What's wrong with this picture?" He answered with a conscious plan of action. Throughout his life, he taught his students to design using the following guidelines:

1. Design for those who don't usually have access to industrial designers. (Those labeled handicapped, the young, the elderly, the poor, women, etc.)
2. Use local and inexpensive materials that can be duplicated by the native people of the region, if possible by those who will be using the product.
3. Include those using the product in the design development.
4. Acknowledge that good design belongs to everyone.

These guidelines are still not widely used today. The majority of design is stuck in the illusion that whatever we do doesn't affect the entire planet. But statistics prove otherwise.[1] Luckily, there is a growing movement among many designers to embrace an entirely new paradigm of design, one that doesn't stop at the end of the production line, but that embraces the entire lifecycle of a given product. If you imagine a designed product as a pebble tossed into a still pond, this new philosophy of design sees not only the pebble but also all the influences it creates – the ever-expanding circles of movement formed through the pebble's impact — as part of the designer's process and responsibility.[6] This represents a quantum leap in design responsibility.

Victor Papenek dedicated the rest of his life to designing items that assisted a broad range of clients. He followed the ancient Finnish tradition of *Kymmenykset,* which was the practice of tithing 10% of one's expertise and time to those in need. The idea was that, if everyone did this, the entire community's needs would be met.[2] Along with encouraging his design students to focus their attention on those usually not served by designers, he also gave many of their designs to the United Nations patent-free to ensure that they would benefit as many people as possible throughout the world. He repeatedly mentioned the radically changing role of designers:

> Our role is changing to that of a "facilitator" who can bring the needs of the people to the attention of manufacturers, government agencies, and the like. The designer then logically becomes no more (and no less) than a tool in the hands of the people...[3]

> It is obvious that the skills of the designer must be made more accessible to all the people. This will mean the restructuring of the role of the designer into that of a community problem-solver. His only allegiance will be to the "direct" clients, the actual users of the devices, tools, products, and environments that he designs. His secondary role will be that of facilitating the production or redesign of these things.[4]

> ...this will mean a new role for designers, no longer as tools in the hands of industry but as advocates for users. [5]

Victor Papenek understood the idea of honoring all life, and lived his life as an expression of this philosophy. His decisions expressed an unwavering desire to express the best of who he knew himself to be, in service to the best of what he saw in others.

He always focused on creating the world he wanted to see by addressing issues no one else seemed to notice. My favorite example is his creation of a 9-cent radio receiver so that people in the most remote rural parts of the world could be connected to the rest of the world.

The design was ingeniously simple. Using an empty frozen concentrate juice can from the garbage (local and easily available), cow dung or a candle for energy, and a transistor radio ear piece, he created a radio receptor that worked for the millions of people who lived within broadcast range of a radio station. Since most rural areas only carried one radio signal, he felt a tuner was unnecessary. My favorite part of the story is the following, because it illustrates so clearly how Papanek honored people.

The cost of each radio receiver was just 9 cents. When he gave the design to the UN, some thought he should include the cost of painting the juice cans a uniform

Although an estimated 100-130 million disabled people worldwide need wheelchairs, less than one percent have access to one. The rest either get around through family and friends, crawl, or lie in bed.

Walt Hays
Wheelchairs Restore Shatterd Lives
http://www.wheelchairfoundation.org/
Timeline Magazine Nov/Dec 2003

How can we design our world such that all people's needs are met – especially those hidden behind doors, perhaps more easily forgotten?

color. He disagreed. Why add even a penny of additional cost to something intended for people with the lowest annual income on the planet? Insightfully, he saw the advantage of asking each owner to personalize his or her own radio. By doing so the person instantly created a work of art and pride of both creativity and ownership. *No longer was this an example of a hand-out, it was a highly original co-creation.*

In Viktor Papenek's thought-provoking 1995 book, <u>The Green Imperative, Natural Design for the Real World</u>, he introduced the idea of DFD – Design for Disassembly, which first emerged around 1990. The idea was to design products so that they could be quickly broken down into their component parts with raw materials separated. This allows for easy recycling or composting. Imagine what the world would look like if all of our products were designed using DFD principles.

Papanek argued that designing things to come apart efficiently is as important as designing them well. One of the side benefits of DFD research is that designers have also begun to design for ease of repair. What could be more honoring of those who's daily life responsibility is to repair products, than to design specifically for ease and efficiency of maintenance? It's time we begin to focus design on all aspects of a product's life-cycle.

Since Papenek's death in 1995, the entire philosophy of "Green Design" has expanded to include many new concepts, some of which are highlighted below. They are important for several reasons:

- The assumptions we make about what is important in life are directly reflected in the way we design the items we use in daily life, as well as the systems we develop that handle the processes of life.
- The focus of design has shifted from only serving the wealthy and specialized industries to a broader base of social architecture.
- It is imperative that we understand the power we bestow upon those who make design decisions for us all, and how we grant that power.
- It is time we accept our responsibility to correct poor unsustainable designs, and empower ourselves and our children to consciously and creatively design our world exactly as we want it, understanding that we no longer have the luxury of living in a way that does not sustain life for future generations.
- The definition of what we mean by the word, "sustainability" has dramatically changed over the last several decades, and therefore so have the solutions proposed.
- By empowering ourselves to design our world, we honor our own innate creativity, our own magnificence, and that of all life.

Traditional Green Design

Green Design embodies several basic ideas:

1. Make the product last as long as possible
2. Make the product out of non-toxic materials
3. Make the product as energy efficient as possible
4. Design the product for disassembly, and parts and materials for recovery

However these guidelines are not always easy to apply and at times contradict each other. Involved in the decision making process are some harsh realities that we rarely recognized until recently. The fact that the product exists at all can be its most unsustainable feature. Having "less impact" is not the same as having NO impact. Likewise, the behavior associated with a product can have more impact than intended, because a less impacting product can still be used in a high-impacting way.

Sustainability Redefined – "Sustainment"

To confuse the issue further, the definition of "sustainability" has been constantly evolving as we have collectively moved from an object-oriented perception of the world to a systems-oriented perception. Seen through the perceptual filter of Systems Theory, for example, a forest isn't merely a grouping of trees and their surrounding bioregion. It is also the interaction, interconnection, and symbiotic relationships of *all aspects* of forest life; much of which we know little about. When seen this way, it is difficult to see where one object (including it's impact on the surrounding environment) ends and another begins. This approach blends the interwoven threads of each expression of forest life into a complex tapestry of what it means to be a forest, revealing a far more detailed design than one would discover by simply studying the individual threads that make up the tapestry.

The EcoDesign Foundation of Australia realized that a new definition of sustainability needed to include a similar perception:

- It would take into account the *context* of the product's use and the ecological impacts that would arise in that context.
- It would involve a determination of which aspects of the man-made world deserve to be made less impacting because only they are inherently sustainable; and which should be abandoned because their very nature precludes sustainability.
- It would see sustainability as a *process*, not just the creation of a less-environmentally impactful product. The process must be on-going, and must include methods for actively sustaining it's sustainability. This means that the process must include the ability for on-going learning, adaptation, and continued or even improved sustainability over time.
- They called this process a "Sustainment," and defined it as "a tangible and significant contribution to the development of more sustainable ways of living and working," that includes "*what* is being sustained, directly and indirectly, and not only just *how* it is being sustained." [6]

The evolution of traditional design to a serious discipline focused on re-examining our assumptions about who we are and how we impact our planet must, by definition, filter down to the rest of us non-design professionals. How can we utilize the knowledge gained over the last 20-30 years regarding sustainable design and embrace it into our own lives and daily decisions? This question is important, because until we are willing to empower each other to take responsibility for the impact our choices make on our environment, we will continue to operate under the mistaken belief that we have no power to create a world that honors the best of who we know ourselves to be.

While we briefly visit some of the sustainable design theories developed over the last few decades, imagine how you might incorporate some of the ideas offered into your own life choices. In other words, ask yourself...

How can my daily life choices be sustainments?

Biomimicry

William McDonough and Michael Braungart describe the complex activities of a cherry tree within its environment:

- It provides food for animals, insects, and microorganisms.
- It enriches the ecosystem, sequestering carbon, producing oxygen, cleaning air and water, and creating and stabilizing soil.
- Among its roots and branches and on its leaves, it harbors a diverse array fo flora and fauna, all of which depend on it and on one another for the functions and flows that support life.
- And when the tree dies, it returns to the soil, releasing, as it decomposes, minerals that will fuel healthy new growth in the same place.[7]

They then invite us to design our buildings and the products of life to fit as sustainably into our environment as the cherry tree fits into its own.

This process provides a beautiful way of honoring what nature has already developed over millions of years of experimentation. Perhaps it is time for us to humbly look to the lessons present in the magnificence of what is already around us.

However, in doing so, it is important to remember the highly personal subjectivity of our own perceptions. How do we determine what model we use and what aspects of that model we emulate? How do we know that our perception of the model chosen is complete? (The complexities involved in the totality of a living system almost guarantee that we will not be able to completely grasp all that is important within that given system.) Additionally, from a systems approach, how do we isolate a particular aspect of a given ecological system – a cherry tree for example – and still maintain the integrity of the lessons available to be learned? Yet despite these questions, Biomimicry offers us one of the best models for creating viable sustainments. In her insightful 1997 book entitled, <u>Biomimicry; Innovation Inspired by Nature,</u> Janine Benyus states the case for Biomimicry beautifully,

> Biomimicry uses an ecological standard to judge the "rightness" of our innovations. After 3.8 billion years of evolution, nature has learned: What works. What is appropriate. What lasts.[8]

Cleaner Production

Cleaner Production addresses manufacturing techniques. The goal is to minimize the ecological impact by constantly striving to lessen the amount of toxic pollutants in the air, water, and soil; to lessen waste; to use resources more efficiently, and to use less energy. Any effort to create sustainability would naturally include these goals.

Ideally, just as much effort would go into making sure that the product being manufactured so carefully also contributed to the sustainability of life on Earth. In the context of sustainments, one would develop a way of extending the life of the product, monitoring and maintaining the sustainability of the product, and servicing it over time. In fact, in the context of sustainments, the product would not even be manufactured unless it was redesigned to ensure that its entire lifecycle promoted cleaner ways of living and working.

Ecodesign

Ecodesign pre-emptively and pro-actively seeks to minimize the ecological impact of the manufacturing, use, and disposal of a product. Obviously, a thorough understanding of those ecological impacts must be made, and from a systems standpoint, this can be challenging. Yet with careful attention to the systems involved, we can get as close as possible to a design that works more co-creatively with the environment. Naturally, the designs will reflect the evolution of our growing body of knowledge over time.

Emissions Trading

Designed as a stop-gap measure, emissions trading in a system whereby companies who can reduce their emissions easily, offer to reduce beyond what is required so that they can sell their excess reductions to companies who find it difficult to meet reduction requirements.

Although well intentioned, this program has significant flaws. It sees reducing emissions as a cost instead of an investment or a savings, even though the reduction of pollutants impacts everyone, especially the company's own employees, lowering healthcare costs over time. Additionally, companies involved in this program have little reason not to pass the cost on to their customers, so ultimately they aren't paying for the emission reductions – we are. In that case, it seems that a more cost-effective strategy would be to actually reduce emissions through design changes rather than delaying the inevitable through emissions trading.

Yet it's a first step. And it signals a new awareness in those companies participating, that their policies actually do contribute to the degradation of the environment. Along with that admission, comes an opportunity to creatively explore alternative ways of doing business that have a more positive impact on the environment.

One UK banking company, HSBC has announced a plan to reach carbon neutrality by 2006. They estimate their 10,000 banks in 76 countries will spend approximately $7 million to account for the approximately 600,000 tons of carbon dioxide the company adds to the atmosphere annually. They intend to reach this goal through a combination of buying green energy, increasing energy efficiency, planting trees, and trading carbon emissions. The only thing missing in this strategy, according to many in the environmental movement, is a commitment to finance only earth-friendly businesses.[9]

Triple Bottom Line Reporting & Extended Producer Responsibility

Developed to encourage a broader view of accounting by including not only the economic value, but also the environmental and social value they add or destroy. It is used to refer to a set of values, issues, and processes companies must address in order to minimize their harmful impact. This valuation requires clarity regarding the company's purpose.

Where environmental and social values meet, businesses work on programs like environmental literacy, training, environmental justice, refugees, and inter-generational equity.

Where economic and social values meet, issues studied are the social impacts of proposed investments, business ethics, fair trade, human and minority rights, and stakeholder capitalism.

While a triple bottom line method of company valuation is a vast improvement over the traditional single bottom line, it still perpetuates a compartmentalized view of sustainability, looking at individual aspects, but still not addressing major structural changes that involve a re-thinking of the entire business. Additionally they could consider, for example, a shift to providing and maintaining products and services facilitating more sustainable lifestyles.

One such innovation is the concept of Extended Producer Responsibility, which maintains that a company is responsible for the product throughout its entire lifecycle. Such a concept forces the producer to design in a way that is adaptively sustainable over time.

Green Purchasing Guides

Guides attempt to offer easier choices to the many millions who want to make sure that their purchases support the sustainability of our planet.

For years I championed the creation of a database that offered people a user-friendly way to make ecologically wise choices within their everyday lives, tied specifically to their own local community services. For example, as communities develop plastic sustainments hand-in-hand with industry, cost-effective plastic recycling could be part of the design. Community members might find that choosing plastic products that work within that closed system supports a healthy environment. I envisioned that this database would connect with other local communities so that resource procurers would know where specific recycled goods that meet their needs were easily obtainable, cutting out the need to truck supplies over large distances.

Until manufacturers align themselves with the idea of sustainments, this type of consumer database is challenging to create. At present, objective information regarding each product is extremely difficult to obtain, because too many variables and motivations are involved, making clear decisions difficult at best. As companies move towards transparency –for the good of all - perhaps this will change.

Ricoh credits their rise in sales to the fact that through their efforts to achieve complete recycling, they increased the quality and elegance of their product. And I am guessing that employee satisfaction mirrors their commitment to environmental sustainability. This story proves, the more bottom lines you feed, the more fish you catch.

Mikela and Philip Tarlow Authors of Digital Aboriginal… from their Newsletter Shape Shifter News – Volume One date October 20, 2002

Additionally, within the context of Sustainments, the issue isn't just about the raw materials used and their waste-management. Perhaps the bigger question is whether the product should exist in the first place.

Life-Cycle Assessment

Life-cycle assessment systems (LCAs) measure the impacts associated with the entire life-cycle of a product. They help us understand the relationships between the various parts of product life, our environment, and our human choices, by focusing more on the interrelationship and integration of the various systems involved.

Conservation

Conserving biodiversity seems a given necessity of "honoring all life." Not only does it honor the rich and diverse expressions of life, but it is logical in the extreme. If nature has taken millions of years to experiment with each life form and system, and if the present state of evolution represents the most adaptive expression to date; it seems crazy not to protect those expressions from careless extinction while there still remains so much we can learn from them.

Yet Conservation alone is not enough. We need to be willing to look beyond what we think is the obvious, and allow ourselves to explore the most subtle system relationships. We also need to factor ourselves into the entire system analysis. We can acknowledge the probability that there is always more to perceive than we are yet perceiving, admit that what we know is less than what we don't know, and approach nature openly seeking new ways of seeing and conserving diversity.

Recycling

Although recycling is often expensive and can use a great amount of energy, it's an idea that has gradually made its way into our waste-prone culture. Many people now include recycling into their daily way of life.

As we become more knowledgeable about how to handle waste with the least amount of energy output, recycling will become less of a controversy and more the norm. The most important impact we can make regarding recycling, however, is to begin designing products with recycling and raw material reclamation built in to the design specifications. In the meanwhile, our communities can work together with manufacturers to develop additional ways of using efficiently recycled materials locally. We can begin that process, as product users, by choosing wisely when we purchase.

Waste = Food

Victor Papanek, William McDonough, Michael Braungart, and many others suggest eliminating the concept of waste entirely. Instead, they propose that we see all "waste" as food for something else. Seen from this point of view, they suggest creating two different closed-loop systems of raw material recycling. The Biological Loop handles all organic material, taking it from growth through the life of the product to it's next use. The Technological Loop handles all non-organic material, like machines, cars, and computers. Since they can't be composted, once the raw materials are extracted from the earth, they need to be designed such that they can always be re-used without adding additional raw material. [10]

Buildings, streets, landscapes and neighborhoods all shape how we perceive the world, how we interact with our neighbors, and how we re-affirm our personal and communal self-worth. The making of places is about power, self-definition, and identity. Because of this, those who determine how these places are made exercise tremendous influence over those who live in or use them. As a priest, architect, teacher, and craftsperson, I have come to believe that what you must focus on is not so much what is designed but how the design responds to the needs, aspirations, and life of those who will use it.

Terrence Curry
Architecture as Ministry - Detroit Community Design Center
http://www.newvillage.net/Journal/Issue3/3curry.html

Ideally, we would design products with long life-spans and multiple uses such that the need to recycle was minimized.

Renewables

Renewable energy includes using the sun, wind, and earth or biomass, to generate energy. Creative solutions abound as we explore the use of magnetics, gyroscopes, fusion, and hydrogen as alternative energy sources. Great advances in solar and wind power generation have made them more reliable and affordable. With energy costs skyrocketing, entire communities are beginning to embrace the concept of using what has always been available to create clean energy.

Even my small town in Oregon has passed an ordinance allowing citizens to sell solar energy back to the local power company, thus creating an incentive for private homes to become solar homes. When this kind of grassroots effort multiplies, curtailing the need to continue creating energy in ways that damage our environment, we all benefit.

Relationships

It is important, however, to see the overall picture. Moving to renewable energy only benefits us when we also curb wasteful energy lifestyles. **As we begin to honor all life, our entire relationship with energy will transform.** Ask yourself the following questions. What do your answers reveal about you and your relationship to all life?

- When was the last time you thanked the electricity, natural gas, or gasoline for running your car, heat, and electrical appliances?
- When was the last time you thought about all of the hundreds or perhaps thousands of people who bring those energy sources to you?
- What is your relationship to life's energy systems? In other words, what assumptions do you hold about energy: your right to use it, the planetary and personal cost, the equality of it's availability and use, and way in which you contribute to the status quo

The mindfulness necessary to shift from seeing every aspect of life on Earth as a right for us to plunder, to a gift for us to honor, is huge. Yet it is the next step in the evolution of our relationship to Earth.

Industrial Ecology

Following on the footsteps of the concept waste = food, Industrial ecology represents a new way of thinking. It includes two aspects:

First, city designs could include areas where industries would be integrated according to their ability to create sustainments. The waste for each would be used as resource material for the others, minimizing transportation of materials and efficiently using the infrastructure of the area.

Second, each product's design creates a sustainment. Ideally the product would be available with reusable or no packaging, the industry would service the product, upgrade it, and then take it back at the end of its lifetime so that the materials could be used again.

Industrial ecologies require careful consideration of all elements of the sustainment process, including the relationship between elements and the entire life-cycle of a product.

Co-Housing

Popular in Northern Europe, but gaining ground within the United States, co-housing refers to a set of principles that encourage sustainable living. They usually include some kind of grouped housing with shared facilities and tools – anything that can be used by many instead of duplicated by all. For example, many co-housing groups share a common well-equipped kitchen and laundry. Many share tools and energy sources, allowing them to conserve funds, their impact on the environment, and energy.

Just as exciting to me, is the social bonding that can occur within such a living arrangement. Even though we never intended to create a co-housing situation, my own neighborhood is a good example of a start in that direction. There are four families in particular who have decided to design our yards, tools, gardens, and childcare such that we support each other. We have consciously chosen to purchase only one set of certain tools, and to work together in mutual support. In many ways, my daughter feels as if she has four homes, (with lots of siblings), instead of one.

As we have moved from the old concept of neighborhoods as community over the last century, our lives have become more isolated, furthering the illusion of separation and increasing our individual loneliness. It's time to move back to the front-porch mentality of friendly housing design in which relationships are encouraged and supported. Well designed Co-housing can be a step in that direction.

Community Design

As we are begin to re-think how we design our cultural structures (education, economics, products, housing, business, democratic politics, etc.) to honor all, it is time to re-think how we design our communities as well.

Most modern communities - whether large metropolis or small country town - are currently designed around the automobile. Transportation has taken the highest priority in community planning, edging infrastructure efficiency and community well-being out of the way. Take a moment to see if this isn't true for your own community. Ask yourself the following questions:

- What takes precedence, ease of traffic flow or ease of community gathering?
- Are your survival needs met as efficiently as possible? What happens when a disaster, such as a flood, occurs? Do you have to rely on outside help, or is the community designed to withstand emergencies such that your basic needs are still met?
- How close is the nearest fresh food grocery store? Can you walk to it or must you take motorized transportation?

- How convenient is the local school to those who use it? Does it require busing? Must parents drive their children or can they walk or bicycle?
- Are recreational facilities and natural settings nearby and accessible?
- How far must employees travel to work? Is the workplace designed such that quality family life is enhanced or hindered? (Some businesses are beginning to design their workspace as a small community complete with school, housing, shops, and recreational facilities that encourage more family and less commute time.)

I remember the flood that washed through our downtown on New Year's day in 1997. It was called a "100 year flood", and we were ill prepared for the outcome. Our water supply was contaminated and it was two weeks before we could safely use tap water again. The National Guard had to deliver bottled water to long lines of waiting citizens. Even though the experience was annoying, it didn't begin to compare with the experience of communities in larger natural disasters.

Yet I began to wonder why my own community wasn't more prepared? Why, for instance, don't we have wells or cisterns placed throughout the neighborhoods, used only for emergency situations? Why don't we make sure that for every three or four homes we have a working fireplace with stored wood, solar and/or wind electricity, and a functioning community garden? Why don't we encourage the collection of rain and grey-water? How about an alternative-powered communication system linking the entire community together?

Instead of merely designing our homes or subdivisions individually why don't we design our communities such that they work as units? Why not take care of their economic well-being by also setting up local currencies and resource management teams to ensure that local natural resources are always protected for the benefit of all?

These are just a few ideas. Each local community could be designed such that its citizens feel empowered knowing that they can handle just about any emergency that comes along. Such a design criteria would go far in lessening the usual feelings of helplessness and victimization that many feel during a natural disaster.

The Natural Step

In 1988 Dr. Karl-Henrik Robèrt, a Swedish cancer doctor and researcher, developed an idea that resulted in The Natural Step, a consensus statement created with 50 ecologists, chemists, physicists, and medical doctors about the conditions that are essential to life. The intent was to step beyond the usual argument between environmental and business interests and to offer accurate information from which a next step towards sustainability could be formulated. When comparing plant and human cells he stated:

> You can't argue with them or negotiate with them. You can't ask them to do anything they can't do. And their complexity is just mind blowing! Since politicians and business people also are constituted of cells, I had a feeling that a broad understanding of these cells might help us reach a consensus on the basic requirements for the continuation of life. [11]

The resulting list of four system conditions necessary to sustain life has now been adopted by many throughout the world. Simply stated, they are:

1. *Substances from the earth's crust must not systematically increase in nature.* This means substituting scarce minerals with others that are more abundant, using all mined materials efficiently, and reducing dependence on fossil fuels.

2. *Substances produced by society must not systematically increase in nature.* This means substituting persistent and unnatural compounds with ones that are normally abundant or break down more easily in nature, and using all substances produced by society efficiently.

3. *The physical basis for the productivity and diversity of nature must not be systematically diminished.* This means drawing resources only from well-managed eco-systems, pursuing the most productive and efficient use of those resources, and avoiding any modification of nature. Natural systems require time to replenish, and we must honor their timing and requirements for optimum health.

4. *We must be fair and efficient in meeting basic human needs.* Last of all, we need to ensure that our use of natural resources is maximally efficient and fair in distribution. The goal is to use our natural resources responsibly so that the needs of all people on whom we have an impact, and the future needs of people who are not yet born, stand the best chance of being met.

This clear guideline is intended to assist with sustainable business and governmental decisions. Using the funnel as a metaphor, Dr. Robèrt likens our current situation to a "resource funnel:"

> I think most people in business understand that we are running into a funnel of declining resources globally. We will soon be 10 billion people on Earth – at the same time as we are running out of forests, crop land, and fisheries. We need more and more resource input for the same crop or timber yield. At the same time, pollution is increasing systematically and we have induced climate change. All that together creates a resource funnel. [11]

He suggests businesses invest in actions that open the funnel by complying with the four systems steps. This will lead to higher profits. Those who ignore the need to open the funnel will face increased costs for resources and eventually – as the public becomes more educated about the issues – a smaller customer base.

Encouragingly, these Four System Conditions have been widely embraced by the business community, because they simply deal with facts – not judgments of right or wrong. Many large corporations have begun the process of re-assessing their corporate decisions to better align with the Four System Conditions including Scandic Hotels, McDonalds, Bank of America, Home Depot, IKEA, and Nike. You can view their progress at http://www.naturalstep.org/learn/case_summaries.php.

Choices that Sustain

Notice what design decisions lead to the creation of sustainments. For example, creating a long-life product that requires maintenance forces the user to take care of it. This change in product treatment - the relationship between the product and the user - fundamentally shifts from a negligent throw-away mentality to one of deep caring and appreciation over time.

Can you remember the 1950's and 1960's image of a car aficionado lovingly caressing the bumper of his favorite rare vehicle while polishing every fingerprint from the surface? That is the level of relationship we are seeking - one in which the service provided both by the product itself and those involved in its creation, maintenance, upgrading, and final return for recycling, is deeply and personally appreciated. It is a level of honoring that is just beginning to seep into our awareness, but one that essentially recognizes the sacredness of all.

Notes

1. See the World Watch Institute for details of our current ecological situation: http://www.worldwatch.org/topics/ and in the Reference section of this book.
2. Design For The Real World, Papanek, page 80.
3. Page 116 Design For The Real World, Papanek.
4. IBID, page 119
5. IBID, page 156
6. http://www.edf.edu.au The EcoDesign Foundation is the source for much of the information in this chapter. The author gratefully acknowledges their contribution both to this book and to the world of sustainable design.
7. William McDonough and Michael Braungart, Cradle to Cradle-Remaking the Way We Make Things, pages 78-79.
8. Janine Benyus (1997) Biomimicry: Innovation Inspired by Nature http://www.biomimicry.org/intro.html
9. BBC News on Dec 6th 2004 (http://news.bbc.co.uk/1/hi/business/4071503.stm)
10. William McDonough and Michael Braungart, Cradle to Cradle-Remaking the Way We Make Things, pages 78-79.
11. The Natural Step – The Science of Sustainability, an interview by Executive Editor Sarah van Gelder, in YES! Magazine, Fall 1998. Reprinted from YES! magazine, PO Box 10818, Bainbridge Island, WA 98110. Subscriptions: 800/937-4451 Web: www.yesmagazine.org Also see www.NaturalStep.org.

14

TRANSPORTATION

The world literally looks different.

Everything is seen at much greater depth.

Everything is alive and radiant with consciousness.

Everything is aware that it is, and it is aware that everything else is aware.

Nothing is innately inert.

Dr. David R. Hawkins
Power vs Force –
The Hidden Determinants of Human Behavior,
page 194

TRANSPORTATION

We have the option of seeing and designing all transportation as a loving Earth embrace...

Essential systems that form the foundation of industrial civilization depend on unfettered access to cheap oil and natural gas. As supply begins to drop and is no longer able to meet demand, less work will be done – which means less materialist economic activity. Alternative energies, conservation, and new energy carriers such as hydrogen will undoubtedly play a role in future energy systems, yet collectively they will not be enough to preserve industrial society as we know it. The possibility for largely positive outcomes demands significant preparation, action, and enduring behavior change.

Peak Oil - Navigating the Coming Energy Crisis
Pachamama Alliance
http://www.pachamama .org/events/index.htm# 2

Not too long ago my entire relationship with cars transformed. For most of my life I have seen cars as transportation vehicles that got me from point A to point B. I did not see them as sexy or exciting. In fact, I saw them as unfortunate necessities of life that I used as little as possible so as not to further pollute our planet.

The change began when I started placing my attention on the fact that cars work at all. Think about it. There are so many things that could go wrong with a car, especially computerized ones, that it is a wonder they continue to function. Yet they do. Why?

The computer itself is an excellent example of this phenomenon. In my early twenties I worked as a tester for the software programs being developed by a major bank. I was very aware of the infinite number of "bugs" that could occur and the incredibly small number of them that we could anticipate and test for. Yet these huge computers worked most of the time.

Somehow, despite all odds, most machines work. This realization led me to ask myself what allows cars to work sometimes, but not all times? Is it possible to consciously influence the outcome? I began to wonder if our *intention* makes them work.

Then I met a friend who was playing with this same concept. Once, when her car broke down at an extremely inconvenient moment, she did something she'd never done before. Instead of getting angry and feeling victimized by circumstances, she took a deep breath and placed her focus within. Allowing herself to merge with the vehicle, she asked it to work... now. Trusting in her ability to create her own reality, she reached down and turned the key. The car started, allowing her to get safely home, and *then* take the car to the shop for repairs.

Choosing My Reality

I, too, have begun playing with my "reality". One day I awoke before a long road trip full of fear. I knew that something would happen on the road that would put our lives in danger. Yet an Inner-Voice told me to trust that all would be well.

The trip took place at the end of April, well into spring weather, and long after we had to legally remove our studded tires. Suddenly a freak snow storm began as we neared Mt. Shasta. Most of the freeway drivers did not carry chains. Those who did immediately pulled over to apply them.

I did not carry chains, and the snow fell so suddenly that within minutes the off-ramps became impassible. There was no choice but to continue driving in the tire tracks of the car in front of me... the only place not covered with snow.

As the quiet of the snow storm descended upon us, time slowed to almost a standstill, and I perceived multiple "doorways" of possible outcomes before me. I saw that some of those possibilities held our death. Whenever a large truck seemed to be sliding towards us, I put my hand up to stop the energy, said "No", and chose another outcome.

I asked my daughter to join me in creating the outcome we wanted. I asked her to imagine that the sun had already melted the snow beneath our tires such that we always found good traction.

She said, "but Mommy, there is no sun."

I told her to act as if it was *already done,* to simply *know* it. I did the same. At that moment, I had the strong sensation that the car was filled with the warmth and love of many unseen beings. I was filled with a calm certainty that not only would we be safe, but that this was a tremendous opportunity to experience life in a new and powerful way. The car was filled with a deep peace and love. I suddenly knew that we were part of a team of support that encompassed everything. I put my hand up to represent the sun, and we drove for the next hour *knowing* we were safe.

I hold that memory with deep fondness. It was one of the first moments in which I consciously experienced what I had previously just conceived. It represented the moment in which I empowered myself to consciously live outside the perceived limits of the world of "circumstances". I am still exploring this idea of life without limits.

Car as Earth Embrace

Several years ago, as I was learning to merge with nature, I chose to also merge with my car. I learned to "feel" the Earth present in the minerals and elements that made up my car. Suddenly my entire experience of "car" transformed from "polluting machine" to an experience of literally being caressed by the Earth while encapsulated in her arms. Being within my car became an experience of love and nurturance.

Whenever I allowed my awareness to embrace my car as the Earth, I was instantly aware of the aliveness of everything. The road was no longer a road; it was the totality of its elements, including the pulsing life of the planet just beneath its surface, the people who's energy helped create it, and those who traveled on it every day. Even that description is inaccurate, because there was no separation between any of the elements, they simply were all Earth expressing. The experience of driving became much like a Disney cartoon in which the flowers sang, the trees beckoned as I passed them by, and the air popped with aliveness. All pulsated with the song of nature, and all beamed perfection.

I practiced allowing my awareness to include this very unusual, but soon-becoming-normal way of perceiving life as often as I remembered. As I did so, my entire life experience transformed. I could no longer make assumptions about anything, as everything was new. I was humbled by the realization of the enormity of my "not-knowing". At the same time, my ability to "lighten up" and simply allow life to unfold increased as I let go of the need to "know" and control outcome. Things that previously seemed important melted into the background. This moment's joy held my attention.

I began to play with this new-found awareness. I wondered if I could merge with the other travelers who shared the road with me. While commuting to the PlaNetwork conference in San Francisco from my sister's home in the East Bay, I decided to test it out. Every morning, as I drove the hour commute, I allowed my awareness to expand beyond my car and the natural surroundings to the people in

Yesterday the Commerce Department reported that the U.S. has already set a record annual trade deficit of $500 billion, due in large part to record oil consumption and skyrocketing prices for that oil. With 4% of the world's population, we consume a quarter of its oil.

New American Dream
Dec 15th, 2004
http://www.newdream.org/emails/ta2.html

Every tree and plant in the meadow seemed to be dancing, those which average eyes would see as fixed and still.

Mevlana Rumi

(1207-1273)

Let us set as our
national goal, in the
spirit of Apollo, with the
determination of the
Manhattan Project, that
by the end of this decade
we will have developed the
potential to meet our own
energy needs without
depending on any foreign
energy source.

--Richard M. Nixon, on
November 7, 1973

the cars around me. I found I could "feel" their individual energy. Each person broadcast a state-of-being quite clearly. I could even feel their energy approach and then fade ahead as they passed me by. WOW. This was far more fun than listening to the radio!

These practices have helped me broaden and explore my world in ways I never felt possible. I often feel like one of the "new world" explorers. But my expeditions take place in what was once perceived as "familiar" territory, and my "new world" remains new every moment.

Now, when I climb into my car, I am embraced by the Earth in loving tenderness. Now, when I drive, my world unfolds in ways that constantly surprise me. Life is a gift when we allow it to be. It truly is that simple.

The Hypercar

I wondered if we could design our world to reflect gratitude for that gift more completely. Many people are working on just that. (See the chapter on Design for more detail.) One such example is the Hypercar being developed at the Rocky Mountain Institute. It is designed to use 85 percent less energy and materials, while delivering superior safety and performance. Amory and Hunter Lovins write:

> It is now possible to make SUVs that emit nothing but hot water, get a hundred miles a gallon equivalent, and perform like a sports car. Over $5 billion has been committed by automakers to this line of development.[1]

E-Traction

The world literally looks
different. Everything is
seen at much greater
depth. Everything is
alive and radiant with
consciousness.
Everything is aware that
it is, and it is aware that
everything else is aware.
Nothing is innately inert.

Dr. David R. Hawkins
Power vs Force – The
Hidden Determinants of
Human Behavior.

Another innovative idea is being developed by a Dutch company who has eliminated the need for the internal combustion engine. They have developed an electric drive motor that is part of the wheel. Power is provided by using a small diesel generator to charge a bank of batteries whenever the brakes are used. Their bus has been dubbed, "The Whisper," because it is so quiet. They are currently testing several versions, including a next-phase more fuel-efficient version of the Whisper, and two SUV models that provide four-wheel drive by using a motor on each wheel. The advantages are impressive: [2]

Even previous to recent improvements, it obtained 6.3 kilometers per liter of diesel fuel.

Noise pollution was reduced from a normal bus of 75 decibels to 58 decibels.

Because of reduced fuel consumption, air pollution is 60% less than a conventional diesel bus. Particulate emissions are 75% less.

Experiments reveal that fuel consumption can be reduced as much as 66.7%. This translates to a difference of approximately 30,000 liters of diesel fuel per bus per year or the equivalent amount of fuel used to operate 30 average passenger cars for a year.

It is estimated that the incremental cost of an E-Traction bus would be approximately US$25,000-$50,000. With a reduced fuel consumption of only 50% (instead of the expected 66.7% that experiments reveal), a fleet of 38 busses would save the equivalent energy produced annually by a giant 2 megawatt wind generator costing well over US$ 2 million each. The cost of the fleet is estimated at between US$950,000 - $1,900,000. This constitutes a minimum savings of $1,100,000 not counting maintenance, environmental impact studies, and the real estate expense of the wind generators.

Design as a Statement of Gratitude

As we broaden our thinking about transportation possibilities, perhaps the first step is to let go of all the ideas we have about cars. If we let go of all judgments – good or bad – about transportation in general, and instead allow ourselves to imagine the possibility of a world in which we are free to enjoy the pleasure of transportation knowing that it costs the environment nothing; what would that look like? Imagine designing a mode of transportation that actually *supports* the environment just as the cherry tree's fruit supports all life around it:

> As it grows, it seeks its own regenerative abundance. But this process is not single-purpose. In fact, the tree's growth sets in motion a number of positive effects. It provides food for animals, insects, and microorganisms. It enriches the ecosystem, sequestering carbon, producing oxygen, cleaning air and water, and creating and stabilizing soil. Among its roots and branches and on its leaves, it harbors a diverse array of flora and fauna, all of which depend on it and on one another for the functions and flows that support life. And when the tree dies, it returns to the soil, releasing, as it decomposes, minerals that will fuel healthy new growth in the same place.[3]

Perhaps we don't know yet how to create that world, but merely imagining it as a possibility sets the energy moving in that direction. Imagine living a life-style that you know *contributes* to the balance of life on Earth, in a deeply spiritual way. One in which you profoundly and consciously receive the gifts of the Earth and then reciprocate that offering – completing the energy cycle full circle – back to its origin in a beneficial way... in every aspect of your life lived. That joy is the promise, I suspect, that honoring all life offers.

At what point is enough enough?

But how do we get there? When faced with the possibility of choosing a world that honors all, one where the experience of all aspects of life are fulfilling, where our human impact actually co-creates with life instead of damages life, why would we choose anything else?

Yet we do. The facts are alarming. Not only do more people drive cars today, but they spend more time in those cars – lots more time: [4]

> In some parts of the USA people spend approximately one-fifth of their driving time in bumper-to-bumper traffic jams.

> Highway usage is growing by approximately 1.5% - now roads designed for 50,000 cars a day frequently carry 150,000.

> Land costs are so high that designers now consider creating multi-level highways.

> Between 1990 and 2000, workers added approximately 26 hours to their commute time, some added up to 44 hours. What kind of family life does that allow for?

> Nationwide traffic has increased five times greater than road capacity, partially due to the lack of real incentives to carpool or use alternative transportation.

> Busses, trains, walking, and bicycles, account for just 2-5 percent of all travel in the USA.

> Of the 100 million households that make 1 billion trips per day in America, 900 million are by car, 65 million by foot or bicycle, and just 19 million are by mass transit. [2]

Most people think of their daily car cost as negligible, but are they really? In his essay entitled, <u>Reinventing the Wheel</u>, Jim Motavalli points out the actual hidden costs:

According to a new analysis by the Clean Car Campaign, a record 18,000 pounds of mercury pollution was released into the environment last year in the U.S. when scrap vehicles were recycled. An estimated 259,000 pounds of mercury have been released into the environment over the past 30 years. Most troubling, according to the analysis, is that an equal amount could be released over the next two decades if programs are not put in place to recover the mercury in vehicles before they are scrapped.

Clean Car Campaign http://www.cleancarcampaign.org/releases/2004 0407mercury.shtml

According to the International Center for Technology Assessment, a gallon of gasoline actually costs $15.14 when billions of federal and state tax breaks, subsidies, regulations, pollution cleanup costs, and other factors are added up. We are all paying a lot more for gasoline than the price at the pump. There's a reason that people in Europe or Japan pay $5 a gallon for gasoline. High prices are among the few things that actually get people off the highway. In the United States, however, one sure way to lose an election is to propose new gasoline taxes, and the highway lobby, which is one of our most powerful, will definitely work against any candidate who's not highway friendly…

A sad consequence of this is that the developing world is not looking at the United States as a model. These countries admire the American transportation system – even though it's an incredible mess – because people abroad form their images from glitzy television shows. India and China are moving very rapidly toward developing a private car-based infrastructure. The implications for global warming are immense and terrifying.[5]

With the price of oil above $50 a barrel, with political instability in the Middle East on the rise, and with little slack in the world oil economy, we need a new energy strategy. Fortunately, the outline of a new strategy is emerging with two new technologies.

These technologies—gas-electric hybrid engines and advanced-design wind turbines—offer a way to wean ourselves from imported oil. If over the next decade we convert the U.S. automobile fleet to gas-electric hybrids with the efficiency of today's Toyota Prius, we could cut our gasoline use in half. No change in the number of vehicles, no change in miles driven— just doing it more efficiently.

Lester R. Brown
The Short Path To Oil Independence: Gas-Electric Hybrids And Wind Power Offer Winning Combination
October 13 , 2004
http://www.earth-policy.org/Updates/Update43.htm

Considering the overwhelming evidence of the impact fossil fuels have on global warming and air pollution, why do we continue to act in such an irresponsible and unloving manner – to ourselves and the rest of life? The latest evidence is even more startling. In a computer study, 95,000 people from 150 countries were asked to download the global climate model of the Met Office's Hadley Centre for Climate Prediction and Research as a screen saver. The article reported:

> David Stainforth of Oxford University, the chief scientist of the latest study, said processing the results showed the Earth's climate is far more sensitive to increases in man-made greenhouse gases than previously realized. The findings indicate a doubling of carbon dioxide from the pre-industrial level of 280 parts per million would increase global average temperatures by between 2C and 11C.
>
> Mr Stainforth said: "An 11C-warmed world would be a dramatically different world… There would be large areas at higher latitudes that could be up to 20C warmer than today… It is possible that even present levels of greenhouse gases maintained for long periods may lead to dangerous climate change… When you start to look at these temperatures, I get very worried indeed."[6]

Even though the Kyoto treaty was an attempt to stabilize the emission of greenhouse gases at 1990 levels, the report warned that is no longer enough. They must now be brought back to much earlier levels. The study concluded that we are already well within the danger zone, as the fifteen hottest years in history took place after 1980.

Vote with your Money

With study after study producing dire predictions, but a reluctance by industries and governments to seriously address the issue, the ball is now in our court. We who drive must vote with our money. We need to constantly ask for alternative non-polluting vehicles, and then purchase them whenever possible. When all else fails, consumer demand usually works on reluctant corporate executives and even politicians.

Though we have a long history of alternative car designs that are safer and less polluting, (some even proto-typed at taxpayer expense yet never produced for the open market); Honda and Toyota have finally begun to break through the gas-barrier

184

with their hybrid designs. Additionally, Honda came out with the Accord 2.2 i-CTDi Sport that offers an amazing 3.07 litres/100 km or 92 miles per gallon fuel economy using diesel, and was available for purchase in the UK in February (Accord i-CTDi – 4dr) and March (5dr) of 2004. [7]

Additionally, we can participate in programs designed to help us move in a healthier direction. The Clean Car Campaign promotes a performance-based standard that is practically achievable by applying the best practices currently used by the auto industry. Its intention is to promote the development of vehicles that are significantly greener than today's in all phases of their life cycle: their production, use, and end-of-life waste management. The goal was to create standards that are practical, affordable, and promote safety. They include the following components:

- <u>fuel efficiency</u> improvements of 1.5 times the fleet average within that vehicle's class;
- <u>tailpipe emissions</u> meeting California's "Super Ultra Low Emission Vehicle" (SULEV) standard;
- <u>clean manufacturing practices</u> that achieve superior environmental performance in the vehicle's manufacture and use of non-toxic recyclable materials. [8]

They even offer a Clean Car Pledge for all of us who wish to put our intentions in writing, clearly indicating our priorities to the industry.

Public Transportation Alternatives

We must be willing to support the development of clean, efficient mass-transit options similar to those developed in Curitiba, Brazil – perhaps even better. With little motivation to focus our attention on this option, we are just beginning to apply our wonderful ingenuity to solving the problem. I have no doubt that we will come up with many highly creative and original ideas. As with the past alternative prototypes, our challenge will be to sustain support as they move from the idea stage to actual manifestation.

Currently Portland, Oregon offers one of the best light rail systems that is actually free within a ten-block radius in the city center, with a future goal of providing the service for free throughout the entire system. The French TGV system and other high-speed rail systems throughout the world are already successful.

Authentic Solutions – Not Band-Aids

Then we need to go a step further. If we intend to design our world in a way that truly honors all, then we must make sure the changes we suggest are authentic. Alternative choices only help if they are produced using non-polluting energy sources. But much of the interest in, for example, hydrogen as an alternative fuel is spurred on by the governments, private parties, and oil industry who hope to benefit by using oil to produce the hydrogen fuel. The same is true of corn-based solutions that use corn grown in large mono-culture crops using petroleum based fertilizers and pesticides. Those plans perpetuate our dependence on fossil fuels. No wonder the oil industry supports them.

Currently the most polluting industrial countries (the leader being the USA) continue to deny the impact of their actions while developing countries eagerly attempt to duplicate the actions of the worst polluters for short-term gain at the expense of their own natural resources and the health of their people.

The model American puts in 1,600 hours to get 7,500 miles: less than five miles per hour. In countries deprived of a transportation industry, people manage to do the same, walking wherever they want to go, and they allocate only 3 to 8 per cent of their society's time budget to traffic instead of 28 per cent. What distinguishes the traffic in rich countries from the traffic in poor countries is not more mileage per hour of life-time for the majority, but more hours of compulsory consumption of high doses of energy, packaged and unequally distributed by the transportation industry.

Ivan Illich,
Energy and Equity,
1973
http://www.pkimaging.c om/mik/infoall/illich/i itext/ienergy.html

185

We need to express our desire to live the "American dream" within the context of honoring all, being clear about whta that means, clear about our boundaries, and unwilling to compromise safety, health, sustainability, the environment, well-being, and love-based decisions for short-term illusory benefits that ultimately don't support life.

Alternative choices surround us. Hydrogen, electric, hybrid, magnetics, solar - you name it and there is probably a transportation vehicle being tested right now using whatever alternative fuel you can think of – yet with very little funding, political backing, or consumer awareness and demand.

Here's where we can make a difference. We can lobby for funding. We can talk to our politicians and friends to help raise awareness that alternative choices exist. We can help raise consumer demand. We can begin to replace our existing gas consuming vehicles with alternative choices. Finally, we can assess our lifestyles to see where walking, bicycling, or public transportation can be substituted for the easy hop in the car. When we think of it as an expression of love for our planet and all life - instead of a loss of freedom - the choice becomes easier.

Notes

1. Where the Rubber Meets the Road, by Amory Lovins and Hunter Lovins from Nature's Operating Instructions edited by Kenny Ausubel with J.P. Harpignies, page 165.
2. From the E-Traction website, http://www.etraction.com/Release%20e-Traction_bus.htm
3. William McDonough and Michael Braungart, Cradle to Cradle, page 78.
4. Reinventing the Wheel, by Jim Motavalli from Nature's Operating Instructions edited by Kenny Ausubel with J.P. Harpignies, pages 176-178.
5. Reinventing the Wheel, by Jim Motavalli from Nature's Operating Instructions edited by Kenny Ausubel with J.P. Harpignies, page 177.
6. Global Warming Is 'Twice As Bad As Previously Thought, by Steve Connor of The Independent U.K. dated January 27, 2005
7. http://www.carpages.co.uk/honda/honda_diesel_sets_new_world_records_12_05_04.asp?switched=on&echo=182432208
8. http://www.cleancarcampaign.org/standards.shtml . The Clean Car Pledge is located at http://www.cleancarcampaign.org/pledge.shtml.

15

EDUCATION

Education is the discovery of who you are
as you interact with the energies of life.

EDUCATION

How can we raise each other?

In order to talk about education we have to first go through a small but very significant perceptual shift. I want you to look deep inside of you for that inner child that we commonly think of as our innocent and vulnerable side. The side that needs to be listened to and nurtured. Try not to let your adult voice get in the way. Completely put yourself into you as a child and allow yourself to feel what that child felt without any adult judgments about it.

Are you there? Now take that inner child back to school. How did you experience school as that child? Was it fun, exciting, and could you hardly wait to get more? Did you feel listened to and as if your thoughts and feelings mattered to the adults and other children alike, as if they thought you truly made a contribution? Did you feel as if you had the whole world available to explore every day?

If you did feel this way then your experience was very different than most. Looking at the stereotypes that we have around school it would seem that most people's experience is not a pleasant one.

Now let's look at those children as adults. How many of them became what they wanted to be when they grew up? How many looked at the entire realm of possibilities and felt they could be anything and do anything they wanted? How many didn't have that dream fade away as they got older and "reality" set in? How many felt pressure to choose something all of a sudden in high school that would determine the rest of their lives?

My children often came home talking about how much they hated school. I saw them go through the same horrible experiences that I remembered from my childhood. I wondered how we could provide our children with educational experiences that truly honored them, that went beyond telling them we believed in their potential, to providing them with the experiences necessary for them to come to that conclusion on their own. And what would this school be like if it inspired everyone participating – students, families, and staff alike – to actively explore the idea of honoring *all* life through every facet of their educational experience?

These question come from a perceptual shift so immense, that the search for their answers requires the creation of an entirely new approach to education; one that acknowledges the interrelatedness of all disciplines and viewpoints. In short, it requires an educational model that mimics real life.

Listening

One of the primary differences in this new approach to education is the willingness to listen to what students have to say. The underlying assumption is that their feedback and desires are essential to an educational system designed to serve their needs.

I had the honor of working with an organization who's goal was to transform education from an often fear-based and coercive experience, to one that honored each person as perfect and complete. I learned much from that experience. As I explored new educational models, I tried them out in my own life. My art students

You begin to see the invisible forest creatures. Not at first by sight, but by tracking them, by seeing the signs and trails that they leave behind, that weave across the landscape in so intricate a manner, like lace. You begin to actually see flow lines, like feng shui, of the animals themselves, of how they affect the landscape. It's a beautiful journey, to explore the land through the eyes of the various mammals that live there.

Awakening Our Senses to Learn - Interview with Wilderness Educator Jon Young

Christina Bertea, Interviewer

Education For Community Building

http://www.newvillage.net/Journal/Issue3/3young.html

were the recipients of my experiments into what worked and what didn't work. Most importantly, I asked each student what worked and didn't work for them individually, and then I listened carefully to the answers. This, I believe, is the necessary dialogue that will transform education on our planet.

HALI

Even though our initial project never completely manifested in the way we intended, we found widespread enthusiasm and eagerness to participate. The idea for the Honoring All Life Institute (HALI) grew from that first effort.

Just as each of us personally explores the question, "What do I want?" in order to make healthy choices in life; HALI asks the same question in the context of education. But we don't just ask it of parents, staff, or even students – we include the entire community in the discussion. Why not? It is arguably one of the primary jobs of any effective educational system to prepare our future voters and social designers to be effective. Thus, HALI is intended to be community based. Much attention will go into asking questions about what is needed, wanted, and what truly serves each community's goals.

Most of all, it is intended to be a *co-creative* exploration. As you read, try to imagine what you would do to enhance these ideas. Many of the concepts presented here are being enacted in various educational settings throughout the world. Hopefully they will provide a springboard for your own experiment in education, both for yourself and the people in your life – no matter what their age. And if you find your passions being ignited by these concepts, please join us.

The HALI Mission

Our mission is to create an educational system that utilizes the unique magnificence of each participant in order to create an enriched learning environment in which the exploration of what it means to "honor all life" can be fully explored.

It is intended to enhance the student's innate ability to explore the richness of life and Self, while developing life skills including: *how* to learn, perceptual awareness, conflict resolution, self-love (which automatically includes the ability to love everyone and everything else), conscious choice-making, integrous self-assessment, creative expression, and gratitude awareness (applied systems theory), all in a context of honoring all expressions of life.

Basic Principles

Like all effective educational models, HALI embraces several potent Principles:

WHOLENESS – Each participant is seen and treated as a whole and complete person - lacking nothing. As a result the child is not seen as an empty container needing to be filled with knowledge. Instead, the purpose of education is to make the child conciously aware of who they *already are* in relation to the universe around them. It embodies both inner and outer exploration, ultimately understanding that they are one and the same. Wholeness, by definition, embraces a partnership model over the old dominator-trance model. Therefore "teachers" are seen as partners in the educational process – facilitators along the way. Likewise, everyone is seen as

What's Wrong with Environmental Education?

In being asked to address the issue of "Environmental Education for school and/or corporation," I would first like to say that I consider "environmental education" a bad idea. I am opposed to teaching anyone, from school child to corporate CEO, that we live in an "environment."

As I say at length in my book EarthDance, we must begin by changing the way we speak of Earthlife. We must abandon the false concept of life on Earth, rather than the more appropriate concept: life of Earth. The Earth is not a non-living planet with some accidental life upon its surface; it is a living planet of which we are an inseparable part. Its life story begins with its crustal elements recycling from and back to its molten depths, continues as they repackage themselves into bacteria, which in turn reorganize the crust and create a new atmosphere as well as the metabolic chemistries of seas and soils. Earthlife is a single complex geobiological process.

Elisabet Sahtouris, Ph.D.
Tachi Kiuchi's Tokyo newsletter, The Bridge March 2002

both a learner and teacher at all times. The concept of Partnership is incorporated into every aspect of the HALI educational context.

RESPONSIBILITY – Each participant takes full responsibility for choices made, and is first accountable to Self, then to the community at large. Together with his support Team (consisting of himself, his teachers, and legal guardians), the Learner is responsible for choosing the topics of active exploration and his programs of participation; determining the skills necessary to accomplish each goal, designing the time-frame, and then commiting himself to meeting those goals.

Self assessment is the best indicator of accomplishment. A student portfolio of work is maintained and constantly updated. But more importantly, the student is required – as in life – to self-assess his success.

Self-assessment is handled uniquely at HALI. At the beginning and end of each day the student meets briefly with a teacher-partner to assess whether the day's goals were accomplished. If not, obstacles are discussed. Blame and make-wrong are never part of this experience. Instead, encouragement and problem solving highlight each meeting. The intention is to create an environment in which self-assessment is a natural and comfortable – even enjoyable – experience.

In the thirty years that the Sudbury models throughout the world have used a similar process instead of grades, their students have entered major universities as easily as those attending traditional schools. Their admissions procedure consists of a personal interview and portfolio review instead of SAT scores and grade-point averages. With the number of home schooled applicants rapidly increasing, universities are quite open to this procedure. Since the HALI system is designed to encourage each student to follow their passions and excel, the percentage of HALI students with the ability to get into top universities should be much higher than most traditional schools.

PASSIONATE EXPLORATION - The learner is free to explore who she is, her passions, and the mysteries of life with all the natural exuberance that adults feel when joyously following their creative passion. Ideally the setting will be richly creative and natural. In fact, following one's passions will be a prerequisite of the entire staff so that everyone models and experiences fulfillment.

COMMUNITY - The student experiences multiple levels of community as an integral part of life, not as a separate entity outside the school/family walls. The school is a community itself, and the "outside" community (the one in which the school is located) is seen as the container for the school – there is no separation. As such, the community is invited to participate and feel partnership with the school as much as possible. Equally, the entire school community is encouraged to experience "school" as having no walls – so that learning takes place in a multitude of real life settings. This "Sense of Place" is an essential element of honoring, as we explore the interconnected, imbeded circles of life that make up our community. Other schools are also included in our definition of "community," resulting in the experience of competition being exchanged for co-creation and partnership.

PARTICIPATION - The student learns though hands-on experiences whenever possible... just as one does in "real" life. Participation and inclusion make learning exciting and joyful.

UNIQUENESS - The learning style of each individual is honored and thoroughly explored.

DEMOCRACY – How can we expect our children to understand and support democracy if they don't experience it in their schools and homes? HALI models the democratic process by allowing each student full voice in all aspects of her educational experience. Conflict resolution is seen as a learning opportunity, and everyone who wishes to participate may do so. Conflicts are handled in the moment, following agreed-upon methods, with each school participant having one vote (no matter what their age). The highest priority is to create a safe space in which inner needs and feelings can be fully explored. Within that safety, the goal is never punishment, but instead – using communication tools like Nonviolent Communication, Compassionate Listening, and Dynamic Facilitation – the intention is understanding, healing, creative resolution, and the honoring of all involved. Daniel Greenberg describes the quality of life in the first democratic school in the USA that he helped create in 1968:

> Lessons learned here become tools for a lifetime. What is mastered is the ability to concentrate and focus attention unsparingly on the task at hand, without regard for limitations--no tiredness, no rushing, no need to abandon a hot idea in the middle to go on to something else. This "lesson" is retained for life...
>
> The absence of fear is what epitomizes democratic schools and makes their atmosphere so unique. At Sudbury we say, "It's one of the things you can't help noticing in the school--that little kids look adults straight in the eye." Adults aren't authority figures, and we are very proud of the beautiful results of age-mixing. It goes without saying that when you mix ages people are going to learn from each other because they have different levels of experience. That happens everywhere. The beauty of age-mixing at democratic schools is that it is without fear. Four year olds walk up to 17 year olds and have no anxiety in relating to them.[1]

New tools in democracy, like Wisdom Councils, the World Café, Open-Space Technology; as well as those tools designed by the students themselves, will be fully explored.

ONENESS – Each participant is an interdependent part of nested wholes. The myriad connections that sustain life will be embraced and explored in all aspects of the HALI experience.

Life-Enriching Education

Before we go on I want to briefly introduce one of the many progressive and creative educational concepts that HALI utilizes. Marshall Rosenberg's Life-Enriching Education ideas incorporate his Nonviolent communication process. Nonviolent Communication (NVC) focuses attention on the feelings and needs that motivate people, and the actions that best meet their needs (at no one's expense.) Rosenberg envisions education that teaches autonomy, interdependence, and the organizational skills necessary to create what he calls, "Life-Enriching systems" in which to live. His stated goal sounds very similar to the experience of Dynamic Facilitation (see the chapter on Co-Creation):

On the practical level, listening with empathy to those with whose positions we disagree increases the chances that they will want to listen to us... Once Judy's experiences were heard fully, magic happened, her heart opened, and a profound shift took place in her.

When we use force, blame and self-righteousness instead, even if we manage to create the outcome we want in the short run, we distance ourselves from those whose actions we want to change. Success in the short run does not lead to the transformation we so wish for, neither in ourselves nor in those we are trying to change.

Miki Kashtan
No Enemies, No Demands
http://www.nonviolentcommunication.com/resources/SC_No_Enemies_No_Demands_M_Kashtan.pdf

To express our needs without blaming others and to listen respectfully to other's needs, without anyone giving up or giving in – and thus create a quality of connection through which everyone's needs can be met. [2]

Addtionally, his description of Life-Enriching Organizations could be describing HALI itself:

Life-Enriching organizations are characterized by fairness and equity in how resources and privileges are distributed. People in positions of leadership serve their constituencies rather than desiring to control them. The nature of laws, rules, and regulations are consensually defined, understood, and willingly followed. [3]

640 million children in developing countries live without adequate shelter: one in three.
400 million children have no access to safe water: one in five.
270 million children have no access to health services: one in seven.
More than 121 million Primary-school-age children are out of school; the majority of them are girls.

Source: Unicef, http://www.unicef.org/sowc05/english/childhood underthreat.html

Life Skills

Now that we know the basic principles of the HALI education system what skills do we want children to gain through this new approach? Of course there are the basic skills we want our children to possess by the time they are adults, those necessary to create a successful and profitable business and to participate fully and confidently in life's rich experiences (basics like reading, math, language skills, computer technology, logic, etc.)...

But in addition to these basics, what skills do children need in order to make their education perfectly customized to their own learning style? How can they shape their own honoring all life perceptual filters? Each of the following ten skills is a new approach that will help students grasp what honoring themselves, their educational process, and all life truly means.

1. **How to learn and honor one's own learning style**
   Learning *how* to learn is one of the most valuable skills one can acquire. It allows each student to self-direct exploration wherever her passion flows. Likewise, learning one's own unique learning *style* offers insights into the best methods of personally gathering knowledge. This is an on-going exploration that will constantly provide the student with new skills and strategies.

2. **How to use design skills in all aspects of life**
   Although rarely acknowledged, the way we live our lives is an expression of design. Our life systems – education, economy, government, community, business, healthcare, etc. – are evolving, living systems of design. A designer's skills include the ability to look at a project from multiple points-of-view, always seeking to think and perceive "outside the box" of common practices, searching for those creative ideas that leap beyond the merely adequate to the sublime. Emphasis will be placed on exploring and creating "sustainments," design that encompasses the full life cycle of any design project. (See the chapter on Design for details.) Design techniques will be incorporated into our skills bank, empowering participants to intentionally choose to design their world as a reflection of their own unique magnificent contribution.

3. **How to listen deeply to one's heart and body**
   Children will be encouraged to pay attention to what their bodies are telling them. For example, when I am humgry what kind of food does my body need? Not what my mind wants but what my body really needs right now to feel it's best. This same skill can be used for the heart. What does my heart tell me when I really listen to it? What really feels right? What honors me and those

around me? Using this skill of listening to their inner selves will help students understand and honor their own needs and those of others.

4. **How to honor ALL life in one's everyday choices**

   Honoring all, means seeing the interconnectedness of all life, and consciously making choices that express one's own heart-felt beliefs in relationship to all aspects of life, while still honoring the aliveness, sustainability, and diversity of all. It means seeing ourselves as Learning-Beings - always open to the possible – and willingly acknowledging that everything (and everyone) is our teacher.

5. **How to see and communicate from the heart**

   Our perceptions are limited by our beliefs, and therefore are always subjective. Learning to be open to seeing beyond previously perceived limitations expands our awareness and experience of life. Learning to honor other's perceptions as unique and valid also honors our own.

   Using the skills developed through differing communication modalities, we explore how to communicate in a manner that validates each other's experience while expressing our own needs and feelings.

6. **How to empower yourself and others to express innate magnificence**

   Only when we feel good about ourselves can we be fully present in the moment, without dragging issues from the past (or fears about tomorrow) into today. Marshall Rosenberg describes this environment so well:

   Students educated in such a judgment-free environment learn because they choose to, not to earn rewards or avoid moralistic judgments or punishment. 5

   They learn for the absolute joy of it. Learning to embrace every aspect of ourselves - even those we have judged - leads to self-acceptance and wholeness. Seeing ourselves as magnificent learning-beings also allows us to see others in the same light. It is from this space that we can truly empower ourselves and others to contribute our best.

7. **Peer to peer learning, reflecting life's realities**

   Adults do not live in a world divided by age groups, they naturally relate to those who resonate with what excites them, regardless of their age. We honor our children when we allow them to do the same.

   Likewise, one of the best methods of learning is to teach. Encouraging participants to share their skills and knowledge not only increases their learning experience while building self-confidence, but it allows them to share their passions with others, one of the most fulfilling experiences humans enjoy.

8. **How to Self-assess and Self-correct**

   Effective adults learn to observe without judgment, to self-assess, and then to make appropriate corrections in whatever they are doing.

   Being an effective kid is just as important. An opportunity to self-assess with a partner (teacher) will take place in the morning and again just before school ends each day. In this way, each student can learn to track her own progress against a set of declared goals that are mutually agreed upon . "Mistakes" or missed deadlines are seen as learning tools or simply as feedback, and not as errors. Accountability is ensured by a description of what was accomplished instead of grades. This way the student participates directly in and takes full responsibility for his own accomplishments based on a comparison of his abilities at the beginning of the assessment period and at the end. *This stresses cooperation and*

My position, more and more, became one of facilitator. I would guide them into new directions and areas; I would hint and suggest and, more often than not, there would be the subtle challenge to push on the present limits. I, in turn, found myself forced to keep up, to constantly press against the invisible envelope of my own assumed limitations. I didn't have to try and give, they demanded and took. They demanded honesty, respect, knowledge and challenge, and, they had fun while doing it.

R. Hawk Starkey, Ph.D.

<u>*Will the Real Teacher Please Stand Up?*</u> *Page 138-9*

Being open to the gifts we offer each other is one of the greatest gifts we can offer to ourselves. Acknowledging those gifts is at the heart of honoring.

eliminates competition as motivation for approval. Rosenberg describes the effect of a typical competitive-based grading system compared to a cooperation-based model:

> …I saw the grading system communicating that competitiveness was to be valued above interdependence. In schools using grades competitively I see students learning that it is not only appropriate but actually expected that one climbs over others in order to attain a high grade. I said that I would prefer to see interdependence stressed in the classroom, to see students learn that their individual welfare is interwoven with the welfare of others. In such a classroom, the stress would not be on competing to get the grade but on everyone cooperating to see that all objectives are reached. [6]

Additionally, HALI encourages the ability to listen to your own heart and then trust your own decisions. Trust can only flourish in an atmosphere free from judgment, so we learn to treat ourselves and others with non-judgmental tenderness.

9. **How to make conscious choices and take full responsibility for them**
   When we are willing to observe free from judgment, an infinite field of possibilities unfolds. This is the ground from which conscious creative choice is possible, and in that space, taking responsibility for our choices becomes natural.

10. **How to create and run a profitable business that expresses the joy and essence of who you are**
    When we ask ourselves, as parents, what skills we want our children to possess, one that tops many lists is being able to take a creative vision from an idea to reality in a profitable way. HALI teaches business that honors all involved. Participants will have many opportunities to learn these skills by opting into student-run businesses. The profits from these businesses will be used to fund special experiences of the students' choice.

These hands-on, real-life business experiences will have tangible feedback. Our evaluation quesitons include:

- Did we create our intended result?
- Did we create a profit – (and how do we *define* profit)?

Our intention isn't just to pretend or create a simulated business, our intention is to assist the student in creating a *real* business that succeeds in producing both life lessons and profit. The idea is to empower students. By the time a student leaves school, our intention is that she would have experienced a vast array of business types and models – all of them profitable – and all of them aimed at providing services or products that honor all. Ideally, all of the business ideas will come from the students themselves.

We plan a broad range of business adventures, hoping to meet each student's passions in the process. An ideal location would allow for a variety of opportunities of student-run business experiences. The intention behind these programs is two-fold: First, to offer the students hands-on experience in all aspects of manifesting their dreams, in a setting that steps beyond practice to actual accountability and success. Second, to empower the students to experience their ability to manifest their dreams for the school (and eventually their lives) as they creatively provide the funds necessary to accomplish their goals. Students will determine the use of all student-earned funds, including scholarships and special events, trips, or equipment, etc. All of these programs will be mentored by experts in each field.

What questions do we ask?

When we allow ourselves to shift our perception such that a new world of possibilities is constantly available, our experience of life dramatically alters. Education no longer seems to be a separate experience relegated to the early years of life – it becomes the description of life itself – and everything (and everyone) becomes your teacher.

Questions become more important than answers, as they form the pathways of discovery. For example, within the context of a school setting, questions shift from "What should we learn?" to deeper issues. Here are a few suggestions:

- *How* do you learn? Not only does this question probe the unique learning style of each individual, but it can go further. How can we constantly expand our learning styles and methodologies, pushing the envelope of the possible? As we expand our perceptual abilities, how does that affect the process of learning itself?

- **What outcome do you wish to achieve?** The idea of focusing on the outcome desired is far from new. But at HALI, were interested in asking the question from a deeper space of inquiry. While skills are important to master, the core of the question can be paraphrased as "**What do you want?**" Another way of asking it is, "**Who do you choose to BE?**" We're not interested in simply discussing professional options (although that discussion will also take place), we want to know:
    a. What kind of human do you want to be?
    b. What do you stand for?
    c. How do your decisions reflect your self-image?
    d. What is important in life?
    e. What contribution do you want to make?
    f. What gifts do you bring?
    g. What excites you to the core of your being?
    h. What talents can you share right now?

We don't just ask these questions of our students, we ask them of everyone, because we are all learners. Likewise, this discussion doesn't just take place once, it is an on-going dialog that is constantly reviewed and updated.

- **What do you need to know and what do you need to do, to accomplish that goal?** We follow the previous questions with this one. In other words, how can we make this real?
    i. What skills do you need?
    j. How will you obtain them? What costs are involved? What materials?
    k. How soon do you want to learn it? What is your timeframe?
    l. How will you know when you have accomplished your goal? How will you be certain that you have mastered the learning ?

WE ARE ALL ONE means that if one of us is suffering, we all are. We may not be able to solve the circumstances of life, nor is that always in a person's best interest; but we can always offer compassion and love instead of indifference. It means that when taking action is clearly an expression of honoring - we do so. WE ARE ALL ONE means treating each other as a divine aspect of God. It means choosing to act from UNITY instead of separation, and to seek a win-win solution whenever possible. Most of all, WE ARE ALL ONE means honoring ALL life's expressions in the scope of our daily decisions.

Along with these basic questions, the way we approach learning differs greatly according to our perceptual filters. For example, a whole systems approach might generate the following questions:

- What systems can you identify?

- How do they relate with each other?

Finally, in our intention to explore what it means to "honor all," HALI includes these timely questions as part of the ever-expanding curriculum:

- How can we design our products, living spaces, food production, economies, and businesses in a way that supports *all* life, at the expense of none?

- How can we make decisions that include the diverse expressions of life in the scope of our deliberations?

- How can we design our own educational and cultural systems such that they support an ever-increasing expansion of our perceptual awareness, with the ultimate goal of honoring and encouraging human creativity?

- How do we make decisions? What do our decisions say about who we are, individually and collectively, and how we perceive the possible?

These questions are obviously appropriate for older learners, but we can begin to integrate their frame-of-reference into all classes. As we do, both students and teachers become learners together.

I have personally witnessed children as young as eight discuss the impact of their decisions, not only on themselves; but on what their decisions say about who they see themselves to be, what they as a group stand for, and the impact their decisions make on the community as a whole. When we offer children the opportunity to explore life's rich nuances of meaning *during* their education instead of afterwards, we create vibrant, participatory, engaged adults. Isn't that the real goal of all education?

How can we raise each other?

As our questions shift, our perception automatically expands, revealing a model of life that is far more complex than previously known. The subtle seen and unseen ways in which we support each other, and life supports us, can no longer be dismissed. **HALI seeks to honor that reality** by actively exploring how education and community can be experienced as one. As a result, we've re-written the old adage, "It takes a village to raise a child," by acknowledging the reciprocal nature of life - that we each have gifts to share and receive – and thereby transforming it into the question: How Can We Raise Each Other?

HALI's answer to that question is embodied in the following concepts:

- **We honor each other's wisdom.** Because we see each being as whole and complete, we do not assume that we have anything to "teach" others, but instead we embrace the reality that we each play the role of teacher and student throughout life. Our goal, therefore, is to facilitate learning. We emphasize *how to learn* and *life skills,* more than teaching merely the accumulation of data.

- **We honor the Oneness of life.** As we learn to perceive the interconnected web of life, we begin to see that what happens to any of us, happens to all of us, whether the effect is obvious or not. Our response to life therefore, is one of creative engagement, actively living the world we envision, through our daily choices. We are no longer willing to play the role of life's victim, nor do we succumb to the illusion of lack. Instead, we actively choose to co-create a life that works for all, whatever that looks like at any given moment.

- **We honor our choices by taking full responsibility for them.** Each of us is free to choose who we are in every moment. Therefore we take full responsibility for our choices and the impact they have in our life and in the world around us.

- **We honor each person's perception as a truth in their life.** All perception is subjective. We are aware that there are as many realities as there are beings experiencing them. Therefore we can let go of being "right" about anything, and simply have fun.

Honoring Children

The test of any theory is always in its application to real-life situations. Not too long ago, Barbara Lynn Kukla, Catherine Fabjance, and Donald T. Beelow had the privilege of applying similar concepts in their own small school called Heartlight Chicago. Unfortunately short-lived, it closed when sponsored funding ended. However, it clearly demonstrated the potential power of education designed to offer learner-led experiential discovery as a potent educational methodology. Most of all, it revealed the power of TRUST in the innate wisdom and loving hearts of all participants in the educational setting. Here is their phenomenal story:

> You can create on paper and with adults all you want, what looks to be an incredible, amazing system of education, but the reality is that in the end, the kids define what it ultimately is. The process was dynamic, fluid and constantly changing, and none of us were completely prepared for how it finally emerged.
>
> Our population was made up of children from diverse backgrounds and educational experiences. These include children labeled gifted, ADHD, Autistic and Dyslexic. They came from affluent and low-income households. They were public, private, charter and home-schooled students. They were white, black and Asian.
>
> The initial class included only one girl, age 6. The boys' ages ranged between 7 and 13 years. The first week a war erupted between the boys. This was not the loving, peaceful, spiritually centered HeartLight Community we envisioned. This was armed conflict and included arms sales and weapons of mass destruction. (Apparently President Bush was looking in the wrong country).
>
> Actually, the weapons were constructed from plastic tubes, which were part of the base of an indoor basketball net. They created weapons and then sold them through the shop, which was one of the rooms in the school. There were two sides and all the boys participated. This resulted in crying, yelling, anger and hurt feelings. As a staff, having a vision for a peaceful and loving self-created community, we were conflicted as to what to do. There was a part of us that wanted to jump in and stop them, while the other part knew we had to let them work through it for a transformation to actually occur. Almost all of the boys individually asked us each day; "Why aren't you stopping us? This is stupid." Our response was always the same; "Why don't you stop yourselves? This is democratic school. It's not up to us to stop you. We are all in charge here."

We decided to hold a democratic meeting to talk about the war. The children said, "The war is stupid, we hate it, nobody wins, and everyone just ends up getting hurt and mad." They decided to call a truce. By the next day they were at it again. We had another democratic meeting, with the staff asking why if its so upsetting to them were they doing it again. One of the students replied, "Because everyone else is doing it." It was then that one of the boys decided to draw up a peace treaty. He researched previously written documents and the war was over. They stopped themselves. If the staff had stopped them, they would've found a way to continue behind our backs. We felt that in the end, it was a week packed full of lessons for life. The children got to experience the reasons for choosing peace rather than war. All this in the first week of school. We as the staff felt blessed to have witnessed this eruption of war and creation of peace within five days.

The democratic meetings became a way of resolving issues and deciding policy at HeartLight. A different child was voted in each week to chair the meeting and record the process. The children nominated themselves to act as either secretary or chairman, and each community member had an equal vote. This included the adult community members. These meetings came at a price however. They were time consuming and boring for this particular population. If you were a fly on the wall, you'd see barefoot children playing with puppets or standing on their heads, while doodling throughout the entire meeting. Jumping off couches was a frequent meeting activity. At times it was almost impossible to read the minutes, due to pictures, distractions and scribbling on the form.

It was decided by the group that after 3 disruptions during a meeting, the disrupting child or adult would have to vacate the room and read or work quietly elsewhere throughout the remainder of the meeting. They would lose their opportunity to vote on any issues brought up during that meeting. This quickly became an easy out for those students bored with the process. Questions began to arise from all of the students; "Why do we have to sit through these meetings? They take too long and are boring." The staff replied that it would be easier for us as well to become a dictatorship rather than a democracy. We could make up all the rules and decide policy and consequences. They would have no voice and would just have to comply with whatever we decided. After a brief discussion, it was unanimously decided to continue with the meetings. They decided they didn't want to lose the privilege of having a voice. Everyone participated from then on.

They even went so far as to form a judicial committee and another group of meetings. We had a jar that was used to collect charges the students or staff called on other members of the community. Several times a week we would hold a meeting of the judicial committee, where consequences for infractions were decided. At first the jar was filled every day, as the children got a taste of power and chose to exercise it regularly. This quickly changed, as we all had charges brought against us, regardless of sex, age or position in the community. The meetings were unbearably long.

At HeartLight, we didn't have a long list of specific rules. Guidelines for behavior included; Respect, Honesty, Responsibility, Awareness, Gratitude and Forgiveness. They had to determine whether their actions reflected these values or not. Most or all of the infractions listed in the jar had to do with lack of respect. It was an amazing thing to witness our youngest female student, who came to us stuttering and timid, find her voice and say to our oldest male student, "You are not respecting me." She received an apology as a result, and from then on, other students called him on his disrespectful attitude as this behavior gradually changed.

Many things happened during our meetings, which were transformational, and life changing. We saw a student melt down due to a charge, and another student step in to nurture her ego with a genuine compliment. The female student expressed that no one liked her or cared. A male student, who up until that point had not spoken up at the meetings, volunteered his support by saying in front of his peers; "I like you and I think you're pretty." That straightened things out and quieted down the group. You could hear a pin drop.

As a democratic community, part of our responsibility was caring for each room in the building. At the end of the day, each adult and child was teamed up for chores to straighten up a specific area. The most common consequence for a personal infraction was doing someone else's chores for the day. This consequence was decided on by a unanimous vote during a democratic meeting.

While this consequence was sufficient in most cases, some charges required more serious consequences. The group decided that serious infractions, involving physical violence against another person, would result in immediate dismissal and suspension for the next day. If this happened more than two times, the community would meet to decide whether or not the student was able to remain successfully in the community. One of the most difficult decisions the community had to make was the expulsion of a well-loved student. They decided that it wasn't healthy for the community to feel unsafe and for that child's self esteem to be diminished on a daily basis. The learning experience throughout this process involved many levels of awareness and responsibility.

Our HeartLight School was open for just 6 months. In that time we experienced first hand what occurs when the responsibility for learning and living is placed squarely in the hands of the children. We had a war, a death (a tadpole), a funeral and a government. We saw auras, meditated, did yoga, played soccer, had a band, put on a show, painted, danced and had several theatrical performances. There was drama on and off the stage with plenty of tears, action and life altering decisions made in unison. This was a group of children, initially drunk with power and off to war, who in the end hugged and held and cried as one. The experience was life changing, wonderful and painful, all at once.

Was there learning? That can only be individually assessed. As grateful directors and founders of the school, we say the lessons learned in that short time were too numerous to document and too grand to articulate in a fashion that any current system of labeling and recording could encompass. Certainly there was growth, but the proof of that remains within each of the 25 children and the many adults fortunate enough to participate.

We feel blessed and honored to have met these children, and shared some of their journey. The doors have closed on this specific school in Palatine, Illinois, (December 2003), but the dream of empowering children has not. We are currently supporting two other schools set to open in September of 2004, and 2005. The story of these last three years does not end here, but begins renewed with a wealth of experience and a host of people now joining with us to create a space where children can realize their personal greatness while developing their passions and discovering their purpose.

Are we brave enough to allow children the opportunity to explore themselves fully? Children want to connect and contribute as much as adults. As we develop our ability to perceive the wholeness of life, not only around us but also *within;* we create the opportunity to blur the lines between student/teacher, school/community, humanity/nature. As a result, we can finally begin to redesign our structures in a way that honors the the nested web of interdependent support systems that constitute life.

A New Beginning

Imagine your first day at school. Instead of telling you what you will learn, the teacher invites you to participate in something new and wonderful...

"Today we are asking you to put on your lab robe and enter the world of the scientist. Here at HALI, you are being asked to participate in a new experiment, with you as both the scientist and the subject of study. We will explore a new way of approaching life, one that has rarely been explored before, so we need to take careful notes to document the progress of our research. And because this is a new way of exploring, we are asking that we each bring our most creative self to this experiment. We need your best ideas. We can guarantee you that this will be the most fun educational journey you can take, because you will be directing it. But it will also stretch you to think in new ways as never before. Are you ready?"

Our best tools already lay within our grasp. All that is necessary is the willingness to let go of ways of perceiving that no longer support life and embrace those that do. It is an act of bravery to step into the unknown. But the path of recognizing that Life always supports Life; and then structuring our educational systems to reflect that realilty doesn't rely on the unknown, because we are provided with excellent teachers everywhere we look, including within our own hearts.

We never stop learning in life. It is our hope that the ideas presented here will inspire you to creatively begin to explore honoring all life within your own educational system.

Place Value

In a continued effort to learn the most effective and fun techniques in teaching various subjects, I have been taking a class lately on how to teach math. In it, we have been using a manipulative called a "Place Value Mat" which consists of a fairly large flat sheet of sturdy paper or felt with one's, ten's, hundred's, and thousand's columns permanently drawn upon the surface. Using tiny snap-together blocks, a student can then re-create most numbers by placing the correct number of blocks in each column. Very quickly, the value of ONE becomes clear.

If the one is in the ten's column, the number is 10 times the value of a one in the one's column. If it is in the hundred's column, it is 100 times the value of a one in the ten's column. You get the point very quickly.

Just as the value of ONE in math was not taught so clearly when I was in school, we have not taught the value of ONE in our communities with any degree of clarity.

ONE person can accomplish the work of 10, 100, or even 1,000 if that person places herself in the most effective situation. When the concepts of co-creation and interdependence are embraced, the illusions of separation and solo effort dissolve into mutually beneficial teamwork. The one in a tens column is only there by virtue of the other nine pieces supporting it. The adding of only one more piece transforms the entire group into a cohesive unit of greater value, still called "One."

Notes

Please see the Reference Section for schools and programs that already support some of the concepts proposed at HALI.

1. R-E-S-P-E-C-T: What Children Get in Democratic Schools, (Mothering - *Issue 103, November/December 2000)*, Daniel Greenberg, http://www.mothering.com/articles/growing_child/education/democratic_schools.html
2. Marshall Rosenberg, Life-Enriching Education – Nonviolent Communication Helps Schools Improve Performance, Reduce Conflict, and Enhance Relationships, Puddle Dancer Press, 2003,   page 3.
3. http://www.nonviolentcommunication.com/books/emotional-intelligence.html Marshall Rosenberg, Life-Enriching Education – Nonviolent Communication Helps Schools Improve Performance, Reduce Conflict, and Enhance Relationships, Puddle Dancer Press, 2003, page 3.
4. http://www.partnershipway.org/pep/newkeys.htm
5. Marshall Rosenberg, Life-Enriching Education – Nonviolent Communication Helps Schools Improve Performance, Reduce Conflict, and Enhance Relationships, Puddle Dancer Press, 2003, page 15.
6. Marshall Rosenberg, Life-Enriching Education – Nonviolent Communication Helps Schools Improve Performance, Reduce Conflict, and Enhance Relationships, Puddle Dancer Press, 2003, page 89.
7. See http://www.tetonscience.org/ and http://www.journeysschool.org/
8. Elisabet Sohtouris, Ph.D, Tachi Kiuchi's Tokyo newsletter, The Bridge March 2002 http://www.ratical.org/LifeWeb/Articles/theBridge0302.html.

16

FOOD

There are people in the world so hungry,
that God cannot appear to them
except in the form of bread.
Mahatma Gandhi

FOOD

When all is seen as One, eating becomes a celebration of the sacred – it is the ritualized eternal dance of giver and receiver that can only be completed through conscious gratitude.

My concepts of food have significantly changed recently. I have come to four realizations regarding the act of feeding ourselves. I share them with you to spark your own inquiry into this most common of everyday events. Together, I believe these four realizations revolutionize our human relationship to food.

Concept One: Food is mostly energy

We are taught that science can literally calculate the quantity and quality of the nutritional value in our foods. But what if we have been looking at only a small part of the potential "value" in our foods? What if we have been missing the most important part? I invite you to see food in an entirely different way…

Food is a vessel that delivers something we can't see, taste, measure, or smell. Yes, it includes those nutrients and molecules we all learned about, but much more is going on. It is something you can't experience unless you are open to it. And once you are, it seems obvious.

Imagine that any food is structured similar to a gelatin capsule. The *form* of the food is represented by the outer gelatin shell. The *energy* of the food resides in the *contents* of the shell, which to our eyes looks empty. Yet we know that space is far from empty. Almost daily the field of quantum physics is revealing more about the potential energy contained in that seemingly "empty" space.

> According to our current understand of physics, every region of space is awash with different kinds of fields composed of waves of varying lengths. Each wave always has at least some energy. When physicists calculate the minimum amount of energy a wave can possess, they find that *every cubic centimeter of empty space contains more energy than the total energy of all the matter in the known universe!* … Bohm's view that space is as real and rich with process as the matter that moves through it reaches full maturity in his ideas about the implicate sea of energy. Matter does not exist independently from the sea, from so-called empty space. It is a part of space.[1]

Most of the nutrition in food is contained *within* the capsule (form), and the capsule itself is merely the container, or delivery mechanism. How we *treat* that container greatly determines the quality of the energy within.

The now-famous studies by Dr. Masaru Emoto indicate the profound affect our emotions have in altering the quality of water. (See the chapter on Nature.) He was able to photographically document the effect our thoughts and words have on water. Since we are all at least 70% water, as is our planet, imagine that effect on us! If his work is substantiated through peer review, it could significantly alter they way we handle food.

Physicists have described life as energy, and interactions as energy exchange. If so, then how far-fetched is it to imagine that the act of eating is actually an energy-exchange ritual?

Concept Two: Consuming the Cosmos

Our food is made up of everything in the cosmos[1]. Take for example, an apple. Contained within that apple are the wind, the rain, the earth, the minerals in

…how we eat determines, to a considerable extent, how the world is used.

Wendell Berry
The Pleasures of Eating from *What Are People For?*

I do not know what I may appear to the world, but to myself I seem to have been only a boy playing on the sea-shore, and diverting myself in now and then finding a smoother pebble or a prettier shell than ordinary, whilst the great ocean of truth lay all undiscovered before me.

Isaac Newton

The average annual growth rate of food production in the developing world declined from 4.2 per cent in the first half of the 90s to 3.5 per cent in the second half…

By 2020, farmers around the globe will need to produce 40 per cent more grain to feed everyone.

Elizabeth John
Focus: When the rain stops falling… Mar 20, 2005
New Straits Times, Malaysia's Premier Newspaper Online
http://www.nst.com.my/Current_News/NST/Sunday/Features/2 0050320105432/Article/indexb _html

the soil, the life both above and below ground, the tree itself, the farmer, the harvester, the packer, the shipper, the grocery store employee, the chef, the food in the bellies of those who touch the food, those who support them, and so on. The energy of all is contained within that apple. To eat mindfully then, one can give thanks for the entire cosmos represented in each bite as it enters the mouth.

Allow yourself to take a moment and contemplate the extraordinary act of consuming the cosmos in every bite. The concept of separation – that things can exist as if in a vacuum, without being continually supported by life in the most thorough, intimate, and persistent manner – is revealed as utter illusion. Everything supports everything!

Fast and Slow Food

Think about the energy surrounding "fast food", about the attitudes and emotions of those who handle it. Are they happy? Do they love what they do? Does their love of life permeate and energize the food they serve? If it did, then the energy surrounding such food would vibrate with vitality.

You can determine the energy of any food by simply placing your hands over the food and allowing yourself to experience the level of aliveness within. Compare the energy of fast food to that of freshly picked fruits or vegetables. The experience is similar to the energy contrast between a live tree and a dead one. Yes, both contain energy, but the quality of the energy is manifestly different.

When food is treated with gratitude and love, its energy is full and alive. This is important, because it can help you choose the best diet for your body's optimum care. Instead of flocking to the latest diet fad, try this. Ask your body what it needs, and then *listen* from deep within for the answer. If the meal is already prepared, place your hands over each item and feel how its aliveness resonates with your body. Be careful here. If you pay attention to your mind, it will reflect the omote of your body's desires (the chemical cravings of your body's neurochemistry.) But if you listen with your heart, your deepest Inner-Being, your body will always indicate what is optimum for that moment – including not eating, if that is appropriate.

Fast food is often produced – from seed to finished product - in an unloving manner. To keep costs at a minimum, fast food is sourced from the least expensive, corporately farmed, often genetically modified, pesticide laden, produce and meat available on the wholesale market. It is usually over-cooked to ensure that all bacteria is dead (no law-suits please), and then presented in packaging that has probably never been thoroughly and independently tested to see if it is safe for human use, let alone Earthly use. It isn't surprising that a Slow-Food movement is growing throughout the world.

The October 2004 Terra Madre Conference sponsored by Slow Foods International, was an international forum for those who seek to grow, distribute, and promote food in ways that respect the environment, defend human dignity, and protect human health. In her speech, Vandana Shiva described the event:

> For me, Terra Madre is a celebration of life's diversities, the Earth's bountiesand her miracles, in which we participate and create the bountiful food that hassustained our societies and communities over millennia.Terra Madre is a tribute to the Earth's caretakers: the small farmers, local producers, peasants and their co-producers — the earthworm, the micoriza,the fungi and

On August 4, 1997, almost a year and a half after the FDA promised a speedy response to the threat of mad cow, new animal feed restrictions took effect....Dead sheep, goats, cattle, deer, mink, elk, dogs, and cats could no longer be fed to cattle...cattle were still allowed to eat: dead horses, pigs, and poultry; cattle blood, gelatin, and tallow; and plate waste collected from restaurants, regardless of what kind of meat those left-overs contained.

Eric Schlosser
Fast Food Nation
pages 273-274

In their natural state cattle eat grass. What does this say about our priorities and intentions regarding the quality of our food? What does this reveal about how we see ourselves – about our own self love?

the eaters of food. I want to thank Carlo for using the term 'co-producer', rather than 'consumer', because a consumer *consumes*, to *consume* means to *destroy*, and so far consumers who have participated in a destructive food chain. We are now inviting all consumers to join life, biodiversity and three-quarters of humanity in the creative act of maintaining the Earth, herd diversity and human life, including the right to food of all human beings across the planet. As co-creators we are all participating ... in one of the biggest transformations of our times—a transformation that reclaims food as food, as the very currency of life, the basis of life, the condition of life, because everything is life only because everything is food. [2]

Terra Madre drew approximately 5,000 people from 130 countries. They were a multi-cultural, multi-colored celebration of that part of humanity who works intimately with the land and lovingly with food. Their Italian hosts insisted on continuing the same level of honor these people show in their daily lives, by ensuring that all guests, whether rich or poor, were treated equally. According to Richard Rathbun, those who were in need even had their plane fares covered. [3]

The intention of the gathering was to creatively address issues like sustaining biodiversity, promoting local and traditional systems, and finding solutions to the degradation caused by conventional agriculture. Those gathered symbolize the wave of change that is washing through our relationship to food, each other, and all life. [3]

Meat

Meat that is honored as a gift and handled with gratitude, similar to the way that many First Nation people (and even predatory animals) handle their food, is vital and alive.

When I merge with trees and animals, I do not experience an attachment to being in a physical form. It seems that only humans have that attachment. Life in general experiences life as ONEness, without concepts of birth and death. Life simply is. Therefore, releasing form when attacked by a predator simply becomes a new moment of now. All physical beings do fight to survive, but when the energy shifts to the point where death is inevitable, the releasing of physical form can be an easy choice, one that is barely noticed by the energy-being involved. Those who are open to these experiences report that the fly continues flying on the same course, regardless of whether its body has been released by a confrontation with a fly-swatter.

This transition with the food we eat, can be handled in an elegant and loving way, one that honors both the animal and the consumer in the process. Yet most meat now produced for consumption on this planet is treated in a manner reminiscent of our worst horror films. I no longer eat most meat because I will not knowingly participate in this process.

Concept Three: Gratitude

I have found that when I consciously allow myself to experience gratitude for my food before eating, my energy merges with an entire universe of oneness represented by the food on my plate. I feel the energy of the rain, sun, and earth that nourished the plants. I feel the life force of all the animals and insects who dwelt upon and within the plant, as well as the unseen energy of the plants themselves. I feel the energy pattern of every hand that touched the food, their intention, and their love. From the farmer to the person harvesting, from the trucker to the store clerk, all of

...the enormous buying power of the fast food giants has given them access to some of the cleanest ground beef. The meatpacking industry is now willing to perform the sort of rigorous testing for fast food chains that it refuses to do for the general public.

Anyone who brings raw ground beef into his or her kitchen today must regard it as a potential biohazard, one that may carry an extremely dangerous microbe, infectious at an extremely low dose...A series of tests conducted by Charles Gerba, microbiologist at the University of Arizona, discovered far more fecal bacteria in the average American kitchen sink than on the average American toilet seat. According to Gerba, "You'd be better off eating a carrot stick that fell in your toilet than one that fell in your sink."

Eric Schlosser
Fast Food Nation
page 221

their energy combines to produce the nourishing love embodied within the food form. When I give gratitude before eating, allowing myself to merge with the universe upon my plate, even the plate is not exempt from conscious gratitude. Everything awakens within me and I fall into and become one with all that is. When I allow myself to feel gratitude for the gift of the food, both in energy and nutrient form, I allow myself to experience the fullness of the gift of consuming the cosmos in every bite.

It is at this point that I have a very difficult time ending my "thanks" and actually proceeding to the eating part of the ritual. And when I do, I often no longer feel hungry. It is as if I have already "consumed" the energy of the food, such that eating becomes almost an after-thought. I suspect this is the journey that the legendary "Breatharians" take. Perhaps they have learned to nourish themselves by simply merging with the love that is the essence of all that is, thus the eating of form is no longer necessary, as the transfer of love has already been accomplished. Here the word, "transfer" isn't really accurate, as the energy of love simply is, everywhere. I imagine that ultimately it is possible to live life consciously aware of the love that emanates from and through all expressions of life, such that all energy transfer (eating) takes place without the need to actually consume the physical form of any food. But to tell the truth, I enjoy the sensual process of eating far to much to by-pass even a moment of its pleasure.

Concept Four: Gifting

Much of the food available for consumption these days is produced with very little consciousness. This is especially true in the meat, dairy, and egg industries. The fact that they are referred to as an "industry", the same word we use to describe the manufacture of machines, indicates the callousness with which we now handle food. We don't even question our tendency to hold food as a commodity, and no longer as a gift of life.

The painful conditions we humans are willing to create for the very animals upon which our sustenance relies, speaks volumes about the lack of consciousness and denial of our own pain that we now endure.

I consciously choose to eat only organically grown local food whenever possible. This doesn't ensure that the food was consciously produced with love, but hopefully it increases the probability. There are many times, however, when I am not sure under what conditions my food was produced. Imagine my joy, then, when I discovered a way to gift healing love and joy back to the same animals that may have suffered to produce the food I eat.

Here is the process. Acknowledgment of pain and reciprocity are two of the most healing forces on the planet. Most people can recall a time when their pain was acknowledged so thoroughly that it disappeared; or when their gift was acknowledged so completely that they felt fully seen – and in that moment, any struggle involved in the creation of the gift was minimized in light of the feeling of self-love that filled their being.

When merging with my food in gratitude, I consciously send that gratitude back to all those who were involved in creating my meal. And since all life is beyond form

Much of the U.S. supply of ordinary crop seeds has become contaminated with strands of engineered DNA, suggesting that current methods for segregating gene-altered seed plants from traditional varieties are failing, according to a pilot study released Monday.

And with a growing number of crop varieties now being engineered to produce not just agricultural chemicals but also potent pharmaceutical and industrial products in their leaves and stems -- many of which are being tested outdoors -- future contamination may pose even more serious health and economic risks, the report warns...

Rick Weiss
Study finds seeds tainted with engineered DNA strands
Washington Post Tuesday, February 24, 2004
http://www.sfgate.com/cgi-bin/article.cgi?file=/c/a/2004/02/24/MNGV356VH11.DTL

and time - expressing as frequencies of energy - I know that my message of love and gratitude is received, whether or not the animal involved is currently alive. With practice, I have been able to feel a connection with the life forms involved in my food, exchange our energy in gratitude, and complete the circle of giving and receiving such that we experience ourselves as one. When this deep connection takes place, I wait until I feel a healing occur, as I consciously acknowledge the gift given and any pain incurred in the process.

Imagine one day walking into a super market and finding people strolling down the aisles in deep meditation, connecting with the energy of the food with the intention of healing and completing the circle of gratitude involved in the production of that food. Until we devise more loving ways of producing our food, I will continue this practice whenever I can. I hope you join me.

Honor and Pleasure

Eating provides one of the greatest pleasures in life. When I am consciously aware as I eat, it feels as if my body is being bathed in love and care. Every cell seems to respond to this all-encompassing nurturance. Seeing food as love helps me to understand why we humans have created so much of our culture around food. Every aspect of food speaks of fulfillment and wholeness. It is a rich language of color, texture, odor, taste, and love energy all wrapped into one!

And in loving my body as well as the food, I am learning to ask my body when and what it wants to eat, *in the moment*. I am learning to listen carefully, beyond the concepts of my mind and the "should's" and "should not's" of our society and the "experts." When I honor my body, I choose to eat only when and what my body wants, trusting in the wisdom of my cells. It is the same trust I felt when birthing my children. When I trust my body, it performs in perfect health.

The wonderful discovery I have made is that I can eat almost anything and find nourishment and love within, *it all depends on how I am willing to perceive and accept the food as it enters my body*. If I am willing to honor the gift of love and life represented therein, it is mine to receive. I choose whole organically grown foods because their production at least attempts to honor all of life. I choose locally grown foods for the same reason. I choose fair-trade products whenever possible because their creation also honors the lives of all who produce the food. And most of all, I choose these foods because I now understand that the true nourishment of food comes from the manner in which it is handled every step of its life from origin to my mouth.

Biodynamic Farming

One of the most holistic farming methods currently in practice was developed by Rudolph Steiner, who also developed the educational methodology know as Waldorf Schools in the USA and Steiner Schools in Europe. Kathryn J. Casternovia, a local Biodynamic (BD) farming expert explains the method:

> BD supplements good farm practices with a spiritual understanding of nature. It is a human service to the Earth. BD is an internationally recognized approach to agriculture in which the farmer or gardener works with the spiritual dimensions of the earth and it's environment, enabling the life processes and ecological interconnections of plants and animals to function at their best. There are 200 BD farms in Holland alone.

Eating with the fullest pleasure - pleasure, that is, that does not depend on ignorance - is perhaps the profoundest enactment of our connection with the world. In this pleasure we experience and celebrate our dependence and our gratitude, for we are living from mystery, from creatures we did not make and powers we cannot comprehend.

Wendell Berry
The Pleasures of Eating
from
What Are People For?

As we move on into this so-called biotech revolution and we start producing more and more transgenic manipulations, we'll start seeing pieces of DNA interacting with each other in ways that are totally unpredictable...

I think this is probably the largest biological experiment humanity has ever entered into.

Ignacio Chapela
http://www.thefuture offood.com/ resources.htm

BD is economically and ecologically sound. It is self-generating, therefore, it decreases production costs. It is modeled after a living organism rather than an industrial model. The farm is self contained and thereby self-sustaining. The farm develops as an individual. A "Being" or "Entity" is actually created that is the individuality of the farm.

Demeter, an international organization, certifies BD farms just as Tilth certifies Organic farms. The criteria for being certified are toward this wholeness and self-sustainability. You may be familiar with some BD products that are on the market: Hauska, Weleda and Wala.

Just because food is certified organic, it does not mean the food has more nutrients or the farm is healthy, especially with the organic industry moving into "corporate" directions… Knowledge of soil building is often overlooked or not understood. The message here is to *know your farmer*.

There are scientific ways to test the *life forces* in foods. One such method is chromatography. Signature patterns can be seen on a lab paper that absorbs the plant liquid. We can also experience the difference ourselves. Good BD practices can produce more flavor, color, fragrance, longer storage capacity as well as visually, they are more beautiful. We can intuitively know as well. When we eat BD food, we KNOW it is good for us; we can experience the *forces* in the food. BD gardening can produce an average of four times more vegetables per acre than the amount grown by farmers using chemical agricultural techniques. The BD method also appears to use 1/2 the water and 1% the energy consumed by commercial agriculture, per pound of vegetable grown.

The BD approach comes from a deeper awareness based on exquisite observation of nature…The task of the farmer is no different than the mystic. The cry of the planet is for humans to realize their oneness with Nature and to learn to live from that realization. If the farmer is able to bring this holistic perspective to the very practical art of farming, a powerful metamorphosis begins to unfold. The farmer becomes the conscious co-creator with the spiritual beings that stand behind the material world. This is the consciousness that the farmer must develop. Food carries sustenance far beyond the vitamins contained within it. Are we willing to farm with an attunement that allows the spiritual world to more fully carry its richness and healing into our crops and livestock? What healing would transpire in the Earth herself if humans consciously took up this work?" Especially for the children, pregnant mothers and men who want to produce off-spring.[4]

Grow Biointensive® Method

Another highly successful method was developed by John Jeavons and his organization, Ecology Action, when he asked himself, "What is the smallest soil surface in which a person can produce everything needed?" He then developed the Grow Biointensive method which, according to 32 years of research:

> when used properly—can reconstruct the soil up to 60 times faster than nature and produce abundant food with 67 to 88% less water, 50 to 100% less purchased nutrient in organic fertilizer form and 99% less energy compared with traditional agriculture; besides, among other advantages it can at the same time increase the soil's fertility and produce between 200 and 400% more calories per area unit. [5]

I began using Jeavon's methods in my small backyard garden decades ago. If practiced correctly, the yields are amazing considering the small space used. Ecology Action estimates the vegetable yield potential is in the range of 2 to 16+ times the USA commercial mechanized levels (with an average of four times), and wheat harvests have been as high as five times the national average.[5] Briefly, the 8-step process includes:

1. Double-digging. The gardener digs twelve inches down and then loosens the soil to a depth of 24 inches. The loosened soil allows roots to penetrate easily, allows more air into the soil, retains moisture without waterlogging, simplifies weeding, and minimizes erosion.

When this year's grain harvest begins in May (2004), world grain stocks will be down to 59 days of consumption—the lowest level in 30 years. The last time stocks were this low, in 1972-74, wheat and rice prices doubled. A politics of scarcity emerged with exporting countries, such as the United States, restricting exports and using food for political leverage.
Hundreds of thousands of people in food-short countries, including Ethiopia and Bangladesh, died of hunger.

Lester R. Brown
World Food Prices Rising: Decades Of Environmental Neglect Shrinking Harvests In Key Countries
http://www.earth-policy.org/Updates/Update39.htm

2. Intensive planting. Plants are arranged in close, hexagonal spacing so that each plant is equidistant from others. When the plants mature, the leaves form a canopied "mini-climate" which retains moisture and retards weed growth.
3. Composting. All plant matter from within the farm is recycled so that the farm becomes a closed-system of constant regeneration. Compost crops are part of the garden.
4. Companion planting. Some plants repel harmful pests; others attract beneficial insects. Many plants have a healthy effect on the soil.
5. Carbon farming. Dual-purpose seed and grain crops which produce a large amount of carbonaceous material are used both for food and for compost.
6. Calorie farming. Potatoes, sweet potatoes, salsify, burdock, garlic, and parsnips produce a large amount of calories per unit of area.
7. Open-pollinated seeds. High yields can be obtained with open-pollinated seeds which have been selected over centuries because of their advantage. This also preserves the world's genetic diversity.
8. A Whole Gardening Method. The Grow Biointensive method is a whole system, and all of the components used together produce the optimum result. If all of the components are not used together, the soil can be depleted instead of enriched because of the method's close planting. [6]

Localization versus Globalization

One of the most shocking aspects of how we now provide food for humanity is the fact that the system we have created for feeding ourselves is inherently destructive. Local farmers, businesses, economies, and communities suffer at the after-affects of large multi-national corporations. Large agricultural corporations can now provide cheaper food to people half way around the world than those same people's neighbor down the street. How is this possible?

When governments subsidize large multi-national agricultural corporations, food is produced on such a mass scale, that even with the costs of shipping great distances and all the other costs factored in, that food can be sold at a lower cost to the purchaser than locally produced food. What does this do to local economies? It devastates them, especially in poorer nations, where farming is the backbone of the economy. [7]

But the picture is even worse. When large corporations come into small communities, they usually bring the money and influence to change laws that favor their own needs. Suddenly locally run businesses must dance to the tune of large corporate regulation in the name of "standardization." What may sound good on the surface, and seem to foster quality control, in essence destroys local businesses. Regulations that serve the large corporations are often too costly for locals to comply with, resulting in failed businesses and job loss. [7]

What happens when most of our survival needs are provided by corporations who's headquarters are out of the community? We lose the human factor, those relationships that allow us to make decisions based on empathy and common concern. When business is local, the economic repercussions of business decisions affect everyone, including the business owners. When business is global, local economies, jobs, and neighborly concerns are replaced by bottom-line decisions that take place halfway around the world. Community money flows out of the area, no longer supporting the very people who's hard work produced it.

What is called food today is not food. It is the by-product of a war economy. We are eating the leftovers of the Second World War. The nitrogen fertilizers that made explosives are now being used to fertilize, but not fertilize, kill, our soil. The chemicals of warfare have been deployed as pesticides and herbicides. Agriculture has been reduced to the consumption and recycling of war waste. No wonder it has reduced to a war against the earth and a war against the farmers…

Because agriculture has become the residual war economy, the alternatives we are building are the economies of peace. They are the biggest peace movement of our times. They are making peace with the earth, they are making peace with all species and, right here in Terra Madre, we are making peace between all cultures.

Vandana Shiva,
Director of Bija Vidyapeeth '
School of Seed' in India, in her
speech at the TERRA
MADRE Conference October
2004, Turino, Italy..

http://www.terramadre

2004.org/eng/discorsi.la
sso

Additionally, decisions that undermine the health of the environment become easier to make when those making the decisions sit in comfortable offices half a world away. What would happen if executives were forced to live in the communities affected by their decisions? What if they were forced to eat the genetically modified, pesticide laden, lifeless food; drink the poisoned water, and live in the polluted villages? When decisions are made from a distance, it becomes easy for a corporate executive to focus only on the facts that support his own desires and beliefs – ignoring those facts that are unpleasant to behold - missing the total picture.

Seed Patents and GMOs

A recent problem undermining the ability of the world to produce enough food for our growing population, is the ever-increasing practice by governments of offering patents on seeds. This highly unethical practice begs the question: who owns the world's seeds? In a report by the Canadian Catholic Organization for Development and Peace the result of this short-sighted practice is discussed:

> Somewhere in the world, a man, woman or child dies of hunger every 3.6 seconds. In this context, more than 1.4 billion people in developing countries depend for their survival on crops they grow from seeds saved from their last harvest. Yet through the World Trade Organization (WTO), powerful corporate interests defend their right to patent seeds, which threatens the food supply and livelihoods of the world's poorest peoples…
>
> Seeds belong to the whole human race. Yet a change to one gene is all that it takes for a corporation to claim ownership. Corn and rice, for instance, were not *invented* but nurtured and bred for millennia, mostly by aboriginal peoples. They are essential foods that they have become cultural and spiritual symbols of the gift of life.
>
> Corporations, by literally stealing community knowledge, and by adding one small step to a centuries-old process, become legal owners of this heritage…New seed strains are not developed in response to farmers' needs. Corporations modify seeds first, and then create "need" by aggressively marketing them to farmers. [8]

Once a farmers growing traditional varieties switches to a patented crop, the farmer must continue to purchase the patented seed, many of which contain a "terminator gene" which makes their own seeds sterile. In the meanwhile, the traditional varieties, seeds that may have been saved for thousands of years from season to season and therefore have evolved with the bioregion, may be lost forever. The report continues:

> This was an "unintended" impact of the Green Revolution, where high-yield but chemically dependent hybrid seeds wiped out three quarters of traditional rice varieties in some Indian states, *increasing* the poverty it was supposed to end. [8]

Additionally, there is mounting evidence that these genetically modified varieties are contaminating traditional seed stock, and perhaps even wild seeds in nature. In lab tests commissioned by the Union of Concerned Scientists, results showed that more than two-thirds of the 36 conventional corn, soy, and canola seed batches tested contained traces of DNA from genetically engineered crop varieties, leading scientists to recommend that the Department of Agriculture conduct a thorough study of the extent of genetic contamination. [9]

Josantony Joseph, Director of The Human Factor, an international development resource centre in Mumbai, India, warns that "when saving and rescuing saved seed becomes a crime, [then] corporations begin to own life."

Why Seed Patents Threaten Food Supply For The World's Poor Canadian Catholic Organization for Development and Peace http://www.devp.org/pdf/seed patents1.pdf

Our current global situation...

Even though it is not in the scope of this book to tackle the large subject of globalization, (and there are many organizations listed in the Reference section that can provide excellent source material), I'd like to include the preface to a new book that sums up the situation quite clearly. It is written by that pioneer of ecological awareness, Lester R. Brown of the Earth Policy Institute, (http://www.earth-policy.org). With permission, here is the Preface from Outgrowing The Earth: The Food Security Challenge In An Age Of Falling Water Tables And Rising Temperatures (W.W. Norton & Co., 2004):

"To live," in Wendell Berry's words:

"We must daily break the body and shed the blood of Creation. When we do this knowingly, lovingly, skillfully, reverently, it is a sacrament. When we do it ignorantly, greedily, clumsily, destructively, it is a desecration. In such desecration we condemn ourselves to spiritual and moral loneliness, and others to want."

David W. Orr
Loving Children

Resurgence Magazine Issue 229 – 2005
http://www.resurgence.org/res urgence/issues/orr000.htm

On hearing his political opponent described as a modest chap, Winston Churchill reputedly responded that "he has much to be modest about." Having just completed a book dealing with the increasingly complex issue of world food security, I too feel that I have a lot to be modest about.

Assessing the world food prospect was once rather straightforward, largely a matter of extrapolating, with minor adjustments, historically recent agricultural supply and demand trends. Now suddenly that is all changing. It is no longer just a matter of trends slowing or accelerating; in some cases they are reversing direction.

Grain harvests that were once rising everywhere are now falling in some countries. Fish catches that were once rising are now falling. Irrigated area, once expanding almost everywhere, is now shrinking in some key food-producing regions.

Beyond this, some of the measures that are used to expand food production today, such as overpumping aquifers, almost guarantee a decline in food production tomorrow when the aquifers are depleted and the wells go dry. The same can be said for overplowing and overgrazing. We have entered an era of discontinuity on the food front, an era where making reliable projections is ever more difficult.

New research shows that a 1 degree Celsius rise in temperature leads to a decline in wheat, rice, and corn yields of 10 percent. In a century where temperatures could rise by several degrees Celsius, harvests could be devastated.

Although climate change is widely discussed, we are slow to grasp its full meaning. Everyone knows the earth's temperature is rising, but commodity analysts often condition their projections on weather returning to "normal," failing to realize that with climate now in flux, there is no normal to return to.

Falling water tables are also undermining food security. Water tables are now falling in countries that contain more than half the world's people. While there is a broad realization that we are facing a future of water shortages, not everyone has connected the dots to see that a future of water shortages will be a future of food shortages. [8]

Perhaps the biggest agricultural reversal in recent times has been the precipitous decline in China's grain production since 1998. Ten years ago, in Who Will Feed China?, I projected that China's grain production would soon peak and begin to decline. But I did not anticipate that it would drop by 50 million tons between 1998 and 2004. Since 1998 China has covered this decline by drawing down its once massive stocks of grain. Now stocks are largely depleted and China is turning to the world market. Its purchase of 8 million tons of wheat to import in 2004 could signal the beginning of a shift from a world food economy dominated by surpluses to one dominated by scarcity.

Overnight, China has become the world's largest wheat importer. Yet it will almost certainly import even more wheat in the future, not to mention vast quantities of rice and corn. It is this potential need to import 30, 40, or 50 million tons of grain a year within the next year or two and the associated emergence of a politics of food scarcity that is likely to put food security on the front page of newspapers.

At the other end of the spectrum is Brazil, the only country with the potential to expand world cropland area measurably. But what will the environmental consequences be of continuing to clear and plow Brazil's vast interior? Will the soils sustain cultivation over the longer term? Will the deforestation in the Amazon disrupt the recycling of rainfall from the Atlantic Ocean to the country's interior? And how many plant and animal species will Brazil sacrifice to expand its exports of soybeans?

Food security, which was once the near-exclusive province of ministries of agriculture, now directly involves several departments of government. In the past, ministries of transportation did not need to think about food security when formulating transport policies. But in densely populated developing countries today, the idea of having a car in every garage one
day means paving over a large share of their cropland. Many countries simply do not have enough cropland to pave for cars and to grow food for their people.

Or consider energy. Energy ministers do not attend international conferences on food security. But they should. The decisions they make in deciding which energy sources to develop will directly affect atmospheric carbon dioxide levels and future changes in temperature. In fact, the decisions made in ministries of energy may have a greater effect on
long-term food security than those made in ministries of agriculture.

Future food security now depends on the combined efforts of the ministries of agriculture, energy, transportation, health and family planning, and water resources. It also depends on strong leadership—leadership that is far better informed on the complex set of interacting forces affecting food security than most political leaders are today.

The choice to honor *all* life automatically forces us to take a broader approach in our decision making processes on all levels, both individually and on the mass scale of multi-national corporations and governmental policy. Perhaps this is a perfect place to apply the Precautionary Principle and first do no harm. (See the chapter of the same name for more detail.) When making decisions that affect quality of life, we need to devise ways in which corporate profits can still take place without doing harm. It is time to create social and business structures that support and honor us all. Meanwhile, what can you do?

Buy locally produced items whenever you can, even if they cost a bit more. Why?

- When you eliminate the need to ship food, you significantly reduce the amount of transportation related pollution and the cost of developing more sources of petroleum.
- Money you spend in your own community supports your neighbors and the health of your community. The money you pay the grocer pays for her children's dental work, which helps pay the dentist's employee's salary, etc. You get the point. Money spent outside the community, say at a Wal-Mart,

Closing the gap in the world grain harvest this year following four consecutive grain harvest shortfalls, each larger than the one before, will not be easy. The grain shortfall of 105 million tons in 2003 is easily the largest on record, amounting to 5 percent of annual world consumption of 1,930 million tons.

Lester R. Brown
World Food Security Deteriorating: Food Crunch In 2005 Now Likely
http://www.earth-policy.org/Updates/Update40.htm

does very little to support the community, no matter what the advertisements say.

- The overall economic health of your community translates to your own economic health and well-being. When you keep money circulating locally, your community can better afford to place attention on quality of life issues: libraries, parks, recreational opportunities, better schools and after school programs, concerts, infrastructure that doesn't harm your environment, etc.

- Farmers who live locally tend to treat the environment with more honor, knowing that whatever they spray on the land affects their own families and their neighbors. Whatever seeps into the water table – they drink. There is a level of accountability involved that far exceeds that of large corporations who's families live in gated communities cushioned from the immediate affect of their decisions.

- Local farmers are a bit more reluctant to use unproven technology, like genetically modified seeds. They know that no matter what Monsanto says about it's ability to keep GMOs from contaminating the general environment, nature doesn't work that way. Wind, insects, and the whims of nature make control impossible. Furthermore, many farming families have spent generations developing special seed strains that are best suited to their location. The work of Kent and Diane Whealy of the Seed Savers Exchange (www.seedsavers.org) comes to mind. Their dedicated efforts to find and collect seed varieties that people have nurtured over generations, most tied to specific bio-regions, may be the saving grace for large parts of our worldwide population if corporate farms ultimately lead to wide-scale starvation. Local genetically specific seeds have a far greater chance of providing reliable food crops than do their genetically bland, pesticide dependent corporate counterparts. Unfortunately, large corporations have been known to influence the passage of laws that force farmers to use only the corporation's seeds – often totally unsuited to the locale, thus requiring chemicals just to maintain their viability.

- Buying locally means you and your neighbors have jobs regulated by your own community decisions. Large corporations tend to eliminate local jobs, and replace them with lower paying jobs that offer few benefits, if any. One common practice is to hire mostly part-time workers, thus side stepping any laws that require employee benefits.

- When you purchase locally, you support community based regulations that support the people in your community, NOT outside interests who are not stakeholders in the quality of life of your community.

- Locally produced food is generally healthier, fresher, and more diverse. Eliminating shipping also eliminates having to grow only those varieties that ship well. Taste, diversity, and nutrition become a critical factors again.

- Best of all, when you purchase locally grown food, you have the pleasure of knowing the people who grew the food you place in your body. When I walk into my local Food Co-op, photos of the people who grow my food are right there in front of me, they are my neighbors and friends. And when I visit the Grower's Market, I don't even need the photos – they are standing with their produce ready to share the result of their labor with me. Buying

On August 4, 1997, almost a year and a half after the FDA promised a speedy response to the threat of mad cow, new animal feed restrictions took effect….Dead sheep, goats, cattle, deer, mink, elk, dogs, and cats could no longer be fed to cattle…cattle were still allowed to eat: dead horses, pigs, and poultry; cattle blood, gelatin, and tallow; and plate waste collected from restaurants, regardless of what kind of meat those left-overs contained.

Eric Schlosser Fast Food Nation pages 273-274

In their natural state cattle eat grass, not corn, and certainly not animal body parts. What does this say about our priorities and intentions regarding the quality of our food? What does this reveal about how we see ourselves – about our own self love?

We
sen(

local means you have the opportunity of knowing the love with which your food was created, the care that went into marketing and distributing it, and ultimately bringing it to your table. And you have the pleasure of knowing exactly who your food money supports and the difference it makes in their lives.

- When buying locally, your monetary exchange comes full circle right before your eyes. You receive life-giving, life-affirming food, and the provider receives your life-supporting money in exchange. What a perfect balance!

Notes

1. Michael Talbot, The Holographic Universe, page 51. He refers to physicist. David Bohm.

2. Vandana Shiva's speech at TERRA MADRE, October 2004.
http://www.terramadre2004.org/eng/discorsi.lasso

3. Richard Rathbun, Terra Madre; Worldwide Gathering of Food Communities, Timeline March/April 2005. See also http://www.slowfood.com/ for more information on Slow Foods.

4. From Biodynamic Agriculture, by Kathryn J. Casternovia, Published in Sentient Times. Kathryn Casternovia, *ELEMENTAL DESIGNS, Inc., Landscape Designs and Consultations for Enchanted Gardens.* 541-482-9362, *natspir@medford.net*

5. http://www.growbiointensive.org/   ECOLOGY ACTION is a small, non-profit organization dedicated to finding practical, environmentally sound solutions to urban and rural food, clothing, shelter, and energy issues through research, development, educational, and outreach programs

6. Mac Lawrence, A Miracle Grows in Kenya, TIMELINE, March/April 2005, page6. Also see Kilili Self Help Project, 260 Marion Ave, Mill Valley, CA 94941. 415-380-0687, Sandra Mardigian.

7. From an interview with Helena Norberg-Hodge of the International Society for Ecology and Culture on Jeff Golden's JEFFERSON EXCHANGE radio show (http://www2.jeffnet.org/Department.asp?DeptID=60), November 29th, 2004. See the Reference section for additional information on Helena's books and website: http://www.isec.org.uk/ SEE RESOURCES FOR FOOD STATISTICS FROM NORBERG-HODGE'S WEBSITE.

8. Why Seed Patents Threaten Food Supply For The World's Poor   Canadian Catholic Organization for Development and Peace http://www.devp.org/pdf/seedpatents1.pdf See also the Organic Consumers Association article entitled Terminator and Traitor seed patents are still being granted, dated 3/12/2001 located at http://www.organicconsumers.org/ge/terminate.cfm which states: 'Terminator technology' refers to plants that have been genetically modified to produce sterile seed; it is designed to prevent farmers from saving and re-planting their seed, forcing them to buy new seeds every year. Terminator has been widely condemned as an immoral technology that threatens global food security, especially for 1.4 billion people who depend on farm-saved seed. In 1999, due to mounting opposition to Terminator seeds, both Monsanto (now Pharmacia) and AstraZeneca (now Syngenta) vowed not to commercialize genetic seed sterilization technology. Syngenta now controls at least six Terminator patents and a host of new patents on genetically modified plants with defective immune systems. If the Gene Giants get their way, warns RAFI, sterility is just one of many traits that could be controlled by the application of external chemicals. 'Traitor' technology or genetic trait-control allows companies to engineer crops that depend on the external application of a chemical in order to develop into fertile, or healthy plants. Using inducible promoter systems, a plant's genetic traits can be turned 'on or off' with the application of an external chemical catalyst. RAFI and other CSOs warn that a new generation of chemically dependent plants will be among the next wave of genetically modified crops unless action is taken to ban them.

9. Rick Weiss, Study finds seeds tainted with engineered DNA strands, Washington Post, Tuesday, February 24, 2004. http://www.sfgate.com/cgi-bin/article.cgi?file=/c/a/2004/02/24/MNGV356VH11.DTL

17

MEDIA

Media must not be considered just another business:
they are special institutions in our society.
Information is the lifeblood of democracy —
and when viewpoints are cut off
and ideas cannot find an outlet, our democracy suffers.
Freepress.net

MEDIA

How can we create a Media that honors all viewpoints?

The Problem

We live in a time when more media choices are available to more people than ever before. Or do we? There are certainly more TV, radio, and publication *choices* available, but is there really much difference between them? Perhaps not. Here's why...

Although most Americans pride themselves on our rich media culture, the truth is that the number of media enterprises has been steadily dwindling, not expanding as the number of TV channels, radio stations, and publications would lead one to believe. Here are the facts: [1]

- Since 1975, two-thirds of independent newspaper owners and one-third of independent television owners have disappeared.
- Only 281 of the nation's 1,500 daily newspapers remain independently owned.
- The three largest newspaper publishers control 25% of daily newspaper circulation worldwide.
- From 1992 to 2002, the percentage of shows on network TV produced by the networks themselves — instead of independent producers — rose from less than 20% to more than 75%.
- Minority ownership of broadcast media is now at a ten-year low — a mere 4% of radio stations and less than 2% of television stations are minority-owned.

Why does this matter?

Even though we (the people) technically own the airwaves (the transmission frequencies used by radio, TV, and satellite broadcasters, cell phone companies, and even remote control devices), our government leases the privilege to use them to various corporations or allows their usage in exchange for the promise to "serve the public interest." The airwaves are part of the Commons,[2] yet those same citizens are rarely involved in the decisions regarding their usage.

Think about it. More Americans obtain their news from commercial media sources than ever before. Even though these statistics are somewhat old, they are revealing: [3]

- 1,669 – The projected number of hours that adults (age 18 and older) will watch television in 2004. This is the equivalent of about 70 days – US. Census Bureau March 11 2003..
- Time per day that TV is on in the average US home: 7 hours 40 minutes – Nielsen Media Research 2000
- Amount of TV the average American watches per day: over 4 hours – Nielsen Media Research 2000
- Number of violent acts the average American child sees on TV by age 18: 200,000 – Senate Judiciary Committee Staff Report " Children, Violence, and the Media" 1999.

When you consider that a few media giants dictate a steady stream of carefully framed information to so many Americans on a constant basis, you begin to get an inkling of the power they hold in their hands to influence public thought and perception. These same viewers will go to the polls and cast votes that will directly influence the power and profits of those media businesses. As our system is currently structured, the odds are high that the media corporations will do everything in their power to influence viewer perceptions in their favor.

Robert W. McChesney describes a perfect example of voter misinformation in his article, On Media and the Election, in which he makes the following observation:

This election was marked by a staggering amount of voter ignorance. Polls show that voters – especially Bush supporters – were grossly misinformed about their candidate's position on a broad range of issues. Surveying supporters of the President, a University of Maryland PIPA/ Knowledge Networks poll found:

- 72% still believe that there were WMD's in Iraq.
- 75% believe that Iraq was providing substantial support for Al Qaeda.
- 66% believe that Bush supports participation in the International Criminal Court.
- 72% believe that he supports the treaty banning land mines.

The catch? None of these statements are true. [4]

Aside from the obvious disconnect between actual fact and perceived truth, this is especially unacceptable in a democratic nation where the major media corporations can donate to the political campaigns of the very people who will set policy regarding governmental regulation of their activities.[5] We seem to have designed a system with built-in conflicts of interest – and it's the public who suffers as a result.

Framing

Much of this disconnect could be attributed to the "framing" of the news, what George Lakoff calls the *context* or mental structures through which the actual information is perceived. Framing could be seen as the deliberate, selective, and repetitious use of image producing words – a kind of verbal perceptual filter - to manipulate a specific outcome. Similar to perceptual filters, frames operate beneath your awareness unless your attention is focused upon them. As a result, most people accept media framing without question, even to their own detriment.

In his book, Don't Think of an Elephant!, Lakoff describes the framing for the word, "relief."

For there to be relief there must be an affliction, an afflicted party, and a reliever who removes the affliction and is therefore a hero. And if people try to stop the hero, those people are villains for trying to prevent relief. When the word *tax* is added to *relief,* the result is a metaphor: Taxation is an affliction. And the person who takes it away is a hero, and anyone who tries to stop him is a bad guy. [6]

Once the media picks up the deliberately repeated metaphor, "Tax Relief", the stage is set for an instant replay of the idea that taxation is an affliction. This is especially self-defeating when the candidate from the opposition uses the same term when discussing taxation. Each time it is repeated – by anyone – *regardless of what is said*, the metaphor is triggered. This is the power of framing.

Lakoff goes on to propose a re-framing of the metaphor, one in which an entirely different light is cast upon the subject. For taxes, he offers two alternate frames: taxes as investments, and taxes as membership in society:

Our parents invested in the future, ours as well as theirs, through their taxes. They invested their tax money in the interstate highway system, the Internet, the scientific and medical establishments, our communications systems, our airline system, the space program. They invested in the future, and we are reaping the tax benefits, the benefits from the taxes they paid. Today we have assets – highways, schools and colleges, the Internet, airlines – that come from the wise investments they made…*Taxes are wise investments for the future…*

The Globalization of humanity is a natural, biological, evolutionary proess. Yet we face an enormous crisis because the most central and important aspect of globalization – its economy – is currently being organized in a manner that so gravely violates the fundamaental principles by which healthy living systems are organized that it threatens the demise of our whole civilization.

E. Sahtouris

The Biology of Globalization, Perspectives on Business and Global Change,

Sept 1997

Taxation is paying your dues, paying your membership fee in America. If you join a country club or a community center, you pay fees. Why? You did not build the swimming pool. You have to maintain it… You may not use the squash court, but you still have to pay your dues. Otherwise it won't be maintained and will fall apart. People who avoid taxes, like corporations that move to Bermuda, are not paying their dues to their country. It is patriotic to be a taxpayer. It is traitorous to desert our country and not pay your dues… There is no such thing as a self-made man. Every business has used the vast American infrastructure, which the taxpayers paid for, to make his money… He got rich on what other taxpayers had paid for: the banking system, the Federal Reserve, the Treasury and Commerce Departments, and the judicial system, where nine-tenths of cases involve corporate law… The wealthy have gotten rich using what previous taxpayers have paid for. They owe the taxpayers of this country a great deal and should be paying it back. [7]

One can see that the importance of framing cannot be over-emphasized. It is imperative that our media be aware of the frames they invoke, and that they intentionally balance the framing of information provided.

Freepress.Net has identified four principal flaws in the media system as it stands today in the United States:

In our commercial system, profit always trumps the public interest. [1]

Our system is designed to be driven by profit. That puts public service in the back seat. Most CEO's feel a primary responsibility to the shareholders. How can we change this so that ALL stakeholders (we – the People), not just the shareholder's needs are considered?

The question assumes a separation of goals that may itself be erroneous. Perhaps what is needed is a re-examination of the underlying assumption that greater profits are only available to those who stress sensationalism and entertainment over neutral and accurate news. That doesn't mean that the presentation needs to be dry and boring. Humans are incredibly creative in their methods of expression. Once the public and shareholders demand a re-examination of the media's intentions, backed by legislation that supports the sacred public trust to receive accurate information – a cornerstone of the democratic process – perhaps the space will be created for a colorfully outrageous, creative expression that better serves the public's needs.

Ownership of media has become incredibly consolidated. [1]

The large media mergers of the last few years have resulted in a massive consolidation of ownership verging on what used to be called a "monopoly". For some reason that word hasn't been uttered often enough and loudly enough to gain the public's outrage. Yet the facts are outrageous. At this point, media owners decide who, what, and when we watch, how it is distributed, and how much we pay.

In recent years, the number of companies who control the majority of the media has been shrinking rapidly, leaving enormous political and economic power in the hands of just a few corporate giants. They include:

2003 Revenues	Company
$17.5 billion	**News Corporation's** holdings include: FOX Network, DirecTV, 34 TV stations, National Geographic Channel, FX, 20th Century Fox, the New York Post, Harper Collins Publishers, Regan Books, and sports teams
$134.2 billion	**General Electric** holdings include: NBC, Telemundo, Universal Pictures,

The State of the First Amendment, a poll conducted by The Freedom Forum First Amendment Center and the Center for Survey Research and Analysis at the University of Connecticut, reveals diminishing support for all of the First Amendment freedoms when compared to a 1997 survey, but most notably the freedom of the press.

More than half of the respondents said they believe the press has too much freedom, and 60 percent said high school students should not be free to print stories about controversial issues without school officials' approval.

Student Press Law Center Fall 1999 - High School Censorship Vol. XX, No. 3 - Page 23

http://www.splc.org/report_detail. asp?id=478&edition=7

	Universal Parks & Resorts, CNBC, Bravo, MSNBC, and vast holdings in numerous other business sectors GE/NBC recently acquired many of the highest-profile media properties previously held by Vivendi.
$26.6 billion	**Viacom** holdings include: CBS and UPN networks, over 35 TV stations, MTV, Showtime, Nickelodeon, BET, Paramount Pictures, Blockbuster Video, over 175 radio stations, Simon & Schuster, and vast billboard holdings
$39.6 billion	**TimeWarner** holdings include: Warner Bros, AOL, CNN, HBO, Time Warner Cable, Turner (TNT, TBS), Cartoon Network, New Line Cinema, Castle Rock Entertainment, Atlantic Recordings, Elektra/Sire, Rhino, Time-Life Books, DC Comics, Fortune, Sports Illustrated, People, and Netscape Communications
$28.4 billion	**The Walt Disney Company** holdings include: ABC, Disney Channel, ESPN, A&E, History Channel, E!, Buena Vista, Touchstone Pictures, 10 TV stations, 60+ radio stations, ESPN Radio, Miramax Films, Hyperion Books, & theme parks
€25.5 billion (roughly $30.1 billion)	**Vivendi Universal** owns: CANAL+, Cineplex Odeon Theatres (42%), MCA Records, PolyGram Records, Vivendi Telecom, and 26.8 million shares of TimeWarner stock Vivendi Universal recently sold its cable and movie properties (Universal Pictures, Sci-Fi Channel, and USA Network) to GE/NBC.
€16.8 billion (roughly $19.8 billion)	**Bertelsmann AG's** holdings include: 11 TV networks, Random House Publishing (which includes Alfred A. Knopf, Ballantine, Doubleday, among many others), BMG Music, Arista Records and RCA Records[8]

Radio giant Clear Channel Communications, Inc. holds the record in both revenue earned and number of stations owned. When one company blankets this much of the airwaves, how can anyone else's voice be heard? [8]

Rank	Company	Stations	Revenue
1.	Clear Channel Communications, Inc.	1,216	$3,423,450,000
2.	Infinity Broadcasting Corp. (Viacom Inc.)	185	$2,186,675,000
3.	Cox Radio Inc. (Cox Enterprises Inc.)	78	$466,850,000
4.	Entercom Communications Corp.	104	$455,100,000
5.	ABC Radio Networks (Walt Disney Co.)	74	$424,625,000
6.	Citadel Broadcasting Corp.	216	$366,125,000
7.	Radio One Inc.	66	$338,100,000
8.	Emmis Communications Corp.	27	$296,775,000
9.	Cumulus Media Inc.	270	$292,975,000
10.	Univision Communications Inc.	57	$290,900,000

Source: Broadcasting & Cable Magazine. http://www.publicintegrity.org/telecom/industry.aspx?act=broadcast

*Our children are being coached and prodded in the arts of petulance and nagging by those whose sole purpose is to turn them into conduits for their parents' money. As the anthropologist Jules Henry once noted, advertising has become an "insolent usurper of parental function, degrading parents to mere intermediaries between children and the market."[121]
...Business Week, no enemy of corporate America, perhaps put it best: "Instead of transmitting a sense of who we are and what we hold important, today's marketing-driven culture is instilling in [children] a sense that little exists without a sales pitch attached and that self-worth is something you buy at a shopping mall."[123]
...The technology of seduction has increased tremendously in sophistication and reach, and corporate seducers have gained new legal rights. Yet the means for parents to contend with these intrusions, and to talk back to the intruders, have scarcely grown at all. In many respects, they have diminished.
Jonathan Rowe and Gary Ruskin The Parent's Bill Of Rights: Helping Moms And Dads Fight Commercialism
Mothering Magazine Issue 116, Jan/Feb 2003
http://www.mothering.com/*

The media don't cover the media. [1]

One of the most useful attributes a person can have is the ability to self-assess; in other words, to clearly see what works and what doesn't work about one's own actions, and then to self-correct in order to meet one's goals. Most businesses fail if they lack this ability. Yet there are two areas within our culture in which we notoriously fail to do just that – self assess. One is within the government structures themselves, and the other is within the media. Who reports media news? Who serves the same watchdog role that a free press is intended to serve within our democracy – for the press itself?

I recall writing letters of protest against the proposed changes to the FCC rules that would have allowed even larger media giants – something that would have affected all Americans in a profound way – yet most of us never heard about the proposed changes. As a result, most Americans didn't even have an opportunity to voice their opinion on a subject that would have deeply impacted the quality of their news; the very news they relied upon to provide them with the necessary information to make intelligent decisions when they vote.

Citizens have been shut out of media policy debates. [1]

Through campaign donations, thorough lobbying, and less emphasis on investigative reporting (especially regarding hot issues and candidates that could affect the bottom-line), media corporations have played a greater role in influencing government. Robert W. McChesney suggests the media sway is even deeper. He reminds us that media corporations, most major local TV stations, and networks made $600 million from presidential TV ads alone, well above previous records while, "subjecting voters to half-truths and distortions from both sides." He writes,

> Political ad revenues cover 10 percent of commercial broadcasting revenue, up from less than three percent in 1992. Overall, federal elections cost nearly $4 billion this year, representing a near 30% increase since 2000. An iron law in commercial broadcasting is you do not do programming that undermines the credibility of your sponsors. The result: more political ads and little-to-no critical journalism that exposes the spin and lies in these TV ads. A more brash insult to our intelligence can hardly be imagined. This also explains why the corporate media giants are as enthusiastic about campaign finance reform as the NRA is regarding gun control. [4]

Furthermore, the nonpartisan Center for Public Integrity offers these facts:

- A new investigation by the Center for Public Integrity has found that the broadcast industry spent more than $222 million lobbying the federal government from 1998 through June 2004—a period of increasingly intense battles over ownership rules.
- In addition, television and radio companies contributed more than $26.5 million to federal candidates and lawmakers during the same period.
- The companies and their principal representative organization—the National Association of Broadcasters—also sponsored 84 trips for lawmakers and regulators at a cost of $165,474, bringing total spending to affect policy and elections by the industry to $248.9 million.
- The volatile political climate also saw 24 individuals with close ties to both the industry and its regulatory overseers make lucrative moves back and forth between the two.

Each week, the typical American child takes in some 38 hours (yes, a full work week) of commercial media, with its endless ads and come-ons.[4] And that's not counting the ads that commandeer their attention from billboards and the Internet, the omnipresent brand logos, and the advertising that increasingly fills the schools.

"Kids and Media @ the New Millennium," The Henry Kaiser Family Foundation, November 1999.

Jonathan Rowe & Gary Ruskin
The Parent's Bill Of Rights: Helping Moms And Dads Fight Commercialism
Mothering Magazine Issue 116, Jan/Feb 2003

http://www.mothering.com/articles/growing_child/consumerism/bill_of_rights.html

- Prior to relaxing media ownership rules in 2003, FCC officials met 71 times behind closed doors with the nation's major broadcasters. In stark contrast, officials held only five such meetings with consumer groups working on the issue.[9]

Even though many people seem to be aware of and often complain about the widespread shift from impartial news to entertainment (sometimes called "infotainment"), the under-representation of local interests, and even entire segments of our population; they don't seem to also be aware of their available options to influence a change. Yet thousands of people are involved in the movement to re-design our media systems. (A website link to a list of media-reform organizations can be found in the Media Reference Section in the back of this book.)

Covert Propaganda

The extent to which the United States government has entered the broadcast media is just now beginning to unfold. Even though our democracy requires a free and *independent* news media, that isn't always the case – and we are often not aware of this vital fact. In a detailed article dated March 13th, 2005, the New York Times revealed just how extensively the government has become involved in the "news." According to the article, the 1948 Smith-Mundt Act stipulates that pro-government "news", like Voice of America, can be broadcast abroad, but not at home. Yet increasingly, government produced news spots that are specifically designed to look, feel, and taste like bona-fide independent news reports are entering the domestic air waves. When it comes to influencing public opinion, the article quotes one senior department official, her department regards such segments as "powerful strategic tools." The article reveals:

> Yet in three separate opinions in the past year, the Government Accountability Office, an investigative arm of Congress that studies the federal government and its expenditures, has held that government-made news segments may constitute improper "covert propaganda" even if their origin is made clear to the television stations. The point, the office said, is whether viewers know the origin. Last month, in its most recent finding, the G.A.O. said federal agencies may not produce prepackaged news reports "that conceal or do not clearly identify for the television viewing audience that the agency was the source of those materials."[10]

Additionally, the article reminds us that Code of Ethics of the Radio-Television News Directors Association states the need to "Clearly disclose the origin of information and label all material provided by outsiders." Who oversees and enforces these laws, especially when the government itself is the source of the breach of conduct? According to the article:

> The Federal Communications Commission does, but it has never disciplined a station for showing government-made news segments without disclosing their origin, a spokesman said. Could it? Several lawyers experienced with F.C.C. rules say yes. They point to a 2000 decision by the agency, which stated, "Listeners and viewers are entitled to know by whom they are being persuaded."
>
> In interviews, more than a dozen station news directors endorsed this view without hesitation. Several expressed disdain for the prepackaged segments they received daily from government agencies, corporations and special interest groups who wanted to use their airtime and credibility to sell or influence.[10]

David Barstow and Robin Stein wrote in The Times on Sunday that at least 20 agencies had made and distributed fake news segments to local TV stations; the administration spent $254 million in its first four years to buy self-aggrandizing puffery from P.R. firms.

The president joked that he could tack on an "I'm George W. Bush and I approved this disclaimer." But then he said he wouldn't - that it was up to local stations to reveal the truth.

Maureen Dowd
A Wink and a Fraud

Op-Ed Columnist
New York Times
March 17, 2005

But evidently stations also have the ability to edit segments at will, before showing them or sending them on for greater distribution. Innocent pressing concerns of time can lead to cutting, but so can personal beliefs or corporate benefits. The article cites many examples of government created "news" where the source ended up in digital neverland.

It isn"t merely a question of whether the government source was clearly cited in a "news" spot, but more important is the *intent*. Is our government using tax-payer money to mislead and covertly propagandize against its own people? According to Freepress.net, the problem is systemic:

> The State Department, Defense Department, Transportation Security Administration and Agriculture Department have produced similar "news" segments for local TV. All told at least 20 federal agencies have quietly used this tactic to cloak the administration's messages as objective television news. And it's all done at the taxpayers' expense. [11]

If only one side of a disputed issue is presented with no possibility of follow-up questions, and it is covertly presented in the guise of independent "news," how can the viewer develop informed opinions and then transfer those outlooks onto their voting ballot? In other words, how can democracy survive?

Suggested Reforms

Freepress.net offers the following suggested reform ideas. [1]

1. Create and support genuine, independent and noncommercial public broadcasting.
2. Independent media of all kinds must be supported.
3. Legislation reversing media ownership consolidation must be enacted.
4. Diversity in media ownership, staffing and representation must be increased.
5. Our broken media regulatory processes must be revamped.
6. Big Media must be accountable to citizens.
7. Require broadcasters to provide free air time for all candidates.
8. Support micro-broadcasting and low power FM.
9. Keep media out of global trade deals.
10. Prevent Big Media from stifling innovation and the free flow of information, on the Internet and elsewhere.

YES! Magazine dedicated its entire Spring 2005 issue to the Media. They highlighted Amy Goodman's independent news program, Democracy Now!, which literally redefines the meaning of "independent." In an interview with Carolyn McConnell, she states her simple philosophy:

> Spotlighting competitive spins on a controversial issue does not constitute good journalism. Facts coupled with a wide range of perspectives on those facts does…Journalism is the only profession explicitly protected by the U.S. Constitution, because journalists are supposed to be the check and balance on government. We're supposed to be holding those in power accountable. We're not supposed to be their megaphone. That's what the corporate media have become…I think what makes Democracy Now! special is that we are a daily, global, grassroots, unembedded news hour committed to airing the voices of people all over the world. [12]

Partnership Media

The importance of hearing the voices of people throughout the world (and our own culture) cannot be underestimated. Yet a recent study by Fairness & Accuracy in

Reporting (FAIR) analyzed on-air news broadcasts over the last few years with the intention of finding if there was a gender/race bias. Not surprisingly, ABC, CBS, NBC, CNN, and FOX all showed a strong white, male, and politically right predisposition. How can the voice of dissent ever hope to be heard? Their statistics reveal the following:

> During the three weeks leading up to the U.S. invasion of Iraq, only 3 percent of U.S. sources on the evening news shows of ABC, CBS, NBC, CNN, Fox, and PBS expressed anti-war opinions – even though more than a quarter of the U.S. public at the time opposed invasion.

> Even National Public Radio fails to give voice to the public: a 2004 FAIR study found that nine of the top 10 most-frequently used sources on NPR were white male government officials. Corporate sources (6 percent) were given almost as much air time as public interest groups (7 percent), and four men were heard for every woman. [13]

No wonder so many of us feel out-of-touch with the mainstream message! The large majority of Americans who fall outside the category of white, male, and right-leaning need to be heard. We need to acknowledge the strong dominator-trace censorship structurally alive within our media system. Such unconscious censorship adversely affects us all – especially within the hugely influential realm of the media. Increasingly our perceptions of all aspects of life on Earth are derived from the media. We owe it to ourselves and all life to shift our awareness and take action.

How can Media Serve ALL Life?

If the purpose of our news media was less to promote private financial agendas, and more to provide balanced reporting without the hidden, carefully framed, or missing language that today often confuses the facts, perhaps the following example of a high level of news accountability could become a reality… for only then can we make informed decisions that benefit us all.

> Imagine Peter Jennings on the network news tonight reciting the latest Commerce Department figures with his polished gravity. Instead of the GDP, however, he is reporting something more like the GPI (Genuine Progress Indicator). The nation's output increased, he says, but parents worked longer hours, and so had less time with their kids. Consumer spending was "up sharply," but much of the difference went for increased medical costs and repairing the rubble left by hurricanes and floods. Utility receipts were up, but resources declined, meaning that part of today's prosperity was taken from our grandchildren. And so on down the line… Suddenly reporters and politicians alike would have to confront the economy that people actually experience. There would be some genuine accountability in Washington, a better sense of cause and effect between what Congress does and what happens in our lives. [14]

Can you imagine a society offering news in such a way that, (to the best of our ability), the whole story is told – both what works and what doesn't – not with shame but with enthusiasm? Because we know that whatever doesn't work can be remedied as we constantly assess and then co-create together.

A media that honors all would be an independent and effective media, one that is designed specifically to support the citizen's right to be thoroughly and impartially informed. It would include the intention to act as a watchdog against manipulation, dishonesty, and ulterior motives; and it would be mindful of the contextual frames invoked by politicians and others to sway public perception.

Most of all, media that honors all would LISTEN. It would listen to the voices of all people, especially those who have been disenfranchised or dismissed as unimportant in the past. It would listen to the voices of all – equally – not just Americans, or corporate executives, or even so-called "experts," because ultimately ALL voices are important and valid. Then it would step beyond the voices of humans and listen to the non-human voices as well, dismissing none as less important than others. It would take a systems approach to information, eagerly combining seemingly unrelated information with the intent to notice overlooked patterns of meaning. It would pro-actively seek out perceptual viewpoints not yet embraced, with the intent of finding new and creative viewpoints and solutions to pressing issues.

We are describing a society that is dedicated to the welfare of its entire being, not just the human element, but the welfare of *all* life, because finally there is no perceived separation between elements that constitute that society. Everything and everyone is perceived as related, not just to each other, but to entire systems nested within systems. In this context, everything matters. As we learn to re-perceive ourselves and our world, we are birthing ourselves anew.

Notes

1. www.Freepress.Net
2. See the chapter on the COMMONS for more information.
3. Facts and Figures about our TV Habit, from TV-Turnoff Network, www.trturnoff.org
4. On Media and the Election, By Robert W. McChesney
5. Broadcast Industry Contributions to Bush Total $523,000 – Source: Federal Election Commission contribution records from January 1998 to September 2004, from http://www.publicintegrity.org/telecom/analysis/InfluenceTracker.aspx?MODE=CONTRECD&RECIPID=648 Broadcast Industry Contributions to Kerry Total $386,000 – Source: Federal Election Commission contribution records from January 1998 to September 2004, from http://www.publicintegrity.org/telecom/analysis/InfluenceTracker.aspx?MODE=CONTRECD&RECIPID=648
6. DON'T THINK OF AN ELEPHANT! George Lakoff, page 4.
7. DON'T THINK OF AN ELEPHANT! George Lakoff, pages 25 -26.
8. This chart is primarily based on information from *Columbia Journalism Review*'s Who Owns What? Site, one of many excellent resources on the web regarding media ownership http://www.freepress.net/ownership/
9. http://www.publicintegrity.org/telecom/report.aspx?aid=406
10. David Barstow and Robin Stein, Under Bush, a New Age of Prepackaged TV News, March 13, 2005, New York Times. (By David Barstow And Robin Stein; Anne E. Kornblut Contributed Reporting For This Article). (NYT)
11. http://www.freepress.net/propaganda/
12. Carolyn McConnell, Going to Where the Silence Is, YES! Magazine Spring 2005 Reprinted from YES! magazine, PO Box 10818, Bainbridge Island, WA 98110. Subscriptions: 800/937-4451 Web: www.yesmagazine.org
13. Julie Hollar, Who's the Expert?, YES! Magazine Spring 2005, page 29. Reprinted from YES! magazine, PO Box 10818, Bainbridge Island, WA 98110. Subscriptions: 800/937-4451 Web: www.yesmagazine.org
14. IF THE GDP IS UP, WHY IS AMERICA DOWN?, by Clifford Cobb, Ted Halstead, and Jonathan Rowe from *The Atlantic Monthly*, October 1995, taken from the Northwest Earth Institute Discussion Course on CHOICES FOR SUSTAINABLE LIVING, © 2000, with permission.

18

COMMUNICATION

Ultimately, listening empathically
does not imply doing what the person wants;
rather, it implies showing respectful acknowledgment
of the individual's inner world.
As we do that, we move from the coercive language we have been taught
to the language of the heart.

Marshall Rosenberg
NonViolent Communication

COMMUNICATION

I remember the situation clearly. I was in a Nonviolent Communication class when it suddenly struck me that there was hardly a thought I had – or a word I said – that wasn't sourced from judgment. I was bowled over with shock. Suddenly years of communication as a parent, friend, wife, and daughter flashed before me – all of them filled with judgment.

For the first time I saw that my way of perceiving and speaking was almost always drawn from this habit. For example, when my adult son came to visit, I immediately jumped into a state of scrutiny in which every nuance of his behavior, every statement made, every facial expression, and even his energy was read, compared with previous data, and then judged. Was he improving, learning, growing, getting "better," advancing, loving himself enough, etc? It wasn't so much the fact that I did what all parents do – assess the condition of their child in order to do their job well – it was the *way* in which I did it that shocked me.

For the first time I began to see what it might feel like to be on the receiving end of that experience. I began imagining what it must be like for my son if he experienced his mother similarly to the way a bug might experience a child examining it under a magnifying glass. Yuck! That was not the experience I wanted my children – nor anyone – to have of me. I had always thought of myself as non-judgmental. Now I realized that to a great extent, that's all I did!

I saw that it was a cultural habit, a way of being that we all do to some extent. It is often praised as "critical thinking." In that context it is a wonderfully useful tool, but when it becomes the modus operandi of our interpersonal interactions, it no longer serves anyone. Surprisingly, a careful analysis of our use of language reveals that it is built into our way of communicating.

So here I was, sitting in a communication class learning to listen to the person speaking, with new ears. As we practiced, I began to notice as judgments arose, as my attention shifted from listening to him, to formulating my reply. I watched as my attention shifted back and forth between us. As my ability to sense this "dance" of connection improved, I was also able to discern when he was fully present or off in his mind, separate and unable to hear me.

I learned to listen for the speaker's deepest feelings and needs, especially those that weren't yet acknowledged. And when I wasn't clear, I learned to guess his feelings and needs while paraphrasing his own words back to him, encouraging him to correct me, until I was truly complete and clear about his experience.

My intention was to remain neutral and open such that I could truly hear what was going on for *him*, not me. I found that if I connected deeply and empathically with his feelings and needs, only then could I understand his motives. Only then could I see beyond his "story" (the details of explanation about why he was choosing to do what he was doing) to the actual needs that he felt would be fulfilled through his choice of actions. Or at least I would have begun to understand, far more clearly, what his perceptions regarding the topic were. And I needed that. We both did. How could I begin to discuss the topic with him until he and I were both clear about those details? We couldn't. How could I begin to explain my own needs and feelings in a manner that he would be willing to listen? I have found that only when I am willing to listen empathically to another's communication, are they willing to listen to mine. One of the best ways of accomplishing this is through Non-Violent Communication.

Nonviolent Communication

Developed by Dr. Marshall Rosenberg[1], Director of the Center for Nonviolent Communication in Geneva, Switzerland, NVC has been perfected over the past 28 years. The process helps people to connect, no matter what the situation, by reminding them to shift their attention from defending their own stance - to listening with the intention of hearing the needs and feelings of the person speaking.

An Example…

As I practiced NVC, several realizations become apparent. I realized that most of the verbal communication I have used in my life has had an underlying judgment built right into the language itself. This realization has forced me to place my awareness on the *intent* behind my words. Even though I think I am aware of my intent, further scrutiny usually reveals that my awareness was casual at best.

Once I saw how easily our language accommodates judgment, I began to practice neutrally observing events, instead of seeing though the lens of judgment. Sound easy? It's much more difficult than it first seems.

When I asked my 9-year-old to do a chore, I instantly learned the difference. I wanted to react to what I perceived as her "failure" to do a specific chore, by telling her how she took me for granted and always expected me to clean up after her. Yet all of that was MY interpretation.

What really happened was that I witnessed her walk by something I had asked her to pick up without giving it her attention. That was it. Everything else was MY perceptual filter that had preconceived the idea that my child took me for granted and didn't appreciate my efforts.

I realized that I needed to give myself some tender loving attention. So I took a moment to go within and remember what a great job I was doing in raising my children, taking care of my house, and all the other things I do every day. I realized that MY need for acknowledgment was not being met – even by me.

Once I gave myself that needed acknowledgment, I was better able to be clear and loving with my child. I was able to tell her how I felt when I witnessed her walking by and not picking up the item I had just asked her to put away – all without adding overtones of judgment. Just the facts. Because my needs were met, I was able to hear what was going on for her at that moment, and to fully connect with her experience.

I was no longer her victim and she was no longer mine. What a change! Like most people, I have no desire to judge those around me, nor myself. Awareness of just how pervasive this habit had become in my life freed me to consciously pay attention to my thoughts and words. What a gift!

Since in order to speak, one must first listen, learn to speak by listening.

Rumi
(1207-1273)

Imprecise Language

I have also noticed my inelegant and imprecise use of language. This is usually tied to my own self-awareness. When I am clear about what I want to say, I speak clearly. I noticed that when I was not clear, or even worse, when I was deliberately evading clarity, I found it extremely difficult to speak from my heart.

Our culture does not always reward honesty or transparency. At times the simplest concepts can be excruciatingly difficult to convey as we trip over our cultural "niceties" and assumptions. It isn't "polite" to speak what you are really thinking. It isn't polite to discuss money. It is invasive to truly inquire about another's feelings, and it is doubly invasive to answer that inquiry with the truth.

Attention and Intention

Something surprising happens we drop all assumptions and allow our hearts to connect by focusing our attention on listening to the feelings and needs supporting what is being spoken. When you are willing to risk failure by guessing what is true for another with the intention of connection, and are willing to paraphrase back what you heard until you are absolutely clear; barriers dissolve and magic occurs. Doors open between hearts, and the magnificence of the "other" becomes a reflection of the magnificence of the Self.

Perhaps there is no greater honoring you can offer another than to simply listen with full *attention* and with full non-judgmental *intention* to understand.

Heart Communication

Beyond verbal communication are all the realms of non-verbal communication. This may seem obvious, but aside from our emphasis on the most cursory visual perceptions, few humans currently place much attention on them. Yet it is a world rich with communication.

As I learned to merge with nature, I expanded my focus to include everything, including humans. Merging with humans is truly a joy, and with practice one can feel deeper and deeper connection, especially if the other person is consciously choosing to merge with you.

When my children were young I taught them to connect with me whenever they wanted. It was a simple process. I asked them to go within their hearts and "feel" my energy there. It was their way of "calling" me.

As a mother I am always connected to my children whether they are physically near or not. I have found that whenever I am absorbed in some activity while my children are elsewhere, and suddenly think of them, it is usually because they are calling me on a subtle level. I then pause and go within. I allow the energy of that child to enter my heart. I actually picture our hearts connecting. Within the connection I can "feel" their energy. I can usually also feel whatever emotion they are experiencing. Sometimes I receive pictures or nuances of information that help me guide them. Whatever happens, I always remind them of their own innate power that resides within their heart. I remind them that they can always trust whatever their heart(Essential Self) tells them. Most of the time I simply send them love.

If you want to go even one more layer, truly dynamic dialogue requires a deep knowledge of the creative process, the cycle of how ideas are formed, dissolved and new ones arise in their place. This cycle has emotional, cognitive and spiritual connotations. It requires a profound ability to be out of control and to surrender to forces of chaos that allow existing knowledge and beliefs to be transformed.

Mikela and Philip Tarlow Authors of Digital Aboriginal... from their Newsletter Shape Shifter News – Volume One date October 20, 2002

232

When we finally do connect later, it is always amazing to see how accurate our connection was. The following essay was written by my daughter, Marika, at my request. She describes *her* experience of this non-local form of communication.

When I was growing up, I had a magic wardrobe. At least, it was magic to me. This wardrobe was in my parent's room and struck me with a mixture of fear and awe every time I looked at it. It was carved out of wood but the wood had been cut in such a way that there were beautiful patterns that looked like devilish faces covering its surface. My brother, my mom and I would lie on my parent's bed and discuss the faces that seemed to stare back at us. The faces seemed to be mocking us with laughter and sinister glee. I would imagine that I could step inside that wardrobe and enter another world full of magical adventures just like the characters in the book The Lion, the Witch, and the Wardrobe. And I did, in fact, try several times to find that world. I would grab my little brother by the hand and pull him into the little space inside. (This was much too scary to do alone). But, of course, we would find ourselves in a tangle of clothes in that cramped space with nowhere to go but out the same face-covered door through which we had come. Eventually, I stopped trying to find that other world through the back of the wardrobe but the sense of fear and awe when standing in front of those faces never left me.

When I was thirteen years old, I suddenly had the opportunity to fulfill a dream I had had since the beginning of the school language program in second grade. A French boy, a year older than me, would come live with us for a month. In exchange, I would be going back to France with him to live with his family for a month as well. Overwhelming excitement drowned out any fear that might have made me hesitate at leaving my family for a month to live with strangers who spoke another language. It wasn't until the trip was at hand that all that fear pushed its way through the excitement and forced me into the reality of what I was doing. I had never been away from my mother for so long, let alone in another country. I see now that I was very young for thirteen and that my mother was hoping not only to introduce me to other parts of the world, but also to give me a little boost in growing up.

However, when the time came I needed some reassuring. I needed something to hold on to so that I would not cry myself to sleep every night with loneliness. So my mother sat me down and elaborated on an idea that she had told me my whole life. She told me that no matter where I am in the world or where she is in the world we can always find each other in our hearts. She told me that all I have to do is look inside myself, concentrate on her, and she would be there. My connection with my mother has always been strong so this idea was very comforting to me. For the whole month I was in France, from the first long plane ride to the last, I felt my mother in the back of my mind like a guardian angel. And I knew that she also had me in the back of her mind. I knew that my mother was somehow aware of my thoughts of her.

But, as the days wore on and I became lonelier and lonelier, this afterthought of my mother was not enough. So, as I lay in bed at night, I began to imagine that I would come to my mother through that magical wardrobe standing in her room. Those same mocking faces in the wood would whisper and call to me and my mind would race through the world until I found them. I would find myself tangled in those same clothes in which I had tried so hard to find an opening to Narnia. Then I would find the door and push into the light of my parents room and mom would be there, ready to embrace me. And my whole body would feel relaxed in her arms and I would fall asleep.

To this day, I remember this as something real. Not so much the faces whispering to me or stepping through the wardrobe into the real room in my parent's house but the feeling of my mother holding me in her arms I remember as real. That feeling remains a part of my memory as though she had been physically standing there in the room with me. Now I realize that I was a very imaginative child who liked very much the drama of magical wardrobes and mocking wooden faces. But all of that was dressing up the real point of what was happening. I was connecting to my mother. Whether that was real or not does not really matter because it was real to me. I changed my own reality. I chose not to be alone.

My mother wanted that trip to France to be a growing experience for me and it was indeed one of the most life changing experiences I have had to date. My trip to France taught me so much about life, people, the incredible size of the world. But most of all it taught me that no matter where I am or how alone I may be physically, I am the one who chooses to wallow in that loneliness or chooses to step through my magic wardrobe and embrace someone I love. Thanks to my mother's little talk about always being a thought away, and my very active imagination, I developed a tool that I can use again and again in my life. This tool is the ability to manipulate my own perception of being alone. How I perceive myself as alone or in the thoughts of my family or loved ones dictates how alone I really am. I am the wardrobe.

Given the subjective nature of our perceptions, I am often awed by the ability we have to communicate at all. Yet we do, and when we open our hearts, that connection transcends space and time.

Merging

Can you imagine what life would be like if we allowed ourselves to connect so deeply that we actually merged? I have had the joy of experiencing this kind of merging, and I believe it will become more common as we allow ourselves to experience deeper levels of perceptual ability.

I understand that this is difficult for some to discuss, but consider it this way. Science is still discovering new perceptual abilities in humans. What if we eventually find that the abilities I'm describing here are nothing more than a holographic effect at the quantum level? Respected scientists from David Bohm, Larry Dossey, Elisabet Sahtouris, Karl Pribram, to Nassim Haramein all have been engaged in the study of holographic theory and discuss non-local events.[2]

I have a friend in New York who I can think of, feel his energy, and then send him a thought message. Sometimes the message is as simple as "call me" or sometimes it is an emotional package, a sort of "snap shot" of my state at the moment. Either way the connection is always made. I believe we all possess this capacity to communicate across distances and even time, for ultimately they are all illusions.[2]

Compassionate Listening

God gave us two ears and only one mouth, that we should listen twice as much as we speak.

universal proverb

I've also had the privilege of studying the methodology of the Compassionate Listening Project. Just as powerful as the Non-Violent Communication teachings, Compassionate Listening asks the listener to place her judgments aside and to listen with the intention of understanding the speaker's point of view. It also concentrates on teaching the listener to create the same compassionate "container" used to listen to others – when listening to our own inner voice – one that is free of judgment, that allows for different points of view at different times, and that is infinitely gentle and forgiving.

Their work in war-torn part of the world, from Bosnia to Palestine, is a powerful force of reconciliation; and a testament to the possibilities available when humans honor each other[3]

Compassionate Mirroring

Perhaps one of the greatest tools is the practice of mirroring the speaker's own magnificence as you listen. This requires an open and accepting heart, and it works miracles. When you allow yourself to truly see the divine within the speaker – no matter what the speaker is saying, or how the speaker is speaking – you allow your own magnificence to connect with the speaker's. At that magical moment, you truly become ONE, as all boundaries between speaker and listener dissolve, and they simply become love recognizing itself.

It is time for humans to explore ourselves as fields of *possibility* instead of limitation. This concept alone could bring about a renaissance in the human experience. **When we see ourselves and each other as fields of possibility, instead of packages of limitations, we allow ourselves to truly honor the very essence of Who We Are.**

Notes

1. Visit http://cnvc.org/, The Center for Nonviolent Communication. Also see H. Holley Humphrey's Practice, Practice, Practice!, An Illustrated Study Guide to Compassionate Communication. You can reach Holley Humphrey at 233 Rogue River Hwy #173, Grants Pass, OR 97527, 541-862-2043, http://www.empathymagic.com/. E-mail: holley@empathymagic.com

2. See Holographic Universe, by Michael Talbot, Harper-Collins, 1991; The Point of it All, By Nassim Haramein, http://www.theresonanceproject.org/home.htm; and Discovering the Living Universe - Scientific Spirituality for a Global Family , Elisabet Sahtouris, Ph.D. 2003 http://www.ratical.org/LifeWeb/Articles/DiscoverLivU.pdf

3. http://www.compassionatelistening.org/

The Face of a Stranger

When the winds of conflict blow across the landscape of our lives

Will we choose to embrace the illusions that we are separate?

I no longer see the face of a stranger.

I have tried, but every face I see looks familiar,

As that of an old friend remembered after years apart.

I gaze into the faces of those I am told are the target of our guns

And all I see is life's jubilant gaze staring back at me.

How can I choose to make an enemy of Life?

When I see with my heart, when I see past the veil of separation,

I see only actors playing their parts on the stage of life.

My soul takes wing, soaring above limiting views

Of right and wrong – good and bad.

I see only love and life glistening with the light of an inner illumination,

Greeting the new dawn of this moment with halleluiahs of recognition, singing

We are the saviors we seek,

We are the peace we long for,

We are the love unconditioned,

We are only a choice away.

March 29, 2003.

19

CONFLICT

Wisdom Of The Dalai Lama...
At the end of the talk someone from the audience asked the Dalai Lama,
"Why didn't you fight back against the Chinese?"
The Dalai Lama looked down, swung his feet just a bit,
then looked back up at us and said with a gentle smile,
"Well, war is obsolete, you know."
Then, after a few moments, his face grave, he said,
"Of course the mind can rationalize fighting back...but the heart,
the heart would never understand.
Then you would be divided in yourself, the heart and the mind,
and the war would be inside you".

CONFLICT

Those with whom we have a strong reaction, are our greatest teachers about ourselves.

One Veteran's Day, as I sunk into the warm waves of my bath water preparing to completely submerge myself in the stillness of this underwater cocoon, I heard a talk show host introduce two Veterans on the radio. Slowly I sank under the surface, shutting off all communication with the outside world.

Then it struck me. I was unconsciously choosing to disconnect myself from anything having to do with the military – just as I had my entire life. After all, I told myself, I am a lover of peace. Yet for the first time I paused. As the speaker began to tell his story, I found myself wanting to hear more. So I listened. For the first time in decades, I paused in my pursuit of peace long enough to actually listen to the life story of a career military man.

Surprisingly, he sounded just like every other person I ever heard talking about the intricate details of his job. His concerns were about the quality of his work and the safety of those he served.

When I allow myself to honor each person enough to really hear his story, I allow myself to experience the multiplicity and depth of that person's reality, and their own creative expression within their perceived reality. Only then can we begin to meet on common ground. Only then can we begin to create a world in which we truly experience ourselves as one.

Righteousness and Greed

A Native American grandfather was talking to his grandson about how he felt. He said, "I feel as if I have two wolves fighting in my heart. One wolf is the vengeful, angry, violent one. The other wolf is the loving, compassionate one."

The grandson asked him, "Which wolf will win the fight in your heart?"

The grandfather answered, "The one I feed."

When I think about war, it is usually about two things…being right and greed, and both come from a position of dominance. Those two issues seem to be the obvious motivations for almost all conflict. Either someone has something someone else wants, like natural resources (oil, water, or land for example); or one group embraces a different belief-structure, and the other group attempts to force them into submission, using the concept of "might proves right" to excuse their willingness to kill and dominate another. Usually a combination of both is in effect. Additionally, violence is often born of self-hate.

But what are the deeper, personal, non-political motivations? What part of us is ignored in order to chose military solutions? It doesn't make much difference whether I hire someone to kill (as in the military), or I do it myself; the choice to use dominant force to solve our problems still remains.

Another Perceptual Filter

Until we shift our perceptions of life from a "dog eat dog" mentality (also known as the "dominator trance") to one of honoring all (or Partnership), we will continue to make choices that diminish our sense of who we are. Personally, I'd rather see myself as a loving, whole, and magnificent being who honors all life and lives in harmony; instead of as a person who solves complex issues through fear and survival motivated domination and force. One choice feels expansive and open, one feels limiting and heavy. We each have the opportunity to choose which we prefer in every moment.

Learning from What Is

Instead of seeing conflict as a "problem", what if we chose to see it as a learning experience? In fact, what if we saw all life as a learning experience... a gift for our own personal growth? When we allow ourselves to see the circumstances of our lives as a gift, a kind of hands-on learning experience, then our questions change...

- What is the lesson you've come to learn here?

- What choice can you make, in this moment, that allows you to experience your own magnificence and that of those around you? Another way of saying this is, "If you chose to honor all in this experience, what would you do?"

- Why did you bring these circumstances into your life? (Asked with great innocence, this last question does not imply blame, but instead is a testament to the wisdom inherent in each individual – a wisdom so vast that life lessons are always handled in the most creative and elegant way possible.)

- If we acknowledge the highly subjective nature of our own perceptions, and thus allow for each person's freedom to experience their own personal subjective "reality", we can ask ourselves possibly the most revealing question of all:

- What about the issues involved; touch you so deeply that you are willing to create a war *within* yourself, between your "position" (or need to be right) and the loving being you know yourself to be?

- What illusion are you attached to that keeps you from seeing your enemy as yourself?

- These are the questions I ask myself whenever conflict arises. I invite you to find the questions that best work for you. They have assisted me in seeing beyond the omote or obvious issue, into the underlying issues waiting to be healed within me. I have found that the core of almost all conflict has nothing to do with what seems to be the easily perceived issue – the one everyone talks about to keep from dealing with the deeper wounds that touch us all.

Asoka

One of the most powerful lessons I ever learned came through viewing the film, "Asoka". I saw it at the beginning of the US invasion of Iraq. It taught me to see war in a new light.

Asoka is the retelling of the transformation from warlord to Buddhist pacifist of one of India's most famous rulers. Following in his grandfather's footsteps, Asoka (299-237 BCE) tried to complete the conquest of the Indian peninsula. Yet he became so disgusted with the cruelty of war that he renounced warfare and embraced Buddhism, sending missionaries throughout the land and beyond. Two of his children became Buddhist saints.

Non-Violence: "The fulfillment of the latent potential of each individual."

Violence: "avoidable compromise of human needs."

Johan Galtung
Definition of Non-Violence from Michael Nagler Compassion – The Radicalism of this Age Yes! Magazine Fall 1998

There is nothing except a tragic death wish to prevent us from reordering our priorities so that pursuit of peace will take precedence over the pursuit of war.

Martin Luther King, Jr.

I know there is anger. I feel it myself. But I don't want my son used as a pawn to justify the killing of others. We as a nation should not use the same means as the people who attacked us.

Oscar Rodriguez, (whose son died in the attack on the World Trade Center Sept. 11, 2001)

I was so upset that my country had invaded Iraq, I felt a need to witness a transformation from war to peace, and intended to watch the film as a kind of deep healing. I was in for a surprise.

I had assumed the story would be about the transformation, but most of it dwelled on the horrors of war. The promised transformation didn't take place until the last few minutes of the film, forcing me to watch hours of gory warfare – exactly the thing I hadn't wanted to watch. I was so furious that the film had been marketed in such a misleading manner, that I couldn't sleep.

Finally I asked my Inner Voice for insight into why this film stirred so much anguish within me. I was thoroughly surprised by the answer I received, and share that dialog below:

My heart cries in pain at the killings that seem to be the desire of humanity... why? Where is the love we are? How can I watch yet another mother cry over her child, another child over his parent, sister, brother?

Must we all devour each other in blood until there is nothing left? Must we devour our planet as well? My sadness knows no bounds as I cry tears for us all... our illusions that lead us to such choices...our stubbornness, our unwillingness to step into our own shoes and be who we are.

How much courage does it take to say I LOVE YOU? How much pain can we endure before there is no more energy left to cry another tear? We have asked ourselves this for millennia...when will we be able to embrace each other at last? When will we be able to *see*? We have all been blind for so many thousands of years... blind to all that is real.

Inner Voice: Dear One, you who choose the eyes of love, do not choose for another. Honor yourself and walk your path, but do not ask that others follow you...only you can choose for yourself.

Instead encourage them to choose their own path, whatever it is. Do you think that the many hundreds of deaths on the battlefield amounted to anything but your awakening? Just as Asoka finally saw the futility of his actions, the emptiness of his life... so you can trust that each will do so in right timing. *Their timing* ... not yours.

When the armies come to slaughter everything in their path, it is your choice to join them or be slaughtered. Which choice honors you - and which does not? That is all you need concern yourself with. Everything else is the choice of those you see as other than yourself. They are not, dear one.

Know this. There is only you on the battlefield. Only you wield the sword, and only you fall at its blade. How many times must you reenact this drama before you understand and choose differently? It may be just in this last bloody moment, as the last breath escapes your lungs in which you choose a different path from the past. Would you then deny yourself that experience if it brought you to your own awakening?

Do not, then, deny it of any other. Honor choice. Honor the divine in all. Choose your path and trust in the unfolding of each person's choice. This is the way of honor.

Do you see now why you had to watch this film? Do you understand the lessons learned? Give gratitude that the advertiser mislead you, for in so doing you have learned to honor others. This is love in one of its highest forms. Know this. Live it. BE it.

Know this also, dear one. Each and every death is over in an instant, but the lesson lasts for eternity. Celebrate then. Give gratitude for the awakening of yet another heart. Rejoice in each person's choice ...for there are no wrong choices... only different ones. What works for you does not for another. Allow. Trust. Let go.

Malnutrition among the youngest Iraqis has almost doubled since the U.S.-led invasion toppled Saddam Hussein, a hunger specialist told the U.N. human rights body Wednesday March 30, 2005 in a summary of previously reported studies on health in Iraq.

Acute malnutrition rates among Iraqi children under five rose late last year to 7.7 per cent from four per cent after the ouster of President Saddam Hussein in April 2003, said Jean Ziegler, the UN Human Rights Commission's special expert on the right to food.

Overall, more than one-quarter of Iraqi children don't have enough to eat, Ziegler told a meeting of the 53-country commission, the top UN rights watchdog, which is halfway through its annual six-week session.

The U.S. delegation and other coalition countries did not respond to the report.

<u>UN Monitor: War on Iraq Has Doubled Malnutrition Among Iraqi Children</u>

Published on Thursday, March 31, 2005 by the Associated Press

http://www.commondreams.org/headlines05/0331-08.htm

Relax into the knowing that all is unfolding in perfection. Yes, even as sons and daughters are being slaughtered in your county's name. Allow yourself to step back from the story and see the larger picture. Let go of the story all together.

What matters if the battleground is now or a thousand years ago? The lessons learned are all that matter. The energy exchanged – the love expressed.

(Rumi wrote,) "Beyond all ideas of right and wrong, there is a field. I'll meet you there." Yes, always! For that is where we truly live. Know this and live it. This is your challenge.

Do you see the veils dropping? Breathe deeply of the new light flooding your heart. Be at peace and choose in this moment who you are, then choose again in the next. That is truly all. Namasté

I share these words with you, trusting that you will take what resonates deeply within, and discard the rest.

Innocence

Ultimately, at a certain level, all participants in war are innocent. We are the victims of our own narrow perceptions of life, acquired through assumptions about life that are native to the cultures in which we live and our own life experiences.

This does not remove our responsibility for the choices we've made, but adds compassion for the highly subjective and selective nature of perception. I would guess that most of us perceive possibly no more than 1% of what is actually happening at any given moment. (In fact, one percent could represent those moments when we are at our *most* aware and open state of perception.) Such a humbling concept opens the heart to compassion for all our miss-perceptions and miss-communications. Only when we surrender to the wisdom of the heart, can we begin to truly perceive and communicate.

Camilo Mejia wrote the following essay while in prison, reprinted with permission from the author and Code Pink, whose Forward appears below. I invite you to read the full essay with an open heart – regardless of your political beliefs - allowing his words to wash over and through you like a gentle rain. Imagine being in his position, what choices would you have made?

> We were delighted to receive a phone call yesterday, February 15, from Camilo Mejia, letting us know that he has just been released from prison. Some of you might remember Camilo, a courageous soldier who spent more than 7 years in the military, 8 months fighting in Iraq, came home for a 2-week furlough, and decided that he could not—in good conscience—return to Iraq. He applied for Conscientious Objector status, and was declared a Prisoner of Conscience by Amnesty International. But the US military convicted him of desertion, and sent him to serve a one-year prison sentence in Fort Sill, Oklahoma. This happened the same day that Spc. Jeremy Sivits was court-martialed and sentenced to a year in prison for abusing Iraqi prisoners at Abu Ghraib, an order Camilo had refused to obey.

Regaining My Humanity
By Camilo Mejia

I was deployed to Iraq in April 2003 and returned home for a two-week leave in October. Going home gave me the opportunity to put my thoughts in order and to listen to what my conscience had to say. People would ask me about my war experiences and answering them took me back to all the horrors—the firefights, the ambushes, the time I saw a young Iraqi dragged by his shoulders through a pool of his own blood or an innocent man was decapitated by our machine gun fire. The time I saw a soldier broken down inside because he killed a child, or an old man on

The first scientific study of the human cost of the Iraq war was done by U.S. and Iraqi researchers, led by the School of Public Health in Baltimore. The team surveyed 1,000 households in 33 randomly chosen areas in Iraq. The researchers found that the risk of violent death was 58 times higher in the period since the invasion, and that most of the victims were women and children. … their final horrifying calculation of more than 100,000 civilian deaths made front-page news in many parts of the world.

… Iraq's child malnutrition rate now roughly equals that of Burundi, a central African nation torn by more than a decade of war. It is far higher than child malnutrition rates in Uganda and Haiti. And this in a country where, just a generation ago, the biggest nutritional problem for young Iraqis was obesity. …

While Iraqis have certainly suffered the most from this war, the cost in lives of U.S. soldiers continues to mount, nearing 1,500 by the end of 2004. Another 10,000 U.S. soldiers have been wounded in action…

Medea Benjamin
Humanitarian Crisis in Iraq Worsens   Feb 25th, 2005

A delegation of military family members whose sons died while fighting in the Iraq war will travel to Jordan from December 27, 2004 to January 4, 2005 to deliver $600,000 worth of humanitarian supplies for refugees from the U.S. attack on Falluja. The November attack, which virtually leveled the city and left some 2,000 Iraqis and 71 U.S. soldiers dead, also created thousands of refugees, who are living without adequate food, water, electricity and healthcare. Most of these refugees are children.

"This delegation is a way for me to express my sympathy and support for the Iraqi people. The Iraq war took away my son's life, and it's taken away the lives of so many innocent Iraqis. It's time to stop the killing and to help the children of Iraq," said Rosa Suarez of Escondido, CA, whose son Jesus was a marine who died in Iraq on March 27, 2003.

In an Internet appeal, the military family members, in collaboration with U.S. peace groups, physicians' organizations, and September 11 families, quickly raised $100,000 in donations from Americans who are concerned about the impact of our government's policies on innocent Iraqi civilians. And humanitarian groups such as the Middle East Children's Alliance and Operation USA contributed $500,000 worth of medical supplies.

Code Pink Press Release December 20th, 2004 http://www.codepinkalert. org/Press_Room_delegatio n.shtml

his knees, crying with his arms raised to the sky, perhaps asking God why we had taken the lifeless body of his son.

I thought of the suffering of a people whose country was in ruins and who were further humiliated by the raids, patrols and curfews of an occupying army.

And I realized that none of the reasons we were told about why we were in Iraq turned out to be true. There were no weapons of mass destruction. There was no link between Saddam Hussein and al Qaeda. We weren't helping the Iraqi people and the Iraqi people didn't want us there. We weren't preventing terrorism or making Americans safer. I couldn't find a single good reason for having been there, for having shot at people and been shot at.

Coming home gave me the clarity to see the line between military duty and moral obligation. I realized that I was part of a war that I believed was immoral and criminal, a war of aggression, a war of imperial domination. I realized that acting upon my principles became incompatible with my role in the military, and I decided that I could not return to Iraq.

By putting my weapon down, I chose to reassert myself as a human being. I have not deserted the military or been disloyal to the men and women of the military. I have not been disloyal to a country. I have only been loyal to my principles.

When I turned myself in, with all my fears and doubts, it did it not only for myself. I did it for the people of Iraq, even for those who fired upon me—they were just on the other side of a battleground where war itself was the only enemy. I did it for the Iraqi children, who are victims of mines and depleted uranium. I did it for the thousands of unknown civilians killed in war. My time in prison is a small price compared to the price Iraqis and Americans have paid with their lives. Mine is a small price compared to the price Humanity has paid for war.

Many have called me a coward, others have called me a hero. I believe I can be found somewhere in the middle. To those who have called me a hero, I say that I don't believe in heroes, but I believe that ordinary people can do extraordinary things.

To those who have called me a coward I say that they are wrong, and that without knowing it, they are also right. They are wrong when they think that I left the war for fear of being killed. I admit that fear was there, but there was also the fear of killing innocent people, the fear of putting myself in a position where to survive means to kill, there was the fear of losing my soul in the process of saving my body, the fear of losing myself to my daughter, to the people who love me, to the man I used to be, the man I wanted to be. I was afraid of waking up one morning to realize my humanity had abandoned me.

I say without any pride that I did my job as a soldier. I commanded an infantry squad in combat and we never failed to accomplish our mission. But those who called me a coward, without knowing it, are also right. I was a coward not for leaving the war, but for having been a part of it in the first place. Refusing and resisting this war was my moral duty, a moral duty that called me to take a principled action. I failed to fulfill my moral duty as a human being and instead I chose to fulfill my duty as a soldier. All because I was afraid. I was terrified, I did not want to stand up to the government and the army, I was afraid of punishment and humiliation. I went to war because at the moment I was a coward, and for that I apologize to my soldiers for not being the type of leader I should have been.

I also apologize to the Iraqi people. To them I say I am sorry for the curfews, for the raids, for the killings. May they find it in their hearts to forgive me.

One of the reasons I did not refuse the war from the beginning was that I was afraid of losing my freedom. Today, as I sit behind bars I realize that there are many types of freedom, and that in spite of my confinement I remain free in many important ways. What good is freedom if we are afraid to follow our conscience? What good is freedom if we are not able to live with our own actions? I am confined to a prison but I feel, today more than ever, connected to all humanity. Behind these bars I sit a free man because I listened to a higher power, the voice of my conscience. (http://www.codepinkalert.org/National_Actions_Camilo.shtml)

Please ask yourself the following questions :

- What can you do to help break the spell of perceptual filters that have us viewing each other as "the other," as "the enemy," or as "less-than" in some way?
- What would it take for you to see each person and yourself as whole and worthy of attention, consideration, and compassion?
- What choices can you make, that reflect the best of who you know yourselves to be – right now… in this next breath?

When conflict is finally seen as the gift it is, the opportunity to heal our deepest wounds, and see further into each other's eyes; then we will no longer avoid it. Instead, when conflict arises, we will eagerly embrace the moment, cherishing the value it holds for us all, welcoming the possibilities that lie just beyond its doorway…if only we are brave enough to open the door and walk through. This courageous act – embracing conflict for the learning it offers, listening with the ears of one who intends to understand – honors the unity of us all.

To My Adversaries, Thankyou!

--Author Unknown

Thank you:

- for shaking me out of my complacency
- for mobilizing my will to introspect
- for mobilizing my will to participate in life, rather than merely allowing life to live me
- for reminding me that I am alive
- for holding a mirror up to my face
- for reminding me of what is most important in life
- for inspiring me to seek love in moments of crisis
- for bringing people together in ways not otherwise accessible
- for inspiring courage, co-operation, uncommon feeling and a renewed sense of community
- for alerting me to the fact that all things and people around me can be destroyed or die, but that there is something within each of us that is immortal, that can never be tarnished, that can never fade, never die, that is always connected to all others and all things
- for illuminating the more extreme emotions that still lie within me, otherwise denied and hidden, that still await my attention, resolution, healing and love
- for inspiring me to actively share my love with those around me
- for causing me to question my beliefs, my values, my biases, my one-eyed stances, my judgments and my blame
- for causing me to seek a bigger picture, a picture that makes sense of the perceived chaos and disorder around me
- for contributing to my evolution of consciousness
- for challenging me to love my enemies
- for helping see that my enemies are but mirror reflections of my own inner devils
- for helping me to love my own inner devils
- for reminding me that each one of us, individually, is a holographic mirror of the whole of Humanity, complete with peace and war, violence and pacifism, love and hatred, likes and dislikes, views and counter-views, angels and devils
- for again bringing the question into the forefront of my consciousness: where is God in all this? (And for bringing me, through my introspection, to again ask myself, where is God not?)

"Mercy entails action, and merciful acts are possible even in the absence of forgiveness, before anyone has tendered an apology and well before reconciliation can even be contemplated. Indeed, mercy may well be the only positive ethical stance that enemies still actively engaged in war can adopt toward one another. Without mercy, without the willingness to desist from punitive and destructive acts that remain within their power, there is no way for leaders in a war to bring the fighting to an end." Meyer-Knapp's closing thoughts: Peace must be dared. Peace is inevitable. Every war will end.
How Wars End
Book Review by Mac Lawrence of Dangerous Peace-Making by Helena Meyer-Knapp
Timeline Nov/Dec 2003

Would she ever consider doing something a little … safer?

"To have a job where you can make things better for people? That's a blessing," she said. *"Why would I do anything else?"*

Jane Ganahl Marla Ruzicka: 26-Year-Old Doing 'The Right Humanitarian Thing' San Francisco Chronicle December 30, 2003

Marla, founder of CIVIC (http://www.civicworldwide.org/) was killed in Iraq doing what she loved

April 17th, 2005

Terror is in the human heart. We must remove this from the heart. Destroying the human heart, both physically and psychologically, is what we should avoid. The root of terrorism is misunderstanding, hatred and violence.

This root cannot be located by the military. Bombs and missiles cannot reach it, let alone destroy it. Only with the practice of calming and looking deeply can our insight reveal and identify this root. Only with the practice of deep listening and compassion can it be transformed and removed. Darkness cannot be dissipated with more darkness. More darkness will only make darkness thicker. Only light can dissipate darkness. Those of us who have the light should display the light and offer it so that the world will not sink into total darkness.

Thich Nhat Hahn in Shanghai, October 19, 2002

- for strengthening my resolve, my vision, my purpose of sharing my God-given gifts with others in whatever way I can
- for reminding me that I, like all others, indeed have a purpose in life, for myself and for others
- for strengthening my certainty that nothing happens or can happen that does not serve a higher purpose, that nothing happens or can happen that is not ultimately a service and an act of Love

To my adversaries:

In the ensuing days, weeks, months, years, in whatever way I respond or others respond to your challenges, collectively or individually, whether from hatred and fear or from love and certainty, whether violent or peaceful, whether destructive or constructive, I wish for you the same awakening to love that you have given me, for I know in my Heart, with utter certainty, that all things are a Service of Love, that all things are part of a larger Plan, that each of us is the same in one respect: we are all here to learn how to Love.

This makes us all brothers and sisters...

20

<u>PEACE AND POLITICS</u>

A belief in the inevitability of war produces war.

War is manifested as a self-fulfilling prophecy ... We have reaped a bitter crop.

There is a better vision of humanity, and of our future.

We reach it through understanding the interdependence

and interconnectedness of all people.

We reach it through compassion. We reach it through cooperation.

Rep. Dennis Kucinich

PEACE AND POLITICS

Honoring All Life is the spirit of democracy in action.
A society that recognizes the inter-dependence of all its parts, makes radically different decisions than one based on the illusion of separation and fear.

The only safe way to overcome an enemy is to make of the enemy a friend.

Gandhi

"We are here to show the world that another world is possible!" the man on stage said, and a crowd of more than 10,000 roared its approval.

What was strange was that we weren't cheering for a specific other world, just the possibility of one. We were cheering for the idea that another world could, in theory, exist.

For the past thirty years, a select group of CEOs and world leaders have met during the last week in January on a mountaintop in Switzerland to do what they presumed they were the only ones capable of doing: determine how the global economy should be governed. We were cheering because it was, in fact, the last week of January, and this wasn't the World Economic Forum in Davos, Switzerland. It was the first annual World Social Forum in Porto Alegre, Brazil. And even though we weren't CEOs or world leaders, we were still going to spend the week talking about how the global economy should be governed. [1]

Patriotism is the principle that will justify the training of wholesale murderers.

Leo Tolstoy

Thus began Naomi Klein's report on the first World Social Forum in Porto Alegre, Brazil; an event held to the delight of thousands of participants every year since. That is not an exaggeration. In its very first year, the WSF was host to 20,000 participants; 4,700 delegates from 117 countries; and 1,870 recognized journalists. Just five years later more than 200,000 people participated. There were 155,000 registered participants; 35,000 of them participated in the Youth Camp; and 6,823 from the press. Approximately 6,872 organizations from 151 countries were involved in 2,500 activities. All together an estimated 500,000 people passed by the event where sixteen languages were translated: Portuguese, English, French, Spanish, Arab, Japanese, Hebrew, German, Italian, Korean, Guarani, Hindu, Quechua, Uolof (Africa), Bahasa (Indonesia), Russian, and libras (brazilian language of signs). In 2006 the WSF will be decentralized throughout the world, and in 2007 it will take place in Africa.

What draws these people together? They come from all walks of life throughout the world, young and old, with diverse economic backgrounds, educational and life experiences, to unite as one voice in declaring:

Another World is Possible

War is only a cowardly escape from the problem of peace.

Thomas Mann

What "other world" do gatherings like these seek? A world of peace that honors all. But the meaning of "peace" has shifted, and can only be understood in the context of our developing perceptual awareness. Peace no longer means simply living *without* war. Peace now incorporates what we have learned about Systems Theory, Partnership, Quantum Physics, democratic systems, and the developing awareness wrought by centuries of experience witnessing the best and worst of human behavior. The concept of peace now requires a re-perceiving of every aspect of life - from the basic assumptions underlying our daily decisions, to a willingness to re-design our societal structures such that they support and promote peace now, *and* in the future.

Learning to say "No"

Gradually people all over the world are waking up from the last several millennia of dominator trance, and are questioning their daily decisions. They are deliberately analyzing what behaviors contribute to the continuing saga of domination as "modus operandi" on the planet. And they are finally taking a stand and saying, "NO." NO, to control and domination in their personal lives; NO, to economic policies that exclude the many and benefit the few; NO to business and governmental policies that disregard the sacredness of all life and the value of the commons to the survival of us all; and NO to the traditional perceptual filters that have kept us locked in ways of perceiving and acting that perpetuate war and honor no one.

Learning to say "Yes"

This is literally a turning point for our species. We are stepping into a new definition of what it means to be human… a definition forged by our own conscious choice to live from a space of love and not from fear. The significance of this still subtle world-wide phenomenon will forever alter the landscape of human possibilities. We are slowly learning to say YES to living in a way that supports all Life (both human and non-human), YES to humbly acknowledging that we have much to learn, YES to caring for each other and providing basic needs, YES to including all in any decision making processes that affect them, YES to the commitment to transparent and accountable governments, businesses, and lives. We are learning to intentionally listen to each other, to see beyond the surface, beyond separation, and to embrace the interdependence of all. The repercussions of this shift of focus will be felt everywhere, especially in the world of politics.

Political Assessment

What changes can you foresee if the political system of each country was carefully scrutinized - by its own people - with the intention to see beyond rhetoric and to discern what decisions truly lead to peace, and which don't? Imagine doing this in the United States. Better yet, imagine doing this in your own daily life.

This re-assessment is especially important for those who feel their best contribution lies within the field of politics. As we finally begin to see ourselves as one interdependent planet, let us declare how we choose to act as a species together… *united for the benefit of all life.*

Politics as an expression of Peace

The following questions are intended as a beginning dialog with our politicians. Of course, as we learn to take full responsibility for our own choices in life, any questions we ask of others must also be asked of ourselves…

- **What is your purpose as a human and as a politician?** Who are we, as a species, willing to declare ourselves to be?

- **What does "peace" mean to you?** Who does it involve? Who isn't involved? Are there beings that can be excluded from your experience of peace and yet still have the situation qualify as peaceful to you?

Do you know what the leading cause of war and terrorism is?

I will tell you. It is seriousness.

Seriousness is the most serious problem we face on the planet today. I'm serious. Think about it. Every terrorist act -- not to mention terror itself -- begins with seriousness. Everywhere we look, we are faced with laugh-threatening seriousness…

Report any serious behavior to the Department of Omland Security.

Swami Beyondananda

I arise in the morning, torn between a desire to save the world, and a desire to savor the world. That makes it hard to plan the day.

E.B. White

- **What do you DO, personally in your day-to-day life, to BE peace?** In other words, if we declare ourselves to be *for peace*, then what thoughts and actions come *from* peace? (One cannot say one is for peace and then automatically resort to force to solve one's perceived problems, including those between our family members.)

- **Who are your constituents?** How do you determine this? Do those who contribute to your campaign receive more attention? How do you keep from being bought? How do you ensure that you represent everyone? Do you include non-humans within your district/state/country as constituents? If not, why not? How many generations into the future will you consider when assessing the impact of your decisions? Are you willing to do this with every decision?

- **How much of your own ego is tied up in your willingness to "serve"?** When you answer this honestly, is a political life really the best choice for you *and* your constituents?

- **How important is it for you to be "right?"** Are you willing to be open to learning different ways of seeing things, to "step outside the box" of your own perceptions?

- **What is important in life?** What are you passionate about? About what do you feel compassion? What do you NOT feel compassionate about?

- **What services are essential to life?** Do you feel they should be available to all? If so, what are you doing to make that your reality? What criteria do you use to determine who's survival needs are met and who's aren't? What are the bottom-line survival needs you feel all people *deserve*? What is the role of government regarding these bottom-line needs? No matter how you answer the previous question, how do you intend to make sure those needs are met at all times?

- **We know that perception is subjective.** How, then, do you honor each person's subjective reality as well as your own?

- **Transparency is considered essential to healthy relationships.** How transparent are you willing to be with your constituents? How do you determine what should be private and what public in life? Does your role as a politician create different criteria for you compared to your constituents? If so, how so?

- **How do you ensure that you thoroughly weigh issues and make informed decisions?** We all reserve the right to change our opinions upon further research or consideration. Our representatives deserve that same option.

- **What system do you use to guarantee that your decisions are born from the latest pertinent data?** How do you ensure that you regularly re-assess decisions based on new information or points-of-view? Re-assessment requires humility. The humility to constantly re-evaluate one's choices is a hallmark of one who intends to find the best option for honoring all,– one who's intention is to expand (not contract) the field of the possible.

I call upon the scientific community in our country, those who gave us nuclear weapons, to turn their great talents now to the cause of mankind and world peace: to give us the means of rendering these nuclear weapons impotent and obsolete.

Ronald Reagan

We need not force a liberal agenda on our society, any more than we need force our political opinions on our children... We can enjoy life instead of banging our heads against the old walls. If we encourage an awake thoughtfulness; democracy and justice will have all the victories our hearts can handle.

Granny D (Doris Haddock) Utne Magazine March-April 2003

What other questions would you want to ask your representatives? A democracy, by definition, requires participation. How can we best support our representatives so that they can truly represent our deepest knowing?

What works and what doesn't work?

As we take a long and discerning look at the structures of our government, let's ask ourselves: What truly works and what doesn't? When we drop the need to be right, or to make others wrong, we can begin to carefully evaluate what works. What points of view have we missed that could lead to creative ideas to handle those things that clearly don't work? The following list is a brief overview of some issues that are counterproductive to a healthy democracy in which each issue is given full attention – including how it fits into the larger picture of our interdependent world...

- **Unrelated Attachments.** The practice of attaching unrelated items to bills in order to sneak unpopular laws (or those that usually benefit some special interest) into creation. Unrelated attachments make it impossible to oppose a portion of a bill without opposing it all.

- **Impossible work loads.** Currently, legislative activities are so demanding that it is impossible for each representative to personally know and understand each piece of legislation brought to a vote – a vote that can significantly affect millions. (A perfect example is all 300+ pages of the Patriot Act which hardly anyone actually read before voting into law.)

- **Campaign financing.** The entire structure of our political campaigns – campaign financing must be revised from the bottom-up. We need to set up our election process such that money is not an issue. Candidates in our current system require huge amounts of funding, which automatically favors wealthy candidates and dissuades impassioned but less famous candidates.

  Several states and communities are actively testing variations on Public Financing of all candidates, and the results have been remarkably promising. What keeps our current politicians from pushing this kind of reform through?

- **Campaign focus.** Political campaigns need to focus on the honesty of the candidate and her willingness to be open, not on who can better develop and fund a slick marketing campaign. The more open a candidate is to examining all points of view and even creatively coming up with additional choices, the greater the odds that the candidate will make choices that honor all. Isn't that the spirit behind representational government in the first place?

- **Campaign Coverage.** The structure of our media must be changed such that all candidates receive in-depth coverage. 30 and 60 second sound bites must be eliminated. *Nothing of any value can be discussed in that small amount of time,* because there is no opportunity for dialog, only proclamation. The public must demand more than a glossing-over of the issues, they must demand substance. What would happen if we insisted that our candidates *must* address each topic for at least 5 minutes whenever they are discussed? Additionally, the media coverage of candidates must be structured in a way that the voices of *all* candidates are heard and accessible. The two-party system automatically censors third and fourth

To announce that there must be no criticism of the president, or that we are to stand by the president, right or wrong, is not only unpatriotic and servile, but is morally treasonable to the American public.

Theodore Roosevelt, 1918

Virtually all the things Nixon did against me that were illegal to keep me from exposing his secret policy are now legal under the Patriot Act. Going into my doctor's office to get information to blackmail me with, wiretaps without warrants, overhearing me--all legal now. The CIA supplied the burglars in my doctor's office with disguises and with cameras and they did a psychological profile on me. That was illegal then, legal now.

Daniel Ellsberg, who publicized the Pentagon Papers 30 years ago, and author of Secrets: A Memoir of Vietnam and the Pentagon Papers, in an interview with Mira Ptacin in Common Dreams Tuesday 29 March 2005 Revelations from an Insider http://www.commondreams.org/views05/0329-20.htm or see http://www.ellsberg.net/

party candidates. Yet their voices represent a huge number of people and often educate us regarding issues concerning us all. They offer valuable alternative points-of-view that can help formulate the main party platforms. We need to hear about all options so that we can make informed decisions when voting. (See the chapter on the Media for additional ideas.)

• **Re-Think the Democratic format.** Perhaps it is time to eliminate the idea of a two-party system. Focusing on just two parties keeps us from hearing about important ideas that affect us all. It perpetuates sameness at the expense of innovation. When power is entrenched in only two groups, there is a natural tendency to pass laws that keep those same people in power… effectively shutting out the voices of those representing differing points of view. Most democracies include more than two parties for just that reason. Why doesn't the USA?

• **Re-Thinking Money.** Are we willing to re-design our concept of money, to create an economy based on abundance and cooperation rather than the existing economy of structured scarcity, hording, and growth at any cost? If not, why? What are our true intentions? There is a growing movement around the world to revisit the idea of "yin" (locally based currencies) and "yang" (cross-cultural and long-distance currencies similar to the EURO and the US Dollar). These yin-yang monetary systems complement each other, allowing local areas to thrive while providing basic needs within the community; and national currencies to provide a method of cross-border trading. Creating currencies tied to tangible value (such as time or specific goods like gold or silver) is another way to help stabilize the economy. (See the Money chapter for more information on this global movement.)

• **Voting Options.** Some democracies are experimenting with the concept of offering a second choice vote at the polls, which offers an automatic run-off without a second election. This eliminates the idea that a voter is "throwing away a vote" if voting for anyone other than the two main candidates. It allows for an instant tally of how many people embrace a third or independent party candidate's policies while still accurately polling the people's choice. There are many variations on this idea, why not examine which ones are working in other parts of the world? Voters need to feel both wanted and honored in the process of sharing their voting choice, and our structures must support that feeling. A culture in which citizens fail to participate can no longer be called a democracy.

• **Re-thinking the Commons.** How can we structure our systems such that we protect what is commonly held by all? This includes looking at ways in which we ask those who wish to pollute the commons to pay for that privilege. What is most sacred to us? Let's prioritize accordingly.

• **Taxes.** How can we structure our tax system such that it becomes a simple and equitable honor to support each other and the infrastructure we all enjoy? Flat taxes disproportionately tax the poor – because 10% of $10,000 has much more of an impact on survival than 10% of $1 million – yet seems fair at higher income levels. Some advocate a tax on those who wish to pollute or own a portion of the Commons, (a tax on those who wish to use what belongs to us all.) For example, those who contribute to air pollution would pay for the privilege. Those funds would then be used to counter-act their pollution or to benefit those who don't degrade the commons. What are your thoughts?

- **What is power?** Our entire idea of power must be re-examined. The idea of "power" meaning "control" harkens from our dominator traditions, and no longer serves us. Let's use the appropriate terms and say "force" if that is what we really mean by "power." Yet we have the choice to use real power, as defined by so many authors today, (David R. Hawkins, Riane Eisler, Gary Zukav, Barbara Marx Hubbard, just to name a few.) These authors define power as the ability to see multiple points of view, to solve problems from a higher level of consciousness or awareness than the perceived limitations that created the issue. True power includes a willingness to remain open to the infinite field of possibilities, and to work from that openness when sourcing solutions. This *willingness* is at the heart of "honoring all," and is born of the realization that we know so little about life. Most importantly, power refers to the ability to manifest and create from an inner unshakable core of BEing, similar to the calm in the center of a storm. *True power is creative, healing, inclusive, and therefore empowering for all.*

- **Governmental Structure.** The structure of our government, every department, and political position must be analyzed in terms of whether it contributes to humanity through compassion and pleasure, or through coercion, domination, and force. This review must include all voices in the process. Perhaps a series of "town hall" type meetings or "Wisdom Councils" could be developed for the purpose.

- **Departmental Intention.** In analyzing our governmental departments, let's also see if they truly intend to accomplish their task. For example, the "Environmental *Protection* Agency" sometimes seems to make policies that are in direct conflict with the title of the department. The same is true of "Homeland Security." Have we asked ourselves what "security" looks like, or how we will know when we are secure? How can we feel secure, for example, when our own policies often hurt more people than they help? Are we willing to tell the truth to ourselves and each other regarding what is so?

Most of all, **there must be a *willingness* to take full responsibility for our government and its decisions**, understanding finally that anything any one of us does, any decision made, affects us all. We can no longer afford the illusion that we are separate beings, and that what happens somewhere "out there" won't affect us. *Everything affects all of us.*

The Ambiguous Vote

In the USA presidential election of 2004, many voters found themselves standing in long lines waiting for the right to cast their ballot. A disproportionate number of those long lines were located in poor or African American neighborhoods, leading some to suspect that there was a deliberate attempt to make it difficult for those more likely to vote for Kerry, to cast their vote. Whether or not that was true for

Taxpayers in the US will pay $207.5 billion for the cost of war in Iraq. For the same amount of money, the following could have been provided:

- *47,133,456 People Receiving Health Care or*

- *27,486,910 Head Start Places for Children or*

- *122,099,681 Children Receiving Health Care or*

- *1,868,579 Affordable Housing Units or*

- *24,422 New Elementary Schools or*

- *40,241,753 Scholarships for University Students or*

- *3,576,505 Music and Arts Teachers or*

- *4,676,000 Public Safety Officers or*

- *367,147,976 Homes with Renewable Electricity or*

- *3,250,796 Port Container Inspectors*

National Priorities Project
17 New South Street, Suite 302
Northampton, MA 01060
Tel: 413-584-9556
http://database.nationalpriorities. org/

you, one can't help but wonder why the process of voting was ever allowed to degenerate into the experience described below:

> We spent the night bringing food and water to those who would end up waiting all night in line. Picture the line like this – families – mothers, fathers, toddlers, children sitting on the floor in long lines down the halls – on the ground here, on a chair there, with the lines not moving fast enough for them even to slide along the floor for 15 minutes at a time. The look was resignation, disgust, acceptance of mistreatment, and only very occasionally rage. Those with young children or without the stomach for obvious disenfranchisement went home in large numbers. Others determined to be counted stuck it out. We saw neighborhood women who were so dismayed at the obvious disrespect for the voters weeping as they brought water, toilet paper, and food. There was a quiet, uneasy sharpness to the collective mood as if everyone knew that history was being made, but it was so ugly that no one really wanted to talk too much about it.[2]

This description of events was not an isolated case, it was echoed by many, especially in large cities.

On January 6th, 2005, Senator Barbara Boxer courageously stood beside Congresswoman Stephanie Tubbs Jones to protest the certification of Ohio's electoral votes by Congress. They weren't hoping to change the outcome, but they were questioning if the witnessed voting irregularities constituted a red-flag regarding the integrity of our democracy. They asked why voters were forced to wait hours in the rain, some until 4am. Why were there only two machines for 1,300 voters in one area? Why were only 2,798 voting machines available for a county that needed 5,000? Of the 68 machines that were held back in a warehouse, why were 42 of them located in predominantly African-American communities? Why, in a precinct in which 638 people voted for Bush, did one machine count 4,258 extra votes for him? That particular machine was caught – how many weren't? Why were 3,000 ballots disqualified after poll workers gave faulty instructions to those voters? In the Columbus area alone an estimated 5,000 to 10,000 voters left polling places out of frustration without having voted – why did we set it up that way? [3]

A year prior to the 2004 election, Senators Boxer, Graham, and Clinton introduced legislation to require that electronic voting systems provide a paper record to verify the vote. Yet the bill was not debated.[3] Why not? Who is served when a simple bill aimed at ensuring the accuracy of our voting process is stalled?

What has happened to our sense of democracy when we allow the most sacred act of voting to become a painful ritual instead of a joy to experience? What has become of us, as a people, when we allow anything to hamper the ability of a voter to freely and easily express her choice with confidence that her vote will be counted?

What does it say about our politicians when so many condone and even actively support redistricting, revamping polling locations, redesigning voting machines and the vote counting process, and generally making it difficult for others to vote; simply to ensure a victory? What does that say about us as a democracy?

...Even after accounting for inflation (constant dollars), the nuclear weapons budget has grown by 84 percent since 1995. The 2005 request is more than one and one-half times the average amount spent on nuclear weapons during the Cold War (in constant dollars) and represents the second highest spending level ever.

http://awakenedwoman.com/ Fiscal 2005 Nuclear Weapons Budget Request

Why? How much is enough?

Who benefits from this kind spending over-kill?

Why is our government involved in the arms-for-profit business at all? How can we say we want peace when we profit through war?

I hate war as only a soldier who has lived it can, only as one who has seen its brutality, its futility, its stupidity.

Dwight D. Eisenhower

Voting As An Act of Love

I volunteered to encourage people to vote in this election. I was struck by the number of eligible voters who were convinced that either their vote would not be counted or that the entire process was useless. It saddened me to see such voter malaise and its subsequent hopelessness sweep our nation.

As a Precinct Leader, I both contacted potential voters and enrolled volunteers to assist me in the effort. On the surface, the voter drive seemed to be a numbers game – a volunteer army descended upon each Precinct with the intention of encouraging every eligible voter to go through the steps necessary to have their vote included in the final tally. In my state, Oregon, that meant reading and understanding the issues, properly marking the ballot, inserting it into a special envelope, and then remembering to sign the outer envelope before either mailing it in on time, or dropping it off at a specified location. There were numerous places along this route where an oversight could cause the ballot to become invalid. Why do we make it so complex?

I believe much more than mere voting was taking place. Each time we approached a voter, we were asking that person to acknowledge his right and privilege to express his own point of view. At the same time, we offered a context – the balloting process – in which the voter's viewpoint could be ritually and ceremonially heard.

In a society stripped of most ceremonial rituals, this is crucial. It was those ceremonial rituals that helped constitute the framework that held indigenous cultures together. The voting ritual feeds our cellular memory of times gone by in which town hall meetings, passing the "talking" stick, and seasonal agrarian-based gatherings knit our community voices together.

On still a deeper level, we offered an invitation to each participant, voter and volunteer alike. It was an invitation to search the silence of their inner-depths, to know their essential BEing, and to celebrate their own magnificence by actively encouraging its expression through the simple act of volunteering and voting.

As a volunteer, the willingness to acknowledge the magnificence of the potential voter before me, whether on the phone or in person, was perhaps one of the greatest gifts I could offer, to both of us. It provided me with the gift of intimate heart-to-heart connection, while offering the voter a witness to his or her personal power, wholeness, and inner light.

When seen from this context, voting becomes an act of love – a conscious affirmation of our shared commonality and the interrelatedness of us all.

Winner Takes All

Another source of voter unhappiness is the inherent lack of representation in our current method of vote counting. In a two-party system, there is often a small difference between the number of votes cast for the winner and loser. Yet only one person can win. This results in a large portion of the voters feeling unrepresented by the party that wins. If there is a third or independent candidate also, the winner could actually end up representing an even smaller portion of the voter's wishes. For example, in a three person race, if the winner receives 40% of the vote and the other two candidates split the remaining 60%; the winner faces a constituency in which

---

Who said this and when?

"The people of England have been led in Mesopotamia into a trap from which it will be hard to escape with dignity and honour. They have been tricked into it by a steady withholding of information. The Baghdad communiques are belated, insincere, incomplete. Things have been far worse than we have been told, our administration more bloody and inefficient than the public knows... We are today not far from a disaster."

Those were the words of T.E. Lawrence (of Arabia fame) in The Sunday Times in August, 1920.

"And," Robert Fisk writes, "every word of it is true today."

Robert Fisk
correspondent for The Independent
www.democracynow.org
January 3rd, 2005

Thanks to instant runoff voting, Mary Robinson in 1990 became the first woman to be elected president of Ireland.

Having received 39% of first choices, she trailed her chief opponent, Fianna Fail candidate Brian Lenihan, by 5%. However, after the elimination of third-place candidate Austin and the second round of counting, Robinson won handily. She gained the votes of 205,565 (77%) of Currie's 267,902 supporters. Her total share then stood at 53%, proving she was clearly preferred over Lenihan.

Robinson was immensely popular as president, both within Ireland and abroad.

FairVote's March Newsletter 2005
http://www.fairvote.org

more than half are not represented by her policies. In such a scenario, how can we begin to suggest that the will of the people is being honored? It is our underlying intention that must be examined here. Do we intend for our government to truly represent the will of all the people, or just those who supported the winner, excluding all the rest?

IRV - Instant Runoff Voting

As voter frustration increases, people are coming up with creative ways of solving this problem. One of the most widely used and popular systems throughout the world is called Instant Runoff Voting (IRV), also known as Ranked Choice Voting (RCV). Here's how it works. Voters choose their candidate choices in order of preference. If no one wins 50% of the votes when the first choices are counted, the candidate with the least number of votes is eliminated. Then the second choice of all voters is added to the remaining candidates' tallies. This process continues until a majority winner is chosen. Many politicians support this voting method, including Governor Howard Dean and Senator John McCain.

In 2002, San Francisco adopted IRV, under the name "Ranked Choice Voting" (RCV) for determining several of its Board of Supervisors positions. Exit polls show high voter enthusiasm for this voting method. The results of the last several San Francisco elections have been carefully analyzed showing the following benefits:

1. *No more December runoff elections.* San Francisco indeed will not hold a December runoff election for the first time since 1998. All winners were definitively determined by Friday, November 5. All winners generally will be identified within 24 hours in future races.

2. *Significant tax savings.* San Francisco avoided runoff elections in four out of 11 supervisor races, which means that the City saved at least $1.2 million in administration and public financing costs this year alone. Avoiding future runoff elections in the City's annual November elections will quickly repay the one-time costs of implementing RCV ($1.6 million to modify the voting equipment's hardware and software and $800,000 for voter education), leading to substantial ongoing savings to San Francisco taxpayers.

3. *Increased votes cast in the decisive election when winners are chosen.* All winning candidates in runoffs had larger vote totals and percentages than winners in 2000. While all winners were ahead after the first round of counting, in several cases their share of the vote was small – meaning that it would not have been clear if they had broad support without conducting an instant runoff; in District 5, for example, Mirkarimi received only 28% of voters' first choices among the 22 candidates. Plurality elections can break down in this way whenever more than two candidates run, thereby allowing potentially unrepresentative, polarizing candidates to win with far less than majority support.

4. *A far greater percentage of voters participated in the final runoff round.* Total runoff turnout in 2000 ranged from 53% to 64% of the November turnout. In 2004, final round RCV turnout ranged from 75% to 90% of first round RCV turnout. · Winning candidates in 2000 received between 5,900 and 10,400 votes. Winning candidates in 2004 received between 10,500 and 13,600, and were ranked on 12,200 to 16,900 ballots.[4]

A Declaration of Humanity

In his speech for the dedication of the University for Peace in Seoul, South Korea on March 3rd, 2003, Dr. Ilchi Lee (creator of Dahn Hak) wrote the following "Declaration of Humanity."

I declare that I am a Spiritual Being, an essential and eternal part of the Soul of Humanity, one and indivisible.
I declare that I am a Human Being whose rights and security ultimately depend on assuring the human rights of all people of Earth.
I declare that I am a Child of the Earth, with the will and awareness to work for goals that benefit the entire community of life on Earth.
I declare that I am a Healer, with the power and purpose to heal the many forms of divisions and conflicts that exist on Earth.
I declare that I am a Protector, with the knowledge and the responsibility to help the Earth recover her natural harmony and beauty.
I declare that I am an Activist, with the commitment and the ability to make a positive difference in my society.[5]

What would the world look like if our political representatives were willing to commit to Dr. Lee's declaration? Would you be willing to make the same declaration, and to offer that option to your children? Instead of just asking our elected officials to look upon their job as representing what is truly best for us all, what if we all took the same responsibility?

The New Principles of Power

There are many organizations dedicated to bringing compassion and spirituality (not religion) into the political realm. The Global Renaissance Alliance, recently re-named the Peace Alliance Foundation, is one such organization. Started in 1998, it is dedicated to the creation of a new political consciousness using the nonviolent principles of Mahatma Gandhi and Dr. Martin Luther King, Jr. The GRA developed "Seven Principles of the New Activist."[6] They offer a wonderful guideline for all who seek to live life from compassion, empowerment, and love.

Additionally, in 1997, Dr. Will Keepin, president of the Satyana Institute and adjunct faculty member of the California Institute of Integral Studies, presented a provisional set of principles intended to be used as a collective inquiry into how to apply spiritual teachings to social change work. They were the result of several years' work with social change leaders in Satyana's "Leading with Spirit" program.[6]

Both sets of principles are wonderful guidelines for politicians and leaders who see themselves as social change artists. Because politicians are placed in positions of power, it is essential that they understand true power, as distinct from force and domination. Equally, because both our ballot vote and our monetary vote are expressions of power, this distinction is important to us all.

In our seeking for economic and political progress, we all go up — or else we all go down.

Franklin D. Roosevelt

'Deep down the consciousness of mankind is one. This is a virtual certainty because even in the vacuum matter is one; and if we don't see this, it's because we are blinding ourselves to it.'

David Bohm
Physicist
from Dan Sewell Ward
http://www.halexandria.org/d ward404.htm

Dr. Will Keepin reminds us that we are urgently called to action in two distinct capacities:

> To serve as hospice workers to a dying culture, and to serve as midwives to an emerging culture. These two tasks are required simultaneously; they call upon us to move through the world with an open heart – meaning we are present for the grief and the pain – as we experiment with new visions and forms for the future. Both are needed. The key is to root our actions in both intelligence and compassion – a balance of head and heart that combines the finest human qualities in our leadership for cultural transformation. [7]

Department of Peace

If you need any further proof that a new level of awareness is seeping into politics, look no further than Rep. Dennis Kucinich's "Department of Peace Legislation." Pending in the U.S. House of Representatives, HR1673, with 53 current co-signers, proposes to create a Department of Peace that would research, facilitate, and articulate nonviolent solutions to domestic and international conflicts. The power of this legislation is beautifully described in Matthew Albracht's article entitled <u>Why Progressives and Conservatives Should Support a Department of Peace</u>:

> The Dept. of Peace would establish nonviolence as an organizing principle of American society, providing the U.S. President with an array of peace-building policy options for domestic and international use. The Department would focus on nonmilitary peaceful conflict resolutions, prevent violence and promote justice and democratic principles to expand human rights. Domestically, the Department would be responsible for developing policies which address issues such as domestic violence, child abuse, mistreatment of the elderly, school and gang violence and other issues of cultural violence. Internationally, the Department would gather research, analyze foreign policy and make recommendations to the President on how to address the underlying causes of war and intervene before violence begins. The Department of Peace would systematically root out the causes of violence by creating new and innovative programs, as well as vastly increasing support of the many existing programs around our nation and the world that are already having a positive impact.[8]

Here is strong evidence that the face of politics and social structures are beginning to change. This idea of structuring government around peaceful living is not new. As Albracht points out later in his article, even George Washington saw the importance of making peace a cornerstone of our government, when he suggested establishing a Peace Academy. The Department of Peace makes the same proposal. Patterned after military academies, the Peace Academy's mission would be to train non-violent conflict specialists in the most cutting-edge ways to wage peace. Programs would explore a "best practices model" for teaching non-violence, conflict resolution, non-violence in the schools, and in our homes to diminish domestic abuse. It would also deploy specialists around the world to quell violence before it escalates.

Reminding us of the skyrocketing cost of the Iraq war, domestic violence, and the mounting incarceration of our own people, Albracht asks us to imagine how much less we would spend on those, and similar issues if the underlying intention for all our government programs was nonviolence. In an April 14th, 2005 interview on CNN, Kucinich compared our current annual military expense of $400 billion with the approximate $8 billion cost of developing a Department of Peace. Just from a pragmatic point of view, which is more cost effective?

Nearly 9 in 10 Americans (86%) say that more of what matters in life better describes their concept of the American dream than more is better (3%).

More than 4 in 5 Americans (85%) say that living in a fair and just society better describes their concept of the American dream than achieving an affluent or wealthy lifestyle (10%).

Nearly 3 in 5 Americans (59%) say that working enough to have a good life (59%) better describes their concept of the American Dream than working hard to get ahead (34%).

Nine in ten Americans (90%) say living in a country dedicated to preserving democratic values, a high quality of life and a healthy future for all better describes their concept of the American Dream than living in the most powerful country in the world (5%).

<u>New American Dream Survey Report - September 2004</u> This summary provides the major findings from a Census-balanced and nationally representative poll of 1,269 American adults ages 18 years of age and older. The "New American Dream Poll" was conducted by Widmeyer Communications of Washington, D.C. for the Center for a New American Dream. The margin of error for the study is +/- 2.7%.

http://www.newdream.org/about/Finalpollreport.pdf

The shift from the old dominator-trance to a partnership social model must begin with a shift in perception and values, and a Department of Peace is an excellent place to begin that shift.

Democracy Defined

As the experiment of democracy begun by humanity in the late 1700's has progressed, it has spun off into many versions and expressions, each experimenting to find the best expression of government "by the people." Even though each country has embraced democratic principles in its own unique way, many of those democracies have united to define the essential principles they hold in common. This is essential. As we move into a global discussion of democratic values, we must align on a common definition of democracy. A clear and detailed definition resulted from the "Toward a Community of Democracies - Ministerial Conference," that took place in Warsaw, Poland, June 27, 2000. Called the <u>Final Warsaw Declaration,</u> it included the following statements: [9]

> Expressing our common adherence to the purposes and principles set forth in the Charter of the United Nations and the Universal Declaration of Human Rights,
>
> Reaffirming our commitment to respect relevant instruments of international law,
>
> Emphasizing the **interdependence between peace, development, human rights and democracy recognizing the universality of democratic values**, we
>
> Hereby agree to respect and uphold the following core democratic principles and practices:
>
> • **The will of the people shall be the basis of the authority of government**, as expressed by exercise of the right and civic duties of citizens to choose their representatives through regular, free and fair elections with universal and equal suffrage, open to multiple parties, conducted by secret ballot, monitored by independent electoral authorities, and free of fraud and intimidation.
>
> • **The right of every person to equal access** to public service and to take part in the conduct of public affairs, directly or through freely chosen representatives.
>
> • **The right of every person to equal protection** of the law, without any discrimination as to race, color, sex, language, religion, political or other opinion, national or social origin, property, birth or other status.
>
> • **The right of every person to freedom of opinion and of expression**, including to exchange and receive ideas and information through any media, regardless of frontiers.
>
> • **The right of every person to freedom of thought, conscience and religion.**
>
> • **The right of every person to equal access to education.**
>
> • **The right of the press to collect, report and disseminate information**, news and opinions, subject only to restrictions necessary in a democratic society and prescribed by law, while bearing in mind evolving international practices in this field.
>
> • **The right of every person to respect for private** family life, home, correspondence, including electronic communications, free of arbitrary or unlawful interference.
>
> • **The right of every person to freedom of peaceful assembly and association**, including to establish or join their own political parties, civic groups, trade unions or other organizations with the necessary legal guarantees to allow them to operate freely on a basis of equal treatment before the law.

An abstract noun can't surrender; it can't do anything really. How do you know when you've won? When the noun gets kicked out of the Oxford English Dictionary? But that's a very useful tool for politicians, to declare an unwinnable war. They can keep it going as long as they like. They can decide when it's won.

Now, you could say that we declared war against Fascism in World War II, but that was only a pseudonym for Nazi Germany. In this case, we have no idea who we're fighting. It's the first time, I think, that a major country has gone to war and not known who the enemy was. Who are they? We have no idea.

*Terry Jones
(of Monty Python fame)
discussing the concept of a
"War on Terrorism"
with Salon.com
TruthOut.org
Jan 21, 2005*

Congressman Jesse Jackson, Jr., … introduced House Joint Resolution 28 for a third consecutive Congress. The resolution proposes to add a new affirmative individual 'right to vote' amendment to the U.S. Constitution. He introduced it with 54 original co-sponsors.

Jackson said, "I first introduced the Voting Rights Amendment on November 6, 2001... During the entire 107th Congress the bill had zero co-sponsors. It was re-introduced in the 108th Congress - with no original co-sponsors - and after two years of hard work 45 members signed on as co-sponsors. The fact that we have 54 original co-sponsors in the 109th Congress shows that the idea of adding a **Voting Rights Amendment** *to the Constitution is growing by leaps and bounds."* *No state should deny the right to vote to a citizen allowed to vote in another state. States have proven ineffective in protecting the individual right to vote. An amendment to the Constitution is the only way to ensure that every citizen's ability to vote is protected.*

http://www.fairvote.org/ index.php

• **The right of persons belonging to minorities or disadvantaged groups to equal protection of the law**, and the freedom to enjoy their own culture, to profess and practice their own religion, and use their own language.

• **The right of every person to be free from arbitrary arrest or detention**; to be free from torture and other cruel, inhumane or degrading treatment or punishment; and to receive due process of law, including to be presumed innocent until proven guilty in a court of law.

• **That the aforementioned rights**, which are essential to full and effective participation in a democratic society, **be enforced by a competent, independent and impartial judiciary** open to the public, established and protected by law.

• **That elected leaders uphold the law** and function strictly in accordance with the constitution of the country concerned and procedures established by law.

• **The right of those duly elected** to form a government, assume office and fulfill the term of office as legally established.

• **The obligation of an elected government to refrain from extra-constitutional actions**, to allow the holding of periodic elections and to respect their results, and to relinquish power when its legal mandate ends.

• **That government institutions be transparent, participatory and fully accountable to the citizenry of the country** and take steps to combat corruption, which corrodes democracy.

• **That the legislature be duly elected and transparent and accountable to the people**.

• **That civilian, democratic control over the military be established and preserved**.

• **That all human rights** -- civil, cultural, economic, political and social -- **be promoted and protected as set forth in the Universal Declaration of Human Rights** and other relevant human rights instruments.

How many of the Warsaw Principles and Practices have been imperiled in the USA through passage of the Patriot Acts I and II, and other similar legislation passed in the wave of emotional reaction to the events of September 11th, 2001? In times of increased national security and threat of terrorism, it is of paramount importance that we boldly uphold and practice those very principles we so willingly fight to protect.

Ever Evolving Democracy

No matter what our political beliefs or how we each vote, we need to come to agreement on what we want our government to advocate – how we want to live – and what we stand for. Yet there seems to be anything but agreement in today's highly-charged, rhetoric-laden, 30-second-sound-bite world.

The US State Department website offers us the following facts regarding the expansion of democracy.

When historians write about U.S. foreign policy at the end of the 20th century, they will identify the growth of democracy--from 30 countries in 1974 to 117 today--as one of the United States' greatest legacies. The United States remains committed to expanding upon this legacy until all the citizens of the world have the fundamental right to choose those who govern them through an ongoing civil process that includes free, fair, and transparent elections. [10]

While taking sole credit for the expansion of democracy in the world is questionable, clearly democracy is an idea who's time has come. The UN Democracy Caucus10 is currently lobbying the General Assembly to open discussion of how best to encourage the growth of democracy through the UN – an idea that has taken many decades to evolve. It is a sign of democracy's global acceptance that there are finally enough democracies active in the UN to make this discussion possible.

Each one of those democracies is a unique expression. Obviously the concept of democracy is complex and constantly changing. The USA cannot afford to hold its concept of democracy as a static idea – something that once achieved, never changes. Instead, just as the business owner constantly reassesses her business - always seeking improvements, corrections of what isn't quite working, and even altering the overall focus of vision as personal growth takes place - we must be willing to do the same.

When democratic ideas were first embraced in our constitution, the only vote belonged to white men who owned land. Since then our ideas of "equality for all" have expanded to include women and people of all races and financial status (even though we are still working out kinks in the actual practice.)

Democratic Accountability

Honoring Self means honoring the core essence of our being. Whether we define "Self" as an individual, a business, a community, or a nation makes no difference, for they are all ultimately extensions of the individual. Just as it is it is imperative that our own individual actions match our beliefs and our rhetoric - if our integrity is to remain intact - the same is true of democratic nations. Yet we are rarely consistent in practice. Not only do many of the provisions of the Patriot Act, for example, contradict the definition of democracy that our government has promoted and exported for hundreds of years, but the same holds true for many nations that profess to be democracies – their actions do not consistently match their words.

Democracy starts at Home

We have to find a way to shift the perception of democracy to something that is alive within each individual, that is real and active in our daily lives. How democratic, for example, are our homes, our relationships, our schools, and our businesses? How can we begin to think that we live in a democracy if our own lives don't reflect democratic ideals and actions? How will our children learn to understand and cherish democracy if they don't experience it directly within their own daily experience? How can we inspire each other to explore what democracy means – and then to share those core beliefs with each other, openly and transparently, so that our government can truly reflect who we see ourselves to be?

Democracy is Free Speech

Essential to the concept of Democracy is the ability to speak freely. Yet the findings of a recent study announced in a press conference on January 31st, 2005, show that most American high school students have a very poor grasp of the First Amendment to the Constitution. In fact, some of the findings are shocking:

> The study suggests that First Amendment values can be taught - that the more students are exposed to news media and to the First Amendment, the greater their understanding of the rights of American citizens. But it also shows that basics about the First Amendment *are not being taught...* Administrators say student learning about the First Amendment is a priority, *but not a high priority.*

While standing vigil holding a candle deep into the night in front of the White House, a reporter commented that his actions wouldn't change the world. AJ Muste replied:

"I don't do this to change the world. I do it to make sure the world doesn't change me.

*AJ Muste
Memorial Institute
www.ajmuste.org*

Today, as we face financial and political crises, it's useful to remember that the ravages of the Great Depression hit Germany and the United States alike. Through the 1930s, however, Hitler and Roosevelt chose very different courses to bring their nations back to power and prosperity.

Germany's response was to use government to empower corporations and reward the society's richest individuals, privatize much of the commons, stifle dissent, strip people of constitutional rights, bust up unions, and create an illusion of prosperity through government debt and continual and ever-expanding war spending.

America passed minimum wage laws to raise the middle class, enforced anti-trust laws to diminish the power of corporations, increased taxes on corporations and the wealthiest individuals, created Social Security, and became the employer of last resort through programs to build national infrastructure, promote the arts, and replant forests.

To the extent that our Constitution is still intact, the choice is again ours.

Thom Hartmann
When Democracy Failed - 2005
The Warnings of History
February 25th, 2005

1. High school students tend to express little appreciation for the First Amendment. Nearly three-fourths say either they don't know how they feel about it or take it for granted.
2. Students are less likely than adults to think that people should be allowed to express unpopular opinions or newspapers should be allowed to publish freely without government approval of stories.
3. Students lack knowledge and understanding about key aspects of the First Amendment. Seventy-five percent incorrectly think that flag burning is illegal. Nearly half erroneously believe the government can restrict indecent material on the Internet.
4. Students who do not participate in any media-related activities are less likely to think that people should be allowed to burn or deface the American flag. Students who have taken more media and/or First Amendment classes are more likely to agree that people should be allowed to express unpopular opinions.
5. Students who take more media and/or First Amendment classes are more willing to answer questions about their tolerance of the First Amendment. Those who have not taken the classes say they "don't know" to First Amendment questions at a much higher rate.
6. Most administrators say student learning about journalism is a priority for their school, but less than 1 in 5 think it is a high priority, and just under a third say it is not a priority at all. Most, however, feel it is important for all students to learn some journalism skills.
7. Most administrators say they would like to see their school expand existing student media, but lack of financial resources is the main obstacle.
8. Students participating in student-run newspapers are more likely to believe that students should be allowed to report controversial issues without approval of school authorities than students who do not participate in student newspapers.
9. Student media opportunities are not universally offered in schools across the country. In fact, more than 1 in 5 schools (21 percent) offer no student media whatsoever.
10. Of the high schools that do not offer student newspapers, 40 percent have eliminated student papers within the past five years. Of those, 68 percent now have no media.
11. Low-income and non-suburban schools have a harder time maintaining student media programs than wealthier and suburban schools.
12. Interestingly, virtually the same percentage of students participate in media activities in schools that offer a high volume of student media, as in those schools with no media programs. Apparently, students interested in journalism find a way to participate in informal media activities, even if their school does not offer formal opportunities. (Italics added by the author.) [12]

What happens when we and our children fail to grasp the essential elements of our democratic way of life? What kind of adult participants in "government of the people, by the people" will they make, and how will they vote (if at all)?

It is our job, as a democracy, to educate the next generation in the privileges they too commonly take for granted or even fail to understand all together. Otherwise, how can we maintain the democratic freedoms our predecessors fought to secure for *our* benefit? Perhaps it is time to re-examine what democracy means and how best we can pass than meaning on to our children; not as a nationalistic, flag-waving, 60-second zealous ourburst; but as an essential element of our relationship to *everything*.

Democracy celebrates Choice

Democratic ideals are constantly evolving as we each grow individually and collectively within our understanding of what the gift of choice really means. What does the concept of choice mean to you? Hand-in-hand with making a choice goes the responsibility for the choice made. Not only must we be willing to listen to each other *without judgment* and truly dialog so that we can come to agreement about what is important as a democratic community, we must be willing to take full responsibility for the manifestation of that agreement. How can we create and maintain systems that support the constant re-assessment and re-creation of democracy anew? How do we keep it alive and developing with our own growth, both personally and collectively? And how do we best facilitate that discussion?

The Renaissance of Democracy

We humans are amazingly creative, and when it comes to the concept of democracy, we exercise that creativity by giving our right to free speech a thorough workout. Here are a few of the many ideas that are being developed in our fervent efforts to keep democracy alive, current, and appropriate to the times…

Wisdom Councils (www.tobe.net) I had the pleasure of witnessing an extraordinary model of democracy in action. The Rogue Valley Wisdom Council met last year, using the principles outlined in Jim Rough's book, Society's Breakthrough! Releasing Essential Wisdom and Virtue in All the People. Combining Dynamic Facilitation (see the chapter on Co-Creation for a detailed account of this powerful group communication method) with a meeting in which issues pertinent to a community are discussed, Jim sees Wisdom Councils as a "whole-system choice-creating conversation," one that has the potential of opening our hearts and minds in a way that could provide new insights, ways of thinking, talking, and deciding that could help create a "new bottom line for society." The power of this form is impressive. Citizens spanning a broad range of backgrounds, education, financial status, and age, who had never met before, experienced the power of flowing with the group energy, the honor of being truly listened to, and the leaps of creativity and insight possible when all perceive an atmosphere of honor and encouraged expression. Jim proposes a quarterly National Wisdom Council with twelve citizens participating in each event, and writes:

> Of course, a National WC is not a complete panacea. It wouldn't do much for old age, illness, death, asteroid collisions with the earth, reversing immediate crises, etc., although it could improve our attitudes about them and spark more innovations. But, because it promises to transform our system of thinking and deciding, our institutions and us, it's hard to imagine issues for which there would not be a breakthrough. [13]

Conversation Cafés (http://www.conversationcafe.org/) Sponsored by the New Road Map Foundation, a non-profit educational and charitable organization teaching people skills to be effective human beings, citizens and agents of social change, the intention of these open and networking Cafés is to generate social engagement so we can have a wise democracy by creating a space in which people can discuss the inner and outer issues of our time. They have created a process that is accessible and works, with a network of 70 ongoing discussion groups in 28 cities, and have trained over 400 "hosts" to facilitate these gatherings. Created by Vicki Robin, President of the New Road Map Foundation and co-author with Joe Dominguez of *Your Money or Your Life*, She writes:

> I envision a culture of conversation — a culture where people talk freely — without fear or taboos — with friends and strangers alike. I once asked a Dane how Denmark had resisted the pressures of globalization. He said two words: study circles. Most Danes throughout their adult lives have the habit of conversation about things that matter in small groups.

> "We can do that here. In Cafés. In Britain in the 1700s the government shut down the Cafés where people met to discuss politics because they were sites of revolutionary thinking. Here, we get our news from the TV, retreat into private sub-cultures through online chats and interact only

Thus, we see, the real battle here is between those who believe that free people can govern themselves - and have the right to keep out powerful interests that would corrupt government - and those who believe that a powerful father-figure is necessary for governance, the people should be kept largely in ignorance, the rich know best, and that We the People will only behave well when, as Hobbes wrote, there is "a common power to keep them all in awe..."

Today's real battles in the halls of government are about the survival of democracy itself.

Thom Hartmann
The Robber Baron's Party: Let's Bring Tea
January 20th, 2005

The rays of the sun are many through refraction, but they have the same source. I cannot therefore detach myself from the wickedest soul (nor may I be denied identity with the most virtuous).

The means may be likened to a seed, the end to a tree; and there is just the same inviolable connection between the means and the end as there is between the seed and the tree.

Mohandas Gandhi

with people who see the world as we do. This is a formula for weakening society enough to allow forces of repression to take over. Conversation Cafés are an attempt to reverse the trend. [14]

Citizens Assembly (http://www.citizensassembly.bc.ca/public) Developed in British Columbia, Canada, this independent, non-partisan group of 161 randomly chosen citizens - one man and one woman from each of the voting districts plus a chairperson - met for one year to discuss how to re-think the electoral process after examining other electoral systems in use around the world. They proposed the adoption of a variation of the Instant-Runoff or Ranked-Choice system they call BC-STV. [15] Their final proposal will go before the voters for approval in approximately six months. If approved, it will be adopted into practice by 2009. This was a unique situation in which randomly chosen citizens were deliberately empowered by the unanimous endorsement of the legislative parties as well as parties and community leaders outside the legislature.

Public Issue Forums (http://www.nifi.org/) National Issues Forums bring people with diverse views together to talk about important issues that concern them deeply. The goal is to find common ground.

They can range from small study circles held in peoples' homes to large community gatherings modeled on New England town meetings. Each forum focuses on a specific issue such as illegal drugs, Social Security, or juvenile crime.

Let's Talk America (http://www.letstalkamerica.org/) The intention of Let's Talk America is to create a national dialogue on the state of our democracy. One includes all voices and viewpoints. Not satisfied with creating simply a place to vent frustration with what currently doesn't work in our democracy, Let's Talk America considers questions essential to the future of our democracy. The discussions include the concept of America's promise, about what freedom, democracy, unity and equality mean to us -- to "we the people." It is a place to listen, speak, ask and learn – a place where your viewpoint and those of others are honored.

National Coalition for Dialogue and Deliberation (http://www.thataway.org/) The National Coalition for Dialogue & Deliberation (NCDD) is a Coalition of 165 organizations and individuals who have collectively involved millions of citizens in public deliberation and civic engagement programs. NCDD's website is an online resource center for organizers and facilitators. Thousands visit the website every day, and 6,000 dialogue and deliberation leaders receive a monthly email update. NCDD utilizes its website and resources to gather and distribute information about the conversations after they occur. This enables project organizers, dialogue practitioners, the public and the media to better understand where, when and how these conversations are taking place as well as what kinds of themes emerge when citizens of different backgrounds talk about their hopes and dreams for the future of our country.

World Café (www.theworldcafe.com) The World Café specializes in designing and hosting large-scale gatherings for up to 1,000 people at a time to learn together in lively dialogue about questions that matter. They image a world in which the job of a Leader includes convening and hosting collaborative conversations among diverse stakeholders to explore core questions and emerging possibilities – and are determined to make that dream a reality. The World Café recognizes that personal

---

There is little new in the tax world: almost every proposal on the table today – from flat taxes to expenditure taxes – has been tried by one or other country. Countries can look and learn from the experiences of their neighbors (see how the UK has drawn from the US on the earned income credit). And herein lies the interest of this conference. What better way to launch the US debate than to look at how countries as diverse as Canada, Russia, Slovakia, UK, Poland, and Ireland have approached reform. It's not difficult to identify the main objectives of most tax reforms:

·A simple tax system .
·A fairer tax system.
·A system that promotes rather than inhibits growth.

And of course a system that delivers the revenues that governments need to finance expenditures. We must never forget that at the end of the day, tax systems are all about collecting tax dollars in the most efficient and fair manner to pay for public services.

Jeffrey Owens
Director
Centre for Tax Policy & Administration, OECD
Fundamental Tax Reform: The Experience Of Oecd Countries Presented at the 67th Annual Meeting of Tax Foundation Washington D.C.

November 18, 2004

http://www.taxfoundation.org/events/conference.html

computing is giving way to interpersonal computing where individual and collective reflection as well as cross-fertilization of ideas can take place across geographic boundaries. These collaborative technologies, used widely in community, corporate, government and educational settings around the globe, invite us to look with new lenses at the strengths of our organizations, and to discover ways in which we can all contribute to a positive future.

Democracy in America Project (http://www.democracycampaign.org/) As many have recognized lately, democracy takes guts. It's a participatory process, not a spectator sport. Democracy in America Project seeks to re-build trust across political divides and restore faith in our democracy by deepening civic dialogue. Their intention is to cross the divide between judgment and misunderstanding by offering a space in which we can truly *listen* to each other. Joseph McCormick, one of the founders, was a national republican politician before realizing that the rhetoric we often use perpetuates and deepens the polarity currently so prevalent in politics today. By creating a context of safety, Democracy in America hopes to:

- Re-connect a broad spectrum group of Americans to the ideals, values, and principles that represent the "spirit of America"
- Provide hope to Americans who feel un-heard by major party candidates
- Create the experience of a living democracy where all voices matter.
- Bring citizens together to take personal responsibility for our government.
- Ignite the voice of We the People by building a network of national networks across America.

The "We the People" National Convention will bring 500 Americans from all fifty states and all walks of life together to begin a national campaign to re-unite Americans from all points of view and ignite the voice of "We the People."

The goal is to awaken an all-inclusive democracy so we can effectively address the issues we most care about in America. Just as the Community of Democracies produced a <u>Final Warsaw Declaration</u> expressing their deepest commonly held beliefs about democracy, the intent of this conference is to produce a "We the People" Statement of shared American ideals, values, and principles. Additionally, a "We the People" Platform will outline where we are, where we want to go, and what we need to do to get there, in a broad range of issues that make up our national expression. The results of this effort will help inform local, state, and national candidates and policy makers regarding the people's will.

In the preliminary conference that took place in March 2004, one of the participants, who spent his entire life seeing ultra-conservative Republicans as the "opposition" or "enemy," was transformed by the experience. He wrote about discovering how almost everyone at the conference, no matter what their current political leanings, shared similar feelings about democracy at the age of twelve. It was the moment of recognition for them all – seeing into each other's eyes as twelve-year-olds, and recognizing themselves in the other's eyes. Suddenly they were no longer "enemies," for they had found common ground on which to stand.

Imagine creating these types of meetings all around our country, and even perhaps around the world, every year. What magic can we create when we stand shoulder-to-

Torture anywhere is an affront to human dignity everywhere. We are committed to building a world where human rights are respected and protected by the rule of law...The United States is committed to the worldwide elimination of torture and we are leading this fight by example.

George W. Bush
in a statement issued
26 June 2003

... a 23-year-old American studying at Oxford, told me that a Pakistani friend at school had asked her if he could just watch her fill out her absentee ballot for the U.S. election. "He said to me, 'It's the closest thing I am going to get to voting. ... I wish I could vote in your election because your government affects my daily life more than my own.' "

Thomas L. Friedman

<u>An American in Paris</u>
January 20, 2005

Op-Ed Columnist,
New York Times

shoulder and declare a common intention to re-imagine and re-create democracy; instead of standing in opposition to each other creating only pain?

The Institute on the Common Good at Regis University

(http://www.regis.edu/regis.asp) The Institute sponsors public and private forums for the discussion of significant social issues. Its intent is to promote the long-term good of the greater community of Denver and the Rocky Mountain West through the discovery of common ground for addressing these issues. Rooted in the tradition of Roman Catholic social teaching, the Institute asserts the dignity and social nature of the human person. Neither liberal nor conservative in its posture, the Institute operates on the belief that a healthy society is committed to the welfare of *all its members*, especially those without a voice, suggesting a balance that avoids the extremes of exclusive individualism or totalitarianism.

The Co-Intelligence Institute

(http://www.co-intelligence.org/index.html) One of the best sources for researching the democratic process, the Co-Intelligence Institute, is the creation of Tom Atlee. He spent nine years exploring the wide range of democratic expressions - from grassroots efforts to multi-national organizations – embraced by humanity. His insights and the wealth of detailed wisdom outlined at his website and in his book, The Tao of Democracy - Using Co-Intelligence to Create a World that Works for All, are a treasure trove of democratic ideas and practices that we can all co-create together. Tom defines Co-Intelligence as follows:

> Healthy communities, institutions and societies -- perhaps even our collective survival -- depend on our ability to organize our collective affairs more wisely, in tune with each other and nature. This ability to wisely organize our lives together -- all of us being wiser together than any of us could be alone -- we call *co-intelligence*.

> Co-intelligence is emerging through new developments in democracy, organizational development, collaborative processes, the Internet and systems sciences like ecology and complexity. Today millions of people are involved in co-creating co-intelligence. Our diverse efforts grow more effective as we discover we are part of a larger transformational enterprise, and as we learn together and from each other. [16]

Co-Creating Together

I love Tom Atlee's definition of Co-Intelligence, because it echoes the essence of what it means to honor *all*. In fact, those who allow themselves to merge deeply with nature often speak of the underlying *Intelligence* that permeates nature.

If our true intention is to live in peace, how better could we design our political systems than to emulate the *co-creative adaptation and mutual support* that is the essential expression of nature? Our emerging understanding of ourselves as co-creators with each other and nature will lead to new ways of perceiving the meaning of democracy, and new tools with which to structure our social systems to reflect those new insights. We now have the understanding, the tools, and the opportunity to co-create human life as a peaceful and democratic expression that honors all.

It is time.

Another world is not only possible, she's on her way. Maybe many of us won't be here to greet her, but on a quiet day, if I listen very carefully, I can hear her breathing.
  Arundhati Roy from Come September, an essay in War Talk

Notes

1. <u>World Social Forum - A Fete for the End of History</u> - Naomi Klein - The Nation (New York) www.thenation.com March 19, 2001
   http://www.nadir.org/nadir/initiativ/agp/free/wsf/fete.htm
2. Charlie Cowan, in a widely distributed e-mail describing his own experience – with permission of the author.
3. From the transcript of the press conference held by Barbara Boxer and Stephanie Tubbs Jones just prior to their historic objection to the Ohio electors in Congress on January 6th, 2005, http://pdamerica.org/newsletter/2005-01-PreSummit/boxer-jones.php
4. From: <u>Evaluation of San Francisco's First Instant Runoff Voting Election</u>, FairVote – The Center for Voting and Democracy (www.FairVote.org) Rob Richie, with Caleb Kleppner and Steven Hill, December 2004http://fairvote.org/sf/SF_EvaluationRCVsuccess.pdf pages 1-4.
5. http://www.healingsociety.org/activities/declaration.html
6. http://www.renaissancealliance.org/ourvis/princ.htm# Henceforth called The Peace Alliance Foundation (501c3), dedicated to the realization of a culture of peace with nonviolence and cooperation as the organizing principles; through education, training, research and collaborative partnerships. (www.peacealliancefound.org) Also see http://www.satyana.org/pdf/lws-2002-2003.pdf, for Dr. Keepin's principles. See also TIMELINE March/April 2002, p. 10, <u>Twelve Principles of Spiritual Leadership.</u>by Dr. Will Keepin.
7. From TIMELINE March/April 2002, p. 10 <u>Twelve Principles of Spiritual Leadership.</u>by Dr. Will Keepin
8. http://www.thepeacealliance.org/press/article.htm, originally published in CommonDreams.org. Also see http://www.dopcampaign.org
9. http://www.demcoalition.org/pdf/warsaw_english.pdf Signed by the following governments: Republic of Albania, People's Democratic Republic of Algeria, Argentine Republic, Republic of Armenia, Australia, Republic of Austria, Azerbaijani Republic, People's Republic of Bangladesh, Kingdom of Belgium, Belize, Republic of Benin, Republic of Bolivia, Bosnia and Herzegovina, Republic of Botswana, Federative Republic of Brazil, Republic of Bulgaria, Burkina Faso, Canada, Republic of Cape Verde, Republic of Chile, Republic of Colombia, Republic of Costa Rica, Republic of Croatia, Republic of Cyprus, Czech Republic, Kingdom of Denmark, Commonwealth of Dominica, Dominican Republic, Republic of Ecuador, Arab Republic of Egypt, Republic of El Salvador, Republic of Estonia, Republic of Finland, Georgia, Federal Republic of Germany, Republic of Guatemala, Republic of Haiti, Hellenic Republic, Republic of Hungary, Republic of Iceland, Republic of India, Republic of Indonesia, Ireland, State of Israel, Italian Republic, Japan, Hashemite Kingdom of Jordan, Republic of Kenya, Republic of Korea, State of Kuwait, Republic of Latvia, Kingdom of Lesotho, Principality of Liechtenstein, Republic of Lithuania, Grand Duchy of Luxembourg, former Yugoslav Republic of Macedonia, Republic of Madagascar, Republic of Malawi, Republic of Mali, Republic of Malta, Republic of Mauritius, Mexico, Republic of Moldova, Principality of Monaco, Mongolia, Kingdom of Morocco, Republic of Mozambique, Republic of Namibia, Kingdom of Nepal, Kingdom of the Netherlands, New Zealand, Republic of Nicaragua, Republic of the Niger, Federal Republic of Nigeria, Kingdom of Norway, Republic of Panama, Papua New Guinea, Republic of Paraguay, Republic of Peru, Republic of the Philippines, Republic of Poland, Portuguese Republic, State of Qatar, Romania, Russian Federation, Saint Lucia, Democratic Republic of Sao Tome and Principe, Republic of Senegal, Republic of Seychelles, Slovak Republic, Republic of Slovenia, Republic of South Africa, Kingdom of Spain, Democratic Socialist Republic of Sri Lanka, Kingdom of Sweden, Swiss Confederation, United Republic of Tanzania, Kingdom of Thailand, Republic of Tunisia, Republic of Turkey, Ukraine, United Kingdom of Great Britain and Northern Ireland, United States of America, Eastern Republic of Uruguay, Bolivarian Republic of Venezuela, Republic of Yemen – signed later by Honduras, Suriname, Guyana, and Yugoslavia. http://www.state.gov/g/drl/rls/26811.htm See also http://www.state.gov/g/drl/democ/21692.htm
10. http://www.state.gov/g/drl/democ/

11. http://www.democracycaucus.net/html/offic.html

12. http://firstamendment.jideas.org/findings/findings.php The John S. and James L. Knight Foundation's High School Initiative seeks to encourage students to use the news media, including student journalism, and to better understand and appreciate the First Amendment. As part of the initiative, the foundation funded this "Future of the First Amendment" research project, focusing on the knowledge and attitudes of high school students, teachers and administrators. Specifically, the study seeks to determine whether relationships exist – and, if so, the nature of those relationships – between what teachers and administrators think, and what students do in their classrooms and with news media, and what they know about the First Amendment. Ultimately, the project surveyed more than 100,000 high school students, nearly 8,000 teachers and more than 500 administrators and principals at 544 high schools across the United States.

13. From Jim Rough's E-Mail to me of 4/6/2004. See www.tobe.net and http://www.mind.net/lance/rvwc/ for more information.

14. Vicki Robins http://www.conversationcafe.org/aboutus.html

15. From http://www.citizensassembly.bc.ca/resources/deliberation/BCSTV-FactSheet.pdf: BC-STV is designed to make every vote count and to reflect voters' support for candidates and parties as closely as possible. It achieves this by ensuring that the share of votes for candidates and parties is reflected in the share of seats won in the Legislature. And it allows voters' second and third (and subsequent) preferences to come into play, if their first choice isn't elected. Designed to make votes count BC-STV is fair because it is proportional. Each party's share of seats in the legislature reflects its share of voter support. This proportionality means voters' views are fairly represented. BC-STV is easy to use and gives voters more choice. Voters rank candidates in the order of their preference (1, 2, 3, etc.) – picking and choosing among candidates from the same party or from several different parties, including independents. Candidates are elected based on voters' choices. BC-STV gives more power to voters. Voters can select and rank candidates from any or all parties – including independents. Since voters choose which candidates from any one party are elected, no party or candidate can count on a "safe seat". So, all candidates must work hard to earn voter support. This ensures effective local representation.

16. http://www.co-intelligence.org/index.html

21

<u>MIRRORS</u>

What do I choose to mirror?

MIRRORS

When we see God in each other we will be able to live in peace.

Mother Teresa

Mirrors have been tremendous tools in my life. When I was learning to love myself, after spending most of my life focusing on what I didn't like about me, I would practice the following whenever I remembered. As soon as I saw my reflection in anything, I would say, "Hello Beautiful!" no matter how I actually felt about myself in the moment.

At the beginning, every reason why I wasn't beautiful and loving came flooding into my mind the second I said, "Hello," but gradually a change began to take place. Over time the flood of "negative" thoughts lessened to a stream. Within two weeks, the flood was gone, replaced by a gentle smile of recognition. I still had thoughts about how I wasn't matching up with my expectations, but a stronger voice began to replace the flood of negative thoughts. (I now know that I was literally re-wiring my neurochemical brain receptors in this process.)

I began to relax into the idea that I truly was beautiful and loving. I know this sounds simplistic, but when your mind has been filled with negative thoughts about yourself all life long, this represents a huge step towards self-acceptance and self-love.

I will probably be wrong much of the time especially since right and wrong tend to evolve and change from year to year but that's ok. I can always apologize and start again. Children are very forgiving. In fact explaining that I've changed my mind about what is right and/or apologizing to my child when I behave unacceptably is probably the most honoring, strengthening thing I can do.

Lynette Louise

Jeff: A Sexually Realized Spiritual Odyssey of Stepping Into Love, www.lynettelouise.com/excerpts.html.

Now whenever I look into the mirror, most of the time I see a beautiful Goddess smiling back at me. She radiates love and acceptance without judgment. She has become my refuge and my deepest friend.

What do I choose to mirror?

This transformation has helped me notice how we all play the role of mirrors for each other. Whenever a friend begins to tell me about an experience in life, I realize I am hearing *her* perceptions of how she holds herself in her mind's eye. The manner in which she tells her story reflects her deepest feelings about who she is and how she feels about her possibilities in life. If I listen openly without judgment, I literally begin to see her through her own eyes. I then have a choice to make. Do I reflect her own self-image back to her, or do I practice something new and exciting?

I realized recently that I can choose what world I want to recognize and live in. In other words, I could believe my own negative thoughts about myself or my friend's thoughts about herself; or I could choose to see both me and my friend through my heart.

When I look at the world and all who inhabit it through my heart, I see their inner light, what I have come to believe is their Essential Self, that eternal Presence that emanates from every thing and every one beneath the "story" of our perceived illusory world. This is the world I can choose to reflect back to my self and my friend.

Imagine what a gift we could offer the world if we all consciously chose to mirror back the light that we see in each other when we look through our hearts. This has become my daily practice.

Take, for example a young adult friend. We had a long conversation the other night in which she discussed what she perceives is working and not working in her life. It was my choice to buy into her perceptions or not.

I can acknowledge her experience without taking it as my own. So I now choose to see my friend through my heart (which is quite easy in her case) and then mirror back to her the light that she is. I don't need to "fix" anything, unless she asks for my assistance. She is perfect, whole, and complete unto herself. What a relief! All I do now is mirror back her own magnificence no matter what illusions are tugging at her sleeve for attention.

I am part and parcel of the whole and cannot find God apart from the rest of humanity.

Gandhi

When I choose to see beyond the ever-changing circumstances and presentations of life, reaffirming the magnificence that I see when perceiving through my heart, I allow myself to truly honor all life.

This can be challenging at times, but we have many role models to remind us. Take for example, the Non-Violent Peaceforce. Created in 1999 by David Hartsough and Mel Duncan, the Peaceforce mission is to build a trained, international civilian peaceforce committed to third-party nonviolent intervention. They were inspired by the thousands of stories in which individual people chose to make a stand for peace and to act as human mirrors for the magnificence of humanity – and all life – in the midst of conflict.

Most famous is the story of the young American, Rachel Corrie, who lost her life in her efforts to stop the destruction of Palestinian homes by Israeli soldiers. But surprisingly, death is rare for these intrepid peace walkers. More often, their non-aligned, apolitical stand for peace has the effect of softening hearts on both sides of the conflict. It is as though the people involved forget who they are, and the peace makers simply remind them of their own inner light, similar to the lesson the Babemba offer us. [1]

Take, for example, the story of Elana Wesley, who participated with an international team in the Balata refugee camp in Palestine 1998. She describes the events:

> As the Israeli forces made their way from house to house, knocking down joint walls between families, the internationals tried to explain to soldiers that the doors were open to adjoining rooms and apartments and there was no need to make holes in walls to gain access…The internationals offered to walk in front of the soldiers so they could enter through doors rather than destroying walls. [2]

The author of the article, Michael N. Nagler, stresses the importance of this offer. It demonstrates the non-partisanship of the internationals who were willing to protect people on both sides of the conflict. They were there to:

> Protect peace, for everyone, and that means getting in the way of violence against anyone – as did the African-American woman from Michigan Peace Teams who covered a fallen Klansman with her own body when he was attacked by an anti-racist mob. [2]

Hartsough and Duncan conducted a feasibility study to document and learn from the many peace teams already in place around the world. The evidence showed that non-violent intervention works. Throughout history people have stepped into the opportunity to mirror back to each other humanity's magnificence. From Gandhi's peace soldiers to the present moment, this movement has grown from individual efforts to carefully coordinated international movements.

Why not turn the restless energies of men (and women) into different channels, creating a disciplined "army of peace"?

…instead of mobilizing what peace theorist Kenneth Boulding would later call "threat power," they would use it for "integrative power."

Michael N. Nagler
Building a New Force
Yes! Magazine

Fall 2002

Can you imagine what the world would look like when we each take it upon ourselves to be a stand for the inner light that shines at the heart of all people?

Imagine an army of peace standing for the best of humanity whenever conflict arises, willing to place their bodies on the line and declare that a better, non-violent way is always available. It's not so far away as one might think. All it takes is a commitment to mirror back the magnificence of each other whenever and where ever we forget who we are. We can start right in our own homes… in our own mirrors.

Notes

1. See the chapter on COMMUNITY for more on the Babemba.
2. Michael Nagler, Building a New Force, YES! Magazine Fall 2002 Reprinted from YES! magazine, PO Box 10818, Bainbridge Island, WA 98110. Subscriptions: 800/937-4451 Web: www.yesmagazine.org and see http://www.nonviolentpeaceforce.org/ for additional information on the Nonviolent Peaceforce

22

<u>FREEDOM</u>

The last of the human freedoms
is to choose one's attitudes.
Victor Frankl

FREEDOM

Freedom is not a function of circumstances,
It is an expression of acceptance and honoring.
When you can see without judgment,
Then you are truly free.

Man's original sin was judgment. That is the only sin which a pure and innocent soul can commit. The immediate, inevitable, and unavoidable consequence of judgment is separation from the object of your judgment, and from God to the degree that the Creator is also part of that which you have judged. Judgments have a way of expanding and multiplying until separation from God becomes a real and monumental problem. A being in separation is unconscious of his Source, and therefore he will endlessly pursue the task of creating himself.

--Glenda Green

The celebration of our nation's birthday in 2003 was particularly powerful for me. After witnessing the strong positioning of opinions regarding the pros and cons of our participation in the Iraq war that seemed to touch a deep wound within us all, causing even more quarreling between citizens; I was somewhat reluctant to attend the public 4th of July celebrations. I feared that tolerance and acceptance for varying points of view would be replaced with yet more judgment and prejudice. While that may have been the experience of some, I experienced the day as a very special and unexpected gift.

Ask just about any USA citizen what one word would describe her country, and I believe most would say, "freedom." As people gathered together in our small southern Oregon town to celebrate their freedom, I asked myself what freedom means to me. As I marched with my group in the parade, I looked into the eyes of my neighbors. Some I knew for years, others were "strangers". Yet something had shifted within me. I no longer cared about the perceived differences between points of view, for they were reflections of an infinite field of choice, and all were merely experiences to be had.

Perhaps the true meaning of freedom, is the willingness to allow all expressions of life to exist without judgment. This willingness to simply accept "what is" offers each of us permission to fully accept ourselves too. I can't think of a more freeing experience.

This year I celebrated "freedom" by consciously choosing to see each person as a whole and complete expression of perfection in that moment. As a result, I was gifted with a new vision of who we are.

I saw people deliberately choose to take a day of rest together and play. I saw people of all walks of life and all beliefs relax their positions enough to simply *be* together in common joy. I saw families walk through the park and share their fun and creativity willingly with others. I saw hundreds prepare long hours, then get up early, walk miles to the beginning of the parade route, and then walk the entire route surrounded by others - all celebrating what is important to each of them in life. I saw a huge variety of those "important aspects of life", and all were celebrated *and received* equally. I saw those with much to share next to those with little. I saw people go out of their way to be kind and caring. I saw exhausted people working for causes they believed in while many honored their work by participating in their endeavors. I saw family members visiting, teasing, playing, and simply BEing together. I saw a fire works display of great beauty and excitement, paid for by those who supported the event, yet enjoyed by all. Together the entire city paused to concentrate on the same experience, as one.

All this I saw from a new standpoint. I was able to play the role of a witness, as if I were from another planet and totally uninvolved emotionally with the events unfolding. Yet because of that distance of emotion, I was able to watch with a keen eye for the unexpected nuance of love expressed. And it was everywhere.

With the little girl sharing her special dessert with the mallard duck who insisted on begging as she sat by the creek in the shade. With the scar-faced young boy who generously shared his family's huge arsenal of fireworks with the family who had few. With the father who playfully attacked his 20-year old son from behind, joyously and publicly proclaiming his love. With the woman who labored for hours in the hot sun until late at night offering magical fairy paintings to the throng that surrounded her stand. With the nursing mother who carried her child in a sling across her back so that she could be comfortable while marching for a cause she believed in. Within the quiet energy bubbles amidst the throng of thousands where time stood still, the creek flowed on, and all nature sang with energy at the joy of mutual celebration. With the faces of those whose eyes met mine in momentary transfixation as I marched in the parade beaming love, seeing only perfection in each face, honoring the beauty that was there.

Spiritual progress is based on acceptance as a matter of free will and choice and thus everyone experiences only the world of their own choosing. The universe is totally free of victims and all eventualities are the unfolding of inner choice and decision.

--Dr. David R. Hawkins
The Eye of the I, page 61

And perhaps just as important, I saw *myself* reflected back to me in all I witnessed, as life unfolding in all its variety and joy. All this I saw as I walked in the parade and crowd. And for this experience and memory, the 4th of July will forever be transformed.

- Instead of hot, frustrated, and angry crowds…

- Instead of tired children and hungry masses…

- Instead of greedy hands asking always for more…

Was I transformed or was it merely my perception, my willingness to see with "new" eyes? When I allow myself to focus on celebrating All That Is, I experience life as celebration. Every event, every moment is transformed. In gratitude I bow to the magnificence of humanity already living in harmony with life. It is all around to be seen. **The invitation is to look with the eyes of love and acceptance instead of judgment and positionality**.

It was with gratitude I ended this day, only to awaken to another beautiful day in paradise. Who could ask for more?

Bless everyone and honor the divine in them. Each is as you.

Each is powerful beyond anyone's comprehension.

Each is a gift of God, and in essence...is God.

Know this whenever you interact with any one, anything.

All is sacred.

Even the chair you are sitting in is sacred.

There is no separation.

This concept is sometimes difficult to grasp with your mind...don't.

Allow it to resonate within your heart, for there lies your wisdom.

When your intention is to honor the person you are with,

The need to be right disappears.

What you are left with,

Is the desire to give that person your full attention.

In so doing, you give yourself full attention also.

The "other" is nothing more, from your standpoint,

Than your own perceptions manifest... learn from them.

23

<u>COMMONS</u>

How can you buy or sell the sky? The land? The idea is strange to us.

If we do not own the freshness of the air and the sparkle of the water,

how can you buy them?

... This we know. The earth does not belong to us; we belong to the earth.

This we know. All things are connected like the blood which unites one family.

All things are connected.

Whatever befalls the earth befalls the sons and daughters of the earth.

We did not weave the web of life; we are merely a strand in it.

Whatever we do to the web, we do to ourselves.

...attributed to Chief Seattle

COMMONS

What we hold in common is, by its very definition, part of who we are.
By honoring the Commons, we honor ourselves and all life.

The term, "the Commons" used to refer to a public area used for grazing a community's cattle. The meaning, however, has expanded far beyond that narrow definition. Today "The Commons" refers to anything that is held by all, with no one person or group of people in control, including the market or the state. It provides the basic support systems of life.

Examples abound, yet most people don't even think of these items as commonly held by all, and therefore attention is rarely paid to these most precious aspects of life. Even worse, most people don't recognize their rights as part owners. Here are a few examples:

- **Water** – Most of us expect local water to be available to those who dwell in the area, as free and available for use as the air we breathe. That freedom is now threatened by transnational corporations. To a large part this is due to IMF and World Bank policies that encourage, and sometimes insist upon privatization of natural resources by multinational companies before providing loans to developing countries. The Spring 2005 issue of YES! magazine reports that in Bolivia, where residents were spending almost *half their wages on water*, a successful protest was mounted against Bechtel Corporation's privatization efforts.[1] Most recently, Uruguayans united to pass a constitutional amendment that guarantees the participation of water users in every aspect of management, declaring water a "public good" never to be privatized. This constitutes the first time a country has outlawed water privatization through direct democracy. Why is that? Why haven't *all* countries taken this obvious step to protect their own people and habitat?

- **Air** – Perhaps the most apparent example of the Commons, most people would chuckle at the idea of having to pay for the right to breathe the air, as it is thought to belong to anyone wise enough to draw breath. Yet industries commonly spew pollution into the air we all breathe with barely a whimper from the rest of us. We are just beginning to pay attention to the silent but increasingly effective voice of nature on the matter, especially as it affects changing global weather patterns and their repercussions.

- **Land** – The concept of land ownership has taken hold over the last 400 years. But most native people and those who shift their view of land from focusing on a specific plot to the view of Earth from space, would argue that the land and water covering our planet belong to all who inhabit this planet equally, just like the air we breathe. This concept is catching on. In record numbers voters in 2004 – including the recent November election – overwhelmingly voted to support land conservation.[2] One novel idea is to create a Land Ownership Tax, by which all who choose to have the privilege of "owning" land (determining how it is used) pay a tax to those who do not. The tax would be collected annually, and distributed equally to the citizens who choose not to "own" land, regardless of their age.

- **Culture** – Each aspect of our culture is held by all and used by all. We are so enmeshed in our cultural identities at the most deep and intrinsic level, that much of what we call "culture" is seen as "reality… the way life is;" with little recognition that there are many other cultural points-of-view and ways of categorizing life's experiences.

  Those diverse perceptions offer us fresh approaches to ways of living our daily lives, yet are threatened by the global insistence on homogeneity. When we export consumer "goods" to other cultures, we also export underlying assumptions about values and what is important in life; yet it is rare to find anyone willing to take responsibility for this aspect of our global economic decisions. Expanding our focus to include all repercussions of our actions will assist us in ensuring that diversity of culture is honored even as we connect globally.

- **Language** – Native language is absorbed into our identity and life-perspective at an extremely early age. Though constantly evolving, each language is held in common by its speakers, a bond that reaches deeply into our perceptual and cultural experiences. In fact, language is a highly proficient revealer of culture. Yet sadly, languages are disappearing at such an accelerated rate that it becoming a worldwide crisis. Statistics show that almost half of the world's languages are in danger because they are no longer taught to the next generation, and another 40% are threatened because fewer children are learning them. Approximately 90% of today's languages could die out by the end of this century. Why does this matter?

  Because just like culture, each language offers us a unique perception of life. Translators understand the wealth of diverse thinking that is lost with each language. A simple example, as mentioned earlier, is the English term "labor" to describe a woman in the process of giving birth. In Spanish, the same experience is referred to as "dar la luz," which means "to give light." Quite a conceptual difference! Additionally, with every language lost, we not only loose a unique perspective of life – one that can often offer insights into problems we currently face – we also loose the accumulated cultural knowledge of those people. Imagine, for example, a first people's knowledge of medicinal herbs. Can we really afford to loose that wisdom at this moment when we face pandemics like AIDS and SARS? What about their concepts of economics, agriculture, socialization, etc.? All offer valuable insights into diverse ways of living.

- **The Airwaves** -- Used by radio, cell phones, satellites, computers, TV, etc.; governments usually lease rights to the airwaves in exchange for what they view as a public good: free access to the broadcasts produced over those airwaves. The chapter on the MEDIA offers greater detail on this subject.

- **Quiet** – This may seem strange, but the quiet of the night and a reasonable quiet during the day is expected by all. The outrage of those who experience violations of this assumed right attest to the underlying assumption of this right.

  Recently, my small community has gathered a grassroots force to protest the creation of a gravel/asphalt pit just outside the city limits, within easy ear-shot of many surrounding rural residents. It would have operated 24 hours a

The *American commons* include tangible assets such as public forests and minerals, intangible wealth such as copyrights and patents, critical infrastructure like the Internet and government research, and cultural resources such as the broadcast airwaves and public spaces.

David Bollier
Public Assets, Private Profits
2001

Collectively, common assets are the basis for our common wealth. Our common assets -- what we share and own together -- are critical to the well-being of current and future generations…What we own in common helps us stay together.

From Redefining Progress –
Our Common Assets
http://www.redefiningprogress.org/programs/commonassets/

day. Many communities have banned the use of snow mobiles and dune buggies not only because they disturb humans, but also the entire bioregion. Examples of our awakening awareness of noise pollution are increasing worldwide.

- **Our shared human story** – No matter what the source, our shared stories and histories belong to all, as do our childhood games, and our shared social public life. This includes the incredibly valuable social activity that takes place on our public streets, and sidewalks, in parks, squares, and all public meeting places; often called "Social Capital." We are just beginning to recognize the value of Social Capital, and its impact in all aspects of life.
- **Human knowledge** – The accumulated and ever-growing knowledge of our species belongs to all. (Think of the freedom you experience when you search for information on the Internet. How can anyone place a value on common knowledge?)
- **The genetic and atomic material that makes up all life**. Although some corporations would like us to think that their tinkering with genetic material allows them to claim title to it, this argument is mainly intellectual; especially when wind and animals spread those genes beyond their intended locale. How can you "own" genetic and atomic material? [3]

The list could go on, but the point is to start noticing how many of these items we take for granted in our daily lives. I invite you to pay attention to any feelings or assumptions you may hold regarding them. Until I heard the Commons described, I'd never really given it much attention. Yet I also know that the elements that constitute the Commons also represent those aspects of life that, perhaps more than anything else, describe and define our common experience on planet Earth. In that sense then, their significance is sacred.

Giving Away the Invisible

Yet we tend to handle them as anything *but* sacred. Even during those times when we focus attention on them, it is usually because we notice a momentary lack of their presence – not because we recognize the valuable role they play in every moment of our lives.

The Commons are virtually invisible to most of us, we don't hear about them in the news, they aren't advertised, we don't focus attention on them, and we don't recognize that they are essential to life. Because we don't recognize the Commons in our everyday awareness, we also don't recognize when they are violated… violations that affects all life, including those who are doing the violating.

We unwittingly give away the rights to what we hold in Common, often without a second thought. We usually are not even aware we are doing so. As a species, we allow activity that pollutes every aspect of the Commons; and we do so without seeing that this is a violation to us ALL. Perhaps if we were truly aware of the Commons as the sacred trust we all share, we would demand that those who choose to use it in a special way or to abuse it, pay the rest of us for that privilege.

Engaging Us as Wholes

Jonathan Rowe of the Tomales Bay Institute has identified three basic attributes of the Commons:

- The Commons is usually present without rules or regulations.
- The Commons requires no advertising, it is simply there to be used.
- The elements of the Commons tend to relate to each being as a whole and equal participant. The resulting experience is usually beneficial. A commons engages people as wholes, and this tends to produce a multiplier of benign effects, especially in terms of social cohesion and trust.

If we want to honor all life, we must recognize and honor the Commons. Yet how can we honor the Commons in a way that all experience a win? Let's look at an easy example – the sky.

The Sky Problem

Even though we already have legislation in place to protect the quality of the air we all breathe, the efficacy and adherence to those laws in often highly questionable. A recent example is the Bush Administration's January 21, 2005 proposal that would grant concentrated animal feeding operations (CAFOs) immunity from clean air standards for the next two years. It also forgives any past fines for violation of those standards. In exchange, the proposal asks those businesses to provide emissions date to the EPA, who considers this data critical in their efforts to monitor potential violators. However the Clean Air Act *already* requires those same businesses to provide the same data while adhering to the law!

If this agreement is approved, the health of farm workers and those living near CAFO facilities will be threatened, along with the local habitat. What is the intent of such a decision? Who's interests are protected here? (Interestingly, one of the possible beneficiaries of such an agreement was also one of the largest contributors to the Bush inauguration celebration.) [4]

Perhaps a deeper question is one we never seem to ask: Who owns the air? Who has the right to make decisions that harmfully impact *all life* for the benefit of a few? It's time to question the *assumptions we all share* that provide authority over the quality of our air to *any* single group of people, especially those who consistently make decisions that potentially harm everyone.

The Sky Trust

To protect the air, Peter Barnes, author of <u>Who Owns the Sky?</u>, suggests we create a Sky Trust. Here are the key elements of such a Trust:

- Carbon emissions cap set initially at 1.346 billion tons, the 1990 level
- Tradable carbon emission permits sold annually to energy companies at the top of the carbon chain.
- All revenue from permit sales goes into a nationwide trust.
- Trust pays equal annual dividends to all U.S. citizens (like the Alaska Permanent Fund).

FDR brought us back to Jefferson's ideals with his third inaugural address, sometimes called his "Four Freedoms speech," on January 6, 1941, when he said:

"The basic things expected by our people of their political and economic systems are simple. They are :

- *Equality of opportunity for youth and for others.*
- *Jobs for those who can work.*
- *Security for those who need it.*
- *The ending of special privilege for the few.*
- *The preservation of civil liberties for all.*
- *The enjoyment of the fruits of scientific progress in a wider and constantly rising standard of living.*

These are the simple, the basic things that must never be lost sight of in the turmoil and unbelievable complexity of our modern world. The inner and abiding strength of our economic and political systems is dependent upon the degree to which they fulfill these expectations."

<u>Branding Progressives</u>
*Thom Hartmann's
Newsletter
Feb 11ᵗʰ, 2005*

Notice FDR failed to mentioned protection of the Commons as one of the basic things expected by our people of their political and economic systems. That's because it was assumed that clean air, water, and unpolluted land was available to all…and always would be. The fallacy of that assumption is now clear.

- Dividends can be placed tax-free in Individual Retirement Accounts or Individual Development Accounts for children.
- Initial price ceiling on carbon emission permits of $25 a ton; ceiling rises 7 percent a year for four years.
- Transition Fund to help those most adversely affected by higher carbon prices. Fund starts at 25 percent of permit revenue, declines 2.5 percent per year.[5]

Paying for the Privilege to Pollute

Based on the successful Alaska Permanent Fund and the Acid Rain Program, he suggests asking anyone who wishes to use any aspect of the Commons in a way that degrades its quality and perpetuity, to pay for that right through a commonly held Public Trust.[6]

Here's how it works:

- We the People recognize that the Commons belong to everyone.

- We then charge a market value for the right to profit from the use of the Commons or to degrade their quality (i.e. pollute).

- The collected funds are distributed equally to every human annually.

- This could result in the following benefits:

- Those who pollute will pay for the right to do so.

- Those who pollute more than others will pay more than others.

- Everyone will then have a financial incentive to conduct business in a healthy and sustainable manner.

- Everyone will also have a financial incentive to live a sustainable lifestyle.

- Yet everyone has a choice.

- Everyone will receive an equal annual dividend from the collected pollution or use tax.

- Those who benefit from the use of the Commons (what belong to everyone) will pay a fee for that right.

By treating the Commons as a public asset, we incorporate its true value into our personal, cultural, business, and political structures and practices. Reflecting on this realization and its impact on corporations, Jonathan Rowe writes in his article, The Hidden Commons:

> A General Electric wouldn't let people dump their trash on its property for free. Why should it get to dump its trash in our common property for free? [7]

In choosing to honor the true value of the Commons, we recognize their essential role in the well-being and survival of us all. The time for us to re-evaluate our priorities and what they say about Who We Are -- individually and as a species – has arrived.

Notes

1. From YES! magazine, PO Box 10818, Bainbridge Island, WA 98110. Subscriptions: 800/937-4451 Web: www.yesmagazine.org

2. Earlier in 2004, 42 ballot measures for land conservation were approved by voters in 22 states raising $821 million for conservation-related purposes. Added to the November results, the total local and state open space funding created at the ballot box in 2004 is now approximately $3.2 billion. Ernest Cook, Trust for Public Land director of Conservation Finance notes, "State legislatures, county commissions and city councils are continuing to give high priority to land conservation, even in tough economic times. This is an acknowledgment that such funds are an investment in the future." A Clear Victory for Land Conservation... Nov 4, 2004, © Copyright 1997-2004 Common Dreams. www.commondreams.org. *The Trust for Public Land, established in 1972, is the only national nonprofit working exclusively to protect land for human enjoyment and well-being. Through LandVote, TPL supports public funding for parks and other protected lands across the United States. Visit TPL on the Web: http://www.tpl.org and http://www.landvote.org.*

3. This list is inspired by the list at the Tomales Bay Institute website: http://www.earthisland.org/tbi/index.cfm

4. http://www.grist.org/news/muck/2005/01/24/factory_farms/   A Big To-Doo-Doo - EPA offers air-pollution immunity to factory farms, By Amanda Griscom Little 24 Jan 2005: Over the past decade, as the meat, dairy, and egg industries have boomed and been consolidated, massive factories -- known as concentrated animal feeding operations, or CAFOs -- have replaced many smaller-scale farms. The huge numbers of chickens, hogs, and heifers in these densely packed facilities produce even huger piles of waste, which in turn produce ammonia, hydrogen sulfide, volatile organic compounds, and particulates. Exactly how much of these pollutants, we don't yet know; CAFOs' emissions haven't been systematically studied... "It's true that much of the consolidation has happened in the last decade, so everybody agrees that additional data collection is appropriate," said Michele Merkel, a former staff attorney in the EPA's enforcement division who filed the agency's first suit against a CAFO for Clean Air Act violations in October 1999, under the Clinton administration. "But the Clean Air Act on its own requires polluting facilities to provide this kind of data. EPA does not need to suspend its enforcement authority while the monitoring takes place."

5. Sky Trust , Peter Barnes www.skybook.org

6. Trusts and the Public Trust Doctrine, By Sally Fairfax, College of Natural Resources, UC Berkeley From a speech given Nov. 14, 2000

7. The Hidden Commons, by Jonathan Rowe, YES! SUMMER 2001 http://www.yesmagazine.com/article.asp?ID=443 . Reprinted from YES! magazine, PO Box 10818, Bainbridge Island, WA 98110. Subscriptions: 800/937-4451 Web: www.yesmagazine.org

24

MONEY

The underlying dynamics of money has remained
mostly invisible to the conscious Western mind.
Money is to a civilization as the DNA code is to a species.
It replicates structures and behavior patterns
that remain active across time and space for generations.
It informs billions of individual and collective decisions, big and small,
of investing and consuming every day.
Bernard Lietaer & Stephen M. Belgin, _Of Human Wealth – Beyond Greed and Scarcity_

MONEY

How can money be an expression and celebration of all life?

According to Bernard Lietaer and Stephen M. Belgin in <u>Of Human Wealth – Beyond Greed and Scarcity</u>, money can be defined as:

> …an agreement within a community to use something as a medium of exchange. As an agreement, money lives in the same space as other social contracts, like marriage or lease agreements…This agreement is valid only within a given *community*. Some currencies are operational only among a small group friends (like chips used in card games), for certain time periods (like the cigarette medium of exchange among front-line soldiers during World War II), or among the citizens of one particular nation (like most "normal" national currencies today).

The first step towards economic and environmental regeneration is to increase the flow of income to consumers. Of course, by 'income' is meant real buying power- not recycled debt for which the people are already responsible in their roles as consumers and taxpayers.

In other words, in a responsible and scientific manner, let us make ourselves financially rich. We cannot be richer financially than we are in real terms, but we can be as rich. Indeed, it would be idiotic to be less rich. Well, yes, this does not say much for the quality of the thinking we have applied to the situation to date, but it is not too late to improve it.

Robert Klinck
<u>*Finance And The Environment*</u>
1991

When I contemplate money, I see it as a matrix of connection between people, ideas, and projects, all empowering each other through the use of money. I imagine how I vote with my money, choosing to support those businesses I truly believe in by purchasing their products and services; (and deliberately choosing not to support those businesses I feel do not honor life). I imagine how the money used to pay my phone bill goes to pay for the food on the dinner tables of phone company employees, which goes to pay for the violin lessons of the grocer's daughter, which also goes to pay for the music teacher's mortgage, etc.

In the process of living life trusting my heart and the natural abundance of life, I am learning some surprising facts about money. This is my own personal experience, but you may glimpse a peek at your own beliefs about money within these concepts.

Money as Energy Balance

When I was an award-winning realtor, I handled what was, to most people, the largest purchase of their lives… their home. It was an honor to guide them through the process. I always sought to find a win-win situation between the buyer and seller, one in which both parties felt honored and satisfied with the entire process including the end result. In so doing, I quickly learned that money is much less a tangible item, and much more a symbol of an exchange of energy.

The seller exchanged the energy of the home, encompassing both the readily apparent or physical aspects of the home and invisible, less apparent - yet just as important intangible aspects of the home (the ambiance, the aesthetics, the subtle energies, the lingering thoughts and feelings of those who lived there, etc.). The buyer exchanged money, a tangible symbol of her time and effort spent acquiring that money, and of energy exchanged through an infinite number of sources.

Money as Life-Blood

You cannot know that life is holy if you are content to live from economic practices that daily destroy life and diminish its possibility.

Wendell Berry

If we approach money as a scarcity to be hoarded, then every time we spend it, we are telling ourselves that we never have enough. Not surprisingly, that becomes our experience. In times when I am feeling only scarcity, I have allowed myself to see money as if it represented my life-blood. Therefore every time I spent it, in my mind I was literally bleeding myself to death. Every monetary transaction became a fearful act instead of a pleasure. What a painful way to choose to live life! Even the momentary pleasure of purchasing some long-sought treasure was overshadowed by the guilt and fear of what I perceived to be my own blood-letting.

Money as Trust

Yet, another choice is available. I've noticed that my attitude towards money and spending alter significantly whenever I experience life *as abundance*. This has been especially obvious whenever I felt secure because I thought I had "enough" money to relax about paying my bills, knowing I could easily pay my monthly debts and still have a little left over with which to play. I began to wonder if I wasn't seeing the story backwards.

Perhaps it wasn't my belief in financial security that allowed me to relax around money, experiencing it with less fear. Perhaps it was my *relaxed attitude* that *created* the security in the first place. I began to notice that there have been people in my life who held the attitude that life would always support them financially, and it always did. Even when one of them lost millions, his response was to simply relax and wait for the millions to return – which always happened. He told me he'd lost millions before, and probably would do so again, but that he was confident money would always come to him, it always supported him.

Somehow, these people managed to develop enough *self-trust* that they were able to relax *all the time* about money, not just when they felt secure.

Money as Cyclical Seasons

I have always been a warm-weather person. I like long sunny days and short cool nights, (especially if I can sleep without a roof over my head under the stars). While others seem to celebrate the summer solstice, it has always been a moment of sadness for me. I didn't understand why this was so until recently.

I perceived the days getting shorter as a loss of something I loved. Seen through the filter of lack, how could I possibly enjoy autumn and winter? Not surprisingly, whenever I experienced financial instability, it was always during this time of year. When I think about it, it is amazing how much my own financial rhythms, body rhythms, and Earth's rhythms align. Fall is the time when the illusion of death is most obvious, surface things whither and seem to die.

Yet I don't have to buy into that illusion. When I shift my focus to gratitude and trust in the abundant cycles of life, I can perceive the perfection of all seasons. Under the surface bleakness of autumn and winter, away from visual validation, life is in gestation. It is actually preparing for birth in the spring. It is my choice to focus on and trust in the regeneration of life even though circumstantial evidence (on the surface) may be missing and even look deceptively contrary to what I know to be true. In the same manner, I can trust in the cycles of money, the natural flow of energy that always cycles back to me, if I am only willing to perceive a deeper reality.

Money as Relationship

As I learned more about money, I wanted to develop a relationship with it that was love-based, like a trusted lover or friend. I was finished with my former relationship that seemed to be based on lack… lack of options, lack of circumstantial evidence, lack of skills, lack of creativity, lack of energy, and most of all lack of trust in myself. Instead I wanted to feel as if money was a most trusted, loving, and generous friend – one I could always count on to be there for me – no matter what. I wanted money to be a blessing in my life, not just an incidental relationship, but an outright

Economics is the study of our optimization (creation, management, allocation and destruction) of our resources. To optimize something is to make the most of it. Our spiritual and intellectual resources are infinite. That means there is more of it than we could ever use up. Our resources in the material world ---such as air, water and land---- are finite. Most of us believe that we have a responsibility to take care of the land, to take care of each other, and to take care of ourselves. Economics is a body of knowledge that helps us do that.

Catherine Austin Fitts,
Economics 101 -
A Curriculum
http://fromtheburbs.blogspot.com /2005/03/economics-101- curriculum-by-catherine.html

The Census Bureau reports that 40 percent of households in our society earn an average of $10.12 per hour, or about $20,000 per year. After housing, food, and clothing are subtracted, these people cannot afford what most of us take for granted, including education, insurance, and health care.

Too much and too long, we seem to have surrendered community excellence and community values in the mere accumulation of material things. Our gross national product ... if we should judge America by that - counts air pollution and cigarette advertising, and ambulances to clear our highways of carnage. It counts special locks for our doors and the jails for those who break them. It counts the destruction of our redwoods and the loss of our natural wonder in chaotic sprawl. It counts napalm and the cost of a nuclear warhead, and armored cars for police who fight riots in our streets. It counts Whitman's rifle and Speck's knife, and the television programs which glorify violence in order to sell toys to our children.

Yet the gross national product does not allow for the health of our children, the quality of their education, or the joy of their play. It does not include the beauty of our poetry or the strength of our marriages; the intelligence of our public debate or the integrity of our public officials. It measures neither our wit nor our courage; neither our wisdom nor our learning; neither our compassion nor our devotion to our country; it measures everything, in short, except that which makes life worthwhile. And it tells us everything about America except why we are proud that we are Americans.

Robert Kennedy
University of Kansas,

March 18, 1968
http://www.mccombs.utexas.edu/facu
lty/Michael.Brandl/Main%20Page
%20Items/Kennedy%20on%20GN
P.htm

expression of the love I experience myself to be. And I wanted to share that love as an expression of who I am – in every choice I made and every action I took.

So I began to look for ways in which I could make money my lover, my friend. What were the characteristics of love that I cherish so much in my human relationships?

- **TRUST.** I can count on my friends to be there when I need them. Once I declare someone my friend, I automatically see these characteristics in them, without the need for some event to prove it true. And perhaps because I come *from* that belief in relating to my friends, they always prove me right. Therefore my ability to trust and rely on my friends has more to do with my choice to see them as trustworthy and reliable, than anything else. I realized that I could relate to money in the same way. I can choose to live my life from the belief that money will always be there for me, even when I don't know how or under what circumstances. It is an issue of TRUST, not trusting something outside myself; but trust in me and in abundance as the natural expression of aliveness and life. Therefore TRUST and abundance become a place I come *from*, not a goal to reach in some distant future.

- **ACCEPTANCE.** When I love someone, I allow myself to see them as total and complete, without judgment. I see what some would call "flaws" and what others might call "talents" as simply what is, and I love and accept it all. We can do the same with money. Without judgment we can observe the energy flow of money. When I make this choice, I am amazed at the power of money, a power *we* give it, to touch so many lives in significant ways.

- **FORGIVENESS.** When my friends treat me in a way that feels less honoring or thoughtless, I look beneath the obvious 'story' to find what part of me is being triggered, what wound of mine am I projecting onto my friend? Money, perhaps more than anything else in our culture, offers this same valuable gift to anyone willing to receive it. It is not money that needs to receive forgiveness, it is *myself*. How I relate to money reveals much about how I relate to life.

- **GRATITUDE & ACCOUNTABILITY.** I naturally nurture and care for those I love. I treat them with honor and gratitude, without expecting anything in return, because the joy of being with them, serving them, and receiving the gift of their presence in my life, is my reward. This is gratitude. Additionally, I willingly choose to be accountable to them for the choices I make, especially those regarding them personally.

I can choose to treat money in a similar manner, with gratitude, honor, and accountability. I can consciously choose to handle it with care, making sure I am honest with myself and others. I can choose to carefully keep track of the money that flows as love-energy through my life, to honor the power of money to transform situations, and to see all money as a gift, just as I see my friends as the gifts they are. In this way I honor money's power and the privilege of participating in its energy flow.

Money as Love

We can choose the focus of money's energy by how we relate to it… as a vehicle of love or a vehicle of fear. I found that when paying bills or making any purchase, if I take a moment to send gratitude to every person who's hands the money has and will touch, then I know that every aspect involved in the energy flow of the money is honored. I can choose to receive the creative energy already present in the money, add my own love energy to it, and then send it on its way, trusting that all who touch it will have the opportunity to receive my gift if they are willing and open to doing so.

When I see money as an energy flow, benefiting every hand it touches, then it is literally an extension of my love traveling from person to person, blessing each one as it moves through her or his life.

In honoring the energy flow of money, I honor all who participate in the giving and receiving of that money. By doing so, I transform the experience from a mere transaction, to a subtle yet powerful healing that literally transforms the experience to a declaration of life AS LOVE.

This concept has taken on a new meaning for me lately. In order to write this book, I used credit cards as a source of abundance. Yet it wasn't until just recently that I realized I was stuck in an illusion that no longer serves me. You see, I was willing to rack-up huge credit card debt, to borrow money from banks, or even my parents because I *allowed* them to be sources of monetary flow for me. But I now realize that the entire Universe is naturally abundant. This realization is profound. Not only does it tremendously expand my sense of the source of my financial well-being to include *everything*, but it also substantially alters my relationship to credit card companies. I now thank them – with heartfelt gratitude – for playing the role of substitute-Universal magnanimity until I was able to see that abundance surrounds me (if I only ALLOW myself to receive it.) Now, my practice is to receive what is already there – all I have to do is focus on it – instead of the illusion of lack.

Money as Flow

Today I awakened into a new world from the one I went to sleep in. Yesterday I understood the concept of scarcity vs. abundance-sufficiency, but it wasn't until today that I saw the level to which scarcity thinking had permeated every thought I had and every action I took.

For example, I had been operating under the idea that I only had a certain amount of money left while I wrote this book. I was carefully counting every penny I spent, always aware that each one depleted my stash. In fact, my thoughts were so narrowly focused on one source of financial support that I would have missed any other opportunities that arose. The only energy attached to the money I spent was fear. I was so attached to the money, I almost wrote "my money".

Yet how could any money (a symbol for value) be "my" money? As money flows from hand to hand, it is more like water, falling upon varied landscapes, flowing through many creeks and rivers, and finally touching many shores as it flows through to the sea. Who can say which water drop touched any particular spot along the way? Could that spot claim ownership of a certain water drop as it sped by? Yet all

Our task is to look at the world and see it whole.

E. F. Schumacher

were nourished by the water. Money simply IS, just as the nourishment intrinsic to food simply is.

We created money and it is we humans who give it value. But once we did, it was no longer ours, for it became a tool – a symbol of value. And now that tool has gotten out of hand. We have forgotten who created it, and in that forgetting, **we have confused the symbol of value, for value itself.** We have forgotten to honor the purpose for which money was originally created – to support life.

Money as Community

When we look at our economic structures – whether local, national, or global – it is obvious that what we have created doesn't work. With only 1% of the USA population holding over 40% of the wealth, our economic structure is severely imbalanced. As more people awaken to the need to re-think the entire concept of our economy they are asking important questions.

It is very different in a world in which the net worth of the world's 358 billionaires roughly equals the aggregate annual incomes of the world's 2.5 billion poorest people. Under conditions of extreme inequality, property rights and living rights come into conflict and the free market becomes an instrument of tyranny rather than an agency of democracy.

David Korten
Property Rights vs Living Rights

- What is the goal of our economic system?
- How does our present economy succeed or fail to meet those goals?
- How and why did we create money?
- Are there alternative ways of meeting our goals that we haven't yet tried – ways that would be far more successful in meeting the needs of all people and the environment?

As humans begin to take full responsibility for the economic policies we use with each other, as our awareness that we have a choice grows, and as we no longer are willing to leave the economics of our lives (and world) for others to mismanage, many new ideas are beginning to emerge.

People are creatively addressing these questions throughout the world. I'd like to highlight just a few of those proposed solutions and tools at the end of this chapter. Check the Reference section for even more ideas. For every one listed, there are hundreds more. I encourage you to search for the ideas (or combination of ideas) that best meet your local needs – then implement them co-creatively within your community.

Our National Choices

Just as with individuals, the decisions a democratic nation makes regarding how money is budgeted reflects its priorities. What does our current budget reveal? The National Priorities Project[1], offers citizens the opportunity to clearly see the priorities we are choosing by offering comparisons of the choices available.

Do these priorities match your own?

Do you feel comfortable being the world's biggest military spender, with over 50% of our budget on national defense when we are already spending 30 times more on defense than what the 'rogue' countries spend (Cuba, Iran, Libya, North Korea, Sudan, Syria). The Pentagon pays for more helicopters, airplanes and warships than all of these countries *combined*, and the capabilities of U.S. weaponry are unrivaled in the world. [1] What does this say about the role we play on this planet? Let's start asking the more subtle question of who are we willing to be – starting from this very next moment.

Security as Motivation

Usually people feel the need to defend themselves when they don't feel safe. With all this military might, why don't we feel safe? Safety is often a function of relationship, the ability to take into consideration the needs of all involved, not just oneself. When everyone's needs are met, the desire to react violently and perhaps irrationally diminishes. Yet how much of our budget is earmarked for making sure that all people are fed, housed, clothed, educated, and medically cared-for? How much is allocated to healing the wound of our international policies such that the desire to harm Americans is eliminated? How much is allocated to protecting the environment whose health directly affects the ability of ALL life to survive? The following are some choice comparisons worth taking into consideration.

Your Tax Dollar

Since the major source of funding for the national budget is our tax revenue, it is important to understand how our contributions break down per dollar spent on taxes. As of April 2005, the breakdown was as follows:

The average household in the U.S. paid $6,296 in federal income taxes in 2004. Here is how that amount was spent: [2]

- Military and Defense: $1,887
- Health: $1,276
- Interest on the Debt (Military): $555
- Interest on the Debt (Non-military): $616
- Income Security: $414
- Education: $231
- Veterans' Benefits: $216
- Nutrition: $169
- Housing: $135
- Natural Resources: $109
- Job Training: $25
- Other: $662

Distribution of Security Dollars:

MILITARY DOMINATES SECURITY SPENDING[3]

- Military = 91%
- Preventive measures [3-1] = 3%
- Homeland security [3-2] = 5%

Close to one-third of the income-tax dollar is spent on national security. This money is divided into military spending, homeland security, and preventive measures such as diplomacy, peacekeeping and development aid. Less than a penny goes to preventive measures that help mitigate conflict and alleviate many of the conditions that produce breeding grounds for terrorists.

MORE ON YOUR TAX DOLLAR...

- Only half of a penny is spent on energy conservation. Safe, reliable and affordable energy alternatives will insure our country against future instability and conflict by reducing our dependence upon fossil fuels.
- Housing assistance accounts for about 2¢ of every tax dollar and made up $36.6 billion in federal outlays last year. By contrast, homeowners with mortgages claimed $70 billion in reduced taxes. Two-thirds of that amount went to those with incomes more than $100,000 a year.[3-3]

- Interest payments on the national debt consume 18.6¢ of every income-tax dollar. While interest rates have remained low, stemming the impact of growing debt, large deficits this year and to come may demand a larger portion of income-tax dollars in the future.
- Veterans' benefits account for about 3.4¢ of the income-tax dollar and include health, education, retirement and other benefits for veterans. Veterans organizations have put forth an alternative budget which indicates that $4.3 billion more is needed in funding. Other changes are required to address rapidly-rising health care costs, special needs of disabled veterans, and other promised benefits for veterans.[3-4]

The 2004 Financial Report of the United States Government was published in December 2004. Under the heading, U.S. Government Structure & Performance - Mission & Organization the report states the following:

> Today, the U.S. Government's most visible mission of managing the security of the Nation, homeland, and economy is still derived from its original mission in the Constitution: "...to form a more perfect union, establish justice, insure domestic tranquility, provide for the common defense, promote general welfare and secure the blessings of liberty to ourselves and our posterity." Since the original mission's inception, other missions have developed as the Congress authorized the creation of other agencies to carry out various objectives established by law. Some of these objectives are to promote health care, foster income security, boost agricultural productivity, provide benefits and services to veterans, facilitate commerce, support housing, support the transportation system, protect the environment, contribute to the security over energy resources, and assist the States in providing education.

Yet the actual spending decisions don't support this statement. The federal government has consistently failed to finance its own mandatory programs for the states, including the much publicized "No Child Left Behind" program. Cuts have taken place in most of the programs dedicated to the above list of objectives, with additional huge cuts requested in the proposed 2006 Budget. In fact, it seems "facilitate commerce" and perhaps "foster income security" (for a few) are the only objectives that are constantly supported. One can make a strong argument that even "boost agricultural productivity" isn't supported, except perhaps in the very short term, if you take into consideration the environmental degradation caused by huge corporate agricultural practices that deplete the clean water supply, destroy the quality of soil with huge mono-crops, pollute the environment with genetically altered bioagents and petroleum based pesticides, etc. Why is there such a disconnect between what we say we stand for and our actual actions?

The Need for Transparency

Not only do our goals not match our actions, but even our bookkeeping is questionable. In both the Total Budget and the Discretionary Budget requests for 2006, the funds requested for the wars in Afghanistan and Iraq were not included. How can Congress begin to intelligently discuss priorities without a full disclosure of funding requests?

In a personal budget, the amount available to spend is generally known, so spending decisions can be made within that limitation. However, when a budget is no longer required to balance, and deficit spending becomes the norm, how can Congress make funding decisions with any integrity? And how can intelligent decisions be made when a large part of the budget is simply not available for discussion? At the very least, if our goal is to truly honor ourselves and each other, we must require that all fiscal discussions be transparent – that they include ALL

In Alaska, residents receive about $1,000 per year as their share of the oil royalty... There are many more natural resources, including surface locations, that people pay top dollar to own or use. Were we to collect all this natural rent, every member of society could receive $4,000-$8,000 per year.

Sharing land rent, this gratis profit, means of course that those few now hoarding it would no longer be able to do so... So the richest and most powerful corporations may at first not see "geonomics" (the policy of paying neighbors for nature) as in their narrow interests. Yet the corollary of sharing Earth's worth (because it is ours) is to quit confiscating labor's wages and capital's interest (because they are not ours). Thus, were we to respect property - both private and public - we'd repeal taxes upon human effort and charge a fee for the use of Mother Earth. Such a formula may be sufficiently balanced to win widespread support and overcome entrenched opposition.

Cutting taxes while disbursing rent is an idea now being promoted by greens in Western Europe. Already, five nations (Sweden, Denmark, the Netherlands, England, and Spain) have begun to implement the collection phase of the geonomic transformation. In the past, advocates included Henry George, author of Progress And Poverty (in the 19th century, it outsold all titles but the Bible), and Tom Paine, the man who christened the 13 colonies "the United States of America."

Jeffery J. Smith,
President of the
Geonomy Society

information necessary to make intelligent decisions based on our vision of who we are – not on a desire to benefit some at the expense of others, (whether intentional or not). In other words, we cannot settle for an "Opps, sorry some people got unintentionally hurt by our policies" attitude, as exemplified by the war-time classification of civilian dead as "collateral damage." This is the backbone of honoring all. We can choose to adopt an attitude that it simply is not acceptable for our cultural structures and policies to allow anyone to suffer for the benefit of a few. Period. This is the backbone of honoring all – not because of a value judgment, but because it brings us greater joy.

Economics that serves all...

Many economic experts throughout the world have rejected the need to continue an economic model that only serves an elite few; and have proposed highly creative solutions for consideration – ones that allow for a relatively easy transition into a system (or group of complementary systems) that more equitably serve us all. I'd like to highlight a few below. See if they can act as inspiration for your own ideas.

Ultimately, our willingness to perpetuate a system that no longer serves us as originally intended, and that is detrimental to survival; without offering methods that can lead to systems more in line with our current level of awareness, makes us complicit in the results. I am no longer willing to play that game.

The Ownership Solution

In 1980 Jeff Gates served as counsel to the Senate Finance Committee, specializing in retirement security. He was able to observe the financial deliberations as both political parties embraced the economic model known as the University of Chicago's "neoliberal" economic model, or the "Chicago Model" for short. Over the years, as he witnessed an ever widening gap develop between those who benefited from the lawmaker's strategies and those who didn't, he has been a clear voice for reason. In a November 2004 article entitled, The Consensus Never Could Have Worked, he outlined many of the serious problems inherent in our current economic reality. He suggests thinking POSIWID: *the purpose of a system is what it does* when trying to distinguish economic theory from real results.

According to Gates, US economic theory has produced results that clearly favor only the few:

> In the U.S., pension funds account for 55-60 percent of the ~\$19,000,000,000,000 in monies under management. Tax subsidies for pensions total ~\$110 billion per year,[1] a fiscal expense surpassed only by national security and interest payments on the national debt. What results does the consensus system create while maximizing returns on those subsidized funds?

> In 1982, the threshold for inclusion in the *Forbes* magazine list of the 400 richest Americans was \$91 million. By 2000, the cut-off had risen to \$725 million as, from 1998-2000, their personal wealth grew an average \$1,920,000 per day (\$240,000 per hour) while the number of billionaires grew from 13 in 1982 to 274 by 2000 and 312 by 2004.[2] During the bull market of 1983 to 1998,

China's eclipse of the United States as a consumer nation should be seen as another milestone along the path of its evolution as a world economic leader. Its record-high domestic savings and its huge trade surplus with the United States are but two of the more visible manifestations of its economic strength. It is now China, along with Japan, that is buying the U.S. treasury securities that enable the United States to run the largest fiscal deficit in history.

The United States, the world's leading debtor nation, is now heavily dependent on Chinese capital to underwrite its fast-growing debt. If China ever decides to divert this capital surplus elsewhere, either to internal investment or to the development of oil, gas, and mineral resources elsewhere in the world, the U.S. economy will be in trouble.

China is no longer just a developing country. It is an emerging economic superpower, one that is writing economic history. If the last century was the American century, this one looks to be the Chinese century.

Lester R. Brown
Eco-Economy Update 2005-1
February 16, 2005
China Replacing The United States As World's Leading Consumer
http://www.earth-policy.org/Updates/Update45.htm

53 percent of capital gains flowed to the topmost 1 percent,[2] confirming that a rising consensus tide lifts all yachts.

Consensus model income patterns reflect similar results. From 1979-1997, the average income of the top quintile of Americans jumped from 9 times the income of the poorest quintile to 15 times.[2] By 1998, the top 1 percent had as much combined annual income as the 100 million citizens with the lowest earnings.[3] By 2000, the top 1 percent claimed 21 percent of national income, up from 14 percent since 1990,[2] as much combined income as the lowest-earning 110 billion and their greatest share since 1929.[2] By 2000, after two centuries of labor-saving progress, Americans were laboring 184 hours longer than in 1970.[2]

As we export our financial theories worldwide, these same policies are producing similar results internationally:

In Indonesia, 62 percent of the stock market value of the world's fourth most populous nation is owned by its most well-to-do 15 families. The comparable figure for the Philippines is 55 percent and 53 percent for Thailand.[4] The world's 200 wealthiest people doubled their net worth in the four years to 1999, to $1,000 billion.[2] The combined income of the topmost one percent worldwide now equals the combined income of the poorest 57 percent (3.2 billion people). [2] Gates points out that these current economic theories destroy virtually all aspects of the social, economic, and ecological support systems upon which we rely for survival, while simultaneously dismissing any concern for our future well-being.

He suggests that the purpose of the existing system has been understood all along, so that either its supporters are incompetent or complicit. He suggests that it is time for business leaders to embrace a monetary system that better reflects the values of citizens, purchasers, communities, ecologies, and democracies.[4]

Analyzing the problem from a systems standpoint, Gates suggests that any possible solution must honor the interdependence of the economic, social, and environmental domains, with an emphasis on meeting people's needs *locally and in human-scale*, while consciously focusing on community wellbeing. He explains the changes needed to create a broader-range of ownership:

Based on experience advising in more than 35 countries, I can state with full confidence that **finance can be designed either for exclusion or inclusion**. Yet we've never asked anyone anywhere, neither here nor abroad, which alternative they prefer...

Economic policy could include both widespread employment of an economy's labor resources and widespread ownership of its capital resources. Yet after two centuries of labor-saving progress, full employment remains this nation's sole economic goal even as the typical American works 184 hours longer each year than in 1970, for just nine percent more pay. So much for 200 years of progress, much of it funded with taxpayer-paid research and development.

Similarly, an "ownership impact report" could be mandated whenever and wherever public policy impacts finance, including World Bank lending policies. Instead, U.S. taxpayers guarantee foreign loans to finance plutocracies abroad while U.S. lawmakers approve $1,140 billion in deficit-financed supply-side investment subsidies with nary a word about who will be supplied. [5]

Gates suggests concrete steps we can begin to take to transition from the "Chicago" model, that has led to such an extreme imbalance of wealth throughout the world, to his "ownership" model that is specifically designed to create "more capitalists, not just more capital." When ownership is held by many, instead of just a few, the effect ripples throughout the economic system. He likens this idea to the original intent of democracy – to place governmental power in the hands of *all* the people, not a just a

I have had the opportunity -- as an investment banker and former Assistant Secretary of Housing responsible under both Bush I and Clinton Administration for the cleanup of some of the S&L, mortgage and real estate related fraud and money-laundering schemes -- to learn more about the black budget business model used in these criminal enterprises.[6] Simply put, we are living in a negative return on investment economy. This means that from the point of view of most people on the planet, the dolphins, the trees and all living things, the world is worse off for our centralized human economic activity, at the crux of which are the central banks and the military-industrial complex they finance.

Catherine Austin Fitts
<u>Mapping the Real Deal :
Where Would Jesus Bank?</u>
Monday, 5 July 2004

6. See, "A Negative Return on Investment Economy – Articles & Documents," at http://www.solari.com/gideon /articles_risk.html and the full article at http://www.scoop.co.nz/ mason/stories/HL0407/S00 040.htm

few. **When capitalism is compromised in favor of a few, democracy is also compromised.**

Creating more Owners...

A first step in this transition is to encourage companies to include their employees, customers, local residents, and others who hold a stake in the company's performance, including the community in which the company resides – as owners. He proposes three methods for doing so. (His comments are in italics.): [6]

- ESOPs – Employee Stock Ownership Plans, which currently exist in more than 11,000 USA companies, already comprising approximately ten percent of the workforce.

- RESOPs – Related Enterprise Stock Ownership Plans which he suggests would expand on the idea of ESOPs by including a firm's suppliers and distributors. *Jamaica Broilers, a chicken processing company, has a broad range of owners. Some of them are traditional investors plus the managers. But they also used the company's buyback of a foreign investor's shares to create ownership not only for their direct employees (that's an ESOP) but also for those working for related enterprises, including those microenterprise employees who grow the chickens and those employed by trucking firms who transport the chickens to market. That's a RESOP.*

- CSOPs – Customer Stock Ownership Plans which would include local residents and offer them a voice in investor-owned utilities. *Imagine living in a utility district for 50 years where every month you have built into your bill a financial return for an absentee investor who may live in an entirely different country. Why do that? Over time, that cash flow could be used to grow capital for you instead. That's a CSOP.*

- GSOCs – General Stock Ownership Corporations in which everyone benefits from local resources. *Trinidad recently discovered what could be as much as 75 trillion cubic feet of natural gas. Who are the natural owners of that natural gas? That resource could be developed so that everyone on the island became a mini-capitalist, ensuring that everyone participates at least a little and none too much. That's a General Stock Ownership Corporation (GSOC).*

- Gates suggests that these inclusive ownership models will lead participants to re-evaluate their relationship to work, while increasing motivation and the awareness that the decisions made directly impact the welfare of their own families and communities. He states:

  Indeed, much of today's violence – physical, psychic and ecological – stems from a pervasive sense of feeling apart from rather than a part of the free enterprise system and its impact on society and nature.

  The very character of democratic free enterprise requires that it include notions of solidarity, mutuality and reciprocity. By turning to broad-based personal ownership as a means for deepening and enriching the relationship that people have with private enterprise, we can do much to ensure that decisions affecting peoples' lives and the environment are no longer resigned to the abstract realm of capital markets or left solely in the hands of a distant and detached financial and managerial elite. Neither left, right nor centrist, this strategy suggests instead the public encouragement of private property patterns that are decentralized, devolved and personalized.

What greater stupidity can be imagined than that of calling jewels, silver, and gold "precious," and earth and soil "base"? People who do this ought to remember that if there were as great a scarcity of soil as of jewels or precious metals, there would not be a prince who would not spend a bushel of diamonds and rubies and a cartload of gold just to have enough earth to plant a jasmine in a little pot, or to sow an orange seed and watch it sprout, grow, and produce its handsome leaves, its fragrant flower, and fine fruit. It is scarcity and plenty that make the vulgar take things to be precious or worthless; they call a diamond very beautiful because it is like pure water, and then would not exchange one for ten barrels of water.

The character of Sagredo in Galileo Galilei's *Dialogo di Galileo Galilei Linceo*, 1632 –
as quoted by Dava Sobel in her historical memoir, *Galileo's Daughter*, Penguin Books, 2000, page 148.

Property is a «property» of free enterprise, much like wet is a property of water. Property patterns are an underutilized tool, a meta-tool if you will, that could be used to evoke a more conscious capitalism, one where a sense of interdependence is immediate, palpable and real. That sense of connectedness, along with newly peoplized feedback loops, could have remarkable implications not only for enterprise performance but also for rebuilding social capital while advancing environmental sustainability.

In many disciplines outside the hard sciences it is said that we live within «fields» of thought and perception – nonmaterial, invisible forces that structure both space and behavior within it. The challenge facing free enterprise lies in creating an organizational field that engages the human conscience. It is in that context that ownership patterns, an invisible field, work their influence for good or ill. [6]

The Solari Solution

In the mid-1990's Catherine Austin Fitts, former partner and member of the board of Dillon Read & Co. Inc., a Wall Street investment bank, and Assistant Secretary of Housing under Bush I, created a financial "toolkit" to help people invest in small businesses, small farms and small real estate portfolios through locally controlled equity databanks and investment advisors called a *solari*, and to help consumers empower themselves both personally and politically by "voting with their money."

She felt it was important to organize locally while networking globally with the intent of implementing financial transparency at the local level - so we are aware of exactly how local money flows, works, and disappears. By working locally, we have a real opportunity to reengineer our economy at the grassroots level, to finance communities with equity and sound currency, reduce debt, create job opportunities and structures for wealth creation while focusing also on healing the environment and all aspects of community.

Her "vote with your money" tools are simple, and she offers a network of support for implementing each step in this grassroots community transformation. Those steps include joining both Solari Circles for networking support and ideas, and Solari Investment Circles to pool savings into local investments with the eventual creation of a Solari Investment Advisor and neighborhood databank. The overall goal is to make local economies the best equity investment worldwide.

The Solari Model allows strategic management and control by local leaders while offering local citizens the opportunity to participate in stock market-type equity and capital gains created from their own deposits, purchases, and focus of attention. Similar models are also used in emerging markets that combine local control with outside global capital. This model proposes to answer the following questions:

- *Why let outside multinational corporations buy up our market and enjoy all the profits from our purchases?* Instead, why not combine our small businesses and profit from financing and modernizing them ourselves?
- *Why let foreign corporations buy up our natural resources and municipal functions?* Why not let the community control and finance their use with capital from a global/local partnership?

- *Why offer our community credit through the use of high-rate credit cards while our deposits earn at extremely low rates at the bank?* Why not pool our capital and allow interest profits to stay and benefit our communities?

Additionally, Solari suggests banking only at locally-based financial institutions that are well managed and community oriented by researching their financial reports, management practices, and history of support for local small businesses. This includes supporting decisions within the community that create and maintain local jobs. It also includes being mindful of the potentially volatile decisions currently being made on the national and international scale that may require the implementation of precautionary measures in investment.

For example, it may be wise to research ways to diversify, to tie local investments to precious metals or offshore deposits in places that promote peace and the honoring of all life. Developing a separated local currency can also be wise. Each community's needs are different, and thus require careful research by its own citizens before determining the best methods for enhancing the strength of the local economy.

The Solari "Popsicle Index"

Solari calls this process of transformation, "Coming Clean," which includes an underlying intent to "first do no harm," a financial manifestation of the Precautionary Principle in action. (See the chapter on the Precautionary Principle for more detail.) This process includes focusing on *local* benefits when making all decisions - shifting our intentions, media coverage, leadership, wealth creation, and community structural design to benefiting local community members *inclusively* (with no exclusions) – while networking globally such that the broader picture supports *all* local communities, and the planet as a whole. They've created a "Solari Index," also known as the "Popsicle Index" explained as follows:

> The Solari Index (or Popsicle Index) is the % of people in a place who believe that a child is safe to leave their home, go to the nearest place to buy a popsicle or a snack and come home alone safely. We like to practice an exercise in which we make a list of all the things that make our Solari Index go up and down – totally 100%. We then look for actions that are under our control that would result in the greatest rise in our Solari Index. Numerous opportunities always emerge. [7]

The Solari Index offers a unique and simple way to measure the efficacy of local financial and community decisions, one that is easy to adopt right now. Imagine the impact of adopting just these two community-wide policies: the Precautionary Principle and the Solari Index whenever we make decisions. This is the opportunity that awaits us whenever we begin to take full responsibility for the condition and experience of our families, communities, and the world.

The Calvert-Henderson Quality of Life Indicators

This Index was developed through a six-year research effort conducted by a multi-disciplinary group of experts, and was first published in 2000 as the first systems approach to defining an overall quality of life indicator. Hazel Henderson and the Calvert Group, an asset management company specializing in socially responsible

Every environmental problem has economic dimensions. A precautionary approach requires thinking about both economics and ethics. We are attempting to define an economics that embodies the values on which the precautionary principle is based . . . giving priority to the health of current and future generations of people, creatures, and ecosystems. This is economic activity that is challenging, exciting, competitive, and at the same time enhances the quality of life in communities.

Nancy Myers
Ethical Economics: Forecaring
http://www.sehn.org/ecoeconomics.ht ml#nm7

The United States has he widest gap of any industrialized country between its rich and its poor. The richest 400 families in the United States now own roughly as much as the bottom 40 percent of families, 100 million people.

MoveOn's 50 Ways to Love Your Country, 2004, page 46.

investing, were the catalyzing forces that brought the effort to fruition. Here, in their own words, is a description of their intention:

> The Calvert-Henderson Quality of Life Indicators are a contribution to the worldwide effort to develop comprehensive statistics of national well-being that go beyond traditional macroeconomic indicators. A systems approach is used to illustrate the dynamic state of our social, economic and environmental quality of life. The dimensions of life examined include: education, employment, energy, environment, health, human rights, income, infrastructure, national security, public safety, re-creation and shelter.
>
> Key decision makers will quickly be brought up-to-speed on the state of each domain. Researchers will be able to download current and historical data streams. Journalists will gain insights from experts in each field who highlight and explain subtle trends that affect our daily lives. It is our hope that all users will use the indicators to help clarify the multiple choices we make in our work, education, leisure, and civic commitments.
>
> The principles guiding the collection of data presented in the Calvert-Henderson models include the following:
>
> - *National Data:* The unit of analysis is the United States. Users are encouraged to extend the unit of analysis to the international arena and/or disaggregate to the local, state, or regional levels.
> - *Annual Data:* The indicators track changes on a yearly basis for simplicity and to avoid seasonal biases.
> - *Federal Government Data:* The United States statistical system provides a wealth of reliable, consistent, and verifiable data for most of the indicators. Wherever possible, authors used federal government data from public use files. Where gaps in federal data were identified, private data were used.
> - *Time Series Data:* Data streams begin and end at periods specified by the authors to reflect salient moments in history for the respective domains. Most of the indicators include the most recent year of data provided by the United States statistical system.
> - *Data and Values:* The data employed in this analysis are not value free. We emphasize that the selection of data draws attention to what each author deemed important to understand the state of the respective domain.
> - *Data and Theory:* Scientific facts or data do not speak for themselves, they are read in light of theory. Hence the teachings that emerge from each indicator are captured in the respective models that represent a theoretical construct through which data can be easily conveyed and perhaps tested in the future.
> - *Stratification of Information:* The Calvert-Henderson models have prioritized information on a given subject based on each author's theoretical understanding of the topic. The authors made critical and often difficult decisions about what to include in the initial model and what could be added in subsequent editions. Recognizing the constraints of developing the first national, comprehensive effort to redefine quality of life using a systems approach, it was understood that there are many layers underneath each model for future exploration. [8]

The Quality of Life Indicators are featured in the new financial TV series, Ethical Marketplace, which highlights ethical and sustainable companies and technologies. (www.ethicalmarketplace.com).

E2M

The E2M concept has been gradually expanding in detail and enthusiastic support since its inception on January 1st, 2000. It was created by Michael Garjian, and represents a new form of capitalism for the new millennia that aims to serve the common good. Here's what it is and how it works.[9]

- E2M is an economic model that uses capitalism to better serve the common good. It has three components.

The contemporary tendency in our society is to base our distribution on scarcity, which has vanished, and to compress our abundance into the overfed mouths of the middle and upper classes until they gag with superfluity. If democracy is to have breadth of meaning, it is necessary to adjust this inequity. It is not only moral, but it is also intelligent. We are wasting and degrading human life by clinging to archaic thinking…

The curse of poverty has no justification in our age. It is socially as cruel and blind as the practice of cannibalism at the dawn of civilization, when men ate each other because they had not yet learned to take food from the soil or to consume the abundant animal life around them. The time has come for us to civilize ourselves by the total, direct and immediate abolition of poverty.

Rev. Martin Luther King Jr. in his last book, Where Do We Go From Here: Chaos or Community? (New York: Harper & Row, 1967).

http://www.progress.org/dividend/cdking.html

- E2M is a refreshing new philosophy of Community Conscious Capitalism based on the belief that entrepreneurs and investors can better serve themselves when they also work to benefit the common good.
- E2M is a certifiable business standard for a new breed of community conscious entrepreneurs who want to be successful while contributing to the common good by including their employees and their communities in the shareholding or profit sharing structure of their companies.
- E2M is an infrastructure that consists of regional economic councils that represent their local communities, much like charitable foundations. These councils work together with entrepreneurs, employees, business enterprises, educational institutions, socially responsible investors, and other individuals to use commerce to create wealth and economic power for the community.
- The current predominant philosophy of capitalism stresses high profits and maximum growth in commerce to satisfy the needs of relatively few investors. E2M seeks adequate profits and sustainable growth to benefit the common good.
- The E2M standard simply calls for entrepreneurs to include their employees and community as owners in their companies. This standard certifies enterprises as E2M compliant if they donate a percentage of their equity and/or profits to their community and make another percentage available to their employees through a stock option or profit sharing plan.
- Corporations must donate 5% to 20% of their corporate stock and/or profits to the community and make another 5% to 20% of their stock available for purchase by their employees.
- A sole proprietorship or partnership must donate 5% to 20% of their profits or 0.5% to 2% of their gross sales, whichever is more, to the community and must share 5% to 20% of their profits with employees.
- The entrepreneurs and/or investors who start the enterprise decide how much to make as a stock or profit contribution. The remaining 60% to 90% of stock/profits, which are not dedicated to the community and employees, are distributed among the entrepreneurs and investors in whatever manner they choose.

It is further claimed that our monetary system, being deeply associated with the Great Mother archetype, is profoundly shaped by its repression, and has therefore become a relentless enforcer of her shadows: greed and scarcity. With this archetype out of balance, a monopoly of Yang-dominated currencies is but one, albeit vital, consequence, and compounds this imbalance by encouraging the Yang coherence with each and every monetary transaction made by individuals, corporations and nations.

Bernard A. Lietaer
Stephen M. Belgin
Of Human Wealth

Banking that Honors All - Grameen

The very poor throughout the world are subject to similar circumstances which keep them mired in poverty. One of those circumstances is a lack of access to credit. The story of Sophia Khatoon was no exception, until she found assistance:

> Sophia Khatoon, a 22 years old skilled furniture-maker in the tiny village of Jobra in Bangladesh, worked 7 long days a week, looked twice her age, and lived in abject poverty. She made stools and chairs out of bamboo, which she had to sell to a money-lender who provided the credit to buy the raw material. The price she received barely covered the costs.

> Dr. Yunus, Professor of Economics at the University in the Southern port city of Chittagong who later founded the Grameen Bank - calculated that effectively Sophia was paying interest at the rate of 10% a day, more than 3,000% a year. Yunus could not reconcile the fact that a woman with such skill who worked so hard, produced such beautiful bamboo furniture and created wealth at such high rate was earning so little. [10]

He realized that the poor throughout the world are trapped in similar stories of exploitation. They work hard, but the resulting wealth generated by their labor is absorbed by the middle-men, money-lenders, and employers. Because they have no traditional "collateral", they have no access to credit - something we take for granted in the western world. Without the options provided by credit, they are continually trapped in debt, poverty, and exploitation.

Yunus offered Sophia a loan of 50 taka (a few dollars), which she paid off in only a few months. The loan helped her establish her own self-employment business which resulted in a seven-fold increase in income, and helped her repay the loan.

Grameen Bank has grown from this modest beginning. Just last year alone it provided US$ 380 million in 3.62 million loans. This year it is expected to lend more than half a billion dollars. Average loan size is a little over $ 100. 10

Since that first loan in 1983, the Grameen Bank of Bangladesh has given out almost 16 million one-time highly specialized loans designed specifically to abolish poverty. With an on-time pay-back rate of 98%, and a default rate of less one-half of one per cent, statistically the Grameen Bank of the poor outperforms all other banks in Bangladesh and most banks throughout the world. The Bank follows six guidelines that have led to its success:

1. It lends only to the landless rural poor.
2. It is women-focused, with women comprising 96% of its customers. Because the Bangladeshi banking system tends to treat women as second class borrowers, the Grameen Bank initially wanted to establish a 50-50 ratio of women and men borrowers. However they soon discovered that women are more effective change agents. When extra income came into households through women, children's diet, family's health and nutrition and the state of repair of the house receive the highest priority. Statistics showed that women were much better credit-risks than men and more responsible managers of meager resources. However, their most compelling reason to lend mostly to women was their first mandate: to lend to the poorest of the poor. In Bangladesh it was not uncommon among the poor for men to abandon their dependent women and children, leaving women consistently marginalized among the poor. Grameen found that their efforts to economically empower women had a dramatic impact on stabilizing families. In fact, studies have shown that one key reason Grameen Bank has succeeded where other programs have failed has been their insistence on economically empowering women, and thereby encouraging them to exercise choice in their lives.
3. The loans are made without collateral or security, something most poor don't possess.
4. The borrower decide the business activity the loan will be utilized for, not the bank. This simple act of trust and acknowledgment of the borrower's wisdom in itself could be healing.
5. The bank helps and supports the borrower in succeeding. This is a step often missing from most start-up businesses. Grameen is structured so that it is in everyone's best interest for the loan to succeed.
6. Borrowers pay as little or as much interest as required to keep the bank self reliant (that is, not dependent on grants or donations).

Access to credit allows the poor to break free from an existing poverty trap (which exists in one form or another in every country), explore their creative potential, and experience wealth, both personally and within their community. It allows them to make a contribution to us all, thereby experiencing their own value and worthiness – everybody wins. Their records indicate what works:

Experience has demonstrated that it takes an utterly destitute (person) six to ten successive loans (one year each) - and a lot of hard work - to cross the poverty line. The first loan is often as little as US$ 50. Average loan size is a little over US$ 100. In the process, the borrower builds a secure self-employment, often employing the whole family.

54% of Grameen borrowers have thus crossed the poverty line and another 27% are very close to it. For those who do not perform as well, poor housing in rain soaked Bangladesh and chronic ill-health are identified as the major reasons. 11

To take a different type of example, the point is often made that African Americans in the United States are relatively poor compared with American Whites, though much richer than people in the third world. It is, however, important to recognize that African Americans have an <u>absolutely</u> lower chance of reaching mature ages than do people of many third world societies, such as China, or Sri Lanka, or parts of India (with different arrangement of health care, education, and community relations). If development analysis is relevant even for richer countries (it is argued in this work that this is indeed so), the presence of such intergroup contrasts within the richer countries can be seen to be an important aspect of the understanding of development and underdevelopment.

Amartya Sen
<u>Development as</u>
<u>Freedom</u>, Winner of the Nobel Prize in Economics 1998

Dr. Sen asks what constitutes "development" and how do we determine it? Our current measurements (GDP, etc.) no longer suffice.

Overall the Grameen Bank has succeeded beautifully, and they continue to devise new programs to address those areas where persistent poverty still lingers. As of July 2004, they had 3.7 million borrowers. With 1,267 branches, providing services in 46,000 villages, Grameen Bank now serves more than 68 percent of the total villages in Bangladesh.

To determine their overall success, they set up incentives that encourage their borrowers to save five percent of the loan amount plus approximately 3 cents per week. Grameen then uses these accumulated savings as an indicator that the poverty level of their borrowers is decreasing. Since 1983 these combined savings have grown from nothing to $108 million US dollars.

From the very beginning the Grameen Bank was designed such that ownership and control would remain in the hands of the people it serves. Upon accumulating sufficient savings, each borrower purchases one share in the bank (for approximately US$3). Today only 8% of the bank shares are owned by the Bangladeshi government, with the remaining 92% owned by the borrowers. Shareholders elect nine of the bank directors while the government appoints the remaining three.

The Board sets an interest rate that allows for a modest profit to be distributed among the shareholders – borrowers as dividends. These rates vary, but have recently been set at 20% for a working-capital loan (those to start a profit making business) and 8% for a home loan. The home loans are cross-subsidized by the working-capital loans. The bank made a profit of US$680,000 last year, making Grameen a model that is totally self-reliant, requiring no assistance to sustain its growth and meet its goal of ending poverty. By placing trust in the poor to run the bank and pay for its development, this model is a perfect example of honoring all involved. It honors their abilities, intelligence, ideas, creativity, and motivation.

Because chronic poor health has been identified as one of the key factors in failure, Grameen is now addressing this issue. They are experimenting with a medical plan in which members pay a premium of US$1.25 per year per family and US 2 cents per clinic visit. They plan to cover 40% of the cost through these fees, with the government covers the remaining 60% combined with others who wish to assist.

Their housing loans are made in the woman's name, and provide approximately US$300 amortized over ten years. More than 350,000 houses have been built using this loan, at 8% interest subsidized from the interest earned through the working-capital loans. But these are not just any type of home, they are specifically designed by local architects using indigenous raw materials that are able to withstand high winds, provide ventilation and offer efficient use of space and aesthetic appeal. The Aga Khan Foundation awarded their prestigious Architecture Award to these designs.

The Grameen Bank model is culturally sensitive and must be adapted to the specific needs of each locale wishing to adopt a similar model of poverty eradication. It is imperative that the local population be involved in every aspect of such an effort.

This need to include all stakeholders in every aspect of the process is becoming one of the major guidelines of setting up structures that honor all. Not only does this high level of inclusiveness ensure that all voices are heard and all needs considered,

Indeed, President Bush 's election promises include partial privatisation of social security and making his earlier tax cuts permanent, which, if adopted, will send the deficits soaring to record levels. What, exactly, this will do to business confidence and currency markets is anybody's guess, but it won't be pretty…

They are all caught between the problems of the present and the mistakes of the past: in Europe, between institutions designed to avoid inflation when the problem is growth and employment; in America, between massive household and government debt and the demands of fiscal and monetary policy; and everywhere, between America's failure to use the world's scarce natural resources wisely and its failure to achieve peace and stability in the Middle East.

*This Can't Go On Forever -
So It Won't
By Joseph Stiglitz
Professor of economics at Columbia University and a Nobel prize winner.
The Guardian U.K.
01 January 2005*

but it also lowers the possibility of failure. Whenever attempts are made to step into a new paradigm of structural design, there is a tendency for those watching the results to draw instant negative conclusions regarding the entire process without a willingness to allow for experimentation as to what works and doesn't work within the overall design. This impatience to draw conclusions can negatively affect all such ventures, no matter how good their intentions. Grameen has found, through their own experience, the efficacy of this high level of inclusiveness. It is a lesson that serves us all.

Eventually, after the Bangladesh Grameen experiment has been fine-tuned, the vision is to "replicate" a customized version of this model wherever poverty exists. The Grameen Trust was set up to provide the necessary training and assistance to economists and bankers in countries wishing to emulate this system. Currently there are over 168 Grameen Bank Replications in 44 countries, with a new one created each week. Ideally, Grameen would like to provide credit to all of the world's 1.3 billion extremely poor by the year 2025.

Creating a Gift Economy

Prior to the development of currencies, people exchanged in a number of ways, but one method used extensively was gift giving. At first gift giving might not seem like an economic structure at all. That is because we all grew up in a culture of currency exchange, one that significantly alters a person's ability to perceive value in gift giving. I recommend reviewing Genevieve Vaughan's 36 Steps Toward a Gift Economy (see the Reference section) as a guideline in exploring the benefits and psychology of gift-giving.

Monetary Instability

There is an additional reason to contemplate change in our way of handling the economies of the world, and it is quickly becoming one of the most important. Our monetary system is now incredibly unstable. According to Lietaer, we have what amount to a global casino of over $1.3 trillion traded each day in foreign exchange markets, over 100 times more than all the trading volume on all the world's stock exchanges together. And most of those, approximately 96% are speculative, do not relate to the "real" economy, and do not reflect actual commodity exchanges or services rendered.[12]

Additionally, because the exchange markets are open 24/7, large fluctuations in currency value can take place over a period of hours. Lietaer feels that any and all currencies are vulnerable.[13]

Taking Economic Responsibility

When we take full responsibility for the economic structures we create, we must also take full responsibility for the outcome. To do so requires that we be clear on the initial intention so that we can ascertain if our intended goals have been achieved. What are the goals of economic systems?

Historically, the development of currencies allowed bartering to broaden its scope from a simple exchange between two people to an exchange between several people – allowing each to obtain what was needed. That's an important distinction – the original goal was to obtain goods necessary for survival. Currencies were given a

---

The point is driven home that the GDP, as a measure of economic well-being, is $7 trillion dollars out of step with economic Reality... The Genuine Progress Indicator (GPI) subtracts important destructive costs and adds in social and economic benefits ignored by the Gross Domestic Product...

For sound economic policy to be formulated and political feedback loops to work better, a more discerning qualitative metric of the economy would be a significant advancement.

The GPI represents a small but important step in this process. The inclusion of multiple stakeholders and the public may be a very worthwhile next step in refining the GPI so as to better represent a shared vision for a better economy.

Redefining Progress
The Genuine Progress
Indicator 1950-2002
(2004 Update)
http://www.redefiningprogress.org
/publications/gpi_march2004upd
ate.pdf

The economy is a subset of the environment. The environment is NOT a subset of the economy.

Ron Castle
Public Eyes TV

value tied to the goods exchanged. They allowed for a broader scale of trading, which also improved the odds of survival. Everybody won.

Yet now that has all changed. Most currencies aren't tied to any value other than the one we give it. Bernard Lietaer, one of the creators of the Euro currency, and author of The Future of Money and Of Human Wealth (with Stephen M. Belgin), writes:

> So long as there remains a scarcity of money, boom and bust periods in the business cycle; or significant numbers of people and indeed entire nations that are deemed unworthy of credit; in essence, as long as there remains a monopoly of interest-bearing, bank-debt national currencies that reinforce the Yang bias in our world, there will always remain a shortage of money, fear of scarcity and greed, and there will be ample, hyper-rational explanations for the continued suffering, disenfranchisement, injustice and destruction we are now experiencing in our world. And those paying jobs that are made available and the salaries that are offered will continue to be skewed in favor of that Yang bias. Our world can no longer afford such conditions. [15]

Yin and Yang Currencies

To counter act that decidedly "Yang bias", many people are now championing the idea of complementary currencies. (Note that we are discussing "complementary" currencies, *not* currencies to replace or compete with the existing national currencies.) Complementary currencies are not new. Throughout history many localities had their own currency, allowing for easy exchange of goods between neighbors, again where all parties involved could benefit from the exchange. Complementary currencies also have recent widespread evidence of their efficacy. They are being adopted at an astounding rate throughout the world. These are what Bernard Lietaer calls "Yin" currencies. There are many new aspects to these Yin currencies.

They allow for a change in *who* issues the currency, from traditional banks, to businesses, private corporations, and local communities. The *conditions* for issuing currencies is also more flexible, including interest-free money. As Lietaer points out, each different type of currency supports different social behaviors – some encourage competition (like our traditional system) while others encourage cooperation. Most importantly, Lietaer reminds us that the choices we make regarding the different aspects of our currencies directly impact our possible futures. If we compare Yin and Yang currencies in general, they support entirely different social behaviors:

Yin currencies have the following features:

- They are based on the concepts of sufficiency and cooperation
- They promote Social Capital – which can be defined as that difficult-to-describe but priceless interaction between people from which networking and creative ideas spring
- They promote Natural Capital
- They are created by the participants using "mutual credit", usually backed by hours or some commodity, controlled through a network and/or cooperation
- They are concerned with community transactions
- They always seek a win-win solution
- Most of all, they are based on *trust* – people's trust in the Universe, the future, the community, each other, and themselves. [17]

The Japanese Ministry of Internal Affairs and Communications (MIC) has started to develop a model of a local currency system, as part of its support measures for regional revitalization, which utilizes information technology (IT) equipment such as basic resident registry cards and cell phones. The ministry also plans to conduct demonstration testing in three areas for about two months from November 2004. The final version of the system will be distributed, free of charge, to local governments that show an interest, next fiscal year (starting in April 2005).

<u>*Ministry to Support Model Local Currency System*</u>

*17 Jan 2005
The Source: Japan for Sustainability*
http://www.via3.net/POOLED/ARTICLES/BF_NEWSART/VIEW.ASP?Q=BF_NEWSART_128216

- Additionally, they increase local wealth by keeping funds circulating locally, they are based on local talent, and they increase the overall financial stability of the region.
- They are usually issued in a careful and gradual pace that accommodates the community's use of them, which often includes the funding of local social programs.
- Depending on how they are set up, yin currencies can promote a more equitable hourly pay for labor and services.

Historically nations developed national currencies primarily for trade across distances. Lietaer refers to these currencies as "Yang". With the development of the banking system, these national currencies were also used for loans, which allowed for the completion of large projects. Yang currencies:

- Are based on the concepts of competition, control, and scarcity
- Promote Financial Capital (whose value is increased by hoarding – not spreading the wealth to benefit all), and Physical Capital
- Called "Fiat", they are created by a central authority, controlled through hierarchy, and backed by nothing (or debt as in the case of US Federal Reserve Notes)
- Are concerned with commercial transactions[17]
- Yang currencies can actually damage local economies by draining money away from the area through large chain stores, resulting in a loss of jobs and local businesses. Just look at the statistics after a Wal-Mart opens in small communities. The end result is the accumulation of wealth in the distant hands of a few who have little or no investment in the well being of the community. Increasingly we are also witnessing the commodifying of natural resources like water, to the profound detriment of the local population.
- Yang funds are over issued so that they can never be completely paid back. This results in an interest payment profit for lenders that can lead to ever increasing debt burden for those acquiring the loans. Social programs are often subsequently cut in an effort to balance the budget.
- In the name of profit, labor is often paid the least the market will allow.

Yang currencies eventually took over, and the use of local currencies waned. In times of economic crisis, however, local currencies have often reappeared quite quickly (as in the 1930's). Unfortunately, when their rapid success became apparent, strong central banking authorities almost always moved quickly to shut them down.

Since the 1930's significant changes have taken place in the financial world, which have led to the volatile world economic picture we experience today. In response, local currencies have made a huge come-back in the last 20 years, expanding from approximately 80 to 6,000+ and growing.

Here's how one such program works, according to its founder, Paul Glover:

> The Ithaca HOUR is Ithaca's $10.00 bill, because ten dollars per hour is the average of wages/salaries in Tompkins County. These HOUR notes, in five denominations, buy plumbing,

---

Last year Ithaca HOURS were visited by a top official of China's central bank, sent from Beijing by the President of the People's Bank of China (their Alan Greenspan) to talk about adopting HOURS as money in China. Wen Tiejun will report directly to the bank's president, who will deliver the report directly to China's Premier.

According to Wen, China is profoundly concerned that the world economy has become dependent on U.S. dollars, which he says (as we've said) is backed by market speculation (98% of daily trade) and military control of foreign oil, rather than by real goods. So China's looking for a new and stable form of money, backed directly by labor, before the dollar bubble breaks

Paul Glover
Chinese Government Studies Ithaca HOURS, January 2001.

Even Alan Greenspan, the governor of the Federal Reserve and the official guardian of the conventional money system says "We will see a return of private currencies in the 21st century.

Bernard Lietaer

carpentry, electrical work, roofing, nursing, chiropractic, child care, car and bike repair, food, firewood, gifts, and thousands of other goods and services. Our credit union accepts them for mortgage and loan fees. People pay rent with HOURS. The best restaurants in town take them, as do movie theater, bowling alleys, two large locally-owned grocery stores, many garage sales, forty farmer's market vendors, the Chamber of Commerce, and 300 other business. [18]

Since that was written, Ithaca has developed an Insurance program for participants that requires a minimum premium payment of $100 *annually*. Lietaer strongly encourages the return to our ancient and reliable dual-currency economic structure. His book, <u>Of Human Wealth – Beyond Greed and Scarcity</u>, outlines in great detail the history of dual-currency cultures and the tremendous benefits experienced by all involved.

The advantages of a dual-currency (yin and yang) approach include the following:

- For the Participating businesses-
  - o Additional clients, because those using the local currency will automatically spend it locally in participating businesses
  - o Visibility as true community supporters, because their participation literally brings money into community projects
  - o Client loyalty
  - o Neighborhood improvements which can significantly impact business
  - o The minimal cost of participation is off-set by the free additional advertising and the advantages listed above
- For Non-Profit Organizations – (their purpose could be described as creating "Social Wealth")-
  - o Increased volunteer activities – because volunteers could be compensated in local currency
  - o Greater recognition
  - o If there is a demurrage feature (simply put – a tax on hoarding), the resulting funds could be distributed to non-profit organizations
- For Members-
  - o For those willing to be paid in local currency, it offers an easier way to combine one's passion with one's job
  - o All members benefit from the improvements to the community
  - o All members experience the joy of community connection
  - o All members experience the power and fulfillment of actively choosing to control the money in their life, instead of feeling as if a victim of the other way around
- For those who are unemployed and under-employed-
  - o The opportunity to turn time into money
  - o The empowerment of being able to full participate in the economic system and to contribute
  - o A great opportunity for additional income
- For those who choose not to participate-
  - o The benefit of all improvements to the community
  - o The well-being of a more united community
  - o The benefit that services that might otherwise be paid for through taxes are instead funded through the local currency

More than 1.5 million families had to declare bankruptcy last year—half because of unexpected and extraordinary medical expenses. Millions more totter on the edge of bankruptcy. The large numbers of bankruptcies is a clear sign about the tenuous state of the economy—millions of Americans who work hard and play by the rules could be pushed at any time to financial ruin by job loss, business failure or major medical expenses..

Tom Matzzie and the MoveOn PAC Team April 12th, 2005

Handheld wireless technology stands ready to enable what's known as the "complementary currency" movement in ways so powerful that the dominance of national currencies such as the dollar and the euro may soon be called into question.

Douglas Rushkoff <u>Open Source Currency - Or, how mobile phones can break the money monopoly</u>. *Oct 13 2004 http://www.thefeature.com /article?articleid=101119*

- For the community as a whole-
  - A more united sense of community
  - A sense that each person supports everyone else in the community
  - A greater ability to better weather any economic storms that affect the national currency
  - The benefit of all community projects that are funded through the local currency[19]

There are millions of people throughout the world gratefully benefiting from a dual (or multiple) currency economy. The statistics prove their efficacy. Their rapid growth in the global economic picture is testimony to their success. And the need to reflect each community's unique attributes (in order to succeed) makes them a rare example of a structure designed specifically to honor all.

Lietaer suggests still another reason to embrace complementary currencies, one that provides the opportunity for a deeper healing. Recalling that many indigenous cultures and psychologists (particularly Jungian trained) promote the understanding of human behavioral through archetypes, Lietaer began to study how our concepts of money fit into traditional archetypal roles.

We have long known that the male/female energy of our western culture is skewed strongly towards the male. Though included in most Indigenous archetypal structures, the Yin has been excluded from those of Western Civilization, where the Father image reigns supreme.

Lietaer suggests that, just as it is time to acknowledge the Great Mother archetypal energy in every aspect of our culture (and selves) in order to balance our societies, it is time to bring a female/yin currency into our culture to balance our expression of community and commodity exchange. Seen from this standpoint, the creation of a Yin currency can be a powerful contributor to deep and lasting cultural healing – one that could significantly impact our ability to honor all life. He writes:

> We now have in our possession readily available tools by which to resolve many of the most pressing problems facing our communities and our planet. These monetary innovations hurt no one; they do not require the re-distribution of wealth or the reallocation of scarce resources that are needed elsewhere. Instead they link unmet needs with unused resources, including human resources, the talents and capabilities that we have within us to each contribute to a better future for the benefit of all.

> If Curitibá, Brazil, a city overwhelmed by poverty and "garbage," in a nation with little resources to assist it, was able to transform its abysmal conditions in less than one generation with simple monetary mechanisms, imagine what is possible for communities, cities and nations of the developed world. Imagine…[20]

Seeing with New Eyes

Many people are taking Lietaer's words to heart. They are imagining a world in which economics adhere to similar ideas as those embraced by the Precautionary Principles (see the chapter of the same name). Which, above all, adheres to the principle, "first do no harm." Yet our economic models rarely take this all important principle into consideration.

Perhaps the person who best brings all these issues about economics and money into focus is Robert Klinck, who concluded his 1991 essay, <u>Finance And The Environment</u>[21] with the following section:

Invisible Prosperity

In early creeds, people were admonished to believe not only in visible reality but in the invisible aspects of reality as well. Ironically, the danger today is the exact opposite: people believe in what is insubstantial while being unable to perceive the physical reality surrounding them.

To clarify the point, let us suppose that the flow of financial credit dried up. There is no question that the direct consequence would be that we would all go begging, and large numbers of us would probably end up starving to death. Yet we would travel to this pathetic end through the valley of abundance. Nothing would have changed in our productive capacity: the fields would still be fertile; the forests would still be growing; the factories and the communications systems and the heritage of millions of inspired men and women would still be in place, along with the knowledge of how to put them to productive ends. Yet without money all of it might as well not exist. We would suffer total deprivation in the midst of the greatest productive potential ever known to man - probably, because of our belief that money (which nowadays could be nothing more than a minute flow of electrons in a computer) is more real than what it represents, without noticing the absurdity of the situation.

While industrialists warn us that we must win the race for the most advanced technology or fall back into "Third World" conditions, while you fret over keeping your job, while you worry about your business crashing before it has a chance to get properly off the ground, while you pray that inflation will not erode your meagre pension, while you worry about your children's ability to make a go of it in a callously competitive world, the productive potential to give everyone a materially comfortable life almost effortlessly is everywhere around us. But we do not see it as it is because our attention is fixed on a wretched money system that drives people mad with cares.

Against the wishes of virtually every conscious person, our beautiful earth is being insensitively ravaged and polluted, and, in a kind of Reichstag fire manoeuvre, power-hungry persons are using these environmental problems for self-serving political ends. When we trace the causes of the present situation to their source, we find a flawed financial system. We need not destroy the money system-indeed, to do so would be a grave error - but it is crucial that we reform it so it becomes the servant, not the master, of our aspirations. [21]

I couldn't agree more. It is our *perception* that needs to shift. Our attention needs to be focused on the abundance and beauty around us, and on how to create systems and structures that reflect that beauty; not on a flawed symbolic system that ultimately serves no one as it desecrates the environment upon which we depend for survival. Once we can see clearly, our intention can embrace honoring *all* life, not just a few privileged humans. What an exciting journey we are just beginning to create!

The GDP, however, is not value free. Leaving social and environmental costs and contributions to the economy off the books does not avoid value judgments. On the contrary, it makes the obvious value judgment that things such as the destruction of farm-land and natural resources, underemployment, longer-commute times, and the loss of free time, count for nothing in assessing how the economy is fairing. The GDP does put a value on such factors: Zero. Keep in mind, this is on top of adding in the value of crime, disaster, and war-related expenditures.

Jason Venetoulis And Cliff Cobb
Redefining Progress The Genuine Progress Indicator

1950-2002 (2004 Update)
page 7
http://www.redefiningprogress.org/publications/gpi_march2004update.pdf

Just in case that wasn't clear, the GDP (Gross Domestic Product) categorizes crime, disaster, and war-related expenditures as valuable.

Notes

1. http://www.nationalpriorities.org/

2. http://www.nationalpriorities.org/TaxDay2005/pdf/us.pdf Notes: The breakdown of the individual income-tax dollar refers to the Federal funds budget outlays and does not include trust fund outlays (such as Social Security). The breakdown is based on fiscal year 2004 actual outlays extracted from the *Budget of the U.S. Government, FY2006, Appendix*. Numbers may not add up to totals due to rounding. *Military and defense* includes the government definition of national defense, other military programs, and the Department of Homeland Security (DHS). *Income security* includes Supplemental Security Income (aimed at elderly, disabled and blind with low income), tax credit programs, TANF, child care spending and other programs aimed at families. *Other* includes the following function and sub-function areas: general science, space and technology; international affairs other than military assistance; energy; agriculture; commerce and housing credit; transportation; community and regional development; labor and social services other than job training; justice; general government; and undistributed offsetting receipts. For more information on the analysis, go to *Where do Your Tax Dollars Go? Notes and Sources* available at www.nationalpriorities.org/TaxDay2005/sources.pdf.

3. http://www.nationalpriorities.org/TaxDay2005/pdf/us.pdf Notes: 1 Preventive measures refer to all non-military forms of international assistance, conduct of foreign affairs, foreign information and exchange activities and international financial programs. 2 Total homeland security outlays in 2004 are not possible to estimate given the presentation of the budget materials by OMB. However, OMB, *Mid-session Review, FY2005* cites discretionary outlays as $29 billion; mandatory outlays as published in the *Public Database, FY2006* add another $434 million. 3 Joint Committee on Taxation. 4 *Independent Budget, FY2006*. For more information and links to sources, go to *Where do Your Tax Dollars go? Notes and Sources* available on the NPP website at www.nationalpriorities.org/TaxDay2005/sources.pdf. National Priorities Project . 17 New South Street, Suite 302 . Northampton, MA 01060 413-584-9556 . info@nationalpriorities.org . www.nationalpriorities.org © 2005 National Priorities Project, Inc.

4. FOOTNOTES:

[i] U.S. Congress Joint Committee of Taxation, *Estimates of Federal Tax Expenditures for Fiscal Years 2002-2006* (U.S. Government Printing Office, January 17, 2002).

[ii] *See* www.forbes.com/richlist. Capital accumulation figures assume that wealth was amassed untaxed over a 40-hour week, 50-week year.

[iii] Edward N. Wolff, "Where has all the Money Gone?," *The Milken Institute Review*, Third Quarter 2001, p. 34.

[iv] Reported in *The Economist*, June 16-22, 2001.

[v] Congressional Budget Office Memorandum, *Estimates of Federal Tax Liabilities for Individuals and Families by Income Category and Family Type for 1995 and 1999* (May 1998).

[vi] IRS 2002 data are available at http://www.house.gov/jec/press/2002/10-24-02.htm.

[vii] Lynnley Browning, "U.S. Income Gap Widening, Study Says," *New York Times*, September 25, 2003, p. C2.

[viii] Juliet S. Schor, *The Overworked American* (New York: Basic Books, 1992) documenting that the annual work year increased by 139 hours from 1969-1989. The Washington, D.C.-based Economic Policy Institute found that the annual hours worked expanded an additional 45 hours from 1989-1994.

[ix] Stijn Claessens, Simeon Djankov and Larry H.P. Lang, "Who Controls East Asian Corporations?" (Washington, D.C.: The World Bank, 1999).

[x] *Ibid.*

xi Branko Milanovic, "True World Income Distribution, 1988 and 1993: First Calculations Based on Household Surveys Alone," *Economic Journal*, January 2002, No. 476, pp. 51-92. At the time that the research was completed, 57 percent of worldwide population totaled ~2.7 billion people. Originally published by the UK Business & Environment Programme Nov 2004

5. <u>Transgenerational Financial Terrorism</u>, Jeff Gates, AlterNet – August 10, 2003. Copyright ©2003 Independent Media Institute.

6. <u>Ownership Patterns, Steps Toward a Conscious Capitalism</u> Jeff Gates, http://www.kat.gr/kat/history/Txt/Ec/conscious_capitalism.htm

7. http://www.solari.com/campaign/coming_clean.htm#CC3   For more information on the Solari Solution and ideas for "Coming Clean" visit their website at http://www.solari.com/campaign/coming_clean.htm#CC3 . They also provide an excellent in-depth analysis of the banking industry and how to "vote" with your banking choices in the article entitled <u>Mapping the Real Deal: Where Would Jesus Bank?</u> by Catherine Austin Fitts dated July 4th, 2004, and located at http://www.scoop.co.nz/mason/stories/HL0407/S00040.htm.

8. <u>Research Methodology</u>, by Patrice Flynn, Ph.D. from: http://www.calvert-henderson.com/meth.htm and

9. From the document <u>E2M - A Second Economic Model (FAQs)</u>, available at http://www.e2m.org/our%20mission/mission.htm

10. http://www.rdc.com.au/grameen/home.html and http://www.grameen-info.org/

11. http://www.rdc.com.au/grameen/Impact.html Please see http://www.grameen-info.org/index.html for up-to-date information on the progress of Grameen replications world wide.

12. Of Human Wealth: Beyond Greed and Scarcity, Bernard Lietaer and Stephen Belgin, Access Foundation 2004, page 194..

13. Of Human Wealth: Beyond Greed and Scarcity, Bernard Lietaer and Stephen Belgin, Access Foundation 2004, page 195.

14. Bernard Lietaer in an interview with By Ravi Dykema, <u>Complementary Currencies for Social Change</u>, NEXUS, July-Aug 2003

15. Bernard A. Lietaer and Stephen M. Belgin, <u>Of Human Wealth – Beyond Greed and Scarcity</u>, (galley edition), page 232.

16. Bernard A. Lietaer and Stephen M. Belgin, <u>Of Human Wealth – Beyond Greed and Scarcity</u>, (galley edition), page 233-234.

17. The Future of Money: Creating New Wealth, Work and a Wiser World by <u>Bernard Lietaer</u>, 2001, pages 272-273 See also Edgar S. Cahn's Time Dollars http://www.timedollar.org/au_staff_td_usa.htm or Ithaca Hours http://www.ithacahours.com/.

18. Paul Glover, <u>Hometown Money: How to Enrich Your Community with Local Currency</u>, in an article entitled <u>Creating Wealth with Local Currency</u>, Augus 1995. http://www.ithacahours.com/

19. Bernard A. Lietaer and Stephen M. Belgin, <u>Of Human Wealth – Beyond Greed and Scarcity</u>, (galley edition), page 233-234

20. Bernard A. Lietaer and Stephen M. Belgin, <u>Of Human Wealth – Beyond Greed and Scarcity</u>, (galley edition), page 233.

21. http://www.socialcredit.com/subpages_resources/environment.htm

25

<u>BUSINESS</u>

Instead of using nature as a mere tool for human purposes,
we can strive to become tools of nature who serve its agenda too.
We can celebrate the fecundity in the world,
instead of perpetuating a way of thinking and making that eliminates it.

—William McDonough and Michael Braungart
<u>Cradle to Cradle</u> page 156

BUSINESS AS AN EXPRESSION OF ALIVENESS

The purpose of business is not to produce wealth,
The purpose of business is to produce joy.

There is a quiet revolution taking place on our planet, it is all around us and touches all our lives, yet you will rarely hear about it in the news. Though this revolution of perception touches all aspects of our lives, this chapter explores its impact on business.

Perhaps the most symbolic example of this change is the growing awareness of the words we use when referring to each other. In the corporate world, humans are referred to as "consumers." From a linear, yang-like perspective, we are seen as giant eating machines, ready to consume whatever pre-packaged natural resource pillage can be the most successfully marketed to our greedily outstretched hands – all for a price. When we see each other as consuming machines, we cease seeing each other at all. This perceptual shift is most easily understood by simply replacing the word "consumer" with "family."

A Whole-Systems Approach

Our perception is shifting from that of an individual business out for it's own profit at the expense of anyone else*; to a Whole Systems Approach, in which every business is seen as part of a web of interactions *between people within their environment* for the benefit of ALL – including the bottom line. In essence, it is an approach that incorporates the desire to honor ALL at the heart of every decision made.

Chaordic

One of the earliest models of this new way of approaching business was pioneered, believe it or not, by the creator of the VISA card, Dee Hock. In 1974 he developed VISA International, following on the foot-steps of his VISA USA of 1970. It was based on the idea of a global system of electronic exchange organized as a for-profit membership program owned by financial institutions around the world. Unlike traditional business hierarchical models, it was decentralized and did not offer stock. Today it is a $1.75 trillion business jointly owned by more than 20,000 financial institutions from over 220 countries and territories around the world.

His experience of creating VISA led to the subsequent book, <u>Birth of the Chaordic Age.</u> [1] The word, Chaordic, is a combination of "chaos" and "order", which he feels describes that space on the edge of chaos that still contains enough order to allow patterns of probability without stifling creativity, adaptation, and learning. It is seen as the space in which most of life evolves and nature thrives – a fundamental organizing principle of life. In other words, when something is chaordic, it honors the creativity and adaptability within us all.

Many organizations have been inspired by this concept of re-thinking how we perceive and structure business. Thousands are banding together to explore the impact of Charodic and Systems Theory on all aspects of human life. Some of those organizations can be found in the References section of this book.

These same theories have begun to filter into the way we approach business education. A wonderful example can be found in Denmark.

KaosPilots – Denmark

Developed by Uffe Elbaek, KaosPilots is an innovative business school that derives its name from Chaos Theory. They have been active since 1991, graduating approximately 30 students in each graduating class. Similar to the way Victor Papanek provided his students with real life design problems that made a contribution to the world (see the Design Chapter), KaosPilot students find themselves encountering hands-on real life consulting projects that are a cornerstone of their curriculum. Over the years the staff and management has developed a set of values they use to screen every decision and initiative they make. They ask, "Is it:

- Playful: It has to be motivational, creative and constructive to be at the KaosPilots.
- Real World: We have to work with authentic projects.
- Streetwise: We should always think about young people - be aware of what's going on out there - at street level.
- Risk-taking: There has to be courage and the willingness to take risks.
- Balanced: There has to be harmony between body and soul, form and content and between economic, human and time resources.
- Compassionate: There always has to be empathy and social responsibility?" [2]

These screening values help them to stay on course with their business goals. Not surprisingly, their graduates are in great demand; a tribute to the training they receive to think creatively outside the normal perceptual assumptions common to most business settings.

Instinctive, Nomadic, and Ever-Changing

It seems to be an idea whose time has come. This changing atmosphere of business is dramatically outlined in Mikela and Philip Tarlow's excellent book, Digital Aboriginal – The Direction of Business Now: Instinctive, Nomadic, and Ever-Changing. Taking this outside-the-box mode of thinking to examine the evolution of business today, Mikela Tarlow had the boldness to compare successful business trends with the culture of Australia's First Nation (Aboriginal) People. She found striking similarities, and backed them up with a broad range of business examples including Anderson Windows, 3-M, Linux, and American Airlines.

She uses American Airlines, in particular, to make a point about the changing thought processes necessary to stay both competitive and successful. Highlighting the story of how American Airlines' computerized reservation system, Sabre, became

According to Mahbub-ul-Haq of Human Development Centre, during the globalization phase about half-a-billion people in South Asia have experienced a decline in their incomes. The income ratio between 20% of the world's poorest and 20% richest was 1:30 in 1960. It increased to 1:61 in 1997. In 1999 it was 1:74 . As for the environment damage there could not be a more convincing evidence of global warming than the recent shattering of a huge ice shelf, Larsen B, weighing 500 million billion tonnes in Antarctica.

Dr Madhav Mehra,
President
World Council for
Corporate Governance
August 2002

more valuable than the airline itself, (once it was developed into an on-line format); she offers the following comparison between the two businesses:[3]

American Airlines	Sabre
Prices rise by limiting volume.	Value rises by increasing volume.
Hard assets dominate.	Intellectual property is highly vulnerable.
Very high barriers to entry.	More level playing field; competition from outsiders.
Fixed rules of operation.	Slippery contexts easily copied; constantly changing.
New directions require large investment.	Small, customized, low investment ideas can be profitable.
Major players create the rules.	Edges drive the market; the center plays catch-up.
Highly skilled staff tend to stay put.	Employees easily break away to start competing ventures.
Predictable ways of getting word out.	Innovative and varied vehicles for visability.
Product is clear and stable.	Product evolves, converging with new areas of market.
Growth is assured through domination.	Growth is assured through alliance and networks.
Well protected and monitored by the law.	Law has not yet arrived in many parts of their town.
Rules of exchange are well defined.	Revolutionary spirit pervades every effort.
Changes in the market happen slowly.	Hit-and-run players can wreak havoc on established markets.
Knowledge is closely guarded.	Knowledge must be shared to facilitate service and growth.
Hierarchies are necessary and useful.	Empowered individuals must be encouraged to bend the rules.

Her entire book is a page-turning "Ah-Ha!" of realizations regarding new ways of perceiving, thinking-about, and manifesting business.

One small example highlights a change in philosophy regarding air conditioning. In ancient China, she reminds us, you paid the doctor only when you were healed. Taking this idea into the business world, Carrier no longer sells air-conditioning equipment, it offers "comfort leases," guaranteeing your comfort as defined by contract. The deal may include making all sorts of ecological upgrades to ensure the lowest cost in providing the greatest comfort. This idea has also taken off in France, where businesses contract for building comfort that include a certain range of temperatures for specific hours of the day. It benefits the provider to use the most

Don't forget until it's too late that the business of life is not business but living.

Bertie Charles Forbes "BC Forbes"

efficient methods possible because the less energy the client uses, the more money the business makes.[4]

Shoe companies are toying with the idea of offering life-time footwear leases in which they purchase your customer loyalty in exchange for providing footwear trade-ins. When a shoe is worn or out-grown, you simply bring it back for an upgrade. The entire design of a shoe is changed by this concept. Suddenly materials must be completely recyclable using DFD (design for disassembly) methodologies. Sturdiness becomes an asset instead of a limitation to higher profits. Current business thinking gets turned on its head.

Another example is what Jim Womack and Dan Jones call "Lean Thinking," used at the Atlanta carpet company, Interface.[5] Instead of selling carpets that must be replaced every few years with new non-compostable carpeting that off-gasses chemicals into the living/work space; the focus has shifted to providing the *service* of providing the benefits carpet offers. By using carpet tiles instead of rolls, individual worn spots can be continually repaired and replaced so that the leased product is always fresh. Additionally, by switching to carbohydrate-based carpets made from DVD-type fully compostable and recyclable fibers, the use of hydrocarbons is severely reduced. It is estimated that resource use will be reduced by 80 percent while jobs will increase. This is a wonderful example of reducing natural resource use, while at the same time providing a higher quality product. Their shift from product to service emphasis increases jobs, benefits the overall economy, and still maintains or even improves profits.

"Not Just a Cup – But a Just Cup"

When I first started writing this book I looked for a model business that already approached their entire operation with the intention of 'honoring all.' I didn't need to look far. As I was attending the annual Bioneers Conference in San Rafael CA, Paul Katzeff - founder of the Thanksgiving Coffee Company along with his wife, Joan – handed me a cup of coffee. As he did so, he pointed to the photograph of a coffee farmer in Nicaragua and said, "He grew the coffee you are drinking right now." How did he know who grew the coffee beans in my cup of coffee? Because Paul and Joan make it their business to grow not only their company, but their relationships, their community, the environment, and the prosperity of all who work with them. Part of the opening statement when you visit their website reads:

> We are as dedicated to environmental and social justice as we are to making great coffee. Thus our site serves as a wealth of information on topics such as shade grown coffee, fair trade coffee, and organic farming, as well as being a great place to learn about and buy our coffee.[6]

Have you encountered many businesses that place as much attention and effort on their environmental and social justice impact as they do on their profit? For those of us used to hearing about the negative impact of globalization in which many are harmed for the benefit of the few[7], this kind of business sounds like a fairy tale. And yet this model is catching on all over the world. Why? Because it is not only successful and profitable, the people involved have the sweet experience every day of knowing that their actions (yes, even in the pursuit of profit) have a positive impact on the world. This revolution is becoming very evident in the world of coffee. A Whole-Systems Approach to the coffee industry shifts the focus from just the

Without relationships, individuals do not exist. But a fundamental dilemma that then arises out of this dialectic relationship between individuals and the larger system is how to identify where the individual begins and ends. The physical, biological, and social sciences show how blurred the boundaries really are. Individual people exist only in relationship with larger communities tht include peple, fungi, bacteria, plants, animals, forests, farms, and cities.

Ted Schettler
Reconciling Human Rights, Public Health, and the Web of Life from Ecological Medicine – Healing the Earth, Healing Ourselves edited by Kenny Ausubel with J.P. Harpignes, page 76.

product, to the product seen within a complex web of relationships – *all* of which are important.

In 1985 Paul Katzeff visited Nicaragua and directly witnessed the conditions in which coffee growers lived. He learned that though a pound of gourmet coffee retails from $10-$15 in the United States, those actually growing the coffee only received 30-50 *cents* of that.

Paul returned to the U.S. and launched Thanksgiving's "Coffee for Peace" program. This involved buying coffee directly from the farmers - thereby cutting out the middlemen who were taking most of the profits - and becoming the first U.S. company to add a surcharge to the price of a product to benefit its producers. The Coffee for Peace program made it possible for the farmers to earn extra money and improve the quality of their lives.

Enter April Pojman, with first hand experience working on coffee fincas (farms) in Bolivia and Ecuador, and a heart committed to social and environmental justice. She established "the Office of Environmental and Social Policy", where all kinds of ideas gestate, and where networking and outreach opportunities now abound.

Imagine how different the world would be if every business had an Office of Environmental and Social Policy, or a Department of Honoring All Life! This was a group of individuals deeply committed to making change happen in the world, and many of Thanksgiving Coffee Company's sustainable policies grew out of their work.

Thanksgiving Coffee's Sustainable Practices Include:

- Thanksgiving's "Coffee for Peace" program described above. This concept is also applied to the many non-profit 'strategic partnerships' Thanksgiving Coffee has made, in which 50% of the sales profits is donated directly to those organizations.

- A 1998 self-initiated environmental audit identified areas in which the company could cut waste and reduce its impact on the Earth resulting in several new initiatives, including: a reduction of over 20,000 gallons of propane use (to date), decreased electricity consumption at a savings of over 43,000 kwh/year, and an increase in recycling that has reduced dumpster trash by 66%. Organic waste had made up 20% of the dumpster trash before starting a vermiculture farm; the worms have now produced over 3,000 pounds of compost from organic waste that is placed on the company's heirloom apple farm (57 trees, 55 varieties) located adjacent to the roasting plant. 5000 hemp and jute coffee sacks are made available to local farmers for mulching purposes annually.

- Partnering with a non-profit organization to plant 70,000 trees in Ethiopia to offset almost 2,000 tons of carbon annually. These measures earned the company the California Environmental Protection Agency Waste Reduction award for 2001 and 2002.

- In 2000, CEO Paul Katzeff designed a 'cupping lab' project, funded by the U.S. Agency for International Development, to provide cooperative coffee farmers with the proper facilities in which to taste, or 'cup,' the coffee beans

Americans believe too much priority is placed on work and making money, and not enough on family and community. Americans want more of what really matters in life.

Nearly all Americans (93%) agree -- more than half agree strongly (52%) -- that Americans are too focused on working and making money and not enough on family and community.

More than 4 in 5 Americans (83%) agree that they wish they had more of what really matters in life.

What Americans say would make them more satisfied with their lives is less stress, more time to spend with friends, and being more active in their communities, NOT more things.

A majority of Americans say that spending more time with family and friends (53%) and having less stress in their lives (52%) would make them much more satisfied with their lives.

Less than 3 in 10 say that having a bigger house or apartment (29%) or nicer

things (16%) would make them much more satisfied.

<u>*New American Dream Survey Report - September 2004*</u>*This summary provides the major findings from a Census-balanced and nationally representative poll of 1,269 American adults ages 18 years of age and older. The "New American Dream Poll" was conducted by Widmeyer Communications of Washington, D.C. for the Center for a New American Dream. The margin of error for the study is +/- 2.7%.*

http://www.newdream.org/about/ Finalpollreport.pdf

they grow. Few of the small farming communities had this opportunity prior to the establishment of the cupping labs; which now provides them with knowledge of how to improve the quality of their beans. These facilities enable small farms to be more competitive in the larger marketplace at a time when coffee prices are the lowest the world has ever seen.

- In September of 2002, Thanksgiving Coffee received a grant from the Mendocino Air Quality Management District to fuel its delivery trucks with biodiesel - an alternative fuel made from vegetable or soybean oil that greatly reduces emissions - making it the first private fleet in the state to use 100% biodiesel in delivery operations.

Social Justice

Thanksgiving Coffee Company adopted the motto "Not Just a Cup, But a Just Cup" in 1989. The decision to do so reflected an evolution in thought process that led to a pioneering role in the specialty coffee industry. In a letter to the author, Ben Corey-Moran, Director of their Campesino Estate Coffee Program wrote:

> We recognize that it is in the best interest of our company to be actively involved in the environmental and social consequences of coffee consumption. These issues affect not just our employees and community, but also the millions of people involved in the cultivation, processing, transportation, trade, roasting, marketing, and sipping of coffee around the world. **Our mission is to enhance the well-being of all we touch, from coffee picker to coffee drinker**.

> Through our products and actions we communicate the values and ideals that are embodied in the name "Thanksgiving." We use the medium of coffee and the environmental and social responsibility issues it embodies to teach people how their purchases impact the rest of the world. **We continually strive to improve our practices in order to model a new corporate paradigm that takes responsibility not only for current actions but for the future well-being of the whole planet.**

The Cooperative Model

As a result of this philosophy, Thankgiving Coffee purchases most of its beans from Coffee Cooperatives, like Las Hermanas in Nicaragua. Co-ops can be found all over the United States, serving a vast array of community needs. According to the National Cooperative Business Association, [7]

- over 120 million people - two of every five people - are members of 48,000 U.S. cooperatives;
- and worldwide some 750,000 cooperatives serve 730 million members.
- In Nicaragua, the need to find solutions to their abundant post-war community problems required a creative re-embracing of this old tried-and-true business model.

Co-ops may be formed for the provision of goods or services to its members or for the marketing of members' products, goods and services to the general public. By working together for their mutual benefit in cooperatives, rural farmers are able to market and process crops and livestock, purchase supplies and services, and to secure credit for their operations.

Why, then, have we lost the option of stepping off the treadmill of economic production. The answer is simple: because if we do not outrun the vast wave of inextinguishable debt and unpayable financial costs constantly arching over us we will be swamped, and, in the short term, superfluous resource conversion is one of the principal means we presently have of racing against the flood of debt.

The picture that emerges from this understanding of the impact of the financial system is of an economy driven largely by financial imperatives rather than by consumer demand for tangible products of the economy, and consequently proliferating unwanted production. The financial pressures tending to make production a goal in itself constitute a powerful incentive to overuse and waste resources. Merely for the sake of distributing income, we must compulsively churn over the resources of the earth.

The effects of this compulsive economic activity on the environment are tremendous. Thousands of deleterious intrusions on nature are justified on the grounds that they put income in people's pockets.

Robert Klinck
Finance And The Environment

The similarities between cooperatives and other businesses are that they both produce and provide services, as well as pay taxes. Cooperatives differ from other businesses in that they are wholly member owned and operate exclusively for the benefit of members, rather than to earn profits for investors. The differences between cooperatives and other businesses are often expressed as three broad principles that characterize all cooperatives and explain how they operate. They are:

- **The user-owner principle**. The member-users own and provide the necessary financing. Members finance cooperatives in several different ways.

- **The user-control principle**. The member-users control the business. They elect the board of directors and approve changes in its structure and operation. The board sets policy and is responsible for business oversight.

- **The user-benefit principle**. Assures that the cooperative's only purpose is to provide and distribute benefits to members based on their use.

Benefits may include a service otherwise not available, advantages from volume purchasing or sales, or distribution of profits based on member use of the cooperative.

The Seven Cooperative Principles are:

1. **Open and voluntary membership** - to all willing to accept the responsibilities of membership; the member service criterion provides for a more localized focus of activity, perhaps explaining why there is a low failure rate for cooperatives.

2. **Democratic member control** - active cooperative members each have one vote.

3. **Limited interest (if any) paid on shares** - this ensures that the operations are focused on servicing the members' needs. In the case of a trading cooperative, surpluses are normally distributed to members in proportion to business done with the cooperative.

4. **Autonomy and Independence** - cooperatives are autonomous, self-help organizations controlled by their members.

5. **Education, training and information** - cooperatives provide education and training for their members, elected representatives, managers and employees so they can contribute effectively to the development of their cooperatives.

6. **Cooperation between cooperatives** - at a local, state, national and international level to enhance the cooperative movement.

7. **Concern for community** - cooperatives work for the sustainable development of their communities through policies accepted by their members.

Mondragón

One of the greatest co-operative success stories is that of MCC, the Mondragón Corporación Cooperativa, in Spain. Started in 1956 with the incorporation of Fagor, at that time manufacturing paraffin stoves and heaters; it has grown into a multinational corporation of co-operatives with widely ranging products and services. According to the February 2001 History of MCC: it is now the seventh largest business group in Spain with regard to sales volumes, and on the basis of employment, it is third. It has a significant impact on the Basque economy, accounting for 4% of the GDP and employing 3.8% of the working population. These percentages are considerably higher with regard to the industrial sector. MCC attributes its consistent growth to its commitment to flexibility, a capacity for constant change and adaptation, and the advantage of being willing to learn from experience. [9]

Co-ops in the United States

In the United States, we use the symbol of two green pine trees within a circle against a gold background to signify a cooperative. The pine tree is an ancient symbol of endurance and productivity; more than one pine signifies cooperation. On this emblem, the trunks of the trees continue into the roots forming a circle, which symbolizes the universal interconnectedness of us all.

You may have seen this symbol before and not realized its significance, because Co-ops are more prevalent in the United States than most people realize. They form one of the core examples of democracy in action within the business forum. More than 30 cooperatives have annual revenue in excess of $1 billion, including such well-known names as Land O'Lakes, Inc., and ACE Hardware. The top 100 co-ops have a combined $125 billion in revenues. They range in size from large enterprises, including U.S. Fortune 500 companies, to single, small local storefronts. [8]

Fair Trade

The worldwide Fair Trade movement supports a new kind of economics based on the concept of creating a win-win situation for all involved. When applied to coffee production it places the concerns of small farmers at the center of business. In return, the coffee companies receive uniquely crafted coffees produced by farmers who know that their efforts are appreciated and are compensated in a way that allows them to meet their needs. Fair Trade products honor those who produce them. Paul Katzeff writes,

> Fair Trade is an economic system that Thanksgiving Coffee Company supports. By trading fairly, we support a new kind of economics that places the concerns of small farmers at the center of the business we do. In turn, we receive uniquely crafted coffees produced by farmers who know that we appreciate the attention and care that they devote to growing the finest coffees in the world. It's what we call "relationship coffee" and it's a way for us to show our respect for the people who work to produce excellent and sustainable coffee.

> Without this work, we all suffer. Without direct relationships with small coffee roasters, small farmers are subject to exploitation by middlemen who pay low and sell high. Without direct relationships, these small farmers are forced to live in poverty. Without Fair Trade we are players in a zero-sum game.

> When small farmers are forced to choose between cutting their forests to earn a quick dollar to feed their children, and preserving their habitat for the future, they choose their children every

The future of business will be created by nimble pods of highly committed individuals in deep relationship. Who has the power in this kind of social landscape?

Mikela and Philip Tarlow,
Authors of Digital Aboriginal – The Direction of Business Now: Instinctive, Nomadic, and Ever-Changing

time. When these farmers are forced into this kind of decision, they are forced to destroy migratory songbird habitats, incalculable biodiversity, and the indigenous forests that are home to the world's delicious and rare coffees.

With Fair Trade we create a new kind of game, a game where coffee farmers are empowered to support their families and communities by producing excellent coffee. This is a game where everyone wins.

This is the vision that leads me to the origins of our coffees time after time. I want coffee to improve the lives of all the people who are part of the "coffee supply chain." I want to honor these farmers as the craftspeople that they are. Fair Trade coffee, certified by TransfairUSA, insures that the farmers get a minimum price of $1.26 per pound, without the need for me to visit every farm personally to set up the trade relationship.

We support the Fair Trade movement as part of our commitment to a sustainable future. Economic justice goes hand-in-hand with social and environmental responsibility and is one of the ways that we express our corporate citizenship.[10]

The International Fair Trade Association is a global network of Fair Trade Organizations (FTOs). Currently counting over 220 FTOs in 59 countries, their membership includes approximately 65% from Asia, the Middle East, Africa and South America, with the rest coming from North America & the Pacific Rim and Europe. They include producer co-operatives and associations, export marketing companies, importers, retailers, national and regional Fair Trade networks and financial institutions, all who agree to a list of standards and monitoring procedures for both business and products. Contrary to the efforts of so-called "Free-Trade", these standards ensure that those producing the products are fairly compensated for their efforts and that their environments do not pay a negative price for the opportunity to do business. (http://www.ifat.org/)

Certified Organic

Both the Thanksgiving Coffee factory itself and the coffee are certified organic. To be "certified organically grown," an independent, third-party certifying program must determine that a coffee is produced without the use of fertilizers, pesticides, insecticides, herbicides, or other potentially harmful chemicals.

Thanksgiving Coffee is certified by third party organizations like OCIA (Organic Crop Improvement Association). OCIA is the largest producer-owned certification organization in the world. It has nearly 40,000 producer members and 300 corporate members in 35 countries. Over 40% of its membership is from developing countries.

OCIA maintains an organic audit trail from farmer to consumer. Each lot of coffee can actually be traced to a specific farm. Farmers must:

- Provide strict resource management
- Use only allowed materials
- Maintain farm/processor history (maps) and documentation
- Adhere to specific crop culture practices.

Finally, a lab analysis is performed prior to shipment.

Certification is a Whole Systems Approach from field to shelf.

In 2002, Thanksgiving Coffee Company was awarded the Governor's Economic and Environmental Leadership Award in the category of Sustainable Practices. California Governor Gray Davis recognized Thanksgiving's...

> pioneering efforts to integrate sound environmental values into management decisions and practices." He added, "We are honoring some of the most innovative companies and organizations in our state. As our award-winners are proving, it is possible to have the best of both worlds; a healthy environment and strong bottom lines.

Exploring Business as Humanity Expressed

Although the Thanksgiving Coffee Company may seem like an extreme example of a company who's staff intend, as a group with total conscious commitment, to engage in business as an expression of the best of humanity; they are not alone. Thousands of people around the world are awakening to this new vision of commerce. They gather in conferences, workshops, and forums annually. Just two of those gatherings are listed below...

- **The World Social Forum** draws thousands of people to Porto Alegre, Brazil in January every year. It represents a bold new model of people gathering for the common good to re-think how humans interact with each other and the rest of the planet. The WSF is a world civil process with an international dimension, focused on alternative proposals to the process of globalization.[11]

- **Bioneers Conference**. Founded by Kenny Ausubel in 1990 - and produced with his wife, Nina Simons – the Bioneers conference was conceived as an educational and economic development program to conserve biological and cultural diversity, support traditional farming, and environmental restoration. It takes place every October in San Rafael, California, and draws people from all over the Americas into lively networks of creativity. In their own words: Our vision of environment encompasses the natural landscape, cultivated landscape, biodiversity, cultural diversity, watersheds, community economics, and spirituality. Bioneers seeks to unite nature, culture and spirit in an Earth-honoring vision, and create economic models founded in social justice. Restoration addresses the premise that "sustainability" is problematic in the context of an environment that is already depleted. As Paul Hawken has noted, sustainability is simply the midpoint between destruction and restoration. The goal of Bioneers is restoration, addressing the interdependent array of economics, jobs, ecologies, cultures, and communities.[12]

Setting Smart Priorities

The issues of how corporations govern themselves and the priorities they make are now at the forefront of debate – not just among those who oppose globalization – but among the executives and shareholders themselves. People from the pensioner in your neighborhood to corporate executives in the Fortune 500 are awakening to the fact that no matter what governments attempt to tell us regarding climate change and pollution, they impact us all – including the bottom line. In a recent article on corporate governance, Dr. Robert Kinloch Massie, Executive Director of CERES, (The Coalition for Environmentally Responsible Economies, named after the Roman goddess of fertility and agriculture), and the largest coalition of investors and NGO's in the United States wrote,

Consider this one example: for every pound of electronics in your pocket or desk, approximately eight thousand pounds of waste was created somewhere in the world. This is not the information age; it is the despoliation age.

Paul Hawken
Brother, Can You Spare a Paradigm? From Nature's Operating Instructions edited by Kenny Ausubel with J.P. Harpignies, page 151.

The world's top 200 companies have twice the assets of 80 percent of the world's people This power was never granted.

Paul Hawken

Brother, Can You Spare a Paradigm? From Nature's Operating Instructions edited by Kenny Ausubel with J.P. Harpignies, page 149.

Companies that do not understand the challenges of sustainability –beginning with climate but including global income disparity, water usage, biodiversity, labor practices and human rights – and firms that do not build such an understanding into their long-term strategies will be viewed as poor risks. Portfolio managers and fund trustees who fail to analyze climate and other sustainability risks will be penalized and probably that has broad significance for corporate management and global capital markets, the two movements have recently begun to merge, both conceptually and politically. More and more people from all perspectives – companies, NGOs and investors –have come to realize that in the 21st century strong corporate governance requires a strategic approach to sustainability.

Companies that fail to understand sustainability, to pursue fair and equitable solutions to climate change, and to anticipate what lies ahead will be caught off guard by unexpected economic risks, environmental hazards and social demands. **Sustainable governance is not an option. It is a fundamental expectation bubbling up from governments, markets and every part of civil society. To restore confidence, to build the structure of trust, companies must commit themselves to openness, transparency and fairness.**

They must do this through innovations in listing exchanges, governance reform and dis-closure through the GRI. Executives and investors who commit themselves to sustainable governance will be in the forefront of history –not just prepared for the future but capable of shaping it to the benefit of all humanity. [13]

At the core of this transformation is the concept of transparency.

Transparency

This is one of the most fundamental concepts of Honoring All. Transparency means the willingness to disclose financial details of all aspects of the business. Shocking as that may seem in a culture where people have difficulty discussing anything regarding finances, including their own income; it is a necessary step when looking at the larger picture.

If our desired goal is to create a business environment that truly honors all involved, including the planet as a whole-system, then secrecy can no longer be encouraged. Salaries, profit margins, etc. must be revealed to those directly involved so that they have access to the pertinent facts necessary to make informed decisions.

The elimination of secrecy goes far to create an atmosphere of trust, the first step in developing a context in which all feel ownership in the successful outcome of the business. It is in this space that true commitment to the desired goal can thrive – a commitment beyond lip-service to actual accountability. This is where people's passions are ignited in common cause. It is where the employee is transformed from merely a "cog in the wheel" to an impassioned dynamo of creativity and energy who feels fully engaged, acknowledged, and responsible.

Profitability

Unlike secrecy, profitability is enthusiastically encouraged. In a whole-systems approach, the success of an honoring-all-life business benefits all. When the intention is to find a decision path that honors all life every step of the way, those profits become the tangible expression of success. They also honor the staff and investors whose efforts made it all possible. The current practice of creating huge disparity between executive salaries and those of the common worker can be eliminated, while still honoring each person for the level of responsibility, time, and effort applied. Within a network of interdependent support, each person's salary, dividend, and bonus goes to support the livelihood of everyone they, in turn, do business with.

Natural Capitalism

Paul Hawken has been a pioneer in the re-thinking of capitalism. As he points out its failures, he also sees a variation of capitalism as part of the solution – a tangible, practical method for healing the woes of our industrial wasteland. He doesn't mince words when he describes capitalism – as it is currently practiced by most – as a "financially profitable, unsustainable aberration in human development." He points out that it

> doesn't fully conform to its own accounting principles, liquidates its capital and calls it income, (while neglecting to) assign any value to the largest stocks of capital it employs; the natural resources and living systems, as well as the social and cultural systems, that are the basis of human capital.[14]

So what changes can be made that will transform this "unsustainable aberration in human development" into something that can be part of the healing process? He calls it "Natural Capitalism." Hawken writes,

> Natural capitalism as a metaphor is an attempt to describe an integrated application and program of the economics of restoration. Rather than being an approach to sustainability, natural capitalism attempts to describe a practical relationship between human beings and the biosphere that will improve the quality of life for all while dramatically reducing our impact on living systems and eventually increasing ecosystem viability and productivity. [14]

Briefly, here are the four main steps:

1. **Radical Resource Productivity.** This means using resources so efficiently that you can obtain "the same amount of utility or work from a product or process while using less material and energy." Currently, according to Amory and Hunter Lovins of the Rocky Mountain Institute, and co-authors with Paul Hawken of Natural Capitalism: Creating the Next Industrial Revolution, Americans use twenty times our body weight per person each day, or a million pounds of resources per American per year to run our industry. Globally, that amounts to about a half trillion tons per year. Yet, they write

   Only about 1 percent of all the materials mobilized in the current economy ever gets embodied in a durable product and is still there six months after its sale. The difference between that 1 percent and something approaching 100 percent is obviously a large business opportunity. [15]

   In 1994 a group of scientists, economists, governmental officials, and business people met and published the "Carnoules Declaration" calling for this leap in resource productivity. Hawken says this beginning to happen right now, companies are designing and developing products that will work 5-100 times harder for us than they do today.

2. **Biomimicry.** This is the art of designing processes, services, and products that both imitate life and are conducive to life. This is significant. It asks the question: What would nature do? Scientists are taking a closer look at the 3.4 billion year experiment called "life on Earth" and are starting to make some amazing discoveries regarding the elegantly simple solutions to problems that

nature has devised. But this revolution in thinking isn't just taking place in processes, services, and products – it's also taking place in the way we think about business itself. When we see business as an imitation of biological and ecosystem processes we realize that in nature, *there is no concept of waste*. Everything serves a purpose and feeds some other part of the overall cycle of life within that system. Thus *everything contributes to life*.

A wonderful example of re-thinking business is when DesignTex asked McDonough and Braungart to assist in the creation of a compostable upholstery fabric to be produced at the Röhner mill in Switzerland. After testing approximately 8,000 chemicals with the assistance of Ciba-Geigy, they found only 38 that weren't toxic or harmful in any way. Luckily those 38 allowed for the mixing of all the colors they needed. They used organic ramie and wool. When the Swiss environmental authorities came to test the water leaving the plant after the dying process, they were shocked to find that it was actually *cleaner* than the drinking-quality water going into the Röhner mill. Evidently the fabric was acting as an additional water filter.

3. **Flow of Services.** Simply put, we can no longer think of business as an episodic producer of goods, but instead need to focus our attention and intention on business as a delivery system of a flow of services. Hawken points out that nature operates in this way. McDonough and Braungart suggest two distinct life cycles we can design within, while making sure they don't contaminate each other:

   a. **Biological Nutrients –** Which includes all organic material that can be used as food for something else in the Biological cycle.

   b. **Technical Nutrients –** Which includes all non-organic materials, like metals and plastics, that can be designed to be used over and over again without returning to the source for more raw materials. Imagine recycling your car and computer parts when you upgrade, and you begin to understand this idea.

4. **Restoration of Natural Capital.** We must not only reorganize the way we do business, we need to restore the Earth and heal the damage already done. When we re-think business as a restorative process, this step is a natural result. It must be incorporated into the very structure of any business process. It's good business to reinvest in the capital that is in short supply.

The State of Grace Document

After going through a divorce, Maureen K. McCarthy realized that there was little support in our culture to view divorce in as a positive growth experience. When she later met her new husband, they both decided that being in what they called a, "state of grace," was more important than maintaining the status quo. They drew up a three page document that was very personal and explicit. It consisted of their own "story of us," which described how they saw each other when things were going smoothly, a list of their own communication styles and warning signs indicating when they each might be out of sync, and a description of how to respond when that happens. They also included a list of questions they have agreed to answer within 24 hours, whenever they need assistance to return to that "state of grace."

The document proved so successful, allowing them to maintain connection and self esteem while exploring new facets of their relationship, that she went on to draw up contracts with many of her friends, family members, and business associates.

In fact, the process has transformed her business experience to the extent that she now uses only State of Grace Documents, even with large global corporations. And, she reports, they have all agreed!

McCarthy and her husband give workshops on the State of Grace Document, and how it shifts relational priorities. Visit http://www.stateofgracedocument.com for additional information. Tools like these are exactly what is needed to transform business into an experience that focuses on relationships, honoring all involved.

Community

Every decision we make, no matter what our position in life, or how seemingly small – affects everyone and every thing. From a systems standpoint, community exists wherever you focus you attention, from the smallest world of the nucleus of an atom to the global community and beyond. How then, can we re-think our ways of perceiving and relating with each other such that all feel empowered, and all contribute?

Designed Learning, a Peter Block Company, develops training workshops to further the themes in his books, which focus on creating partnership within both the business and community settings. His work is highlighted in the chapter on Community, because from an honoring all life standpoint, business and community are the same. As more people shift their focus from the old paradigm of domination and control, to a new paradigm in which we are all co-creating together, honoring through conscious partnership and recognition of the gifts and value we each bring to the community, we are literally transforming every aspect of our world.

You can also find many supporting organizations listed in the Reference section. The list includes some of the most famous organizations involved in this business revolution and some of the lesser-known but just as powerfully transformative organizations. Those who dedicate their lives to creating a world that honors all, by that very definition, see themselves as part of an all-inclusive team working for the benefit of everyone and every thing. Gone is the idea that we must compete against each other. We are all in this together, and when anyone "wins", we all do.

A Choice that Serves All

The winner of the 2004 Global Social Venture Competition was the Rotterdam School of Management's Eco-Friendly Agricultural Products. They manufacture biodegradable, water-absorbent organic fertilizer to provide plant nutrition and conserve water in arid regions. The team leader, Vasu Bhat, commenting on their success stated that he was motivated by the promise of profit, but even more excited by the prospect of providing a benefit to underserved communities. Careful analysis revealed that for every one dollar they make, the community would receive five dollars.

The retailing behemoth, whose $10 billion annual profits are based on low prices, low expenses and its relentless pace of store openings, announced it will shut the doors here May 6 after workers voted to make this the first unionized Wal-Mart in North America.

The closure will leave 190 bitter employees out of work, the town uneasy over the future of unions, and the mayor angry at the company.

The world's largest retail chain has fiercely and successfully resisted unionization attempts at its 3,600 stores in the United States. Its closest call ended in Texas in 2000 when the store eliminated its meat department after 11 meat cutters voted to join a union. While union membership in the United States dropped to 12.5 percent of workers in 2004, according to the U.S. Department of Labor, it was 28.6 percent in Canada.

Doug Struck Wal-Mart Leaves Bitter Chill, Quebec Store Closes After Vote to Unionize Washington Post Foreign Service April 14, 2005

As noted in a Jungle Magazine article on Bhat's win, when you think about it; if you have two businesses with equal profits, but one contributes to the quality of life, both socially and environmentally, while the other has a negative impact in those areas; which one would you invest in?[16]

Hopefully, investors, employees, and those who use products will soon all agree that the question isn't a fair one; because in the final analysis there is no competition. When business ventures are approached from the desire to honor all, everybody and every thing wins. It's that simple. What we do, who we experience ourselves to be, and how we treat each other becomes a celebration of life's magnificence.

Notes

1. Birth of the Chaordic Age, published in November, 1999, by Berrett-Koehler, San Francisco, California
2. FROM: http://www.kaospilot.dk/docs/Values.asp
3. Digital Aboriginal – The Direction of Business Now: Instinctive, Nomadic, and Ever-Changing, by Mikela Tarlow with Philip Tarlow, pages 23-24.
4. Digital Aboriginal – The Direction of Business Now: Instinctive, Nomadic, and Ever-Changing, by Mikela Tarlow with Philip Tarlow, pages 223.
5. Interface Carpets http://www.interfaceinc.com/ Vision Statement: To be the first company that, by its deeds, shows the entire industrial world what sustainability is in all its dimensions: People, process, product, place and profits — by 2020 — and in doing so we will become restorative through the power of influence.
6. All Thanksgiving Coffee Company quotes are taken from their library-like website that offers extensive information on sustainable business practices and why they choose to practice them. www.ThanksgivingCoffee.com
7. Read the overview (see resources at the back of this book) taken from www.nic.coop, the domain designed specifically for "bona fide cooperatives and cooperative service organizations that ascribe to the Cooperative Principles of the ICA." Source : ICA News, No. 5/6, 1995.
8. See information in the resources at the back of this book from the Global Exchange Website: http://www.globalexchange.org/index.html
9. Mondragón Corporación Cooperativa From pages 34-38 of MCC History: http://www.mondragon.mcc.es/ing/quienessomos/historia.html
10. Thanksgiving Coffee Company website: http://www.thanksgivingcoffee.com/justcup/fairtrade/why.lasso
11. World Social Forum: http://www.forumsocialmundial.org.br/home.asp
12. Bioneers: www.Bioneers.org (see resources at the back of this book) From: http://bioneers.org/whoweare/press.php by Wren Farris, Communications Coordinator wren@bioneers.org
13. CERES Global Agenda 2003, SUSTAINABILITY CORPORATE GOVERNANCE by DR Robert Kinloch Massie
14. Paul Hawken, Natural Capitalism: Brother, Can you Spare a Paradigm? From Nature's Operating Instructions, Edited by Kenny Ausubel with J.P. Harpignies, pages 149-150.
15. Amory and Hunter Lovins, Where the Rubber Meets the Road From Nature's Operating Instructions, Edited by Kenny Ausubel with J.P. Harpignies, page 164.
16. http://www.mbajungle.com/magazine.cfm?INC=inc_article.cfm&artid=3308&template=0 Jungle Magazine, Executive Summary, Jo Napolitano and Elizabeth Herr, Good as Gold, August 12, 2004.

26

OWNERSHIP

Ownership is the decision to become the author of our own experience.
It is to be cause rather than effect.
The willingness to bring our own value to what we participate in.
Peter Block

OWNERSHIP

How can you purchase that which is already yours?

Our laws and beliefs are based on an assumption that we all understand a common concept of "ownership." The right to "own" something seems to be a cornerstone of Western culture, but what exactly does it mean? For many people, ownership offers controlling rights. In other words, when you own something, you can then choose if it is used, how it is used, and when it is used. You control it.

A Deeper Need

It seems that we humans want to feel we are in control at all times. Our notion of ownership goes well beyond property. We fight constantly over ownership, even of beliefs and concepts. Perhaps what looks like a need to feel superior to another, is actually based on a fear that we won't survive. I have already experienced a similar dichotomy in my own life. I notice that I own a house, but don't. I notice that "my" children are mine by law, but they are really their own. I notice that anything I can claim I own is not really mine. In fact, the entire concept of ownership seems to be based on empty air.

Molecular Soup

All matter is made up from the same molecular "soup" from which all has materialized on Earth, including the dinosaurs. Even the very molecules that make up your body are not yours, you just borrow them. Once you no longer need them, they will return to the molecular "soup", ready for the next temporary user.

Even when you own, for example a simple cup, what do you own? The elements making up the cup are part of the elemental soup of the cosmos, available to all. The cup could easily have existed before you were born, and could also just as easily exist after you die. For that matter, it could break tomorrow, be tossed into the garbage, and again become part of the elemental soup. So what was owned?

Who owns the store?

It is as if we sit in a candy store counting out pennies to see how much we can buy, drooling all the while as we imagine our soon to be purchased prize, while ignorant of the fact that we own the candy store and all its contents. (In fact, it could be said that we ARE the candy store and all its contents.) Do you see the problem?

It is not that we have a lack; it is that we have abundance, and do not realize it because our focus has been on an illusion of lack.

This concept can be difficult to grasp, because our entire culture sees "lack" as normal. It is like asking a fish to see water, when water is all the fish has ever experienced. Only by removing the water, can the fish clearly understand what it has known, quite intimately, all along. When we allow ourselves to see beyond the circumstances and details of this very moment, perhaps even this lifetime, what do we see?

We live in a lush and abundant world. There is enough food, clothing, shelter, water, and livelihood for everyone. The issue is not lack as much as choice and distribution. We choose to live in a world in which most of the world's resources are used by a very small portion of the population. Currently only 6% of the world's population uses over half the world's resources. If you were designing the way the world worked, would you choose that as your reality? If your answer is, "No," then how can you live your life so that your voice and vote are heard?

Scarcity or Abundance

It is so easy for us to feel that we are victims of the system, yet the system is human made. We have a choice: do we choose to come from scarcity or abundance? Our choice determines all our perceptions and subsequent actions.

Those who choose to honor all life, choose to see life AS abundant. In fact, to them life simply IS abundance. Therefore, they actively seek to provide all with that same experience; to ensure that the necessities of life are readily available, sustainably produced in a way that honors and supports the diverse expressions of life on Earth. By doing so, their life becomes an expression and celebration of life's magnificence.

Sharing

So often, when children are learning to socialize with their peers, adults will tell them to share. Yet even that concept assumes ownership. You cannot share something that isn't yours. A slight shift of perception, however, allows for the possibility of seeing everything as yours *and* everyone else's. Seen from that perception, sharing would be automatic, because ownership would no longer be in question.

How can we, as an evolving human species, create a world in which ownership is no longer an issue, in which humans are no longer preoccupied with control? Since the need to control usually comes from a survival fear, what if we structured our society such that all knew their necessities of life were automatically met? Would the idea of ownership disappear?

Until we are each willing to face our deeply ingrained fears regarding ownership and scarcity, how can we ever allow ourselves to experience the peace and joy of unconditionally loving each other and ourselves?

Language

Here's a first step. What would life would be like if we eliminated the "owning" words from our vocabulary? For example:

- Instead of MY house… the house.
- Instead of MY wife, husband, or child… call them by name.
- Instead of MY (any body part goes here)… THIS (body part), etc.

What a subtle but powerful difference! When I honor each thing or being in life by giving it back it's ownership, such that I claim nothing as mine… the energy shift within me is striking. I feel a freedom I haven't allowed before. At the same time, I offer freedom to those with whom I speak and OF WHOM I speak.

True Ownership

Now let's make a new definition of ownership. To truly own something, it must be taken deeply within you, it must be allowed to course through your veins with your blood, until you and it become one in complete merging. This is a level of

Once emancipated from debt psychosis, an economy's limitations are bound only by its availability of manpower and its own physical resources.

James Gibb Stuart
Emancipation From Debt Psychosis and author of
The Money Bomb

ownership most people feel about their place within a family or a community. It is the same energy that allows them to be willing to fight for a cause or a homeland. It is because they see themselves *as* that cause, as an expression of it living through them.

When we truly own something, we take complete care of it. We take complete responsibility for our experience of and the value we place on it. What if we held our planet in that light? I have belonged to the same community for almost two decades. I feel it deeply within my being, and my partnership with the people in this community leads me to constantly include them and their well being into my thoughts. But what of the land on which we live, the air we breathe, the water we drink, and the waste we produce?

A Sense of Place

When we truly feel as if the environment is part of who we are, we have a well developed sense of place. Not only are we aware that we breathe the same air, drink the same water, eat the same molecules, and experience the same events; but we also support each other completely.

Yet rarely do we live that way. A deep sense of ownership, or sense of place, includes a responsibility for how we live within that place. Nothing is seen as outside of that sense of responsibility. For example, human waste is handled in a manner that shows complete ownership of it and complete honor for the land upon which we live. It isn't shipped off to be handled by someone else, it is handled right beneath our feet.

Ownership as Awareness

Used in this way, the term ownership takes on a completely different meaning. It implies full responsibility, and requires that we own all that we do, think, and say.

I am slowly beginning to see the subtle ways in which my sense of ownership or lack thereof, permeates every choice I make. It is the dawning of "ownership" in me. As this awareness begins to unfold before my eyes, separation melts away.

For example, when I take ownership of my body, I relate to it in an entirely different way than when I simply use it as a vehicle that moves me through life. I become aware that my thoughts affect the quality of my bodily experience, and thus I begin to take ownership of the thoughts I have regarding my body. My speech, too, reflects those thoughts. What does my language reveal about how I think and feel?

Ownership requires that I pay full attention to every aspect of how I relate to my body. It also requires that I take full responsibility for feeding it and handling my waste in a mindful manner. Full ownership requires that everything I do regarding my body, honors both myself and all who encounter me. Can you imagine how we would design our world if every person took ownership – full responsibility – for just that? **Imagine what would happen if we extended that sense of ownership to include everything**.

27

<u>CONSCIOUS</u>
<u>CREATION</u>

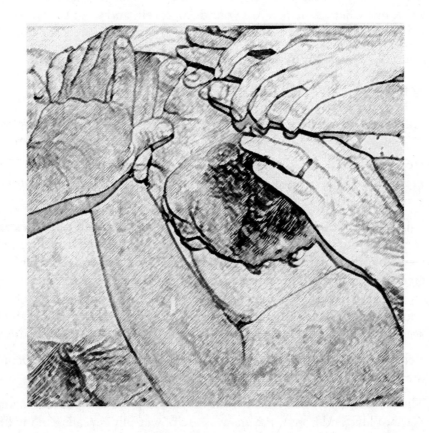

Reality is wrong.
Dreams are for real.

Tupac Shakur

CONSCIOUS CREATION

What makes sense at one level of perception often no longer stands as valid at another.
We are more powerful than we realize, in our ability to comprehend and create reality.

There is a concept that has been floating around our culture that, when watered down to a sentence or two, looses its meaning so completely that people scratch their heads in confusion and wonder what is meant; or assume they understand something other than what was intended.

I'd like to take a moment to clarify this concept of subconscious creation as I see it. Please simply allow these ideas to wash over you as a wave washes over the shore. Just as the wave deposits only a few items on the beach, I ask you to release any attachments to these thoughts, and simply see how they land without judgment. You will know what resonates with your deepest self, and what to discard back into the sea of possibilities.

"Why did you create __(blank)__ in your life?"

I have heard this statement used to blame another for their circumstances in life. Yet the concept originating this statement is far from blaming. In fact, it is just the opposite… it is a huge affirmation of the wisdom and magnificence of each human being.

How then, did it get so convoluted? When statements are taken out of the context in which they make sense, they usually loose their original intent of meaning. This is a perfect example.

I spent many years asking myself why I created the health-related experiences I had as a child. How did those experiences serve me? I asked myself in the most loving way, honoring and recognizing my inner wisdom, and trusting that I wouldn't have given myself those experiences if they hadn't been absolutely vital to my own soul growth. Additionally, I wouldn't have created those opportunities for growth if I hadn't been capable of handling them. Within that context, those questions can be seen as intelligent, loving, and even supportive of my own inner growth.

Yet the minute I ask those same questions in the context of judgment and blame, they sound far from loving and supportive. They sound cruel.

The truth is, that when I ask myself those questions without judgment, and from a place of love and honor, the answers are powerfully revealing in my life. I am able to see the progression of experiences I have given myself specifically to lead me to a moment in time when a great Ah-ha occurred, and all the pieces of the puzzle fell into place, revealing – as if magically – the wisdom of those combined experiences.

Based on these assumptions, I can now fully support each person on their life journey of discovery, treating them as the wise and whole person I know them to be whenever they are in touch with their inner-self. In that context, the question of "Why did you create so-and-so in your life?" takes on a completely new meaning.

Instead of indicating judgment and blame, it indicates my immense honor and trust in that person's wisdom. Worded differently, the question might read,

"What life-lesson are you exploring in this moment, that makes this particular experience so valuable?"

We each create our own reality.

All too often, I hear this statement used in a blaming way, dismissing the pain of another's experience. When said through judgment, this statement can excuse and justify *any* behavior. It is the exact *opposite* of taking responsibility. Yet there is another perceptual context in which this statement can offer a deeper insight into our own experience.

Studies in perception indicate that we all create our *experience* of reality – by choosing filters through which we perceive life. I can experience an event as joyful while my friend could experience it as boring. The actual event remains the same, but our filters differ, leading us to perceive the event differently. One could say, then, that our filters determine our experience of reality.

Additionally, whatever we place our attention on, determines our filter; and we all seem to make choices that deliberately reinforce our beliefs about ourselves. Therefore, if I constantly choose to see myself as capable and intelligent, I will perceive my experiences of life as proof that my perception is correct. If I choose to see myself as indecisive and full of self-doubt, I will perceive each event as a reinforcement of the perception also.

If I believe myself to be loved by many, I will surround myself with those who love me – constantly reinforcing that belief. I might even perceive that strangers act in a loving manner towards me, simply because of that belief. That in turn may induce strangers to actually treat me in a loving manner, because I am perceived as non-threatening. Therefore, in a way then, I do create my own reality. We each do.

The power of attention and intention on reality

We could take this even further. When I focus all my *attention* and *intention* on a goal, several things happen. I create a perceptual filter for that goal. I then perceive everything through that filter, such that my experience relates directly to my goal. I am alert and able to respond quickly to opportunities that arise precisely because my attention is on the goal.

Some quantum physicists and spiritually-focused people might say that I am creating an energy field with my consciously focused intention – one that can actually create desired results. The physicists would say that my intentions operate on the implicate order in which a field of infinite possibilities exists and all is one. Each spiritual discipline has a different name for this implicate order, and it really doesn't matter what you call it. What is important to note, however, is that many humans throughout history from widely varying walks of life and hugely varying perceptual filters have all developed incredibly similar explanations for the phenomenon of creation – how we manifest from the void into our experience of physical reality. All of them agree that we have the ability to use our focused intention in this way. It is important to remember that we are *all* doing this, and thus are all impacting each other's experience of reality. This is what is meant when people say we "draw an experience to us". They are noticing this phenomenon.[1]

Creating New Perceptual Realities

I encourage you to play with practicing the art of creating your own reality. It is one of the greatest learning experiences I can imagine. Why? Because once you set your *intention* and focus your *attention* on a goal, several things happen.

1. **ALLOW RESISTANCE TO SURFACE.** Every bit of resistance you hold in the form of a thought, feeling, or belief, will surface for you to examine. This is a gift. It brings into sharp focus all of the obstacles that have kept you from manifesting your goal in the past. Though this stage of the experience may be uncomfortable, it is very enlightening. I mean that literally. Once you see the thoughts, patterns, feelings, and beliefs that have kept you from accomplishment, you can choose to jettison them. Even though they may have been totally appropriate as survival skills in the past, they no longer serve you.

   It is essential that this is done with the utmost tenderness and love for yourself and the choices you've made. NO judgments. All choices are simply that – choices. They are opportunities to learn. Seen from this context, one choice is no better than another. No goals are better than others, either. It is important to remember that this process is on-going. I like to think of my experience of self as an onion. I keep peeling back layers of thoughts, beliefs, and concepts that no longer serve me. There is always another layer beneath. After awhile, I have learned to just smile and enjoy the experience of exploring myself. It is rich and full and often comical.

2. **CHOOSE A NEW FOCUS.** Once you are aware of those thoughts, feelings, and beliefs that sabotage your desire to create your goal, you can practice the lessons offered by those studying neurochemistry – you can re-wire your brain's neuroreceptors so that more receptors exist for the neurochemical soup associated with the new thoughts and feelings you want to experience. This will automatically lead you to enjoy doing those very things that help accomplish your goal. Affirmations are wonderfully effective tools here. Instead of telling yourself how _____ you are (in a negative way), fill in the blank with whatever you desire to feel about yourself (in a positive way). Why not remind yourself you are magnificent, unconditionally loving, receptive, honoring, brilliant, etc.?

3. **FEEL YOUR NEW CHOICE.** Once you've decided to perceive yourself in a new way by constantly choosing the path that truly brings you JOY (that makes your heart sing), it is essential that you allow yourself to experience how that new choice feels. Take a few moments and allow the feeling of that experience to fill your being. This shifts your choice from a mental exercise to an actual experience you can draw upon whenever you wish.

4. **LET GO OF CONTROL.** It is also crucial that you let go of the need to control *how* the manifestation takes place. I say this in all humility. From everything I have learned about perception, we know so little about *anything*. Yet at the implicate level, all is possible and all is one. The operating verb here is TRUST.

5. **TRUST THE PROCESS.** More than anything else, you have to trust yourself to manifest what you desire in the perfect way and perfect timing. Many would suggest trusting God, the Universe, Spirit, or the divine within all life. It doesn't matter what word you use, the concept is the same, and trust is the necessary action.

Once you surrender into TRUST, you can simply let go and allow life to manifest in all its wildly creative and juicy ways. It is really the journey – the *process* – that is the gift in life. The goal is just the prop, the arbitrary end-point upon which we focus our attention and intention as we play the game. In other words, I don't have to wait for some far-off day when I live my life *honoring all*, to feel that I've accomplished my goal.

Only this moment of NOW exists. Everything else is my story, my creative way of caressing the joy of what simply, elegantly, and perfectly IS. I can *be* "honoring all" right now with my next breath, and the next one after that. As I practice, it becomes easier. It becomes the perceptual filter through which I perceive and interact with reality. When there is no separation, I *am* the realty, and I live it with every choice I make, in every moment.

Notes

1.   There are quantum physics explanations for this, as so beautifully illustrated in the film, What the #$*! Do we (k)now!? (www.WhattheBleep.com) See the chapter Avoiding the Void, for a more detailed description of this experience through the eyes of physics. Also read Michael Talbot's Holographic Universe., and any of the Scientists mentioned in the References section in the back of this book.

28

<u>SELF</u>

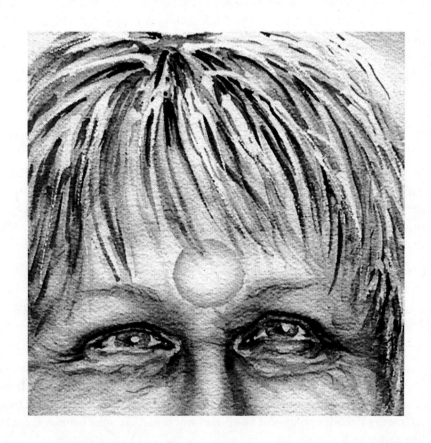

Love your rhythm and rhythm your actions
in obedience to its law, and your poetry as well;
You are a universe of universes,
And your soul a fountain of song.
Rubén Darío

SELF

When you honor Self, you can't help but honor All.
Self-Honoring includes the acknowledgment that in this moment,
you are free to choose how you think, act, and perceive your world.
Create the world you choose to live in as an expression of who you know yourself to be
Your Essential Self — beyond personality and identity.

The "U" in universe stands for you. You are the Universe, looking in the mirror. When you observe the Universe, you are observing Urself.

John Archibald Wheeler
Physicist

When I was ten years old I was told that I had scoliosis, a curvature of the spine that could get worse as I grew. My parents did everything possible to help me, beginning with a set of special exercises. They even had a small swimming pool built in our backyard so I could exercise my back daily — no small feat for a middle-class household in the suburbs. I was told I was the first kid on the west coast to wear a new body brace. I was embarrassed to wear the big clunky thing. Because it was so awkward, I had to wear special clothes, which didn't help my self esteem. I remember being called a "cripple" by one of the kids in my class the very first day I wore it to school. In my mind, it seemed that I had crossed an invisible barrier between being seen as "normal," and being seen as "less than." I hated it. From that moment on no one seemed to see ME, they just saw the brace.

By the time I was twelve the curve was spiraling, so the doctors decided to perform surgery. They placed me in a stretching contraption similar to the medieval torture device called "the rack," and turned the crank while I screamed. Then they cast my body from my hips to just under my chin and the back of my head while I hung in that stretched position. Surgery was performed through the cast.

I was in the body-cast for approximately four months. I was not allowed to get out of bed, or even to sit up. It was very humiliating. Again, I felt like an object of pity and it seemed that no one really saw ME. I remember everyone telling me how brave I was, but I couldn't understand why they would say that. To me, I didn't have much choice in the matter, so there was nothing brave about it. It was just my life.

I can see so many moments during this period of my life where I made decisions about who I was and what I deserved that didn't serve me later in life. I feel great compassion for myself during that time. I also realize that I spent most of the following decades trying NOT to feel my body. It was a survival technique, and I learned it well.

Be strong, O my heart,
Put your fancy away,
And stand where you are
In yourself.

Kabir

Until the past decade, I was not able to see this experience as anything but as a victim. As long as I saw myself as a victim, I couldn't see any gifts that the experience provided. Yet there were many. I remember lying in bed alone at home with nothing to do and no one to talk to. My parents were at work and my siblings were at school. As a result, my two favorite pastimes were thinking and meditating.

Most of the issues important in the life of a 12 year old girl fell away for me, and I began contemplating the meaning of life. Although I could draw no conclusions, I was able to still myself enough to observe that most of what humans thought important (at least from the standpoint of a young teenager), was not. I was constantly amazed at the topics that occupied the minds of my friends. Even the adults paying their requisite visit to see how I was, seemed locked into lives that were wrapped around illusions. I remember realizing that their visits were less for me and more out of a sense of duty to my parents and social custom. I received a minute or two of their attention, and most of that time was spent trying *not* to see me. It seemed all they could see was my condition. I made many judgments about others during this time. Much time would pass before I got off my intellectual high-horse and humbled myself to the reality of how little I actually knew about anything.

Seeing is Honoring

There was one magical being in my life at that time, my piano teacher. Of course, I could no longer play the piano as I was stuck in bed, but she wrote daily and visited often. Her letters were simple, often containing the wonders of the Universe and nothing else: a small stone, a bird's feather, a leaf. It was she who really understood my experience and knew what I needed… not pity but adventure. And so she gave it to me, in the form of nature's gifts. It was up to me to provide the rest of the story, and my vivid imagination had no problem filling in the blanks. Most of all she gave me acceptance and love. I felt fully seen and honored.

Honor was the essential difference between her visits and that of other adults. She *wanted to see ME*, whereas most adults had no desire to connect with me at all. Their own fears about illness, finances, the fear that their own child could become ill; all those thoughts kept them from wanting to connect. I could see it in their faces and hear it in their voices.

Carl Rogers describes the impact of empathy on its recipients:

> When…someone really hears you without passing judgment on you, without trying to take responsibility for you, without trying to mold you, it feels damn good…When I have been listened to and when I have been heard, I am able to reperceive my world in a new way and go on. It is astonishing how elements that seem insoluble become soluble when someone listens. [1]

It was exactly this kind of empathic listening that my piano teacher offered to me. As a result, I felt honored and seen. If I had known about Dr. Rosenberg's Non-Violent Communication methods then, and had the courage, I would have wanted to reach out and soothe the fears of my adult visitors, even though their stated intention was to soothe mine.

Re-Perceiving Healing

This ability to "re-perceive my world in a new way and go on", is exactly the gift that honoring Self provides. It re-contextualizes one's entire experience of life. It would be decades before I learned to love myself enough to do so.

Learning to re-perceive my own healing took most of my life. It required an entirely new definition of "healing", one that shifted the meaning from a momentary "fixing" of something that was previously broken, to that of a *process* similar to the following statement by holistic physician and psychiatrist George L. Hogben:

> Healing may be defined as a miraculous unfolding of consciousness for one's being in the world. We learn who we are, what and who really matter to us, how to express ourselves fully and openly. Ultimately, the healing journey leads to an intimate union with God through the experience of the flow of God's spirit within. It is a slow, arduous passage, unique for each individual, filled with danger and risk, triumph and joy, and finally, peace, trust, awe, reverence, love, tenderness. [2]

You, yourself, as much as anybody in the entire universe, deserve your love and affection.

--Buddha

And, since every aspect of our experience is a manifestation in the mind, it is the creator of the world we know. These qualities—truth, absolute, eternal, essence, creator—are amongst those traditionally associated with God. From this perspective, the statement "I am God" is not so puzzling or deluded after all. Although it might be more accurate to say that "I am" is God, or possibly, "God is consciousness".

Peter Russell
Reality and Consciousness: Turning the Superparadigm Inside Out

I love this definition of healing, because it incorporates deep total healing, of the transformational kind. This is the healing I now seek for any wound that I uncover. Yet when I was young, my scope of what "healing" meant was vastly different.

The doctors told me I was "healed", and I believed them. What they really meant was that the surgery was successful. It was not within their realm of reality to contemplate healing beyond a very limited definition. They didn't take into consideration the emotional, spiritual, environmental, or mental influences that could have been involved. As a result, neither did I.

The Self is the total field and all its contents as well. Consciousness is the quality by which the Self is known, knowable, and expressed. God is All That Is, without any exclusion —sight, sound, space, objects, form, formless, visible, invisible, solid, liquid, without dimension or location, and everywhere equal. There is no opposite to God. God is both Allness and voidness, equally form and nonform.

Dr. David R. Hawkins,
The Eye of the I

During and after surgery I experienced a lot of physical pain. I learned to remove awareness from my back such that the surface remained numb for decades. It wasn't until I committed to over a year of weekly massages combined with the conscious choice to experience my entire body that the feeling in my back returned. With it came a new appreciation for the joys of physical bodies. Instead of avoiding physical sensations, I was finally able to revel in them.

Yet I still thought of "healing" as "fixing", and was constantly frustrated that I could not "heal" my back, but simply honor and begin to accept it. I say "begin to accept it" because I now realize that as long as I desired more, I wasn't really accepting it at all. I had an agenda: the straightening of my back. I still didn't see it as beautiful, and I certainly didn't show it off. It wasn't until I started thinking about the word, "willing", that I began to see how stuck I truly was.

Willingness

A wonderful friend of mine ends his radio talk show each day with the words, "Do what you can do." I love that simple line. Yet I would add a slight change, for first I would ask you to choose who you are *willing to be,* as that will determine what you are willing to do. And I use the word *willing,* because it implies that through your choice, you will ensure that your life will actually embrace and express that declaration in all you think, speak, and do. To me, its not about what I "can" do, because there are many things I can do. But the heart of the matter is, what am I *willing* to do?

So the question remains, "what am I willing to do to heal my back?" Am I willing to release all old ideas that no longer serve my healing? Am I willing to look deeper than ever before to discover hidden beliefs that have kept me stuck throughout my life (and perhaps even life*times*)? **Am I willing to allow for the outrageous idea that perhaps there is *nothing* to heal** – that perhaps my physical presentation has been the most perfect growth-producing presentation I could have chosen?

If my answer is YES, then the experience of scoliosis, for me, has been one of the greatest gifts I ever received. It has pushed me to experience more at an earlier age, and then to continue that process of self-discovery throughout my life. I am immeasurably grateful.

Another gift of scoliosis has been the opportunity to carefully examine how I see myself in life. How do I *choose* to see me? Remember that the first day I wore the back brace my friend called me a "cripple"? I had the choice to see myself as she did, or as whole and healthy. The circumstances didn't change, only my *experience* of myself changed. Her name-calling was a tremendous gift in disguise. It prompted me to examine the filters through which I saw myself.

I recently read an article in the New York Times about patients with ALS, commonly called Lou Gehrig's disease. Some choose to end their lives when they can no longer breathe on their own, but others seem to shift their perception of what constitutes "quality of life". One of their physicians, Dr. Bach, asks

> "Do you know what happiness is?" … citing a survey that showed patients on ventilators tend to rank their level of satisfaction with life at 5.1 out of a possible score of 7; the average person in the same surveys has a score of 5.5. **"Happiness is reality divided by expectations."**[3]

What a wonderful statement. When I allow myself to accept life however it is presented, and then actively and willingly choose WHO I am in that context, my happiness increases. One of the patients on a ventilator, Dr. Lodish, states

> Much of this boils down to whether or not one can hang on to who one is…In fundamental ways, I feel totally unchanged. Quintessentially, I have found that ambulation, movement, swallowing, eating, talking, breathing, and self care are not me. They are substantial physical losses; but they are not me. [3]

It is specifically because Dr. Lodish identifies himself as more than this body and its functions, that he is able to embrace and love all aspects of his life. The changes in his physical body have not diminish his own self love.

Self Love

Just like Dr. Lodish, we have the choice of declaring our own self love in every moment of life. Who are you in this moment? Your answer will create your life.

Are you willing to unconditionally love *yourself?* We are conditioned to serve others, especially if we grow up female. Your answer to this question determines the rest of your life. If you are not willing to love yourself, how can you possibly know how to love others?

You must first experience love in the core of your being. It is who you are. I have yet to meet a human who is not love. Even the most fear-laden, seemingly hateful being, was once a small child seeking love. That child is still present, though perhaps buried beneath pain and self-hatred.

Those of us who seek to see the light in each being must first see the light in ourselves. That is where the work resides, for we have all grown up in a culture of domination and pain, where self-love was confused with conceit and self-delusion. In actuality, the conceited person behaves that way precisely because he doesn't love himself. If he did, there would be no need to try to prove to the world his own worth. When you truly love yourself, your own worth is self evident, as is the worth of all. There is no "better than", because when bathed in love, there is no separation… there is only unity and oneness.

That is the secret to self love. It doesn't lead to conceit. On the contrary, it leads to wholeness and oneness with all. Self love and love of all, are synonymous. Love is love. It has no opposite. It is the source and essence of everything.

Don't Should on me.

As I've learned to love myself, I've begun to see the ways in which I haven't acted in a loving way towards myself and others. Some of these realizations have been

That which we call genius is simply the willingness to be lost in the Oneness of All without definitions of self, sense of direction, or expectation of discovery.

Dr. David Bohm
Physicist

If we hate ourselves we can never love others, for love is the gift of oneself. How will you make a gift of that which you hate?

William Sloane Coffin

shocking, as I've slowly realized that many of my actions have had the exact opposite affect than what I desired. Here is one example.

At one of my recent birthdays I received a totally unexpected yet absolutely perfect gift. The entire day was a celebration of the senses, yet hidden under my joy was the ever-present sadness that my birthday celebration did not match my expectations. I realized later that the extent to which I held on to my expectations matched my inability to be fully present in the moment. I was denying myself the experience of appreciating the pleasures of the moment whenever my attention was focused on loneliness or disappointment. What a subtle but effective way of not honoring myself!

I realized I held many expectations of how those "who love me" *should* act. I believed there was a connection between their actions and their love. I saw everything they did through a test: Did their actions indicated enough appreciation for me?

As a result, I learned that many of my closest friends and family members sometimes felt as if on trial when around me… were they "doing it right?" With great sorrow I saw how I have tested many of the people I love in this way.

With gratitude I understood just how insidious the belief of unworthiness can be. When I re-focused my attention from looking for reasons to validate the unloving beliefs I held about myself to focusing attention on the gifts beneath my perceived circumstances, those hidden gifts were finally revealed.

I am not your teacher, your teacher is within you, and all around you. Learn to see the Beauty in You.

--Yogi Bhajan

Approval and Value come from Within

Another realization I made was that I had always looked outside myself for approval. This meant that I was always a puppet of everyone else's thoughts and actions. I could feel elated one moment and totally devastated the next… all based on how I *perceived* the circumstances around me, especially how others reacted to me. My perception was always through the lens of being an unappreciated victim, so that is exactly what I experienced. I did not approve of myself. If I did, I wouldn't have been motivated to search outside myself for approval.

As long as I insisted on judging my value based on what I perceived as other's reactions, I would never be able to truly experience my own value, to see the contribution I made by simply BEing me.

I realized that I don't want anyone to *ever* feel they have to perform in a certain way for me, *for any reason*. **Honoring all life means I honor each person's choice – including my own. It means that I choose not to manipulate anyone's choice in any way.**

Life as an Onion

I've noticed that just when I think I've understood something – life hands me another layer of the story. As I peel back one layer of meaning and experience the lessons learned, I am always guaranteed another level of meaning awaits. It is a humbling and now joyous realization.

The circumstances of my life have absolutely nothing to do with anything, because I create all meaning in my life; I draw all conclusions, in fact… I write the script. I *am* responsible for how I think and act and I wouldn't have it any other way. Realizing this has given me a tremendous sense of freedom. I always have the *choice* in any moment to create anew.

My self-worth is never in question because it simply is. Put another way, the very concept of self-worth is based on the erroneous belief that there is something other than self-worth to experience. Yet when I remember that "I" am One with all, there is no "self" to find worthy or unworthy. There is no judgment to be made. Self simply is and Self has no boundaries.

I am not worthy of love… I am love.

Finally I perceive that I am free to truly celebrate the part of me that expresses in any way. I am free from the need to identify a "me" at all. As a result I am also free from fear about how this identity is perceived, and free to live life fully engaged in the creative moment of now. Suddenly *every moment* has become a celebration of *all*, and *nothing is excluded.*

> "…Our deepest fear is not that we are inadequate. Our deepest fear is that we are powerful beyond measure. It is our light, not our darkness, that most frightens us. We ask ourselves, who am I to be brilliant, gorgeous, talented, fabulous? Actually, who are you *not* to be? You are a child of God. Your playing small doesn't serve the world. There's nothing enlightened about shrinking so that other people won't feel insecure around you. We are all meant to shine, as children do. We were born to make manifest the glory of God that is within us. It's not just in some of us; it's in everyone. And as we let our own light shine, we unconsciously give other people permission to do the same. As we're liberated from our own fear, our presence automatically liberates others…"[5]

Children as Teachers

Who do you want to be? What attributes do you most value in others? Now declare them to be yours too. Be like a child and hold the wisdom of a child. Children live completely in the moment, and when you watch them pretend to be something…can you truly question whether they experience that moment as anything other than what they are pretending? Their experience IS exactly what they pretend, regardless of what you and I perceive them to be. Hence, suddenly my daughter becomes a unicorn. In that moment, in her reality, she IS a unicorn.

Think about it. What power of creation we each hold! Simply pretend to be the person you want to be… and you are!

- Do you want to be beautiful? See your own beauty.
- Do you want to be loved? Love yourself and see the love surrounding you everywhere. (It has always been there.)
- Do you want to have fulfilling and deep relationships with others? Be that relationship with yourself, and you will automatically open the space within to have the same kind of relationship with others. This is not magic. When you are deeply open to yourself, you are also open to others. When you are forgiving and tender with yourself, you are the same with others. Love is always inclusive, never exclusive.
- Do you want to BE unconditional love? Be unconditional love in your every thought, word, and action. Start with yourself.
- Do you want to be enlightened? How would an enlightened person be? BE enlightened right now.

To attain this additional blessing, you must realize that 'for righteousness sake' means 'for love's sake'. Whenever you stand firmly in the midst of a hardship, holding and expressing the love that you are, you will witness illusions falling away. Through being the love that you are, you are empowered to transcend your sufferings."

Glenda Green,
Love Without End

Life can be seen as complex, as simple, and all the stages in between. It is *all* true. You choose your own perception of life. Then live it.

Re-writing the Story

A few years ago, I was dismissed from a dream job that I thought would amount to my life's work. For a while I was devastated. Then, after I allowed myself to experience feelings of anger and grieving, I did something new. I re-wrote the story of the event.

The part of the experience I kept missing was that I, in a sense, "hired" those involved to fire me so that I could get on with writing this book. They did their job. After I allowed myself to feel the emotions that flowed through me in waves, I had a choice. I could feel like a victim of the circumstances, or I could re-write the story, telling it the way I wanted to perceive it.

I became aware that my energy would serve the planet better by writing this book. It had been gestating inside me for almost a year (or lifetimes – depending on your perception), and it was ready to be birthed. So the new story was that I needed to write this book, therefore I arranged my life such that my job disappeared, no new job was available, and thus I was clearly available to write. No judgments, no make-wrong, no attachments, just a thought, "my life was following this path, and now its following another." This slight shift of perception allowed me to experience the exact same circumstances in a different way.

I now saw a new path in my life. Others could handle the job I was previously doing, but only I could write this book at this time, in this way. This was my true job at the moment, and the Universe had merely stepped in and made a slight adjustment to my job description. All that was left to do was to trust the change, embrace it, and whole-heartedly plunge into the adventure. Who is that "Universe" I referred to above? Give it any name you'd like, including Self. It really doesn't matter. What matters is that I accepted life's energy flow instead of fighting it. I flowed *with* the current, and thus was able to harness the power of that flow. It was a lot easier and a lot more fun than fighting what IS.

Once I chose to re-write my "story" from the stand point of choice; in other words, seeing myself as choosing to write a book instead of choosing to do my previous job, I was instantly transformed from a victim to the creator of my own life. Importantly, *none of the circumstances changed at all.*

Gratitude for Lessons Learned

On New Year's Eve, I paused for a moment to honor the previous 365 days and all they had taught me. I would like to share that journal entry with you now.

> I have learned to see myself as more than this body and name. As my perceptual abilities have increased, because I chose to focus attention on them this year, I have begun to see that I am an integral part of all life. The reverse is also true. I can point to no boundary between the molecules that make up what is commonly referred to as "me", and those that make up all life. We energy BEings breathe each other in, digest each other, and influence each other simply by our consciousness. Therefore, this year the definition of what constitutes "me" expanded to encompass more than my imagination can hold… the field of all possibilities and the manifestation of all that is.

If you want to hold the beautiful one, hold yourself to yourself.

When you kiss the Beloved, touch your own lips with your own fingers.

The beauty of every woman and every man is your own beauty.

Rumi
RUMI Like This – 43 Odes- Versions by Coleman Barks #2061

As the field of all possibilities has unfolded before me, the limitations of how I experience this world – my perceptions – have continued to expand. No longer held by the belief that all that can be perceived falls within the limits of scientific inquiry, my sense of space, matter, light, and time have all expanded beyond what I previously thought possible. Entire worlds now open themselves before me. Life literally sings when I allow it to. For this I am deeply grateful.

In previous years I have participated in a ritual at year's end where I wrote down thoughts I no longer wanted (those I held as negative or as no longer serving me) so that I could burn them in a physical ceremony honoring my 'letting go" of the negative. This year I will do just the opposite. Instead of judging any of my thoughts as "not serving me" or "negative", I want to honor them all for the great teachers they have been. Instead of passing judgment over any of my thoughts, beliefs, ideas, or actions, I want to finally call home to myself all parts of me that I have previously neglected, forgotten, shunned, ignored, hidden, shamed, judged, or disowned. (That includes all manifestations of those characteristics that I see in others.) **The dis-membering of this BEing is over, the re-membering has begun**. Today I love and celebrate ALL, not just that which I judge to be worthy, but ALL, for **I have learned that all is important and worthy. There is no less-than in life. Life is love expressed**. That means ALL LIFE, not just some of it. Therefore, tonight at this ceremony marking a passage of linear time, I embrace ALL into my BEing. I acknowledge that I am whole and complete, lacking nothing. I celebrate the ONEness, Beauty, and Perfection of ALL.

This year I have finally found my voice. It has taken a long time to warm up and get ready to speak, but that moment has finally arrived. In embracing my voice, I let go of the ownership of it, or any other part or concept of "me". What speaks through me, what lives and breathes this BEing is beyond my understanding; and at the same time, is simply and perfectly unconditional love. It is the voice of the ONE that now speaks, especially when I allow it consciously to do so.

This year I have learned more about trust. It seems to be the heartbeat of all manifestation, and is synonymous with love.

This year I have allowed myself to experience vulnerability, fear, and larger wounds than ever before. This willingness has also allowed greater forgiveness, understanding, connection, and healing to take place on a more conscious level of awareness than ever before. **I am beginning to see that all wounds are missed-perceptions; and that all healing – no matter what form it takes – is the result of a shift in perception.** The first step in creating that shift is the willingness to do so. The second it to tell the truth.

This BEing has learned to see the love that has always been present, the support, the ONEness, the unity, and the Perfection. And these experiences were not held as if "outside" the self, but instead, the entire concept of separation, of duality, of anything other than All-That-Is began to look as illusory as smoke.

Therefore, on this night of recognition, (as subjectively chosen as all moments are that we hold separately as more significant than others); I celebrate this BEing's recognition of the humor, folly, and joy of life; the impossibility of ever understanding anything, and the equally real knowingness that all is already known. This BEing bows in eternal gratitude for the magnificence of ALL, and celebrates the love that binds all experience/ experiencer together in that spiral dance called life. All is magic. All is illusion. All is love. All is ONE. All simply and perfectly IS.

If you are irritated by every rub, how will you be polished?

*Mevlana Rumi
(1207-1273)*

*Namaste means:
I honour that place in you where the whole Universe resides. And when I am in that place in me and you are in that place in you, there is only one of us.*

–Anonymous

Notes

1. NON-VIOLENT COMMUNICATION, A LANGUAGE OF COMPASSION, by Marshall Rosenberg, ©1999 by Puddle Dancer Press, page 119
2. THE TWELVE STAGES OF HEALING, Donald Epstein quotes holistic physician and psychiatrist George L. Hogben in SPIRITUAL ASPECTS OF THE HEALING ARTS, pg. 4
3. LOVE WITHOUT END, Glenda Green, page 238
4. Living for Today, Locked in a Paralyzed Body, By John Schwartz and James Estrin, © New York Times, November 7, 2004
5. Marianne Williamson, Return to Love. Nelson Mandela used this quote in his inaugural address.

BELOVED

When the sky,
like the softness of my innermost being
caresses the stars on a moonless night,
I remember the beloved's sighs
in the gentle north wind.

The quivering leaf
beholds the majesty of the smallest ant,
as the beauty of the beloved's perfection
sends tears of joy
at the witnessing of such wonder.

Then, all I know disappears
into the swelling of my pulsing heart,
and I stand, naked before God,
surrendering my ego
on the alter of aliveness.

Tenderly, the Beloved calls me to the mirror
where I behold my own reflection
in his face.
"This is the truth you have been seeking",
he replies,
to my unasked questions of doubt.

And while the "I" that was
melts into the All that is,
we smile at the simple joy
of embracing our ONEness.

29
SERVICE

Anybody who has ever mattered,
Anybody who's ever been happy,
Anybody who's ever given any gift into the world
Has been a divinely selfish soul,
Living for his own best interest.
No exceptions.

Richard Bach , Illusions

SERVICE

In true service, giver and receiver are the same.

The goals of service are inclusive and nourishing: to honor diversity, protect the environment, and enrich our nation's educational, social, and economic policies so that they enhance human dignity. On a personal level, volunteering—the very act of caring and doing—makes a substantial difference in our individual lives because it nourishes the moral intelligence required for critical judgment and mature behavior.

Arthur I. Blaustein
Serve Your Community *from* MoveOn's 50 Ways to Love Your Country, *2004, page 105-106.*

Service is deeply rooted in the dominator model of religions and cultures. Those in service learned to subjugate their own needs for the needs of others. We romanticize this notion in film and literature. In fact, the concept of service has become so engrained in our culture, that one can often hear the dictum, "God first, others second, me third". Most often the God in this quote refers to a deity, often male, outside of self, whose desires were dictated to the masses through a strictly controlled hierarchy of male leaders.

Yet there is another way of seeing service, that honors the very essence of the concept. In his book, *Illusions*, Richard Bach places the following words into the mouth of his Reluctant Messiah, "Anybody who has ever mattered, anybody who's ever been happy, anybody who's ever given any gift into the world has been a divinely selfish soul, living for his own best interest. No exceptions."[1] This seemingly incendiary statement inspires further analysis.

All Giving is Reciprocal

I believe Richard Bach is stating that when one truly looks at the concept of giving, there is always a gift in return. It could be as simple as a great feeling of having contributed, or it could be the joy of knowing that for the moment, suffering in a given instance has been reduced. No matter what the circumstances, the gift of giving or serving can always be found to provide the giver with some reciprocal gift in return. Check this out yourself. Look at instances in your life where you feel you were of service or truly gave of yourself. What did you receive in return?

Those who make service a regular part of their lives will be the first to tell you of the multitude of blessings they receive in return. Additionally, the quality of balance in the energy exchanged seems to determine the experience of completion and wholeness for the parties involved. In other words, true service empowers the receiver, it offers a way in which the separation between giver and receiver blur such that the energy exchanged feels balanced to all involved.

Giving as an Expression of Oneness

I believe Bach's quote can lead us to a deeper meaning of service. If we allow ourselves to see our lives as players on a stage, then the people in our lives are players also. They are not just the role they are playing at any one moment, but also something bigger that includes any number of roles. We all are. Moreover, just as actors are aware of the overall storyline and the need for each role to be performed a certain way – so that the main character can learn; perhaps on that deep level of awareness that unites us all, we can each become aware of the "storyline" being performed in our everyday lives.

A playwright adds characters only when needed to further the storyline. We can see the players in our lives as gifts to further our life lessons or storyline. They are the mirrors that reflect Self, just as the characters in a play allow the protagonist to understand himself through his interaction with them.

In this context, when we choose to *serve* another player on the stage, many gifts are available to us, including:

1. An opportunity to learn
2. Recognition of our wholeness and abundance (for surely we must already have if we are able to give)
3. Access to the divine energy of interconnectedness, our Oneness, that level of awareness outside the roles we seem to be playing.

The opportunity available here is to see the beggar on the street, the friend in need, the charity, the sick, etc. as a *gift* to each of us. It is not about our experiencing how wonderful we are (although that is a by-product of service); it's about recognizing how wonderful the recipient is in offering us a deeper experience of the magnificence of our lives. Who then is serving whom?

A Tsunami of Reciprocity

When a good friend of mine returned from relief work in Sri Lanka following the December 2004 earthquake and tsunami, he brought back several stories from the experience that beautifully illustrate true service.

Amidst all the pain and suffering that everyone experienced in the tiny Tamil-controlled village in which he was working, he was most impressed with the people's ability to express joy in the moment, even though most of them lost family, belongings, shelter, food, access to potable water, and had been relying on international aide for their most basic needs for quite awhile. He wrote:

> A lady and I were in the main community tent in the Refugee Camp (kind of an irony considering they're in their own country and are refugees), and it was an absolutely smoldering hot day. It was even hotter inside the tent. Out of no where this little girl appeared and handed us a plastic bottle which she had filled with water. She also brought her own little cup, and offered it to us so we could re-hydrate ourselves. This simple offering was unbelievably kind, but what made it more special was that water was a rare commodity there. Water was trucked in about three times a day into a few medium-sized containers. It was used very sparingly. Nevertheless, this sweet little girl offered us water with her *own* cup!!

> In another story, there was a smaller girl (about thigh high), who came around offering five cookies (which we probably gave her). She offered *all 5 cookies* to our entire group without keeping one to herself! I mean, cookies for a little girl here is something to googoo gaga over. She was willing to give us (who had everything by comparison) all that she had. You could tell just by looking into her eyes what absolute selfless love she had towards us when she was offering these cookies. They have nothing, and are still willing to offer us anything they get.

> What a truly humbling and life changing experience those two incidents were! I have never seen such an example of pure, unhindered, selfless love in my entire life.

What a perfect example of reciprocity in action! My friend risked his life to enter Tamil country (he is Singhalese, but has lived most of his life in the USA) in a selfless act of courage to help people who some Sri Lankans would consider "the enemy," only to receive one of the greatest gifts of his life: "pure, unhindered, selfless love." Although many of the relief workers came from cultures that often judge success through accumulation of material objects, the gifts offered by those *receiving* the international aide was just as great – perhaps even life transforming.

There was a time when I was in need of self-development and so I gave myself a lot of people to teach. I was immature so I reached for responsibility and challenge. I was alone and so I opened my arms for people to hug. I am not altruistic. In fact I don't even believe in altruism. I believe that the greatest thing I can do for myself is to help someone else out of my own selfish need to experience the helping. And the beauty of it is when I help my children while blanketed with that attitude I'm never foolish enough to go and miss the fun part because I'm too busy worrying about what I will get back. I get to love my children because it feels good and for no other reason than that.

Lynette Louise,
Jeff: A Sexually Realized Spiritual Odyssey of Stepping Into Love,
www.lynettelouise.com/excerpts.html.

The energy of Honoring All is always expansive, so is the energy of true service.

Community service helps us to integrate our idealism and realism. An idealist without a healthy dose of realism tends to become a naïve romantic. A realist without ideals tends to become a cynic. Service helps us put our ideals to work in a realistic setting.

Arthur I. Blaustein
Serve Your Community
from
MoveOn's 50 Ways to Love Your Country, 2004, page 105-106

One of the greatest ways we can honor all life is to be a stand, in every action, for the magnificence of each person. *Therefore, the highest service we can offer anyone is whatever allows them to experience their own magnificence.* It's not about what WE think they need, it's about what honors and enhances their experience of themselves.

For example, a habitual drunk may think that another drink is what he needs. Since I don't know the context of his life, for all I know, I might choose to drink if I was in his position also. Yet sometimes the biggest gift we can offer another person is simply to listen without judgment and with a keen intent on understanding what is real for that person. It could be possible that the greatest gift I could give that person - one that offers him the highest experience of his own self-worth - may be to simply sit down with him and listen to his story as a witness to his journey. The quest and privilege is to participate in that experience without judgment. In so doing, we can experience our own magnificence, as well as his. If, when we give, the recipient doesn't feel included, loved, and more whole through the experience, then we have failed to serve.

Every Moment as an Expression of Service

Let's look even closer at this phenomenon. In order to perceive a giver and receiver, one must assume separation. However, once you embrace the experience of ONEness, the illusion of separation disappears, and with it, the idea of giver/receiver.

Honoring All Life then becomes an acknowledgment of the divinity in all. Service becomes a choice, not a rescue operation, and certainly not an act of noblesse oblige (giving out of a sense of duty.)

A conscious person's thoughts shift from, "how can I serve?" to "how do I declare who I am in this moment, and in so doing, express the ONEness of All-That-Is?" The actions may look the same, but one comes from a space of a "have" helping a "have-not" hierarchy (separation), while the other comes from a space of honoring and ONEness, the very essence of which naturally expresses as an action that serves.

Thus, if I am choosing to define myself as unconditional love, then every action becomes a service expressing unconditional love. If I am choosing to define myself as abundance, then every action comes *from* abundance. And when the intention of my actions is to empower an experience of life's magnificence for everyone and everything I meet, then every action *is* service. It is a natural expression of who we are.

Awakening to Social Justice

The beauty of human beings is never more apparent than when we serve each other. Because I've lived in such privilege compared to most people, I was not aware of the prevalence of social injustice through out the world. Even in my own country, although I knew society was stratified and unjust at times, I didn't fully understand that the system is often set up as a no-win experience for many people. I still cannot honestly say I understand the fullness of that experience.

Yet with new-found compassion I can begin to address what I perceive as social injustice as it comes within my field of awareness. Knowing that my world is a reflection of myself, I can take responsibility for the world I have helped create, by beginning to do whatever I can to create a world that truly reflects my intention to honor all. I can make choices that bring me joy and reflect the abundance and love I know to be real. Most importantly, I can focus my attention on choices that reflect the world I want to live in – while releasing attention on judging what I don't want.

Here are a few of the programs that have touched my heart in the past few years. I mention them because they are examples of people taking responsibility for the quality of their lives in innovative and multi-disciplinary ways. These programs represent a new wave of service in which those served are seen as whole, complete beings, honored fully for the gift they bring to us all. I am deeply moved by their courage and self-love – a love and trust of the human spirit so strong that its rippling effect moves throughout each community privileged to be a part of their world, changing lives in its wake.

Literacy for Environmental Justice (LEJ)[3]

I met Dana Lanza and the LEJ kids at the Bioneers Conference in 2003. There they were, beaming a joy for life I rarely see in teens, let alone kids from the inner city. They were part of a panel discussing the impact of environmental and social injustice on their lives, and the kids were some of the most articulate, empowered speakers presents that day. And why not? Since it's inception in 1998, LEJ has led over 5,000 public school students in neighborhood improvement initiatives, hosted workshops and conferences on youth empowerment, community involvement, and environmental justice.

Living in one of the most polluted areas of the San Francisco Bay, which just happens to also be one of the most beautiful, the kids told stories about what their lives were like living in what was formerly one of the Navy's dumping grounds.

They discussed the fact that Hunters Point produces much of the city's electricity at the Hunters Point Power Plant, and that their 21 schools and more than 38 community centers are located within 3 miles of the Hunters Point Shipyard. Both of these businesses deal with toxins, yet there are no emergency response or evacuation plans currently in place in the event of a toxic environmental exposure.

They told stories of how their neighborhoods are low on grocery stores that offer fresh healthy produce, but high on little half-boarded-up neighborhood stores that offer alcoholic drinks and tobacco products. They pointed out that a single mother with toddlers would have to ride several buses, making multiple transfers, for at least an hour just to go grocery shopping for high-quality fruits and vegetables. How likely would it be, under those circumstances, for her to trail her children through the bus system and return home carrying groceries in her arms? How can she afford to do so when most of the jobs at both the power plant and shipyard – two of the larger employment opportunities in the area - require skills that most residents don't possess and for which training doesn't exist?

Because the power plant is the largest stationary polluter in San Francisco, the students have developed a program aimed at shutting it down. Through their efforts

Don't ask yourself what the world needs.

Ask yourself what makes you come alive, and then go do that.

Because what the world needs is people who have come alive.

Harold Thurman Whitman

involving an organized march, hosting an Earth Day Renewable Energy Fair, and conducting a youth-led environmental justice training for over twenty-five State Representatives from five separate agencies, they have persuaded the initiation of an environmental justice mandate for SF power plants.

LEJ defines Environmental Justice as "the right of all people to their basic needs: clean water, healthy food, non-toxic communities, open space, safe energy, and equitable educational and job opportunities." Isn't that what we all want?

What is especially powerful about Dana's programs is that they are often youth-led, highly creative, always educational, and exceptionally empowering. Because LEJ programs involve hands-on learning experiences in usable life-skills, they provide a wonderful model for educational programs wishing to honor both the participants and their specific location.

La Donna Redmond and the Institute for Community Resource Development (ICRD), Chicago, Ill.

From 1984 to 1994, California built 21 prisons, and only one state university...the prison system realized a 209% increase in funding, compared to a 15% increase in state university funding.

The Justice Policy Institute (1996)

The U.S. has both the largest prison population and the highest rate of incarceration in the world, including China and Russia. The U.S. incarcerates people at a rate more than 15 times that of Japan, and its prison population is more than eight times that of Italy, France, the UK, Spain, and Australia combined.

International Socialist Review

http://www.thirdworldtraveler.com/Prison_System/Prison_System.html

The Institute's mission is to rebuild the local food system. ICRD projects include: building grocery stores that bring access to sustainable products to urban communities of color, organizing farmers markets, converting vacant lots to urban farm sites and distributing local grown produce to restaurants. LaDonna Redmond is president and CEO of the ICRD. Redmond began researching the food system in order to feed her severely allergic son. She found that her African-American neighborhood of Austin on Chicago's West Side offered $200 sneakers, semiautomatic weapons, heroin, but no organic tomatos. The entire community of approximately 117,000 residents is served by only one major supermarket, but many fast food restaurants. The connection between lack of healthy food and the community's high rate of obesity, diabetes, and hypertension became clear. Along with starting a local farmers market, prompting the Chicago Public Schools to re-evaluate access to junk food, and starting ICRD, she and her husband also grew 40,000 lbs. of produce in the urban garden they helped create.

A recent recipient of a W.K. Kellogg Foundation grant, Redmond has teamed up with five Chicago universities to study Austin's broader food needs. Says Redmond, "Eating is a political act."

Ella Baker Center for Human Rights[4]

Named after one of the less-known but highly effective civil rights heros who believed in empowering individuals to speak out, the Ella Baker Center for Human Rights (EBC) has a three-part mission:

1. to document, expose and challenge human rights abuses in the United States criminal justice system;
2. to build power in communities most harmed by government-sanctioned violence; and
3. to develop and advocate for proactive, community-based solutions to systemic "criminal injustice."

The Ella Baker Center provides grassroots organizing, direct-action mobilizing, media advocacy, public education, cultural activism, policy reform and legal services.[12]

The creative approach to finding solutions to problems inherent in our social systems at the Ella Baker Center is inspiring. Take, for example, their Books Not Bars "Alternatives for Youth" Campaign, a statewide effort to transform the California prison system for youth. Citing the failure of the current system to rehabilitate youth who get into trouble, the Books Not Bars program intends to replace that system with a model that truly works, one based on helping and rehabilitating kids instead of punishing, abusing, and humiliating them.

Using Missouri's successful new model as a guide, the plan includes the following: replacing youth prisons with small-scale regional residential programs run by youth advocates, with no more than 40 beds at each location. Since the desire is to rehabilitate instead of humiliate, youth will receive counseling, educational assistance, therapy, and job training at the same current cost per youth that California now spends. Most importantly the kids experience no violence, no chemical weapons, and no cages that tell them they are unworthy to be treated with honor and tenderness. Missouri's new program yields a low 15 percent repeat-offender rate compared to California's current rate of 91 percent.

If we were not so single minded about keeping our lives moving, and for once could do nothing, perhaps a huge silence might interrupt this sadness of never understanding ourselves and of threatening ourselves with death.

Perhaps the earth can teach us, as when everything seems dead in winter and later proves to be alive.

Pablo Neruda

Prison statistics in the USA are not pretty. We hold the unfortunate title of being the country that imprisons more of its own citizens than any other, including those governments labeled "evil" by our own government. When we learn to treat our prison population with honor, seeing them as whole people – many of whom are from a cultural structure that doesn't always serve their best interests – then perhaps they will begin to see themselves as whole and worthy of honor too. Only people who love themselves are able to truly love others, because their actions aren't constant reactions to their own inner pain.

Many people don't realize just how terrible our prison system is, and many more don't want to know. Here are some statistics:

On December 31, 2003, there were 2,085,331 people in U.S. prisons and jails. That's a rise of 2.6% during the 12 previous months. Federal prisons are growing almost 5 times faster than state prison populations.

As of that same date, the U.S. incarceration rate was 714 per 100,000 residents. But when the statistics are broken down by race, it becomes clear that incarceration is not an equal opportunity punishment.

U.S. incarceration rates by race, June 30, 2003:

- Whites: 376 per 100,000
- Latinos: 997 per 100,000
- Blacks: 2,526 per 100,000

Gender is an important "filter" on the who goes to prison or jail, June 30, 2003:

- Females: 119 per 100,000
- Males: 1,331 per 100,000

Look at just the males by race, and the incarceration rates become even more frightening, June 30, 2003:

- White males: 681 per 100,000
- Latino males: 1,778 per 100,000

- Black males: 4,834 per 100,000

When the statistics are restricted to only males aged 25-29 by race, the situation becomes even more clear. As of June 30, 2003 the rate was:

- For White males ages 25-29: 1,607 per 100,000.
- For Latino males ages 25-29: 3,719 per 100,000.
- For Black males ages 25-29: 12,809 per 100,000. (That's 12.8% of Black men in their late 20s.)

In an international comparison, for example South Africa under Apartheid when it was internationally condemned as a racist society, the rates reveal:

- South Africa under apartheid (1993), Black males: 851 per 100,000
- U.S. (2003), Black males: 4,834 per 100,000

What does it mean that a leader of the "free world" locks up its Black males at a rate 5.7 times higher than the most openly racist country in the world?[3] What does that say about the equality of our democracy or our core beliefs about each other? What a prime opportunity to re-design our society so that all feel included and honored!

A further look at the statistics reveal lessons about who we are willing to jail. The US Federal Bureau of Prisons (BOP) offers the following September 2004 statistics on types of Offenses (calculated for those with offense-specific information available): [5]

Drug Offenses	88,619	(54.1%)
Weapons, Explosives, Arson	20,128	(12.3%)
Immigration	17,745	(10.8%)
Robbery	10,204	(6.2%)
Extortion, Fraud, Bribery	7,191	(4.4%)
Burglary, Larceny, Property Offenses	7,051	(4.3%)
Homicide, Aggravated Assault, and Kidnapping Offenses	5,363	(3.3%)
Miscellaneous	3,251	(2.0%)
Sex Offenses	1,702	(1.0%)
Banking and Insurance, Counterfeit, Embezzlement	1,072	(0.7%)
Courts or Corrections (e.g., Obstructing Justice)	728	(0.4%)
Continuing Criminal Enterprise	614	(0.4%)
National Security	97	(0.1%)

Note how roughly only 27.2% were incarcerated for violent crimes (weapons, explosives, arson, robbery, burglary, homicide, kidnapping, assault, sex offenses). Over half were jailed as a result of the so-called "war on drugs" that has done nothing to lower drug use but has succeeded in ruining many lives while filling our jails.

Additionally, with the increasing use of low-wage prison labor by major corporations, the economic benefits of filling our jails becomes ethically questionable.

It is time we ask how we can best serve each other rather than dismiss and negate each other. Only then can we experience our full potential.

The Center for Young Women's Development and Lateefah Simon.[6]

Founded in 1993, this San Francisco based collective of service providers work primarily with young and adult women in the juvenile and criminal justice systems. Since 1997 CYWD has honored the intelligence and wisdom of those they serve by asking them to assume responsibility for its direction. Thus, CYWD became one of the first youth run social service organizations in the nation.

The successful transformation for those involved, from young previously incarcerated women who worked the street economies and may not have finished school, to community leaders who actively participate in social solutions, has made this model highly insiring and effective. As they serve each other, they create a space in which deep healing and collective envisioning can walk hand-in-hand.

The outgoing Executive Director, Lateefah Simon, is a dynamic example of self-empowerment. Named a 2003 MacArthur Fellow, she is a tireless voice for the too-often over-looked young women caught within our dominator-trance culture that sometimes issues policies without first looking at the broader picture.

As a result, some programs simply ignore them, while other policies seem designed to deliberately dis-empower young women of color. For example, with little incentive to stay in school, young low-income women are often pressured to produce an income any way they can. For many that means engaging in activities that lead to incarceration. Yet when released, those very same young women who desperately need the comfort and support of family members in order to pull their lives together, find that they can no longer live with their parents if they are receiving federal housing aid. CYWD works to create alternatives that keep young women from feeling they have no choice but to return once more to life on the streets.

Their programs range from a sister-to-sister outreach program offering support and mentoring for those currently incarcerated, (who often also experienced violence and need healing themselves); to employment training; criminal justice education; and various networking programs to empower and educate each other.

When things look most bleak, CYWD provides young women the caring attention needed to heal, learn from personal experience, and intelligently create a brighter future.

Notes

1. Page 170, Illusions by Richard Bach
2. William Shakespeare Topic: Proverbs Source: As You Like It (Jaques at II, vii)
3. http://www.lejyouth.org/ Literacy for Environmental Justice
4. http://www.ellabakercenter.org/page.php?pageid=56 Statistics as of December 31, 2003 from Bureau of Justice Statistics, November 2004, NCJ 205335, [PDF] Table 1 on page 2. (http://www.ojp.usdoj.gov/bjs/pub/pdf/p03.pdf) Statistics as of June 30, 2003 from http://www.ojp.usdoj.gov/bjs/abstract/pjim03.htm, Tables 1, 14 and 15; Calculation for rates by race uses Table 13 and Census Bureau population estimates http://www.census.gov/popest/national/asrh/NC-EST2003/NC-EST2003-03.pdf [PDF] for 2003. South Africa figures from http://www.druglibrary.org/schaffer/other/sp/abb.htm, Americans Behind Bars: The International Use of Incarceration 1992-1993 by Marc Mauer, Assistant Director, The Sentencing Project, September 1994. All references to Blacks and Whites are for what the Bureau of Justice Statistics and U.S. Census refer to as "non-Hispanic Blacks" and "non-Hispanic Whites".) Additonally, the following statistics reflect the imbalance these policies create regarding the quality of our democracy:

   a.   There are nearly four million persons currently or permanently disenfranchised as a result of laws that take away the voting rights of felons and ex-felons.
   b.   No other democracy besides the US. disenfranchises convicted offenders for life. Many democratic nations, including Denmark, France, Israel and Poland, permit prisoners to vote as well.
   c.   Nearly three-quarters (73 percent) of the disenfranchised are not in prison but are on probation, on parole or have completed their sentences.
   d.   1.4 million African American men -- 13 percent of the adult African American male population -- have lost the right to-vote, a rate of disenfranchisement that is seven times the national average. By comparison, in the 1996 general election 4.6 million African American men voted.
   e.   In Florida one in three African American men has permanently lost the right to vote.
   f.   In five states Iowa, Mississippi, New Mexico, Virginia, and Wyoming one in four black men (24% to 28%) have permanently lost the right to vote.
   All above statistics are from http://www.thirdworldtraveler.com/Prison_System/Prison_System.html

5. FEDERAL BUREAU OF PRISONS http://www.bop.gov/fact0598.html#Inst
6. http://www.cywd.org/about_us/staff.html

30

THANK YOU FOR BEING YOU

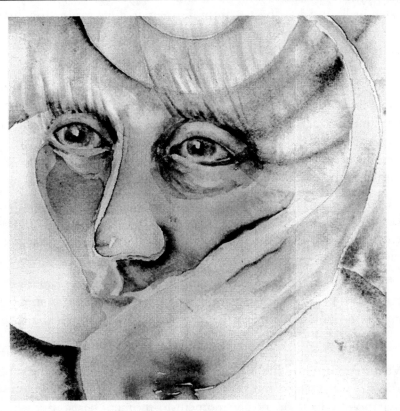

Thank you for all I have learned by being with you,
interacting with you, and having you in my life.
Everything I experienced from you has been a gift
and has provided value and context in my life.

THANK YOU FOR BEING YOU

There isn't a molecule on Earth that does not support us.
We have the choice at every moment to experience our environment
as a wonderland of pulsating energy… of love.

One Breath Time

Every day we do things, we are things that have to do with peace.

If we are aware of our life…, our way of looking at things, we will know how to make peace right in the moment, we are alive.

Thich Nhat Hanh

Israeli artist Emilio Mogilner's life has led him to make some powerful changes in the way he approaches art. No longer willing to separate the choices we make, individually and as a species, from his own creative expression, his art has become a metaphor for who we choose to be *in this moment*. Painting only what he can within one held breath, he exemplifies our planetary "last gasp." Metaphorically representing our own self-suffication through addictive thinking, narrowly focused perceptions, and spiritual denial, his paintings also powerfully express the creative possibility contained within one focused moment. And what a moment! As his oxygen runs out, his body shifts to survival mode, technique and contemplated actions are replaced by the transcendent energy of pure creativity. He states, "This is the only breath that I have for survival…This is the only breath that can lead the human race to social and environmental revolution." [1]

Seeing an opportunity to shift perceptions, Mogilner now leads "1 Breath Time" workshops with children and adults of Arab, Palestinian, and Jewish backgrounds in which he assists them in visualizing their core beliefs and revealing their essential life mission.

Offering one of the most simple and direct methods to reach one's essential Self, his workshops help open that space in which we can see our commonality and the interconnection of all life with understanding and compassion for all involved.

Perceiving the Essence

When our vision of life is brought down to the essential aspects of one moment, with survival at stake, our perception can't help but change. Honoring All Life is an invitation to do so on a daily, moment-to-moment basis. But what does that look like in everyday reality?

In the chapter on Transportation, we touched on the idea of seeing deeper into form, specifically cars. I'd like to take that discussion a bit further, focusing on the gift offered.

When driving, if I focus on each object within my view, I am forced to really see it. It is no longer part of a massive visual panorama, it now becomes a living subject of deeply focused attention. Instead of seeing just the surface presentation, I allow myself to see with "new eyes," focusing on the molecules and energy of each object.

Suddenly a street sign becomes molecules of metal mined from the Earth. Windows become silicon sand particles from our beaches. Motor vehicles become Earth-based materials (dead dinosaurs - oil, metals, and other natural resources) caressing the human within while serving humanity by moving individuals through space. In fact, the entire environment becomes a planetary life-dance, with humanity being served in a most generous manner.

Whether I agree with a particular choice of natural resource use or not, I can still recognize the service rendered, and celebrate with genuine gratitude. **The energy with which we humans encounter our environment and the attitudes we each bring to any given situation significantly alter the quality of that experience.**

David Suzuki[2] likes to remind us that we are made of the same elements as everything else; we eat the same recycled molecules, breathe the same atmospheric elements that all Earth life has respirated throughout history, use the by-products of photosynthesis every time we consume any form of energy, and circulate the same water through the mostly-water life-forms on this mostly-water planet. Seen through his scientific perceptual filter, the interconnectedness of all expressions of life stand blatantly revealed. As he says, "We ARE the environment." If that is so, then coloring our perception of life with anything other than gratitude, clouds that truth.

Honoring all life requires approaching each situation with a *neutral* stance, neither pro nor con, but simply accepting of what is. Thus, whether I agree that petroleum-based vehicles are a life-supporting choice of locomotion or not, honoring all life requires that I *consciously acknowledge the gift* inherent in our use of natural resources to produce such vehicles. When I see a car as Earth protectively encapsulating a human while facilitating movement, the energy involved is significantly different than if I see that same car as symbolic of all that is wrong with the world. When I acknowledge the gift of the molecules and energy involved in the creation and use of that car, the energetic experience is very different than when I resent the car and see it as a vile and disgusting material form that I wish did not exist.

Where does this lead us? When we humans allow ourselves to see life straight-on, without judgments of right and wrong, we effect the energy present in profound ways. We are then free to see the gifts bestowed upon us by all life.

Acknowledging the Service Offered

Think about the horse for a moment. Although humans often refer to the need to "control" the horse, and "show him who's boss", the reality is quite different. The horse is a huge animal out-weighing the human riding by multiples of pounds. The idea of "controlling" a horse is an illusion. The only reason the horse allows the human to ride is either through fear of pain or through willingness. When you think about the thousands of years the horse has served humanity, gratitude seems the only appropriate reaction.

The Gratitude Shift

So what does it mean to feel gratitude for what is? It requires a shift of perception from judging things, to simply acknowledging them with gratitude. It calls us to appreciate the gift of the present moment and the lessons available in that moment. Thus, a car can be seen as a reminder of many things:

• That Earth's natural resources serve and support us daily

• That there is always the opportunity to make choices that reflect the best of who we are.

• The fond memories we already carry regarding our experiences in cars.

Out of those realizations, I am free to choose many things whenever a car is the focus of my attention:

• I can choose to send gratitude directly back to the Earth for the use of natural resources and the support to fulfill my desires (whatever they are). This recognition of support is a new concept for any humans - the realization that *the Earth – in fact everything – supports each of us in a very intimate and immediate manner every single moment.*

• I can recognize that my thoughts and actions do not yet fully express my desire to support life in all ways. In that knowing, I can change my focus of attention to creating what DOES fill my heart with joy.

• I can choose to feel gratitude for these reminders and renew my efforts to honor all life.

Feeling the Energy

Beyond awareness of my reactions to various forms, I can also choose to bring my awareness to the energy of each form. When I do, I find that the energy of all form is neutral – or put another way – is simply love.

It seems that only humans emanate a vast range of emotions. And boy do we ever! When my heart is open, I can often feel the emotional energy of others so strongly that they sometimes seem to shout at me. Even then, I can choose to hold the experience as a gift. We always have the option of choosing to see each being with compassion, and when we do, we experience our own self-compassion. **When we choose to consciously see everything/everyone without judgment, we automatically see through the eyes of compassion. What greater form of honoring can we offer?**

My Inner-Voice confirmed these thoughts:

Your practice of seeing all as perfect as you drove home Monday was a beautiful example of oneness revealed. Literally everything you saw danced in aliveness and love. Every person revealed his/her inner light, whether acknowledged by that person consciously or not. Every blade of grass sang hosannas of love to the sun, air, and earth. Life vibrated with life. Do you understand the dance your heart witnessed? It was not unique, but simply revealed. It is the dance that celebrates all life, the joyous "song of nature," and it is literally the embodiment of all that is.

When you thanked each thing for BEing, you accepted fully what is; you saw through the illusion of outer appearance and witnessed the energy that is the signature of existence. This is the energy beyond form, for it comes from the unmanifest divine.

When you perform the simple act of acknowledging this energy, you break the illusion of form and the significance humans place on it. Allow yourself to practice this honoring often. It is your next step in awareness.

Notice that you came home and ceased seeing your own daughter and son in this light. It is the result of your habit of seeing those associated with you as less-than, for your old habit saw yourself as "less-than". Know that your children are the magnificence of the Universe, the ONEness of All-That-Is, as are you. Everything/Everyone is. There is no separation anywhere, anytime. All simply IS. All is sacred. Let this seep deeply into your being.

We *are* the Process

A friend of mine killed herself recently. She was one of those vibrantly alive people who willingly shared her enthusiastic caring for people and life in a larger-than-life way. Where others wrote letters to the editor about injustices or causes they believe in, she created non-profit organizations and wrote one-woman plays that she hoped to tour nationwide. She was always wanting to "save the world," and in many ways I believe her effervescent love touched so many hearts that her mission was accomplished. Yet I wonder if she ever understood that it was not what she DID, but *who* she *was* that really made a difference in our lives.

Ultimately, that is what will be remembered about us all – not what we did or said – but who we were. It is the *process*, the way in which we live moment-to-moment, that is more important than what we accomplish when all those moments are summed; *who we choose to be* in every moment is far more important than what we do.

A perfect example of this is a woman, now called Amma, who was born in India in 1953. Recognizing the suffering and pain that lies within every human – no matter what their story – she has dedicated her life to offering what she can to alleviate suffering. For thirty years she has traveled around the world offering the simplest of gestures – a hug – to anyone who comes to her. While each person probably finds a uniquely individual healing within her arms – one exclusive to their needs and situation (ranging from the experience of infectious illness, poverty, loss, disillusionment, and *all* other experiences of the human condition), all find acceptance and love.

> Once a press reporter asked Amma how was it possible for her to embrace each and every one in the same loving way, even if they were diseased or unpleasant. Amma replied, " When a bee hovers over a garden of varied flowers, what it beholds is not the difference between the flowers but the honey within them. Similarly Amma sees the same Supreme Self in each and every one." [3]

What better gifts can we offer each other than those: acceptance, love, and gratitude for the gifts therein? I believe Amma is expressing what is at the heart of all humans: unconditional love and acceptance – a simple recognition of What IS.

The Next Step

My next experiment will involve using this walking meditation daily. What will life look like if I actively choose to thank everything and everyone for simply and perfectly BEing?

Every night before sleeping I practice thanking everything within my perception for its gift. Included within this group are my children, my body; the air I breathe; the water I drink; the bed, pillow, and sheets I sleep on; every molecule of my house; and all who support and make those experiences and things possible. I have expanded

this practice to include the systems of life — those interconnected cycles of being and manifestation, energy flows, and relationships that constitute my experience of life. As I allow myself to sink into the realization that everything affects everything, I remember that I am supported by all life — that in a very real sense...I literally AM the expression of all life — we each are.

Therefore, let us honor each other and ALL life by offering the following:

- Unconditional love to all (including self)

- Gratitude for all (on all levels of perception)

- The willingness to live our lives as an expression of that love and gratitude in every choice we make — with every breath we take.

This new experiment, then, takes my daily practice just a step further. It is the step I have been shy and reluctant to pursue because it demands that I tell the truth about what I know of life, by actively and openly offering gratitude to all I meet. So I now offer all who have walked beside me in this lifetime the statements with which I began this book:

> **Thank you for BEing YOU**. Thank you for all I have learned by being with you, interacting with you, having you in my life — whether I experienced it as fun or difficult; positive or negative; challenging to everything I embrace, or as an ecstatic affirmation of what I embrace as real. Everything I experienced from you has been a gift and has provided value and context in my life.

> **I love you**. Underneath everything that has been said and done between us, is love. I recognize that the core of our beings IS love. I appreciate the richness and magnificence I experience in both you AND me when I allow myself to simply and fully BE present with you.

If I say this to people, what will they think? At this point, any fears I hold about how this practice will be judged by some are far outweighed by my growing need to simply acknowledge the beauty and perfection of life around me — all life.

The Gift Realized

This morning I visited our local Grower's Market. It was alive with activity. Vendors were selling their wares – food and crafts they lovingly grew or created. Friends were busy meeting and catching up on each other's life story. The air hummed with joy and abundance. As I walked through the stalls, I almost burst into tears at the love I felt. The light and love that is the essence of humanity radiated so brightly through everyone. What a *privilege* it is to participate in this adventure together!

This is who we are. At this point I can no longer separately define the following words: love, acceptance, trust, gratitude.

They all hold the same meaning, and at our essence,… they describe us and all of life. These, I am sure, are the lyrics to the Song of Nature; our song… the one that bursts forth from our hearts whenever we allow ourselves to simply BE.

I share these words with you, trusting that you will take what resonates deeply within, and discard the rest.

Notes

1. Paul Schmelzer, <u>Last Gasp - One breath for revolution</u>, Adbusters Magazine. http://www.adbusters.org/magazine/54/features/breath.html . Also see Mogilner's website: www.1breathtime.com.
2. See David Suzuki's books, <u>The Sacred Balance</u> and <u>You Are The Earth.</u>
3. From her website: **http://www.amma.org/amma/index.html**

REFERENCES & RESOURCES

The following resource list is included as an example of various Perceptual Filters. Please keep in mind that any statistics included are those of the people who created them. They are part of their experience of reality, and will become part of yours only if you so choose. The following resource list is by no means complete and is organized by chapter alphabetically. Most descriptions came directly from the websites cited. Please use these sources as signposts pointing you in the direction you may want to go for further research. If I've missed some of the best resources, please forgive me. I encourage you to use this section as a springboard to your own passionate inquiry into how to live honoring all.

AVOIDING THE VOID

SCIENTISTS

DEAN RADIN   Consciousness Research
Senior Scientist at the IONS Campus and author of *The Conscious Universe*. http://www.psiresearch.org/CRL.htm and http://www.ions.org/

NASSIM HARAMEIN Physics
http://www.theresonanceproject.org/home.htm

DR. ELISABET SAHTOURIS: Evolution biologist
For her writings, see http://www.ratical.org/LifeWeb/

DR. WILL KEEPIN Mathematical physics, Transpersonal Psychology, Eastern Meditation Disciplines, Applied Systems Analysis, and Environmental Science
http://www.satyana.org/about.html
The Satyana Institute is a non-profit service and training organization. Their mission is to support individuals, communities, and organizations to combine inner work of the heart with outer service in the world.

F. DAVID PEAT Physics
http://www.fdavidpeat.com/index.htm

DAVID BOHM Physics http://www.david-bohm.net/

DR. KARL H. PRIBRAM Holonomic Brain Theory
Brain/behavior research, Neurophysiology and Physiological Psychology
http://www.georgetown.edu/departments/psychology/faculty/pribram.html

DR. HUMBERTO MATURANA - Cognition
http://www.inteco.cl/biology/ and
http://www.matriztica.org/

DR. FRANCISCO VARELA - Cognition
http://web.ccr.jussieu.fr/varela/

Articles on Neurophenomenology and First person Methods
http://web.ccr.jussieu.fr/varela/human_consciousness/articles.html

THE MIND AND LIFE INSTITUTE
http://www.mindandlife.org/index.html The Mind and Life Institute is dedicated to fostering dialogue and research at the highest possible level between modern science and the great living contemplative traditions, especially Buddhism. It builds on a deep commitment to the power and value of both of these ways of advancing knowledge and their potential to alleviate suffering.

CENTER FOR CONSCIOUSNESS STUDIES
http://consciousness.arizona.edu/

JOHN E MACK INSTITUTE
http://www.johnemackinstitute.org/
The John E. Mack Institute explores the ways in which perceptions and beliefs about reality shape the human condition.

UNIION OF CONCERNED SCIENTISTS
http://www.ucsusa.org/global_security/nuclear_weapons/page.cfm?pageID=1384 UCS is an independent nonprofit alliance of more than 100,000 concerned citizens and scientists. We augment rigorous scientific analysis with innovative thinking and committed citizen advocacy to build a cleaner, healthier environment and a safer world.

The following scientists contributed to the film, What the Bleep Do We Know?
http://www.whatthebleep.com/scientists/

WILLIAM A. TILLER   Physics and Psychoenergetics
http://www.tiller.org/

JOSEPH DISPENZA Neurology, Neurophysiology and Brain function   www.drjoedispenza.com

CANDACE PERT   Physiology, Molecular Biology, Biophysics
http://www.candacepert.com/

AMIT GOSWAMI Physics
http://darkwing.uoregon.edu/~its/

JOHN HAGELIN Physics   http://www.hagelin.org/
Author of *Manual for a Perfect Government*.

FRED ALAN WOLF Physics   http://www.fredalanwolf.com/

DAVID ALBERT The Philosophical Foundations of Physics
Author of *Quantum Mechanics and Experience* and *Time and Chance*.

MASARU EMOTO
http://www.masaru-emoto.net/english/entop.html
Although his techniques have yet to go through peer review, Dr. Emoto's work offers a possible evidence that thoughts and feelings affect PHYSICAL reality.

STUART HAMERHOFF Brain/Mind Science
http://www.quantumconsciousness.org/

JEFFREY SATINOVER Psychiatry
http://www.satinover.com/

ANDREW B NEWBERG   Co-authored, *Why God Won't Go Away: Brain Science and the Biology of Belief* and *The Mystical Mind: Probing the Biology of Belief*. Both books explore the relationship between neuroscience and spiritual experience.

DR. DANIEL MONTI Psychiatry and Human Behavior
http://www.jeffersonhospital.org/cim/article5017.html

DR. BRUCE LIPTON http://www.brucelipton.com/index.php
Author of THE NEW BOOK! BIOLOGY OF BELIEF :
Unleashing the Power of Consciousness, Matter and Miracles

BUSINESS

**ACKOFF CENTER FOR ADVANCEMENT OF SYSTEMS
APPROACHE**S   http://www.acasa.upenn.edu/

MANAGEMENT WISDOM
http://www.managementwisdom.com/index.html
Exploring the ideas of W. Edwards Deming and other
pioneers in systems thinking and its application.

*All of the information below is taken, with permission, from
the **Global Exchange** Website:*
http://www.globalexchange.org/index.html

Top Ten Reasons to Oppose
the Free Trade Area of the Americas
http://www.globalexchange.org/campaigns/ftaa/topten.html.pf

*In recent years, representatives from 34 countries have
been working to expand the North American Free Trade
Agreement (NAFTA) to Central America, South America and
the Caribbean. The Free Trade Area of the Americas (FTAA)
is another example of the free-market fundamentalism that
has created a global race-to-the-bottom that threatens the
environment, families' livelihoods, human rights, and
democracy. Once again, a sweeping "free trade" agreement
is in the works that puts commercial interests above all other
values.*

1. The FTAA Expands a Proven Disaster

The FTAA is essentially an expansion of NAFTA. But NAFTA
has proven to be a nightmare for working families and the
environment. A look at NAFTA's legacy shows why these
kinds of "free trade" agreements should be opposed.
Working families suffer: In the US, more than 765,000
jobs have disappeared as a result of NAFTA. When these laid
off workers find new jobs, they earn 23 percent less on
average than at their previous employment. In Mexico,
manufacturing wages fell 21 percent from 1995 to 1999, and
have only started to recover. The percentage of Mexicans
living in poverty has also grown since NAFTA went into
effect. **The environment suffers:** In the maquiladora
zones along the US-Mexico border, the increased pollution
and the improper disposal of chemical wastes have
dramatically raised rates of hepatitis and birth defects.
NAFTA should be repealed, not expanded.

2. The Agreement Is Being Written Without Citizen
Input

Despite repeated calls for the open and democratic
development of trade policy, the FTAA negotiations have
been conducted without citizen input. A process has been
set up to solicit citizens' views, but there is no real
mechanism to incorporate the public's concerns into the
actual negotiations. The public has been given nothing more
than a suggestion box. At the same time, however,
hundreds of corporate representatives are advising the US
negotiators and have advance access to the negotiating

texts. While citizens are left in the dark, corporations are
helping to write the rules for the FTAA.

3. The Agreement Will Undermine Labor Rights and
Cause Further Job Loss

The NAFTA experience demonstrates how basic labor rights
and the interests of working families are eroded by "free
trade" agreements that lack enforceable labor protections.
Corporations move high-paying jobs to countries with lower
wages and bust unionization drives with threats to transfer
production abroad. According to a Cornell University study,
since NAFTA two-thirds of manufacturing and
communications companies faced with union organizing
campaigns threatened workers with moving their jobs
abroad. This "race-to-the-bottom" will accelerate under the
FTAA as corporations pit exploited workers in Mexico against
even more desperate workers in countries such as Haiti and
Guatemala. Already, Mexico is losing maquiladora jobs to
countries with cheaper wages. In the last two years, some
280,000 jobs have vanished with the closure of more than
350 maquiladoras.

4. The Agreement Will Exacerbate Environmental
Destruction

The export-driven growth model promoted by "free trade"
agreements and the policies of the World Bank and the IMF
have destroyed ecosystems around the world. Under this
unsustainable model, many countries in the Global South cut
down their forests, overfish their waters and exploit other
natural resources to pay off foreign debts. Since NAFTA, 15
US wood product companies have set up operations in
Mexico, and logging there has increased dramatically. In the
Mexican state of Guerrero, 40 percent of the forests have
been lost in the last eight years, and massive clear cutting
has led to soil erosion and habitat destruction.

5. The Agreements Will Hurt Family Farmers

NAFTA has been a disaster for small farmers in the US and
Mexico. By favoring the interests of agribusiness
corporations over the needs of family farmers, NAFTA's
model of export-oriented agriculture has slashed farmers'
income. Between 1995 and 2000, the prices US farmers
receive for corn declined 33 percent, 42 percent for wheat,
and 34 percent for soybeans. No wonder that since NAFTA
went into effect 33,000 small farmers in the US have gone
out of business more than six times the pre-NAFTA rate. In
Mexico, the price farmers receive for corn has plummeted 45
percent in three years as agribusiness giants dump their
subsidized corn there. At least half a million farmers have
left their land. The FTAA threatens to make this crisis worse
by encouraging even more overproduction.

6. The Agreement Will Lead to Privatization of
Essential Services   The FTAA is expected to force
countries to privatize services such as education, health
care, energy and water. Such privatization would especially
harm working class communities and communities of color.
In some countries, these privatizations are already
occurring, and those least able to pay for vital services are
the ones who suffer the most. When the Bolivian city of
Cochabamba privatized its water utility, water rates
increased 200 percent. In the ensuing protests, police shot
and killed a 17-year-old student.

7. The Agreement Will Jeopardize Consumer and
Environmental Protections   NAFTA includes

unprecedented ways for corporations to attack our laws through so-called "investor-to-state" lawsuits. Such suits, established by NAFTA's Chapter 11, allow corporations to sue governments for compensation if they feel that any government action, including the enforcement of public health and safety laws, cuts into their profits. Already, Chapter 11 lawsuits have been used to repeal a Canadian law banning a chemical linked to nervous system damage, and to challenge California's phase-out of a gas additive, MTBE, that is poisoning the state's ground water. Negotiators want to include these anti-democratic lawsuits in the FTAA.

8. The Agreement Will Spread the Use of GMOs

US trade negotiators are trying use the FTAA to force other countries to accept the use of genetically modified organisms (GMOs). But environmental groups warn that these technologies haven't been adequately tested, and food security experts say GMOs could increase hunger in poor nations. Farmers have traditionally saved their seeds from year to year, but as multinational corporations patent GM seeds these farmers will be forced to pay for seeds, pushing them further into dependency.

9. The Agreement Will Increase Poverty and Inequality
"Free trade" is not working for the majority of the world. During the most recent period of rapid growth in global trade and investment-1960 to 1998-inequality worsened internationally and within countries. Without debt cancellation and rules to curtail rampant capital speculation, countries in the Global South will remain dominated by the Global North, inequality will increase, and the hope of achieving sustainable development will be farther off.

There Are Proven Alternatives Policy makers and pundits often try to convince us that corporate globalization is inevitable. In fact, the current economic processes known as "globalization" have been defined and driven by a very small number of corporations. Now people around the world are creating an alternative grassroots globalization. Citizens' groups from across the Western Hemisphere have written an "Alternative Agreement for the Americas" that offers a picture of what socially responsible and environmentally sustainable trade would look like. You can find the document on the www.hsa-asc.org website. To learn more about the FTAA and what you can do to stop it, visit our background section, or contact us at 415-255-7296 or ftaa@globalexchange.org.

Top Reasons to Oppose the WTO
http://www.globalexchange.org/campaigns/wto/OpposeWTO.html.pf

1. The WTO Is Fundamentally Undemocratic
The policies of the WTO impact all aspects of society and the planet, but it is not a democratic, transparent institution. The WTO rules are written by and for corporations with inside access to the negotiations. For example, the US Trade Representative gets heavy input for negotiations from 17 "Industry Sector Advisory Committees." Citizen input by consumer, environmental, human rights and labor organizations is consistently ignored. Even simple requests for information are denied, and the proceedings are held in secret. Who elected this secret global government?

2. The WTO Will Not Make Us Safer
The WTO would like you to believe that creating a world of "free trade" will promote global understanding and peace. On the contrary, the domination of international trade by rich countries for the benefit of their individual interests fuels anger and resentment that make us less safe. To build real global security, we need international agreements that respect people's rights to democracy and trade systems that promote global justice.

3. The WTO Tramples Labor and Human Rights
WTO rules put the "rights" of corporations to profit over human and labor rights. The WTO encourages a 'race to the bottom' in wages by pitting workers against each other rather than promoting internationally recognized labor standards. The WTO has ruled that it is illegal for a government to ban a product based on the way it is produced, such as with child labor. It has also ruled that governments cannot take into account "non commercial values" such as human rights, or the behavior of companies that do business with vicious dictatorships such as Burma when making purchasing decisions.

4. The WTO Would Privatize Essential Services
The WTO is seeking to privatize essential public services such as education, health care, energy and water. Privatization means the selling off of public assets – such as radio airwaves or schools – to private (usually foreign) corporations, to run for profit rather than the public good. The WTO's General Agreement on Trade in Services, or GATS, includes a list of about 160 threatened services including elder and child care, sewage, garbage, park maintenance, telecommunications, construction, banking, insurance, transportation, shipping, postal services, and tourism. In some countries, privatization is already occurring. Those least able to pay for vital services – working class communities and communities of color – are the ones who suffer the most.

5. The WTO Is Destroying the Environment
The WTO is being used by corporations to dismantle hard-won local and national environmental protections, which are attacked as "barriers to trade." The very first WTO panel ruled that a provision of the US Clean Air Act, requiring both domestic and foreign producers alike to produce cleaner gasoline, was illegal. The WTO declared illegal a provision of the Endangered Species Act that requires shrimp sold in the US to be caught with an inexpensive device allowing endangered sea turtles to escape. The WTO is attempting to deregulate industries including logging, fishing, water utilities, and energy distribution, which will lead to further exploitation of these natural resources.

6. The WTO is Killing People
The WTO's fierce defense of 'Trade Related Intellectual Property' rights (TRIPs)—patents, copyrights and trademarks—comes at the expense of health and human lives. The WTO has protected for pharmaceutical companies' 'right to profit' against governments seeking to protect their people's health by providing lifesaving medicines in countries in areas like sub-saharan Africa, where thousands die every day from HIV/AIDS. Developing countries won an important victory in 2001 when they affirmed the right to produce generic drugs (or import them if they lacked production capacity), so that they could provide essential lifesaving medicines to their populations less expensively. Unfortunately, in September 2003, many new conditions were agreed to that will make it more difficult for countries to produce those drugs. Once again, the WTO demonstrates that it favors corporate profit over saving human lives.

7. The WTO is Increasing Inequality
Free trade is not working for the majority of the world. During the most recent period of rapid growth in global trade and investment

(1960 to 1998) inequality worsened both internationally and within countries. The UN Development Program reports that the richest 20 percent of the world's population consume 86 percent of the world's resources while the poorest 80 percent consume just 14 percent. WTO rules have hastened these trends by opening up countries to foreign investment and thereby making it easier for production to go where the labor is cheapest and most easily exploited and environmental costs are low.

8. The WTO is Increasing Hunger Farmers produce enough food in the world to feed everyone – yet because of corporate control of food distribution, as many as 800 million people worldwide suffer from chronic malnutrition. According to the Universal Declaration of Human Rights, food is a human right. In developing countries, as many as four out of every five people make their living from the land. But the leading principle in the WTO's Agreement on Agriculture is that market forces should control agricultural policies-rather than a national commitment to guarantee food security and maintain decent family farmer incomes. WTO policies have allowed dumping of heavily subsidized industrially produced food into poor countries, undermining local production and increasing hunger.

9. The WTO Hurts Poor, Small Countries in Favor of Rich Powerful Nations The WTO supposedly operates on a consensus basis, with equal decision-making power for all. In reality, many important decisions get made in a process whereby poor countries' negotiators are not even invited to closed door meetings – and then 'agreements' are announced that poor countries didn't even know were being discussed. Many countries do not even have enough trade personnel to participate in all the negotiations or to even have a permanent representative at the WTO. This severely disadvantages poor countries from representing their interests. Likewise, many countries are too poor to defend themselves from WTO challenges from the rich countries, and change their laws rather than pay for their own defense.

10. The WTO Undermines Local Level Decision-Making and National Sovereignty The WTO's "most favored nation" provision requires all WTO member countries to treat each other equally and to treat all corporations from these countries equally regardless of their track record. Local policies aimed at rewarding companies who hire local residents, use domestic materials, or adopt environmentally sound practices are essentially illegal under the WTO. Developing countries are prohibited from creating local laws that developed countries once pursued, such as protecting new, domestic industries until they can be internationally competitive. California Governor Gray Davis vetoed a "Buy California" bill that would have granted a small preference to local businesses because it was WTO-illegal. Conforming with the WTO required entire sections of US laws to be rewritten. Many countries are even changing their laws and constitutions in anticipation of potential future WTO rulings and negotiations.

11. There are Alternatives to the WTO Citizen organizations have developed alternatives to the corporate-dominated system of international economic governance. Together we can build the political space that nurtures a democratic global economy that promotes jobs, ensures that every person is guaranteed their human rights to food, water, education, and health care, promotes freedom and security, and preserves our shared environment for future generations.

The Tide is Turning Against Free Trade and the WTO!

International opposition to the WTO is growing. Massive protests in Seattle of 1999 brought over 50,000 people together to oppose the WTO—and succeeded in shutting the meeting down. When the WTO met in 2001, the Trade negotiators were unable meet their goals of expanding the WTO's reach. The WTO met in Cancún, Mexico this past September 10–14, and met thousands of activists in protest and scoring a major victory for democracy. Developing countries refused to give in to the rich countries' agenda of WTO expansion – and caused the talks to collapse.

Top Ten Reasons to Oppose the IMF
http://www.globalexchange.org/campaigns/wbimf/TopTenIMF.html

What is the IMF?

http://www.globalexchange.org/campaigns/wbimf/TopTenIMF.html.pf   The International Monetary Fund and the World Bank were created in 1944 at a conference in Bretton Woods, New Hampshire, and are now based in Washington, DC. The IMF was originally designed to promote international economic cooperation and provide its member countries with short term loans so they could trade with other countries (achieve balance of payments). Since the debt crisis of the 1980's, the IMF has assumed the role of bailing out countries during financial crises (caused in large part by currency speculation in the global casino economy) with emergency loan packages tied to certain conditions, often referred to as structural adjustment policies (SAPs). The IMF now acts like a global loan shark, exerting enormous leverage over the economies of more than 60 countries. These countries have to follow the IMF's policies to get loans, international assistance, and even debt relief. Thus, the IMF decides how much debtor countries can spend on education, health care, and environmental protection. The IMF is one of the most powerful institutions on Earth – yet few know how it works.

1.   The IMF has created an immoral system of modern day colonialism that SAPs the poor

The IMF – along with the WTO and the World Bank – has put the global economy on a path of greater inequality and environmental destruction. The IMF's and World Bank's structural adjustment policies (SAPs) ensure debt repayment by requiring countries to cut spending on education and health; eliminate basic food and transportation subsidies; devalue national currencies to make exports cheaper; privatize national assets; and freeze wages. Such belt-tightening measures increase poverty, reduce countries' ability to develop strong domestic economies and allow multinational corporations to exploit workers and the environment A recent IMF loan package for Argentina, for example, is tied to cuts in doctors' and teachers' salaries and decreases in social security payments.. The IMF has made elites from the Global South more accountable to First World elites than their own people, thus undermining the democratic process.

2.   The IMF serves wealthy countries and Wall Street

Unlike a democratic system in which each member country would have an equal vote, rich countries dominate decision-making in the IMF because voting power is determined by the amount of money that each country pays into the IMF's quota system. It's a system of one dollar, one vote. The U.S. is the largest shareholder with a quota of 18 percent. Germany, Japan, France, Great Britain, and the US combined control about 38 percent. The disproportionate amount of power held by wealthy countries means that the interests of bankers, investors and corporations from industrialized countries are put above the needs of the world's poor majority.

3. The IMF is imposing a fundamentally flawed development model

Unlike the path historically followed by the industrialized countries, the IMF forces countries from the Global South to prioritize export production over the development of diversified domestic economies. Nearly 80 percent of all malnourished children in the developing world live in countries where farmers have been forced to shift from food production for local consumption to the production of export crops destined for wealthy countries. The IMF also requires countries to eliminate assistance to domestic industries while providing benefits for multinational corporations – such as forcibly lowering labor costs. Small businesses and farmers can't compete. Sweatshop workers in free trade zones set up by the IMF and World Bank earn starvation wages, live in deplorable conditions, and are unable to provide for their families. The cycle of poverty is perpetuated, not eliminated, as governments' debt to the IMF grows.

4. The IMF is a secretive institution with no accountability

The IMF is funded with taxpayer money, yet it operates behind a veil of secrecy. Members of affected communities do not participate in designing loan packages. The IMF works with a select group of central bankers and finance ministers to make polices without input from other government agencies such as health, education and environment departments. The institution has resisted calls for public scrutiny and independent evaluation.

5. IMF policies promote corporate welfare

To increase exports, countries are encouraged to give tax breaks and subsidies to export industries. Public assets such as forestland and government utilities (phone, water and electricity companies) are sold off to foreign investors at rock bottom prices. In Guyana, an Asian owned timber company called Barama received a logging concession that was 1.5 times the total amount of land all the indigenous communities were granted. Barama also received a five-year tax holiday. The IMF forced Haiti to open its market to imported, highly subsidized US rice at the same time it prohibited Haiti from subsidizing its own farmers. A US corporation called Early Rice now sells nearly 50 percent of the rice consumed in Haiti.

6. The IMF hurts workers

The IMF and World Bank frequently advise countries to attract foreign investors by weakening their labor laws – eliminating collective bargaining laws and suppressing wages, for example. The IMF's mantra of "labor flexibility" permits corporations to fire at whim and move where wages are cheapest. According to the 1995 UN Trade and Development Report, employers are using this extra "flexibility" in labor laws to shed workers rather than create jobs. In Haiti, the government was told to eliminate a

statute in their labor code that mandated increases in the minimum wage when inflation exceeded 10 percent. By the end of 1997, Haiti's minimum wage was only $2.40 a day. Workers in the U.S. are also hurt by IMF policies because they have to compete with cheap, exploited labor. The IMF's mismanagement of the Asian financial crisis plunged South Korea, Indonesia, Thailand and other countries into deep depression that created 200 million "newly poor." The IMF advised countries to "export their way out of the crisis." Consequently, more than US 12,000 steelworkers were laid off when Asian steel was dumped in the US.

7. The IMF's policies hurt women the most

SAPs make it much more difficult for women to meet their families' basic needs. When education costs rise due to IMF-imposed fees for the use of public services (so-called "user fees") girls are the first to be withdrawn from schools. User fees at public clinics and hospitals make healthcare unaffordable to those who need it most. The shift to export agriculture also makes it harder for women to feed their families. Women have become more exploited as government workplace regulations are rolled back and sweatshops abuses increase.

8. IMF Policies hurt the environment

IMF loans and bailout packages are paving the way for natural resource exploitation on a staggering scale. The IMF does not consider the environmental impacts of lending policies, and environmental ministries and groups are not included in policy making. The focus on export growth to earn hard currency to pay back loans has led to an unsustainable liquidation of natural resources. For example, the Ivory Coast's increased reliance on cocoa exports has led to a loss of two-thirds of the country's forests.

9. The IMF bails out rich bankers, creating a moral hazard and greater instability in the global economy

The IMF routinely pushes countries to deregulate financial systems. The removal of regulations that might limit speculation has greatly increased capital investment in developing country financial markets. More than $1.5 trillion crosses borders every day. Most of this capital is invested short-term, putting countries at the whim of financial speculators. The Mexican 1995 peso crisis was partly a result of these IMF policies. When the bubble popped, the IMF and US government stepped in to prop up interest and exchange rates, using taxpayer money to bail out Wall Street bankers. Such bailouts encourage investors to continue making risky, speculative bets, thereby increasing the instability of national economies. During the bailout of Asian countries, the IMF required governments to assume the bad debts of private banks, thus making the public pay the costs and draining yet more resources away from social programs.

10. IMF bailouts deepen, rather then solve, economic crisis

During financial crises – such as with Mexico in 1995 and South Korea, Indonesia, Thailand, Brazil, and Russia in 1997 – the IMF stepped in as the lender of last resort. Yet the IMF bailouts in the Asian financial crisis did not stop the financial panic – rather, the crisis deepened and spread to more countries. The policies imposed as conditions of these loans were bad medicine, causing layoffs in the short run and undermining development in the long run. In South Korea, the IMF sparked a recession by raising interest rates, which led to more bankruptcies and unemployment. Under the IMF imposed economic reforms after the peso bailout in 1995, the number of Mexicans living in extreme poverty increased more than 50 percent and the national average minimum wage fell 20 percent.

A list of other organizations working for democratic, socially responsible, and environmentally sustainable trade policies.

THE ALLIANCE FOR RESPONSIBLE TRADE
http://www.art-us.org/

THE HEMISPHERIC SOCIAL ALLIANCE (HSA)
http://www.asc-hsa.org/rubrique.php3?id_rubrique=11

CITIZEN'S TRADE CAMPAIGN
http://www.citizenstrade.org/

PUBLIC CITIZEN'S GLOBAL TRADE WATCH
http://www.citizen.org/trade/

JOBS WITH JUSTICE   http://www.jwj.org/

ALTERNATIVE FOR THE AMERICAS
http://www.web.net/comfront/alts4americas/eng/eng.html
A 54-page document outlining a progressive vision of socially responsible and environmentally sustainable international commerce, dated 1998.

Also see the 2002, 103-page full document: http://www.asc-hsa.org/castellano/download/42_Alternativas%20ene%2020 03%20english.pdf

This document addresses the major topics on the official agenda of current trade negotiations. They should be considered as a complete package of proposals for positive economic integration.

THE DEVELOPMENT GROUP FOR ALTERNATIVE POLICIES
http://www.developmentgap.org/

INSTITUTE FOR CENTRAL AMERICAN DEVELOPMENT STUDIES   http://www.icadscr.com/

CENTER FOR CORPORATE POLICY
http://www.corporatepolicy.org/

U.S. TRADE REPRESENTATIVE   http://www.ustr.gov/
The official government website of US trade negotiators

FREE TRADE AREA OF THE AMERICAS
http://www.ftaa-alca.org/   The official website.

HELSINKI PROCESS   http://www.helsinkiprocess.fi/

CITIZEN'S GLOBAL PLATFORM
http://www.globalplatform.fi/

COOPERATIVES

MONDRAGÓN CORPORACIÓN COOPERATIVA
http://www.mondragon.mcc.es/ing/quienessomos/historia.html

INTERNATIONAL CO-OPERATIVE ALLIANCE (ICA)
www.ica.coop
ICA has 236 member organisations from over 93 countries, representing approximately 725 million individuals worldwide. The ICA celebrated its Centennial in 1995 with the adoption of a new Statement of the Co-operative Identity including revised Co-operative Principles. These are:

1.   Voluntary and Open Membership
2.   Democratic Member Control
3.   Member Economic Participation
4.   Autonomy and Independence
5.   Education, Training and Information
6.   Co-operation among Co-operatives
7.   Concern for Community

NATIONAL COOPERATIVE BUSINESS ASSOCIATION (NCBA) http://www.ncba.coop/
Together, NCBA and its members represent more than **48,000 cooperatives, and the 120 million Americans** that own and control those cooperatives. The following overview and statistics come from the NCBA website:

Cooperatives Are...

In many ways, they are like any other business; but in several important ways they're unique and different.

Cooperatives—

o   Are owned and democratically controlled by their members-the people who use the co-op's services or buy its goods-not by outside investors;

o   Co-op members elect their board of director from within the membership.

o   Return surplus revenues (income over expenses and investment) to members proportionate to their use of the cooperative, not proportionate to their "investment" or ownership share.

o   Are motivated not by profit, but by service-to meet their members' needs for affordable and high quality goods or services;

o   Exist solely to meet the serve their members.

o   Pay taxes on income kept within the co-op for investment and reserves. Surplus revenues from the co-op are returned to individual members who pay taxes on that income.

Co-op Statistics

o   More than 30 cooperatives have annual revenue in excess of $1 billion, including such well-known names as Land O'Lakes, Inc., and ACE Hardware. The top 100 co-ops have a combined $125 billion in revenues.

o   Cooperatives range in size from large enterprises, including U.S. Fortune 500 companies, to single, small local storefronts.

o   270 telephone cooperatives provide service to two million households.

o   Some 250 purchasing cooperatives offer group buying and shared services to more than 50,000 independents businesses.

o   10,000 U.S. credit unions have 83 million members and assets in excess of $600 billion.

o   Cooperatives operate in every industry including agriculture, childcare, energy, financial services, food retailing and distribution, health care, insurance, housing, purchasing and shared services, telecommunications, and others.

o   About 30 percent of farmers' products in the U.S. are marketed through 3,400 farmer-owned cooperatives.

o   Nearly 1,000 rural electric cooperatives own and maintain nearly half of the electric distribution lines in the U. S., cover 75 percent of the land mass and provide electricity to 36 million people.

o   More than 1,000 mutual insurance companies, with more than $80 billion in net written premiums, are owned by their policyholders.

o   More than 6,400 housing cooperatives provide homes for more than one million households.

o   U.S. co-ops serve some 120 million members, or 4 in 10 Americans.

—   Statistics gathered from various sources as of October 2003.

THANKSGIVING COFFEE COMPANY
http://www.thanksgivingcoffee.com/justcup/fairtrade/why.lasso

WORLD SOCIAL FORUM:
http://www.forumsocialmundial.org.br/home.asp

BIONEERS   http://www.bioneers.org/

CHAORDIC COMMONS
http://www.chaordic.org/commons/CC-Princ.html

KAOSPILOTS   http://www.kaospilot.dk/docs/Values.asp

BUSINESS FOR SOCIAL RESPONSIBILITY
http://www.bsr.org/

DIGITAL ABORIGINAL: http://www.digitalaboriginal.com/

SOCIAL VENTURES NETWORK   http://www.svn.org/

CERES: http://www.ceres.org/
Our 85-member coalition and 70-plus partner companies share a core belief that environmental responsibility and corporate value are strongly linked, that the bedrock for sound corporate governance is measurement and disclosure, and that investors need complete and transparent information about a company's financial, social and environmental performance.

GLOBAL REPORTING INITIATIVE
http://www.globalreporting.org/
The Global Reporting Initiative (GRI) is a multi-stakeholder process and independent institution whose mission is to develop and disseminate globally applicable Sustainability Reporting Guidelines.

http://www.ceres.org/sustreporting/gri.php

The GRI's Sustainability Reporting Guidelines first released in draft form in 1999, represent the first global framework for comprehensive sustainability reporting, encompassing the **"triple bottom line"** of economic, environmental and social issues. In 2004, in part due to the efforts of Ceres, its Coalition and the Ceres companies, there are over 600 organizations who report using the GRI.

SUSTAINABLE HARVEST http://www.sustainableharvest.org/

FAIR TRADE FEDERATION:
http://www.fairtradefederation.com/

FTF Principles and Practices

FTF members are committed to the following principles and practices in their trading relationships:

FAIR WAGES
Producers are paid fairly for their products, which means that workers are paid at least that country's minimum wage. Since the minimum wage is often not enough for basic survival, whenever feasible, workers are paid a **living wage**, which enables them to cover basic needs, including food, shelter, education and health care for their families. Paying fair wages does not necessarily mean that products cost the consumer more. Since Fair Trade Organizations bypass exploitative middlemen and work directly with producers, they are able to cut costs and return a greater percentage of the retail price to the producers.

COOPERATIVE WORKPLACES
Cooperatives and producer associations provide a healthy alternative to large-scale manufacturing and sweatshops conditions, where unprotected workers earn below minimum wage and most of the profits flow to foreign investors and local elites who have little interest in ensuring the long term health of the communities in which they work. Fair Trade Organizations work primarily with small businesses, worker owned and democratically run cooperatives and associations which bring significant benefits to workers and their communities.

CONSUMER EDUCATION
Fair Trade Organizations educate consumers about the importance of purchasing fairly traded products which support living wages and healthy working conditions. By defining fair trade and conducting business in a manner that respects workers' rights and the environment, the fair trade movement strives to educate consumers about the often **hidden human costs of their "bargains."** They also educate consumers and policy makers about inequities in the global trading system.

ENVIRONMENTAL SUSTAINABILITY
Fair Trade Organizations encourage producers to engage in **environmentally friendly practices** which manage and use local resources sustainably. Many FTF members work directly with producers in regions of high biodiversity to develop products based on sustainable use of their natural resources, giving communities an incentive to preserve their natural environments for future generations.

FINANCIAL AND TECHNICAL SUPPORT
Small-scale farmers and artisans in the developing world lack access to affordable financing, impeding their profitability. FTF members that buy products directly from producers often provide financial assistance either through direct loans, prepayment or by linking producers with sources of financing. Unlike many commercial importers who often wait 60-90 days before paying producers, Many FTOs ensure prepayment so that producers have sufficient funds to cover raw materials and basic needs during production time. They also often provide other critical technical assistance and support such as market information, product feedback and training in financial management. Unlike commercial importers, FTOs establish **long term relationships** with their producers and help them adapt production for changing trends.

RESPECT FOR CULTURAL IDENTITY
Fair Trade Organizations encourage the production and development of products based on producers' cultural traditions adapted for Western markets. They seek to promote producers' artistic talents in a way that **preserves cultural identity.**

PUBLIC ACCOUNTABILITY
FTF members' finances, management policies, and business practices are **open to the public** and monitoring by the Fair Trade Federation.

Additional FAIR TRADE sites can be found at GLOBAL EXCHANGE
http://www.globalexchange.org/campaigns/fairtrade/links.html

SPIRIT IN BUSINESS:
http://www.spiritinbusiness.org/new/content/home.php

WORLD BUSINESS ACADEMY:
http://www.worldbusiness.org/

THE CONFERENCE BOARD:
http://www.conference-board.org/

SOCIETY FOR ORGANIZATIONAL LEARNING (SOL):
http://www.solonline.org/
The Society for Organizational Learning, is a nonprofit global membership organization that connects researchers, organizations, and consultants to create and implement knowledge for fundamental innovation and change. SoL was founded in 1997 as an outgrowth of the MIT Center for Organizational Learning. Peter Senge, author of The Fifth Discipline: the Art and Practice of the Learning Organization, was the founding chairperson.

ASSOCIATION FOR SPIRIT AT WORK:
http://www.spiritatwork.org/

LASSALLE INSTITUT:
http://www.lassalle-institut.org/indexeng.php

AKADEMIE HEILIGENFELD
http://www.akademie-heiligenfeld.de/

CENTER FOR CORPORATE SOCIAL RESPONSIBILITY
http://www.centreforcsr.org.sg/

ENCOUNTER OF WORLD VIEWS FOUNDATION:
http://www.encounterofworldviews.org/index2.php

EUROPEAN BAHA'I BUSINESS FORUM: http://www.ebbf.org/

ETHICAL MARKET PLACE
http://www.ethicalmarketplace.com/ *Ethical Marketplace*© is a new TV series about the revolution that is happening in the business and investment in the world – the new **"triple bottom line"**- respecting people and the environment while earning a profit. Also see
http://www.mediaventure.org/ethical_market.html

GLOBAL CHALLENGES NETWORK, Germany:
http://www.gcn.de/

HEARTLAND INSTITUTE, USA:
http://www.thoughtleadergathering.com/home.php

HEARTMATH LLC, USA: http://www.heartmath.com/

INNOVEST GROUP, USA: http://www.innovestgroup.com/

NET IMPACT, USA: http://www.net-impact.org/
Net Impact is a powerful and influential network of over 10,000 MBA students and professionals committed to using the power of business to create a better world.

PROGRESSIO FOUNDATION, Netherlands:
http://www.progressiofoundation.org/

RUDOLF STEINER FOUNDATION:
http://www.rsfoundation.org/

WORLD SPIRIT FORUM:
http://www.worldspiritforum.org/en/index.php. The WSF World Spirit Forum is an annual world congress for spiritually oriented leaders and participants from various fields such as science, economy, religion, culture, society and sports. The WSF World Spirit Forum defines itself as an independent but complementary event to the World Economic Forum in Davos.

CONTEMPORARY SLAVERY

ANIT-SLAVERY SOCIETY
http://www.anti-slaverysociety.addr.com/index.htm

Scale of African slavery revealed:
FROM: http://news.bbc.co.uk/2/hi/africa/3652021.stm

In Africa, children are twice as likely to be trafficked as women. The BBC's Imogen Foulkes in Geneva says the report found that **89% of the countries had trafficking to and from neighboring countries, but 34% also had a human trade to Europe.** Friday, 23 April, 2004

U.S. DEPARTMENT OF STATE REPORT
http://www.state.gov/g/tip/
Annually, at least 600,000 – 800,000 people, mostly women and children, are trafficked across borders worldwide, including 14,500 – 17,500 persons into the United States

CONTEMPORARY SLAVERY AND INVOLUNTARY SERVITUDE – GOVERNMENT RESOURCES
http://library.louisville.edu/government/subjects/humanrights/contslavery.html from University Libraries

For more Links, see THE FEMINIST SEXUAL ETHICS PROJECT
http://www.brandeis.edu/projects/fse/Pages/linkscontemporaryslavery.html#anchor_UN

Inclusiveness

WORLD ECONOMIC FORUM Global Corporate Citizenship Initiative
http://www.weforum.org/site/homepublic.nsf/Content/Global+Corporate+Citizenship+Initiative

LOHAS http://www.lohas.com/page/home.html
Lifestyles of Health and Sustainability (LOHAS) describes a $226.8 billion U.S. marketplace
http://www.lohasjournal.com/app/cda/nbp_cda.php

SOCIAL ACCOUNTABILITY 800 (SA8000)
www.cepaa.org   In 1996, SAI helped create Social Accountability 8000 (SA8000), a voluntary standard for workplaces based on ILO (International Labor Organization) and other human rights conventions.

ACCOUNTABILITY 1000 (AA1000)
http://www.accountability.org.uk/

AA1000 is intended to improve the accountability and overall performance of business firms by enhancing the quality of social and ethical accounting, auditing and reporting.

SUSTAINABLE VILLAGE   http://www.sustainablevillage.com/
The Sustainable Village is a "social enterprise." We donate/invest all profits for microfinance and microenterprise

projects in developing countries.

HAL Principles of Practice*

This Honoring All Life Business Guide* is offered as inspiration for creation of your own guiding principles:

1. **Provide survival and expression needs.** Ensure that all people have their survival (water, food, shelter, health care, etc.) and expressive (creative, spiritual, physical, and mental) needs met in a way that profits all stakeholders, and at the expense of none.

2. **Honor Interdependence.** Ensure that all human impact on the planet sustains, supports, and restores Life. All aspects of Earth (including the human) shall be seen as interdependent systems of aliveness – ultimately as ONE.

3. **Promote current and future Diversity.** Promote the health and diversity of all; not only now but for generations to come.

4. **Humbly learn from conflict.** Resolve conflict creatively, cooperatively, and non-violently by willingly and gratefully seeing conflict as an indication that there is more to perceive and understand – and then actively pursuing that understanding.

5. **Practice Transparency.** Freely and transparently exchange information and ideas, except in cases where it will cause more harm than good.

HAL Principles of Organization*

1. **Be Inclusive.** Anyone is free to participate as long as they are willing to own and follow the purpose and Principles of Practice adopted by the group.

2. **Follow your Passions.** Encourage people to participate in those organizations and projects that follow their passions. By doing so, we honor the gifts they offer and we benefit from their enthusiasm and creativity; while they experience deep fulfillment and acknowledgment of their value.

3. **Take full Responsibility.** Honor each group by encouraging full ownership of the goals, self-organization in any time or manner consistent with the goals, and self-assessment.

4. **Model Democracy.** Deliberations, discussions, and decisions should come from the entire group, honoring each person's input as valuable – including dissenting voices.

5. **Empower Magnificence.** Domination in any form is seen as counterproductive. Empower each other to work from the deepest most essential part of your being – your still, calm core of inner wisdom and love.

6. **Work Locally.** If it seems necessary to create a position of authority, do so from the most local level. Likewise, always perform all necessary functions and use resources from the most local level possible.

7. **Encourage Particpatory Design.** Encourage all stakeholders to participate in the design process.

* The Chaordic Commons Principles were the inspiration for the HAL Business Guide.

COMMONS

GEONOMY SOCIETY:
http://www.progress.org/geonomy/   If "economy" is literally "management of the household", then geonomy is "management of the planet". So far this year, four states have introduced geonomic bills: Connecticut, Maryland, Minnesota, and Oregon. In Oregon SJR 1 would go on the ballot at the next regular general election. If passed by voters, it would amend the Oregon Constitution to allow cities and counties to replace the uniform ad valorem property tax with one having different tax rates for land and for buildings. A local taxing district could set the rate on improvements at zero, creating a pure site-value tax in lieu of the conventional property tax. (From http://www.progress.org/geonomy/geonom134.htm, THE GEONOMIST, Vol. 13, No. 4, Editor: Jeffery Johnson Smith.)

TOMALES BAY INSTITUTE:
http://www.earthisland.org/tbi/

The mission of the Tomales Bay Institute is to develop an intellectual framework that includes the commons as well as the market and the state, and to inject that expanded framework into America's vision of possibilities.

EARTH RIGHTS INSTITUTE: http://www.greentax.net/

INTERNATIONAL UNION FOR LAND VALUE TAXATION AND FREE TRADE: http://www.interunion.org.uk/
All Citizens should have Equal Rights to the values of Common Property, and enjoy Individual Rights to the full Results of their Lawful Exertions; Domestic and Foreign Trade and Industry should compete as freely and efficiently as possible,

- without damaging nature,

- without injuring human health or life,

- without private capture of publicly created values,

- without private withholding of rent of *Common Property*.

REDEFINING PROGRESS – Environmental Tax Reform – A Market Based Solution
http://www.redefiningprogress.org/programs/sustainableeconomy/ETR.htm
The tax system offers many options for reducing uncertainty and better allocating environmental costs. In its broadest sense, "environmental tax reform" means lowering taxes on payroll, capital formation and clean energy technology, and financing those reductions with higher taxes on activities that hurt the environment. In addition, a portion of the revenues from environmental tax reform can be used to provide: transition for energy-intensive companies; assistance to low-income households; and incentives for business to achieve energy efficiency and develop cleaner technologies and processes.
There is solid proof that environmental tax reform and other market-based initiatives work. At the national level, taxes on ozone-depleting chemicals have reduced environmental destruction and provided a boost to clean technologies. States are increasingly adopting environmental tax initiatives, and nine European nations have changed their tax policies with measurable environmental and economic benefits. TAX POLICY COUNCIL
http://www.redefiningprogress.org/programs/sustainableeconomy/taxpolcoun.htm   REDEFINING PROGRESS –

Common Assets Program
http://www.redefiningprogress.org/programs/commonassets/
CREATIVE COMMONS   http://creativecommons.org/

SKY TRUST INITIATIVE:
http://www.usskytrust.org/
Guiding Principles of the Sky Trust:

o   The sky belongs to all of us equally.

o   The sky does not belong to private corporations or the federal government.

o   Pollution must be limited to what the sky can safely absorb.

o   Once limits are set, companies should pay for pollution permits. The money they pay should go into a trust.

o   The trust should pay equal dividends to all citizens.

COMMON ASSETS:
http://www.commonassets.org/template.php
Common assets are the invaluable assets we inherit as a community, rather than as individuals. Some are physical, others are social and human-made. They include the atmosphere, oceans and rivers, the electromagnetic spectrum, our democratic political system, roads and parking spaces, landscapes and soundscapes, wilderness and wild animals, our monetary and financial systems, our store of scientific knowledge, our languages and cultures, the Internet and many more. These assets, diverse as they are, share several notable traits:

o   They are all inherited - no individual or corporation made them.

o   Their economic value is enormous (probably greater than the value of all private and state-owned assets combined).

o   Their biological value is inestimable.

o   We have a collective responsibility to preserve these inheritances and pass them on, undiminished, to future generations (our heirs).

In most cases, no one is managing these assets on behalf of future generations.
In most cases, our common ownership of (and common responsibility for) these assets is not legally recognized. Common Assets brings local, regional and national movements together to activate the American public to defend the commons from misuse, privatization and destruction.

ALASKA PERMANENT FUND:
http://www.apfc.org/ What is the Alaska Permanent Fund?

GLOBAL COMMONS INSTITUTE: http://www.gci.org.uk/

CENTER FOR SCIENCE AND ENVRIONMENT (India):
http://www.cseindia.org/

DAVID BOLLIER: http://www.bollier.org/ and
http://www.silenttheft.com/ the website for his book,
Silent Theft: The Private Plunder Of Our Common Wealth.

ON THE COMMONS   http://www.onthecommons.org/

FRIENDS OF THE COMMONS
http://www.friendsofthecommons.org/

SECTION Z,   http://www.sectionz.info/ISSUE_5/
prepared by Ecotrust and called "Let's Reclaim the Commons." http://www.sectionz.info/ISSUE_5/content.html

CORNELL PARTICIPATORY ACTION RESEARCH NETWORK
http://www.einaudi.cornell.edu/cparn/about/purpose.asp

SOCIETY FOR PARTICIPATORY RESEARCH IN ASIA
http://www.pria.org/index.htm

SIMPLE LIVING –AWAKENING EARTH DUANE ELGIN
http://www.simpleliving.net/awakeningearth/

OREGON PROGRESS BOARD
http://egov.oregon.gov/DAS/OPB/
http://egov.oregon.gov/DAS/OPB/docs/2005report/05BBPR_PR.pdf or CONTACT: Jeff Tryens or Rita Conrad (503) 378-3201)

COMMUNICATION

COMPASSIONATE LISTENING PROJECT:
http://www.compassionatelistening.org/ Also read Hwoschinsky, Carol Listening with the Heart – A Guide For Compassionate Listening The Compassionate Listening Project, 2001.

CENTER FOR NONVIOLENT COMMUNICATION:
http://www.cnvc.org/ Also read Rosenberg, Marshall B. Nonviolent Communication – A Language of Compassion PuddleDancer Press 1999.

DAYS OF DIALOGUE
http://www.ci.la.ca.us/dodialogue/dialogue.htm

NATIONAL COALITION FOR DIALOGUE AND DELIBERATION
http://thataway.org/conference/index.html

THE DIALOGUE GROUP
http://www.thedialoguegrouponline.com/

STUDY CIRCLES http://www.studycircles.org/

ETHIC DIALOGUE
http://www.uky.edu/ILC/html/dialogues.html

DIALOGOS   http://www.thinkingtogether.com/index.html

GLOBAL DIALOGUE INSTITUTE
http://global-dialogue.com/

COLLECTIVE WISDOM INITIATIVE
http://www.collectivewisdominitiative.org/papers/laberge_wholesystems.htm#co_creative   We believe there exists a field of collective consciousness — often seen and expressed through metaphor — that is real and influential, yet invisible. It is our shared work, therefore, to perceive the existence of and to develop our inherent aptitude for collective wisdom. We are conductors and conduits of a collective knowing.

DIALOGUE ON LEADERSHIP
http://www.dialogonleadership.org/

LIVING DIRECTORY
http://www.livingdirectory.net/ Friendly Favors (FF) is a Web based community online since August 1999, consisting presently of 46,306 participants, living in 171 countries.

- They are a diverse group of good people envisioning a world that works for all.

- They support each other's projects by sharing our know-how, connections and resources.

- They report generosity and encourage goodwill by giving referrals and Thankyou's.

Participation is FREE and by invitation. Unsponsored applicants receive a unique number and password to login, and once in can use Find and Events to locate and personally meet sponsoring members (FF Sponsors or Networkers) that may agree to invite you into our network's web of trust.

ECO Earth Communication Office -
http://www.oneearth.org/

A KID'S EYE-VIEW OF SPEAKING COMPASSION – Nonviolent Communication for Kids by Kids (Video).
Holley Humphrey at 233 Rogue River Hwy #173, Grants Pass, OR 97527, 541-862-2043,
http://www.empathymagic.com/.
E-mail: holley@empathymagic.com.

GAMES FOR SPEAKING COMPASSION – A Fun Way to Teach Nonviolent Communication.

Holley Humphrey at 233 Rogue River Hwy #173, Grants Pass, OR 97527, 541-862-2043,
http://www.empathymagic.com/.
E-mail: holley@empathymagic.com

COMMUNITY

ABUNDANCE SWAP   http://www.abundanceswap.org/

GREENMAPS –   http://www.greenmap.org/
Green Map System is a global eco-cultural movement, energized by local knowledge, action and responsibility.

COMMUNITY INDICATORS PROJECT
http://www.redefiningprogress.org/projects/indicators/

COMMUNITY SCORECARD –   http://www.scorecard.org/
Scorecard is the web's most popular resource for information about pollution problems and toxic chemicals.

THE AHWAHNEE PRINCIPLES
http://www.lgc.org/ahwahnee/econ_principles.html

NEW URBANISM
http://www.newurbanism.org/pages/416429/index.htm

GREAT LAND USE ARTICLES FROM LGC:
http://www.lgc.org/freepub/land_use/articles/index.html

NORTHWEST ENVIRONMENTAL WATCH – produces an incredibly detailed report on the Pacific North West from BC to Northern California entitled: **Cascadia Scorecard 2004:**
http://www.northwestwatch.org/

THE NORTHWEST ENVIRONMENT WATCH also offers suggestions (http://www.northwestwatch.org/reforms) to curb urban sprawl.

BREAD FOR THE JOURNEY
http://www.breadforthejourney.org/index.htm

FOUNDATION FOR GLOBAL COMMUNITY
http://www.globalcommunity.org

GLOBAL COMMUNITY
http://www.globalcommunity.org/flash/wombat.shtml

PROJECT FOR PUBLIC SPACES
http://www.pps.org/info/aboutpps/staff/jwalljasper

GOVERNING MAGAZINE   http://governing.com/ .

DAMANHUR http://www.damanhur.info/en/html/home.asp
http://www.damanhurusa.com/

WATTS GARDEN CLUB   http://wattsgardenclub.org/

OREGON PROGRESS BOARD
http://egov.oregon.gov/DAS/OPB/
http://egov.oregon.gov/DAS/OPB/docs/2005report/05BBPR
PR.pdf or CONTACT: Jeff Tryens or Rita Conrad (503) 378-3201)

PETER BLOCK COMMUNITY ENGAGEMENT
http://www.peterblock.com/commun.html

VILLAGE EARTH   http://www.villageearth.org/index.htm
INTERNATIONAL INSTITUTE FOR SUSTAINABLE
DEVELOPMENT   http://www.colostate.edu/Orgs/IISD/

INSTITUTE FOR LOCAL SELF-RELIANCE
New Rules Project   http://www.newrules.org/

NEW VILLAGE.

http://www.newvillage.net/

CONFLICT

IRAQ BODY COUNT
http://www.iraqbodycount.net/
http://www.iraqbodycount.net/database/

The IRAQ BODY COUNT Database

This is a human security project to establish an independent and comprehensive public database of media-reported civilian deaths in Iraq resulting directly from military action by the USA and its allies. This database includes up to 7,350 deaths which resulted from coalition military action during the "major-combat" phase prior to May 1st 2003. In the current occupation phase the database includes all deaths which the Occupying Authority has a binding responsibility to prevent under the Geneva Conventions and Hague Regulations. This includes civilian deaths resulting from the breakdown in law and order, and deaths due to inadequate health care or sanitation.

Results and totals are continually updated and made immediately available on this page and on various **IBC counters** which may be freely displayed on any website, where they will be automatically updated without further intervention. Casualty figures are derived solely from a comprehensive survey of online media reports. Where these sources report differing figures, the range (a minimum and a maximum) are given. All results are independently reviewed and error-checked by at least three members of the Iraq Body Count project team before publication.

Reported Minimum As Of 4/13/05 17,384

Reported Maximum As Of 4/13/05 19,770

CIVIC WORLDWIDE   (Campaign for Innocent Victims in Conflict)   http://www.civicworldwide.org/
CIVIC is a small organization working to obtain U.S.

Government assistance for communities and families in need, while helping to shine a spotlight on the human costs of war.

The humanitarian situation in Iraq remains serious. CIVIC seeks to mitigate the impact of the conflict and its aftermath on the people of Iraq by ensuring that timely and effective life-saving assistance is provided to those in need. We have kept the stories of families harmed in both Iraq and Afghanistan on the agenda both on the ground and in the halls of Congress. In the short time we have been operating, we have succeeded in putting laws in place that will assist those we identified in our field survey work.

CIVIC also works to promote public understanding, engagement and support for the human dimension in wars. Civilian casualties and injuries are the most unacceptable consequence of all wars - threatening the survival and dignity of millions of ordinary men, women and children. We believe it is a moral and humanitarian duty for each death and injury to be recorded, publicized, and given the weight it deserves. **Marla Ruzicka,** Founder

COUNTING THE COST http://www.countingthecost.org/

JOINT REPORT ON CIVILIAN CASUALTIES AND CLAIMS

RELATED TO U.S. MILITARY OPERATIONS

Presented by the Occupation Watch Center in Baghdad and the National Association for the Defense of Human Rights in Iraq
http://www.civicworldwide.org/pdfs/compensationreport.pdf

DESIGN

The ECODESIGN FOUNDATION
http://www.edf.edu.au
SUSTAINMENTS
http://www.edf.edu.au/MenuSust.htm

William McDonough and Michael Braungart, Read Cradle to Cradle-Remaking the Way We Make Things, North Point Press. Also visit their website: http://www.mbdc.com/

BIOMIMICRY: Janine Benyus Read Biomimicry: Innoviation Inspired by Nature, 1997. Also visit: http://www.biomimicry.org/intro.html
Nature as Model - Biomimicry is a new science that studies nature's models and then imitates or takes inspiration from these designs and processes to solve human problems, e.g., a solar cell inspired by a leaf.
Nature as Mentor - Biomimicry uses an ecological standard to judge the "rightness" of our innovations. After 3.8 billion years of evolution, nature has learned: What works. What is appropriate. What lasts.
Nature as Measure - Biomimicry is a new way of viewing and valuing nature. It introduces an era based not on what we can extract from the natural world, but on what we can learn from it.
BIOMIMICRY GUILD functions within an ecosystem~ we are subject to the same biological rules that govern the interactions of organisms that coexist in a common habitat. We are striving to evolve organizational dynamics that mimic mature ecosystems. As such, we:
1. Consider waste as a resource.

2. Diversify and cooperate to fully use the habitat.

3. Gather and use energy efficiently.

4. Optimize rather than maximize.

5. Use materials sparingly.

6. Don't foul our nest.

7. Don't draw down resources.

8. Remain in balance with biosphere.

9. Run on information.

10. Shop locally.

See examples of Applied Biomimicry In Action at:
http://www.biomimicry.net/case_studies_materials.html and
http://www.biomimicry.net/case_studies_processes.html

LEADERSHIP IN ENERGY AND ENVIRONMENTAL DESIGN (LEED)
http://www.usgbc.org/

ELEMENTS   http://elements.bnim.com/index.html

HEALTHY BUILDING NETWORK
http://www.healthybuilding.net

ARCHITECTURE FOR HUMANITY
http://www.architectureforhumanity.org

ASHLAND SCHOOL OF ENVIRONMENTAL TECHNOLOGY http://www.greeninventor.org/index.html
Ashland School of Environmental Technology (ASET) is a nonprofit organization established in Ashland Oregon to provide hands on education and inspiration to students while simultaneously developing simple positive solutions to global environmental problems. We believe that solutions are contained in the problems we face, and to be effective, these solutions must address multiple problems. Society has spent too many generations solving problems in a linear fashion only to find that each solution resulted in a multiplicity of future problems.

STRAWJET PROJECT
http://www.greeninventor.org/strawjet_sum2.html
Developing technologies for fabricating load bearing, insulating construction materials from surplus straw. This innovative design offers a solution to the need for better housing in a world of diminishing resources. The true significance of this technology is the universal availability of straw on a continuously renewable basis.

ALTERNATIVES TO PVC:
http://www./pvc/PVCFreeAlts.html

HOLISTIC MANAGEMENT:
http://www.holisticmanagement.org/

GLOBAL IDEAS BANK – Check out this great concept in sharing new ideas   www.globalideasbank.org

Brown, Lester R., **Plan B – Rescuing a Planet under Stress and a Civilization in Trouble**, Earth Policy Institute, W.W. Norton & Company, New York, 2003

Papanek, Victor Design for the Real World – Human Ecology and Social Change, Pantheon-Random House, 1972.

Papanek, Victor The Green Imperative, Thames and Hudson, London 1995

DESIGN FOR DISASSEMBLY

- o http://www.co-design.co.uk/design.htm
- o http://dfe-sce.nrc-cnrc.gc.ca/dfestra7/dfestra7/dfestra7_2_e.html
- o http://www.npd-solutions.com/dfe.html
- o http://villa.lakes.com/eltechno/TVAdfd.html

SUSTAINABLE CITY http://www.sustainable-city.org/

EDUCATION

HONORING ALL LIFE INSTITUTE (HALI)
http://www.honoringalllife.org/HALI.php

NATIONAL ASSOCIATION OF INDEPENDENT SCHOOLS (NAIS) http://www.nais.org/

SUDBURY EDUCATION RESOURCE NETWORK
http://www.sudburynetwork.org/perspectives.htm

http://www.sudval.org/ Sudbury Valley School.

BLUE MOUNTAIN CHARTER SCHOOL,
COTTAGE GROVE OREGON
http://www.bluemountainschool.com/index.cfm

WALDORF EDUCATION http://www.awsna.org/

GREAT IDEAS IN EDUCATION:
http://www.great-ideas.org/

PATHS OF LEARNING http://www.pathsoflearning.net/

NATIONAL COALITION OF ALTERNATIVE COMMUNITY SCHOOLS   http://www.ncacs.org/

ASCD SYSTEMS THINKING CURRICULUM
http://www.haven.net/patterns/index.html
This systems thinking and chaos theory forum explores the new evolutionary cosmology and the emergence of new science which includes the human spirit. It recognizes the importance of creativity and imagination in a re-enchantment of learning and teaching. It supports the development of a design culture in which we learn to create our futures.

FREE THE CHILDREN http://www.freethechildren.org/

MONTESSORI EDUCATION http://www.amshq.org/

REGGIO EMILIA EDUCATION
http://zerosei.comune.re.it/inter/

LEARNING TAPESTRY:
http://www.learningtapestry.com/index.html

BRAIN GYM: http://www.braingym.org/ and http://www.braingym.com/

FREECHILD PROJECT:
http://www.freechild.org/unschooling.htm

UNSCHOOLING: http://www.unschooling.com/

LEARNING IN FREEDOM: http://learninfreedom.org/

DO SOMETHING http://www.dosomething.org/

THE EDUCO INTERNATIONAL ALLIANCE (EIA)
http://www.educointernational.org/index.htm

EDCOUSA http://www.educocolorado.org/

THE AL RABY SCHOOL FOR COMMUNITY AND ENVIRONMENT http://alraby.cps.k12.il.us/

MULTIPLE INTELLIGENCES

DR. THOMAS ARMSTRONG:
http://www.thomasarmstrong.com/multiple_intelligences.htm

The theory of multiple intelligences was developed in 1983 by Dr. Howard Gardner, professor of education at Harvard University. It suggests that the traditional notion of intelligence, based on I.Q. testing, is far too limited. Instead, Dr. Gardner proposes eight different intelligences to account for a broader range of human potential in children and adults. These intelligences are:

Linguistic intelligence   ("word smart")

Logical-mathematical intelligence ("number/reasoning smart")

Spatial intelligence   ("picture smart")

Bodily-Kinesthetic intelligence ("body smart")

Musical intelligence   ("music smart")

Interpersonal intelligence ("people smart")

Intrapersonal intelligence   ("self smart")

Naturalist intelligence   ("nature smart")

One of the most remarkable features of the theory of multiple intelligences is how it provide eight different potential pathways to learning. If a teacher is having difficulty reaching a student in the more traditional linguistic or logical ways of instruction, the theory of multiple intelligences suggests several other ways in which the material might be presented to facilitate effective learning. Whether you are a kindergarten teacher, a graduate school instructor, or an adult learner seeking better ways of pursuing self-study on any subject of interest, the same basic guidelines apply. Whatever you are teaching or learning, see how you might connect it with:

- words (linguistic intelligence)
- numbers or logic (logical-mathematical intelligence)
- pictures (spatial intelligence)
- music (musical intelligence)
- self-reflection (intrapersonal intelligence)
- a physical experience (bodily-kinesthetic intelligence)
- a social experience (interpersonal intelligence), and/or
- an experience in the natural world. (naturalist intelligence)

MULTIPLE INTELLIGENCES:
http://www.newhorizons.org/strategies/mi/front_mi.htm

ECOLITERACY: http://www.ecoliteracy.org/ The Center for Ecoliteracy is dedicated to education for sustainable living by fostering a profound understanding of the natural world, grounded in direct experience.

EARTHFORCE
http://www.earthforce.org/
Earth Force launched in 1994 to address two emerging national trends among young people identified by The Pew Charitable Trust:

1. Their overwhelming desire to act on behalf of the

environment

2. Their desire to help their communities through voluntary service

Since its creation Earth Force has developed a series of tools designed to assist educators in facilitating youth-driven civic action with their students. Community Action and Problem Solving (CAPS) was the first program developed, and is the basis for Earth Force programming today.

Through GREEN partnerships students in more than 47 communities around the United States protect and improve their local rivers and streams.

THE THREE PILARS: EDUCATION, BUSINESS, COMMUNITY

http://www.centralrangesllen.org.au/gardner2005

KIDS WITH CAMERAS
http://www.kids-with-cameras.org/home/

FACTS ABOUT MARKETING TO CHILDREN

From: New American Dream

http://www.newdream.org/kids/facts.php 877.68.DREAM

Advertising Expenditures Spiral

In 2001 US advertising expenditures topped $230 billion, more than doubling the $105.97 billion spent in 1980. (1)

Given that the 2000 Census reports 105 million households in America, this means that advertisers spend, an average of $2,190 per year to reach one household. (2)

Ad Industry Spends Billions to Target Kids

Marion Nestle, chair of the Department of Nutrition and Food Studies at New York University, estimates that $13 billion a year is spent marketing to American children - by food and drink industries alone. Food advertising makes up about half of all advertising aimed at kids. (3)

Channel One's twelve-minute in-classroom broadcast, featuring 2 minutes of commercials for every 10 minutes of news, is compulsory on 90% of the school days in 80% of the classrooms in 40% of U.S. middle and high schools. Companies pay up to $195,000 for a 30-second ad, knowing that they have a captive audience of 8 million students in 12,000 classrooms across the country. (4)

Little Big Spenders – Children and Teen Spending Skyrockets

Children's spending has roughly doubled every ten years for the past three decades, and has tripled in the 1990's. Kids 4-12 spent $2.2 billion in 1968, and $4.2 billion in 1984. By 1994 the figure climbed to $17.1 billion, and by 2002 their spending exceeded $40 billion. Kids' direct buying power is expected to exceed $51.8 billion by 2006. (5)

Older kids, 12-19, spent a record $155 billion of their own money in 2001, (6) up from $63 billion just four years earlier. (7)

The "Nag" Factor Works – Kids Influence on Parents' Purchases Continues to Grow

In the 1960's, children influenced about $5 billion of their parents' purchases. By 1984 that figure increased ten-fold to $50 billion. (8) By 1997 it had tripled to $188 billion. Kids marketing expert James McNeal estimates that by 2000,

children 12 and under influenced family purchases to the tune of $500 billion. (9)

Kids are Glued to the Tube and Bombarded by Commercials

It's estimated the average child sees more than 20,000 commercials every year - that works out to at least 55 commercials per day. (10)

Children spend a daily average of 4 hours and 40 minutes in front of a screen of some kind - two and a half hours of which are watching television. (11)

47% of children have a television set in their bedroom. (12)

Creating Brand-Conscious Babies

At six months of age, the same age they are imitating simple sounds like "ma-ma," babies are forming mental images of corporate logos and mascots. (13)

According to recent marketing industry studies, a person's "brand loyalty" may begin as early as age two. (14)

At three years of age, before they can read, one out of five American children are already making specific requests for brand-name products. (15)

Experts say a lifetime customer may be worth $100,000 to a retailer, making effective "cradle to grave" strategies extremely valuable. (16)

What Do Kids Really Want?

According to a Kaiser Family Foundation study, children who use the most media tend to be the least contented. (17)

In the Art/Essay Contest "What Do Kids Really Want That Money Can't Buy?" sponsored by the Center for a New American Dream, the most common answers were "love," "happiness," "peace on earth," and "friends." Significant numbers of children also wanted time with family, a clean environment, a world where people treat each other with respect, a chance to see lost loved ones, help for suffering people, health, and time to play.

Footnotes

(1) McCann-Erickson U.S. Advertising Volume Reports and Bob Coen's Insider's Report for December 2001 (www.mccann.com/insight/bobcoen.html. Accessed 5/8/02.)

(2) Ibid., and U.S. Census reports.

(3) Marion Nestle and Margo Wootan as quoted in "Spending on Marketing to Kids Up $5 Billion In Last Decade," The Food Institute Report, April 15, 2002.

(4) Center for Commercial-Free Public Education, "Channel One." www.commercialfree.org/channelone.html. Accessed 6/5/02.

(5) James McNeal, The Kids' Market: Myths and Realities, Ithaca: Paramount Market Publishing, Inc., 1999, and The U.S. Kids Market, a 2002 report from Packaged Facts available at MarketResearch.com.

(6) National Institute on Media and the Family "Children and Advertising Fact Sheet" 2002. www.mediaandthefamily.org/research/fact/childadv.shtml. Accessed 5/8/02

(7) Peter Zolo, "Talking to Teens," American Demographics, November 1995.

(8) James McNeal, "Tapping the Three Kids' Markets," American Demographics, April 1998.

(9) Kim Campbell and Kent Davis-Packard, "How ads get kids to say I want it!" Christian Science Monitor, September 18, 2000.

(10) American Academy of Pediatrics, "Television and the Family" fact sheet. www.aap.org/family/tv1.htm. Accessed 5/9/02.

(11) Annenberg Public Policy Center, "Media In The Home 2000: The Fifth Annual Survey of Parents and Children", http://www.appcpenn.org/reports/2000/

(12) Ibid.

(13) James McNeal and Chyon-Hwa Yeh. "Born to Shop," American Demographics, June 1993, pp 34-39.

(14) Cited in "Brand Aware," Children's Business, June 2000.

(15) "New Poll Shows Marketing to Kids Taking Its Toll on Parents, Families." Center for a New American Dream, 1999. www.newdream.org/campaign/kids/press-release.html

(16) James McNeal and Chyon-Hwa Yeh, "Born to Shop," American Demographics, June 1993.

(17) Kaiser Family Foundation, "Kids & Media @ The New Millennium," 39. see www.kff.org/content/1999/1535/

SOCIETY FOR ORGANIZATIONAL LEARNING (SoL)
http://www.solonline.org/

Guiding Principles of SoL

DRIVE TO LEARN - All human beings are born with an innate, lifelong desire and ability to learn, which should be enhanced by all organizations.

LEARNING IS SOCIAL - People learn best from and with one another, and participation in learning communities is vital to their effectiveness, well-being and happiness in any work setting.

LEARNING COMMUNITIES - The capacities and accomplishments of organizations are inseparable from, and dependent on, the capacities of the learning communities which they foster.

ALIGNING WITH NATURE - It is essential that organizations evolve to be in greater harmony with human nature and with the natural world.

CORE LEARNING CAPABILITIES - Organizations must develop individual and collective capabilities to understand complex, interdependent issues; engage in reflective, generative conversation; and nurture personal and shared aspirations.

CROSS-ORGANIZATIONAL COLLABORATION - Learning communities that connect multiple organizations can significantly enhance their capacity for profound individual and organizational change.

BRAIN, CHILD MAGAZINE http://www.brainchildmag.com/

MOTHERING MAGAZINE   http://www.mothering.com/ It is a treasure!

GEE-WOW!   http://www.ecocenter.org/education.shtml

ORGANIZATIONS EMPOWERING YOUTH

YES! http://www.yesworld.org/aboutyes.html

TAKING IT GLOBAL http://www.takingitglobal.org

GLOBAL YOUTH ACTION NETWORK
http://www.youthlink.org/gyanv3/home.html

GREENCORPS http://www.greencorps.org/

INFORMAL EDUCATION HOMEPAGE   Excellent!
http://www.infed.org/index.htm

ALTERNATIVE EDUCATION RESOURCE ORGANIZATION (AERO) http://www.educationrevolution.org/

GREAT IDEAS IN EDUCATION
http://www.great-ideas.org/

NATIONAL COALITION OF ALTERNATIVE COMMUNITY SCHOOLS http://ncacs.org/

NATIONAL SOCIETY FOR EXPERIENTIAL EDUCATION
http://www.nsee.org/

RETHINKING SCHOOLS http://www.rethinkingschools.org/

NATIONAL ASSOCIATION OF MULTICULTURAL EDUCATION
http://www.nameorg.org/

ECOVILLAGE TRAINING CENTER AT THE FARM
http://www.thefarm.org/etc/

SECOND NATURE   http://www.secondnature.org/
NORDIC PROJECTS – IDEA BANK FOR SCHOOLGROUNDS
http://home.c2i.net/swan/
TOOLS FOR PARTICIPATORY PLANNING
http://home.c2i.net/swan/medvirkning.htm#oversikt
CREATING BETTER CITIES WITH CHILDREN AND YOUTH
http://www.unesco.org/most/guic/guiccbccy.htm
ARCHITECTURE IN EDUCATION
http://home.c2i.net/swan/workshop.htm
The most effective way to make children and youth more conscious and responsible for their surrounding architecture and environment, is to give them a chance to participate in planning processes and projects that will have a direct and concrete influence on their daily surroundings: the school.
ECO-SCHOOLS   http://www.eco-schools.org/
FOUNDATION FOR ENVIRONMENTAL ORGANIZATION
http://www.eco-schools.org/aboutus/fee.htm
FEE - is an umbrella non-governmental organization.

o   LEARNING ABOUT FORESTS (LeAF) An international programme for schools, aiming to support teachers and pupils to go to forests, learn from them and in them, and to learn further by sharing experiences internationally

o   YOUNG REPORTERS FOR THE ENVIRONMENT (YRE)

o   ECO-SCHOOLS

ECOSCHOOL DESIGN   http://www.ecoschools.com/

EVERGREEN   http://www.evergreen.ca/

GREEN TEACHER MAGAZINE
http://www.greenteacher.com/ Education for Planet Earth

NORTH AMERICAN ASSOCIATION FOR ENVIRONMENTAL EDUCATION http://naaee.org/

NATIONAL WILDLIFE FEDERATION SCHOOLYARD HABITATS http://www.nwf.org/schoolyardhabitats/

INSTITUTE FOR PEOPLE'S EDUCATION AND ACTION
http://www.peopleseducation.org/

NEW GAMES   http://www.inewgames.com/default.htm

PHYSICAL GAMES FOR COOPERATIVE PLAY
http://northonline.sccd.ctc.edu/eceprog/games.html

THE T.R.E.A.T.Y. TOTAL IMMERSION SCHOOL
http://www.russellmeans.com/school.html
This unique program created a revolutionary approach to teaching by focusing on culturally centered private schools for grades K through 3 for the indigenous population.

MAORI TOTAL IMMERSION COURSES
http://jan.ucc.nau.edu/~jar/NALI8.html
http://www.forachange.co.uk/index.php?stoid=41
http://www.nativeweb.org/resources.php?name=Maori&type=1&nation=209
http://www.uatuahine.hawaii.edu/hana/si98/jar/nabe.html

ENCOMPASS http://www.encompassfamilies.org/home/
Natural Learning Rhythms is a powerful approach that combines the best of child development and family dynamics.

NATURAL LEARNING RHYTHM COOPERATIVE GAMES
Everyone Wins!
http://www.encompassfamilies.org/store/products/everyone_wins.html

Win-Win Games for All Ages
http://www.encompassfamilies.org/store/products/win_win.html

GREEN DOVE PEACE EDUCATION LINKS
http://www.greendove.net/education.htm

CONNEXIONS http://cnx.rice.edu/

STREET KIDS INTERNATIONAL http://www.streetkids.org/

FRITJOF CAPRA, Creativity and Leadership in Learning Communities, http://www.ecoliteracy.org/pdf/creativity.pdf
see also: http://www.fritjofcapra.net/index.html

HEARTLIGHT LEARNING COMMUNITY SOUTH AFRICA
http://www.heartlight.co.za/

The HeartLight Difference	
Conventional System	**HeartLight Model**
Curriculum Focused	Learner Centered
IQ learning	Total Living
Isolated Subjects	Integrated Learning
Academic Content	Relevant Life Challenges
Content Memorisation	Demonstrated Competence
Teacher-Directed Instruction	Learner-Led Projects
Written Examinations	Life-Role Performances
Grade-Level Progression	On-going Advancement

FOOD

CENTER FOR INFORMED FOOD CHOICES
http://www.informedeating.org/ The Center for Informed Food Choices (CIFC) advocates for a diet based on whole, unprocessed, local, organically grown plant foods. CIFC believes that: placing these foods at the center of the plate is crucial for promoting public health, protecting the environment, and assuring the humane treatment of animals and food industry workers…CIFC believes that making personal dietary improvements is just one component of social change… They advocate for social and political reforms that will support people in making healthy food choices over the long term, as well as in creating a more just, humane, and sustainable food system.

INTERNATIONAL SOCIETY FOR ECOLOGY AND CULTURE's Local Food Toolkit

FROM: http://www.isec.org.uk/factsheet.html
ISEC's Local Food Toolkit describes how the globalization of the food supply—supported by government policies—has been disastrous for consumers, farmers, local economies, and the environment. We also outline the many benefits of shifting course and supporting local food systems instead. This supplemental fact sheet provides a range of statistics supporting the Toolkit's arguments, and debunking some of the myths of global food.

Global Food and the Environment

Biodiversity
- Over 75% of the planet's agricultural biodiversity has already been lost. [1]
- 90% of the crop varieties that were grown a century ago are no longer commercially produced. [2]
- Each year genetic diversity in crops decreases by 2% worldwide; the number of livestock breeds decreases by 5%. [3]
- 9 crops supply 75% of the world's food, and 3 crops provide 50%. [4]
- 1/2 the vegetable servings eaten in the US in 1996 came from only 3 vegetables: lettuce (mostly iceberg), potatoes, and tomatoes. [5]
- In the last 80 years, the number of produce varieties produced on at least 1% of Iowa farms has fallen from 24 to 4. [6]

Food Miles and Global Warming
- Global warming is already underway. Temperatures in Antarctica have risen 2.5o C in the last 50 years—causing the recent collapse of two ice shelves over 1,000 square miles in area [7]—and the North Pole melted last year, for the first time in 50 million years. [8]
- The global food system is one of the single most important causes of increased greenhouse gases [9]; in the US it accounts for almost a fifth of the nation's energy consumption. [10]
- Per capita, the US uses more energy for food production, processing and distribution than Asia and Africa use for all activities combined. [11]
- The typical plate of food in the U.S. has traveled 1,500 miles from source to table, 22% more than in 1980. [12]
- International trade in agriculture has increased 70% since 1990, 200% since 1980, and 1800% since 1970 (a 19 fold increase). [13]
- Domestic transportation of grain products doubled between 1978 and 1995 while consumption remained constant [14]; agricultural products now account for close to 1/3 of all domestic freight transportation. [15]

Air Pollution
- Factory farms, especially intensive livestock operations, have been associated with air pollution—including release of ammonia nitrogen—and impact neighboring communities with problems ranging from respiratory illnesses to declining property values. [16]

- Factory farming of animals is responsible for 30% of acid rain in Netherlands. [17]

Water Pollution and Waste
- Irrigation practices in the US so wasteful – accounting for a full 2/3 of all groundwater used [18]- that millions of acres of farmland must be abandoned each year due to salinization.[19]
- Hog, chicken and cattle waste has polluted 35,000 miles of rivers in 22 states and contaminated groundwater in 17 states. [20]
- Abnormally high levels of nitrates have been found in 10% of the drinking wells near hog and chicken operations. [21]
- In 1999, a large waste lagoon burst and dumped 22 million gallons of hog waste into North Carolina's New River—that's twice the quantity of oil spilled from the Exxon Valdez. [22]
- In 2002, Cargill—one of the world's largest agribusinesses—was charged with illegally dumping hog waste through valves and holding ponds into Missouri's Loutre river, contaminating five miles of the river and killing 53,000 fish. [23]

Erosion
- Since World War II, 37% of the world's cropland has been eroded [24], and topsoil is currently being destroyed 17 times faster than it can be regenerated. [25]
- The UN Food and Agriculture Organization predicts that 140 million hectares (350 million acres) of high quality soil will be gone by 2010, mostly from the food-short regions of Africa and Asia. [26]

Genetic Engineering
- The impacts of GE documented so far include damage to vital organs and the immune system, increased pesticide resistance in insects and weeds, and DNA transfer to non-engineered varieties. [27]
- 75% of all GE crops worldwide are grown in the US. [28]
- Over half of all cotton and soybeans grown in the US are genetically modified. Over four dozen GE foods are now being grown or sold in the US [29] and several dozen more are in the final stages of development. [30]
- Most processed food items in the US now have GE ingredients. [31]
- Research has shown GE potatoes to cause damage to the vital organs and immune system of laboratory rats. [32]
- In 1989, a genetically engineered dietary supplement killed 37 Americans and permanently disabled 5,000 others. [33]
- The claims that genetically engineered seed would reduce pesticide use have proven false: for most commercial crops, pesticide use has not decreased and for some crops it has actually increased. [34]

Global Food and Human Health
- Over 1/4 of meals consumed in US are 'fast food'. [35]
- In the US, 1/5 of all meals are consumed in a car. [36]
- The US Surgeon-General reports that almost 2/3 of Americans are now significantly overweight (compared with 55% in the early 1990s, and 46% in the late 1970s), and the proportion is rising steadily. Each year, the obesity epidemic costs the medical system $117 billion in bills and causes 300,000 premature deaths. [37]
- 3/4 of all antibiotics used in the United States are for livestock, mostly in the absence of disease—this has the effect of increasing pathogenic antibiotic resistance. [38]
- Despite the prolific use of antibiotics, factory farms and meat processing plants are breeding grounds for bacteria like E. coli and salmonella. [39] In 2002 alone, ConAgra was forced to recall 19 million pounds of beef contaminated at one of its meat-packing plants with a deadly strain of E. coli.

[40]
- The rate of food-borne illnesses in the US is soaring. Salmonella cases have doubled since 1980, and similar increases are reported for other food borne bacteria. [41]

Chemicals
- In the US, the use of pesticides has increased 33 fold since 1945. [42]
- In California, use of carcinogenic pesticides increased 127% between 1991 and 1998, while reproductive and developmental toxicants, groundwater contaminants, and acutely toxic pesticides increased as well. [43]
- Globally, pesticides kill 20-40,000 farmers each year. [44]
- The documented health effects of pesticide exposure include: leukemia, brain tumors, prostate cancer, sterility, birth defects, damage to the immune system, and cognitive disorders such as impairment of memory and psychomotor speed, anxiety, irritability, and depression. [45]
- These chemical inputs simply aren't working as predicted: in the U.S., the quantity of crops lost to pests has increased 20% since the introduction of pesticides [46], and $40 billion a year is now spent on pesticides to save an estimated $16 billion in crops. [47]

Politics and Economics of Global Food

Disappearing Farms and Local Economies
- While 40% of Americans were employed in farming in 1910, today that figure is less than 2% [48], and the number of farmers in the US has declined by 65% since 1950. [49]
- Family farmers in the US typically lose more money than they make [50]—their average income declined by over 60% between 2000 and 2001 alone. [51]
- When 235,000 US farms failed during the mid-1980s, roughly 60,000 other rural businesses also went under. One agricultural region, McPherson County in Nebraska, has lost two-thirds of its population—as well as 19 post offices, 58 school districts, and 3 entire towns—since 1920. [52]
- Farmers' prospects are so bleak that in many regions suicide has become their leading cause of death. [53]
- The National Retail Planning Forum in England found that each new supermarket eliminates 276 more jobs than it creates. [54]

Global Food and the South
- The world already produces more than enough to provide a healthy diet for everyone on the planet. [55] The problem is not that there is a food deficit, it is the unequal distribution of food and the control of food by profit-driven corporations that leads to world hunger.
- There are currently 840 million people in the world who are hungry. [56]
- In 1979, 92% of China's population lived on the land; China's abandonment of collectivized agriculture and efforts to integrate rapidly into the global economy have reduced the number to less than 40% today. In one year alone, 10 million Chinese peasants left their farms. [57] Free market reforms in China have already led hundreds of thousands of farmers, mostly women, to commit suicide. [58]
- Largely because so many farmers in the South have been pulled from the land, there are now 20 more Third World cities with populations over 10 million than there were in 1970. [59]
- India is a net exporter of food, even though 400 million of its people go hungry every day; it has been a net exporter of food even during its worst famines. [60]

Poverty and Inequality
- While the inflation-adjusted income of the bottom 60% of

American households has stagnated since 1970, the income of the top fifth has risen by over 50% and that of the top 5% has almost doubled. [61]

- Today, the richest tenth of the world's population earns 118 times more than the poorest tenth—a gap almost twice as wide as twenty years ago. [62]

Centralization

- A handful of massive agribusinesses now dominate farming: the largest 6% of farms currently capture almost 60% of all farming revenue. [63]

- The average farm size in the US has increased by 25% since 1970, while the number of farms decreased by 40% in the same time period. [64]

- In 1995, the top 4 supermarkets controlled 24% of industry sales; in 2000 they controlled 42% and in the coming years, it is expected to climb to over 50%. [65]

- In 1980, not one of the world's 7,000 major sources of planting seed held an identifiable share of the commercial seed market. By 1999, the top 10 seed companies held 1/3 of the world's market. [66]

- Nine companies sell 90% of the world's pesticides [67] and in the US four companies slaughter 80% of all cattle. [68]

- The top four wholesalers control almost half of the market for Florida tomatoes, and the top two account for three quarters of all fresh-cut salad sold in supermarkets. [69]

- This concentration gives farmers fewer and fewer places to sell their harvests by enabling powerful middlemen, such as wholesalers and supermarkets, to squeeze out all of the profits. By 1990, only 9 cents of every dollar spent on domestically produced food in the US went to the farmer, while middlemen, marketers, and input suppliers took the rest. [70]

Subsidies and Regulations

- In 2000, 3/4 of government agricultural subsidies went to the largest 15% of farms, and the largest 7% of farms received 43%. [71]

- In addition, large farms receive greater tax incentives for capital purchases to expand their operations, while exemptions from federal labor laws give them the advantage of low-wage farm labor. [72]

- Farm subsidy recipients include wealthy hobby farmers like David Rockefeller, Ted Turner, basketball star Scottie Pippen and several members of Congress. Meanwhile, the average family farmer earns a negative income. [73]

Benefits of Localization

Environmental Benefits

- A study in Iowa showed that food distributed through local food programs reduced the distance traveled by the average meal from 1500 miles, down to 45 miles. [74]

- The same study calculated that buying produce from a supermarket resulted in 17 times more carbon dioxide being released into the atmosphere than buying from a farmers' market. [75]

- Simply buying 10% of our most common fruits and vegetables locally would save more than 300,000 gallons of fossil fuel and keep up to 8 million pounds of CO_2 from being emitted. [76]

Economic Benefits

- Buying direct from local farmers generates 44% more revenue for the local economy than purchasing food at supermarkets. [77]

- There are now over 2,800 registered farmers' markets in the US, at which nearly 20,000 farmers sell their produce. [78]

- In Massachusetts, a $470 share in a Community Supported Agriculture (CSA) project was shown to provide the equivalent of $700 worth of produce from a supermarket. [79]

- In direct marketing initiatives, farmers take home 80-90% of each dollar the consumer spends, as opposed to an average of 9% when consumers buy from supermarkets. [80]

Health Benefits

- Fresh, organic vegetables have significantly higher levels of vitamin C, iron, magnesium and phosphorus than conventional vegetables [81]. For some nutrients, they are on average ten times more nutritious than regular supermarket vegetables. [82]

Productivity

- The idea that factory farms produce more food is a myth: the total productive output of food per acre on small, diversified farms is up to 1,000 percent higher per unit area than on large farms. [83]

References

1) FAO 1996. State of the World's Plant Genetic Resources. Rome: FAO.

2) Tuxill. 2000. "The Biodiversity That People Made." World Watch. 13 (3): 24-35.

3) Mooney, Pat 1999. The ETC century: Erosion, technological transformation and corporate concentration in the 21st century. In: Development Dialogue 1999 (1-2).

4) Withgott, Jay. 2001. "Saving Seeds, Saving Cultures." BioMedNet. 19 March 2001.

5) Schueller, Gretel. 2001. "Eat Local." Discover. 22(5).

6) Pirog, Richard et al. 2001. Food, Fuel and Freeways: An Iowa Perspective on How Far Food Travels, Fuel Usage, and Greenhouse Gas Emissions. Iowa State University, Leopold Center for Sustainable Agriculture. September.

7) Vidal, John. 2002. "Antarctica sends 500 billion tonne warning of the effects of global warming." The Guardian. March 20, 2002.

8) Smith, Gar. 2000. "Goodbye North Pole?" Earth Island Journal. 15(4).

9) Shrybman, Steven 1999. Trade, Agriculture and Global Warming: How Agricultural Trade Policies are Fuelling Global Warming. Draft document for discussion. Ottawa: West Coast Environmental Law Association.

10) Pimentel, D. and M. Pimental 1996. Food, Energy, and Society. Niwot: Colorado University Press.

11) Schueller, G. 2001. "Eat Local." Discover. 22(5).

12) Pirog, Richard et al. 2001. Food, Fuel and Freeways: An Iowa Perspective on How Far Food Travels, Fuel Usage, and Greenhouse Gas Emissions. Iowa State University, Leopold Center for Sustainable Agriculture. September. See also Hora, Matthew and Jody Tick 2001. From Farm to Table: Making the Connection in the Mid-Atlantic Food System. Washington: Capital Area Food Bank.

13) FAO statistics tables, 2000.

14) USDA 1998. Transportation of U.S. Grains: A Modal Share Analysis, 1978-95. Washington, DC: USDA.

15) Klindworth, K. 1999. Agricultural Transportation Challenges for the 21st Century: A Framework for Discussion. USDA AMS Transportation and Marketing Programs. Cited in Hora and Tick 2001.

16) Donham, K. 1998. "Community and Environmentally Acceptable Livestock Production: Defining the Challenge". Presentation at Animal Feeding Operations and Ground Water Conference. November.

17) Norberg-Hodge, Helena, Todd Merrifield and Steven Gorelick. Bringing the Food Economy Home: Local Alternatives to Global Agribusiness. Kumarian Press, Bloomfield, CT. 2002.

18) Pimentel, David et al. (1997). "Water Resources: Agriculture, the Environment, and Society." BioScience. 47: 97-106.

19) Hora, M. and J. Tick 2001. From Farm to Table: Making the Connection in the Mid-Atlantic Food System. Washington: Capital Area Food Bank.

20) Sierra Club website. Keep Animal Waste out of our Waters: Stop Factory Farm Pollution. www.sierraclub.org/factoryfarms.

21) Rudo, Kenneth. Memo to Dennis McBride, State Health Director, RE: Nitrate Well Water Testing Program Adjacent to Intensive Livestock Operations. August 14, 1998.

22) Hogwatch. 2002. "Environmental Impacts of Hog Factories in North Carolina." Accessed: 25 April, 2002. Available: [http://www.hogwatch.org/html/gtf/fctsht/gtf_fctsht_envimpct.html].

23) Krebs, A.V. (ed.) 2002. "Cargill to pay $1 million fine and costs for polluting central Missouri river with illegal dumpings of hog wastes." Argibusiness Examiner. Issue #147, March 11, 2002.

24) Mooney, Pat 1999. The ETC century: Erosion, technological transformation and corporate concentration in the 21st century. In: Development Dialogue 1999 (1-2).

25) International Union of Geological Sciences, Geoindicators: Tools for Assessing Rapid Environmental Change. On-line: http://www.gcrio.org/geo/title.html Excerpted from: Berger, A. and W. Iams. Geoindicators. Assessing rapid environmental changes in earth systems. A.A.Balkema/Roterdam/Brookfield 1996. P. 466.

26) UN Food and Agriculture Organization, 2002. Available: http://www.acnatsci.org/research/kye/kye82002.html. Accessed: November 21, 2002.

27) Ibid.

28) USDA 2001. Agricultural Biotechnology Briefing Room. Available: http://www.ers.usda.gov/Briefing/biotechnology/ Accessed: May 20, 2002.

29) Cummins, Ronnie. Hazards of Genetically Engineered Foods and Crops – Why We Need a Global Moratorium. Factsheet. Little Marais, MN: Organic Consumers Association.

30) Ibid.

31) Ibid.

32) Ibid.

33) Ibid.

34) For example, see Fernandez-Cornejo, Jorge and William McBride 2000. Genetically Engineered Crops for Pest Management in U.S. Agriculture. USDA Agricultural Economics Report No. 786. Washington: USDA Economic Research Service. Available: http://www.ers.usda.gov/publications/aer786/aer786e.pdf.

35) Schlosser, E. 2001. Fast Food Nation: The Dark Side of the All-American Meal. New York: Perennial.

36) Primedia 2002. What's Cooking: The Food Industry Looks to Shifts in the Country's Demographic Composition, Social Behaviour and Attitudes to Grow Dormant Sales. Primedia Company American Demographics. March.

37) Cited in: Gumbel, A. 2002. Fast Food Nation: An Appetite for Litigation. The Independent. United Kingdom. June 4.

38) Mellon, M,, C. Benbrook and K. Lutz Benbrook 2001. Hogging It: Estimates of Antimicrobial Abuse in Livestock. Cambridge, MA: Union of Concerned Scientists. Available: http://www.ucsusa.org/index.html.

39) Tauxe, R. 1997. "Emerging Foodborne Diseases: An Evolving Public Health Challenge", Emerging Infectious Diseases. 3(4) October-December.

40) Graham, Judith. "Two US Meat Inspectors Warned USDA in February Concerning Possible Con-Agra E-Coli Contaminated Beef; Agency Took No Action Until Late June. From Agribusiness Examiner #177 July 26, 2002.

41) Tauxe, R. 1997. "Emerging Foodborne Diseases: An Evolving Public Health Challenge", Emerging Infectious Diseases. 3(4) October-December.

42) Schueller, Gretel. 2001. "Eat Local." Discover. 22(5).

43) PANNA 2000. "Hooked on Poison: Pesticide Use in California 1991-1998. San Francisco: PANNA. Available: www.panna.org.

44) Postel, S. 1998. Controlling toxic chemicals. In: State of the World 1988. New York: WorldWatch Institute.

45) Solomon, Gina, O.A. Ogunseitan, and Jan Kirsch. 2000. Pesticides and Human Health: A Resource Guide for Health Care Professionals. Santa Monica, CA: Physicians for Social Responsibility.

46) Ableman, Michael 1993. From the Good Earth. New York: Harry Abrams Inc.

47) Altieri, Miguel A. 2000. "Modern Agriculture: Ecological impacts and the possibilities for truly sustainable farming." Agroecology in Action. July 30, 2000.

48) USDA Economic Research Service 2000. Using Historical Statistics of the U.S., Colonial Times to 1970. Series D 1-10, p. 126-127. Census and BLS. Cited in: Hora, Matthew and Jody Tick 2001. From Farm to Table: Making the Connection in the Mid-Atlantic Food System. Washington, DC: Capital Area Food Bank.

49) USDA 2001. Trends in US Agriculture. Available: www.usda.gov/nass/pubs/trends/index.htm.

50) USDA National Commission on Small Farms 1998. A Time to Act. A report of the USDA National Commission on Small Farms. Available: http://www.reeusda.gov/smallfarm/report.htm.

51) USDA 2001. USDA Agricultural Income and Financial Outlook. Washington DC: USDA.

52) Nicholas D. Kristof, op. cit., p. 18.

53) See for example: Lee, M. 1999. "Study Shows Suicide High Among Farmers", Tulsa World, September 12; and Lee, M. 1989. "High Suicide Rate Linked to Farm Financial Stress", Tulsa World, September 16; Lewis, P. 1989. "Preventable Agricultural Deaths in Oklahoma 1983-1988: Self Inflicted or Suicides", Agricultural Engineering Department, Oklahoma State University. Unpublished.

54) National Retail Planning Forum cited in Pretty, Jules 2001. Some benefits and drawbacks of local food systems. Briefing note for Sustain AgriFood Network. November 2. Essex, UK.

55) Rosset, P. 1999. "Why Genetically Altered Food Won't Conquer Hunger." New York Times. September 1, 1999.

56) FAO, 2002. State of Food and Security in the World. Rome, Italy; FAO. Available at http://www.fao.org/docrep/005/Y7352E/Y7352E00.htm/.

57) Dyer, Joel. Harvest of Rage. Boulder, CO: Westview Press, 1998, p.110.

58) MacLeod, Callum 2001. Farmers' wives paying a terrible price for progress. The Independent. August 11. Section A

59) David Morris, "Unmanageable Megacities", Utne Reader, September-October 1994, p. 80.

60) UN Food and Agriculture Office http://www.fao.org/DOCREP/003/X8731E/x8731e07.htm#P4_37.

61) Homer-Dixon, Thomas. 2001. The Ingenuity Gap. Toronto: Alfred A. Knopf. 340.

62) Weller, C.E., and A. Hersh 2002. Free markets and poverty. The American Prospect. 13(1).

63) USDA National Commission on Small Farms 1998. A Time to Act. A report of the USDA National Commission on Small Farms. Available: http://www.reeusda.gov/smallfarm/report.htm.

64) National Agricultural Statistics Service 2000. Trends in U.S. Agriculture: A Walk Through the Past and a Step Into the New Millennium. Washington, DC: United States Department of Agriculture.

65) A.C. Nielsen. 2000. "An Update on Retail Consolidation." Consumer Insight Magazine. 2(2). [Available: http://www.acnielsen.com/pubs/ci/2000/q2]; and Arthur Andersen Corporate Finance. 2001. Food Retail Industry Consolidation – Halftime Report. Chicago: Arthur Andersen. [Available: http://www.andersen.com/website.nsf/content/IndustriesProductsRetailResourcesMASurvey].

66) Mooney, Pat 1999. The ETC century: Erosion, technological transformation and corporate concentration in the 21st century. In: Development Dialogue 1999 (1-2).

67) Ibid.

68) USDA National Commission on Small Farms 1998. A Time to Act: A Report of the USDA National Commission on Small Farms. Available: http://www.reeusda.gov/smallfarm/report.htm.

69) Calvin, Linda et al. 2001. U.S. Fresh Fruit and Vegetable Marketing: Emerging Trade Practices, Trends, and Issues. (Agricultural Economic Report No. 795.) Washington, DC: Market and Trade Economics Division, Economic Research Service, U.S. Department of Agriculture.

70) Stewart Smith, "Farming Activities and Family Farms: Getting the Concepts Right", presented to US Congress symposium "Agricultural Industrialization and Family Farms", October 21, 1992.

71) USDA 2001. USDA Agricultural Income and Financial Outlook. Washington DC: United States Department of Agriculture.

72) USDA National Commission on Small Farms 1998. A Time to Act. A report of the USDA National Commission on Small Farms. Available: http://www.reeusda.gov/smallfarm/report.htm.

73) Reidl, B. 2001. Ag Legislation Would Be a Boon to Rich Farmers, Analysts Say. Washington, DC. Heritage Foundation.

74) Pirog, R. T. Van Pelt, K. Enshayan and E. Cook 2001. Food, Fuel and Freeways: An Iowa Perspective on How Far Food Travels, Fuel Usage, and Greenhouse Gas Emissions. Leopold Center for Sustainable Agriculture, Iowa State University.

75) Ibid.

76) Ibid.

77) Hill, Caroline, Sarah Higginson, and Julie Lewis. 2001. "Leaky Bucket Causing a Stir." Plugging the Leaks (New Economics Foundation). July 2001.

78) USDA Agriculture Marketing Service 2002. USDA AMS Farmers Markets website. Available: www.ams.usda.gov/farmersmarkets/facts.htm.

79) ATTRA 2000. Available: www.attra.org/attra-pub/csa.html.

80) Pretty, Jules 2001. Some Benefits and Drawbacks of Local Food Systems. Briefing note for Sustain AgriFood Network. November 2.

81) Worthington, V. 2001. Nutritional Quality of Organic Versus Conventional Fruits, Vegetables and Grains. Journal of Alternative and Complementary Medicine. 7(2):161-173.

82) Organic Retailers and Growers Association 1999. Press release: Is our food supplying us with adequate nutrition? Study performed by the Australian Government Analytical Laboratory and commissioned by the Organic Retailers and Growers Association. 3 November.

83) Rosset, P. 1999. The Multiple Functions and Benefits of Small Farm Agriculture in the Context of Global Trade Negotiations. Policy Brief #4. Oakland: Institute for Food and Development Policy. September.

ECOVILLAGE MOVEMENT

ECOVILLAGE NETWORK OF THE AMERICAS
http://ena.ecovillage.org/English/index.html

GLOBAL ECOVILLAGE NETWORK – EUROPE
http://www.gen-europe.org

GLOBAL ECOVILLAGE NETWORK – OCEANIA AND ASIA
http://genoa.ecovillage.org

BIODYNAMICS

BIODYNAMIC FARMING AND GARDENING ASSOCIATION
http://www.biodynamics.com

http://www.giodynamic.org.uk

http://www.biodynamic.org.nz

http://www.biodynamic.net

ATTRA – National Sustainable Agriculture Information Service http://www.attra.org

RUDOLF STEINER COLLEGE
http://www.steinercolege.org/biodynamics.html

DEMETER http://www.demeter-usa.org/biodyn.htm

ORGANIC & LOCAL FARMING

ALTERNATIVE FARMING SYSTEMS INFORMATION CENTER
http://www.nal.usda.gov/afsic/

TILTH   http://www.tilth.org/index.html
Oregon Tilth is a non-profit research and education organization certifying organic farmers, processors, retailers and handlers throughout Oregon, the United States, and internationally.

CENTER FOR INTEGRATED AGRICULTURAL SYSTEMS
http://www.cias.wisc.edu/

FOOD CIRCLES NETWORKING PROJECT
http://foodcircles.missouri.edu/

LOCAL HARVEST
http://www.localharvest.org/about.jsp

FOUNDATION FOR LOCAL FOOD INITIATIVES
http://www.localfood.org.uk/

ORGANIC ALLIANCE   http://www.allorganiclinks.com/

ORGANIC FARMING RESEARCH FOUNDATION

GREEN PEOPLE
http://www.greenpeople.org/
Community supported agriculture (CSA) is where a group of folks buy seasonal shares of a farmer's produce, in essence, they have a stake in the farm. The farmers fresh fruits and vegetables are normally delivered each week to a location where each "buying group" then further divides the food into individual shares. CSA's support organic farming, permaculture and biodynamic farming methods for sustainable agriculture.
http://www.greenpeople.org/search2nd.cfm?type=Community_Supported_Agriculture

THE GREEN GUIDE
http://www.thegreenguide.com/issue.mhtml

ORGANIC CONSUMERS ASSOCIATION
http://www.organicconsumers.org/

THE INTERNATIONAL WWOOF
ASSOCIATIONhttp://www.wwoof.org/ is dedicated to helping those who would like to volunteer on organic farms internationally.

ORGANIC RESEARCH
http://www.organic-research.com/farms/index.asp

HEIFER INTERNATIONAL
http://www.heifer.org/index.htm
Heifer International has a unique and successful approach to ending hunger and poverty. Since 1944, Heifer has provided food- and income-producing animals and training to millions of resource-poor families in 115 countries.

Giving **microcredit** in the form of livestock promotes self-reliance, which builds self-esteem and helps families lift themselves out of poverty. Heifer's grassroots approach lets people and communities make their own decisions about how to improve their lives. As partners work together to overcome obstacles, they strengthen their communities and foster democracy.

HEIFER GLOBAL VILLAGE
http://www.howellnaturecenter.org/challengeprograms/globalvillage.htm Through education that emphasizes experience, participants gain a greater awareness of world hunger, poverty, and population issues. Groups participate in discussions on world hunger, sustainable development, and other global issues. A visit to the Heifer Global Village will take you to houses that represent Nepal, rural America, Africa, Urban Slums, Thailand, and Shantytowns.

SLOW FOOD   http://www.slowfood.com/

TERRA MADRE CONFERENCE 2004
http://www.terramadre2004.org/welcome_en.lasso
Check here to read the speeches from Carlo Petrini, Alice Waters, Winona La Duke, The Prince of Wales, Vandana Shiva, Frei Betto (of Zero Hunger), Francis Fru NGang

THE FUTURE OF FOOD – FILM
http://thefutureoffood.com/ "The Future of Food provides an excellent overview of the key questions raised by consumers as they become aware of GM foods... [The film] draws questions to critical attention about food production that need more public debate." --- Film Review by Thomas J. Hoban, **Nature Biotechnology Magazine**, March 2005, Volume 23 No. 3

NATURE BIOTECHNOLOGY MAGAZINE
http://www.nature.com/nbt/index.html Nature Biotechnology is a monthly journal covering the science and business of biotechnology. It publishes new concepts in technology/methodology of relevance to the biological, biomedical, agricultural and environmental sciences as well as covers the commercial, political, ethical, legal, and societal aspects of this research

INSTITUTE FOR COMMUNITY RESOURCE DEVELOPMENT – CHICAGO The Institute's mission is to rebuild the local food system. ICRD projects include: building grocery stores that bring access to sustainable products to urban communities of color, organizing farmers markets, converting vacant lots to urban farm sites and distributing local grown produce to restaurants. LaDonna Redmond is president and CEO of the ICRD. Redmond began researching the food system in order to feed her severely allergic son. She found that her African-American neighborhood of Austin on Chicago's West Side offered $200 sneakers, semiautomatic weapons, heroin, but no organic tomatoes. The entire community of approximately 117,000 residents is served by only one major supermarket, but many fast food restaurants. The connection between lack of healthy food and the community's high rate of obesity, diabetes, and hypertension became clear. Along with starting a local farmers market, prompting the Chicago Public Schools to re-evaluate access to junk food, and starting ICRD, she and her husband also   grew 40,000 lbs. of produce in the urban garden they helped create. A recent recipient of a **W.K. Kellogg Foundation** grant, Redmond has teamed up with five Chicago universities to study Austin's broader food needs. **Says Redmond, "Eating is a political act."** *Institute for Community Resource Development farms, Ladonna Redmond, 4429 W. Fulton Street, 200 N. Kenneth Avenue, Chicago; 773-261-7339* http://www.wkkf.org/Programming/Extra.aspx?CID=4&ID=2 25

ORGANIC CONSUMERS ASSOCIATION
http://www.organicconsumers.org/index.htm

RAINFOREST ALLIANCE
http://www.rainforest-alliance.org/

SEATTLE AUDUBON SOCIETY
http://www.seattleaudubon.org/shadecoffee/

SMITHSONIAN MIGRATORY BIRD CENTER
http://nationalzoo.si.edu/ConservationAndScience/Migratory Birds/Coffee/

SONGBIRD FOUNDATION
http://www.songbird.org/coffee/coffee_index.htm

COMMUNITY ALLIANCE WITH FAMILY FARMERS (CAFF)
http://www.caff.org/ The Community Alliance with Family Farmers is building a movement of rural and urban people to foster family-scale agriculture that cares for the land, sustains local economies and promotes social justice

COMMUNITY FOOD SECURITY COALITION
http://www.foodsecurity.org/

FOODROUTES NETWORK
http://www.foodroutes.org/ When you buy local food, you vote with your food dollar. This ensures that family farms in your community will continue to thrive and that healthy, flavorful, plentiful food will be available for future generations.

INSTITUTE FOR AGRICULTURE AND TRADE POLICY
http://www.iatp.org/ worldwide

UNITED FARMWORKERS
http://www.ufw.org/

MENDOCINO COUNTY - MEASURE H – BANS GROWING GENETICALLY ALTERED PLANTS AND ANIMALS
http://www.gmofreemendo.com/

LEOPOLD CENTER FOR SUSTAINABLE AGRICULTURE
http://www.leopold.iastate.edu/

DEEP ECOLOGY PLATFORM
http://www.deepecology.org/deepplatform.html

MEDIA

"A popular Government, without popular information, or the means of acquiring it, is but a Prologue to a Farce or a Tragedy; or, perhaps both... A people who mean to be their own Governors must arm themselves with the power which knowledge gives." -- James Madison

The following MEDIA RESOURCES are from
http://www.freepress.net/ownership/resources.php

WHO OWNS THE MEDIA?

CJR: Who Owns What? http://www.cjr.org/tools/owners/
The Columbia Journalism Review's resource page on "who owns what." The focus is on major media companies' holdings. Also included are links to relevant articles on media ownership issues. This resource is generally up-to-date.

CPI: Well Connected Databases
http://www.openairwaves.org/telecom/default.aspx
The Center For Public Integrity has an online broadcast ownership database searchable by area, call sign and company name, in addition to databases on radio rankings and FCC travel.

API: Convergence Tracker
http://www.mediacenter.org/convergencetracker/search/index.cfm The American Press Institute runs an extensive convergence tracker at their Media Center which features an interactive map of the U.S. illustrating strategic partnerships among daily newspapers, online and broadcast media.

MediaChannel: Eye on Media Ownership
http://www.mediachannel.org/ownership/
This page features various articles on media cartels, including a graphically illustrated ownership chart of the top six media conglomerates that can be accessed directly

The Nation: Big Ten
http://www.thenation.com/special/bigten.html
The Nation profiles "the big ten" media conglomerates (current as of Dec. 20, 2001) and links to a related article by NYU professor and media analyst, Mark Crispin Miller.

FRONTLINE: Media Giants
http://www.pbs.org/wgbh/pages/frontline/shows/cool/giants/ PBS "The Merchants of Cool" provides another ownership map of the top media giants (as of February, 2001) with an interesting interface.

NOW Foundation: Who Controls the Media?
http://www.nowfoundation.org/issues/communications/tv/mediacontrol.html The National Organization for Women Foundation has created a chart titled, "Who controls the Media?" With a focus on television, the chart includes good background information on parent companies, networks owned and cable interests, plus information on other significant players.

Corporations.org: Media Reform Info. Center
http://www.corporations.org/media/
The Media Reform Information Center features a basic graph depicting media concentration overtime from 1983 to 2001 along with lists of relevant links. In 1983, 50 corporations controlled the vast majority of all news media in the U.S. In 2004, Bagdikian's revised and expanded book, The New Media Monopoly, (http://www.benbagdikian.com/), shows that only 5 huge corporations -- Time Warner, Disney, Murdoch's News Corporation, Bertelsmann of Germany, and Viacom (formerly CBS) -- now control most of the media industry in the U.S. General Electric's NBC is a close sixth.

FAIR: Corporate Ownership http://www.fair.org/media-woes/corporate.html Fairness and Accuracy in Reporting offers a collection of links to investigative articles, studies and analysis of media ownership-related issues, including their annual report on "How Power Shapes the News."

MEDIA, POLITICS AND MONEY

CJR: Media Money
http://www.cjr.org/archives.asp?url=/00/3/mediamoney.asp
An in-depth analysis written in 2000 by Charles Lewis concerning the relationships between media industry contributions to politicians, lobbying costs and policy objectives. The article, from the Columbia Journalism Review, includes breakdowns of donors and recipients, such as amounts donated (including junkets) from particular companies and amounts received by individual politicians.

CRP: Capital Eye
http://www.capitaleye.org/mediacontribs.6.2.03.asp
Provided a graph of media campaign contributions.

The Center for Responsive Politics' OpenSecrets.org
http://www.opensecrets.org/
is dedicated to investigating the relationship between money and politics and is a great entry point for investigating the impact that powerful industries have on the U.S. political process. They focus on numerous issues involving the "money in politics" angle, including media ownership. The CRP's newsletter, Capital Eye, has looked at the top 25 media companies in terms of both campaign contributions and lobbying activity.

Federal Election Commission http://www.fec.gov/
For basic information on who is giving and who is receiving campaign contributions, the Federal Election Commission's website is a good resource, though not tailored specifically to media.

CPI: Well Connected .
http://www.openairwaves.org/telecom/

The Center For Public Integrity has issued a study that focuses on the cozy relationship between the FCC and the telecommunications industry. The study links to searchable databases of information on local media markets, including radio, television, telephone and cable companies. On their homepage, the Center For Public Integrity provides special investigative reports on corporate and governmental abuses of power

INTERLOCKING BOARDS OF DIRECTORS

Eat the State: Directors' Fees http://eatthestate.org/03-20/DirectorsFees.htm
An Eat the State article from 1999, based on a Project Censored article, traces connections between media companies and other corporations via overlapping boards of directors.

FAIR: Interlocking Directorates
http://www.fair.org/media-woes/interlocking-directorates.html FAIR provides an excellent resource on interlocking boards of directors for major media companies. Though this information is current as of June, 2001, FAIR also provides links to the current boards of directors of media companies' corporate parents, including Disney, GE, Time Warner, News Corp. http://www.fair.org/index.php

CENTER FOR MEDIA AND DEMOCRACY
http://www.prwatch.org/prwissues/

For a thorough list of MEDIA REFORM ORGANIZATIONS and their links, see:
http://www.freepress.net/orgs/results.php?phrase=&quickstate=any&qscope=

NEWS SOURCES

DEMOCRACY NOW! **Amy Goodman**
http://www.democracynow.org/

TOMPAINE.COM http://www.tompaine.com/

LINK TV http://www.worldlinktv.org/

COMMON DREAMS http://www.commondreams.org/

INFORMATION CLEARING HOUSE
http://www.informationclearinghouse.info/

GLOBAL PUBLIC MEDIA http://www.globalpublicmedia.com/

PUBLIC EYES TV http://www.publiceyestv.org/

INSTITUTE FOR GLOBAL COMMUNICATIONS
http://www.igc.org/index.html

ANTI-RACISM NET http://www.antiracismnet.org/main.html

ALERTNET
http://www.foundation.reuters.com/disaster/alertnet_summary.htm

INDEPENDENT MEDIA CENTER
http://www.indymedia.org/en/index.shtml

TRUTH OUT http://www.truthout.org/

GRIST http://www.grist.org/

GOOGLE NEWS
http://news.google.com/nwshp?hl=en&gl=us

ALTERNATIVE RADIO http://www.alternativeradio.org/

ALTERNET http://www.alternet.org/

ENVIRONMENTAL NEWS NETWORK http://www.enn.com/

NATIONAL PUBLIC RADIO http://www.npr.org/

TIDEPOOL http://www.tidepool.org/

CENTER FOR AMERICAN PROGRESS
http://www.americanprogressaction.org/site/pp.asp?c=klLW
JcP7H&b=83210

ESSENTIAL NEWS LINKS http://www.democracycircles.org/

TERRA DAILY http://www.terradaily.com

SPACE DAILY http://spacedaily.com/

THE SCIENTIST http://www.the-scientist.com/

UTNE.COM http://utne.com/ Excellent!

VILLAGE VOICE http://www.villagevoice.com/

WIRETAP http://www.alternet.org/wiretap/

FREE SPEECH
http://www.freespeech.org/fsitv/fscm2/genx.php?name=ho
me

ZNET http://www.zmag.org/ZNET.htm

PACIFICA RADIO http://www.pacifica.org/stations/

CHRISTIAN SCIENCE MONITOR http://www.csmonitor.com/

THE ECONOMIST http://www.economist.com

MOTHER JONES http://www.motherjones.com/

COUNTER PUNCH   http://www.counterpunch.org/

FIELDNOTES
http://www.shambhalainstitute.org/Fieldnotes/Issue3/

STAY FREE MAGAZINE http://www.stayfreemagazine.org/

PUBLIC LIBRARY OF SCIENCE
http://www.publiclibraryofscience.com/

BEYOND THE ORDINARY – RADIO
http://www.beyondtheordinary.net/BTO-PreLoad-4.html

SCIENCE AND DEVELOPMENT NETWORK
http://www.scidev.net/

HUMAN MEDIA http://www.humanmedia.org

POSITIVE NEWS, worldwide publication:
http://www.positivenews.org.uk/index.php

NEW WAYS OF PERCEIVING MEDIA

BOOTSTRAP INSTITUTE   http://bootstrap.org/
Imagine what we can accomplish together
The Bootstrap Institute was conceived by **Dr. Douglas C.
Engelbart**. He garnered fame through his invention of the
computer mouse and is credited with pioneering online
computing and email, and other inventions and innovations.
MEDIA VENTURE COLLECTIVE
http://www.mediaventure.org/call.html?&PHPSESSID=0a625
65e6ccdd591d3507de77c8a95cc

FIRST AMENDMENT RIGHTS & EDUCATION

FUTURE OF THE FIRST AMENDMENT
http://firstamendment.jideas.org/index.html

Key Findings Published JAN 31 2005:
http://firstamendment.jideas.org/findings/findings.php

FIRST AMENDMENT STANDARDS IN EDUCATION
http://firstamendment.jideas.org/standards/standards.php

J-IDEAS http://www.jideas.org/

REPORTER SAFETY
REPORTERS WITHOUT BORDERS   http://www.rsf.org/
More than a third of the world's people live in countries
where there is no press freedom. Reporters Without Borders
works constantly to restore their right to be informed.
**Fourty-two media professionals lost their lives in
2003 for doing what they were paid to do -- keeping
us informed. Today, more than 130 journalists
around the world are in prison simply for doing their
job.** In Nepal, Eritrea and China, they can spend years in jail
just for using the "wrong" word or photo. Reporters Without
Borders believes imprisoning or killing a journalist is like
eliminating a key witness and threatens everyone's right to
be informed. It has been fighting such practices for more
than 18 years. Reporters Without Borders' maintains this
trilingual (French, English and Spanish) website in order to
keep a daily tally of attacks on press freedom as they occur
throughout the world.
Every year, on 3 May, Reporters Without Borders celebrates
World Press Freedom Day. On this occasion, it publishes a
full report of the status of press freedom in more than 150
countries. In addition, the association offers news staffs
around the world an opportunity to support incarcerated
journalists through its "sponsorship" programme.

Free Wireless Access Model
CHAMPAIGN-URBANA COMMUNITY WIRELESS NETWORK
http://www.cuwireless.net/

MONEY

INSTITUTE OF ECOLONOMICS   The mission of the
Institute of Ecolonomics is to demonstrate that creating a
symbiotic relationship between a strong economy and a
healthy ecology is the only formula for a sustainable future.
http://www.ecolonomics.org/

THE PROSPERITY GAME
http://www.choosingprosperity.com/game/ Elyse Hope
Killoran of Choosing Prosperity developed The Prosperity
Game, first introduced by **Abraham-Hicks**
(http://www.choosingprosperity.com/abraham-hicks.htm),
teachers of Deliberate Creation. It is a simple, fun, and
empowering way to activate one's ability to create prosperity
- from the inside-out. *(From Shaktari – I cannot recommend
this game enough. Try it with a partner. It is a joyous way
to re-think your relationship to money – and ultimately all
life.)*

JEFF GATES AND THE SHARED CAPITALISM INSTITUTE:
http://www.sharedcapitalism.org/

The mission of the Shared Capitalism Institute is to catalyze
critically needed progress at the local, regional, national and
global levels toward a more equitable and sustainable form
of free enterprise

Facts From Jeff's Website Showing
WHY THIS IS AN ISSUE:
http://www.sharedcapitalism.org/scfacts.html

o The financial wealth of the top one percent of households now exceeds the combined wealth of the bottom 95 percent. [Note 1]

o The wealth of the Forbes 400 richest Americans grew by an average $940 million each from 1997-1999 [Note 2] while over a recent 12-year period the net worth of the bottom 40 percent of households declined 80 percent. [Note 3]

o For the well-to-do, that's an average increase in wealth of $1,287,671 per day. [Note 4] If that were wages earned over a 40-hour week, that would be $225,962 an hour or 43,876 times the $5.15 per hour minimum wage.

o The Federal Reserve found in its latest survey of consumer finances that although median family net worth rose 17.6 percent between 1995 and 1998, family wealth was "substantially below" 1989 levels for all income groups under age 55. [Note 5]

o From 1983-1997, only the top five percent of households saw an increase in their net worth while wealth declined for everyone else. [Note 6]

o As of 1997, the median household financial wealth (marketable assets less home equity) was $11,700, $1,300 lower than in 1989. [Note 7]

o Anticipated Social Security payments are now the largest single "asset" for a majority of Americans. Funded by a levy on jobs, the Social Security payroll tax is now the largest tax paid by a majority of Americans (the largest for 90 percent of GenXers), funded with a flat tax of 12.4 percent on earnings up to $72,600.

o For the first time since the Great Depression, the national savings rate turned negative (during the first quarter of 1999). [Note 8]

o What about the largest intergenerational transfer of wealth in history -- that $12 trillion in the hands of baby-boomers' parents? Current wealth patterns indicate that one-third of that pending transfer will go to 1 percent of the boomers ($1.6 million each). Another third will go to the next 9 percent ($336,000). The final slice will be divided by the remaining 90 percent (an average $40,000 apiece). [Note 9]

A Boom for Whom?

o The richest 400 Americans hold wealth equivalent to one-eighth of the GDP. [Note 10]

o The average wealth of the Forbes 400 was $200 million in 1982, just after the enactment of the Reagan-Bush "supply-side" tax package - paid for with $872 billion in deficit financing. [Note 11] By 1986, their average wealth was $500 million.

o In 1982, inclusion on the Forbes 400 required personal wealth of $91 million. The list then included 13 billionaires. By 1999, $625 million was required for inclusion on a list that included 268 billionaires. [Note 12]

o The federal debt was $909 billion in 1980. At the close of the Reagan-Bush era, the debt was $4,202 billion. It currently hovers around $5,700 billion. [Note 13]

o Government debt securities are owned dominantly by upper-crust households. The latest figures show that tax-exempt interest was reported on 4.9 million personal tax returns for 1997, about 4 percent of all taxpayers. Total tax-exempt interest income was $48.5 billion in 1997. [Note 14]

o The combined net worth of the Forbes 400 topped $1 trillion in September 1999, up from $738 billion 12 months earlier, for an average one-year increase of $655 million each ($12.6 million per week). [Note 15]

o Less than one-fifth of that increase ($48.4 billion) would have been enough to bring every American up to the official poverty line, leaving each of the Forbes 400 with an average one-year increase of $534 million ($10.2 million per week).

o While the number of households expanded 3 percent from 1995 to 1998, households with a net worth of $10 million or more grew 44.7 percent. [Note 16]

o Eighty-six percent of stock market gains between 1989 and 1997 flowed to the top ten percent of households while 42 percent went to the most well-to-do one percent. [Note 17]

o If Congress adopts Martin Feldstein's proposal for the partial privatization of Social Security, the U.S. Treasury will pump budget surpluses equal to 2.3 percent of the national payroll into the stock market each year. That's $100 billion-plus per year in tax revenues to boost stock prices. [Note 18]

In a Nation of Equals

o In 1998 the top-earning one percent had as much income as the 100 million Americans with the lowest earnings. [Note 19]

o From 1983-1995, only the top 20 percent of households saw any real increase in their income while the middle-earning 20 percent, if they lost their jobs, had enough savings to maintain their standard of living for 1.2 months (36 days), down from 3.6 months in 1989. [Note 20]

o Economist Robert Frank reports that the top one percent captured 70 percent of all earnings growth since the mid-1970's. [Note 21]

o The Federal Reserve found that "median income between 1989 and 1998 rose appreciably only for families headed by college graduates." [Note 22]

o On an inflation-adjusted basis, the median hourly wage in 1998 was 7 percent lower than in 1973 - when Richard Nixon was in the White House. [Note 23]

o The pay gap between top executives and production workers grew from 42:1 in 1980 to 419:1 in 1998 (excluding the value of stock options). [Note 24]

o Executive pay at the nation's 365 largest companies rose an average 481 percent from 1990 to 1998 while corporate profits rose 108 percent. [Note 25]

o Had the typical worker's pay risen in tandem with executive pay, the average production worker would now earn $110,000 a year and the minimum wage would be $22.08.

o   Business Week reports that in 1998 the average large company chief executive was paid $10.6 million, a 36 percent jump over 1997. [Note 26] That omits unexercised stock options.

o   Compensation expert Graef Crystal identifies five CEOs who each saw their wallets widen by more than $232 million in 1998 as they exercised their stock options. For a 40-hour week, that's $116,000 per hour.

In the Pursuit of Happiness

o   The work year has expanded by 184 hours since 1970, an additional 4-1/2 weeks on the job for the same or less pay. [Note 27]

o   Household working hours reached 3,149 in 1998, roughly 60 hours a week for the typical family, moving Americans into first place worldwide in the number of hours worked, nudging aside the workaholic Japanese. [Note 28]

o   According to the Bureau of Labor statistics, the typical American now works 350 hours more per year than a typical European -- almost nine full weeks.

o   More than 65 million anti-depressant prescriptions were written in 1998.

o   Parents spend 40 percent less time with their children today than they did thirty years ago. [Note 29]

o   A 40-hour week at today's minimum wage of $5.15 per hour nets a pre-tax annual income of $10,300. That's $6,355.00 below the official 1998 poverty line for a family of four.

o   Had increases in the minimum wage kept pace with inflation since the 1960s, the minimum wage would now exceed the earnings of nearly 30 percent of U.S. workers. [Note 30]

o   The after-tax income flowing to the middle 60 percent of households in 1999 is the lowest recorded since 1977. Among the bottom fifth of households, average after-tax income fell nine percent from 1977 to 1999.

o   In New York, the highest-income five percent of families gained nearly $108,000 in average income per family from the late 1970s to the late 1990s, while the lowest-income 20 percent of New Yorkers lost $2,900. [Note 31]

o   The Census Bureau reports that the pretax median income was $1,001 higher in 1998 than in 1989. For the decade of the 1990s, that's an average annual raise, adjusted for inflation, of $111.22, or 0.3 percent.

o   According to the Census Bureau, the top fifth of households now claim 49.2 percent of national income while the bottom fifth gets by on 3.6 percent. [Note 32]

o   Except for inflation adjustments, today's poverty formula remains unchanged since 1965 when it was designed by Lyndon Johnson to address severe nutritional deprivation but only if "the housewife is a careful shopper, a skillful cook and a good manager who will prepare all the family's meals at home."

o   The national poverty rate remains above that for any year in the 1970's.

o   One in every four preschoolers in the United States now lives in poverty. [Note 33]

o   Bill Clinton reported a 12.7 percent poverty rate in September 1999, the lowest level in a decade.

o   Raising the poverty threshold to $19,500 (as recommended by the Census Bureau) boosts the poverty rate to a record-high 17 percent, leaving 46 million Americans short of that minimal level.

o   In 1998, the nation's three primary income security programs -- Social Security, Medicare and civil service pensions -- consumed $805.2 billion in federal tax revenues. [Note 34] Meanwhile, the U.S. General Accounting Office (GAO) reports that we need $112 billion to repair dilapidated public schools.

o   In 1973, the United States imprisoned 350,000 people nationwide. By 1998, the prison population was 1.8 million or roughly 674 people in prison per 100,000, while Europe-wide the imprisonment rate is 60 to 100 per 100,000. Florida now spends more on corrections than on colleges. California spent nine percent of its 1998 budget on prisons as it responded to an 8-fold increase in its prison population over the past two decades. The Rand Corporation projects that California's prison spending will top 16 percent by 2005.

Whose Wealth of Nations?

o   In 1998, Disney CEO Michael Eisner received a pay package totaling $575.6 million, 25,070 times the average Disney worker's pay. [Note 35]

o   In the same year (1998) when one American (Bill Gates) amassed more wealth than the combined net worth of the poorest 45 percent of American households, [Note 36] a record 1.4 million Americans filed for bankruptcy -- 7,000 bankruptcies per hour, 8 hours a day, 5 days a week. [Note 37] Personal bankruptcy filings topped 1.3 million in 1999.

o   Since 1992, mortgage debt has grown 60 percent faster than income while consumer debt (mostly auto loans and credit cards) has grown twice as fast. The fastest growing segment of the credit card market consists of low-income holders, with the average amount owed growing 18 times faster than income. [Note 38]

o   Nine years into the longest economic expansion in the nation's history, labor's share of the national income remains two to four percentage points below the levels reached in the late 1960's and early 1970's. [Note 39]

o   Household debt as a percentage of personal income rose from 58 percent in 1973 to an estimated 85 percent in 1997.

o   In 1997, 142,556 people reported adjusted gross income of $1 million or more, according to the IRS, up from 86,998 for 1995. [Note 40]

o   For 1999, the Congressional Budget Office (CBO) projects that the top one percent will report average before-tax income of $786,000 and average after-tax income of $516,000. [Note 41]

o   The top one percent pocketed, on average, an annual tax cut of $40,000 since 1977, an amount exceeding the average annual income of the middle fifth of households. [Note 42]

o If the richest one percent of the population had received the same share of the nation's after-tax income in 1999 as it did in 1977, it would have received $271 billion less in 1999 -- $226,000 less per household. [Note 43]

o Between 1977 and 1999, the after-tax income of the top one percent grew faster (115 percent) than their before-tax income (96 percent). [Note 44]

o In 1998, 9,257 new and existing homes sold for $1 million or more, triple the number of million-dollar homes on the market in 1995. Annual mortgage interest payments on a newly purchased $1 million home total $79,247 (assuming 10 percent down and a 30-year adjustable rate mortgage at 8 percent). The home mortgage interest deduction for someone in the top 39.6-percent tax bracket saves on that house $31,382 a year in federal income taxes. When that saving is added to the $40,000 average annual tax cut allowed the top one percent since 1977, that $1 million home costs $7,865 per year, or $655 per month.

o Federal tax law allows a personal income tax deduction on home mortgage interest costs up to $1 million. If that limit were reduced to $300,000, the CBO calculates that federal tax receipts would increase by $40.8 billion over nine years. In 1998, four percent of new mortgages exceeded $300,000.

o For every age group under 55, home ownership remains below where it was in the early 1980s. [Note 45]

Minorities and Foundations

o The percentage of black households with zero or negative net worth (31.3 percent) is double that of whites. [Note 46]

o As of 1997, the net worth of white families was 8 times that of African-Americans and 12 times that of Hispanics. The median financial wealth of African-Americans (net worth less home equity) is $200 while that of Hispanics is zero. [Note 47]

o The poverty rate among blacks, 26.1 percent, is 2.5 times greater than the rate for whites. For Hispanics, the rate is 25.6 percent.

o Black applicants were granted less than one percent of total home mortgages approved between 1930 and 1960. [Note 48]

o Only in 1999 did home ownership among blacks recover ground lost since 1983.

o Black-owned small businesses were three times as likely as whites to have their loan applications turned down in the 1990s. [Note 49]

o The United States has 18,000 black farmers, down from 925,000 in 1920. Less than one percent of farmers are black, and they are abandoning farming at three times the rate of whites. In 1999, the Agriculture Department gave its long-delayed assent to a class-action settlement to compensate black farmers who have complained for decades at being shut out of federal loan programs due to racism. [Note 50]

o In 1865, blacks owned 0.5 percent of the nation's net worth. In 1990, their net worth totaled 1 percent. [Note 51]

o Black students scored 144 points less on the SAT than white students where the parents of both earn over $70,000. When black test scores are compared to those of white students with the same family wealth, the "achievement gap" disappears. [Note 52]

o If your financial wealth is $225,000 (about 20 times the national median) and you give $1,500 to charity, how large a donation would be required for Bill Gates to experience a similar dent in his net worth? According to Wired magazine, $6.7 billion. That's almost seven times the amount he pledged in September 1999 to provide 20,000 minority scholarships over the next two decades. [Note 53] With the December 1999 completion of Windows 2000, the value of Gates's personally held Microsoft shares rose to more than $130 billion, almost 12 times the $11 billion or so in securities owned by all 33 million African-Americans combined.

o If an entry-level Forbes 400 member gives away $1 million of their income, how much would a median-level household need to donate to make a similar financial sacrifice? A bit less than $60.

Making the World Safe for Plutocracy

o The world's 200 richest people more than doubled their net worth in the four years to 1999, to more than $1 trillion, for an average $5 billion each. [Note 54] Their combined wealth (the top seven are Americans) equals the combined annual income of the world's poorest 2.5 billion people. [Note 55]

o Microsoft co-founders Bill Gates and Paul Allen plus Berkshire Hathaway's Warren Buffet have a net worth larger than the combined GDP of the 41 poorest nations and their 550 million people. [Note 56]

o Warren Buffet's 1999 net worth ($31 billion) equals the GDP of Kuwait.

o The wealth of the world's 84 richest individuals exceeds the GDP of China with its 1.3 billion people. [Note 57]

o If the value of Bill Gates's Microsoft stock continues to grow at the same pace as it has since Microsoft's 1986 initial public offering (58.2 percent a year), Wired projects he will become a trillionaire in March 2005, at the age of 49, and his Microsoft holdings will top $1 quadrillion (one million billion) in March 2020, at the age of 64. The Gross World Product for 1998 was $39,000 billion.

o The UN Development Program (UNDP) reports that 80 countries have per capita incomes lower than a decade ago. [Note 58] Sixty countries have been growing steadily poorer since 1980. [Note 59]

o Three billion people live on less than $2 per day while 1.3 billion of those get by on less than $1 per day. [Note 60]

o In 1960, the income gap between the fifth of the world's people living in the richest countries and the fifth in the poorest countries was 30 to 1. By 1990, the gap had widened to 60 to 1. By 1998, it had grown to 74 to 1. [Note 61]

o   With global population expanding 80 million each year, World Bank President Jim Wolfensohn cautions that, unless we address this "challenge of inclusion," 30 years hence we will have 5 billion people living on less than $2 per day.

o   The UNDP reports that two billion people suffer from anemia, including 55 million in industrial countries. Current trends suggest that in three decades we could inhabit a world where 3.7 billion people suffer from anemia.

o   UNDP's assessment of today's development trends: "Development that perpetuates today's inequalities in neither sustainable nor worth sustaining." [Note 62]

o   In Indonesia, 61.7 percent of the stock market's value is held by the nation's 15 richest families. The comparable figure for the Philippines is 55.1 percent and 53.3 percent for Thailand. [Note 63]

A Closer Look at Globalization

o   The world's 200 largest corporations account for 28 percent of global economic activity while employing less than one-quarter of one percent of the global workforce.

o   The World Bank estimates that $100 billion to $150 billion has flowed out of the former Soviet Union since the fall of the Berlin Wall. As of July 1999, one-third of Russians were living below the official poverty line of $38 per month.

o   The UNDP identifies six core ingredients as minimal conditions for a decent life: safe drinking water (1.3 billion people lack access to clean water), [Note 64] adequate sanitation, sufficient nutrition, primary health care, basic education (one in seven children of primary school age is out of school), [Note 65] and family planning services for all willing couples. UNDP calculates the cost at $35 billion each year for the next 15 years. That's about what the United States spent in 1999 to maintain its nuclear readiness, a decade after the fall of the Berlin Wall. For the world community to bear the cost would require 1/7 of 1 percent of global GDP; the United States contributes to the UN 0.09 percent of its GDP. [Note 66]

o   Every jet fighter sold by a developed country to a developing country costs the schooling of three million children. [Note 67] The cost of a submarine denies safe drinking water to 60 million people.

o   In the 1997 fiscal year, the United States exported $8.3 billion of arms to non-democratic countries.

o   The Clinton-Gore Administration is calling for a $110 billion increase in the Pentagon budget, including a 50 percent increase in weapons procurement through 2004; Republican Congressional leaders insist on considerably more funds for military remobilization.

o   What if those individuals who have captured the most wealth in the global economy were to bear this $35 billion development cost? An annual 3.5 percent levy on the $1 trillion in assets owned by the world's 200 wealthiest people would raise the requisite funds.

Three-quarters of those people live in OECD countries; one-third of them reside in the United States. [Note 68]

o   Experts report that the well-to-do have hidden at least $8 trillion in tax havens. [Note 69]

o   If the international community identified the owners of that $8 trillion -- held in an estimated 1.5 million offshore corporations (up from 200,000 just since the late 1980s) -- an annual "freeloader levy" of 3.5 percent, less than the typical sales tax, could generate $280 billion each year. That's 165 times the current budget for all UN development programs. Or 93 times the UN's annual expenditure for peacekeeping operations, now raised pass-your-hat style. That's enough to build 140,000 schools at $2 million apiece. That's also the bulk of the $300 billion that environmental researchers at Cambridge and Sheffield Universities report would be required each year to "save the planet." [Note 70]

o   Eighty percent of the world's people live in developing countries.

o   Ninety-five percent of the next generation's children will be born to women there.

o   Seventy percent of those women live on less than $1 per day.

o   Ninety percent of those women labor on average 35 hours more per week than the typical paid workman. None of their work is reflected in the GDP.

o   Women in developing countries produce 80 percent of the food and receive 10 percent of the agricultural assistance.

o   Seventy percent are illiterate.

o   For every year that women attend school beyond the fourth grade, the birth rate declines 20 percent.

o   Fifty percent of women over age 18 can neither read nor write.

o   Less than one percent of the world's assets are held in the name of women.

END NOTES

1) Edward N. Wolff, "Recent Trends in Wealth Ownership," a paper for the conference on "Benefits and Mechanisms for Spreading Asset Ownership in the United States," New York University, December 10-12, 1998. In 1995, the financial wealth of the top one percent was greater than the bottom 90 percent.

2) Forbes 400, October 11, 1999.

3) Edward N. Wolff, "Recent Trends in Wealth Ownership," Ibid. The period cited was 1983 to 1995, based on the Federal Reserve's 1995 Survey of Consumer Finances.

4) Forbes 400 wealth was $624 billion in 1997, $738 billion in 1998 and $1 trillion-plus in 1999. See www.forbes.com.

5) Federal Reserve Bulletin, January 2000, p. 6.

6) Ibid., p. 10.

7) Median household financial wealth was less than $10,000 in 1995. The $11,700 figure is based on a 12-percent growth projection in Wolff, "Recent Trends in Wealth Ownership," Ibid.

8) Albert B. Crenshaw, "Taking Reduced Saving Into Account," The Washington Post National Weekly Edition, June 28, 1999, p. 21.

9) Near Karlen, "And the Meek Shall Inherit Nothing," The New York Times, July 29, 1999, p. B1.

10) See www.forbes.com.

11) Joint Committee on Taxation, General Explanation of the Economic Recovery Tax Act of 1981, p. 401.

12) Forbes 400, September 13, 1982; Forbes 400, October 11, 1999.

13) Economic Report of the President (February 1999), p. 419.

14) "Tax Report," The Wall Street Journal, July 21, 1999, p. 1

15) Forbes 400, October 11, 1999 (see www.forbes.com).

16) Louis Uchitelle, "More Wealth, More Stately Mansions," The New York Times, June 6, 1999, p. A 16, citing research by Prof. Edward N. Wolff.

17) David Wessel, "U.S. Stock Holdings Rose 20% in 1998," The Wall Street Journal, March 15, 1999, p. A6..

18) Feldstein, chairman of Reagan's Council of Economic Advisers, was a key architect of supply-side economics.

19) Congressional Budget Office Memorandum, Estimates of Federal Tax Liabilities for Individuals and Families by Income Categoy and Family Type for 1995 and 1999, May 1998.

20) Edward N. Wolff, Ibid., p. 10.

21) Robert Frank, Luxury Fever (New York: Simon & Schuster, 1999).

22) Federal Reserve Bulletin, January 2000, p. 53.

23) Median earnings based on Commerce Department's Bureau of Economic Analysis data reported in State of Working America 1998-99; labor's share of non-farm business sector income based on Bureau of Labor Statistics data reported in Economic Report of the President (February 1999), at p. 384.

24) Business Week, "49th Annual Executive Pay Survey," April 19, 1999.

25) A Decade of Executive Excess: The 1990s (Boston: United for a Fair Economy and Institute for Policy Studies, 1999).

26) Business Week, "49th Annual Executive Pay Survey," April 19, 1999.

27) Juliet S. Schor, The Overworked American (New York: Basic Books, 1992) indicating that the annual work year increased by 139 hours from 1969-1989. The Washington, D.C.-based Economic Policy Institute found that the annual hours worked expanded by 45 hours from 1989-1994.

28) Steven Greenhouse, "So Much Work, So Little Time," The New York Times, September 5, 1999, p. WK1.

29) Charles Handy, The Hungry Spirit (New York: Broadway, 1998), p. 17.

30) See Joel Blau, Illusions of Prosperity: America's Working Families in an Age of Economic Insecurity (New York: Oxford University Press, 1999).

31) "State Income Inequality Continues to Grow in Most States in the 1990s, Despite Economic Growth and Tight Labor Markets," report by the Economic Policy Institute and the Center for Budget and Policy Priorities, Washington, D.C., January 18, 2000.

32) See www.census.gov ("income" at Table H-2).

33) Tamar Levin, "Study Finds That Youngest U.S. Children are Poorest, The New York Times, March 15, 1998, p. Y 18.

34) Economic Report of the President (February 1999), p. 421.

35) It was only after strenuous objection from institutional investors that Eisner agreed to remove his personal attorney from the compensation committee of Disney's board of directors.

36) Professor Edward N. Wolff cited in "A Scholar Who Concentrates... on Concentrations of Wealth," Too Much, Winter 1999, p.8.

370 Doug Henwood, "Debts Everywhere," The Nation, July 19, 1999, p. 12.

38) Ibid.

39) Louis Uchitelle, "As Class Struggle Subsides, Less Pie for the Workers," The New York Times, December 5, 1999, p. BU4 (reporting on research by Professor Edward N. Wolff).

40) "Tax Report," The Wall Street Journal, July 28, 1999, p. 1.

41) CBO Memorandum, Estimates of Federal Tax Liabilities for Individuals and Families by Income Category and Family Type for 1995 and 1999, May 1998.

42) Issac Shapiro and Robert Greenstein, "The Widening Income Gulf," Washington, D.C., Center for Budget and Policy Priorities, September 4, 1999, citing CBO figures.

43) Isaac Shapiro and Robert Greenstein, Ibid.

44) Ibid.

45 Homeowners are also now much more highly leveraged than in the 1980s, with down payments at record lows and mortgage levels at record highs. Lou Uchitelle, "In Home Ownership Data, A Hidden Generation Gap," The New York Times, September 26, 1999, p. BU4.

46) Edward N. Wolff, Ibid.

47) Ibid., p. 41, table 6.

48) Results of 1991 Federal Reserve Board study analyzing 1990 Home Mortgage Disclosure Act data.

49) "Credit Gap in Black and White," FOMC Alert, Financial Markets Center, May 18, 1999, p. 11.

50) "15,000 Black Farmers File Claims in Racial Settlement," The New York Times, September 21, 1999, p. A25.

51) Dalton Conley, Being Black, Living in the Red, (Berkeley: University of California Press, 1999).

52) Ibid.

53) Evan L. Marcus, "The World's First Trillionaire," Wired, September 1999, p. 163.

54) United Nations Human Development Report 1999, Ibid.

55) United Nations Human Development Report 1998 (New York: Oxford University Press, 1998).

56) "Rich Comparison," The Wall Street Journal, July 30, 1999, p. 1.

57) United Nations Human Development Report 1998, Ibid.

58) United Nations Human Development Report 1999 (New York: Oxford University Press, 1999), p. 2.

59) Ibid. at p. v.

60) Ibid., at p. 3.

610 United Nations Human Development Report 1999, Ibid., p. 28.

62) United Nations Human Development Report 1996 (New York: Oxford University Press, 1996), p. 4.

63) Stijn Claessens, Simeon Djankov and Larry H.P. Lang, "Who Controls East Asian Corporations?" (Washington, D.C.: The World Bank, 1999).

64) United Nations Human Development Report 1999, Ibid., p. 28.

65) Ibid.

66) Mahbub ul Haq, "Charter of Human Development Initiative," State of the World Forum (San Francisco, October 3, 1996).

67) See Oscar Arias, "Stopping America's Most Lethal Export," New York Times, June 23, 1999, p. A23.

68) United Nations Human Development Report, 1998, p. 30.

69) The IMF estimates that the amount in offshore tax havens grew from $3.5 trillion in 1992 to $4.8 trillion in 1997. Other estimates put the amount as high as $13.7 trillion. See Douglas Farah, "A New Wave of Island Investing," The Washington Post National Weekly Review, October 18, 1999, p. 15. Alan Cowell and Edmund L. Andrews, "Undercurrents at a Safe Harbor," The New York Times, September 24, 1999, p. C1.

70) The Times (London), September 23, 1999.

LIVING ECONOMIES http://www.stable-money.com/tiki-index.php **PATHWAY TO LIVING ECONOMIES** – PDF Collaborative Working Document http://www.svn.org/Initiatives/fall-2001/PDF_livingeconomies.pdf

BOOKS

Brown, Lester **Eco-Economy** – Building an Economy for the Earth EARTH POLICY INSTITUTE, W.W. Norton & Company NY 2001

Lietaer, Bernard A. and Belgin, Stephen M. **Of Human Wealth** – Beyond Greed & Scarcity (Galley Edition), Human Wealth Book and Talks, 2003

Lietaer, Bernard A. **The Future of Money** – Creating New Wealth, Work and a Wiser World, Century, The Random House Group Limited, London, 2001.

Hwoschinsky, Paul **True Wealth** – An Innovative Guide to Dealing with Money in Our Lives, Ten Speed Press, 1990.

Roads, Michael J. **More Than Money, True Prosperity** - A Wholistic Guide To Having It All, SilverRoads, 2003.

COMPLEMENTARY CURRIENCIES

BERNARD LIETAER ACCESS FOUNDATION: http://access.dreamteamtech.com/

TRANSACTION http://www.transaction.net/money/cc/cc01.html

COMPLEMENTARY ECONOMICS: http://www.skaggs-island.org/sustainable/awcomplementaryecon.html Arthur Warmoth, Ph.D. Sonoma State University, Skaggs Island Foundation "Complementary economics" deals with those areas of economics that are ignored or inadequately understood by conventional economics (and economists), which is essentially the economics of markets, of manufacturing and trade. Conventional economics pays insufficient attention to the question of the nature of money as such. Furthermore, it ignores or provides a distorted image of a large arena of economic activity that cannot be traded in markets. This economic arena is sometimes referred to as public goods and services. However, there is no widely accepted term to refer in a comprehensive way to these collectively consumed goods and services, as well as to our collectively held natural and social assets. Recently some commentators have begun to refer to this economic arena as "the commons."

MARGRIT KENNEDY: http://www.margritkennedy.de/english/index.html Money allows the exchange of goods and services and, in doing so, becomes one of the most genial inventions of humankind. However, few people understand how money functions. If they did understand, we would have a quite different monetary system immediately - one which would bring more social justice, better opportunities for a healthy environment and higher stability of currencies.

CHIEMGAUER: http://www.chiemgau-regional.de/

SALT SPRING ISLAND CURRENCY http://www.saltspringdollars.com/welcome.htm

LETS SYSTEM http://www.gmlets.u-net.com/ A LETSystem is a trading network supported by its own internal currency. It is self-regulating and allows its users to manage and issue their own 'money supply' within the boundaries of the network.

The key points include:

- **co-operation:** no-one owns the network.

- **self-regulation:** the network is controlled by its users.

- **empowerment:** all network users may 'issue' the 'internal currency'.

- **money:** money, as a means of exchange, is an integral feature.

LETSystem recording services keep track of transactions. The word "LETS" was chosen to highlight an invitation (let's) and a culture of consent. LETS embodies the 'Law of Two Feet' - *"If you like it, you walk in. If you don't, then you walk away"*.

TIME DOLLARS

NEW ENGLAND TIME BANKS   http://www.mtdn.org/ Join 1000s of others across Maine, the US and the world who have become part of the growing international Time Dollar movement: A movement that values all human beings as equals; honors human decency, kindness and compassion and encourages love and sharing. It's about TIME!

TIME DOLLAR USA http://www.timedollar.org/au_staff_td_usa.htm

ITHACA HOURS http://www.ithacahours.com/ and http://www.ithacahours.org/

Here in Ithaca, New York, we've begun to gain control of the social and environmental effects of commerce by issuing over $105,000 of our own local paper money, to thousands of residents, since 1991. We call our local currency Ithaca "HOURS" because this encourages us to think about the value of everyone's time. The name reminds us that the real source of money's value is created by people -- their time, skills, and energy. Every time we use HOURS, we:

- Strengthen our commitment to the people who live here.

- Add to our local spending power.

- Reduce the need to transport goods and for excess packaging.

- Create jobs for ourselves and our neighbors.

- Help set a standard for a living wage.

Doing business locally often turns into doing business with friends.

We're Making a Community while Making a Living.

TOM GRECO JR. and the COMMUNITY INFORMATION RESOURCE CENTER http://circ2.home.mindspring.com/ CIRC is a networking hub and information source dedicated to building a better world.

TOM GRECO JR and **REINVENTING MONEY**: http://reinventingmoney.com/ The mission of this site is to demystify money by presenting the best leading-edge ideas on monetary and non-monetary exchange. It is a resource devoted to the advancement of economic democracy, self-determination, and global harmony.

LIVING ECONOMIES – NEW ZEALAND http://www.stable-money.com/tiki-index.php

LOCAL EXCHANGE SYSTEMS IN ASIA, AFRICA, AND LATIN AMERICA http://www.appropriate-economics.org/

VIA3.NET   http://www.via3.net/default.asp

CC WORLD TALK http://ccit.wji.com/tiki-read_article.php?articleId=49

COMPLEMENTARY CURRENCY RESOURCE CENTER http://complementarycurrency.org/

COMPLEMENTARY CURRENCY DATABASE http://complementarycurrency.org/ccDatabase/les_public.html

CYCLOS COMPLEMENTARY CURRENCY SOFTWARE http://project.cyclos.org .

PAYCIRCLE   http://www.paycircle.org/

GOLD MONEY BILL – NEW HAMPSHIRE http://www.goldmoneybill.org/

MONEYFILES.ORG http://www.moneyfiles.org/usapower.jpgs

The following graph shows the purchasing power of the US Dollar in the 20th Century. This graph is re-printed with permission from MoneyFiles.org. Graph by Bud Wood based on data from "Dirty Little Secrets of the 20th Century" by James Dunnigan. © 2002 Bud Wood.

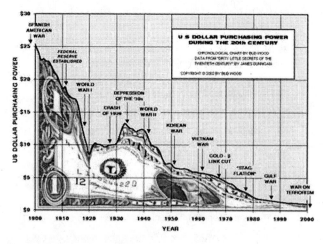

FINANCIAL SENSE ON-LINE http://www.financialsense.com/index.html

ANTI-COUNTERFEIT OPTIONS:

ALDERTECH INTERNATIONAL INC. http://www.saltspringdollars.com/antiframe.htm

RE-THINKING ECONOMIC WELLBEING

REDEFINING PROGRESS - The Genuine Progress Indicator 1950-2002 (2004 Update), http://www.redefiningprogress.org/publications/gpi_march2004update.pdf *For a brief explanation of the GPI, see:* http://www.redefiningprogress.org/projects/gpi/

Nation's Economic Health Overstated by $7 Trillion: Genuine Progress Indicator Tells the Real Story. *For a press release explaining the March 2004 GPI Report,:* http://www.redefiningprogress.org/media/releases/040311_gpi.html

HAZEL HENDERSON: http://www.hazelhenderson.com/

THE DARWIN PROJECT http://www.thedarwinproject.com/ In the Descent of Man Charles Darwin wrote only twice of "survival of the fittest" — but 95 times about love! 92 times about moral sensitivity. And 200 times about brain and mind. Suppression over 100 years of the real Darwin has led to the social, political, economic, scientific, educational, moral and spiritual mess we are in today. The mission of The Darwin Project is to speed the shift in our homes, schools, and the media from only teaching destructive "first-half" Darwinism to the inspiring liberation of Darwin's long lost completing half — along with all the fields of modern science that support and expand Darwin's original full vision to reveal caring, love, moral evolution, and education as the prime drivers for human evolution. See specifically **http://www.thedarwinproject.com/philanthropy/philanthropy.html** on the economics of philanthropy.

ALLIANCE FOR A CARING ECONOMY (ACE) http://www.partnershipway.org/html/acepage.htm

KENAN INSTITUTE http://www.kenan-flagler.unc.edu/KI/

CENTER ONF BUDGET AND POLICY PRIORITIES http://www.cbpp.org/

CAPITAL OWNERSHIP GROUP http://cog.kent.edu/

CLUB OF BUDAPEST USA   http://www.cobusa.org/

INVESTING AND BANKING WEBSITES

Socially Responsible Investment Funds (SRI)

(**NOTE**: Paul Hawken has recently had the Natural Capital Institute (http://www.naturalcapital.org/intro.html) research SRI Funds. He was disappointed to find that few screen thoroughly for environmental responsibility. Hawken writes, "In the US, there are funds that make real contributions to corporate reform and accountability:
Portfolio 21(http://www.portfolio21.com/),
Calvert(http://www.calvertgroup.com/),
Domini(http://www.domini.com/),
Citizens(http://www.citizensfunds.com/content/approaches.asp),

Walden
(http://www.waldenassetmgmt.com/investment/usequity.html), and
Women's Equity(http://www.womens-equity.com/)
are rightfully considered leaders."
FROM: Is Your Money Where Your Heart Is? The Truth About SRI Mutual Funds,
http://www.dragonflymedia.com/portal/featured_stories/200410/hawken_paul.html)

GRAMEEN BANK TO THE POOR
http://www.grameen-info.org/

USA BUDGET

http://www.pipa.org/OnlineReports/budget/030705/Report03_07_05.pdf
As Congress undertakes the process of making up a discretionary budget in response to the Administration's recently proposed budget for FY 2006, the question arises of how well the proposed discretionary budget aligns with the priorities of the American public. To find out, the Program on International Policy Attitudes conducted a unique type of survey. Respondents were presented the major items of the discretionary budget, including a breakdown of the

proposed funding for each item, and given an opportunity to redistribute the funds as they saw fit. They were also given the opportunity, if they wished, to reallocate some funds to deficit reduction (though the amount of the deficit was not provided). **What this reveals is how the budget would look if Americans could each specify where their own tax dollars would go.**
For more information about this methodology, go to www.knowledgenetworks.com/ganp.

Fiscal Year 2006 Federal Budget Trade-Offs
(SOURCE: http://database.nationalpriorities.org/cgi-bin/WebObjects/NPP.woa/13/wo/tUNzjk1N4QxK9XmRcArFtw/0.0.1.3.12.1)

$89 billion in tax cuts for the wealthiest 5% this year could be spent on the people of United States instead. If that money were used to support state and local programs, the residents of United States could have $88.7 billion, which could provide:

20,134,182 People Receiving Health Care or

1,536,329 Elementary School Teachers or

11,741,691 Head Start Places for Children or

52,157,797 Children Receiving Health Care or

798,208 Affordable Housing Units or

10,432 New Elementary Schools or

17,190,227 Scholarships for University Students or

1,527,790 Music and Arts Teachers or

1,997,465 Public Safety Officers or

156,836,034 Homes with Renewable Electricity or

1,388,655 Port Container Inspectors

Notes and Sources:

Tax Cuts:

Each state's share is based on how much they received in federal aid to states for fiscal year 2003, the most recent year the data is available.

$225 billion in tax cuts this year: According to the Center on Budget and Policy Priorities, the Bush Administration's tax cuts (from 2001 through 2004) will cost $225 billion in revenues for fiscal year 2005 (the current fiscal year). For more information about the long-term cost of the Bush Administration's tax cuts, see CBPP's report, Extending the tax cuts would cost $2.1 trillion through 2015.

$55 billion in tax cuts for the wealthiest 1%: According to the Tax Policy Center (Table T05-0067), the wealthiest 1% would receive 24.6% of the tax cuts this year.

$89 billion in tax cuts for the wealthiest 5%: According to the Tax Policy Center (Table T05-0067), the wealthiest 5% would receive 39.4% of the tax cuts this year.

Trade-Offs:

Elementary School Teachers, Music and Arts Teachers, Public Safety Officers, Police Officers, Firefighters, Nurses, and any other occupation: Each state's number is based on the average amount of annual pay an elementary school teacher receives, plus 25% for other expenses associated with employment such as benefits. These numbers were forecasted for 2004 from data for 1999 through 2003 from the Occupational Employment and Wage Estimates.

Head Start Places for Children: We calculated cost per child numbers for each state based on state numbers from the Administration of Children and Families' Head Start Bureau. These numbers have been adjusted for inflation to provide a 2004 estimate.

People or Children Receiving Health Care: The state numbers are based on the Centers for Medicare and Medicaid Data Compendium. They represent the average Medicaid outlays per person or per child in each state for 1999 and 2000, and then are forecasted for 2004.

Elementary Schools: The cost of a new elementary school is based on the median amount spent on a 65,000 square foot elementary school in 2003, as reported by the School Planning and Management's 9th Annual Construction Report. A 65,000 square foot elementary school can accommodate roughly 500 students. Regional differences in cost are reflected in each states totals.

Scholarships for University Students: The number for each state is based on the cost of tuition and fees at that state's flagship university for the 2003-2004 academic year. Data on tuition and fees are available at the National Center for Education Statistics' College Opportunities On-Line (COOL).

Affordable Housing Units: The number for each state is based on Census 1990 and 2000 housing values. We have taken the average of the median and lower quartile values, and forecasted for 2004. This may be a fairly rough estimate of what is would cost to build affordable housing, but does constitute a good estimate of an inexpensive housing unit in each state.

Housing Vouchers: On average, each housing voucher is worth $6,665. While there is some variation between cities, we used the national average for each state because it represented the best guide for the value of a housing voucher. This amount is from the Congressional Budget Office.

Students receiving Pell Grants of $4050: The maximum Pell Grant award is currently set at $4050. We used that number for each of the states and for the United States as a whole. Information on the Federal Pell Grant Program can be found at the Office of Postsecondary Education at the US Department of Education.

Copyright 2004 National Priorities Project

17 New South Street, Suite 302

Northampton, MA 01060

Tel: 413-584-9556

fax: 413-586-9647

info@nationalpriorities.org

NATURE

NATURE'S OPERATING INSTRUCTIONS – THE TRUE BIOTECHNOLOGIES, edited by Kenny Ausubel with J.P. Harpignies, The Collective Heritage Institute, 2004. The Bioneers Series.

Wendell Berry offered the following advice during a commencement address delivered in June 1989 at the College of the Atlantic in Bar Harbor, Maine. His words are even more potent today, as they offer a perceptual shift in how we see our species in relation to Nature:

1. Beware the justice of Nature.
2. Understand that there can be no successful human economy apart from Nature or in defiance of Nature.
3. Understand that no amount of education can overcome the innate limits of human intelligence and responsibility. We are not smart enough or conscious enough or alert enough to work responsibly on a gigantic scale.
4. In making things always bigger and more centralized, we make them both more vulnerable in themselves and more dangerous to everything else. Learn, therefore, to prefer small-scale elegance and generosity to large-scale greed, crudity, and glamour.
5. Make a home. Help to make a community. Be loyal to what you have made.
6. Put the interest of the community first.
7. Love your neighbors--not the neighbors you pick out, but the ones you have.
8. .Love this miraculous world that we did not make, that is a gift to us.
9. As far as you are able make your lives dependent upon your local place, neighborhood, and household-- which thrive by care and generosity--and independent of the industrial economy, which thrives by damage.
10. Find work, if you can, that does no damage. Enjoy your work. Work well.

ECOLOGICAL MEDICINE – HEALING THE EARTH, HEALING OURSELVES, edited by Kenny Ausubel, founder of the Bioneers, with J.P. Harpignies, The Collective Heritage Institute, 2004. The Bioneers Series.

RADICAL ECOLOGY – THE SEARCH FOR A LIVABLE WORLD, Carolyn Merchant, Routledge, 1992. Revolutionary Thought/ Radical Movements Series.

See the **World Watch Institute** for details of our current ecological situation: http://www.worldwatch.org/topics/ With permission, here is an overview from their research library:

Climate Change

The Earth's atmosphere is now warming at the fastest rate in recorded history, a trend that is projected to cause extensive damage to forests, marine ecosystems, and agriculture. Human communities are also threatened by climate change as seas rise, storms become more intense, and episodes of drought and flooding increase. The scientific evidence is now compelling that recent climate change is caused at least in part by human activities, especially the burning of fossil fuels, which has driven atmospheric carbon dioxide concentrations to their highest levels in 420,000 years. Worldwatch publications have increased public understanding of the risks of climate change and provided guidance on effective policies to reduce dependence on the fossil fuels that cause it. Researchers ·Christopher Flavin ·Janet L. Sawin

Materials

Most of the wood, metal, plastic, and minerals consumed in industrial countries is used only once, then discarded. This wasteful practice contributes to environmental ills from shrinking forests to changes in climate. Worldwatch research showcases creative ways to cut materials use radically, without reducing our quality of life. "Zero-waste" factories, products designed for easy disassembly and remanufacturing, and the creative combination of leasing and recycling are among the cutting edge concepts analyzed by Institute researchers. These and other innovations change the way we think about materials, and offer the potential for major reductions in the environmental harm created by our material world. Researchers ·Gary Gardner

Transportation

The automobile dominated the world's roads in the last century, eventually polluting many communities and helping to change the global climate. Air travel, the fastest-growing form of transportation, also contributes to pollution and climate change. Today, with the environmental and social costs of road and air traffic well documented, and with natural gas and renewable sources of energy beginning to replace oil, we can envision a new generation of rail, bus, and cycle facilities, as well as 'walkable' communities that give people more choice while causing less damage to the environment. Researchers ·Gary Gardner ·Molly O'Meara Sheehan

Consumption

Overhauling the "consume and dispose" engine that drives today's industrial economies is a multi-pronged challenge. Subsidies for extraction and harvesting of metals, timber, and other virgin materials; advertising that equates self-worth with ownership of goods; land use policies that promote materials-intensive sprawl-these are just a few of the engines that drive excessive consumption. Worldwatch research has documented the environmental damage caused by intensive consumption of fossil fuels, livestock products, paper, and other materials and products. Future research will explore how the procurement policies of governments, corporations, and other institutions might be changed to jump-start the market for "green" products. Researchers ·Gary Gardner ·Lisa Mastny

Globalization and Governance

Globalization poses enormous environmental dangers, from the spread of invasive species to global warming, but it also offers important opportunities, such as the use of the Internet to spur cross-border activism and the diffusion of environmentally beneficial technologies. The Institute's Global Governance Project works to strengthen the role of international institutions and policies in promoting sustainable development. The project is exploring how the world's environmental treaties can be structured to work in concert, how institutions of trade and finance can support environmentally sustainable development, and how strong partnerships can be forged between non-governmental organizations, businesses, national governments, and international institutions. Researchers ·Chris Bright ·Hilary French ·Lisa Mastny ·Molly O'Meara Sheehan ·Zoë Chafe

Sustainable Economics

The spread of industrialism in the last two centuries has made life easier and longer for a growing share of humanity. But it is also taking a great toll on the health of the planet. Sustainable economics is about making the global economy sustainable without sacrificing the benefits of industrialism. One focus of Worldwatch work on economics has been government spending and taxation policies. Currently, governments subsidize environmentally harmful activities such as driving, logging, and mining, tilting the economy in the direction of resource waste and pollution. Taxing harmful activities instead would force consumers and companies to pay the full environmental costs of their actions and free up billions of dollars to support wind power, recycling, and other technologies and practices essential to building a sustainable industrial economy. Researchers ·Lisa Mastny ·Michael Renner

Water

Water scarcity may be the most underappreciated global environmental challenge of our time. In the Middle East, China, India, and the United States, groundwater is being pumped faster than it is being replenished, and rivers such as the Colorado and Yellow River no longer reach the sea year round. Over the next quarter century, the number of people in countries unable to meet their domestic, industrial, and agricultural water needs is expected to balloon substantially. Worldwatch research on water focuses on practical policies to ensure more efficient use and equitable access to water, to minimize international and intersectoral conflict over this vital resource, and to avoid groundwater contamination. Researchers ·Anne Platt McGinn ·Sandra Postel

Pollution

Despite growing support from the chemical industry and environmentalists for phasing out several highly toxic and long-lived substances, new compounds continue to be introduced into global commerce at a rapid rate. Because the health effects of such substances often become apparent only long after their introduction, Worldwatch research emphasizes avoiding the use of toxic chemicals. It shows how industry leaders, farmers, public health officials, and community members have adopted safe and economical alternatives to toxics, in the process realizing countless health and environmental benefits. Researchers ·Anne Platt McGinn ·Molly O'Meara Sheehan

NATIONAL PRIORITIES PROJECT
http://database.nationalpriorities.org/cgi-

bin/WebObjects/NPP.woa/17/wo/H4KPDneaLlYuuvc35SxGs0/6.0.1.3.12   Report:

ENERGY

The Numbers in United States:

Total Energy Consumption (BBtu) 96,275,334

Gasoline Consumption per Capita (Gallons) 463

Renewables Share of Total Energy 5%

Fossil Fuel R & D Programs $67,630,552

Renewable Energy R & D Programs $148,773,877

Nationally, consumption of all forms of energy has increased on average about 2% per year. The U.S. is becoming more efficient over time where we produce more with less energy input, but our efficiency does not compare to the improvements gained by other countries such as Japan and those of the European Union. Federal government priorities may explain part of this quandary. Each year, more federal money is put into research and development (R & D) of fossil fuels such as coal, oil, and gas, than into energy-efficiency and conservation programs.

As our total consumption of energy increases, we consume proportionately fewer renewables such as wind, solar and geothermal than fossil fuels and nuclear power. Renewable energy makes up 5.5% of total energy consumed, down from around 8% in the mid-1980s. Hydroelectric, the production of which has some negative environmental consequences, makes up more than 40% of all renewable energy.

Our heavy reliance on fossil fuels remains a critical problem. The burning of fossil fuels releases greenhouse gases which are the main cause of global warming and more immediately adversely affect our health. Competition and conflict over fossil fuels, in particular oil, has led to geopolitical problems and war.

Sources

Btu - British thermal units, a standard of measurement for energy (BBtu - billions of Btu). Energy consumption statistics, Energy Information Administration, 2001, with graph indicating past decade; share of renewable energy as a proportion of total energy consumed includes hydroelectric and biomass, share would be less than 1% without; spending data on R & D, the Consolidated Federal Funds Reports, 2003; for more information on the environmental impact and connection between oil and conflict, see FPIF & SEEN, Oil Change: Petropolitics Briefing Book, January, 2004, and M.T. Klare, Resource Wars: the New Landscape of Global Conflict, Metropolitan Books, 2001.

Quick Report generated on February 01, 2005 at www.nationalpriorities.org

Copyright 2004 National Priorities Project

PEER – PUBLIC EMPLOYEES FOR ENVIRONMENTAL RESPONSIBILITY http://www.peer.org/index.html

COLORADO GREEN WINDFARM
http://www.ppmenergy.com/news/rel_031027_Lamar.pdf

EARTH SHARE   http://www.earthshare.org/

ENVIRONMENTAL LAW INSTITUTE
http://www2.eli.org/index.cfm

ENVIRONMENTAL DEFENCE
http://www.environmentaldefense.org/home.cfm

NEW ENERGY MOVEMENT
http://www.newenergymovement.org/index.htm

APOLLO ALLIANCE http://www.apolloalliance.org/

The Apollo Alliance Ten-Point Plan
for Good Jobs and Energy Independence

1. Promote Advanced Technology & Hybrid Cars
2. Invest In More Efficient Factories
3. Encourage High Performance Building
4. Increase Use of Energy Efficient Appliances
5. Modernize Electrical Infrastructure
6. Expand Renewable Energy Development
7. Improve Transportation Options
8. Reinvest In Smart Urban Growth
9. Plan For A Hydrogen Future
10. Preserve Regulatory Protections
CLIMATE SOLUTIONS http://www.climatesolutions.org/

NATIONAL BIODIESEL BOARD http://www.biodiesel.org/

DATABASE OF STATE INCENTIVES FOR RENEWABLE
ENERGY   http://www.dsireusa.org/

ENVIRONMENT CANADA
http://www.ec.gc.ca/water/en/info/facts/e_quantity.htm

.INDIGENOUS PEOPLES

CENTER FOR WORLD INDIGENOUS STUDIES
http://www.cwis.org

Latest Version Of The Draft United Nations
Declaration On The Rights Of Indigenous
Peoples: UN Document :
E/CN.4/Sub.2/1993/29/Annex I
23 August 1993 Original: ENGLISH
GE.93-85003 (E):
http://www.un.org/esa/socdev/unpfii/pfii/draftdec.htm

CENTER FOR WORLD INDIGENOUS STUDIES
http://www.cwis.org/fwdp/drft9329.html

UN SUMMIT OF THE ELDERS 1995:
http://www.ratical.org/many_worlds/6Nations/EldersSummit
.html

INDIGENOUS PEOPLE'S COUNCIL ON BIOCOLONIALISM
http://www.ipcb.org/

PACHAMAMA ALLIANCE
http://www.pachamama.org/

RELIGIOUS ENVRIONMENTALISM

NATIONAL RELIGIOUS PARTNERSHIP FOR THE
ENVIRONMENT
http://www.nrpe.org/

EXPANDED CONSCIOUSNESS

MICHAEL J. ROADS: www.MichaelRoads.com

JOANNA MACY: http://www.joannamacy.net/

FOUNDATION FOR DEEP ECOLOGY
http://www.deepecology.org/directory.html

THE GAIA FOUNDATION
http://www.gaiawest.iinet.net.au/index.html

INSTITUTE OF NOETIC SCIENCES, USA:
http://www.ions.org/

SANTA BARBARA INSITUTE FOR THE INTERDISCIPLINARY
STUDY OF CONSCIOUSNESS, USA:
http://www.sbinstitute.com/

WORLDWIDE RECOGNITION EXCHANGE NETWORK
(WwREN) http://www.gaiawest.iinet.net.au/WwREN.htm

SACRED EARTH NETWORK
http://www.sacredearthnetwork.org/

ECOLOGICAL FOOTPRINT WEBSITES

http://www.mec.ca/Apps/ecoCalc/ecoCalc.jsp;jsessionid=2Q
rjuBEjgyGxlTW20eCyDd

http://www.earthday.net/footprint/index.asp

http://www.bestfootforward.com/footprintlife.htm

Ranking the Ecological Impact of Nations
http://www.ecouncil.ac.cr/rio/focus/report/english/footprint/
ranking.htm

Redefining Progress – 2002 Ecological Impact
http://www.redefiningprogress.org/publications/ef1999.pdf

BIOMIMICRY WEBSITES

PAX SCIENTIFIC http://www.paxscientific.com/tech.html

BIOMIMICRY: http://www.biomimicry.org/intro.html

BIOMIMICRY GUILD
http://www.biomimicry.org/guildFrame.html

WATER

Water Facts from
http://www.ec.gc.ca/water/en/info/facts/e_quantity.htm

About 70% of the earth is covered in water.

The total amount of water in the world is approximately 1.4 billion km3, of which 97.5% is saltwater and 2.5% is fresh water.

Of the 35 million km3 of freshwater on earth, about 24.4 million km3 are locked up in the form of glacial ice, permafrost, or permanent snow. Groundwater and soil moisture account for 10.7 million km3. Freshwater lakes and marshlands hold about 1.0 million km3. Rivers, the most visible form of fresh water account for 0.002 million km3 or about less than 0.01% of all forms of fresh water.

The major source of fresh water is evaporation off the surface of the oceans, approximately 505 000 km3 a year. Another 72 000 km3 evaporates from land surfaces annually. Approximately 80% of all precipitation (about 458 000 km3) falls on the oceans, the remaining 20% (119 000 km3) falls over land. The difference between precipitation onto land surfaces and evaporation from those surfaces is runoff and groundwater recharge – approximately 47 000 km3 per year.

Brazil is the country with the most renewable fresh water. Canada is third after Russia.

Ninety-nine percent of surface freshwater by volume is in lakes and only one percent in rivers.

Of all fresh water not locked up in ice caps or glaciers, some 20% is in areas too remote for humans to access and of the remaining 80% about three-quarters comes at the wrong time and place – in monsoons and floods – and is not always captured for use by people. The remainder is less than 0.08 of 1% of the total water on the planet.

Expressed another way, if all the earth's water were stored in a 5-litre container, available fresh water would not quite fill a teaspoon.

There are some 100 million lakes between 1 hectare (0.01 km2) and 1 km2 in area and about one million lakes which are greater than 1 km2 in area.

The lake with the largest surface area in the world is the Caspian Sea (about 436 000 km2) followed by Lake Superior (about 82 300 km2).

The deepest lake is Lake Baikal (about 1 700 metres deep) followed by Lake Tanganyika (about 1 400 metres deep).

The largest river basin in the world, by drainage basin size and by discharge, is the Amazon.

The Nile River is the world's longest river. It flows 6 670 kilometres from its headwaters to the Mediterranean Sea.

Although 60% of the world's population live in Asia, the continent has only 36% of the world's water resources.

Water stress begins when there is less than 1 700 m3 of water per person per year for all major functions (domestic, industrial, agricultural, and natural ecosystems) and becomes severe when there is less than 1 000 m3 per person.

Currently, 600 million people face water scarcity. Depending on future rates of population growth, **between 2.7 billion and 3.2 billion people may be living in either water-scarce or water-stressed conditions by 2025.**

At times, the flow is so low in some of the world's largest rivers – the Amu Darya and Syr Darya in central Asia, the Yellow River in China, the Colorado River in the United States, the Indus River between India and Pakistan – **that they do not reach the sea.**

The Aral Sea was once the world's fourth largest lake; now it's the site of aquatic ruin. It's lost two-thirds of its surface area, some 60 000 fishing jobs have been wiped out, and people living in the salty and toxic surroundings suffer from a variety of ailments.

The world's wetland area was halved during the 20th century. In some locations wetlands are worth as much as $20 000 per hectare (0.01 km2).

The most devastating floods have occurred on the Yellow River in China. In 1887, 900 000 lives were lost and in 1938, 870 000. In each of 1911, 1931, and 1935 at least 100 000 lives were lost in the Yangtze River basin in China.

More than 2 200 major and minor water-related natural disasters occurred in the world between 1990 and 2001. Asia and Africa were the most affected continents, with floods accounting for half of these disasters.

SEAFLOW   http://www.seaflow.org/
Examples of man-made ocean noise include:

• The 85,000 plus ships in our global fleet

• Air guns used in seismic exploration

• Advanced technology used to locate fish

• Remotely operated research vehicles

• Recreational vehicles

• Military active sonars which pose the greatest threat right now.

FOUNDATION FOR WATER AND ENERGY EDUCATION:
http://www.fwee.org/hlogic.html

MASARU EMOTO:
http://www.masaru-emoto.net/english/entop.html

AIR

FOR A DESCRIPTION OF ATMOSPHERIC POLLUTANTS AND THEIR EFFECTS:
http://www.mhhe.com/biosci/ap/dynamichuman2/content/respiratory/reading7.mhtml

SUSTAINABILITY IN COMMUNITY

NORTHWEST EARTH INSTITUTE
http://www.nwei.org/index.html
Current offerings include:

• Voluntary Simplicity, an eight-session course addressing the distractions of modern society that keep us from caring for ourselves, our relationships, and our environment

• Exploring Deep Ecology, a nine-session course addressing core values and how they affect the way we view and treat the earth

• Discovering a Sense of Place, a nine-session course focusing on knowing and protecting our place

• Choices for Sustainable Living, a nine-session course exploring the meaning of sustainable living and the ties between lifestyle choices and their impact on the earth

• Globalization and Its Critics, Globalization, a nine-session course, explores how global trade is affecting the environment, local economies, and social and cultural customs throughout the world

SUSTAINABLE ROBERTSFORS
http://www.hallbara.robertsfors.se/engelsk/indexeng.html

ALLIANCE FOR SUSTAINABILITY
http://allianceforsustainability.net/

ALTERNATE CHOICES TO PLASTIC

EARTHSHELL   http://www.earthshell.com/

BIOPLASTIC
http://www.bioplastic.org/

http://web-japan.org/trends/science/sci031212.html

http://www.innovations-report.com/html/reports/materials_science/report-17893.html

http://202.221.217.59/print/business/nb06-2004/nb20040623a3.htm

GREEN PLASTIC http://web-japan.org/trends01/article/030213sci_index.html

BIOTEC   http://www.biotec.de/engl/index_engl.htm

NATUREWORKS PLA
http://www.natureworksllc.com/corporate/nw_pack_home.asp

CENTER FOR RENEWABLE ENERGY AND SUSTAINABLE TECHNOLOGY http://www.crest.org/

NATIONAL RENEWABLE ENERGY LABORATORY http://www.nrel.gov/

GLOBAL WARMING MYTHS & FACTS

In April 2005 Environmental Defense published a peer-reviewed report produced by scientists to clarify the scientific community's unity regarding global warming. Written by **Dr.James Wang,** Scientist, Climate And Air Program, Environmental Defense; and **Dr. Michael Oppenheimer,** Professor of Geosciences and International Affairs, Princeton University; it was intended to assist the USA Congress in its policy decisions. The full report can be found at:

http://www.environmentaldefense.org/documents/4418_MythsvFacts_05.pdf

DECLARATION OF INTERDEPENDENCE

This We Know

We are the earth, through the plants and animals that nourish us.

We are the rains and the oceans that flow through our veins.

We are the breath of the forests of the land, and the plants of the sea.

We are human animals, related to all other life as descendants of the firstborn cell.

We share with these kin a common history, written in our genes.

We share a common present, filled with uncertainty.

And we share a common future, as yet untold.

We humans are but one of thirty million species weaving the thin layer of life enveloping the world.

The stability of communities of living things depends upon this diversity.

Linked in that web, we are interconnected -- using, cleansing, sharing and replenishing the fundamental elements of life.

Our home, planet Earth, is finite; all life shares its resources and the energy from the sun, and therefore has limits to growth.

For the first time, we have touched those limits.

When we compromise the air, the water, the soil and the variety of life, we steal from the endless future to serve the fleeting present.

This We Believe

Humans have become so numerous and our tools so powerful that we have driven fellow creatures to extinction, dammed the great rivers, torn down ancient forests,

poisoned the earth, rain and wind, and ripped holes in the sky.

Our science has brought pain as well as joy; our comfort is paid for by the suffering of millions.

We are learning from our mistakes, we are mourning our vanished kin, and we now build a new politics of hope.

We respect and uphold the absolute need for clean air, water and soil.

We see that economic activities that benefit the few while shrinking the inheritance of many are wrong.

And since environmental degradation erodes biological capital forever, full ecological and social cost must enter all equations of development.

We are one brief generation in the long march of time; the future is not ours to erase.

So where knowledge is limited, we will remember all those who will walk after us, and err on the side of caution.

This We Resolve

All this that we know and believe must now become the foundation of the way we live.

At this turning point in our relationship with Earth, we work for an evolution: from dominance to partnership; from fragmentation to connection; from insecurity, to interdependence.

FROM:
http://www.davidsuzuki.org/About_us/Declaration_of_Interdependence.asp

DAVID SUZUKI FOUNDATION http://www.davidsuzuki.org/ The David Suzuki Foundation works through science and education to protect the diversity of nature and our quality of life, now and for the future. With a goal of achieving sustainability within a generation, the Foundation collaborates with scientists, business and industry, academia, government and non-governmental organizations. We seek the best research to provide innovative solutions that will help build a clean, competitive economy that does not threaten the natural services that support all life.

PARTNERSHIP

PEACE BETWEEN THE SHEETS
http://reuniting.info
Marnia Robinson and **Gary Wilson.** This is a highly recommended, informative, and funny website.

THE KAREZZA METHOD OR MAGNETATION, by J. WILLIAM LLOYD (1931) Similar to Peace Between the Sheets, this classic is highly recommended by many. 64 pages, ISBN 0-7873-0565-0

HUMAN AWARENESS INSTITUTE http://www.hai.org/

PEOPLE-CENTERED DEVELOPMENT FORUM (**David Korten**) http://www.pcdf.org/

AFRICAN GENDER INSTITUTE **http://web.uct.ac.za/org/agi/about.htm** See

gender related links at
http://web.uct.ac.za/org/agi/links%20gws.htm

Men's Resource Center
http://www.mensresourcecenter.org/index.html

The mission of the Men's Resource Center is to support men, challenge men's violence, and develop men's leadership in ending oppression in our lives, our families, and our communities.

Men's Resources International
http://www.mensresourcesinternational.org/

OUR MISSION is to promote positive masculinity and end men's violence.

OUR APPROACH is to support the development of men's programs in diverse communities, and build a global network of these organizations working in alliance with women to prevent violence and promote peace.

OUR PROGRAMS focus on developing leadership skills and increasing program sustainability for community-based men's programs at all stages of development. We do this by providing personalized and affordable programs.

Gender Statistics

GENDER STATS – WORLD BANK
http://genderstats.worldbank.org/home.asp

CEDAW

FROM: http://www.womenstreaty.org/why.htm
What is the CEDAW Treaty for the Rights of Women?
The Treaty for the Rights of Women is the most comprehensive international agreement on the basic human rights of women. Created in 1979 as the UN Convention on the Elimination of All Forms of Discrimination Against Women (CEDAW), it is an important tool for all those who seek to end abuses of women and girls, such as those committed by the Taliban in Afghanistan.

Because of the CEDAW Treaty, millions of girls are now receiving primary education who were previously denied access; measures have been taken against sex slavery, domestic violence and trafficking of women; women's health care services have improved, saving lives during pregnancy and childbirth; and millions of women have secured loans or the right to own or inherit property.

Exactly how does the treaty work?

The treaty commits ratifying nations to overcoming barriers to discrimination against women in the areas of legal rights, education, employment, health care, politics and finance. Like all human rights treaties, the CEDAW Treaty sets benchmarks within traditional enforcement mechanisms that respect sovereignty and democracy. In many of the 179 countries that have ratified the treaty, it has guided the passage and enforcement of national law. For example:

Uganda, South Africa, Brazil, Australia and others have incorporated treaty provisions into their constitutions and domestic legal codes; Ukraine, Nepal, Thailand and the Philippines all passed new laws to curb sexual trafficking;

India developed national guidelines on workplace sexual assault after the Supreme Court, in ruling on a major rape case, found that CEDAW required such protections;

Nicaragua, Jordan, Egypt and Guinea all saw significant increases in literacy rates after improving access to education for girls and women; and After ratification, Colombia made domestic violence a crime and required legal protection for its victims.

Much remains to be done:

Sex trafficking: at least 4 million women and girls are sold into sexual slavery each year;

Education: two-thirds of the world's 799 million illiterate adults are women;

Maternal mortality: 510,000 women die each year from pregnancy-related complications;

HIV/AIDS: women are four times more vulnerable than men, and 1.3 million die each year;

Violence: an estimated 25 to 30 percent of all women experience domestic violence;

Discrimination: millions of women lack full legal and political rights; and

Female genital mutilation: 130 million women are victims.

How would U.S. ratification help women around the world?

The United States has long been a world leader on human rights. But U.S. failure to ratify the treaty allows other countries to distract attention from their neglect of women and undermines the powerful principle that human rights of women are universal across all cultures and religions. Until the United States ratifies, our country cannot credibly demand that others live up to their obligations under this treaty. Our failure to ratify puts us in the company of Sudan, Iran and Somalia; every other industrialized country has ratified the treaty.

Ratification does not require any change in U.S. law and would be a powerful statement of our continuing commitment to ending discrimination against women worldwide. The U.S. already has laws consistent with the CEDAW Treaty. Under the terms of the treaty, the U.S. would submit regular reports to an advisory committee, which would provide an important opportunity to spotlight our best practices and assess where we can do better.

The United States has a bipartisan tradition of support for international standards through human rights treaties. Presidents Reagan, Bush and Clinton ratified similar treaties on genocide, torture, race and civil and political rights. This treaty continues that proud tradition.

What is the treaty's U.S. status?

Treaty approval requires a two-thirds vote in the U.S. Senate, or 67 votes. Ratification does not require consideration by the House of Representatives.

The treaty is languishing in the Senate Foreign Relations Committee under Chairman Senator Richard Lugar (R-IN), who has indicated he is waiting for the Bush Administration to complete a review of the treaty. In 2002, the State Department notified the Senate Foreign Relations Committee that the CEDAW Treaty for the Rights of Women was "generally desirable and should be ratified." Nevertheless, the Administration has not yet taken further action on the treaty; it awaits a Justice Department review about what Reservations, Understandings and Declarations may be necessary.

A coalition of over 190 U.S. religious, civic, and community organizations remain committed to supporting ratification. They include the AARP, American Nurses Association, National Education Association, National Coalition of Catholic Nuns, American Bar Association, The United Methodist Church, YWCA, and Amnesty International. In addition, a bipartisan consensus of U.S. voters has consistently supported human rights for women, showing overwhelming support for efforts to secure the rights of women and girls in Afghanistan and elsewhere.

UN CEDAW SITE:
http://www.un.org/womenwatch/daw/cedaw/

PEACE & POLITICS

PEACE

INTERNATIONAL FELLOWSHIP OF RECONCILIATION
http://www.ifor.org/

PRAXIS PEACE INSTITUTE http://www.praxispeace.org/

USA DEPT OF PEACE CAMPAIGN
http://www.thepeacealliance.org/main.htm

MISSION- The (cabinet-level) Department shall-- (1) hold peace as an organizing principle, coordinating service to every level of American society; (2) endeavor to promote justice and democratic principles to expand human rights; (3) strengthen nonmilitary means of peacemaking; (4) promote the development of human potential; (5) work to create peace, prevent violence, divert from armed conflict, use field-tested programs, and develop new structures in nonviolent dispute resolution; (6) take a proactive, strategic approach in the development of policies that promote national and international conflict prevention, nonviolent intervention, mediation, peaceful resolution of conflict, and structured mediation of conflict; (7) address matters both domestic and international in scope; and (8) encourage the development of initiatives from local communities, religious groups, and nongovernmental organizations.

THE PEACE ALLIANCE FOUNDATION
http://www.thepeacealliance.org/main.htm

The Peace Alliance Foundation's mission is to identify and reveal a Culture of Peace based on the organizing principles of nonviolence and cooperation. It holds that all of our systems of foreign policy, education, politics, business, health, and social welfare can and must be united in seeking, teaching and living peace. The Foundation recognizes that the seeds of such a culture already exist and that revealing them is of primary importance to the development of a sustainable and productive future.

MINISTRY FOR PEACE, UK
http://www.ministryforpeace.org.uk/index.php

The goal of *ministry for peace* is to reduce violence in all its forms and to convince people that the use of direct violence as a means to achieve ends is uncivilised and counterproductive. Their programme is educational, not party political. It is designed to foster a culture of peace and to embed non-violent methods and approaches into all public institutions.

RESOURCE CENTER FOR NONVIOLENCE
http://www.rcnv.org/

<u>Nonviolence Guidelines</u>
<u>For All Participants In RCNV Actions</u>

1) We will not harm anyone, but will be nonviolent in words and actions.
2) We will treat every person with respect.
3) We will not damage or deface property.
4) We will not carry any weapons.
5) We will not bring or use any alcohol or drugs, other than for medical purposes.
6) We will not resist arrest.

THE SPIRITUAL ALLIANCE TO STOP INTIIMATE VIOLENCE http://www.saiv.net/
Breaking cycles of violence in families and the family of nations. Intimate violence is a major global problem. We all know of the suffering that results from domestic violence, rape, child abuse, female infanticide, and other brutal practices. What is less known is the link between violence in the home and violence in the world.

<u>Victims of Intimate Violence are More Prone to Violent Behavior</u> The aftermath of violent homes is a higher risk for depression, substance abuse, and violent behaviors – even if the violence is directed at another family member. The effects are not only emotional, but physical. Research from Harvard University and McLean Hospital shows that the brain neurochemistry of adults who grow up in violence and neglect is often optimized for the fight-or-flight response.

<u>The Link Between Intimate Violence and International Violence</u> In her germinal book The Chalice & The Blade and her award-winning The Power of Partnership, Riane Eisler shows that throughout history, and cross culturally, the most violently despotic and warlike cultures have been those where violence in homes is culturally condoned. We see this connection in Hitler's Germany and Stalin's Soviet Union. We see it in the Taliban, and other cultures that feed terrorism and war today. Logic alone tells us that early training to accept violence as a means of imposing one's will on others is useful to violent and repressive regimes.

<u>Engaging Religious Leaders</u>
It is estimated that over 80% of the world's population belongs to a major religion. These people often look to their spiritual leaders for guidance. Yet religious leaders have been mostly silent on the issue of intimate violence.

The greatest opportunity to reduce violence in the world is being missed. SAIV is working to change this.

LYSISTRATA PROJECT – Kathryn Blume
www.LysistrataProject.com www.TheAccidentalActivist.com

WORLD MILLENNIUM PEACE SUMMIT:
http://www.rcgg.ufrgs.br/mwps_ing.htm

AMNESTY INTERNATIONAL
http://www.amnestyusa.org/news/index.do

GLOBAL PEACE ORGANIZATIONS LISTINGS
nswas.com/links/frames/world.htm

CENTER FOR THE NEW AMERICAN DREAM
http://www.newdream.org/index.php

EVOLVE – BARBARA MARX HUBBARD
http://www.evolve.org/pub/doc/index2.html

OREGON PEACEWORKS
http://www.oregonpeaceworks.org/site/index.php

NEW PARADIGM INSTITUTE – DANNY SHEEHAN
http://www.newparadigminstitute.org/index.html

WOMEN'S INTERNATIONAL LEAGUE FOR PEACE AND FREEDOM   http://www.wilpf.org/

COUNCIL FOR A PARLIAMENT OF WORLD RELIGIONS
http://www.cpwr.org/

CORRYMEELA COMMUNITY Ireland
http://www.corrymeela.org/

SULHA PEACE PROJECT http://www.metasulha.org/sulha/
Sulha is an indigenous, middle eastern way of reconciliation.

GLOBAL ALLIANCE OF INTERFAITH ACTION
http://www.gaiaweb.org/

THE PEACEMAKER COMMUNITY
http://www.peacemakercommunity.org/

WOMEN'S ACTION FOR NEW DIRECTIONS (WAND)
http://www.wand.org/

EDUCATION FOR PEACE IN IRAQ (EPIC)
http://www.epic-usa.org/

NONVIOLENT PEACEFORCE
http://www.nonviolentpeaceforce.org/

FOREIGN POLICY RESEARCH INSTITUTE
http://www.fpri.org/

Founded in 1955, FPRI is devoted to bringing the insights of scholarship to bear on the development of policies that advance U.S. national interests. They add perspective to events by fitting them into the larger historical and cultural context of international politics. They conduct research on pressing issues. Each week, FPRI transmits by email a succinct analysis of some critical international issue. These bulletins are emailed to some 18,000 key people in 85 countries directly, and reach thousands more indirectly by postings on the Internet. Frequently, they are reprinted in or quoted by newspapers around the world. They are often invited to testify on Capitol Hill, comment on national radio and television, and consult informally with U.S. government officials.

MINISTRY FOR PEACE
http://www.ministryforpeace.org.uk/

The Ministry for Peace campaign wishes to see:

▪The creation of a Ministry for Peace

▪The promotion of peace and non-violence education in schools

▪The funding of peace workers to transform conflict in all areas of society

▪The active promotion of a Culture of Peace in the UK

▪The development of a 'Programme for a Peaceful City ' by every UK city

TRANSCEND http://www.transcend.org/

To work for peace is to work against violence ... Whether as direct violence or as the indirect slow, grinding violence of social structures that do not deliver sufficient nutrition and health at the bottom of world society, enormous suffering, dukkha, is the effect. To work for peace is to build sukha, liberation, well-ness in a world with peace with nature, between genders, generations and races, where the excluded are included but not by force, and where classes, nations and states serve neither direct nor structural violence. In such a world they would all pull together for better livelihood for all. That would be true globalization, unlike the present reduction of that term to represent only state and corporate elites in a handful countries.

Protective Accompaniment
Peaceforce workers accompany vulnerable leaders and negotiators in conflict zones. Accompaniment has been used successfully in places such as Guatemala where assassinations of human rights leaders terrorized efforts to re-establish civil society. Since 1985, when international accompaniment was first provided on a small-scale, accompaniment has been put into practice throughout the world by organisations like Peace Brigades International (PBI). In PBI's history, neither accompaniers nor activists have been killed while this strategy has been employed.
International Presence
Large numbers of Peaceforce workers create an international presence in vulnerable villages, borders, and areas of conflict. Presence is akin to accompaniment but expanded to an entire community. It is appropriate when violence is one-sided and/or parties are impossible to separate and it seeks to reduce the risk of violence rather than to protect any particular individual or group. Past instances of international presence have prevented villages from being attacked during conflicts in Nicaraguan villages in the 1980s.
Witnessing
By making sure "the whole world is watching," Peaceforce will deter violence by making violent action politically unacceptable. Peaceforce members will monitor events in conflict areas, and disseminate information internationally to the media and general public. In addition to traditional media, Peaceforce will project real-time digital photography to their worldwide monitoring system via the Internet.
Interpositioning
Peaceforce workers may place themselves between opposing groups in an attempt to prevent violence, thus creating cooling off time and a space for local groups to peacefully resolve their conflicts. As conflicts do not necessarily have a separation of parties and often have more than two contending sides, interpositioning is not always possible.

INTERNATIONAL PEACE BUREAU
http://www.ipb.org/web/index.php

POSITIVE FUTURES NETWORK,

http://www.yesmagazine.org/

publisher of **YES! magazine** - *A Journal of Positive Futures.*

THE INTERNATIONAL FORUM FOR THE LITERATURE AND CULTURE OF PEACE
http://www.iflac.com/

Ada Aharoni, IFLAC-LENA President (Dr. Aharoni's home page: http://www.new-horizon.up.co.il/)

NUCLEAR WAR

"Today, the United States has deployed approximately 4,500 strategic, offensive nuclear warheads. Russia has roughly 3,800. The strategic forces of Britain, France, and China are considerably smaller, with 200–400 nuclear weapons in each state's arsenal. The new nuclear states of Pakistan and India have fewer than 100 weapons each. North Korea now claims to have developed nuclear weapons, and US intelligence agencies estimate that Pyongyang has enough fissile material for 2–8 bombs.

How destructive are these weapons? The average US warhead has a destructive power 20 times that of the Hiroshima bomb. Of the 8,000 active or operational US warheads, 2,000 are on hair-trigger alert, ready to be launched on 15 minutes' warning...

There is no way to effectively contain a nuclear strike—to keep it from inflicting enormous destruction on civilian life and property, and there is no guarantee against unlimited escalation once the first nuclear strike occurs. We cannot avoid the serious and unacceptable risk of nuclear war until we recognize these facts and base our military plans and policies upon this recognition."

From _Apocalypse Soon_, by Robert S. McNamara (Robert S. McNamara was U.S. secretary of defense from 1961 to 1968 and president of the World Bank from 1968 to 1981.) Originally from Foreign Policy - May/June 2005 Issue. From TruthOut.org:
http://www.truthout.org/docs_2005/050505B.shtml and http://www.foreignpolicy.com/story/cms.php?story_id=2829&page=0 Does this policy honor anyone or anything?

CENTER FOR ARMS CONTROL AND NON-PROLIFERATION
http://www.armscontrolcenter.org/index.php

THE ALLIANCE FOR NUCLEAR ACCOUNTABILITY
http://ananuclear.org/

POLITICS

FREEDOM HOUSE
http://www.freedomhouse.org/index.htm

THE DEMOCRACY COLLABORATIVE
http://www.democracycollaborative.org/

DEMOCRACY COALITION PROJECT
http://www.demcoalition.org/2005_html/home.html

MOVE ON http://www.moveon.org/front/
MoveOn is working to bring ordinary people back into politics. MoveOn is a catalyst for a new kind of grassroots involvement, supporting busy but concerned citizens in finding their political voice.

TRANSNATIONAL RADICAL PARTY
http://www.radicalparty.org/welcome2.html

CENTER FOR CONSTITUTIONAL RIGHTS
http://www.ccr-ny.org/v2/home.asp

WORLD SOCIAL FORUM
http://www.forumsocialmundial.org.br/index.php?cd_language=2

http://www.forumsocialmundial.org.br/main.php?id_menu=4&cd_language=2

BRENNAN CENTER http://www.brennancenter.org/

LEAGUE OF WOMEN VOTERS http://www.lwv.org/

MOVING IDEAS http://www.movingideas.org/

DEMOCRACY MATTERS
http://www.democracymatters.org/

CIVICUS Index Project
http://www.civicus.org/new/CSI_overview.asp?c=FD8912
The CIVICUS Civil Society Index
The CIVICUS Civil Society Index (CSI) is an action-research project that aims to assess the state of civil society in countries around the world, with a view to creating a knowledge base and an impetus for civil society strengthening initiatives.

CO-INTELLIGENCE INSITUTE
http://www.co-intelligence.org/index.html

"Together we can be wiser than any of us can be alone. We need to know how to tap that wisdom." **Tom Atlee** is the author of **The Tao of Democracy** - **Using Co-Intelligence to Create a World that Works for All**

WORLD POLICY INSTITUTE
http://www.worldpolicy.org/

COMMUNITY OF DEMOCRACIES
http://www.santiago2005.org/html/what.html

DEMOCRACY CAUCUS
http://www.democracycaucus.net/html/about.html

The Campaign for a United Nations Democracy Caucus is dedicated to the promotion and fulfillment of the principles of democracy and human rights embodied in the Universal Declaration of Human Rights and the Warsaw Declaration of the Community of Democracies.

COUNCIL FOR A COMMUNITY OF DEMOCRACIES
http://www.ccd21.org/

THE KUDIRAT INITIATIVE FOR DEMOCRACY
http://www.kind.org/

TRANSPARENCY INTERNATIONAL
http://www.transparency.org/

UN DEMOCRACY CAUCUS
http://www.democracycaucus.net/html/home.html

INSTITUTE FOR DEMOCRACY AND ELECTORAL ASSISTANCE (IDEA) INTERNATIONAL
http://www.idea.int/publications/pub_electoral_main.htm

AFRICA ACTION   http://www.africaaction.org/index.php

CLUB OF ROME
http://www.clubofrome.org/ The Club of Rome is a global think tank and centre of innovation and initiative.

PEOPLE CENTERED DEVELOPMENT FORUM
http://www.pcdf.org/

DEMOCRACY FOR AMERICA
http://www.democracyforamerica.com/

CITIZEN DEMOCRACY PROJECT
http://www.citizendemocracy.net/

LETS TALK AMERICA http://www.letstalkamerica.org/

DEMOCRACY IN AMERICA PROJECT
http://www.democracycampaign.org/declaration.html

NATIONAL ISSUES FORUM http://www.nifi.org/

RECLAIM DEMOCRACY http://www.reclaimdemocracy.org/

INSTITUTE FOR POLICY STUDIES
http://www.ips-dc.org/

CENTER FOR AMERICAN PROGRESS
http://www.americanprogress.org/site/c.biJRJ8OVF/b.8473/
The Center for American Progress is a nonpartisan research
and educational institute dedicated to promoting a strong,
just and free America that ensures opportunity for all.

http://www.americanprogress.org/site/pp.asp?c=biJRJ8OVF
&b=310260

PEOPLE FOR THE AMERICAN WAY
http://www.pfaw.org/pfaw/general/

DEMOCRACY CAMPAIGN
http://www.democracycampaign.org/index.html

PUBLIC CITIZEN http://www.citizen.org/

NETHERLANDS INSTITUTE FOR MULTIPARTY DEMOCRACY
http://www.nimd.org
The IMD is an institute *of* political parties *for* political parties.

PACIFIC ENVIRONMENT http://www.pacificenvironment.org/

CENTER FOR RESPONSIVE POLITICS

http://www.opensecrets.org/

CENTER FOR WISE DEMOCRACY
http://www.wisedemocracy.org/

ROGUE VALLEY WISDOM COUNCIL
http://www.mind.net/lance/rvwc/

PROJECT VOTE SMART   http://www.vote-smart.org/

As a national library of factual information, Project Vote
Smart covers your candidates and elected officials in five
basic categories: biographical information, issue positions,
voting records, campaign finances and interest group
ratings.

INTERNATIONAL FOUNDATION FOR ELECTION
SYSTEMS (IFES)   http://www.ifes.org/

As one of the world's premier democracy and governance
assistance organizations, IFES provides targeted technical
assistance to strengthen transitional democracies... We
possess the expertise and flexibility to develop
comprehensive solutions to complex problems of
democratization anywhere and at any time.

ELECTION ACCESS   http://www.electionaccess.org/

IFES is the first mainstream democracy organization
committed to ensuring that people with disabilities have free
and equal access to electoral systems. The website is
organized into five sections: Laws and Regulations, Rights
and Standards , Best Practices,

Publications, and Contacts and Links.

ELECTIONS & ACCOUNTABILITY

PUBLIC CAMPAIGN http://www.publicampaign.org/

ALLIANCE FOR BETTER CAMPAIGNS
http://www.bettercampaigns.org/

CLEAN ELECTIONS INSTITUTE http://www.azclean.org/

THE INSTITUTE ON MONEY IN STATE POLITICS
http://www.followthemoney.org/

CENTER FOR GOVENMENTAL STUDIES http://www.cgs.org/

OPEN DEBATES   http://www.opendebates.org/

INITIATIVE AND REFERENDUM INSTITUTE
http://www.iandrinstitute.org/

COMMON CAUSE   http://www.commoncause.org

WHITE HOUSE FOR SALE
http://www.whitehouseforsale.org/

CAMPAIGN FINANCE INFORMATION CENTER
http://www.campaignfinance.org/

CAMPAIGN FINANCE INSTITUTE http://www.cfinst.org/

CITIZENS FOR RESPONSIBILITY AND ETHICS IN
WASHINGTON (CREW)
http://www.citizensforethics.org/index.php

FANNIE LOU HAMER PROJECT http://www.flhp.org/

VOTING METHODS

INSTANT RUNOFF VOTING DEMO
http://www.chrisgates.net/irv/index.html
This demo is the best explanation I've found yet. It is highly
recommended.

WIKIPEDIA – VOTING METHODS EXPLAINED Excellent !
http://en.wikipedia.org/wiki/Voting_methods

FEDERAL BUDGET & POLICIES

NATIONAL PRIORITIES PROJECT
http://www.nationalpriorities.org/
Since 1983, the National Priorities Project (NPP) has been
the only group in the country that focuses on the impacts of
federal tax and spending policies at the community level...

For a number of years, NPP has focused on the trade-offs
between military spending and tax breaks with social
spending. This has enabled us to build bridges between the
peace community and the many groups fighting for social
and economic justice, expanding the number of groups who
will work on both community needs and peace.

2002: Launched the **NPP Database, the first interactive
database providing state-level data on socio-
economic needs and federal expenditures on such
issues as hunger, education, housing,
poverty/income and military spending. It allows the
user to create customized tables, graphs and reports.**
For more info click on the DATABASE:
www.nationalpriorities.org/database.

For a **2004 Federal Budget Year in Review** see
http://www.nationalpriorities.org/yir/yir2004.pdf

Military Spending In United States 2004

The Numbers in United States:

Cost of the Military $251,760,371,755

Cost of Nuclear Weapons $10,668,177,672

Cost of War in Iraq $152,595,000,000

Defense Contracts $201,229,509,585

Military spending consumes 26 cents out of every individual income tax dollar. It makes up about 20% of total federal spending and over half of the discretionary budget.

The United States is the world's biggest military spender, accounting for over 40% of world military spending, and amounting to more than 30 times what the 'rogue' countries spend (Cuba, Iran, Libya, North Korea, Sudan, Syria). The Pentagon pays for more helicopters, airplanes and warships than all of these countries combined, and the capabilities of U.S. weaponry are unrivaled in the world.

A recent Congressional Budget Office study predicts the costs of the military will continue to increase well into the future. Current Pentagon plans will bring defense spending to levels higher than at anytime since World War II.

Many Americans are willing to pay a high price for the military if they believe it buys them real security. However, highly respected critics argue that the Bush Administration's policy of unilateralism and first strike is actually a 'terror-generator.' They suggest alternatives, including stopping the arms trade and safeguarding nuclear materials, which are far less costly and far more likely to bring greater national security than the current policy.

Sources

The 'cost' of military, nuclear weapons and war in Iraq (in terms of taxpayer money to pay for these programs)are the state's share based on IRS data. The total amount of allocated by Congress so far for Iraq is around $150 billion. Defense contracts are Dept. of Defense procurement contracts for 2003, Consolidated Federal Funds Report. World military information and projections are based on the federal budget; the Center for Defense Information; and Congressional Budget Office, 'The long-term implications of current defense plans: summary update for FY2004,' July, 2003. Figures are adjusted for inflation (in $2003).

Quick Report generated on February 01, 2005 at www.nationalpriorities.org

Copyright 2004 National Priorities Project
http://database.nationalpriorities.org/cgi-bin/WebObjects/NPP.woa/17/wo/H4KPDneaLlYuuvc35SxGs0/6.0.1.3.12

2006 Budget Impact on the USA

The President's budget request for fiscal year 2006 would cut total spending on discretionary domestic services by 7%, not including homeland security, while at the same time increasing military spending by 2%, after adjusting for inflation.[1] **Military spending does not include the cost of the wars in Iraq or Afghanistan.**

Discretionary spending on federal grants to state and local governments would be cut under this budget proposal by 9%, after adjusting for inflation.[2]

The budget proposal includes cuts of $12.4 billion for discretionary grants to state and local governments, including:

o $1.6 billion for community and economic development;

o $234.4 million for low-income home energy assistance; and

o $387.4 million for the Clean Water State Revolving Fund.

Programs constituting **the No Child Left Behind Act** (NCLB) would remain **underfunded by $13.1 billion**. The NCLB legislation authorizes funding each year for its programs.[3]

While taxpayers in the U. S. would lose local services, they will pay increasingly more for the Pentagon, including:

o $19.2 billion for the proposed increase in military spending; and

o $152.6 billion for what Congress has so far allocated for the Iraq War.[4]

Domestic Spending Squeezed

.The President's budget does not provide full information about discretionary spending in the future. It lays the

foundation for steeper declines in domestic spending with continued increases in military spending. The Center on Budget and Policy Priorities estimates that **domestic discretionary spending would decrease by 16% in real terms by 2010.**[5] **Military spending would increase by 6%.**

FY2006 Discretionary Spending*

Domestic 40%

Military 52%

Other Security 8%

* does not include funding for wars in Iraq or Afghanistan

Priorities that would impact the nation...

Veterans: This budget proposes to charge annual medical fees and increase pharmaceutical co-payments for higher-income veterans. More than $400 million in "savings" would be shifted onto veterans for medical care.

Children: The budget request does not allocate the funding authorized in the No Child Left Behind Act, leaving states and local school districts to come up with the necessary funding to meet the many federal mandates of the Act.

Healthy environment: All natural resources and environmental funding would be cut by close to 10%. Funding for a variety of important services would

be cut, including the National Park Service and Environmental Protection Agency state grants.

Low-income families: The budget proposes to reduce the number of families eligible for the Food Stamp program. Three million fewer people would receive Food Stamps by 2010. Community and economic development, home energy

assistance and other services aimed at low- and moderate-income Americans are also targeted for reduction.

Safe communities: State and local law enforcement assistance would be <u>eliminated</u> (from a current level of $1.2 billion) and the Community Oriented Policing Services (COPS) would be nearly eliminated, suffering a cut of 95%.

Students: Federal funding for vocational and adult education would be cut in half. Vocational and adult education programs prepare students for postsecondary careers and technical education, and provide adults with basic skills and literacy training.

Taxpayers: Net interest payments on the **debt will go up nearly 20%** to $211 billion. While we must pay this money regardless of what happens during the budget process, **it signifies the payment we are making for poor fiscal discipline** over the past four years. The President's budget to extend tax breaks in future years will create fiscal problems for generations to come.

Oregon
http://www.nationalpriorities.org/impact05/or.pdf
February 2005

The President's budget request for fiscal year 2006 would cut total spending on discretionary domestic services by 7%, not including homeland security, while at the same time increasing military spending by 2%, after adjusting for inflation.[1] **Military spending does not include the cost of the wars in Iraq or Afghanistan.**

Discretionary spending on federal grants to state and local governments would be cut under this budget proposal by 9%, after adjusting for inflation.[2]

In Oregon, the budget proposal includes cuts of $155.3 million for discretionary grants to state and local governments, including:

o $20.0 million for community and economic development;

o $2.9 million for low-income home energy assistance; and

o $4.4 million for the Clean Water State Revolving Fund.

In Oregon, programs constituting the No Child Left Behind Act (NCLB) would remain **underfunded by $124.4 million**. The NCLB legislation authorizes funding each

year for its programs. However, the budget would **underfund them nationwide in fiscal year 2006 by $13.1 billion.**[3]

While taxpayers in Oregon would lose local services, they will pay increasingly more for the Pentagon, including:

o $156.5 million for the proposed increase in military spending; and

o $1.3 billion for what Congress has so far allocated for the Iraq War.[4]

Notes:

1 All information and figures, unless otherwise noted, are based on an analysis of the *Budget of the U.S. Government, FY2006*, all volumes available at www.whitehouse.gov/omb.
2 For more information on state breakdowns and programs, go to www.nationalpriorities.org/budget.

3 Based on authorizations made in PL 107-110.
4 State breakdowns based on IRS data; Iraq estimate based on analysis of relevant legislation as of February 10, 2005.
5 See http://www.cbpp.org/2-9-05bud.htm.

UNIVERSAL DECLARATION OF HUMAN RIGHTS:

On December 10, 1948 the General Assembly of the United Nations adopted and proclaimed the Universal Declaration of Human Rights the full text of which appears in the following pages. Following this historic act the Assembly called upon all Member countries to publicize the text of the Declaration and "to cause it to be disseminated, displayed, read and expounded principally in schools and other educational institutions, without distinction based on the political status of countries or territories."

PREAMBLE

Whereas recognition of the inherent dignity and of the equal and inalienable rights of all members of the human family is the foundation of freedom, justice and peace in the world,

Whereas disregard and contempt for human rights have resulted in barbarous acts which have outraged the conscience of mankind, and the advent of a world in which human beings shall enjoy freedom of speech and belief and freedom from fear and want has been proclaimed as the highest aspiration of the common people,

Whereas it is essential, if man is not to be compelled to have recourse, as a last resort, to rebellion against tyranny and oppression, that human rights should be protected by the rule of law,

Whereas it is essential to promote the development of friendly relations between nations,

Whereas the peoples of the United Nations have in the Charter reaffirmed their faith in fundamental human rights, in the dignity and worth of the human person and in the equal rights of men and women and have determined to promote social progress and better standards of life in larger freedom,

Whereas Member States have pledged themselves to achieve, in co-operation with the United Nations, the promotion of universal respect for and observance of human rights and fundamental freedoms,

Whereas a common understanding of these rights and freedoms is of the greatest importance for the full realization of this pledge,

Now, Therefore THE GENERAL ASSEMBLY proclaims THIS UNIVERSAL DECLARATION OF HUMAN RIGHTS as a common standard of achievement for all peoples and all nations, to the end that every individual and every organ of society, keeping this Declaration constantly in mind, shall strive by teaching and education to promote respect for these rights and freedoms and by progressive measures, national and international, to secure their universal and effective recognition and observance, both among the peoples of Member States themselves and among the peoples of territories under their jurisdiction.

Article 1.

All human beings are born free and equal in dignity and rights.They are endowed with reason and conscience and should act towards one another in a spirit of brotherhood.

Article 2.

Everyone is entitled to all the rights and freedoms set forth in this Declaration, without distinction of any kind, such as race, colour, sex, language, religion, political or other opinion, national or social origin, property, birth or other status. Furthermore, no distinction shall be made on the basis of the political, jurisdictional or international status of the country or territory to which a person belongs, whether it be independent, trust, non-self-governing or under any other limitation of sovereignty.

Article 3.

Everyone has the right to life, liberty and security of person.

Article 4.

No one shall be held in slavery or servitude; slavery and the slave trade shall be prohibited in all their forms.

Article 5.

No one shall be subjected to torture or to cruel, inhuman or degrading treatment or punishment.

Article 6.

Everyone has the right to recognition everywhere as a person before the law.

Article 7.

All are equal before the law and are entitled without any discrimination to equal protection of the law. All are entitled to equal protection against any discrimination in violation of this Declaration and against any incitement to such discrimination.

Article 8.

Everyone has the right to an effective remedy by the competent national tribunals for acts violating the fundamental rights granted him by the constitution or by law.

Article 9.

No one shall be subjected to arbitrary arrest, detention or exile.

Article 10.

Everyone is entitled in full equality to a fair and public hearing by an independent and impartial tribunal, in the determination of his rights and obligations and of any criminal charge against him.

Article 11.

(1) Everyone charged with a penal offence has the right to be presumed innocent until proved guilty according to law in a public trial at which he has had all the guarantees necessary for his defence.

(2) No one shall be held guilty of any penal offence on account of any act or omission which did not constitute a penal offence, under national or international law, at the time when it was committed. Nor shall a heavier penalty be imposed than the one that was applicable at the time the penal offence was committed.

Article 12.

No one shall be subjected to arbitrary interference with his privacy, family, home or correspondence, nor to attacks upon his honour and reputation. Everyone has the right to the protection of the law against such interference or attacks.

Article 13.

(1) Everyone has the right to freedom of movement and residence within the borders of each state.

(2) Everyone has the right to leave any country, including his own, and to return to his country.

Article 14.

(1) Everyone has the right to seek and to enjoy in other countries asylum from persecution.

(2) This right may not be invoked in the case of prosecutions genuinely arising from non-political crimes or from acts contrary to the purposes and principles of the United Nations.

Article 15.

(1) Everyone has the right to a nationality.

(2) No one shall be arbitrarily deprived of his nationality nor denied the right to change his nationality.

Article 16.

(1) Men and women of full age, without any limitation due to race, nationality or religion, have the right to marry and to found a family. They are entitled to equal rights as to marriage, during marriage and at its dissolution.

(2) Marriage shall be entered into only with the free and full consent of the intending spouses.

(3) The family is the natural and fundamental group unit of society and is entitled to protection by society and the State.

Article 17.

(1) Everyone has the right to own property alone as well as in association with others.

(2) No one shall be arbitrarily deprived of his property.

Article 18.

Everyone has the right to freedom of thought, conscience and religion; this right includes freedom to change his religion or belief, and freedom, either alone or in community with others and in public or private, to manifest his religion or belief in teaching, practice, worship and observance.

Article 19.

Everyone has the right to freedom of opinion and expression; this right includes freedom to hold opinions without interference and to seek, receive and impart information and ideas through any media and regardless of frontiers.

Article 20.

(1) Everyone has the right to freedom of peaceful assembly and association.

(2) No one may be compelled to belong to an association.

Article 21.

(1) Everyone has the right to take part in the government of his country, directly or through freely chosen representatives.

(2) Everyone has the right of equal access to public service in his country.

(3) The will of the people shall be the basis of the authority of government; this will shall be expressed in periodic and genuine elections which shall be by universal and equal suffrage and shall be held by secret vote or by equivalent free voting procedures.

Article 22.

Everyone, as a member of society, has the right to social security and is entitled to realization, through national effort and international co-operation and in accordance with the organization and resources of each State, of the economic, social and cultural rights indispensable for his dignity and the free development of his personality.

Article 23.

(1) Everyone has the right to work, to free choice of employment, to just and favourable conditions of work and to protection against unemployment.

(2) Everyone, without any discrimination, has the right to equal pay for equal work.

(3) Everyone who works has the right to just and favourable remuneration ensuring for himself and his family an existence worthy of human dignity, and supplemented, if necessary, by other means of social protection.

(4) Everyone has the right to form and to join trade unions for the protection of his interests.

Article 24.

Everyone has the right to rest and leisure, including reasonable limitation of working hours and periodic holidays with pay.

Article 25.

(1) Everyone has the right to a standard of living adequate for the health and well-being of himself and of his family, including food, clothing, housing and medical care and necessary social services, and the right to security in the event of unemployment, sickness, disability, widowhood, old age or other lack of livelihood in circumstances beyond his control.

(2) Motherhood and childhood are entitled to special care and assistance. All children, whether born in or out of wedlock, shall enjoy the same social protection.

Article 26.

(1) Everyone has the right to education. Education shall be free, at least in the elementary and fundamental stages. Elementary education shall be compulsory. Technical and professional education shall be made generally available and higher education shall be equally accessible to all on the basis of merit.

(2) Education shall be directed to the full development of the human personality and to the strengthening of respect for human rights and fundamental freedoms. It shall promote understanding, tolerance and friendship among all nations, racial or religious groups, and shall further the activities of the United Nations for the maintenance of peace.

(3) Parents have a prior right to choose the kind of education that shall be given to their children.

Article 27.

(1) Everyone has the right freely to participate in the cultural life of the community, to enjoy the arts and to share in scientific advancement and its benefits.

(2) Everyone has the right to the protection of the moral and material interests resulting from any scientific, literary or artistic production of which he is the author.

Article 28.

Everyone is entitled to a social and international order in which the rights and freedoms set forth in this Declaration can be fully realized.

Article 29.

(1) Everyone has duties to the community in which alone the free and full development of his personality is possible.

(2) In the exercise of his rights and freedoms, everyone shall be subject only to such limitations as are determined by law solely for the purpose of securing due recognition and respect for the rights and freedoms of others and of meeting the just requirements of morality, public order and the general welfare in a democratic society.

(3) These rights and freedoms may in no case be exercised contrary to the purposes and principles of the United Nations.

Article 30.

Nothing in this Declaration may be interpreted as implying for any State, group or person any right to engage in any activity or to perform any act aimed at the destruction of any of the rights and freedoms set forth herein.

From: http://www.un.org/Overview/rights.html

PRECAUTIONARY PRINCIPLE

SEHN - SCIENCE AND ENVIRONMENTAL HEALTH NETWORK http://www.sehn.org/
Since 1998, SEHN has been the leading proponent in the United States of the Precautionary Principle as a new basis for environmental and public health policy.

MARIN COUNTY CALIFORNIA ORDINANCE 2004
http://www.sehn.org/rtfdocs/MarinCounty.doc

MULTNOMAH COUNTY OREGON ORDINANCE (Includes Portland, Oregon) 2004
http://www.sehn.org/rtfdocs/ToxicsResolution.pdf

CITY OF SAN FRANCISCO ORDINANCE 2003
http://www.sehn.org/rtfdocs/SF_ordinance.doc

NEW YORK LEGISLATION 2003
http://www.sehn.org/rtfdocs/NY_legislation.doc

US GOVERNMENT FOOD SAFETY AND INSPECTION SERVICE

HEALTH CARE WITHOUT HARM
http://www.noharm.org/

COMMONWEAL http://www.commonweal.org/index.html
Commonweal is a nonprofit health and environmental
research institute in Bolinas, California.

THE COLLABORATIVE ON HEALTH AND THE ENVIRONMENT
http://www.cheforhealth.org/

CENTER FOR HEALTH, ENVIRONMENT AND JUSTICE (CHEJ)
http://www.chej.org/

CHEJ is the only national environmental organization
founded and led by grassroots leaders. After winning the
federal relocation of residents victimized by toxic waste at
Love Canal, Lois Gibbs and other local activists were
inundated with calls from people around the country who
were facing similar threats and wanted help. CHEJ was
founded in 1981 to address this need. For a full
understanding of the services CHEJ offers see:
http://www.chej.org/UsersGuide.pdf

ALLIANCE FOR HUMAN RESEARCH PROTECTION
http://www.ahrp.org/

US FOOD AND DRUG ADMINISTRATION
http://www.fda.gov/medwatch/index.html

HEALTHY SKEPTICISM
http://www.healthyskepticism.org/index.htm

INSTITUTE FOR HEALTH FREEDOM
http://www.forhealthfreedom.org/

NATIONAL VACCINE INFORMATION CENTER
http://www.909shot.com/

NO FREE LUNCH
http://www.nofreelunch.org/factsfallacies.htm

Pharmaceutical Facts

o   The "Research-based" pharmaceutical industry spends
    more on marketing and administration than it does on
    research and development. (Families USA)
    http://www.familiesusa.org/site/PageServer

o   U.S. Drug spending increased 17.1% to $154.5 billion
    dollars in 2001. One-quarter of this increase was due to
    a shift to the use of more expensive drugs. (National
    Institute for Health Care Management)
    http://www.nihcm.org/

o   Pharmaceutical industry profits were 18.5% of revenue
    in 2001. For the remainder of Fortune 500 companies,
    median profits were 3.5% (FamiliesUSA).
    http://www.familiesusa.org/site/PageServer

o   Since 1995, R&D staff of U.S. brand name drug
    companies have decreased by 2%, while marketing
    staff have increased by 59%. Currently, 22% of staff
    are employed in research and development, while 39%
    are in marketing. (PhRMA Industry Profile 2000;
    percentages calculated by Sager and Socolar)
    http://dcc2.bumc.bu.edu/hs/ushealthreform.htm

o   In a study by Avorn, et al, forty-six per-cent of
    physicians reported that drug reps are moderately to
    very important in influencing their prescribing habits
    Am Journal of Med, 1982
    http://www.nofreelunch.org/required.htm.

o   In a study by Lurie, et al, one-third of medical residents
    reported that they change their practice based on
    information provided by drug reps (Journal of Gen Int
    Med, 1990 http://www.nofreelunch.org/required.htm).

o   In a study by Steinman, et al, 61% of medical residents
    stated that industry promotions did not influence their
    own prescribing, but only 16% believed other
    physicians to be similarly uninfluenced. Am Journal of
    Med, 2000 http://www.nofreelunch.org/required.htm

o   Two and one-half billion dollars were spent on
    advertising to consumers in 2000. Increases in the
    sales of the 50 drugs most heavily advertised to
    consumers were responsible for almost half (47.8%) of
    the $20.8 billion increase in spending in 2000.(NIHCM
    http://www.nihcm.org/)

o   In 2000, Merck spent $161 million on advertising for
    Vioxx. That is more than Pepsico spent advertising
    Pepsi. ($125 million), and more than Anheuser-Busch
    spent advertising Budweiser.($146 million). The
    increase in Vioxx sales in 2000 accounted for 5.7% of
    the 1 year increase in drug spending. (NIHCM
    http://www.nihcm.org/)

o   A study by Westfall, et al, found that 96% of physicians
    and staff had taken samples for personal or family use
    in the preceding year. JAMA, 1997 -
    http://www.nofreelunch.org/required.htm

o   According to industry estimates, drug companies spent
    $15.7 billion dollars on promotion in 2000. $7.2 billion
    dollars worth of free samples were distributed that
    year(IMS Health http://www.ims-
    global.com/index.html).

o   A study by Chew, et al , found that in the treatment of
    hypertension, over 90% of physicians would dispense a
    sample that differed from their preferred drug choice.
    (JGIM, 2000 http://www.nofreelunch.org/required.htm)

o   The AMA generates $20 million in annual income by
    selling detailed personal and professional information
    on all doctors practicing in the United States to the
    pharmaceutical industry (NY Times, November 16, 2000
    http://www.nytimes.com/2000/11/16/science/16PRES.h
    tml?ex=1103864400&en=e72f88d181c14408&ei=5070
    &oref=login).

NORTHWEST ENVIRONMENT WATCH
http://www.northwestwatch.org
We monitor the Northwest's progress toward a sustainability
with a tool the Cascadia Scorecard,
(http://www.northwestwatch.org/scorecard/) an index of
seven key trends critical to the future of the Northwest.

In February 2004, Northwest Environment Watch (NEW), in
partnership with Washington Toxics Coalition
(http://www.watoxics.org/pages/root.aspx), released a
report on levels of toxic flame retardants (PBDEs) found in
the bodies of Puget Sound mothers. The analysis is the first
set of results from a larger NEW study on body burdens in
northwesterners. We released the final report on PBDEs in
the Northwest on September 29, 2004; please go to
http://www.northwestwatch.org/toxics/ And read
more about our pollution monitoring project go to
**http://www.northwestwatch.org/scorecard/pollutio
n.asp.**

The report found high levels of toxic flame retardants in every woman tested. Levels of the chemicals—called PBDEs, or polybrominated diphenyl ethers—were found in milk samples donated by nine Puget Sound women at levels 20 to 40 times higher than levels found in European and Japanese women. The report confirms other US studies documenting rapidly rising concentrations of widely used flame retardants in people and the environment.

HEALTH ACTION CENTER
http://www.healthactioncenter.com/action/

UNION OF CONCERNED SCIENTISTS

http://www.ucsusa.org/ UCS is an independent nonprofit alliance of more than 100,000 concerned citizens and scientists. They augment rigorous scientific analysis with innovative thinking and committed citizen advocacy to build a cleaner, healthier environment and a safer world.

They have produced several public statements and warnings.

STOP WASTE
http://www.stopwaste.org/home/index.asp
A brief synopsis of their goals includes:

o   75% diversion from landfills by the year 2010

o   specific quantitative and/or qualitative goals for all programs.

o   The Agency's waste prevention and recycling programs are integral to a society. Agency programs are linked with other resource conservation efforts and with local and countywide social and economic development programs.

o   Helps create an aware and educated public that has adopted the values and behaviors associated with conservation and

o   Establishes durable, economically sustainable markets for discarded materials that are recovered

o   Creates jobs and other forms of social betterment for the residents of Alameda County.

Other Green Purchasing Links/Resources from http://www.stopwaste.org/home/index.asp?page=532

COSMETICS

NOT TOO PRETTY   http://www.nottoopretty.org/

Very informative site regarding harmful chemicals in cosmetics. Montiors actions worldwide.

FRAGRANCE PRODUCTS INFORMATION NETWORK
http://www.fpinva.org/ A comprehensive web site on health, environmental, and regulatory aspects related to fragrance

BODY BURDEN REPORTS

CDC's New Report http://www.cdc.gov/exposurereport/
A direct link to the Centers for Disease Control's National ReportS on Human Exposure to Environmental Chemicals. CDC tested hundreds of Americans.

Collaborative on Health and the Environment (CHE)-
http://www.cheforhealth.org and CHE's Science Page -

http://www.protectingourhealth.org. Describes the health effects of some of the chemicals covered in the CDC report.

EWG/Commonweal Body Burden Report
http://www.ewg.org - With Mt. Sinai School of Medicine in New York, the Environmental Working Group and Commonweal tested nine Americans for 210 chemicals found in consumer products and industrial pollution. The EWG/Commonweal report provides a personal view of chemical body burden testing and its implications for public health.

Pesticide Action Network's Pesticide Backgrounder
http://www.panna.org - Describes the types of pesticides found in the CDC report, sources of exposure and health effects, with detailed fact sheets on 7 key chemicals and direct links to PANNA's pesticide database for 32 pesticides.

Physicians for Social Responsibility's *Bearing the Burden: Health Implications of Environmental Pollutants in Our Bodies*
http://www.envirohealthaction.org/bearingtheburden -
Provides information on the known and potential health effects of human exposure to the chemicals studied in the CDC report.

CHEMICAL BODY BURDEN
http://www.chemicalbodyburden.org/
Before we are even born, synthetic chemicals and heavy metals of all kinds begin building up in our bodies. This chemical "body burden" is the focus of the information you will find on this web site. The information on this site has been developed through the collaboration of health professionals, scientists, citizens groups and environmental organizations concerned about the chemical body burden we all carry and its health effects - known and unknown. The information you find here will make clear the magnitude of the human experiment we are all part of and what can be done to make change.

ON-LINE COMMUNITY MONITORING HANDBOOK
http://www.oztoxics.org/cmwg/index.html

The handbook is an initiative of the Community Monitoring Working Group (CMWG) established by the International POPS Elimination Network (IPEN)
It is a community resource to support the implementation of the Stockholm Convention on Persistent Organic Pollutants (2001) and the phase out and elimination of persistent and bioaccumulative chemicals.
INTERNATIONAL POPS ELIMINATION NETWORK
http://ipen.ecn.cz/
IPEN is a global network of public interest non-governmental organizations united in support of a common POPs Elimination Platform. The mission of IPEN is to work for the global elimination of persistent organic pollutants, on an expedited yet socially equitable basis.

CENTERS FOR DISEASE CONTROL AND PREVENTION
http://www.cdc.gov/exposurereport/2nd/ The *Report* is the second in a series of publications that provide an ongoing assessment of the exposure of the U.S. population to environmental chemicals using biomonitoring. Released Jan 31, 2003.

PRINCIPLES OF ENVIRONMENTAL JUSTICE

411

Adopted today, October 27, 1991, in Washington, D.C., and re-affirmed October 2002.
http://www.ejrc.cau.edu/princej.html

ENVIRONMENTAL JUSTICE RESOSURCE CENTER
http://www.ejrc.cau.edu/Welcome.html

PARTNERS IN HEALTH
http://www.pih.org/index.html
Their mission is to provide a preferential option for the poor in health care. When their patients are ill and have no access to care, their team of health professionals, scholars, and activists will do whatever it takes to make them well—just as we would do if a member of our own families—or we ourselves—were ill.

GREEN AND SAFE PRODUCTS

THE GREEN GUIDE   http://www.thegreenguide.com/

GREEN GUIDE PRODUCT REPORT
http://www.thegreenguide.com/reports/

THE GREEN REPORT – GENERAL CLEANING PRODUCTS
http://www.newdream.org/consumer/greensealcleaner.html
A superior green cleaner is one that lessens its environmental impacts at every stage of its life cycle, including its packaging.
o Product should be **BIODEGRADABLE AND NON-TOXIC** to *both* humans and aquatic life.
o **EDTA and NTA–avoid** purchasing products with these ingredients. Instead choose builders such as sodium citrate, sodium bicarbonate, sodium carbonate, or sodium silicate
o **PHOSPHATES**–choose products with a phosphate concentration of 0.5% by weight or less. Those without are the best!
o Product should be **CONCENTRATED** and able to work in cold water.
o **AVOID** products containing **CHLORINE BLEACH** or **SODIUM HYPOCHLORITE.**
o **VOC CONCENTRATION**S—choose products with a VOC concentration **no more than 10%** of the weight of the product, when diluted for use as directed.
o Generally try to **avoid ingredients derived from petroleum.** Choose **SURFACTANTS** derived from vegetable oil when possible. Avoid those with nonylphenol ethoxylate. Look for d-limonene and pine oil **SOLVENTS.**
o Favor products with a **NEUTRAL pH.**
o **PACKAGING** –choose products in recycled containers with recyclable HDPE or PET. Choose those shipped in recycled and recyclable cardboard boxes and other recyclable and refillable containers.
See the website for the full report.

MAKE YOUR OWN CLEANING PRODUCTS Many websites offer cleaning recipes. Here are a few:
http://environment.about.com/od/householdcleaners/

http://www.ci.greensboro.nc.us/env_svcs/hhw/HHWrecipes.html

http://www.makingindiagreen.org/springclean.htm

http://www.earthshare.org/tips/friendlyclean.html

http://www.deliciousorganics.com/Controversies/cleaningproducts.htm

MEDICAL INSURANCE

INSTITUTE OF MEDICINE OF THE NATIONAL ACADEMIES
http://www.iom.edu/report.asp?id=12313
COVERING EVERYONE: The United States spends $41 billion per year on "uncompensated" care for people with no insurance, while the economy loses between $65 billion and $130 billion in productivity. More than 18,000 25- to 64-year-olds die every year because they don't have health insurance.

In their report, **Hidden Costs, Value Lost: Uninsurance in America**, the Committee concludes that the estimated benefits across society in health years of life gained by providing the uninsured with the kind and amount of health services that the insured use are likely greater than the additional social costs of doing so. The potential economic value to be gained in better health outcomes from uninterrupted coverage for all Americans is estimated to be between $65 and $130 billion each year. Obtain a PDF version here: http://www.iom.edu/file.asp?id=12327

LAW

COMPREHENSIVE LAW
http://www.fcsl.edu/faculty/daicoff/The%20Comprehensive%20Law%20Movement.htm

TRANSFORMING PRACTICES
http://transformingpractices.com/
Mission: to explore sources of meaning and pleasure in law practice, by continuing the conversation begun in **Steven Keeva's** *Transforming Practices: Finding Joy and Satisfaction in the Legal Life* (an ABA Journal Book published by Contemporary Books, 1999).

RESTORATIVE JUSTICE
http://www.restorativejustice.com
http://www.aic.gov.au/
http://www.restorativejustice.org/
http://www.context.org/ICLIB/IC38/SvGldr2.htm
http://www.justice.govt.nz/pubs/reports/1998/restorative_justice/index.html
http://www.fcrjquaker.org/
http://www.restorativejustice.org.nz/
http://www.sfu.ca/crj/

MEDIATION
www.mediate.com
www.hofstra.edu/Law/isct
www.mediationinlaw.org

PEACE-MAKING
INSTITUTE FOR MULTI-TRACK DIPLOMACY
http://www.imtd.org/

GROUP PEACE
www.grouppeace.com

COMMONWAY www.commonway.org

TRANSFORMATIVE LAW
http://www.transformingpractices.com/

CONTEMPLATIVE MIND LAWYERS RETREAT
http://www.contemplativemind.org/programs/law/events.html

THE PROJECT ON INTEGRATING LAW, POLITICS, AND SPIRITUALITY

http://www.renaissancelawyer.com/Vectors/lawpoliticsspirituality.htm

PRECAUTIONARY PRINCIPLE AROUND THE WORLD

AUSTRALIA http://www.aph.gov.au/library/pubs/rn/1997-98/98rn04.htm

RIO DECLARATION http://www.gdrc.org/u-gov/precaution-7.html

EU FOOD AND SAFETY http://www.gdrc.org/u-gov/precaution-7.html

INTERNATIONAL LAW

http://europa.eu.int/comm/justice_home/ejn/interim_measures/interim_measures_int_en.htm

http://www.aspenpublishers.com/Product.asp?catalog_name=Aspen&category_name=&product_id=9041117857&cookie%5Ftest=1

http://www.ingentaconnect.com/content/kli/euro/2004/00000010/f0000002/2004022

http://www.journal.law.mcgill.ca/abs/vol49/3ellis.html

http://www.uea.ac.uk/env/cserge/pub/wp/gec/gec_1994_11.htm

http://www.britannica.com/eb/article?tocId=224613

http://www.findarticles.com/p/articles/mi_qa3970/is_200410/ai_n9460054

http://www.legal500.com/devs/uk/ev/ukev_044.htm

AT SEA
http://www.ecologic.de/modules.php?name=News&file=article&sid=572

http://www.inderscience.com/search/index.php?action=record&rec_id=6264&prevQuery=&ps=10&m=or

EUROPEAN CHEMICAL INDUSTRY
http://www.cefic.be/Position/sec/pp_sec05.htm
The chemical industry subscribes to the Precautionary Principle as an important policy guidance in environment matters. The interpretation of the Precautionary Principle must be worked out in accordance with the idea of sustainable development. It must not lead to paralysis. The Precautionary Principle has to deal with situations where science and technology cannot provide a full response to issues, leaving a degree of uncertainty in terms of the effects of certain activities, technologies and products.

CEFIC supports the Precautionary Principle as stated in Article 130r of the EU Treaty and within the context of the various paragraphs of this Article.

CEFIC calls for a reasonable, balanced, proportionate and science-based understanding of the principle as a guide to law-making and policy development. The Chemical Industry initiative, Responsible Care which is a separate voluntary commitment of the chemical industry is in harmony with this approach.

PRECAUTIONARY PRINCIPLE IN WILDLIFE CONSERVATION
http://www.traffic.org/briefings/precautionary.html

USA FOOD SAFETY
http://www.biointegrity.org/Advisory.html **U.S. Law Requires That GE Foods Be Proven Safe**

1. U.S. food safety law has mandated the precautionary approach since 1958. In that year, Congress passed the Food Additive Amendment to the Food, Drug and Cosmetic Act requiring that new additives to food be demonstrated safe through standard scientific testing before they are marketed. (21 U.S.C. Sec. 321).

2. An official Senate report described the intent of the amendment as follows: "While Congress did not want to unnecessarily stifle technological advances, it nevertheless intended that additives created through new technologies be proven safe before they go to market. S. Rep. 2422, 1958 U.S.C.C.A.N. 5301-2. (emphasis added) This clearly shows that the precautionary principle is the cornerstone of food safety law in the United States.

3. However, although the Bush Administration is legally required to uphold the precautionary principle at home and honor it abroad, it is doing neither. Instead, it claims that the principle is an illegitimate restraint on business and trade - and that the US is free to disregard it and to resist its application by the EU. As reported in the New York Times on May 18, "The Bush administration believes the precautionary principle is an unjustified constraint on business and does not even recognize the existence of the doctrine."

4. If the U.S. government was following the law, not only would it respect the EU's precautionary policy on GE foods, it would have prevented these foods from coming to market in America until they had been proven safe.

GESUNDHEIT INSTITUTE – PATCH ADAMS
http://www.patchadams.org/flash.htm

SCHOOL FOR DESIGNING A SOCIETY
http://www.designingsociety.com/

ALTERNATIVE MEDICINE HOMEPAGE
http://www.pitt.edu/~cbw/altm.html

NEW OUTLOOKS IN SCIENCE

The Santa Fe Institute is devoted to creating a new kind of scientific research community, one emphasizing multidisciplinary collaboration in pursuit of understanding the common themes that arise in natural, artificial, and social systems. **Murray Gell-Mann** http://www.santafe.edu/

FACULTY OF 1000 - BIOLOGY
http://www.facultyof1000.com/home
Faculty of 1000 will be run by scientists for scientists, and will provide a rapidly updated consensus map of the important papers and trends across biology.

FACULTY of 1000 - ECOLOGY
http://www.facultyof1000.com/about/members/8032
Ecologists and conservation biologists will be able to quickly and easily identify important articles of relevance to them in a range of journals, and read evaluations of the articles by experts in the field.

INTEGRAL INSTITUTE
http://www.integralinstitute.org/integral.html
Integral Institute is dedicated to the proposition that partial and piecemeal approaches to complex problems are ineffective. Accordingly, there are four main goals for the Institute:

o *Integrate the largest amount of research from the largest number of disciplines*

o *Develop practical products and services from this research*

o *Apply this integrated knowledge and method of problem solving to critical and urgent issues*

o *Create the world's first Integral Learning Community—with national and international communities of Integral Practice, as well as with Integral University.*

SEEING THE WHOLE - SYSTEMS THEORY

PEGASUS COMMUNICATIONS offers the following simple explanation of systems theory:

http://www.pegasuscom.com/aboutst.html
Pegasus Communications is dedicated to providing resources that help individuals, teams, and organizations understand and address the challenges they face in managing the complexities of a changing world.

- **WHAT IS SYSTEMS THINKING?**
  Systems thinking offers you a powerful new perspective, a specialized language, and a set of tools that you can use to address the most stubborn problems in your everyday life and work. Systems thinking is a way of understanding reality that emphasizes the relationships among a system's parts, rather than the parts themselves. Based on a field of study known as system dynamics, systems thinking has a practical value that rests on a solid theoretical foundation.

- **Why Is Systems Thinking Important?**
  Why is systems thinking valuable? Because it can help you design smart, enduring solutions to problems. In its simplest sense, systems thinking gives you a more accurate picture of reality, so that you can work with a system's natural forces in order to achieve the results you desire. It also encourages you to think about problems and solutions with an eye toward the long view—for example, how might a particular solution you're considering play out over the long run? And what unintended consequences might it have? Finally, systems thinking is founded on some basic, universal principles that you will begin to detect in all arenas of life once you learn to recognize them.

- **What Are Systems?**
  What exactly is a system? A system is a group of interacting, interrelated, and interdependent components that form a complex and unified whole. Systems are everywhere—for example, the R&D department in your organization, the circulatory system in your body, the predator/prey relationships in nature, the ignition system in your car, and so on. Ecological systems and human social systems are living systems; human-made systems such as cars and washing machines are nonliving systems. Most systems thinkers focus their attention on living systems, especially human social systems. However, many systems thinkers are also interested in how human social systems affect the larger ecological systems in our planet.

- Systems have several defining characteristics:
  • **Every system has a purpose within a larger system.** Example: The purpose of the R&D department in your organization is to generate new product ideas and features for the organization.
  • **All of a system's parts must be present for the system to carry out its purpose optimally.** Example: The R&D system in your organization consists of people, equipment, and processes. If you removed any one of these components, this system could no longer function.
  • **A system's parts must be arranged in a specific way for the system to carry out its purpose.** Example: If you rearranged the reporting relationships in your R&D department so that the head of new-product development reported to the entry-level lab technician, the department would likely have trouble carrying out its purpose.
  • **Systems change in response to feedback.** The word feedback plays a central role in systems thinking. Feedback is information that returns to its original transmitter such that it influences that transmitter's subsequent actions. Example: Suppose you turn too sharply while driving your car around a curve. Visual cues (you see a mailbox rushing toward you) would tell you that you were turning too sharply. These cues constitute feedback that prompts you to change what you're doing (jerk the steering wheel in the other direction somewhat) so you can put your car back on course.
  • **Systems maintain their stability by making adjustments based on feedback.** Example: Your body temperature generally hovers around 98.6 degrees Fahrenheit. If you get too hot, your body produces sweat, which cools you back down.

- **Systems Thinking as a Perspective: Events, Patterns, or System?**
  Systems thinking is a perspective because it helps us see the events and patterns in our lives in a new light—and respond to them in higher leverage ways. For example, suppose a fire breaks out in your town. This is an **event**. If you respond to it simply by putting the fire out, you're reacting. (That is, you have done nothing to prevent new fires.) If you respond by putting out the fire and studying where fires tend to break out in your town, you'd be paying attention to **patterns**. For example, you might notice that certain neighborhoods seem to suffer more fires than others. If you locate more fire stations in those areas, you're adapting. (You still haven't done anything to prevent new fires.) Now suppose you look for the **systems**—such as smoke-detector distribution and building materials used—that influence the patterns of neighborhood-fire outbreaks. If you build new fire-alarm systems and establish fire and safety codes, you're creating change. Finally, you're doing something to prevent new fires!

This is why looking at the world through a systems thinking "lens" is so powerful: It lets you actually make the world a better place.

- **Systems Thinking as a Special Language** As a language, systems thinking has unique qualities that help you communicate with others about the many systems around and within us: • It emphasizes wholes rather than parts, and stresses the role of interconnections—including the role we each play in the systems at work in our lives.
  • It emphasizes circular feedback (for example, A leads to B, which leads to C, which leads back to A) rather than linear cause and effect (A leads to B, which leads to C, which leads to D, . . . and so on).
  • It contains special terminology that describes system behavior, such as reinforcing process (a feedback flow that generates exponential growth or collapse) and balancing process (a feedback flow that controls change and helps a system maintain stability).

- **Systems Thinking as a Set of Tools**
  The field of systems thinking has generated a broad array of tools that let you (1) graphically depict your understanding of a particular system's structure and behavior, (2) communicate with others about your understandings, and (3) design high-leverage interventions for problematic system behavior.

- These tools include causal loops, behavior over time graphs, stock and flow diagrams, and systems archetypes—all of which let you depict your understanding of a system—to computer simulation models and management "flight simulators," which help you to test the potential impact of your interventions.

Whether you consider systems thinking mostly a new perspective, a special language, or a set of tools, it has a power and a potential that, once you've been introduced, are hard to resist. The more you learn about this intriguing field, the more you'll want to know!

Livio, Mario The Golden Ratio – The Story of PHI, the World's Most Astonishing Number Broadway Books, NY, 2002

Capra, Fritjof The Web of Life – A new Scientific Understanding of Living Systems Anchor Books, 1996

http://www.fritjofcapra.net/

WHAT IS SYSTEMS THEORY?:
http://pespmc1.vub.ac.be/SYSTHEOR.html

INTERNATIONAL SOCIETY FOR THE SYSTEMS SCIENCES: http://www.isss.org/lumLVB.htm Ludwig von Bertalanffy (1901--1972) ...developed a kinetic theory of stationary open systems and the General System Theory, was one of the founding fathers and vice-president of the Society for General System Theory, and one of the first who applied the system methodology to psychology and the social sciences ...

BUCKMINSTER FULLER INSTITUTE: http://www.bfi.org/ The Buckminster Fuller Institute is committed to a successful and sustainable future for 100% of humanity. Founded in 1983 and inspired by the **Design Science** principles pioneered by the late Buckminster Fuller, BFI serves as an information resource for concerned citizens around the world.

SOCIETY FOR CHAOS THEORY IN PSYCHOLOGY AND LIFE SCIENCES   http://www.societyforchaostheory.org/

WIKIPEDIA – SYSTEMS THEORY
http://en.wikipedia.org/wiki/Systems_theory

CENTER FOR HUMAN EMERGENCE
http://www.humanemergence.org/home.html

INTEGRAL INSTITUTE http://integralinstitute.org/

SERVICE
SOCIAL JUSTICE

ELLA BAKER CENTER FOR HUMAN RIGHTS
http://www.ellabakercenter.org/index.html Programs include the following:

BOOKS NOT http://ellabakercenter.org/page.php?pageid=20 RECLAIMING THE FUTURE
http://www.ellabakercenter.org/page.php?pageid=233BAY AREA POLICE WATCH or their families.
http://www.ellabakercenter.org/page.php?pageid=56 FREEDOM FIGHTER MUSIC
http://ellabakercenter.org/page.php?pageid=180

LITERACY FOR ENVIRONMENTAL JUSTICE
http://www.lejyouth.org/evntspg.htm Their mission is to foster an understanding of the principles of environmental justice* and urban sustainability in young people in order to promote the long-term health of their communities. Literacy for Environmental Justice (LEJ) is an urban environmental education and youth empowerment organization created specifically to address the unique ecological and social concerns of Bayview Hunters Point, San Francisco, and the surrounding communities of Mission, Potrero Hill, Visitacion Valley, and Excelsior.

LEJ engages urban youth in traditional environmental problems by drawing concrete linkages between the state of human health, the environment, and urban quality of life. Experiences has taught them that once these inter-relationships are recognized many young people feel compelled to become involved in the cause of creating a 'livable' city. Students leave their programs with skills and a shared experience of positive and visible work.

INSTITUTE FOR COMMUNITY RESOURCE DEVELOPMENT – CHICAGO The Institute's mission is to rebuild the local food system. ICRD projects include: building grocery stores that bring access to sustainable products to urban communities of color, organizing farmers markets, converting vacant lots to urban farm sites and distributing local grown produce to restaurants. Institute for Community Resource Development farms, Ladonna Redmond, 4429 W. Fulton Street, 200 N. Kenneth Avenue, Chicago; 773-261-7339

CENTER FOR YOUNG WOMEN'S DEVELOPMENT
http://www.cywd.org/about_us/staff.html Their innovative approach and successful programs have gained them national and international recognition. Their determination to honor each person's potential led them to staff their organization almost entirely with young women 26 and under, who have moved up through their programs into leadership roles. Their new successful model for youth development is an organization run by and for the young women they serve.

415

TRANSPORTATION

CONSUMERS FOR AUTO RELIABILITY AND SAFETY
http://www.carconsumers.com/

GREENERCARS.COM
http://www.greenercars.com/indexplus.html

GREEN CAR JOURNAL http://greencars.com/

GREEN VEHICLE GUIDE – EPA
http://www.epa.gov/greenvehicles/

HYPERCAR, INC. .http://www.hypercar.com/index.html
Hypercar was founded around the vision of enabling automakers to profitably produce sustainable vehicles for everyone. Through the application of lightweighting and whole-system design, hypercars respond to regulatory challenges and meet customer demand for safe, cleaner, greener cars.

E-TRACTION
http://www.etraction.com/   A leading Dutch research institute (T.N.O.) confirmed that a newly developed light-weight bus equipped with the (patent pending) e-Traction system achieved 14.8 MPG, approximately 3 times the mileage of the most fuel efficient conventional diesel buses. The centerpiece of the e-Traction system is the electric, direct-drive wheel hub motor that the company claims will revolutionize the way vehicles will be operated in the future. (From a Nov 2, 2004 press release at the website.)

RENEWABLE FUELS ASSOCIATION
http://www.ethanolrfa.org/
The voice of the Ethanol Industry.

BETTER WORLD CLUB
http://www.betterworldclub.com/
Better World Club, Inc. is dedicated to balancing economic goals with social and environmental responsibility. Better World supports a cleaner environment and alternative modes of transportation through their Emergency Roadside Assistance, Travel Products and Services, and Insurance Products and Services.

Importantly, we act as an advocate on behalf of the consumer and demonstrate our social and environmental commitment by donating an amount equal to 1% of our annual revenues toward environmental clean-up efforts and by providing unique eco-friendly travel alternatives.

PATRIOT'S ENERGY PLEDGE
http://www.saveabarrel.org/ The Patriot's Energy Pledge is a civic campaign to help Americans reduce our dependence on oil, by taking personal steps to meet our transportation needs in more fuel-efficient ways.

THE CLEAN CAR PLEDGE AND INDUSTRY CHALLENGE
http://actionnetwork.org/campaign/clean_car_pledge?source =edac1 **Sign the Clean Car Pledge**. Over 100,000 people have taken the Clean Car Pledge so far, and you can, too. The Clean Car Campaign will collect your Pledge and deliver it to U.S. auto companies reminding them that consumers want cars that are cleaner and more fuel efficient. The Clean Car Campaign, an Environmental Defense partner, is a coalition of organizations dedicated to promoting a progressive and profound transformation of the motor vehicle industry. Through its Clean Car Standard,

(http://www.cleancarcampaign.org/standards.shtml), the Campaign challenges industry to develop and market vehicles in the near-term that are signficantly cleaner than today's in their production, use, and end-of-life disposition.

The Clean Car Standard is a performance-based standard that is practically achievable by applying the best practices currently used by the global auto industry. The standard is intended to promote the near-term development of vehicles that are significantly greener than today's in their production, use and end-of-life disposition. Meeting these standards should complement other important values of practicality, affordability and safety. The standard includes the following components:

1. fuel efficiency improvements of 1.5 times the fleet average within that vehicle's class;

2. tailpipe emissions meeting California's "Super Ultra Low Emission Vehicle" (SULEV) standard;

3. clean manufacturing practices that achieve superior environmental performance in the vehicle's manufacture and use of non-toxic recyclable materials.

For more information see:
http://www.cleancarcampaign.org/standards.shtml

AMERICAN COUNCIL FOR AN ENERGY EFFICIENT ECONOMY
http://www.aceee.org/ The American Council for an Energy-Efficient Economy is a nonprofit organization dedicated to advancing energy efficiency as a means of promoting both economic prosperity and environmental protection. ACEEE fulfills its mission by

- Conducting in-depth technical and policy assessments

- Advising policymakers and program managers

- Working collaboratively with businesses, public interest groups, and other organizations

- Organizing conferences and workshops

- Publishing books, conference proceedings, and reports

- Educating consumers and businesses

ECOLOGY CENTER   http://www.ecocenter.org/
The Ecology Center (EC) is a membership-based, nonprofit environmental organization based in Ann Arbor, Michigan. Founded by community activists after the country's first Earth Day in 1970, the Center is now a regional leader in the struggle for clean air, safe water, healthy communities, and environmental justice.

GREEN CAR CONGRESS
http://www.greencarcongress.com/2005/02/association_of_.html

CARBON CALCULATOR
http://www.ucsusa.org/general/special_features/page.cfm?p ageID=1535   Find out how much less you'd pollute and your savings at the pump if you had cleaner car technology choices.

PLANETWALK http://www.planetwalk.org/ Planetwalk is a non-profit educational organization dedicated to raising environmental consciousness and promoting earth stewardship. For twenty-two years, Dr. Francis gave up the use of motorized vehicles as an expression of his personal commitment to creating a sustainable world, walked across the United States, sailed and walked through the Caribbean and continued his walk through South America. In 1972, after seeing an oil spill in San Francisco Bay, Dr. Francis gave up the use of motorized vehicles. A year later, he made a vow of silence that lasted 17 years. Not only did Francis not talk, he earned a Bachelor, Masters, and a Doctorate while he walked across the country. In 1991, Dr. Francis was named a United Nations Environment Programme Goodwill Ambassador to the World's Grassroots Communities.

INTERNATIONAL CLEARING HOUSE FOR HYDROGEN COMMERCE http://www.ch2bc.org/

HYBRID CARS.COM http://www.hybridcars.com/ HybridCars.com is part web journal, part online community, and part hybrid market research organization. HybridCars.com works closely with the University of Michigan's Office for the Study of Automotive Transportation in developing surveys and other research projects related to the emerging hybrid market

NEW MEXICO HYDROGEN BUSINESS COUNCIL http://www.nmhbc.org/

INTERGALACTIC HYDROGEN http://www.h2go.info/

Intergalactic Hydrogen is a vehicle conversion and technology advancement enterprise with over 30 years of experience in the areas of engine and vehicle research, development and deployment. Our specialties include engine tuning, fuel system integration, and the design and installation of complete hydrogen fuel systems.Tai W. Robinson, President, 9851 S. Borg Dr., Sandy, UT 84092 801-201-7370 airtai@cs.com

W. Fred Robinson, Founder, PO BOX 772528, Steamboat Springs, CO 80477 970-736-8451 intergalactici@aol.com

DENNIS WEAVER'S DRIVE TO SURVIVE http://www.electrifyingtimes.com/drivetosurvive.html

OTHER REFERENCE MATERIALS

Arrien, Angeles The Four-Fold Way – Walking the Paths of the Warrior, Teacher, Healer and Visionary Harper 1992

Bach, Richard Illusions – The Adventures of a Reluctant Messiah Dell 1989

Berry, Wendell What are People For? North Point Press, San Francisco 1990

Braden, Gregg The Isaiah Effect – Decoding the Lost Science of Prayer and Prophecy Three Rivers Press, 2000

Green, Glenda Love Without End – Jesus Speaks Spiritis Publishing 1999

Hawkins, David R. Power vs. Force – The Hidden Determinants of Human Behavior Hay House, 1995

Hawkins, David R. The Eye of the I – From Which Nothing Is Hidden Veritas, 2001

Hawkins, David R. I – Reality and Subjectivity Veritas, 2003

Hubbard, Barbara Marx Conscious Evolution – Awakening the Power of Our Social Potential New World Library, 1998

Hubbard, Barbara Marx Emergence – The Shift from Ego to Essence Hampton Roads, 2001

Shlain, Leonard Art & Physics – Parallel Visions in Space, Time & Light Quill William Morrow, NY 1991

Daniel Quinn. Ishmael: An Adventure of the Mind and Spirit, Bantun/Turner, 1992.

Ivan Illich, **Energy and Equity, 1973**, in which he states:

"The advocates of an energy crisis believe in and continue to propagate a peculiar vision of man. According to this notion, man is born into perpetual dependence on slaves which he must painfully learn to master. If he does not employ prisoners, then he needs machines to do most of his work. According to this doctrine, the well-being of a society can be measured by the number of years its members have gone to school and by the number of energy slaves they have thereby learned to command. This belief is common to the conflicting economic ideologies now in vogue. It is threatened by the obvious inequity, harriedness, and impotence that appear everywhere once the voracious hordes of energy slaves outnumber people by a certain proportion. The energy crisis focuses concern on the scarcity of fod der for these slaves. I prefer to ask whether free men need them.

The energy policies adopted during the current decade will determine the range and character of social relationships a society will be able to enjoy by the year 2000. A low-energy policy allows for a wide choice of life-styles and cultures. If, on the other hand, a society opts for high energy consumption, its social relations must be dictated by technocracy and will be equally degrading whether labeled capitalist or socialist."

http://www.cogsci.ed.ac.uk/~ira/illich/texts/energy_and_equity/energy_and_equity.html

For more juicy quotes from Illich, see http://www.pkimaging.com/mik/infoall/illich/iitext/ienergy.html . . .

TO HONOR ALL LIFE

ask

"Does this choice honor all?"

Some suggestions:

- **Be Open, notice that you always have a choice.**
  When we humbly realize how little we know, we are free to perceive new possibilities. In truth, the field of possibilities is infinite. Creativity is a product of intention and humility.

- **Come *from* what you want, instead of striving to reach it.**
  If you want joy in your life – BE that joy, focus on the joy around you. If you want love, BE loving. When you clearly know WHO you want to be, (who you are at the core of your being – your Essential Self), simply BE that person *now*. If you want to be non-judgmental, then accept everything and everyone with every breath you take, especially yourself. If you want to experience abundance, then BE the expression of abundance in your every thought, word, and action. Simply BE the magnificently loving person you know yourself to be, and let go of the need to analyze and "get better." Enlightenment is BEing your inner light. Choose YOU now.

- ***Everything* is a gift and is worthy of attention.**
  There isn't one molecule on Earth that doesn't support you, even if the circumstances seem to reflect the opposite. Look deeper and see the incredible gift of this moment. Give it your full attention.

- **Gratitude reciprocates and acknowledges the gift.**
  The energy of giving and receiving are one. Acknowledging the gift completes the giving/receiving circle of energy. Reciprocity touches and balances every detail of life.

- **Flow with the energy of life – don't fight it.**
  It's easier to flow with the current rather than fight it; and it's always easier (and more enjoyable) to eat ripe fruit rather than fruit before its time. We are the same. When we surrender to and trust the right-timing of our life's unfolding, the fullness of the possible awakens within. Acting at cusp is most powerful.

- **Take full responsibility.**
  When we perceive the rich variety of choice available in every moment, we are free to choose with total commitment. The opportunity to take full responsibility and own the results of our choices simply awaits our acknowledgment. Responsibility is not a synonym for "blame," it's just the opposite. Responsibility is alive to the infinitely possible, in which the interconnection of ALL is acknowledged. It is the ultimate statement of creativity and freedom.

FULL GRATITUDE

This section is entitled GRATITUDE instead of the traditional "Acknowledgments" because I want to make a point of going far beyond merely acknowledging those of you who have contributed to the creation of this book. Each of you has provided me with experiences that have allowed me to know my Inner-Self, and for that gift I have no words sufficient to express my joy.

This book is truly a co-creative collaboration, verified by the many editors who assisted in its birthing. They include Marika Belew, Susan Brook, Janet Greek, Seth Belew, Nina Kelly, Akiva, Alaya Ketani, Dominic Allamano, Tiki McClure, Jeanine Landheer, Helene Enslow, Kirsten Liegmann, and Maria Katsantones.

The **Honoring All Life Foundation** grew out of the process of writing this book. Those who have supported that effort must also be included in this list: Helene Enslow, (who helped develop the initial Seeing from the Heart(SM) workshop), Bill Kauth, Kim Keller, William Cerf, Angelika Austin, Mark Vicente, Ed Keller. Special thanks to David Spinney for skillfully coaching me through the website creation process and designing a website that thoroughly reflects our intention.

I am extremely grateful to Michael and Treenie Roads. Michael's books have inspired me since the late 1980's, and the Roadsway Re*treat provided me with a tangible way of experiencing my own power, and hence the ONEness of all. The term, "Honoring All Life," was inspired by Michael's quote:

If you Honour Self,
You Honour Life,
If you Honour Life,
Life will Honour You.

I would like to acknowledge the tremendous gift given me by Neale Donald Walsch, when he appointed me Director of HeartLight, Ashland; and "gave" the entire HeartLight concept to Dr. William Spady and the remaining HeartLight International concept team, including James Colen, Scott Kiere, Deborah Oliff, Linda Lee Ratto, Pam Spady, and me. Through my experience as one of the original participants, I grew in ways I could not have imagined. I will always be grateful for that incredible journey. I would like to thank everyone involved for the tremendous gift of your authentic selves. In knowing you, I have found me. You have provided the perfect mirror upon which my own self reflected, forcing me to grow, to open, and to celebrate all aspects of life.

I thank the Earth In Focus team. Your dedication to creating a workshop to heal the Human-Earth relationship contributed greatly to my awareness of the need to take full responsibility for the impact of my everyday decisions. A special thanks to Bill Kauth for his abundant generosity, his open heart, and his willingness to share all he knows and is, for the benefit of us all.

My entire Nonviolent Communication class taught me much about communication, empathy, and compassion. Most of all, you were willing to be vulnerable, allowing me to access my own vulnerability…and therein my own empowerment. Marshall Rosenberg, Joanne Lescher and Holley Humphrey, thank you for being the wonderful teachers that you are.

To my women's group, our seven years of weekly empowerment sessions taught me the meaning of sisterhood, compassion, and friendship.

My publishers, Grant Plowman and Linda Nichols of Interactive Media Publishing, have been my staff of support, always willing to be a never-ending source of creative ideas while offering calm professionalism in the center of the storm.

My neighbors have taught me the joy of co-creating community together. Watching our children grow while exploring our definition of neighborhood in the true sense of community, has been a gift I never expected yet will always treasure.

To each author quoted, I offer my humble gratitude. You have been my teachers and my inspiration. As I do not believe I have "seen further", but have instead perhaps seen deeper into mySelf, I nevertheless offer you this tribute originally written by Sir Issac Newton:

If I have seen further it is by standing on the shoulders of giants.

How can I begin to thank my birth family for all they have provided me? My gratitude to Barbara and Raymond Park, my parents, has no end. To my sister, Janet Garvin, and my twin brother, Jeff Park, I can only say, "thank you for being you." Your love has always sustained me.

Most of all, I want to thank my children, Marika, Seth, and Kesa; and my former husband, Bill Belew. You have provided me with the compassion to look deeply within, the courage to speak my truth, and the willingness to honor mySelf by learning to honor us all. I am in awe of your magnificence.

To all of you, I offer my gratitude and joy. I celebrate our dance together knowing that our energy exchange has fed us all and ultimately helped us to see our own reflection in each other's eyes. The joy of experiencing our ONEness has no bounds.

ABOUT THE AUTHOR

Shaktari L. Belew has worn many hats and played many roles in her lifetime. She served on the Board of HeartLight International, seeking to explore and create a new paradigm of heart-led education throughout the world. It was during this highly creative time that she began to develop the ideas that led to this book. Her formal education is in Developmental Psychology and Fine Arts/Art History, yet she has had successful careers as a realtor, systems analyst, counseling kinesiologist, and educator. Perhaps it was this wide variety of experience that peaked her curiosity about how we perceive.

Her years of teaching fine arts and perception brought her tremendous joy as well as many humbling lessons. They are the source of the experiences offered through the POWER OF PERCEPTION[SM] workshops.

Shaktari created the Honoring All Life Foundation as an active exploration of what it means to honor all, specifically through empowering people to experience their own innate magnificence and that of all life.

ABOUT THE HONORING ALL LIFE FOUNDATION

The Honoring All Life Foundation is intent on exploring an emerging new reality that includes all life in our designs, decisions, and plans. It serves as a networking tool to connect those with ideas to those who manifest them. It invites each person to fully embrace the power and responsibility of their daily choices, and to become deliberate creators of their own reality. Most of all, it is a celebration of who we know our deepest selves to be.

We can choose to create a world that honors all - right now – with our next breath, our next thought, our next action.

Our programs are designed to explore new ways of perceiving the possible:

The POWER OF PERCEPTION Workshops ask **How and what do we allow ourselves to see?** Though seemingly simple, the answer to this question literally determines your sense of reality. The POWER OF PERCEPTION Workshops provide a safe space in which to explore, develop, and embrace our sensorial experiences in new ways. Using current findings in brain research, perception, and Systems Theory, these general-exploration or topic-specific workshops provide a richly experiential, hands-on opportunity to dive deeply into your own perceptual process, and to become aware of the choices you make - moment to moment - that define your sense of reality. If you are ready to honestly explore life's fullness, you are ready for this workshop.

Honoring All Life Institute (HALI) asks How can we educate a Whole Person in a Whole World?

HALI seeks to create an educational context that taps our inner passions, nurtures our ability to tenderly self-assess and create new choices, celebrates our individual and collective magnificence, and actively explores life that honors all. Our proto-type educational experience will serve all ages and erase the illusory dividing line between school and community.

Awareness Media Spots - Creating fertile ground for new ideas.

Imagine watching a 30 or 60-second media spot that doesn't sell you anything. Instead it creatively captivates your attention, enticing you to initiate a state of introspection in relation to the given topic, ultimately asking you to reflect on two questions: Is there another more inclusive and loving choice for humanity? Do your daily choices reflect the highest expression of who you choose to be - in this moment - regarding this topic?

Ultimately we want to leave the viewer aroused, informed, and empowered to express him/herself in a way that truly brings joy to life. With each media spot, we invite the viewer to share creative ideas with us, by providing an internet site that acts as a network – sorting ideas to those who can actively implement them in the given field.

In My Village – Building joy-centered communities.

In My Village invites participants to explore their own relationship to joy as they work together to create the kind of community they long to live in. It asks a simple but deeply profound question, the answer of which lies at the core of all mindful community manifestation: "What do you truly want?" Above all, In My Village is a co-creative exploration of who we see ourselves to be – individually and collectively - one that hopefully embraces an ever-expanding perception of our potential and possibilities.

Earth Embrace Clubs - Empowering children to fully participate in and design their world.

Like parenting skills, sustainable design is one of the core elements that seem to be missing from the educational opportunities we offer all but the select few in our society. Yet we ask each generation to design the human interaction with our planet in ways that deeply affect the well being of us all.

Earth Embrace Clubs offer design curriculum that incorporates the lessons of sustainability while offering hands-on fun experiences for kids of all ages. Five easy-to-remember questions run though each project - questions that strengthen our ability to discern sustainable design. The five questions are:

1. What natural resources were used to make the object?
2. What energy was used to obtain the natural resources?
3. Does it function as intended?
4. Can it be designed so that it becomes food for something else?
5. Does it truly contribute to the joy and well-being of the world?

We are developing an on-line searchable database for use in classrooms and after school settings worldwide. Our intent is to provide environmental and design awareness to a broad range of people in a fun and inexpensive environment. Anyone who has the desire can start an Earth Embrace Club, all that is required is passion and access to the internet.

The **Honoring All Life Foundation** is a non-profit organization under IRC Section 501(c)(3). If you would like to receive our NEWSLETTER "New Perceptions", co-create our projects, or support our programs, visit our website or write to the author at Shaktari@HonoringAllLife.org

You can make a tax deductible contribution by simply visiting our website **http://www.HonoringAllLife.org/** and pressing the **DONATE** button. (As with any donation, you should consult with your CPA or tax advisor as to the proper treatment in your tax return. ID# 51-0428894.)

The Honoring All Life Foundation gratefully accepts donations that truly honor YOU. We invite you to donate as a declaration of WHO YOU ARE – an affirmation of your own magnificence and that of the world around you. The power of a donation made in that spirit touches lives in innumerable ways, and knows no bounds.